50 World's Greatest Essays

50 World's Greatest Essays

RUPA

Published by
Rupa Publications India Pvt. Ltd 2023
7/16, Ansari Road, Daryaganj
New Delhi 110002

Sales Centres:
Bengaluru Chennai
Hyderabad Jaipur Kathmandu
Kolkata Mumbai Prayagraj

P-ISBN: 978-93-5702-984-1
E-ISBN: 9978-93-5702-971-1

First impression 2023

10 9 8 7 6 5 4 3 2 1

Printed in India

CONTENTS

1

WHY I WRITE

George Orwell

From a very early age, perhaps the age of five or six, I knew that when I grew up I should be a writer. Between the ages of about 17 and 24 I tried to abandon this idea, but I did so with the consciousness that I was outraging my true nature and that sooner or later I should have to settle down and write books.

I was the middle child of three, but there was a gap of five years on either side, and I barely saw my father before I was eight. For this and other reasons I was somewhat lonely, and I soon developed disagreeable mannerisms which made me unpopular throughout my schooldays. I had the lonely child's habit of making up stories and holding conversations with imaginary persons, and I think from the very start my literary ambitions were mixed up with the feeling of being isolated and undervalued. I knew that I had a facility with words and a power of facing unpleasant facts, and I felt that this created a sort of private world in which I could get my own back for my failure in everyday life. Nevertheless the volume of serious—i.e. seriously intended—writing which I produced all through my childhood and boyhood would not amount to half a dozen pages. I wrote my first poem at the age of four or five, my mother taking it down to dictation. I cannot remember anything about it except that it was about a tiger and the tiger had 'chair-like teeth'—a good enough phrase, but I fancy the poem was a plagiarism of Blake's 'Tiger, Tiger'. At eleven, when the war of 1914–18 broke out, I wrote a patriotic poem which was printed in the local newspaper, as was another, two years later, on the death of Kitchener. From time to time, when I was a bit older,

I wrote bad and usually unfinished 'nature poems' in the Georgian style. I also attempted a short story which was a ghastly failure. That was the total of the would-be serious work that I actually set down on paper during all those years.

However, throughout this time I did in a sense engage in literary activities. To begin with there was the made-to-order stuff which I produced quickly, easily and without much pleasure to myself. Apart from school work, I wrote *vers d'occasion*, semi-comic poems which I could turn out at what now seems to me astonishing speed—at fourteen I wrote a whole rhyming play, in imitation of Aristophanes, in about a week—and helped to edit school magazines, both printed and in manuscript. These magazines were the most pitiful burlesque stuff that you could imagine, and I took far less trouble with them than I now would with the cheapest journalism. But side by side with all this, for fifteen years or more, I was carrying out a literary exercise of a quite different kind: this was the making up of a continuous 'story' about myself, a sort of diary existing only in the mind. I believe this is a common habit of children and adolescents. As a very small child I used to imagine that I was, say, Robin Hood, and picture myself as the hero of thrilling adventures, but quite soon my 'story' ceased to be narcissistic in a crude way and became more and more a mere description of what I was doing and the things I saw. For minutes at a time this kind of thing would be running through my head: 'He pushed the door open and entered the room. A yellow beam of sunlight, filtering through the muslin curtains, slanted on to the table, where a match-box, half-open, lay beside the inkpot. With his right hand in his pocket he moved across to the window. Down in the street a tortoiseshell cat was chasing a dead leaf', etc. etc. This habit continued until I was about 25, right through my non-literary years. Although I had to search, and did search, for the right words, I seemed to be making this descriptive effort almost against my will, under a kind of compulsion from outside. The 'story' must, I suppose, have reflected the styles of the various writers I admired at different ages, but so far as I remember it always had the same meticulous descriptive quality.

When I was about 16 I suddenly discovered the joy of mere words, i.e. the sounds and associations of words. The lines from *Paradise Lost*—

So hee with difficulty and labour hard
Moved on: with difficulty and labour hee.

which do not now seem to me so very wonderful, sent shivers down my backbone; and the spelling 'hee' for 'he' was an added pleasure. As for the need to describe things, I knew all about it already. So it is clear what kind of books I wanted to write, in so far as I could be said to want to write books at that time. I wanted to write enormous naturalistic novels with unhappy endings, full of detailed descriptions and arresting similes, and also full of purple passages in which words were used partly for the sake of their own sound. And in fact my first completed novel, *Burmese Days*, which I wrote when I was thirty but projected much earlier, is rather that kind of book.

I give all this background information because I do not think one can assess a writer's motives without knowing something of his early development. His subject matter will be determined by the age he lives in—at least this is true in tumultuous, revolutionary ages like our own—but before he ever begins to write he will have acquired an emotional attitude from which he will never completely escape. It is his job, no doubt, to discipline his temperament and avoid getting stuck at some immature stage, in some perverse mood; but if he escapes from his early influences altogether, he will have killed his impulse to write. Putting aside the need to earn a living, I think there are four great motives for writing, at any rate for writing prose. They exist in different degrees in every writer, and in any one writer the proportions will vary from time to time, according to the atmosphere in which he is living. They are:

(i) Sheer egoism. Desire to seem clever, to be talked about, to be remembered after death, to get your own back on the grown-ups who snubbed you in childhood, etc., etc. It is humbug to pretend this is not a motive, and a strong one. Writers share this characteristic with scientists, artists, politicians, lawyers, soldiers, successful businessmen—in short, with the whole top crust of humanity. The great mass of human beings are not acutely selfish. After the age of about thirty they almost abandon the sense of being individuals at all—and live chiefly for others, or are simply smothered under drudgery. But there is also the minority of gifted, willful people who are determined to live their own lives to the end, and writers belong in this class. Serious writers, I should say, are on the whole more vain and self-centered than journalists, though less interested in money.

(ii) Aesthetic enthusiasm. Perception of beauty in the external world, or, on the other hand, in words and their right arrangement. Pleasure in the impact of one sound on another, in the firmness of good prose or the rhythm of a good story. Desire to share an experience which one feels is valuable and ought not to be missed. The aesthetic motive is very feeble in a lot of writers, but even a pamphleteer or writer of textbooks will have pet words and phrases which appeal to him for non-utilitarian reasons; or he may feel strongly about typography, width of margins, etc. Above the level of a railway guide, no book is quite free from aesthetic considerations.

(iii) Historical impulse. Desire to see things as they are, to find out true facts and store them up for the use of posterity.

(iv) Political purpose.—Using the word 'political' in the widest possible sense. Desire to push the world in a certain direction, to alter other peoples' idea of the kind of society that they should strive after. Once again, no book is genuinely free from political bias. The opinion that art should have nothing to do with politics is itself a political attitude.

It can be seen how these various impulses must war against one another, and how they must fluctuate from person to person and from time to time. By nature—taking your 'nature' to be the state you have attained when you are first adult—I am a person in whom the first three motives would outweigh the fourth. In a peaceful age I might have written ornate or merely descriptive books, and might have remained almost unaware of my political loyalties. As it is I have been forced into becoming a sort of pamphleteer. First I spent five years in an unsuitable profession (the Indian Imperial Police, in Burma), and then I underwent poverty and the sense of failure. This increased my natural hatred of authority and made me for the first time fully aware of the existence of the working classes, and the job in Burma had given me some understanding of the nature of imperialism: but these experiences were not enough to give me an accurate political orientation. Then came Hitler, the Spanish Civil War, etc. By the end of 1935 I had still failed to reach a firm decision. I remember a little poem that I wrote at that date, expressing my dilemma:

A happy vicar I might have been
Two hundred years ago
To preach upon eternal doom
And watch my walnuts grow;
But born, alas, in an evil time,
I missed that pleasant haven,
For the hair has grown on my upper lip
And the clergy are all clean-shaven.
And later still the times were good,
We were so easy to please,
We rocked our troubled thoughts to sleep
On the bosoms of the trees.
All ignorant we dared to own
The joys we now dissemble;
The greenfinch on the apple bough
Could make my enemies tremble.
But girl's bellies and apricots,
Roach in a shaded stream,
Horses, ducks in flight at dawn,
All these are a dream.
It is forbidden to dream again;

We maim our joys or hide them:
Horses are made of chromium steel
And little fat men shall ride them.
I am the worm who never turned,
The eunuch without a harem;
Between the priest and the commissar
I walk like Eugene Aram;
And the commissar is telling my fortune
While the radio plays,
But the priest has promised an Austin Seven,
For Duggie always pays.
I dreamt I dwelt in marble halls,
And woke to find it true;
I wasn't born for an age like this;
Was Smith? Was Jones? Were you?

The Spanish war and other events in 1936-37 turned the scale and thereafter I knew where I stood. Every line of serious work that I have written since 1936 has been written, directly or indirectly, against totalitarianism and for democratic socialism, as I understand it. It seems to me nonsense, in a period like our own, to think that one can avoid writing of such subjects. Everyone writes of them in one guise or another. It is simply a question of which side one takes and what approach one follows. And the more one is conscious of one's political bias, the more chance one has of acting politically without sacrificing one's aesthetic and intellectual integrity.

What I have most wanted to do throughout the past ten years is to make political writing into an art. My starting point is always a feeling of partisanship, a sense of injustice. When I sit down to write a book, I do not say to myself, 'I am going to produce a work of art'. I write it because there is some lie that I want to expose, some fact to which I want to draw attention, and my initial concern is to get a hearing. But I could not do the work of writing a book, or even a long magazine article, if it were not also an aesthetic experience. Anyone who cares to examine my work will see that even when it is downright propaganda it contains much that a full-time politician would consider irrelevant. I am not able, and do not want, completely to abandon the world view that I acquired in childhood. So long as I remain alive and well I shall continue to feel strongly about prose style, to love the surface of the earth, and to take a pleasure in solid objects and scraps of useless information. It is no use trying to suppress that side of myself. The job is to reconcile my ingrained likes and dislikes with the essentially public, non-individual activities that this age forces on all of us.

It is not easy. It raises problems of construction and of language, and it raises in a new way the problem of truthfulness. Let me give just one example of the cruder kind of difficulty that arises. My book about the Spanish civil war, *Homage to Catalonia*, is of course a frankly political book, but in the main it is written with a certain detachment and regard for form. I did try very hard in it to tell the whole truth without violating my literary instincts. But among other things it contains a long chapter, full of newspaper quotations and the like, defending the Trotskyists who were accused of plotting with Franco. Clearly such a chapter, which after a year or two would lose its interest for any ordinary reader, must ruin the book. A critic whom I respect read me a lecture about it. 'Why did you put in all that stuff?' he said. 'You've turned what might have been a good book into journalism.' What he said was true, but I could not have done otherwise. I happened to know, what very few people in England had been allowed to know, that innocent men were being falsely accused. If I had not been angry about that I should never have written the book.

In one form or another this problem comes up again. The problem of language is subtler and would take too long to discuss. I will only say that of late years I have tried to write less picturesquely and more exactly. In any case I find that by the time you have perfected any style of writing, you have always outgrown it. *Animal Farm* was the first book in which I tried, with full consciousness of what I was doing, to fuse political purpose and artistic purpose into one whole. I have not written a novel for seven years, but I hope to write another fairly soon. It is bound to be a failure, every book is a failure, but I do know with some clarity what kind of book I want to write.

Looking back through the last page or two, I see that I have made it appear as though my motives in writing were wholly public-spirited. I don't want to leave that as the final impression. All writers are vain, selfish and lazy, and at the very bottom of their motives there lies a mystery. Writing a book is a horrible, exhausting struggle, like a long bout of some painful illness. One would never undertake such a thing if one were not driven on by some demon whom one can neither resist nor understand. For all one knows that demon is simply the same instinct that makes a baby squall for attention. And yet it is also true that one can write nothing readable unless one constantly struggles to efface one's own personality. Good prose is like a windowpane. I cannot say with certainty which of my motives are the strongest, but I know which of them deserve to be followed. And looking back through my work, I see that it is invariably where I lacked a political purpose that I wrote lifeless books and was betrayed into purple passages, sentences without meaning, decorative adjectives and humbug generally.

2

A MODEST PROPOSAL

Jonathan Swift

It is a melancholy object to those, who walk through this great town, or travel in the country, when they see the streets, the roads, and cabbin-doors crowded with beggars of the female sex, followed by three, four, or six children, all in rags, and importuning every passenger for an alms. These mothers, instead of being able to work for their honest livelihood, are forced to employ all their time in stroling to beg sustenance for their helpless infants who, as they grow up, either turn thieves for want of work, or leave their dear native country, to fight for the Pretender in Spain, or sell themselves to the Barbadoes.

I think it is agreed by all parties, that this prodigious number of children in the arms, or on the backs, or at the heels of their mothers, and frequently of their fathers, is in the present deplorable state of the kingdom, a very great additional grievance; and therefore whoever could find out a fair, cheap and easy method of making these children sound and useful members of the commonwealth, would deserve so well of the publick, as to have his statue set up for a preserver of the nation.

But my intention is very far from being confined to provide only for the children of professed beggars: it is of a much greater extent, and shall take in the whole number of infants at a certain age, who are born of parents in effect as little able to support them, as those who demand our charity in the streets.

As to my own part, having turned my thoughts for many years upon this important subject, and maturely weighed the several schemes of our projectors, I have always found them grossly mistaken in their computation. It is true, a child just dropt from its dam, may be supported by her milk, for a solar year, with little other nourishment: at most not above the value of two shillings, which the mother may certainly get, or the value in scraps, by her lawful occupation of begging; and it is exactly at one year old that I propose to provide for them in such a manner, as, instead of being a charge upon their parents, or the parish, or wanting food and raiment for the rest of their lives, they shall, on the contrary, contribute to the feeding, and partly to the clothing of many thousands.

There is likewise another great advantage in my scheme, that it will prevent those voluntary abortions, and that horrid practice of women murdering their bastard children, alas! too frequent among us, sacrificing the poor innocent babes, I doubt, more to avoid the expence than the shame, which would move tears and pity in the most savage and inhuman breast.

The number of souls in this kingdom being usually reckoned one million and a half, of these I calculate there may be about two hundred thousand couple, whose wives are breeders; from which number I subtract thirty thousand couple, who are able to maintain their own children, (although I apprehend there cannot be so many under the present distresses of the kingdom) but this being granted, there will remain a hundred and seventy thousand breeders. I again subtract fifty thousand, for those women who miscarry, or whose children die by accident or disease within the year. There only remain a hundred and twenty thousand children of poor parents annually born. The question therefore is, How this number shall be reared and provided for? which, as I have already said, under the present situation of affairs, is utterly impossible by all the methods hitherto proposed. For we can neither employ them in handicraft or agriculture; they neither build houses, (I mean in the country) nor cultivate land: they can very seldom pick up a livelihood by stealing till they arrive at six years old; except where they are of towardly parts, although I confess they learn the rudiments much earlier; during which time they can however be properly looked upon only as probationers; as I have been informed by a principal gentleman in the county of Cavan, who protested to me, that he never knew above one or two instances under the age of six, even in a part of the kingdom so renowned for the quickest proficiency in that art.

I am assured by our merchants, that a boy or a girl, before twelve years old, is no saleable commodity, and even when they come to this age, they will not yield above three pounds, or three pounds and half a crown at most, on the exchange; which cannot turn to account either to the parents or kingdom, the charge of nutriments and rags having been at least four times that value.

I shall now therefore humbly propose my own thoughts, which I hope will not be liable to the least objection.

I have been assured by a very knowing American of my acquaintance in London, that a young healthy child well nursed, is, at a year old, a most delicious nourishing and wholesome food, whether stewed, roasted, baked or boiled; and I make no doubt that it will equally serve in a fricasee or a ragoust.

I do therefore humbly offer it to publick consideration, that of the hundred and twenty thousand children, already computed, twenty thousand may be reserved for breed, whereof only one fourth part to be males; which is more than we allow to sheep, black cattle or swine, and my reason is, that these children are seldom the fruits of marriage, a circumstance not much regarded by our savages, therefore, one male will be sufficient to serve four females. That the remaining hundred thousand may, at a year old, be offered in sale to the persons of quality and fortune, through the kingdom, always advising the mother to let them suck plentifully in the last month, so as to render them plump, and fat for a good table. A child will make two dishes at an entertainment for friends, and when the family dines alone, the fore or hind quarter will make a reasonable dish, and seasoned with a little pepper or salt, will be very good boiled on the fourth day, especially in winter.

I have reckoned upon a medium, that a child just born will weigh 12 pounds, and in a solar year, if tolerably nursed, encreaseth to 28 pounds.

I grant this food will be somewhat dear, and therefore very proper for landlords, who, as they have already devoured most of the parents, seem to have the best title to the children.

Infant's flesh will be in season throughout the year, but more plentiful in March, and a little before and after; for we are told by a grave author, an eminent French physician, that fish being a prolifick dyet, there are more children born in Roman Catholick countries about nine months after Lent, than at any other season; therefore, reckoning a year after Lent, the markets will be more glutted than usual, because the number of Popish infants, is at least three to one in this kingdom, and therefore it will have one other collateral advantage, by lessening the number of Papists among us.

I have already computed the charge of nursing a beggar's child (in which list I reckon all cottagers, labourers and four-fifths of the farmers) to be about two shillings per annum, rags included; and I believe no gentleman would repine to give ten shillings for the carcass of a good fat child, which, as I have said, will make four dishes of excellent nutritive meat, when he hath only some particular friend, or his own family to dine with him. Thus the squire will learn to be a good landlord, and grow popular among his tenants, the mother will have eight shillings neat profit, and be fit for work till she produces another child.

Those who are more thrifty (as I must confess the times require) may flay the carcass; the skin of which, artificially dressed, will make admirable gloves for ladies, and summer boots for fine gentlemen.

As to our City of Dublin, shambles may be appointed for this purpose, in the most convenient parts of it, and butchers we may be assured will not be wanting; although I rather recommend buying the children alive, and dressing them hot from the knife, as we do roasting pigs.

A very worthy person, a true lover of his country, and whose virtues I highly esteem, was lately pleased in discoursing on this matter, to offer a refinement upon my scheme. He said, that many gentlemen of this kingdom, having of late destroyed their deer, he conceived that the want of venison might be well supplied by the bodies of young lads and maidens, not exceeding fourteen years of age, nor under twelve; so great a number of both sexes in every county being now ready to starve for want of work and service: and these to be disposed of by their parents if alive, or otherwise by their nearest relations. But with due deference to so excellent a friend, and so deserving a patriot, I cannot be altogether in his sentiments; for as to the males, my American acquaintance assured me from frequent experience, that their flesh was generally tough and lean, like that of our schoolboys, by continual exercise, and their taste disagreeable, and to fatten them would not answer the charge. Then as to the females, it would, I think, with humble submission, be a loss to the publick, because they soon would become breeders themselves: and besides, it is not improbable that some scrupulous people might be apt to censure such a practice, (although indeed very unjustly) as a little bordering upon cruelty, which, I confess, hath always been with me the strongest objection against any project, how well soever intended.

But in order to justify my friend, he confessed, that this expedient was put into his head by the famous Psalmanaazor, a native of the island Formosa, who came from thence to London, above twenty years ago, and in conversation told my friend, that in his country, when any young person happened to be put to death, the executioner sold the carcass to persons of quality, as a prime dainty; and that, in his time, the body of a plump girl of fifteen, who was crucified for an attempt to poison the Emperor, was sold to his imperial majesty's prime minister of state, and other great mandarins of the court in joints from the gibbet, at four hundred crowns. Neither indeed can I deny, that if the same use were made of several plump young girls in this town, who without one single groat to their fortunes, cannot stir abroad without a chair, and appear at a playhouse and assemblies in foreign fineries which they never will pay for, the kingdom would not be the worse.

Some persons of a desponding spirit are in great concern about that vast number of poor people, who are aged, diseased or maimed; and I have been desired to employ my thoughts what course may be taken, to ease the nation of so grievous an incumbrance. But I am not in the least pain upon that matter, because it is very well known, that they are every day dying, and rotting, by cold and famine, and filth, and vermin, as fast as can be reasonably expected. And as to the young labourers, they are now in almost as hopeful a condition. They cannot get work, and consequently pine away from want of nourishment, to a degree, that if at any time they are accidentally hired to common labour, they have not strength to perform it, and thus the country and themselves are happily delivered from the evils to come.

I have too long digressed, and therefore shall return to my subject. I think the advantages by the proposal which I have made are obvious and many, as well as of the highest importance.

For first, as I have already observed, it would greatly lessen the number of Papists, with whom we are yearly overrun, being the principal breeders of the nation, as well as our most dangerous enemies, and who stay at home on purpose with a design to deliver the kingdom to the Pretender, hoping to take their advantage by the absence of so many good Protestants, who have chosen rather to leave their country, than stay at home and pay tithes against their conscience to an episcopal curate.

Secondly, The poorer tenants will have something valuable of their own, which by law may be made liable to a distress, and help to pay their landlord's rent, their corn and cattle being already seized, and money a thing unknown.

Thirdly, Whereas the maintainance of a hundred thousand children, from two years old, and upwards, cannot be computed at less than ten shillings a piece per annum, the nation's stock will be thereby encreased fifty thousand pounds per annum, besides the profit of a new dish, introduced to the tables of all gentlemen of fortune in the kingdom, who have any refinement in taste. And the money will circulate among our selves, the goods being entirely of our own growth and manufacture.

Fourthly, The constant breeders, besides the gain of eight shillings sterling per annum by the sale of their children, will be rid of the charge of maintaining them after the first year.

Fifthly, This food would likewise bring great custom to taverns, where the vintners will certainly be so prudent as to procure the best receipts for dressing it to perfection; and consequently have their houses frequented by all the fine gentlemen, who justly value themselves upon their knowledge in good eating; and a skilful cook, who understands how to oblige his guests, will contrive to make it as expensive as they please.

Sixthly, This would be a great inducement to marriage, which all wise nations have either encouraged by rewards, or enforced by laws and penalties. It would encrease the care and tenderness of mothers towards their children, when they were sure of a settlement for life to the poor babes, provided in some sort by the publick, to their annual profit instead of expence. We should soon see an honest emulation among the married women, which of them could bring the fattest child to the market. Men would become as fond of their wives, during the time of their pregnancy, as they are now of their mares in foal, their cows in calf or sows when they are ready to farrow; nor offer to beat or kick them (as is too frequent a practice) for fear of a miscarriage.

Many other advantages might be enumerated. For instance, the addition of some thousand carcasses in our exportation of barrel'd beef: the propagation of swine's flesh, and improvement in the art of making good bacon, so much wanted among us by the great destruction of pigs, too frequent at our tables; which are no way comparable in taste or magnificence to a well grown, fat yearling child, which roasted whole will make a considerable figure at a Lord Mayor's feast, or any other publick entertainment. But this, and many others, I omit, being studious of brevity.

Supposing that one thousand families in this city, would be constant customers for infants flesh, besides others who might have it at merry meetings, particularly at weddings and christenings, I compute that Dublin would take off annually about twenty thousand carcasses; and the rest of the kingdom (where probably they will be sold somewhat cheaper) the remaining eighty thousand.

I can think of no one objection, that will possibly be raised against this proposal, unless it should be urged, that the number of people will be thereby much lessened in the kingdom. This I freely own, and was indeed one principal design in offering it to the world.

I desire the reader will observe, that I calculate my remedy for this one individual Kingdom of Ireland, and for no other that ever was, is, or, I think, ever can be upon Earth. Therefore let no man talk to me of other expedients: Of taxing our absentees at five shillings a pound: Of using neither clothes, nor houshold furniture, except what is of our own growth and manufacture: Of utterly rejecting the materials and instruments that promote foreign luxury: Of curing the expensiveness of pride, vanity, idleness and gaming in our women: Of introducing a vein of parsimony, prudence and temperance: Of learning to love our country, wherein we differ even from Laplanders, and the inhabitants of Topinamboo: Of quitting our animosities and factions, nor acting any longer like the Jews, who were murdering one another at the very moment their city was taken: Of being a little cautious not to sell our country and consciences for nothing: Of teaching landlords to have at least one degree of mercy towards their tenants. Lastly, of putting a spirit of honesty, industry, and skill into our shopkeepers, who, if a resolution could now be taken to buy only our native goods, would immediately unite to cheat and exact upon us in the price, the measure, and the goodness, nor could ever yet be brought to make one fair proposal of just dealing, though often and earnestly invited to it.

Therefore I repeat, let no man talk to me of these and the like expedients, till he hath at least some glympse of hope, that there will ever be some hearty and sincere attempt to put them into practice.

But, as to myself, having been wearied out for many years with offering vain, idle, visionary thoughts, and at length utterly despairing of success, I fortunately fell upon this proposal, which, as it is wholly new, so it hath something solid and real, of no expence and little trouble, full in our own power, and whereby we can incur no danger in disobliging England. For this kind of commodity will not bear exportation, and flesh being of too tender a consistence, to admit a long continuance in salt, although perhaps I could name a country, which would be glad to eat up our whole nation without it.

After all, I am not so violently bent upon my own opinion, as to reject any offer, proposed by wise men, which shall be found equally innocent, cheap, easy, and effectual. But before something of that kind shall be advanced in contradiction to my scheme, and offering a better, I desire the author or authors will be pleased maturely to consider two points. First, As things now stand, how they will be able to find food and raiment for a hundred thousand useless mouths and backs. And secondly, There being a round million of creatures in humane figure throughout this kingdom, whose whole subsistence put into a common stock, would leave them in debt two million of pounds sterling, adding those who are beggars by profession, to the bulk of farmers, cottagers and labourers, with their wives and children, who are beggars in effect; I desire those politicians who dislike my overture, and may perhaps be so bold to attempt an answer, that they will first ask the parents of these mortals, whether they would not at this day think it a great happiness to have been sold for food at a year old, in the manner I prescribe, and thereby have avoided such a perpetual scene of misfortunes, as they have since gone through, by the oppression of landlords, the impossibility of paying rent without money or trade, the want of common sustenance, with neither house nor clothes to cover them from the inclemencies of the weather, and the most inevitable prospect of intailing the like, or greater miseries, upon their breed for ever.

I profess in the sincerity of my heart, that I have not the least personal interest in endeavouring to promote this necessary work, having no other motive than the publick good of my country, by advancing our trade, providing for infants, relieving the poor and giving some pleasure to the rich. I have no children, by which I can propose to get a single penny; the youngest being nine years old, and my wife past child-bearing.

3

DEATH OF THE MOTH

Virginia Woolf

Moths that fly by day are not properly to be called moths; they do not excite that pleasant sense of dark autumn nights and ivy-blossom which the commonest yellow-underwing asleep in the shadow of the curtain never fails to rouse in us. They are hybrid creatures, neither gay like butterflies nor sombre like their own species. Nevertheless the present specimen, with his narrow hay-coloured wings, fringed with a tassel of the same colour, seemed to be content with life. It was a pleasant morning, mid-September, mild, benignant, yet with a keener breath than that of the summer months. The plough was already scoring the field opposite the window, and where the share had been, the earth was pressed flat and gleamed with moisture. Such vigour came rolling in from the fields and the down beyond that it was difficult to keep the eyes strictly turned upon the book. The rooks too were keeping one of their annual festivities; soaring round the tree tops until it looked as if a vast net with thousands of black knots in it had been cast up into the air; which, after a few moments sank slowly down upon the trees until every twig seemed to have a knot at the end of it. Then, suddenly, the net would be thrown into the air again in a wider circle this time, with the utmost clamour and vociferation, as though to be thrown into the air and settle slowly down upon the tree tops were a tremendously exciting experience.

The same energy which inspired the rooks, the ploughmen, the horses and even, it seemed, the lean bare-backed downs, sent the moth fluttering from side to side of his square of the window-pane.

One could not help watching him. One was, indeed, conscious of a queer feeling of pity for him. The possibilities of pleasure seemed that morning so enormous and so various that to have only a moth's part in life, and a day moth's at that, appeared a hard fate, and his zest in enjoying his meagre opportunities to the full, pathetic. He flew vigorously to one corner of his compartment, and, after waiting there a second, flew across to the other. What remained for him but to fly to a third corner and then to a fourth? That was all he could do, in spite of the size of the downs, the width of the sky, the far-off smoke of houses, and the romantic voice, now and then, of a steamer out at sea. What he could do he did. Watching him, it seemed as if a fibre, very thin but pure, of the enormous energy of the world had been thrust into his frail and diminutive body. As often as he crossed the pane, I could fancy that a thread of vital light became visible. He was little or nothing but life.

Yet, because he was so small, and so simple a form of the energy that was rolling in at the open window and driving its way through so many narrow and intricate corridors in my own brain and in those of other human beings, there was something marvellous as well as pathetic about him. It was as if someone had taken a tiny bead of pure life and decking it as lightly as possible with down and feathers, had set it dancing and zig-zagging to show us the true nature of life. Thus displayed one could not get over the strangeness of it. One is apt to forget all about life, seeing it humped and bossed and garnished and cumbered so that it has to move with the greatest circumspection and dignity. Again, the thought of all that life might have been had he been born in any other shape caused one to view his simple activities with a kind of pity.

After a time, tired by his dancing apparently, he settled on the window ledge in the sun, and, the queer spectacle being at an end, I forgot about him. Then, looking up, my eye was caught by him. He was trying to resume his dancing, but seemed either so stiff or so awkward that he could only flutter to the bottom of the window-pane; and when he tried to fly across it he failed. Being intent on other matters I watched these futile attempts for a time without thinking, unconsciously waiting for him to resume his flight, as one waits for a machine, that has stopped momentarily, to start again without considering the reason of its failure. After perhaps a seventh attempt he slipped from the wooden ledge and fell, fluttering his wings, on to his back on the window sill. The helplessness of his attitude roused me. It flashed upon me that he was in difficulties; he could no longer raise himself; his legs struggled vainly. But, as I stretched out a pencil, meaning to help him to right himself, it came over me that the failure and awkwardness were the approach of death. I laid the pencil down again.

The legs agitated themselves once more. I looked as if for the enemy against which he struggled. I looked out of doors. What had happened there? Presumably it was midday, and work in the fields had stopped. Stillness and quiet had replaced the previous animation. The birds had taken themselves off to feed in the brooks. The horses stood still. Yet the power was there all the same, massed outside indifferent, impersonal, not attending to anything in particular. Somehow it was opposed to the little hay-coloured moth. It was useless to try to do anything. One could only watch the extraordinary efforts made by those tiny legs against an oncoming doom which could, had it chosen, have submerged an entire city, not merely a city, but masses of human beings; nothing, I knew, had any chance against death. Nevertheless after a pause of exhaustion the legs fluttered again. It was superb this last protest, and so frantic that he succeeded at last in righting himself. One's sympathies, of course, were all on the side of life. Also, when there was nobody to care or to know, this gigantic effort on the part of an insignificant little moth, against a power of such magnitude, to retain what no one else valued or desired to keep, moved one strangely. Again, somehow, one saw life, a pure bead. I lifted the pencil again, useless though I knew it to be. But even as I did so, the unmistakable tokens of death showed themselves. The body relaxed, and instantly grew stiff. The struggle was over. The insignificant little creature now knew death. As I looked at the dead moth, this minute wayside triumph of so great a force over so mean an antagonist filled me with wonder. Just as life had been strange a few minutes before, so death was now as strange. The moth having righted himself now lay most decently and uncomplainingly composed. O yes, he seemed to say, death is stronger than I am.

4

SHOOTING AN ELEPHANT

George Orwell

In Moulmein, in Lower Burma, I was hated by large numbers of people—the only time in my life that I have been important enough for this to happen to me. I was sub-divisional police officer of the town, and in an aimless, petty kind of way anti-European feeling was very bitter. No one had the guts to raise a riot, but if a European woman went through the bazaars alone somebody would probably spit betel juice over her dress. As a police officer I was an obvious target and was baited whenever it seemed safe to do so. When a nimble Burman tripped me up on the football field and the referee (another Burman) looked the other way, the crowd yelled with hideous laughter. This happened more than once. In the end the sneering yellow faces of young men that met me everywhere, the insults hooted after me when I was at a safe distance, got badly on my nerves. The young Buddhist priests were the worst of all. There were several thousands of them in the town and none of them seemed to have anything to do except stand on street corners and jeer at Europeans.

All this was perplexing and upsetting. For at that time I had already made up my mind that imperialism was an evil thing and the sooner I chucked up my job and got out of it the better. Theoretically—and secretly, of course—I was all for the Burmese and all against their oppressors, the British. As for the job I was doing, I hated it more bitterly than I can perhaps make clear. In a job like that you see the dirty work of Empire at close quarters. The wretched prisoners huddling in the stinking cages of the lock-ups, the grey, cowed faces of the long-term convicts, the scarred buttocks of the men who had been flogged with bamboos—all these oppressed me with an intolerable sense of guilt. But I could get nothing into perspective. I was young and ill-educated and I had had to think out my problems in the utter silence that is imposed on every Englishman in the East. I did not even know that the British Empire is dying, still less did I know that it is a great deal better than the younger empires that are going to supplant it. All I knew was that I was stuck between my hatred of the empire I served and my rage against the evil-spirited little beasts who tried to make my job impossible. With one part of my mind I thought of the British Raj as an unbreakable tyranny, as something clamped down, in saecula saeculorum, upon the will of prostrate peoples; with another part I thought that the greatest joy in the world would be to drive a bayonet into a Buddhist priest's guts. Feelings like these are the normal by-products of imperialism; ask any Anglo-Indian official, if you can catch him off duty.

One day something happened which in a roundabout way was enlightening. It was a tiny incident in itself, but it gave me a better glimpse than I had had before of the real nature of imperialism—the real motives for which despotic governments act. Early one morning the sub-inspector at a police station the other end of the town rang me up on the phone and said that an elephant was ravaging the bazaar. Would I please come and do something about it? I did not know what I could do, but I wanted to see what was happening and I got on to a pony and started out. I took my rifle, an old .44 Winchester and much too small to kill an elephant, but I thought the noise might be useful in terrorem. Various Burmans stopped me on the way and told me about the elephant's doings. It was not, of course, a wild elephant, but a tame one which had gone 'must'. It had been chained up, as tame elephants always are when their attack of 'must' is due, but on the previous night it had broken its chain and escaped. Its mahout, the only person who could manage it when it was in that state, had set out in pursuit, but had taken the wrong direction and was now twelve hours' journey away, and in the morning the elephant had suddenly reappeared in the town. The Burmese population had no weapons and were quite helpless against it. It had already destroyed somebody's bamboo hut, killed a cow and raided some fruit-stalls and devoured the stock; also it had met the municipal rubbish van and, when the driver jumped out and took to his heels, had turned the van over and inflicted violences upon it.

The Burmese sub-inspector and some Indian constables were waiting for me in the quarter where the elephant had been seen. It was a very poor quarter, a labyrinth of squalid bamboo huts, thatched with palmleaf, winding all over a steep hillside. I remember that it was a cloudy, stuffy morning at the beginning of the rains. We began questioning the people as to where the elephant had gone and, as usual, failed to get any definite information. That is invariably the case in the East; a story always sounds clear enough at a distance, but the nearer you get to the scene of events the vaguer it becomes. Some of the people said that the elephant had gone in one direction, some said that he had gone in another, some professed not even to have heard of any elephant. I had almost made up my mind that the whole story was a pack of lies, when we heard yells a little distance away. There was a loud, scandalized cry of 'Go away, child! Go away this instant!' and an old woman with a switch in her hand came round the corner of a hut, violently shooing away a crowd of naked children. Some more women followed, clicking their tongues and exclaiming; evidently there was something that the children ought not to have seen. I rounded the hut and saw a man's dead body sprawling in the mud. He was an Indian, a black Dravidian coolie, almost naked, and he could not have been dead many minutes. The people said that the elephant had come suddenly upon him round the corner of the hut, caught him with its trunk, put its foot on his back and ground him into the earth. This was the rainy season and the ground was soft, and his face had scored a trench a foot deep and a couple of yards long. He was lying on his belly with arms crucified and head sharply twisted to one side. His face was coated with mud, the eyes wide open, the teeth bared and grinning with an expression of unendurable agony. (Never tell me, by the way, that the dead look peaceful. Most of the corpses I have seen looked devilish.) The friction of the great beast's foot had stripped the skin from his back as neatly as one skins a rabbit. As soon as I saw the dead man I sent an orderly to a friend's house nearby to borrow an elephant rifle. I had already sent back the pony, not wanting it to go mad with fright and throw me if it smelt the elephant.

The orderly came back in a few minutes with a rifle and five cartridges, and meanwhile some Burmans had arrived and told us that the elephant was in the paddy fields below, only a few hundred yards away. As I started forward practically the whole population of the quarter flocked out of the houses and followed me. They had seen the rifle and were all shouting excitedly that I was going to shoot the elephant. They had not shown much interest in the elephant when he was merely ravaging their homes, but it was different now that he was going to be shot. It was a bit of fun to them, as it would be to an English crowd; besides they wanted the meat. It made me vaguely uneasy. I had no intention of shooting the elephant—I had merely sent for the rifle to defend myself if necessary—and it is always unnerving to have a crowd following you. I marched down the hill, looking and feeling a fool, with the rifle over my shoulder and an ever-growing army of people jostling at my heels. At the bottom, when you got away from the huts, there was a metalled road and beyond that a miry waste of paddy fields a thousand yards across, not yet ploughed but soggy from the first rains and dotted with coarse grass. The elephant was standing eight yards from the road, his left side towards us. He took not the slightest notice of the crowd's approach. He was tearing up bunches of grass, beating them against his knees to clean them and stuffing them into his mouth.

I had halted on the road. As soon as I saw the elephant I knew with perfect certainty that I ought not to shoot him. It is a serious matter to shoot a working elephant—it is comparable to destroying a huge and costly piece of machinery—and obviously one ought not to do it if it can possibly be avoided. And at that distance, peacefully eating, the elephant looked no more dangerous than a cow. I thought then and I think now that his attack of 'must' was already passing off; in which case he would merely wander harmlessly about until the mahout came back and caught him. Moreover, I did not in the least want to shoot him. I decided that I would watch him for a little while to make sure that he did not turn savage again, and then go home.

But at that moment I glanced round at the crowd that had followed me. It was an immense crowd, two thousand at the least and growing every minute. It blocked the road for a long distance on either side. I looked at the sea of yellow faces above the garish clothes—faces all happy and excited over this bit of fun, all certain that the elephant was going to be shot. They were watching me as they would watch a conjurer about to perform a trick. They did not like me, but with the magical rifle in my hands I was momentarily worth watching. And suddenly I realized that I should have to shoot the elephant after all. The people expected it of me and I had got to do it; I could feel their two thousand wills pressing me forward, irresistibly. And it was at this moment, as I stood there with the rifle in my hands, that I first grasped the hollowness, the futility of the white man's dominion in the East. Here was I, the white man with his gun, standing in front of the unarmed native crowd—seemingly the leading actor of the piece; but in reality I was only an absurd puppet pushed to and fro by the will of those yellow faces behind. I perceived in this moment that when the white man turns tyrant it is his own freedom that he destroys. He becomes a sort of hollow, posing dummy, the conventionalized figure of a sahib. For it is the condition of his rule that he shall spend his life in trying to impress the 'natives', and so in every crisis he has got to do what the 'natives' expect of him. He wears a mask, and his face grows to fit it. I had got to shoot the elephant. I had committed myself to doing it when I sent for the rifle. A sahib has got to act like a sahib; he has got to appear resolute, to know his own mind and do definite things. To come all that way, rifle in hand, with two thousand people marching at my heels, and then to trail feebly away, having done nothing—no, that was impossible. The crowd would laugh at me. And my whole life, every white man's life in the East, was one long struggle not to be laughed at.

But I did not want to shoot the elephant. I watched him beating his bunch of grass against his knees, with that preoccupied grandmotherly air that elephants have. It seemed to me that it would be murder to shoot him. At that age I was not squeamish about killing animals, but I had never shot an elephant and never wanted to. (Somehow it always seems worse to kill a large animal.) Besides, there was the beast's owner to be considered. Alive, the elephant was worth at least a hundred pounds; dead, he would only be worth the value of his tusks, five pounds, possibly. But I had got to act quickly. I turned to some experienced-looking Burmans who had been there when we arrived, and asked them how the elephant had been behaving. They all said the same thing: he took no notice of you if you left him alone, but he might charge if you went too close to him.

It was perfectly clear to me what I ought to do. I ought to walk up to within, say, twenty-five yards of the elephant and test his behavior. If he charged, I could shoot; if he took no notice of me, it would be safe to leave him until the mahout came back. But also I knew that I was going to do no such thing. I was a poor shot with a rifle and the ground was soft mud into which one would sink at every step. If the elephant charged and I missed him, I should have about as much chance as a toad under a steam-roller. But even then I was not thinking particularly of my own skin, only of the watchful yellow faces behind. For at that moment, with the crowd watching me, I was not afraid in the ordinary sense, as I would have been if I had been alone. A white man mustn't be frightened in front of 'natives'; and so, in general, he isn't frightened. The sole thought in my mind was that if anything went wrong those two thousand Burmans would see me pursued, caught, trampled on and reduced to a grinning corpse like that Indian up the hill. And if that happened it was quite probable that some of them would laugh. That would never do.

There was only one alternative. I shoved the cartridges into the magazine and lay down on the road to get a better aim. The crowd grew very still, and a deep, low, happy sigh, as of people who see the theatre curtain go up at last, breathed from innumerable throats. They were going to have their bit of fun after all. The rifle was a beautiful German thing with cross-hair sights. I did not then know that in shooting an elephant one would shoot to cut an imaginary bar running from ear-hole to ear-hole. I ought, therefore, as the elephant was sideways on, to have aimed straight at his ear-hole, actually I aimed several inches in front of this, thinking the brain would be further forward.

When I pulled the trigger I did not hear the bang or feel the kick—one never does when a shot goes home—but I heard the devilish roar of glee that went up from the crowd. In that instant, in too short a time, one would have thought, even for the bullet to get there, a mysterious, terrible change had come over the elephant. He neither stirred nor fell, but every line of his body had altered. He looked suddenly stricken, shrunken, immensely old, as though the frightful impact of the bullet had paralysed him without knocking him down. At last, after what seemed a long time—it might have been five seconds, I dare say—he sagged flabbily to his knees. His mouth slobbered. An enormous senility seemed to have settled upon him. One could have imagined him thousands of years old. I fired again into the same spot. At the second shot he did not collapse but climbed with desperate slowness to his feet and stood weakly upright, with legs sagging and head drooping. I fired a third time. That was the shot that did for him. You could see the agony of it jolt his whole body and knock the last remnant of strength from his legs. But in falling he seemed for a moment to rise, for as his hind legs collapsed beneath him he seemed to tower upward like a huge rock toppling, his trunk reaching skyward like a tree. He trumpeted, for the first and only time. And then down he came, his belly towards me, with a crash that seemed to shake the ground even where I lay.

I got up. The Burmans were already racing past me across the mud. It was obvious that the elephant would never rise again, but he was not dead. He was breathing very rhythmically with long rattling gasps, his great mound of a side painfully rising and falling. His mouth was wide open—I could see far down into caverns of pale pink throat. I waited a long time for him to die, but his breathing did not weaken. Finally I fired my two remaining shots into the spot where I thought his heart must be. The thick blood welled out of him like red velvet, but still he did not die. His body did not even jerk when the shots hit him, the tortured breathing continued without a pause. He was dying, very slowly and in great agony, but in some world remote from me where not even a bullet could damage him further. I felt that I had got to put an end to that dreadful noise. It seemed dreadful to see the great beast Lying there, powerless to move and yet powerless to die, and not even to be able to finish him. I sent back for my small rifle and poured shot after shot into his heart and down his throat. They seemed to make no impression. The tortured gasps continued as steadily as the ticking of a clock.

In the end I could not stand it any longer and went away. I heard later that it took him half an hour to die. Burmans were bringing dash and baskets even before I left, and I was told they had stripped his body almost to the bones by the afternoon.

Afterwards, of course, there were endless discussions about the shooting of the elephant. The owner was furious, but he was only an Indian and could do nothing. Besides, legally I had done the right thing, for a mad elephant has to be killed, like a mad dog, if its owner fails to control it. Among the Europeans opinion was divided. The older men said I was right, the younger men said it was a damn shame to shoot an elephant for killing a coolie, because an elephant was worth more than any damn Coringhee coolie. And afterwards I was very glad that the coolie had been killed; it put me legally in the right and it gave me a sufficient pretext for shooting the elephant. I often wondered whether any of the others grasped that I had done it solely to avoid looking a fool.

5

SELF-RELIANCE

Ralph Waldo Emerson

'Ne te quæsiveris extra.'

'Man is his own star; and the soul that can
Render an honest and a perfect man,
Commands all light, all influence, all fate;
Nothing to him falls early or too late.
Our acts our angels are, or good or ill,
Our fatal shadows that walk by us still.'
—*Epilogue to Beaumont and Fletcher's Honest Man's Fortune*

Cast the bantling on the rocks,
Suckle him with the she-wolf's teat;
Wintered with the hawk and fox,
Power and speed be hands and feet.

I read the other day some verses written by an eminent painter which were original and not conventional. The soul always hears an admonition in such lines, let the subject be what it may. The sentiment they instill is of more value than any thought they may contain. To believe your own thought, to believe that what is true for you in your private heart is true for all men,—that is genius. Speak your latent conviction, and it shall be the universal sense; for the inmost in due time becomes the outmost,—and our first thought is rendered back to us by the trumpets of the Last Judgment. Familiar as the voice of the mind is to each, the highest merit we ascribe to Moses, Plato and

Milton is, that they set at naught books and traditions, and spoke not what men, but what they thought. A man should learn to detect and watch that gleam of light which flashes across his mind from within, more than the luster of the firmament of bards and sages. Yet he dismisses without notice his thought, because it is his. In every work of genius we recognize our own rejected thoughts: they come back to us with a certain alienated majesty. Great works of art have no more affecting lesson for us than this. They teach us to abide by our spontaneous impression with good-humored inflexibility then most when the whole cry of voices is on the other side. Else, to-morrow a stranger will say with masterly good sense precisely what we have thought and felt all the time, and we shall be forced to take with shame our own opinion from another.

There is a time in every man's education when he arrives at the conviction that envy is ignorance; that imitation is suicide; that he must take himself for better, for worse, as his portion; that though the wide universe is full of good, no kernel of nourishing corn can come to him but through his toil bestowed on that plot of ground which is given to him to till. The power which resides in him is new in nature, and none but he knows what that is which he can do, nor does he know until he has tried. Not for nothing one face, one character, one fact, makes much impression on him, and another none. This sculpture in the memory is not without preëstablished harmony. The eye was placed where one ray should fall, that it might testify of that particular ray. We but half express ourselves, and are ashamed of that divine idea which each of us represents. It may be safely trusted as proportionate and of good issues, so it be faithfully imparted, but God will not have his work made manifest by cowards. A man is relieved and gay when he has put his heart into his work and done his best; but what he has said or done otherwise shall give him no peace. It is a deliverance which does not deliver. In the attempt his genius deserts him; no muse befriends; no invention, no hope.

Trust thyself: every heart vibrates to that iron string. Accept the place the divine providence has found for you, the society of your contemporaries, the connection of events. Great men have always done so, and confided themselves childlike to the genius of their age, betraying their perception that the absolutely trustworthy was seated at their heart, working through their hands, predominating in all their being. And we are now men, and must accept in the highest mind the same transcendent destiny; and not minors and invalids in a protected corner, not cowards fleeing before a revolution, but guides, redeemers and benefactors, obeying the Almighty effort, and advancing on Chaos and the Dark.

What pretty oracles nature yields us on this text, in the face and behavior of children, babes, and even brutes! That divided and rebel mind, that distrust of a sentiment because our arithmetic has computed the strength and means opposed to our purpose, these have not. Their mind being whole, their eye is as yet unconquered, and when we look in their faces we are disconcerted. Infancy conforms to nobody: all conform to it, so that one babe commonly makes four or five out of the adults who prattle and play to it. So God has armed youth and puberty and manhood no less with its own piquancy and charm, and made it enviable and gracious and its claims not to be put by, if it will stand by itself. Do not think the youth has no force, because he cannot speak to you and me. Hark! in the next room his voice is sufficiently clear and emphatic. It seems he knows how to speak to his contemporaries. Bashful or bold, then, he will know how to make us seniors very unnecessary.

The nonchalance of boys who are sure of a dinner, and would disdain as much as a lord to do or say aught to conciliate one, is the healthy attitude of human nature. A boy is in the parlor what the pit is in the playhouse; independent, irresponsible, looking out from his corner on such people and facts as pass by, he tries and sentences them on their merits, in the swift, summary way of boys, as good, bad, interesting, silly, eloquent, troublesome. He cumbers himself never about consequences about interests; he gives an independent, genuine verdict. You must court him: he does not court you. But the man is, as it were, clapped into jail by his consciousness. As soon as he has once acted or spoken with éclat he is a committed person, watched by the sympathy or the hatred of hundreds, whose affections must now enter into his account. There is no Lethe for this. Ah, that he could pass again into his neutrality! Who can thus avoid all pledges, and having observed, observe again from the same unaffected, unbiased, unbribable, unaffrighted innocence, must always be formidable. He would utter opinions on all passing affairs, which being seen to be not private, but necessary, would sink like darts into the ear of men, and put them in fear.

These are the voices which we hear in solitude, but they grow faint and inaudible as we enter into the world. Society everywhere is in conspiracy against the manhood of everyone of its members. Society is a joint-stock company, in which the members agree, for the better securing of his bread to each shareholder, to surrender the liberty and culture of the eater. The virtue in most request is conformity. Self-reliance is its aversion. It loves not realities and creators, but names and customs.

Whoso would be a man must be a nonconformist. He who would gather immortal palms must not be hindered by the name of goodness, but must explore if it be goodness. Nothing is at last sacred but the integrity of your own mind. Absolve you to yourself, and you shall have the suffrage of the world. I remember an answer which when quite young I was prompted to make to a valued adviser, who was wont to importune me with the dear old doctrines of the church. On my saying, What have I to do with the sacredness of traditions, if I live wholly from within? my friend suggested: 'But these impulses may be from below, not from above.' I replied: 'They do not seem to me to be such; but if I am the Devil's child, I will live then from the Devil.' No law can be sacred to me but that of my nature. Good and bad are but names very readily transferable to that or this; the only right is what is after my constitution, the only wrong what is against it. A man is to carry himself in the presence of all opposition, as if everything were titular and ephemeral but he. I am ashamed to think how easily we capitulate to badges and names, to large societies and dead institutions. Every decent and well-spoken individual affects and sways me more than is right. I ought to go upright and vital, and speak the rude truth in all ways. If malice and vanity wear the coat of philanthropy, shall that pass? If an angry bigot assumes this bountiful cause of Abolition, and comes to me with his last news from Barbadoes, why should I not say to him: 'Go love thy infant; love thy wood-chopper: be good-natured and modest: have that grace; and never varnish your hard, uncharitable ambition with this incredible tenderness for black folk a thousand miles off. Thy love afar is spite at home.' Rough and graceless would be such greeting, but truth is handsomer than the affectation of love. Your goodness must have some edge to it,—else it is none. The doctrine of hatred must be preached as the counteraction of the doctrine of love when that pules and whines. I shun father and mother and wife and brother, when my genius calls me. I would write on the lintels of the door-post, *Whim*. I hope it is somewhat better than whim at last, but we cannot spend the day in explanation. Expect me not to show cause why I seek or why I exclude company. Then, again, do not tell me, as a good man did to-day, of my obligation to put all poor men in good situations. Are they my poor? I tell thee, thou foolish philanthropist, that I grudge the dollar, the dime, the cent, I give to such men as do not belong to me and to whom I do not belong. There is a class of persons to whom by all spiritual affinity I am bought and sold; for them I will go to prison, if need be; but your miscellaneous popular charities; the education at college of fools; the building of meeting-houses to the vain end to which many now stand; alms to sots; and the thousand-fold Relief Societies;—though I confess with shame I sometimes succumb and give the dollar, it is a wicked dollar which by and by I shall have the manhood to withhold.

Virtues are, in the popular estimate, rather the exception than the rule. There is the man and his virtues. Men do what is called a good action, as some piece of courage or charity, much as they would pay a fine in expiation of daily non-appearance on parade. Their works are done as an apology or extenuation of their living in the world,—as invalids and the insane pay a high board. Their virtues are penances. I do not wish to expiate, but to live. My life is for itself and not for a spectacle. I much prefer that it should be of a lower strain, so it be genuine and equal, than that it should be glittering and unsteady. I wish it to be sound and sweet, and not to need diet and bleeding. I ask primary evidence that you are a man, and refuse this appeal from the man to his actions. I know that for myself it makes no difference whether I do or forbear those actions which are reckoned excellent. I cannot consent to pay for a privilege where I have intrinsic right. Few and mean as my gifts may be, I actually am, and do not need for my own assurance or the assurance of my fellows any secondary testimony.

What I must do is all that concerns me, not what the people think. This rule, equally arduous in actual and in intellectual life, may serve for the whole distinction between greatness and meanness. It is the harder, because you will always find those who think they know what is your duty better than you know it. It is easy in the world to live after the world's opinion; it is easy in solitude to live after our own; but the great man is he who in the midst of the crowd keeps with perfect sweetness the independence of solitude.

The objection to conforming to usages that have become dead to you is, that it scatters your force. It loses your time and blurs the impression of your character. If you maintain a dead church, contribute to a dead Bible-society, vote with a great party either for the government or against it, spread your table like base housekeepers,—under all these screens I have difficulty to detect the precise man you are. And, of course, so much force is withdrawn from your proper life. But do your work, and I shall know you. Do your work, and you shall reinforce yourself. A man must consider what a blindman's-buff is this game of conformity. If I know your sect, I anticipate your argument. I hear a preacher announce for his text and topic the expediency of one of the institutions of his church. Do I not know beforehand that not possibly can he say a new and spontaneous word? Do I not know that, with all this ostentation of examining the grounds of the institution, he will do no such thing? Do I not know that he is pledged to himself not to look but at one side,—the permitted side, not as a man, but as a parish minister? He is a retained attorney, and these airs of the bench are the emptiest affectation. Well, most men have bound their eyes with one or another handkerchief, and attached themselves to some one of these communities of opinion. This conformity makes them not false in a few particulars, authors of a few lies, but false in all particulars. Their every truth is not quite true. Their two is not the real two, their four not the real four; so that every word they say chagrins us, and we know not where to begin to set them right. Meantime nature is not slow to equip us in the prison-uniform of the party to which we adhere. We come to wear one cut of face and figure, and acquire by degrees the gentlest asinine expression. There is a mortifying experience in particular which does not fail to wreak itself also in the general history; I mean 'the foolish face of praise,' the forced smile which we put on in company where we do not feel at ease in answer to conversation which does not interest us. The muscles, not spontaneously moved, but moved by a low usurping willfulness, grow tight about the outline of the face with the most disagreeable sensation.

For nonconformity the world whips you with its displeasure. And therefore a man must know how to estimate a sour face. The bystanders look askance on him in the public street or in the friend's parlor. If this aversation had its origin in contempt and resistance like his own, he might well go home with a sad countenance; but the sour faces of the multitude, like their sweet faces, have no deep cause, but are put on and off as the wind blows and a newspaper directs. Yet is the discontent of the multitude more formidable than that of the senate and the college. It is easy enough for a firm man who knows the world to brook the rage of the cultivated classes. Their rage is decorous and prudent, for they are timid as being very vulnerable themselves. But when to their feminine rage the indignation of the people is added, when the ignorant and the poor are aroused, when the unintelligent brute force that lies at the bottom of society is made to growl and mow, it needs the habit of magnanimity and religion to treat it godlike as a trifle of no concernment.

The other terror that scares us from self-trust is our consistency; a reverence for our past act or word, because the eyes of others have no other data for computing our orbit than our past acts, and we are loth to disappoint them.

But why should you keep your head over your shoulder? Why

drag about this corpse of your memory, lest you contradict somewhat you have stated in this or that public place? Suppose you should contradict yourself; what then? It seems to be a rule of wisdom never to rely on your memory alone, scarcely even in acts of pure memory, but to bring the past for judgment into the thousand-eyed present, and live ever in a new day. In your metaphysics you have denied personality to the Deity; yet when the devout motions of the soul come, yield to them heart and life, though they should clothe God with shape and color. Leave your theory, as Joseph his coat in the hand of the harlot, and flee.

A foolish consistency is the hobgoblin of little minds, adored by little statesmen and philosophers and divines. With consistency a great soul has simply nothing to do. He may as well concern himself with the shadow on the wall. Speak what you think now in hard words, and to-morrow speak what to-morrow thinks in hard words again, though it contradict everything you said to-day.—'Ah, so you shall be sure to be misunderstood.'—Is it so bad, then, to be misunderstood? Pythagoras was misunderstood, and Socrates, and Jesus, and Luther, and Copernicus, and Galileo, and Newton, and every pure and wise spirit that ever took flesh. To be great is to be misunderstood.

I suppose no man can violate his nature. All the sallies of his will are rounded in by the law of his being, as the inequalities of Andes and Himmaleh are insignificant in the curve of the sphere. Nor does it matter how you gauge and try him. A character is like an acrostic or Alexandrian stanza;—read it forward, backward or across, it still spells the same thing. In this pleasing, contrite wood-life which God allows me, let me record day by day my honest thought without prospect or retrospect, and, I cannot doubt, it will be found symmetrical, though I mean it not, and see it not. My book should smell of pines and resound with the hum of insects. The swallow over my window should interweave that thread or straw he carries in his bill into my web also. We pass for what we are. Character teaches above our wills. Men imagine that they communicate their virtue or vice only by overt actions, and do not see that virtue or vice emit a breath every moment.

There will be an agreement in whatever variety of actions, so they be each honest and natural in their hour. For of one will, the actions will be harmonious, however unlike they seem. These varieties are lost sight of at a little distance, at a little height of thought. One tendency unites them all. The voyage of the best ship is a zigzag line of a hundred tacks. See the line from a sufficient distance, and it straightens itself to the average tendency. Your genuine action will explain itself, and will explain your other genuine actions. Your conformity explains nothing. Act singly, and what you have already done singly will justify you now. Greatness appeals to the future. If I can be firm enough to-day to do right, and scorn eyes, I must have done so much right before as to defend me now. Be it how it will, do right now. Always scorn appearances, and you always may. The force of character is cumulative. All the foregone days of virtue work their health into this. What makes the majesty of the heroes of the senate and the field, which so fills the imagination? The consciousness of a train of great days and victories behind. They shed an united light on the advancing actor. He is attended as by a visible escort of angels. That is it which throws thunder into Chatham's voice, and dignity into Washington's port, and America into Adams's eye. Honor is venerable to us because it is no ephemeris. It is always ancient virtue. We worship it to-day because it is not of to-day. We love it and pay it homage, because it is not a trap for our love and homage, but is self-dependent, self-derived and therefore of an old immaculate pedigree, even if shown in a young person.

I hope in these days we have heard the last of conformity and consistency. Let the words be gazetted and ridiculous henceforward. Instead of the gong for dinner, let us hear a whistle from the Spartan fife. Let us never bow and apologize more. A great man is coming to eat at my house. I do not wish to please him; I wish that he should wish to please me. I will stand here for humanity, and though I would make it kind, I would make it true. Let us affront and reprimand the smooth mediocrity and squalid contentment of the times, and hurl in the face of custom, and trade, and office, the fact which is the upshot of all history, that there is a great responsible Thinker and Actor working wherever a man works; that a true man belongs to no other time or place, but is the center of things. Where he is, there is nature. He measures you, and all men, and all events. Ordinarily, everybody in society reminds us of somewhat else, or of some other person. Character, reality, reminds you of nothing else; it takes place of the whole creation. The man must be so much, that he must make all circumstances indifferent. Every true man is a cause, a country and an age; requires infinite spaces and numbers and time fully to accomplish his design;—and posterity seem to follow his steps as a train of clients. A man Cæsar is born, and for ages after we have a Roman Empire. Christ is born, and millions of minds so grow and cleave to his genius, that he is confounded with virtue and the possible of man. An institution is the lengthened shadow of one man; as Monachism, of the hermit Antony; the Reformation, of Luther; Quakerism, of Fox; Methodism, of Wesley; Abolition, of Clarkson. Scipio, Milton called 'the height of Rome'; and all history resolves itself very easily into the biography of a few stout and earnest persons.

Let a man then know his worth, and keep things under his feet. Let him not peep or steal, or skulk up and down with the air of a charity-boy, a bastard or an interloper, in the world which exists for him. But the man in the street, finding no worth in himself which corresponds to the force which built a tower or sculptured a marble god, feels poor when he looks on these. To him a palace, a statue, a costly book, have an alien and forbidding air, much like a gay equipage, and seem to say like that, 'Who are you, Sir?' Yet they all are his, suitors for his notice, petitioners to his faculties that they will come out and take possession. The picture waits for my verdict: it is not to command me, but I am to settle its claims to praise. That popular fable of the sot who was picked up dead drunk in the street, carried to the duke's house, washed and dressed and laid in the duke's bed, and, on his waking, treated with all obsequious ceremony like the duke, and assured that he had been insane, owes its popularity to the fact that it symbolizes so well the state of man, who is in the world a sort of sot, but now and then wakes up, exercises his reason, and finds himself a true prince.

Our reading is mendicant and sycophantic. In history, our

imagination plays us false. Kingdom and lordship, power and estate, are a gaudier vocabulary than private John and Edward in a small house and common day's work; but the things of life are the same to both; the sum total of both is the same. Why all this deference to Alfred, and Scanderbeg, and Gustavus? Suppose they were virtuous; did they wear out virtue? As great a stake depends on your private act to-day, as followed their public and renowned steps. When private men shall act with original views, the luster will be transferred from the actions of kings to those of gentlemen.

The world has been instructed by its kings, who have so magnetized the eyes of nations. It has been taught by this colossal symbol the mutual reverence that is due from man to man. The joyful loyalty with which men have everywhere suffered the king, the noble or the great proprietor to walk among them by a law of his own, make his own scale of men and things, and reverse theirs, pay for benefits not with money but with honor, and represent the law in his person, was the hieroglyphic by which they obscurely signified their consciousness of their own right and comeliness, the right of every man.

The magnetism which all original action exerts is explained when we inquire the reason of self-trust. Who is the Trustee? What is the aboriginal Self, on which a universal reliance may be grounded? What is the nature and power of that science-baffling star, without parallax, without calculable elements, which shoots a ray of beauty even into trivial and impure actions, if the least mark of independence appear? The inquiry leads us to that source, at once the essence of genius, of virtue and of life, which we call Spontaneity or Instinct. We denote this primary wisdom as Intuition, whilst all later teachings are tuitions. In that deep force, the last fact behind which analysis cannot go, all things find their common origin. For the sense of being which in calm hours rises, we know not how, in the soul, is not diverse from things, from space, from light, from time, from man, but one with them, and proceeds obviously from the same source whence their life and being also proceed. We first share the life by which things exist, and afterwards see them as appearances in nature, and forget that we have shared their cause. Here is the fountain of action and of thought. Here are the lungs of that inspiration which giveth man wisdom, and which cannot be denied without impiety and atheism. We lie in the lap of immense intelligence, which makes us receivers of its truth and organs of its activity. When we discern justice, when we discern truth, we do nothing of ourselves, but allow a passage to its beams. If we ask whence this comes, if we seek to pry into the soul that causes, all philosophy is at fault. Its presence or its absence is all we can affirm. Every man discriminates between the voluntary acts of his mind, and his involuntary perceptions, and knows that to his involuntary perceptions a perfect faith is due. He may err in the expression of them, but he knows that these things are so, like day and night, not to be disputed. My willful actions and acquisitions are but roving;—the idlest reverie, the faintest native emotion, command my curiosity and respect. Thoughtless people contradict as readily the statement of perceptions as of opinions, or rather much more readily; for, they do not distinguish between perception and notion. They fancy that I choose to see this or that thing. But perception is not whimsical, it is fatal. If I see a trait, my children will see it after me, and in course of time, all mankind,—although it may chance that no one has seen it before me. For my perception of it is as much a fact as the sun.

The relations of the soul to the divine spirit are so pure, that it is profane to seek to interpose helps. It must be that when God speaketh he should communicate, not one thing, but all things; should fill the world with his voice; should scatter forth light, nature, time, souls, from the center of the present thought; and new date and new create the whole. Whenever a mind is simple, and receives a divine wisdom, old things pass away,—means, teachers, texts, temples, fall; it lives now, and absorbs past and future into the present hour. All things are made sacred by relation to it,—one as much as another. All things are dissolved to their center by their cause, and, in the universal miracle, petty and particular miracles disappear. If, therefore, a man claims to know and speak of God, and carries you backward to the phraseology of some old moldered nation in another country, in another world, believe him not. Is the acorn better than the oak which is its fullness and completion? Is the parent better than the child into whom he has cast his ripened being? Whence, then, this worship of the past? The centuries are conspirators against the sanity and authority of the soul. Time and space are but physiological colors which the eye makes, but the soul is light; where it is, is day; where it was, is night; and history is an impertinence and an injury, if it be anything more than a cheerful apologue or parable of my being and becoming.

Man is timid and apologetic; he is no longer upright; he dares not say 'I think,' 'I am,' but quotes some saint or sage. He is ashamed before the blade of grass or the blowing rose. These roses under my window make no reference to former roses or to better ones; they are for what they are; they exist with God to-day. There is no time to them. There is simply the rose; it is perfect in every moment of its existence. Before a leaf-bud has burst, its whole life acts; in the full-blown flower there is no more; in the leafless root there is no less. Its nature is satisfied, and it satisfies nature, in all moments alike. But man postpones, or remembers; he does not live in the present, but with a reverted eye laments the past, or, heedless of the riches that surround him, stands on tiptoe to foresee the future. He cannot be happy and strong until he too lives with nature in the present, above time.

This should be plain enough. Yet see what strong intellects dare not yet hear God himself, unless he speak the phraseology of I know not what David, or Jeremiah, or Paul. We shall not always set so great a price on a few texts, on a few lives. We are like children who repeat by rote the sentences of grandames and tutors, and, as they grow older, of the men and talents and characters they chance to see,—painfully recollecting the exact words they spoke; afterwards, when they come into the point of view which those had who uttered those saying, they understand them, and are willing to let the words go; for, at any time, they can use words as good when occasion comes. If we live truly, we shall see truly. It is as easy for the strong man to be strong, as it is for the weak to be weak. When we have new perception, we shall gladly disburden the memory of its hoarded treasures as old rubbish. When a man lives with God, his voice shall be as sweet as the murmur of the brook and the rustle of the corn.

And now at last the highest truth on this subject remains unsaid; probably cannot be said; for all that we say is the far-off remembering of the intuition. That thought, by what I can now nearest approach to say it, is this. When good is near you, when you have life in yourself, it is not by any known or accustomed way; you shall not discern the footprints of any other; you shall not see the face of man; you shall not hear any name;—the way, the thought, the good, shall be wholly strange and new. It shall exclude example and experience. You take the way from man, not to man. All persons that ever existed are its forgotten ministers. Fear and hope are alike beneath it. There is somewhat low even in hope. In the hour of vision, there is nothing that can be called gratitude, nor properly joy. The soul raised over passion beholds identity and eternal causation, perceives the self-existence of Truth and Right, and calms itself with knowing that all things go well. Vast spaces of nature, the Atlantic Ocean, the South Sea,—long intervals of time, years, centuries,—are of no account. This which I think and feel underlay every former state of life and circumstances, as it does underlie my present, and what is called life, and what is called death.

Life only avails, not the having lived. Power ceases in the instant of repose; it resides in the moment of transition from a past to a new state, in the shooting of the gulf, in the darting to an aim. This one fact the world hates, that the soul becomes; for that forever degrades the past, turns all riches to poverty, all reputation to shame, confounds the saint with the rogue, shoves Jesus and Judas equally aside. Why, then, do we prate of self-reliance? Inasmuch as the soul is present, there will be power not confident but agent. To talk of reliance is a poor external way of speaking. Speak rather of that which relies, because it works and is. Who has more obedience than I masters me, though he should not raise his finger. Round him I must revolve by the gravitation of spirits. We fancy it rhetoric, when we speak of eminent virtue. We do not yet see that virtue is Height, and that a man or a company of men, plastic and permeable to principles, by the law of nature must overpower and ride all cities, nations, kings, rich men, poets, who are not.

This is the ultimate fact which we so quickly reach on this, as on every topic, the resolution of all into the ever-blessed ONE. Self-existence is the attribute of the Supreme Cause, and it constitutes the measure of good by the degree in which it enters into all lower forms. All things real are so by so much virtue as they contain. Commerce, husbandry, hunting, whaling, war eloquence, personal weight, are somewhat, and engage my respect as examples of its presence and impure action. I see the same law working in nature for conservation and growth. Power is in nature the essential measure of right. Nature suffers nothing to remain in her kingdoms which cannot help itself. The genesis and maturation of a planet, its poise and orbit, the bended tree recovering itself from the strong wind, the vital resources of every animal and vegetable, are demonstrations of the self-sufficing, and therefore self-relying soul.

Thus all concentrates: let us not rove; let us sit at home with the cause. Let us stun and astonish the intruding rabble of men and books and institutions, by a simple declaration of the divine fact. Bid the invaders take the shoes from off their feet, for God is here within. Let our simplicity judge them, and our docility to our own law demonstrate the poverty of nature and fortune beside our native riches.

But now we are a mob. Man does not stand in awe of man, nor is his genius admonished to stay at home to put itself in communication with the internal ocean, but it goes abroad to beg a cup of water of the urns of other men. We must go alone. I like the silent church before the service begins, better than any preaching. How far off, how cool, how chaste the persons look, begirt each one with a precinct or sanctuary! So let us always sit. Why should we assume the faults of our friend, or wife, or father, or child, because they sit around our hearth, or are said to have the same blood? All men have my blood, and I have all men's. Not for that will I adopt their petulance or folly, even to the extent of being ashamed of it. But your isolation must not be mechanical, but spiritual, that is, must be elevation. At times the whole world seems to be in conspiracy to importune you with emphatic trifles. Friend, client, child, sickness, fear, want, charity, all knock at once at thy closet door, and say, 'Come out unto us.' But keep thy state; come not into their confusion. The power men possess to annoy men, I give them by a weak curiosity. No man can come near me but through my act. 'What we love that we have, but by desire we bereave ourselves of the love.'

If we cannot at once rise to the sanctities of obedience and faith, let us at least resist our temptations; let us enter into the state of war, and wake Thor and Woden, courage and constancy, in our Saxon breasts. This is to be done in our smooth times by speaking the truth. Check this lying hospitality and lying affection. Live no longer to the expectation of these deceived and deceiving people with whom we converse. Say to them, O father, O mother, O wife, O brother, O friend, I have lived with you after appearances hitherto. Henceforward I am the truth's. Be it known unto you that henceforward I obey no law less than the eternal law. I will have no covenants but proximities. I shall endeavor to nourish my parents, to support my family, to be the chaste husband of one wife,—but these relations I must fill after a new and unprecedented way. I appeal from your customs. I must be myself. I cannot break myself any longer for you, or you. If you can love me for what I am, we shall be the happier. If you cannot, I will still seek to deserve that you should. I will not hide my tastes or aversions. I will so trust that what is deep is holy, that I will do strongly before the sun and moon whatever inly rejoices me, and the heart appoints. If you are noble, I will love you; if you are not, I will not hurt you and myself by hypocritical attentions. If you are true, but not in the same truth with me, cleave to your companions; I will seek my own. I do this not selfishly, but humbly and truly. It is alike your interest, and mine, and all men's however long we have dwelt in lies, to live in truth. Does this sound harsh to-day? You will soon love what is dictated by your nature as well as mine, and, if we follow the truth, it will bring us out safe at last. But so may you give these friends pain. Yes, but I cannot sell my liberty and my power, to save their sensibility. Besides, all persons have their moments of reason, when they look out into the region of absolute truth; then will they justify me, and do the same thing.

The populace think that your rejection of popular standards is a rejection of all standard, and mere antinomianism; and the bold sensualist will use the name of philosophy to gild his crimes. But the law of consciousness abides. There are two confessionals, in one or the other of which we must be shriven. You may fulfill your round of duties by clearing yourself in the direct, or in the reflex way. Consider whether you have satisfied your relations to father, mother, cousin, neighbor, town, cat and dog; whether any of these can upbraid you. But I may also neglect this reflex standard, and absolve me to myself. I have my own stern claims and perfect circle. It denies the name of duty to many offices that are called duties. But if I can discharge its debts, it enables me to dispense with the popular code. If any one imagines that this law is lax, let him keep its commandment one day.

And truly it demands something godlike in him who has cast off the common motives of humanity, and has ventured to trust himself for a taskmaster. High be his heart, faithful his will, clear his sight, that he may in good earnest be doctrine, society, law, to himself, that a simple purpose may be to him as strong as iron necessity is to others!

If any man consider the present aspects of what is called by distinction society, he will see the need of these ethics. The sinew and heart of man seem to be drawn out, and we are become timorous, desponding whimperers. We are afraid of truth, afraid of fortune, afraid of death and afraid of each other. Our age yields no great and perfect persons. We want men and women who shall renovate life and our social state, but we see that most natures are insolvent, cannot satisfy their own wants, have an ambition out of all proportion to their practical force, and do lean and beg day and night continually. Our housekeeping is mendicant, our arts, our occupations, our marriages, our religion, we have not chosen, but society has chosen for us. We are parlor soldiers. We shun the rugged battle of fate, where strength is born.

If our young men miscarry in their first enterprises, they lose all heart. If the young merchant fails, men say he is ruined. If the finest genius studies at one of our colleges, and is not installed in an office within one year afterwards in the cities or suburbs of Boston or New York, it seems to his friends and to himself that he is right in being disheartened, and in complaining the rest of his life. A sturdy lad from New Hampshire or Vermont, who in turn tries all the professions, who teams it, farms it, peddles, keeps a school, preaches, edits a newspaper, goes to Congress, buys a township and so forth, in successive years, and always, like a cat, falls on his feet, is worth a hundred of these city dolls. He walks abreast with his days, and feels no shame in not 'studying a profession,' for he does not postpone his life, but lives already. He has not one chance, but a hundred chances. Let a Stoic open the resources of man, and tell men they are not leaning willows, but can and must detach themselves; that with the exercise of self-trust, new powers shall appear; that a man is the word made flesh, born to shed healing to the nations, that he should be ashamed of our compassion, and that the moment he acts from himself, tossing the laws, the books, idolatries and customs out of the window, we pity him no more, but thank and revere him,—and that teacher shall restore the life of man to splendor, and make his name dear to all history.

It is easy to see that a greater self-reliance must work a revolution in all the offices and relations of men; in their religion; in their education; in their pursuits; their modes of living; their association; in their property; in their speculative views.

1. In what prayers do men allow themselves! That which they call a holy office is not so much as brave and manly. Prayer looks abroad and asks for some foreign addition to come through some foreign virtue, and loses itself in endless mazes of natural and supernatural, and mediatorial and miraculous. Prayer that craves a particular commodity,—anything less than all good,—is vicious. Prayer is the contemplation of the facts of life from the highest point of view. It is the soliloquy of a beholding and jubilant soul. It is the spirit of God pronouncing his works good. But prayer as a means to effect a private end is meanness and theft. It supposes dualism and not unity in nature and consciousness. As soon as the man is at one with God, he will not beg. He will then see prayer in all action. The prayer of the farmer kneeling in his field to weed it, the prayer of the rower kneeling with the stroke of his oar, are true prayers heard throughout nature, though for cheap ends. Caratach, in Fletcher's Bonduca, when

admonished to inquire the mind of the god Audate, replies,—

> 'His hidden meaning lies in our endeavors;
> Our valors are our best gods.'

Another sort of false prayers are our regrets. Discontent is the want of self-reliance; it is infirmity of will. Regret calamities, if you can thereby help the sufferer; if not, attend your own work, and already the evil begins to be repaired. Our sympathy is just as base. We come to them who weep foolishly, and sit down and cry for company, instead of imparting to them truth and health in rough electric shocks, putting them once more in communication with their own reason. The secret of fortune is joy in our hands. Welcome evermore to gods and men is the self-helping man. For him all doors are flung wide: him all tongues greet, all honors crown, all eyes follow with desire. Our love goes out to him and embraces him, because he did not need it. We solicitously and apologetically caress and celebrate him, because he held on his way and scorned our disapprobation. The gods love him because men hated him. 'To the persevering mortal,' said Zoroaster, 'the blessed Immortals are swift.'

As men's prayers are a disease of the will, so are their creeds a disease of the intellect. They say with those foolish Israelites, 'Let not God speak to us, lest we die. Speak thou, speak any man with us, and we will obey.' Everywhere I am hindered of meeting God in my brother, because he has shut his own temple doors, and recites fables merely of his brother's, or his brother's brother's God. Every new mind is a new classification. If it prove a mind of uncommon activity and power, a Locke, a Lavoisier, a Hutton, a Betham, a Fourier, it imposes its classification on other men, and lo! a new system. In proportion to the depth of the thought, and so to the number of the objects it touches and brings within reach of the pupil, is his complacency. But chiefly is this apparent in creeds and churches, which are also classifications of some powerful mind acting on the elemental thought of duty, and man's relation to the Highest. Such is Calvinism, Quakerism, Swedenborgism. The pupil takes the same delight in subordinating everything to the new terminology, as a girl who has just learned botany in seeing a new earth and new seasons thereby. It will happen for a time, that the pupil will find his intellectual power has grown by the study of his master's mind. But in all unbalanced minds, the classification is idolized, passes for the end, and not for a speedily exhaustible means, so that the walls of the system blend to their eye in the remote horizon with the walls of the universe; the luminaries of heaven seem to them hung on the arch their master built. They cannot imagine how you aliens have any right to see,—how you can see; 'It must be somehow that you stole the light from us.' They do not yet perceive that light, unsystematic, indomitable, will break into any cabin, even into theirs. Let them chirp awhile and call it their own. If they are honest and do well, presently their neat new pinfold will be too strait and low, will crack, will lean, will rot and vanish, and the immortal light, all young and joyful, million-orbed, million-colored, will beam over the universe as on the first morning.

2. It is for want of self-culture that the superstition of Traveling, whose idols are Italy, England, Egypt, retains its fascination for all educated Americans. They who made England, Italy, or Greece venerable in the imagination did so by sticking fast where they were, like an axis of the earth. In manly hours, we feel that duty is our place. The soul is no traveler; the wise man stays at home, and when his necessities, his duties, on any occasion call him from his house, or into foreign lands, he is at home still; and shall make men sensible by the expression of his countenance, that he goes the missionary of wisdom and virtue, and visits cities and men like a sovereign, and not like an interloper or a valet.

I have no churlish objection to the circumnavigation of the globe, for the purposes of art, of study and benevolence, so that the man is first domesticated, or does not go abroad with the hope of finding somewhat greater than he knows. He who travels to be amused, or to get somewhat which he does not carry, travels away from himself, and grows old even in youth among old things. In Thebes, in Palmyra, his will and mind have become old and dilapidated as they. He carries ruins to ruins.

Traveling is a fool's paradise. Our first journeys discover to us the indifference of places. At home I dream that at Naples, at Rome, I can be intoxicated with beauty, and lose my sadness. I pack my trunk, embrace my friends, embark on the sea, and at last wake up in Naples, and there beside me is the stern fact, the sad self, unrelenting, identical, that I fled from. I seek the Vatican, and the palaces. I affect to be intoxicated with sights and suggestions, but I am not intoxicated. My giant goes with me wherever I go.

3. But the rage of traveling is a symptom of a deeper unsoundness affecting the whole intellectual action. The intellect is vagabond, and our system of education fosters restlessness. Our minds travel when our bodies are forced to stay at home. We imitate; and what is imitation but the traveling of the mind? Our houses are built with foreign taste; our shelves are garnished with foreign ornaments; our opinions, our tastes, our faculties, lean, and follow the Past and the Distant. The soul created the arts wherever they have flourished. It was in his own mind that the artist sought his model. It was an application of his own thought to the thing to be done and the conditions to be observed. And why need we copy the Doric or the Gothic model? Beauty, convenience, grandeur of thought and quaint expression are as near to us as to any, and if the American artist will study with hope and love the precise thing to be done by him considering the climate, the soil, the length of the day, the wants of the people, the habit and form of the government, he will create a house in which all these will find themselves fitted, and taste and sentiment will be satisfied also.

Insist on yourself; never imitate. Your own gift you can present every moment with the cumulative force of a whole life's cultivation; but of the adopted talent of another, you have only an extemporaneous, half possession. That which each can do best, none but his Maker can teach him. No man yet knows what it is, nor can, till that person has exhibited it. Where is the master who could have taught Shakespeare? Where is the master who could have instructed Franklin, or Washington, or Bacon, or Newton? Every great man is a unique. The Scipionism of Scipio is precisely that part he could not borrow. Shakespeare will never be made by the study of Shakespeare. Do that which is assigned to you, and you cannot hope too much or dare too much. There is at this moment for you an utterance brave and grand as that of the colossal chisel of Phidias, or trowel of the Egyptians, or the pen of Moses, or Dante, but different from all these. Not possibly will the soul all rich, all eloquent, with thousand-cloven tongue, deign to repeat itself; but if you can hear what these patriarchs say, surely you can reply to them in the same pitch of voice; for the ear and the tongue are two organs of one nature. Abide in the simple and noble regions of thy life, obey thy heart, and thou shalt reproduce the Foreworld again.

4. As our Religion, our Education, our Art look abroad, so does our spirit of society. All men plume themselves on the improvement of society, and no man improves.

Society never advances. It recedes as fast on one side as it gains on the other. It undergoes continual changes; it is barbarous, it is civilized, it is Christianized, it is rich, it is scientific; but this change is not amelioration. For everything that is given, something is taken. Society acquires new arts, and loses old instincts. What a contrast between the well-clad, reading, writing, thinking American, with a watch, a pencil and a bill of exchange in his pocket, and the naked New Zealander, whose property is a club, a spear, a mat and an undivided twentieth of a shed to sleep under! But compare the health of the two men, and you shall see that the white man has lost his aboriginal strength. If the traveler tell us truly, strike the savage with a broad ax, and in a day or two the flesh shall unite and heal as if you struck the blow into soft pitch, and the same blow shall send the white to his grave.

The civilized man has built a coach, but has lost the use of his feet. He is supported on crutches, but lacks so much support of muscle. He has a fine Geneva watch, but he fails of the skill to tell the hour by the sun. A Greenwich nautical almanac he has, and so being sure of the information when he wants it, the man in the street does not know a star in the sky. The solstice he does not observe; the equinox he knows as little; and the whole bright calendar of the year is without a dial in his mind. His notebooks impair his memory; his libraries overload his wit; the insurance office increases the number of accidents; and it may be a question whether machinery does not encumber; whether we have not lost by refinement some energy, by a Christianity entrenched in establishments and forms, some vigor of wild virtue. For every Stoic was a Stoic; but in Christendom where is the Christian?

There is no more deviation in the moral standard than in the standard of height or bulk. No greater men are now than ever were. A singular equality may be observed between great men of the first and of the last ages; nor can all the science, art, religion and philosophy of the nineteenth century avail to educate greater men than Plutarch's heroes, three or four and twenty centuries ago. Not in time is the race progressive. Phocion, Socrates, Anaxagoras, Diogenes, are great men, but they leave no class. He who is really of their class will not be called by their name, but will be his own man, and, in his turn, the founder of a sect. The arts and inventions of each period are only its costume, and do not invigorate men. The harm of the improved machinery may compensate its good. Hudson and Bering accomplished so much in their fishing boats, as to astonish Parry and Franklin, whose equipment exhausted the resources of science and art. Galileo, with an opera-glass, discovered a more splendid series of celestial phenomena than any one since. Columbus found the New World in an undecked boat. It is curious to see the periodical disuse and perishing of means and machinery, which were introduced with loud laudation a few years or centuries before. The great genius returns to essential man. We reckoned the improvements of the art of war among the triumphs of science, and yet Napoleon conquered Europe by the bivouac, which consisted of falling back on naked valor, and disencumbering it of all aids. The Emperor held it impossible to make a perfect army, says Las Casas, 'without abolishing our arms, magazines, commissaries and carriages, until, in imitation of the Roman custom, the soldier should receive his supply of corn, grind it in his handmill, and bake his bread himself.'

Society is a wave. The wave moves onward, but the water of which it is composed does not. The same particle does not rise from the valley to the ridge. Its unity is only phenomenal. The persons who make up a nation to-day, next year die, and their experience with them.

And so the reliance on Property, including the reliance on governments which protect it, is the want of self-reliance. Men have looked away from themselves and at things so long, that they have come to esteem the religious, learned and civil institutions as guards of property, and they deprecate assaults on these, because they feel them to be assaults on property. They measure their esteem of each other by what each has, and not by what each is. But a cultivated man becomes ashamed of his property, out of new respect for his nature. Especially he hates what he has, if he see that it is accidental,—came to him by inheritance, or gift, or crime; then he feels that it is not having; it does not belong to him, has no root in him, and merely lies there, because no revolution or no robber takes it away. But that which a man is, does always by necessity acquire, and what the man acquires is living property, which does not wait the beck of rulers, or mobs, or revolutions, or fire, or storm, or bankruptcies, but perpetually renews itself wherever the man breathes. 'Thy lot or portion of life,' said the Caliph Ali, 'is seeking after thee; therefore be at rest from seeking after it.' Our dependence on these foreign goods leads us to our slavish respect for numbers. The political parties meet in numerous conventions; the greater the concourse, and with each new uproar of announcement, The delegation from Essex! The Democrats from New Hampshire! The Whigs of Maine! the young patriot feels himself stronger than before by a new thousand of eyes and arms. In like manner the reformers summon conventions, and vote and resolve in multitude. Not so, O friends! will the god deign to enter and inhabit you, but by a method precisely the reverse. It is only as a man puts off all foreign support, and stands alone, that I see him to be strong and to prevail. He is weaker by every recruit to his banner. Is not a man better than a town? Ask nothing of men, and in the endless mutation, thou only firm column must presently appear the upholder of all that surrounds thee. He who knows that power is inborn, that he is weak because he has looked for good out of him and elsewhere, and so perceiving, throws himself unhesitatingly on his thought, instantly rights himself, stands in the erect position, commands his limbs, works miracles; just as a man who stands on his feet is stronger than a man who stands on his head.

So use all that is called Fortune. Most men gamble with her, and gain all, and lose all, as her wheel rolls. But do thou leave as unlawful these winnings, and deal with Cause and Effect, the chancelors of God. In the Will work and acquire, and thou hast chained the wheel of Chance, and shalt sit hereafter out of fear from her rotations. A political victory, a rise of rents, the recovery of your sick, or the return of your absent friend, or some other favorable event, raises your spirits, and you think good days are preparing for you. Do not believe it. Nothing can bring you peace but yourself. Nothing can bring you peace but the triumph of principles.

6

ON THE PLEASURE OF HATING

William Hazlitt

There is a spider crawling along the matted floor of the room where I sit (not the one which has been so well allegorized in the admirable *Lines to a Spider*, but another of the same edifying breed); he runs with heedless, hurried haste, he hobbles awkwardly towards me, he stops—he sees the giant shadow before him, and, at a loss whether to retreat or proceed, meditates his huge foe—but as I do not start up and seize upon the straggling caitiff, as he would upon a hapless fly within his toils, he takes heart, and ventures on with mingled cunning, impudence and fear. As he passes me, I lift up the matting to assist his escape, am glad to get rid of the unwelcome intruder, and shudder at the recollection after he is gone. A child, a woman, a clown or a moralist a century ago, would have crushed the little reptile to death—my philosophy has got beyond that—I bear the creature no ill-will, but still I hate the very sight of it. The spirit of malevolence survives the practical exertion of it. We learn to curb our will and keep our overt actions within the bounds of humanity, long before we can subdue our sentiments and imaginations to the same mild tone. We give up the external demonstration, the brute violence, but cannot part with the essence or principle of hostility. We do not tread upon the poor little animal in question (that seems barbarous and pitiful!) but we regard it with a sort of mystic horror and superstitious loathing. It will ask another hundred years of fine writing and hard thinking to cure us of the prejudice and make us feel towards this ill-omened tribe with something of 'the milk of human kindness,' instead of their own shyness and venom.

Nature seems (the more we look into it) made up of antipathies: without something to hate, we should lose the very spring of thought and action. Life would turn to a stagnant pool, were it not ruffled by the jarring interests, the unruly passions, of men. The white streak in our own fortunes is brightened (or just rendered visible) by making all around it as dark as possible; so the rainbow paints its form upon the cloud. Is it pride? Is it envy? Is it the force of contrast? Is it weakness or malice? But so it is, that there is a secret affinity, a hankering after, evil in the human mind, and that it takes a perverse, but a fortunate delight in mischief, since it is a never-failing source of satisfaction. Pure good soon grows insipid, wants variety and spirit. Pain is a bittersweet, wants variety and spirit. Love turns, with a little indulgence, to indifference or disgust: hatred alone is immortal. Do we not see this principle at work everywhere? Animals torment and worry one another without mercy: children kill flies for sport: every one reads the accidents and offences in a newspaper as the cream of the jest: a whole town runs to be present at a fire, and the spectator by no means exults to see it extinguished. It is better to have it so, but it diminishes the interest; and our feelings take part with our passions rather than with our understandings. Men assemble in crowds, with eager enthusiasm, to witness a tragedy: but if there were an execution going forward in the next street, as Mr Burke observes, the theater would be left empty. A strange cur in a village, an idiot, a crazy woman, are set upon and baited by the whole community. Public nuisances are in the nature of public benefits. How long did the Pope, the Bourbons and the Inquisition keep the people of England in breath, and supply them with nicknames to vent their spleen upon! Had they done us any harm of late? No: but we have always a quantity of superfluous bile upon the stomach, and we wanted an object to let it out upon. How loth were we to give up our pious belief in ghosts and witches, because we liked to persecute the one, and frighten ourselves to death with the other! It is not the quality so much as the quantity of excitement that we are anxious about: we cannot bear a state of indifference and ennui: the mind seems to abhor a vacuum as much as ever nature was supposed to do.

Even when the spirit of the age (that is, the progress of intellectual refinement, warring with our natural infirmities) no longer allows us to carry our vindictive and head strong humours into effect, we try to revive them in description, and keep up the old bugbears, the phantoms of our terror and our hate, in imagination. We burn Guy Fawx in effigy, and the hooting and buffeting and maltreating that poor tattered figure of rags and straw makes a festival in every village in England once a year. Protestants and Papists do not now burn one another at the stake: but we subscribe to new editions of *Fox's Book of Martyrs*; and the secret of the success of the Scotch Novels is much the same—they carry us back to the feuds, the heart-burnings, the havoc, the dismay, the wrongs and the revenge of a barbarous age and people—to the rooted prejudices and deadly animosities of sects and parties in politics and religion, and of contending chiefs and clans in war and intrigue. We feel the full force of the spirit of hatred with all of them in turn. As we read, we throw aside the trammels of civilization, the flimsy veil of humanity. 'Off, you lendings!' The wild beast resumes its sway within us, we feel like hunting animals, and as the hound starts in his sleep and rushes on the chase in fancy the heart rouses itself in its native lair, and utters a wild cry of joy, at being restored once more to freedom and lawless unrestrained impulses. Every one has his full swing, or goes to the Devil his own way. Here are no Jeremy Bentham Panopticons, none of Mr Owen's impassable Parallelograms (Rob Roy would have spurred and poured a thousand curses on them), no long calculations of self-interest—the will takes its instant way to its object, as the mountain-torrent flings itself over the precipice: the greatest possible good of each individual consists in doing all the mischief he can to his neighbour: that is charming, and finds a sure and sympathetic chord in every breast! So Mr Irving, the celebrated preacher, has rekindled the old, original, almost exploded hell-fire in the aisles of the Caledonian Chapel, as they introduce the real water of the New River at Sadler's Wells, to the delight and astonishment of his fair audience. *'Tis pretty, though a plague*, to sit and peep into the pit of Tophet, to play at *snap-dragon* with flames and brimstone (it gives a smart electrical shock, a lively fillip to delicate constitutions), and to see Mr Irving, like a huge Titan, looking as grim and swarthy as if he had to forge tortures for all the damned! What a strange being man is! Not content with doing all he can to vex and hurt his fellows here, 'upon this bank and shoal of time,' where one would think there were heartaches, pain, disappointment, anguish, tears, sighs and groans enough, the bigoted maniac takes him to the top of the high peak of school divinity to hurl him down the yawning gulf of penal fire; his speculative malice asks eternity to wreak its infinite spite in, and calls on the Almighty to execute its relentless doom! The cannibals burn their enemies and eat them in good-fellowship with one another: meek Christian divines cast those who differ from them but a hair's-breadth, body and soul into hellfire for the glory of God and the good of His creatures! It is well that the power of such persons is not coordinate with their wills: indeed it is from the sense of their weakness and inability to control the opinions of others, that they thus 'outdo termagant,' and endeavour to frighten them into conformity by big words and monstrous denunciations.

The pleasure of hating, like a poisonous mineral, eats into the heart of religion, and turns it to rankling spleen and bigotry; it makes patriotism an excuse for carrying fire, pestilence and famine into other lands: it leaves to virtue nothing but the spirit of censoriousness, and a narrow, jealous, inquisitorial watchfulness over the actions and motives of others. What have the different sects, creeds, doctrines in religion been but so many pretexts set up for men to wrangle, to quarrel, to tear one another in pieces about, like a target as a mark to shoot at? Does any one suppose that the love of country in an Englishman implies any friendly feeling or disposition to serve another bearing the same name? No, it means only hatred to the French or the inhabitants of any other country that we happen to be at war with for the time. Does the love of virtue denote any wish to discover or amend our own faults? No, but it atones for an obstinate adherence to our own vices by the most virulent intolerance to human frailties. This principle is of a most universal application. It extends to good as well as evil: if it makes us hate folly, it makes us no less dissatisfied with distinguished merit. If it inclines us to resent the wrongs of others, it impels us to be as impatient of their prosperity. We revenge injuries: we repay benefits with ingratitude. Even our strongest partialities and likings soon take this turn. 'That which was luscious as locusts, anon becomes bitter as coloquintida;' and love and friendship melt in their own fires. We hate old friends: we hate old books: we hate old opinions; and at last we come to hate ourselves.

I have observed that few of those whom I have formerly known most intimate, continue on the same friendly footing, or combine the steadiness with the warmth of attachment. I have been acquainted with two or three knots of inseparable companions, who saw each other 'six days in the week;' that have been broken up and dispersed. I have quarrelled with almost all my old friends, (they might say this is owing to my bad temper, but) they have also quarrelled with one another. What is become of 'that set of whist-players,' celebrated by ELIA in his notable *Epistle to Robert Southey, Esq.* (and now I think of it—that I myself have celebrated in this very volume) 'that for so many years called Admiral Burney friend?' They are scattered, like last year's snow. Some of them are dead, or gone to live at a distance, or pass one another in the street like strangers, or if they stop to speak, do it as coolly and try to cut one another as soon as possible. Some of us have grown rich, others poor. Some have got places under Government, others a *niche* in the *Quarterly Review*. Some of us have dearly earned a name in the world; whilst others remain in their original privacy. We despise the one, and envy and are glad to mortify the other. Times are changed; we cannot revive our old feelings; and we avoid the sight, and are uneasy in the presence of, those who remind us of our infirmity, and put us upon an effort at seeming cordiality which embarrasses ourselves, and does not impose upon our *quondam* associates. Old friendships are like meats served up repeatedly, cold, comfortless and distasteful. The stomach turns against them. Either constant intercourse and familiarity breed weariness and contempt; if we meet again after an interval of absence, we appear no longer the same. One is too wise, another too foolish, for us; and we wonder we did not find this out before. We are disconcerted and kept in a state of continual alarm by the wit of one, or tired to death of the dullness of another. The *good things* of the first (besides leaving strings behind them) by repetition grow stale, and lose their startling effect; and the insipidity of the last becomes intolerable. The most amusing or instructive companion is best like a favorite volume, that we wish after a time to *lay upon the shelf*; but as our friends are not willing to be laid there, this produces a misunderstanding and ill-blood between us. Or if the zeal and integrity of friendship is not abated, or its career interrupted by any obstacle arising out of its own nature, we look out for other subjects of complaint and sources of dissatisfaction. We begin to criticize each other's dress, looks, general character. 'Such a one is a pleasant fellow, but it is a pity he sits so late!' Another fails to keep his appointments, and that is a sore that never heals. We get acquainted with some fashionable young men or with a mistress, and wish to introduce our friend; but be is awkward and a sloven, the interview does not answer, and this throws cold water on our intercourse. Or he makes himself obnoxious to opinion; and we shrink from our own convictions on the subject as an excuse for not defending him. All or any of these causes mount up in time to a ground of coolness or irritation; and at last they break out into open violence as the only amends we can make ourselves for suppressing them so long, or the readiest means of banishing recollections of former kindness so little compatible with our present feelings. We may try to tamper with the wounds or patch up the carcase of departed friendship; but the one will hardly bear the handling, and the other is not worth the trouble of embalming! The only way to be reconciled to old friends is to part with them for good: at a distance we may chance to be thrown back (in a waking dream) upon old times and old feelings: or at any rate we should not think of renewing our intimacy, till we have fairly *spit our spite* or said, thought, and felt all the ill we can of each other. Or if we can pick a quarrel with some one else, and make him the scape-goat, this is an excellent contrivance to heal a broken bone. I think I must be friends with Lamb again, since he has written that magnanimous Letter to Southey, and told him a piece of his mind!—I don't know what it is that attaches me to H—— so much, except that he and I, whenever we meet, sit in judgment on another set of old friends, and 'carve them as a dish fit for the Gods'. There was L [Leigh Hunt], John Scott, Mrs [Montagu], whose dark raven locks make a picturesque background to our discourse, B——, who is grown fat, and is, they say, married, R[ickman]; these had all separated long ago, and their foibles are the common link that holds us together. We do not affect to condole or whine over their follies; we enjoy, we laugh at them, till we are ready to burst our sides, '*sans* intermissions for hours by the dial.' We serve up a course of anecdotes, *traits*, master-strokes of character, and cut and hack at them till we are weary. Perhaps some of them are even with us. For my own part, as I once said, I like a friend the better for having faults that one can talk about. 'Then,' said Mrs [Montagu], 'you will cease to be a philanthropist!' Those in question were some of the choice-spirits of the age, not 'fellows of no mark or likelihood'; and we so far did them justice: but it is well they did not hear what we sometimes said of them. I care little what any one says of me, particularly behind my back, and in the way of critical and analytical discussion: it is looks of dislike and scorn that I answer with the worst venom of my pen. The expression of the face wounds me more than the expressions of the tongue. If I have in one instance mistaken this expression, or resorted to this remedy where I ought not, I am sorry for it. But the face was too fine over which it mantled, and I am too old to have misunderstood it! ...I sometimes go up to ——'s; and as often as I do, resolve never to go again. I do not find the old homely welcome. The ghost of friendship meets me at the door, and sits with me all dinner-time. They have got a set of fine notions and new acquaintances. Allusions to past occurrences are thought trivial, nor is it always safe to touch upon more general subjects. M. does not begin as he formerly did every five minutes, 'Fawcett used to say,' &c. That topic is something worn. The girls are grown up, and have a thousand accomplishments. I perceive there is a jealousy on both sides. They think I give myself airs, and I fancy the same of them. Every time I am asked, 'If I do not think Mr Washington Irving a very fine writer?' I shall not go again till I receive an invitation for Christmas Day in company with Mr Liston. The only intimacy I never found to flinch or fade was a purely intellectual one. There was none of the cant of candour in it, none of the whine of mawkish sensibility. Our mutual acquaintance were considered merely as subjects of conversation and knowledge, not all of affection. We regarded them no more in our experiments than 'mice in an air-pump:' or like malefactors, they were regularly cut down and given over to the dissecting-knife. We spared neither friend nor foe. We sacrificed human infirmities at the shrine of truth. The skeletons of character might be seen, after the juice was extracted, dangling in the air like flies in cobwebs; or they were kept for future inspection in some refined acid. The demonstration was as beautiful as it was new. There is no surfeiting on gall: nothing keeps so well as a decoction of spleen. We grow tired of every thing but turning others into ridicule, and congratulating ourselves on their defects.

We take a dislike to our favourite books, after a time, for the same reason. We cannot read the same works for ever. Our honey-moon, even though we wed the Muse, must come to an end; and is followed by indifference, if not by disgust. There are some works, those indeed that produce the most striking effect at first by novelty and boldness of outline, that will not bear reading twice: others of a less extravagant character, and that excite and repay attention by a greater nicety of details, have hardly interest enough to keep alive our continued enthusiasm. The popularity of the most successful writers operates to wean us from them, by the cant and fuss that is made about them, by hearing their names everlastingly repeated, and by the number of ignorant and indiscriminate admirers they draw after them:—we as little like to have to drag others from their unmerited obscurity, lest we should be exposed to the charge of affectation and singularity of taste. There is nothing to be said respecting an author that all the world have made up their minds about: it is a thankless as well as hopeless task to recommend one that nobody has ever heard of. To cry up Shakespear as the God of our idolatry, seems like a vulgar national prejudice: to take down a volume of Chaucer, or Spenser, or Beaumont and Fletcher, or Ford, or Marlowe, has very much the look of pedantry and egotism. I confess it makes me hate the very name of Fame and Genius, when works like these are 'gone into the wastes of time,' while each successive generation of fools is busily employed in reading the trash of the day, and women of fashion gravely join with their waiting-maids in discussing the preference between the *Paradise Lost* and Mr Moore's *Loves of the Angels*. I was pleased the other day on going into a shop to ask, 'If they had any of the *Scotch Novels*?' to be told—'That they had just sent out the last, *Sir Andrew Wylie*!'—Mr Galt will also be pleased with this answer! The reputation of some books is raw and *unaired*: that of others is worm-eaten and mouldy. Why fix our affections on that which we cannot bring ourselves to have faith in, or which others have long ceased to trouble themselves about? I am half afraid to look into *Tom Jones*, lest it should not answer my expectations at this time of day; and if it did not, I would certainly be disposed to fling it into the fire, and never look into another novel while I lived. But surely, it may be said, there are some works that, like nature, can never grow old; and that must always touch the imagination and passions alike! Or there are passages that seem as if we might brood over them all our lives, and not exhaust the sentiments of love and admiration they excite: they become favourites, and we are fond of them to a sort of dotage. Here is one:

'— Sitting in my window
Printing my thoughts in lawn, I saw a God,
I thought (but it was you), enter our gates;
My blood flew out and back again, as fast
As I had puffed it forth and sucked it in
Like breath; then was I called away in haste
To entertain you: never was a man
Thrust from a sheepcote to a sceptre, raised
So high in thoughts as I; you left a kiss
Upon these lips then, which I mean to keep
From you for ever. I did hear you talk
Far above singing!'

A passage like this, indeed, leaves a taste on the palate like nectar, and we seem in reading it to sit with the Gods at their golden tables: but if we repeat it often in ordinary moods, it loses its flavour, becomes vapid, 'the wine of *poetry* is drank, and but the lees remain.' Or, on the other hand, if we call in the air of extraordinary circumstances to set it off to advantage, as the reciting it to a friend, or after having our feelings excited by a long walk in some romantic situation, or while we

'—play with Amaryllis in the shade,
Or with the tangles of Neaera's hair'—

we afterwards miss the accompanying circumstances, and instead of transferring the recollection of them to the favourable side, regret what we have lost, and strive in vain to bring back 'the irrevocable hour'—wondering in some instances how we survive it, and at the melancholy blank that is left behind! The pleasure rises to its height in some moment of calm solitude or intoxicating sympathy, declines ever after, and from the comparison and conscious falling-off, leaves rather a sense of satiety and irksomeness behind it... 'Is it the same in pictures?' I confess it is, with all but those from Titian's hand. I don't know why, but an air breathes from his landscapes, pure, refreshing, as if it came from other years; there is a look in his faces that never passes away. I saw one the other day. Amidst the heartless desolation and glittering finery of Fonthill, there is a portfolio of the Dresden Gallery. It opens, and a young female head looks from it; a child, yet woman grown; with an air of rustic innocence and the graces of a princess, her eyes like those of doves, the lips about to open, a smile of pleasure dimpling the whole face, the jewels sparkling in her crisped hair, her youthful shape compressed in a rich antique dress, as the bursting leaves contain the April buds! Why do I not call up this image of gentle sweetness, and place it as a perpetual barrier between mischance and me?—It is because pleasure asks a greater effort of the mind to support it than pain; and we turn after a little idle dalliance from what we love to what we hate!

As to my old opinions, I am heartily sick of them. I have reason, for they have deceived me sadly. I was taught to think, and I was willing to believe, that genius was not a bawd, that virtue was not a mask, that liberty was not a name, that love had its seat in the human heart. Now I would care little if these words were struck out of the dictionary, or if I had never heard them. They are become to my ears a mockery and a dream. Instead of patriots and friends of freedom, I see nothing but the tyrant and the slave, the people linked with kings to rivet on the chains of despotism and superstition. I see folly join with knavery, and together make up public spirit and public opinions. I see the insolent Tory, the blind Reformer, the coward Whig! If mankind had wished for what is right, they might have had it long ago. The theory is plain enough; but they are prone to mischief, 'to every good work reprobate.' I have seen all that had been done by the mighty yearnings of the spirit and intellect of men, 'of whom the world was not worthy,' and that promised a proud opening to truth and good through the vista of future years, undone by one man, with just glimmering of understanding enough to feel that he was a king, but not to comprehend how he could be king of a free people! I have seen this triumph celebrated by poets, the friends of my youth and the friends of men, but who were carried away by the infuriate tide that, setting in from a throne, bore down every distinction of right reason before it; and I have seen all those who did not join in applauding this insult and outrage on humanity proscribed, hunted down (they and their friends made a byword of), so that it has become an understood thing that no one can live by his talents or knowledge who is not ready to prostitute those talents and that knowledge to betray his species, and prey upon his fellow- man. 'This was some time a mystery: but the time gives evidence of it.' The echoes of liberty had awakened once more in Spain, and the mornings of human hope dawned again: but that dawn has been overcast by the foul breath of bigotry, and those reviving sounds stifled by fresh cries from the time-rent towers of the Inquisition—man yielding (as it is fit he should) first to brute force, but more to the innate perversity and dastard spirit of his own nature which leaves no room for farther hope or disappointment. And England, that arch-reformer, that heroic deliverer, that mouther about liberty, and tool of power, stands gaping by, not feeling the blight and mildew coming over it, nor its very bones crack and turn to a paste under the grasp and circling folds of this new monster, Legitimacy! In private life do we not see hypocrisy, servility, selfishness, folly and impudence succeed, while modesty shrinks from the encounter, and merit is trodden under foot? How often is 'the rose plucked from the forehead of a virtuous love to plant a blister there!' What chance is there of the success of real passion? What certainty of its continuance? Seeing all this as I do, and unravelling the web of human life into its various threads of meanness, spite, cowardice, want of feeling and want of understanding, of indifference towards others, and ignorance of ourselves,—seeing custom prevail over all excellence, itself giving way to infamy—mistaken as I have been in my public and private hopes, calculating others from myself, and calculating wrong; always disappointed where I placed most reliance; the dupe of friendship, and the fool of love;—have I not reason to hate and to despise myself? Indeed I do; and chiefly for not having hated and despised the world enough.

7

STREET HAUNTING: A LONDON ADVENTURE

Virginia Woolf

No one perhaps has ever felt passionately towards a lead pencil. But there are circumstances in which it can become supremely desirable to possess one; moments when we are set upon having an object, an excuse for walking half across London between tea and dinner. As the foxhunter hunts in order to preserve the breed of foxes, and the golfer plays in order that open spaces may be preserved from the builders, so when the desire comes upon us to go street rambling the pencil does for a pretext, and getting up we say: 'Really I must buy a pencil,' as if under cover of this excuse we could indulge safely in the greatest pleasure of town life in winter—rambling the streets of London.

The hour should be the evening and the season winter, for in winter the champagne brightness of the air and the sociability of the streets are grateful. We are not then taunted as in the summer by the longing for shade and solitude and sweet airs from the hayfields. The evening hour, too, gives us the irresponsibility which darkness and lamplight bestow. We are no longer quite ourselves. As we step out of the house on a fine evening between four and six, we shed the self our friends know us by and become part of that vast republican army of anonymous trampers, whose society is so agreeable after the solitude of one's own room. For there we sit surrounded by objects which perpetually express the oddity of our own temperaments and enforce the memories of our own experience. That bowl on the mantelpiece, for instance, was bought at Mantua on a windy day. We were leaving the shop when the sinister old woman plucked at our skirts and said she would find herself starving one of these days, but, 'Take it!' she cried, and thrust the blue and white china bowl into our hands as if she never wanted to be reminded of her quixotic generosity. So, guiltily, but suspecting nevertheless how badly we had been fleeced, we carried it back to the little hotel where, in the middle of the night, the innkeeper quarrelled so violently with his wife that we all leant out into the courtyard to look, and saw the vines laced about among the pillars and the stars white in the sky. The moment was stabilized, stamped like a coin indelibly among a million that slipped by imperceptibly. There, too, was the melancholy Englishman, who rose among the coffee cups and the little iron tables and revealed the secrets of his soul—as travellers do. All this—Italy, the windy morning, the vines laced about the pillars, the Englishman and the secrets of his soul—rise up in a cloud from the china bowl on the mantelpiece. And there, as our eyes fall to the floor, is that brown stain on the carpet. Mr Lloyd George made that. 'The man's a devil!' said Mr Cummings, putting the kettle down with which he was about to fill the teapot so that it burnt a brown ring on the carpet.

But when the door shuts on us, all that vanishes. The shell-like covering which our souls have excreted to house themselves, to make for themselves a shape distinct from others, is broken, and there is left of all these wrinkles and roughnesses a central oyster of perceptiveness, an enormous eye. How beautiful a street is in winter! It is at once revealed and obscured. Here vaguely one can trace symmetrical straight avenues of doors and windows; here under the lamps are floating islands of pale light through which pass quickly bright men and women, who, for all their poverty and shabbiness, wear a certain look of unreality, an air of triumph, as if they had given life the slip, so that life, deceived of her prey, blunders on without them. But, after all, we are only gliding smoothly on the surface. The eye is not a miner, not a diver, not a seeker after buried treasure. It floats us smoothly down a stream; resting, pausing, the brain sleeps perhaps as it looks.

How beautiful a London street is then, with its islands of light, and its long groves of darkness, and on one side of it perhaps some tree-sprinkled, grass-grown space where night is folding herself to sleep naturally and, as one passes the iron railing, one hears those little cracklings and stirrings of leaf and twig which seem to suppose the silence of fields all round them, an owl hooting, and far away the rattle of a train in the valley. But this is London, we are reminded; high among the bare trees are hung oblong frames of reddish yellow light—windows; there are points of brilliance burning steadily like low stars—lamps; this empty ground, which holds the country in it and its peace, is only a London square, set about by offices and houses where at this hour fierce lights burn over maps, over documents, over desks where clerks sit turning with wetted forefinger the files of endless correspondences; or more suffusedly the firelight wavers and the lamplight falls upon the privacy of some drawing-room, its easy chairs, its papers, its china, its inlaid table and the figure of a woman, accurately measuring out the precise number of spoons of tea which——She looks at the door as if she heard a ring downstairs and somebody asking, is she in?

But here we must stop peremptorily. We are in danger of digging deeper than the eye approves; we are impeding our passage down the smooth stream by catching at some branch or root. At any moment, the sleeping army may stir itself and wake in us a thousand violins and trumpets in response; the army of human beings may rouse itself and assert all its oddities and sufferings and sordidities. Let us dally a little longer, be content still with surfaces only—the glossy brilliance of the motor omnibuses; the carnal splendour of the butchers' shops with their yellow flanks and purple steaks; the blue and red bunches of flowers burning so bravely through the plate glass of the florists' windows.

For the eye has this strange property: it rests only on beauty; like a butterfly it seeks colour and basks in warmth. On a winter's night like this, when nature has been at pains to polish and preen herself, it brings back the prettiest trophies, breaks off little lumps of emerald and coral as if the whole earth were made of precious stone. The thing it cannot do (one is speaking of the average unprofessional eye) is to compose these trophies in such a way as to bring out the more obscure angles and relationships. Hence after a prolonged diet of this simple, sugary fare, of beauty pure and uncomposed, we become conscious of satiety. We halt at the door of the boot shop and make some little excuse, which has nothing to do with the real reason, for folding up the bright paraphernalia of the streets and withdrawing to some duskier chamber of the being where we may ask, as we raise our left foot obediently upon the stand: 'What, then, is it like to be a dwarf?'

She came in escorted by two women who, being of normal size, looked like benevolent giants beside her. Smiling at the shop girls, they seemed to be disclaiming any lot in her deformity and assuring her of their protection. She wore the peevish yet apologetic expression usual on the faces of the deformed. She needed their kindness, yet she resented it. But when the shop girl had been summoned and the giantesses, smiling indulgently, had asked for shoes for 'this lady' and the girl had pushed the little stand in front of her, the dwarf stuck her foot out with an impetuosity which seemed to claim all our attention. Look at that! Look at that! she seemed to demand of us all, as she thrust her foot out, for behold it was the shapely, perfectly proportioned foot of a well-grown woman. It was arched; it was aristocratic. Her whole manner changed as she looked at it resting on the stand. She looked soothed and satisfied. Her manner became full of self-confidence. She sent for shoe after shoe; she tried on pair after pair. She got up and pirouetted before a glass which reflected the foot only in yellow shoes, in fawn shoes, in shoes of lizard skin. She raised her little skirts and displayed her little legs. She was thinking that, after all, feet are the most important part of the whole person; women, she said to herself, have been loved for their feet alone. Seeing nothing but her feet, she imagined perhaps that the rest of her body was of a piece with those beautiful feet. She was shabbily dressed, but she was ready to lavish any money upon her shoes. And as this was the only occasion upon which she was not afraid of being looked at but positively craved attention, she was ready to use any device to prolong the choosing and fitting. Look at my feet, she seemed to be saying, as she took a step this way and then a step that way. The shop girl good-humouredly must have said something flattering, for suddenly her face lit up in ecstasy. But, after all, the giantesses, benevolent though they were, had their own affairs to see to; she must make up her mind; she must decide which to choose. At length, the pair was chosen and, as she walked out between her guardians, with the parcel swinging from her finger, the ecstasy faded, knowledge returned, the old peevishness, the old apology came back, and by the time she had reached the street again she had become a dwarf only.

But she had changed the mood; she had called into being an atmosphere which, as we followed her out into the street, seemed actually to create the humped, the twisted, the deformed. Two bearded men, brothers, apparently, stone-blind, supporting themselves by resting a hand on the head of a small boy between them, marched down the street. On they came with the unyielding yet tremulous tread of the blind, which seems to lend to their approach something of the terror and inevitability of the fate that has overtaken them. As they passed, holding straight on, the little convoy seemed to cleave asunder the passers-by with the momentum of its silence, its directness, its disaster. Indeed, the dwarf had started a hobbling grotesque dance to which everybody in the street now conformed: the stout lady tightly swathed in shiny sealskin; the feeble-minded boy sucking the silver knob of his stick; the old man squatted on a doorstep as if, suddenly overcome by the absurdity of the human spectacle, he had sat down to look at it—all joined in the hobble and tap of the dwarf's dance.

In what crevices and crannies, one might ask, did they lodge, this maimed company of the halt and the blind? Here, perhaps, in the top rooms of these narrow old houses between Holborn and Soho, where people have such queer names, and pursue so many curious trades, are gold beaters, accordion pleaters, cover buttons or support life, with even greater fantasticality, upon a traffic in cups without saucers, china umbrella handles and highly-coloured pictures of martyred saints. There they lodge, and it seems as if the lady in the sealskin jacket must find life tolerable, passing the time of day with the accordion pleater, or the man who covers buttons; life which is so fantastic cannot be altogether tragic. They do not grudge us, we are musing, our prosperity; when, suddenly, turning the corner, we come upon a bearded Jew, wild, hunger-bitten, glaring out of his misery; or pass the humped body of an old woman flung abandoned on the step of a public building with a cloak over her like the hasty covering thrown over a dead horse or donkey. At such sights the nerves of the spine seem to stand erect; a sudden flare is brandished in our eyes; a question is asked which is never answered. Often enough these derelicts choose to lie not a stone's thrown from theatres, within hearing of barrel organs, almost, as night draws on, within touch of the sequined cloaks and bright legs of diners and dancers. They lie close to those shop windows where commerce offers to a world of old women laid on doorsteps, of blind men, of hobbling dwarfs, sofas which are supported by the gilt necks of proud swans; tables inlaid with baskets of many coloured fruit; sideboards paved with green marble the better to support the weight of boars' heads; and carpets so softened with age that their carnations have almost vanished in a pale green sea.

Passing, glimpsing, everything seems accidentally but miraculously sprinkled with beauty, as if the tide of trade which deposits its burden so punctually and prosaically upon the shores of Oxford Street had this night cast up nothing but treasure. With no thought of buying, the eye is sportive and generous; it creates; it adorns; it enhances. Standing out in the street, one may build up all the chambers of an imaginary house and furnish them at one's will with sofa, table, carpet. That rug will do for the hall. That alabaster bowl shall stand on a carved table in the window. Our merrymaking shall be reflected in that thick round mirror. But, having built and furnished the house, one is happily under no obligation to possess it; one can dismantle it in the twinkling of an eye, and build and furnish another house with other chairs and other glasses. Or let us indulge ourselves at the antique jewellers, among the trays of rings and the hanging necklaces. Let us choose those pearls, for example, and then imagine how, if we put them on, life would be changed. It becomes instantly between two and three in the morning; the lamps are burning very white in the deserted streets of Mayfair. Only motor-cars are abroad at this hour, and one has a sense of emptiness, of airiness, of secluded gaiety. Wearing pearls, wearing silk, one steps out on to a balcony which overlooks the gardens of sleeping Mayfair. There are a few lights in the bedrooms of great peers returned from Court, of silk-stockinged footmen, of dowagers who have pressed the hands of statesmen. A cat creeps along the garden wall. Love-making is going on sibilantly, seductively in the darker places of the room behind thick green curtains. Strolling sedately as if he were promenading a terrace beneath which the shires and counties of England lie sun-bathed, the aged Prime Minister recounts to Lady So-and-So with the curls and the emeralds the true history of some great crisis in the affairs of the land. We seem to be riding on the top of the highest mast of the tallest ship; and yet at the same time we know that nothing of this sort matters; love is not proved thus, nor great achievements completed thus; so that we sport with the moment and preen our feathers in it lightly, as we stand on the balcony watching the moonlit cat creep along Princess Mary's garden wall.

But what could be more absurd? It is, in fact, on the stroke of six; it is a winter's evening; we are walking to the Strand to buy a pencil. How, then, are we also on a balcony, wearing pearls in June? What could be more absurd? Yet it is nature's folly, not ours. When she set about her chief masterpiece, the making of man, she should have thought of one thing only. Instead, turning her head, looking over her shoulder, into each one of us she let creep instincts and desires which are utterly at variance with his main being, so that we are streaked, variegated, all of a mixture; the colours have run. Is the true self this which stands on the pavement in January, or that which bends over the balcony in June? Am I here, or am I there? Or is the true self neither this nor that, neither here nor there, but something so varied and wandering that it is only when we give the rein to its wishes and let it take its way unimpeded that we are indeed ourselves? Circumstances compel unity; for convenience sake a man must be a whole. The good citizen when he opens his door in the evening must be banker, golfer, husband, father; not a nomad wandering the desert, a mystic staring at the sky, a debauchee in the slums of San Francisco, a soldier heading a revolution, a pariah howling with scepticism and solitude. When he opens his door, he must run his fingers through his hair and put his umbrella in the stand like the rest.

But here, none too soon, are the second-hand bookshops. Here we find anchorage in these thwarting currents of being; here we balance ourselves after the splendours and miseries of the streets. The very sight of the bookseller's wife with her foot on the fender, sitting beside a good coal fire, screened from the door, is sobering and cheerful. She is never reading, or only the newspaper; her talk, when it leaves bookselling, which it does so gladly, is about hats; she likes a hat to be practical, she says, as well as pretty. O no, they don't live at the shop; they live in Brixton; she must have a bit of green to look at. In summer a jar of flowers grown in her own garden is stood on the top of some dusty pile to enliven the shop. Books are everywhere; and always the same sense of adventure fills us. Second-hand books are wild books, homeless books; they have come together in vast flocks of variegated feather, and have a charm which the domesticated volumes of the library lack. Besides, in this random miscellaneous company we may rub against some complete stranger who will, with luck, turn into the best friend we have in the world. There is always a hope, as we reach down some grayish-white book from an upper shelf, directed by its air of shabbiness and desertion, of meeting here with a man who set out on horseback over a hundred years ago to explore the woollen market in the Midlands and Wales; an unknown traveller, who stayed at inns, drank his pint, noted pretty girls and serious customs, wrote it all down stiffly, laboriously for sheer love of it (the book was published at his own expense); was infinitely prosy, busy and matter-of-fact, and so let flow in without his knowing it the very scent of hollyhocks and the hay together with such a portrait of himself as gives him forever a seat in the warm corner of the mind's inglenook. One may buy him for eighteen pence now. He is marked three and sixpence, but the bookseller's wife, seeing how shabby the covers are and how long the book has stood there since it was bought at some sale of a gentleman's library in Suffolk, will let it go at that.

Thus, glancing round the bookshop, we make other such sudden capricious friendships with the unknown and the vanished whose only record is, for example, this little book of poems, so fairly printed, so finely engraved, too, with a portrait of the author. For he was a poet and drowned untimely, and his verse, mild as it is and formal and sententious, sends forth still a frail fluty sound like that of a piano organ played in some back street resignedly by an old Italian organ-grinder in a corduroy jacket. There are travellers, too, row upon row of them, still testifying, indomitable spinsters that they were, to the discomforts that they endured and the sunsets they admired in Greece when Queen Victoria was a girl. A tour in Cornwall with a visit to the tin mines was thought worthy of voluminous record. People went slowly up the Rhine and did portraits of each other in Indian ink, sitting reading on deck beside a coil of rope; they measured the pyramids; were lost to civilization for years; converted negroes in pestilential swamps. This packing up and going off, exploring deserts and catching fevers, settling in India for a lifetime, penetrating even to China and then returning to lead a parochial life at Edmonton, tumbles and tosses upon the dusty floor like an uneasy sea, so restless the English are, with the waves at their very door. The waters of travel and adventure seem to break upon little islands of serious effort and lifelong industry stood in jagged column upon the floor. In these piles of puce-bound volumes with gilt monograms on the back, thoughtful clergymen expound the gospels; scholars are to be heard with their hammers and their chisels chipping clear the ancient texts of Euripides and Aeschylus. Thinking, annotating, expounding goes on at a prodigious rate all around us and over everything, like a punctual, everlasting tide, washes the ancient sea of fiction. Innumerable volumes tell how Arthur loved Laura and they were separated and they were unhappy and then they met and they were happy ever after, as was the way when Victoria ruled these islands.

The number of books in the world is infinite, and one is forced to glimpse and nod and move on after a moment of talk, a flash of understanding, as, in the street outside, one catches a word in passing and from a chance phrase fabricates a lifetime. It is about a woman called Kate that they are talking, how 'I said to her quite straight last night...if you don't think I'm worth a penny stamp, I said...'

But who Kate is, and to what crisis in their friendship that penny stamp refers, we shall never know; for Kate sinks under the warmth of their volubility; and here, at the street corner, another page of the volume of life is laid open by the sight of two men consulting under the lamp-post. They are spelling out the latest wire from Newmarket in the stop press news. Do they think, then, that fortune will ever convert their rags into fur and broadcloth, sling them with watch-chains, and plant diamond pins where there is now a ragged open shirt? But the main stream of walkers at this hour sweeps too fast to let us ask such questions. They are wrapt, in this short passage from work to home, in some narcotic dream, now that they are free from the desk, and have the fresh air on their cheeks. They put on those bright clothes which they must hang up and lock the key upon all the rest of the day, and are great cricketers, famous actresses, soldiers who have saved their country at the hour of need. Dreaming, gesticulating, often muttering a few words aloud, they sweep over the Strand and across Waterloo Bridge whence they will be slung in long rattling trains, to some prim little villa in Barnes or Surbiton where the sight of the clock in the hall and the smell of the supper in the basement puncture the dream.

But we are come to the Strand now, and as we hesitate on the curb, a little rod about the length of one's finger begins to lay its bar across the velocity and abundance of life. 'Really I must—really I must'—that is it. Without investigating the demand, the mind cringes to the accustomed tyrant. One must, one always must, do something or other; it is not allowed one simply to enjoy oneself. Was it not for this reason that, some time ago, we fabricated the excuse, and invented the necessity of buying something? But what was it? Ah, we remember, it was a pencil. Let us go then and buy this pencil. But just as we are turning to obey the command, another self disputes the right of the tyrant to insist. The usual conflict comes about. Spread out behind the rod of duty we see the whole breadth of the river Thames—wide, mournful, peaceful. And we see it through the eyes of somebody who is leaning over the Embankment on a summer evening, without a care in the world. Let us put off buying the pencil; let us go in search of this person—and soon it becomes apparent that this person is ourselves. For if we could stand there where we stood six months ago, should we not be again as we were then—calm, aloof, content? Let us try then. But the river is rougher and greyer than we remembered. The tide is running out to sea. It brings down with it a tug and two barges, whose load of straw is tightly bound down beneath tarpaulin covers. There is, too, close by us, a couple leaning over the balustrade with the curious lack of self-consciousness lovers have, as if the importance of the affair they are engaged on claims without question the indulgence of the human race. The sights we see and the sounds we hear now have none of the quality of the past; nor have we any share in the serenity of the person who, six months ago, stood precisely where we stand now. His is the happiness of death; ours the insecurity of life. He has no future; the future is even now invading our peace. It is only when we look at the past and take from it the element of uncertainty that we can enjoy perfect peace. As it is, we must turn, we must cross the Strand again, we must find a shop where, even at this hour, they will be ready to sell us a pencil.

It is always an adventure to enter a new room for the lives and characters of its owners have distilled their atmosphere into it, and directly we enter it we breast some new wave of emotion. Here, without a doubt, in the stationer's shop people had been quarrelling. Their anger shot through the air. They both stopped; the old woman—they were husband and wife evidently—retired to a back room; the old man whose rounded forehead and globular eyes would have looked well on the frontispiece of some Elizabethan folio, stayed to serve us. 'A pencil, a pencil,' he repeated, 'certainly, certainly.' He spoke with the distraction yet effusiveness of one whose emotions have been roused and checked in full flood. He began opening box after box and shutting them again. He said that it was very difficult to find things when they kept so many different articles. He launched into a story about some legal gentleman who had got into deep waters owing to the conduct of his wife. He had known him for years; he had been connected with the Temple for half a century, he said, as if he wished his wife in the back room to overhear him. He upset a box of rubber bands. At last, exasperated by his incompetence, he pushed the swing door open and called out roughly: 'Where d'you keep the pencils?' as if his wife had hidden them. The old lady came in. Looking at nobody, she put her hand with a fine air of righteous severity upon the right box. There were pencils. How then could he do without her? Was she not indispensable to him? In order to keep them there, standing side by side in forced neutrality, one had to be particular in one's choice of pencils; this was too soft, that too hard. They stood silently looking on. The longer they stood there, the calmer they grew; their heat was going down, their anger disappearing. Now, without a word said on either side, the quarrel was made up. The old man, who would not have disgraced Ben Jonson's title-page, reached the box back to its proper place, bowed profoundly his good-night to us, and they disappeared. She would get out her sewing; he would read his newspaper; the canary would scatter them impartially with seed. The quarrel was over.

In these minutes in which a ghost has been sought for, a quarrel composed, and a pencil bought, the streets had become completely empty. Life had withdrawn to the top floor, and lamps were lit. The pavement was dry and hard; the road was of hammered silver. Walking home through the desolation one could tell oneself the story of the dwarf, of the blind men, of the party in the Mayfair mansion, of the quarrel in the stationer's shop. Into each of these lives one could penetrate a little way, far enough to give oneself the illusion that one is not tethered to a single mind, but can put on briefly for a few minutes the bodies and minds of others. One could become a washerwoman, a publican, a street singer. And what greater delight and wonder can there be than to leave the straight lines of personality and deviate into those footpaths that lead beneath brambles and thick tree trunks into the heart of the forest where live those wild beasts, our fellow men?

That is true: to escape is the greatest of pleasures; street haunting in winter the greatest of adventures. Still as we approach our own doorstep again, it is comforting to feel the old possessions, the old prejudices, fold us round; and the self, which has been blown about at so many street corners, which has battered like a moth at the flame of so many inaccessible lanterns, sheltered and enclosed. Here again is the usual door; here the chair turned as we left it and the china bowl and the brown ring on the carpet. And here—let us examine it tenderly, let us touch it with reverence—is the only spoil we have retrieved from all the treasures of the city, a lead pencil.

8

SUCH, SUCH WERE THE JOYS

George Orwell

I

Soon after I arrived at St Cyprian's (not immediately, but after a week or two, just when I seemed to be settling into the routine of school life) I began wetting my bed. I was now aged eight, so that this was a reversion to a habit which I must have grown out of at least four years earlier. Nowadays, I believe, bed-wetting in such circumstances is taken for granted. It is normal reaction in children who have been removed from their homes to a strange place. In those days, however, it was looked on as a disgusting crime which the child committed on purpose and for which the proper cure was a beating. For my part I did not need to be told it was a crime. Night after night I prayed, with a fervour never previously attained in my prayers, 'Please God, do not let me wet my bed! Oh, please God, do not let me wet my bed!', but it made remarkably little difference. Some nights the thing happened, others not. There was no volition about it, no consciousness. You did not properly speaking do the deed: you merely woke up in the morning and found that the sheets were wringing wet.

After the second of third offence I was warned that I should be beaten next time, but I received the warning in a curiously roundabout way. One afternoon, as we were filing out from tea, Mrs Wilkes the Headmaster's wife, was sitting at the head of one of the tables, chatting with a lady of whom I knew nothing, except that she was on an afternoon's visit to the school. She was an intimidating, masculine-looking person wearing a riding-habit, or something that I took to be a riding-habit. I was just leaving the room when Mrs Wilkes called me back, as though to introduce me to the visitor.

Mrs Wilkes was nicknamed Flip, and I shall call her by that name, for I seldom think of her by any other. (Officially, however, she was addressed as Mum, probably a corruption of the 'Ma'am' used by public schoolboys to their housemasters' wives.) She was a stocky square-built woman with hard red cheeks, a flat top to her head, prominent brows and deep-set, suspicious eyes. Although a great deal of the time she was full of false heartiness, jollying one along with mannish slang ('*Buck* up, old chap!' and so forth), and even using one's Christian name, her eyes never lost their anxious, accusing look. It was very difficult to look her in the face without feeling guilty, even at moments when one was not guilty of anything in particular.

'Here is a little boy,' said Flip, indicating me to the strange lady, 'who wets his bed every night. Do you know what I am going to do if you wet your bed again?' she added, turning to me, 'I am going to get the Sixth Form to beat you'.

The strange lady put on an air of being inexpressibly shocked, and exclaimed 'I-should-*think*-so!' And here there occurred one of those wild, almost lunatic misunderstandings which are part of the daily experience of childhood. The Sixth Form was a group of older boys who were selected as having 'character' and were empowered to beat smaller boys. I had not yet learned of their existence, and I mis-heard the phrase 'the Sixth Form' as 'Mrs Form'. I took it as referring to the strange lady—I thought, that is, that her name was Mrs Form. It was an improbable name, but a child has no judgement in such matters. I imagined, therefore, that it was she who was to be deputed to beat me. It did not strike me as strange that this job should be turned over to a casual visitor in no way connected with the school. I merely assumed the 'Mrs Form' was a stern disciplinarian who enjoyed beating people (somehow her appearance seemed to bear this out) and I had an immediate terrifying vision of her arriving for the occasion in full riding kit and armed with a hunting-whip. To this day I can feel myself almost swooning with shame as I stood, a very small, round-faced boy in short corduroy knickers, before the two women. I could not speak. I felt that I should die if 'Mrs Form' were to beat me. But my dominant feeling was not fear or even resentment: it was simply shame because one more person, and that a woman, had been told of my disgusting offence.

A little later, I forget how, I learned that it was not after all 'Mrs Form' who would do the beating. I cannot remember whether it was that very night that I wetted my bed again, but at any rate I did wet it again quite soon. Oh, the despair, the feeling of cruel injustice, after all my prayers and resolutions, at once again waking between the clammy sheets! There was no chance of hiding what I had done. The grim statuesque matron, Margaret by name, arrived in the dormitory specially to inspect my bed. She pulled back the clothes, then drew herself up, and the dreaded words seemed to come rolling out of her like a peal of thunder:

'REPORT YOURSELF to the Headmaster after breakfast!'

I put REPORT YOURSELF in capitals because that was how it appeared in my mind. I do not know how many times I heard that phrase during my early years at St Cyprian's. It was only very rarely that it did not mean a beating. The words always had a portentous sound in my ears, like muffled drums or the words of the death sentence.

When I arrived to report myself, Flip was doing something or other at the long shiny table in the ante-room to the study. Her uneasy eyes searched me as I went past. Sambo was a round-shouldered, curiously oafish-looking man, not large but shambling in gait, with a chubby face which was like that of an overgrown baby, and which was capable of good humour. He knew, of course, why I had been sent to him, and had already taken a bone-handled riding-crop out of the cupboard, but it was part of the punishment of reporting yourself that you had to proclaim your offence with your own lips. When I had said my say, he read me a short but pompous lecture, then seized me by the scruff of the neck, twisted me over and began beating me with the riding-crop. He had a habit of continuing his lecture while he flogged you, and I remember the words 'you dir-ty lit-tle boy' keeping time with the blows. The beating did not hurt (perhaps, as it was the first time, he was not hitting me very hard), and I walked out feeling very much better. The fact that the beating had not hurt was a sort of victory and partially wiped out the shame of the bed-wetting. I was even incautious enough to wear a grin on my face. Some small boys were hanging about in the passage outside the door of the ante-room.

'D'you get the cane?'

'It didn't hurt.' I said proudly.

Flip had heard everything. Instantly her voice came screaming after me:

'Come here! Come here this instant! What was that you said?'

'I said it didn't hurt,' I faltered out.

'How dare you say a thing like that? Do you think that is a proper thing to say? Go in and REPORT YOURSELF AGAIN!'

This time Sambo laid on in real earnest. He continued for a length of time that frightened and astonished me—about five minutes, it seemed—ending up by breaking the riding-crop. The bone handle went flying across the room.

'Look what you've made me do!' he said furiously, holding the broken crop.

I had fallen into a chair, weakly snivelling. I remember that this was the only time throughout my boyhood when a beating actually reduced me to tears, and curiously enough I was not even now crying because of the pain. The second beating had not hurt very much either. Fright and shame seemed to have anaesthetized me. I was crying partly because I felt that this was expected of me, partly from genuine repentance, but partly also because of a deeper grief which is peculiar to childhood and not easy to convey: a sense of desolate loneliness and helplessness, of being locked up not only in a hostile world but in a world of good and evil where the rules were such that it was actually not possible for me to keep them.

I knew the bed-wetting was (a) wicked and (b) outside my control. The second fact I was personally aware of, and the first I did not question. It was possible, therefore, to commit a sin without knowing that you committed it, without wanting to commit it, and without being able to avoid it. Sin was not necessarily something that you did: it might be something that happened to you. I do not want to claim that this idea flashed into my mind as a complete novelty at this very moment, under the blows of Sambo's cane: I must have had glimpses of it even before I left home, for my early childhood had not been altogether happy. But at any rate this was the great, abiding lesson of my boyhood: that I was in a world where it was not possible for me to be good. And the double beating was a turning-point, for it brought home to me for the first time the harshness of the environment into which I had been flung. Life was more terrible, and I was more wicked, than I had imagined. At any rate, as I sat snivelling on the edge of a chair in Sambo's study, with not even the self-possession to stand up while he stormed at me, I had a conviction of sin and folly and weakness, such as I do not remember to have felt before.

In general, one's memories of any period must necessarily weaken as one moves away from it. One is constantly learning new facts, and old ones have to drop out to make way for them. At twenty I could have written the history of my schooldays with an accuracy which would be quite impossible now. But it can also happen that one's memories grow sharper after a long lapse of time, because one is looking at the past with fresh eyes and can isolate and, as it were, notice facts which previously existed undifferentiated among a mass of others. Here are two things which in a sense I remembered, but which did not strike me as strange or interesting until quite recently. One is that the second beating seemed to me a just and reasonable punishment. To get one beating, and then to get another and far fiercer one on top of it, for being so unwise as to show that the first had not hurt—that was quite natural. The gods are jealous, and when you have good fortune you should conceal it. The other is that I accepted the broken riding-crop as my own crime. I can still recall my feeling as I saw the handle lying on the carpet—the feeling of having done an ill-bred clumsy thing, and ruined an expensive object. I had broken it: so Sambo told me, and so I believed. This acceptance of guilt lay unnoticed in my memory for twenty or thirty years.

So much for the episode of the bed-wetting. But there is one more thing to be remarked. This is that I did not wet my bed again—at least, I did wet it once again, and received another beating, after which the trouble stopped. So perhaps this barbarous remedy does work, though at a heavy price, I have no doubt.

II

St Cyprian's was an expensive and snobbish school which was in process of becoming more snobbish, and, I imagine, more expensive. The public school with which it had special connexions was Harrow, but during my time an increasing proportion of the boys went on to Eton. Most of them were the children of rich parents, but on the whole they were the un-aristocratic rich, the sort of people who live in huge shrubberied houses in Bournemouth or Richmond, and who have cars and butlers but not country estates. There were a few exotics among them—some South American boys, sons of Argentine beef barons, one or two Russians, and even a Siamese prince, or someone who was described as a prince.

Sambo had two great ambitions. One was to attract titled boys to the school, and the other was to train up pupils to win scholarships at public schools, above all at Eton. He did, towards the end of my time, succeed in getting hold of two boys with real English titles. One of them, I remember, was a wretched drivelling little creature, almost an albino, peering upwards out of weak eyes, with a long nose at the end of which a dewdrop always seemed to be trembling. Sambo always gave these boys their titles when mentioning them to a third person, and for their first few days he actually addressed them to their faces as 'Lord So-and-so.' Needless to say he found ways of drawing attention to them when any visitor was being shown round the school. Once, I remember, the little fair-haired boy had a choking fit at dinner, and a stream of snot ran out of his nose on to his plate in a way horrible to see. Any lesser person would have been called a dirty little beast and ordered out of the room instantly: but Sambo and Flip laughed it off in a 'boys will be boys' spirit.

All the very rich boys were more or less undisguisedly favoured. The school still had a faint suggestion of the Victorian 'private academy' with its 'parlour boarders', and when I later read about that kind of school in Thackeray I immediately saw the resemblance. The rich boys had milk and biscuits in the middle of the morning, they were given riding lessons once or twice a week, Flip mothered them and called them by their Christian names, and above all they were never caned. Apart from the South Americans, whose parents were safely distant, I doubt whether Sambo ever caned any boy whose father's income was much above £2,000 a year. But he was sometimes willing to sacrifice financial profit to scholastic prestige. Occasionally, by special arrangement, he would take at greatly reduced fees some boy who seemed likely to win scholarships and thus bring credit on the school. It was on these terms that I was at St Cyprian's myself: otherwise my parents could not have afforded to send me to so expensive a school.

I did not at first understand that I was being taken at reduced fees; it was only when I was about eleven that Flip and Sambo began throwing the fact in my teeth. For my first two or three years I went through the ordinary educational mill: then, soon after I had stated Greek (one started Latin at eight, Greek at ten), I moved into the scholarship class, which was taught, so far as classics went, largely by Sambo himself. Over a period of two or three years the scholarship boys were crammed with learning as cynically as a goose is crammed for Christmas. And with what learning! This business of making a gifted boy's career depend on a competitive examination, taken when he is only twelve or thirteen is an evil thing at best, but there do appear to be preparatory schools which send scholars to Eton, Winchester, etc. without teaching them to see everything in terms of marks. At St Cyprian's the whole process was frankly a preparation for a sort of confidence trick. Your job was to learn exactly those things that would give an examiner the impression that you knew more than you did know, and as far as possible to avoid burdening your brain with anything else. Subjects which lacked examination-value, such as geography, were almost completely neglected, mathematics was also neglected if you were a 'classical', science was not taught in any form—

indeed it was so despised that even an interest in natural history was discouraged—and even the books you were encouraged to read in your spare time were chosen with one eye on the 'English paper'. Latin and Greek, the main scholarship subjects, were what counted, but even these were deliberately taught in a flashy, unsound way. We never, for example, read right through even a single book of a Greek or Latin author: we merely read short passages which were picked out because they were the kind of thing likely to be set as an 'unseen translation'. During the last year or so before we went up for our scholarships, most of our time was spent in simply working our way through the scholarship papers of previous years. Sambo had sheaves of these in his possession, from every one of the major public schools. But the greatest outrage of all was the teaching of history.

There was in those days a piece of nonsense called the Harrow History Prize, an annual competition for which many preparatory schools entered. It was a tradition for St Cyprian's to win it every year, as well we might, for we had mugged up every paper that had been set since the competition started, and the supply of possible questions was not inexhaustible. They were the kind of stupid question that is answered by rapping out a name of quotation. Who plundered the Begams? Who was beheaded in an open boat? Who caught the Whigs bathing and ran away with their clothes? Almost all our historical teaching ran on this level. History was a series of unrelated, unintelligible but—in some way that was never explained to us—important facts with resounding phrases tied to them. Disraeli brought peace with honour. Clive was astonished at his moderation. Pitt called in the New World to redress the balance of the Old. And the dates, and the mnemonic devices. (Did you know, for example, that the initial letters of 'A black Negress was my aunt: there's her house behind the barn' are also the initial letters of the battles in the Wars of the Roses?) Flip, who 'took' the higher forms in history, revelled in this kind of thing. I recall positive orgies of dates, with the keener boys leaping up and down in their places in their eagerness to shout out the right answers, and at the same time not feeling the faintest interest in the meaning of the mysterious events they were naming.

'1587'

'Massacre of St Bartholomew!'

'1707?'

'Death of Aurangzeeb!'

'1713?'

'Treaty of Utrecht!'

'1773?'

'Boston Tea Party!'

'1520?'

'Oo, Mum, please, Mum—'

'Please, Mum, please Mum! Let me tell him, Mum!'

'Well! 1520?'

'Field of the Cloth of Gold!'

And so on.

But history and such secondary subjects were not bad fun. It was in 'classics' that the real strain came. Looking back, I realize that I then worked harder than I have ever done since, and yet at the time it never seemed possible to made quite the effort that was demanded of one. We would sit round the long shiny table, made of some very pale-coloured hard wood, with Sambo goading, threatening, exhorting, sometimes joking, very occasionally praising, but always prodding, prodding away at one's mind to keep it up to the right pitch of concentration, as one keeps a sleepy person awake by sticking pins in him.

'Go on, you little slacker! Go on, you idle, worthless little boy! The whole trouble with you is that you're bone and horn idle. You eat too much, that's why. You wolf down enormous meals, and then when you come here you're half asleep. Go on, now, put your back into it. You're not *thinking*. Your brain doesn't sweat.'

He would tap away at one's skull with his silver pencil, which, in my memory, seems to have been about the size of a banana, and which certainly was heavy enough to raise a bump: or he would pull the short hairs round one's ears, or, occasionally, reach out under the table and kick one's shin. On some days nothing seemed to go right, and then it would be 'All right, then, I know what you want.

You've been asking for it the whole morning. Come along, you useless little slacker. Come into the study.' And then whack, whack, whack and back one would come, red-wealed and smarting—in later years Sambo had abandoned his riding-crop in favour of a thin rattan cane which hurt very much more—to settle down to work again. This did not happen very often, but I do remember, more than once, being led out of the room in the middle of a Latin sentence, receiving a beating and then going straight ahead with the same sentence, just like that. It is a mistake to think such methods do not work. They work very well for their special purpose. Indeed, I doubt whether classical education ever has been or can be successfully carried on without corporal punishment. The boys themselves believed in its efficacy. There was a boy named Beacham, with no brains to speak of, but evidently in acute need of a scholarship. Sambo was flogging him towards the goal as one might do with a foundered horse. He went up for a scholarship at Uppingham, came back with a consciousness of having done badly, and a day or two later received a severe beating for idleness. 'I wish I'd had that caning before I went up for the exam,' he said sadly—a remark which I felt to be contemptible, but which I perfectly well understood.

The boys of the scholarship class were not all treated alike. If a boy were the son of rich parents to whom the saving of fees was not all-important, Sambo would goad him along in a comparatively fatherly way, with jokes and digs in the ribs and perhaps an occasional tap with the pencil, but no hair-pulling and no caning. It was the poor but 'clever' boys who suffered. Our brains were a gold-mine in which he had sunk money, and the dividends must be squeezed out of us. Long before I had grasped the nature of my financial relationship with Sambo, I had been made to understand that I was not on the same footing as most of the other boys. In effect there were three castes in the school. There was the minority with an aristocratic or millionaire background, there were the children of the ordinary suburban rich, who made up the bulk of the school, and there were a few underlings like myself, the sons of clergyman, Indian civil servants, struggling widows and the like. These poorer ones were discouraged from going in for 'extras' such as shooting and carpentry, and were humiliated over clothes and petty possessions. I never, for instance, succeeded in getting a cricket bat of my own, because 'Your parents wouldn't be able to afford it'. This phrase pursued me throughout my schooldays. At St Cyprian's we were not allowed to keep the money we brought back with us, but had to 'give it in' on the first day of term, and then from time to time were allowed to spend it under supervision. I and similarly-placed boys were always choked off from buying expensive toys like model aeroplanes, even if the necessary money stood to our credit. Flip, in particular, seemed to aim consciously at inculcating a humble outlook in the poorer boys. 'Do you think that's the sort of thing a boy like you should buy?' I remember her saying to somebody—and she said this in front of the whole school: 'You know you're not going to grow up with money, don't you? Your people aren't rich. You must learn to be sensible. Don't get above yourself!' There was also the weekly pocket-money, which we took out in sweets, dispensed by Flip from a large table. The millionaires had a sixpence a week, but the normal sum was threepence. I and one or two others were only allowed twopence. My parents had not given instructions to this effect, and the saving of a penny a week could not conceivably have made any difference to them: it was a mark of status. Worse yet was the detail of the birthday cakes. It was usual for each boy, on his birthday, to have a large iced cake with candles, which was shared out at tea between the whole school. It was provided as a matter of routine and went on his parents' bill. I never had such a cake, though my parents would have paid for it readily enough. Year after year, never daring to ask, I would miserably hope that his year a cake would appear. Once or twice I even rashly pretended to my companions that this time I *was* going to have a cake. Then came tea-time, and no cake, which did not make me more popular.

Very early it was impressed upon me that I had no chance of a decent future unless I won a scholarship at a public school. Either I won my scholarship, or I must leave school at fourteen and become, in Sambo's favourite phrase 'a little office boy at forty pounds a year'. In my circumstances it was natural that I should believe this. Indeed, it was universally taken for granted at St Cyprian's that unless you went to a 'good' public school (and only about fifteen schools came under this heading) you were ruined for life. It is not easy to convey to a grown-up person the sense of strain, of nerving oneself for some terrible, all-deciding combat, as the date of the examination crept nearer—eleven years old, twelve years old, then thirteen, the fatal year itself! Over a period of about two years, I do not think there was ever a day when 'the exam', as I called it, was quite out of my waking thoughts. In my prayers it figured invariably: and whenever I got the bigger portion of a wishbone, or picked up a horseshoe, or bowed seven times to the new moon, or succeeded in passing through a wishing-gate without touching the sides, then the wish I earned by doing so went on 'the exam' as a matter of course. And yet curiously enough I was also tormented by an almost irresistible impulse *not* to work. There were days when my heart sickened at the labours ahead of me, and I stood stupid as an animal before the most elementary difficulties. In the holidays, also, I could not work. Some of the scholarship bonus received extra tuition from a certain Mr Batchelor, a likeable, very hairy man who wore shaggy suits and lived in a typical bachelor's 'den'—book-lined wall, over-whelming stench of tobacco—somewhere in the town. During the holidays Mr Batchelor used to send us extracts from a wad of work once a week. Somehow I could not do it. The empty paper and the black Latin dictionary lying on the table, the consciousness of a plain duty shirked, poisoned my leisure, but somehow I could not start, and by the end of the holidays I would only have sent Mr Batchelor fifty or a hundred lines. Undoubtedly part of the reason was that Sambo and his cane were far away. But in term-time, also, I would go through periods of idleness and stupidity when I would sink deeper and deeper into disgrace and even achieve a sort of feeble, snivelling defiance, fully conscious of my guilt and yet unable or unwilling—I could not be sure which—to do any better. Then Sambo or Flip would send for me, and this time it would not even be a caning.

Flip would search me with her baleful eyes. (What colour were those eyes, I wonder? I remember them as green, but actually no human being has green eyes. Perhaps they were hazel.) She would start off in her peculiar, wheedling, bullying style, which never failed to get right through one's guard and score a hit on one's better nature.

'I don't think it's awfully decent of you to behave like this, is it? Do you think it's quite playing the game by your mother and father to go on idling your time away, week after week, month after month? Do you want to throw all your chances away? You know your people aren't rich, don't you? You know they can't afford the same things as other boys' parents. How are they to send you to a public school if you don't win a scholarship? I know how proud your mother is of you. Do you want to let her down?'

'I don't think he wants to go to a public school any longer,' Sambo would say, addressing himself to Flip with a pretence that I was not there. 'I think he's given up that idea. He wants to be a little boy at forty pounds a year.'

The horrible sensation of tears—a swelling in the breast, a tickling behind the nose—would already have assailed me. Flip would bring out her ace of trumps:

'And do you think it's quite fair to us, the way you're behaving? After all we've done for you? You do know what we've done for you, don't you?' Her eyes would pierce deep into me, and though she never said it straight out, I did know. 'We've had you here all these years—we even had you here for a week in the holidays so that Mr Batchelor could coach you. We don't want to have to send you away, you know, but we can't keep a boy here just to eat up our food, term after term. I don't think it's very straight, the way you're behaving. Do you?'

I never had any answer except a miserable 'No, Mum,' or 'Yes, Mum,' as the case might be. Evidently it was not straight, the way I was behaving. And at some point or other the unwanted tear would always force its way out of the corner of my eye, roll down my nose and splash.

Flip never said in plain words that I was a non-paying pupil, no doubt because vague phrases like 'all we've done for you' had a deeper emotional appeal. Sambo, who did not aspire to be loved by his pupils, put it more brutally, though, as was usual with him in pompous language. 'You are living on my bounty' was his favourite phrase in this context. At least once I listened to these words between blows of the cane. I must say that these scenes were not frequent, and except on one occasion they did not take place in the presence of other boys. In public I was reminded that I was poor and that my parents 'wouldn't be able to afford' this or that, but I was not actually reminded of my dependent position. It was a final unanswerable argument, to be brought forth like an instrument of torture when my work became exceptionally bad.

To grasp the effect of this kind of thing on a child of ten or twelve, one has to remember that the child has little sense of proportion or probability. A child may be a mass of egoism and rebelliousness, but it has not accumulated experience to give it confidence in its own judgements. On the whole it will accept what it is told, and it will believe in the most fantastic way in the knowledge and powers of the adults surrounding it. Here is an example.

I have said that at St Cyprian's we were not allowed to keep our own money. However, it was possible to hold back a shilling or two, and sometimes I used furtively to buy sweets which I kept hidden in the loose ivy on the playing-field wall. One day when I had been sent on an errand I went into a sweet-shop a mile or more from the school and bought some chocolates. As I came out of the shop I saw on the opposite pavement a small sharp-faced man who seemed to be staring very hard at my school cap. Instantly a horrible fear went through me. There could be no doubt as to who the man was. He was a spy placed there by Sambo! I turned away unconcernedly, and then, as though my legs were doing it of their own accord, broke into a clumsy run. But when I got round the next corner I forced myself to walk again, for to run was a sign of guilt, and obviously there would be other spies posted here and there about the town. All that day and the next I waited for the summons to the study, and was surprised when it did not come. It did not seem to me strange that the headmaster of a private school should dispose of an army of informers, and I did not even imagine that he would have to pay them. I assumed that any adult, inside the school or outside, would collaborate voluntarily in preventing us from breaking the rules. Sambo was all-powerful; it was natural that his agents should be everywhere. When this episode happened I do not think I can have been less than twelve years old.

I hated Sambo and Flip, with a sort of shamefaced, remorseful hatred, but it did not occur to me to doubt their judgement. When they told me that I must either win a public-school scholarship or become an office boy at fourteen, I believed that those were the unavoidable alternatives before me. And above all, I believed Sambo and Flip when they told me they were my benefactors. I see now, of course, that from Sambo's point of view I was a good speculation. He sank money in me, and he looked to get it back in the form of prestige. If I had 'gone off'; as promising boys sometimes do, I imagine that would have got rid of me swiftly. As it was I won him scholarships when the time came, and no doubt he made full use of them in his prospectuses. But it is difficult for a child to realize that a school is primarily a commercial venture. A child believes that the school exists to educate and that the school-master disciplines him either for his own good, or from a love of bullying. Flip and Sambo had chosen to befriend me, and their friendship included canings, reproaches and humiliations, which were good for me and saved me from an office stool. That was their version, and I believed in it. It was therefore clear that I owed them a vast debt of gratitude. But I was *not* grateful, as I very well knew. On the contrary, I hated both of them. I could not control my subjective feelings, and I could not conceal them from myself. But it is wicked, is it not, to hate your benefactors? So I was taught, and so I believed. A child accepts the codes of behaviour that are presented to it, even when it breaks them. From the age of eight or even earlier, the consciousness of sin was never far away from me. If I contrived to seem callous and defiant, it was only a thin cover over a mass of shame and dismay. All through my boyhood I had a profound conviction that I was no good, that was wasting my time, wrecking my talents, behaving with monstrous folly and wickedness and ingratitude—and all this, it seemed, was inescapable, because I lived among laws which were absolute, like the law of gravity, but which it was not possible for me to keep.

III

No one can look back on his schooldays and say with truth that they were altogether unhappy.

I have good memories of St Cyprian's, among a horde of bad ones. Sometimes on summer afternoons there were wonderful expeditions across the Downs to a village called Birling Gap, or to Beachy Head, where one bathed dangerously among the boulders and came home covered with cuts. And there were still more wonderful mid-summer evenings when, as a special treat, we were not driven off to bed as usual but allowed to wander about the grounds in the long twilight, ending up with a plunge into the swimming bathe at about nine o'clock. There was the joy of waking early on summer mornings and getting in an hour's undisturbed reading (Ian Hay, Thackeray, Kipling and H.G. Wells were the favourite authors of my boyhood) in the sunlit, sleeping dormitory. There was also cricket, which I was no good at but with which I conducted a sort of hopeless love affair up to the age of about eighteen. And there was the pleasure of keeping caterpillars—the silky green and purple puss-moth, the ghostly green poplar-hawk, the privet-hawk, large as one's third finger, specimens of which could be illicitly purchased for sixpence at a shop in the town—and, when one could escape long enough from the master who was 'taking the walk', there was the excitement of dredging the dew-ponds on the Downs for enormous newts with orange-coloured bellies. This business of being out for a walk, coming across something of fascinating interest and then being dragged away from it by a yell from the master, like a dog jerked onwards by the leash, is an important feature of school life, and helps to build up the conviction, so strong in many children, that the things you most want to do are always unattainable.

Very occasionally, perhaps once during each summer, it was possible to escape altogether from the barrack-like atmosphere of school, when Brown, the second master, was permitted to take one or two boys for an afternoon of butterfly hunting on a common a few miles away. Brown was a man with white hair and a red face like a strawberry, who was good at natural history, making models and plaster casts, operating magic lanterns, and things of that kind. He and Mr Batchelor were the only adults in any way connected with the school whom I did not either dislike or fear. Once he took me into his room and showed me in confidence a plated, pearl-handled revolver—his 'six-shooter', he called it—which he kept in a box under his bed, and oh, the joy of those occasional expeditions! The ride of two or three miles on a lonely little branch line, the afternoon of charging to and fro with large green nets, the beauty of the enormous dragonflies which hovered over the tops of the grasses, the sinister killing-bottle with its sickly smell, and then tea in the parlour of a pub with large slices of pale-coloured cake! The essence of it was in the railway journey, which seemed to put magic distances between yourself and school.

Flip, characteristically, disapproved of these expeditions, though not actually forbidding them. 'And have you been catching *little butterflies*?' she would say with a vicious sneer when one got back, making her voice as babyish as possible. From her point of view, natural history ('bug-hunting' she would probably have called it) was a babyish pursuit which a boy should be laughed out of as early as possible. Moreover it was somehow faintly plebeian, it was traditionally associated with boys who wore spectacles and were no good at games, it did not help you to pass exams, and above all it smelt of science and therefore seemed to menace classical education. It needed a considerable moral effort to accept Brown's invitation. How I dreaded that sneer of *little butterflies*! Brown, however, who had been at the school since its early days, had built up a certain independence for himself: he seemed to handle Sambo, and ignored Flip a good deal. If it ever happened that both of them were away, Brown acted as deputy headmaster, and on those occasions instead of reading the appointed lesson for the day at morning chapel, he would read us stories from the Apocrypha.

Most of the good memories of my childhood, and up to the age of about twenty, are in some way connected with animals. So far as St Cyprian's goes, it also seems, when I look back, that all my good memories are of summer. In winter your nose ran continually, your fingers were too numb to button your shirt (this was an especial misery on Sundays, when we wore Eton collars), there was the daily nightmare of football—the cold, the mud, the hideous greasy ball that came whizzing at one's face, the gouging knees and trampling boots of the bigger boys. Part of the trouble was that in winter, after about the age of ten, I was seldom in good health, at any rate during term-time. I had defective bronchial tubes and a lesion in one lung which was not discovered till many years later. Hence I not only had a chronic cough, but running was a torment to me. In those days however, 'wheeziness', or 'chestiness', as it was called, was either diagnosis imagination or was looked on as essentially a moral disorder, caused by overeating. 'You wheeze like a concertina,' Sambo would say disapprovingly as he stood behind my chair; 'You're perpetually stuffing yourself with food, that's why.' My cough was referred to as a 'stomach cough', which made it sound both disgusting and reprehensible. The cure for it was hard running, which, if you kept it up long enough, ultimately 'cleared your chest'.

It is curious, the degree—I will not say of actual hardship, but of squalor and neglect—that was taken for granted in upper-class schools of the period. Almost as in the days of Thackeray, it seemed natural that a little boy of eight or ten should be a miserable, snotty-nosed creature, his face almost permanently dirty, his hands chapped, his nails bitten, his handkerchief a sodden horror, his bottom frequently blue with bruises. It was partly the prospect of actual physical discomfort that made the thought of going back to school lie in one's breast like a lump of lead during the last few days of the holidays. A characteristic memory of St Cyprian's is the astonishing hardness of one's bed on the first night of term. Since this was an expensive school, I took a social step upwards by attending it, and yet the standard of comfort was in every way far lower than in my own home, or, indeed, than it would have been in a prosperous working-class home. One only had a hot bath once a week, for instance. The food was not only bad, it was also insufficient. Never before or since have I seen butter or jam scraped on bread so thinly. I do not think I can be imagining the fact that we were underfed, when I remember the lengths we would go in order to steal food. On a number of occasions I remember creeping down at two or three o'clock in the morning through what seemed like miles of pitch-dark stairways and passages—barefooted, stopping to listen after each step, paralysed with about equal fear of Sambo, ghosts and burglars—to steal stale bread from the pantry. The assistant masters had their meals with us, but they had somewhat better food, and if one got half a chance it was usual to steal left-over scraps of bacon rind or fried potato when their plates were removed.

As usual, I did not see the sound commercial reason for this underfeeding. On the whole I accepted Sambo's view that a boy's appetite is a sort of morbid growth which should be kept in check as much as possible. A maxim often repeated to us at St Cyprian's was that it is healthy to get up from a meal feeling as hungry as when you sat down. Only a generation earlier than this it had been common for school dinners to start off with a slab of unsweetened suet pudding, which, it was frankly said, 'broke the boys' appetites.' But the underfeeding was probably less flagrant at preparatory schools, where a boy was wholly dependent on the official diet, than at public schools, where he was allowed—indeed, expected—to buy extra food for himself. At some schools, he would literally not have had enough to eat unless he had bought regular supplies of eggs, sausages, sardines, etc.; and his parents had to allow him money for this purpose. At Eton, for instance, at any rate in College, a boy was given no solid meal after mid-day dinner. For his afternoon tea he was given a miserable supper of soup or fried fish, or more often bread and cheese, with water to drink. Sambo went down to see his eldest son at Eton and came back in snobbish ecstasies over the luxury in which the boys lived. 'They give them fried fish for supper!' he exclaimed, beaming all over his chubby face. 'There's no school like it in the world.' Fried fish! The habitual supper of the poorest of the working class! At very cheap boarding schools it was no doubt worse. A very early memory to mine is of seeing the boarders at a grammar school—the sons, probably, of farmers and shopkeepers—being fed on boiled lights.

Whoever writes about his childhood must beware of exaggeration and self-pity. I do not claim that I was a martyr or that St Cyprian's was a sort of Dotheboys Hall. But I should be falsifying my own memories if I did not record that they are largely memories of disgust. The overcrowded, underfed underwashed life that we led *was* disgusting, as I recall it. If I shut my eyes and say 'school', it is of course the physical surroundings that first come back to me: the flat playing field with its cricket pavilion and the little shed by the rifle range, the draughty dormitories, the dusty splintery passages, the square of asphalt in front of the gymnasium, the raw-looking pinewood chaplet at the back. And at almost every point some filthy detail obtrudes itself. For example, there were the pewter bowls out of which we had our porridge. They had overhanging rims, and under the rims there were accumulations of sour porridge, which could be flaked off in long strips. The porridge itself, too, contained more lumps, hairs and unexplained black things than one would have thought possible, unless someone were putting them there on purpose. It was never safe to start on that porridge without investigating it first. And there was the slimy water of the plunge bath—it was twelve or fifteen feet long, the whole school was supposed to go into it every morning, and I doubt whether the water was changed at all frequently—and the always-damp towels with their cheesy smell: and, on occasional visits in the winter, the murky sea-water of the local Baths, which came straight in from the beach and on which I once saw floating a human turd. And the sweaty smell of the changing-room with its greasy basins, and, giving on this, the row of filthy, dilapidated lavatories, which had no fastenings of any kind on the doors, so that whenever you were sitting there someone was sure to come crashing in. It is not easy for me to think of my schooldays without seeming to breathe in a whiff of something cold and evil-smelling—a sort of compound of sweaty stockings, dirty towels, faecal smells blowing along corridors, forks with old food between the prongs, neck-of-mutton stew, and the banging doors of the lavatories and the echoing chamber-pots in the dormitories.

It is true that I am by nature not gregarious, and the WC and dirty handkerchief side of life is necessarily more obtrusive when great numbers of human beings are crushed together in a small space. It is just as bad in an army, and worse, no doubt, in a prison. Besides, boyhood is the age of disgust. After one has learned to differentiate, and before one has become hardened—between seven and eighteen, say—one seems always to be walking the tight-rope over a cesspool. Yet I do not think I exaggerate the squalor of school life, when I remember how health and cleanliness were neglected, in spite of the hoo-ha about fresh air and cold water and keeping in hard training. It was common to remain constipated for days together. Indeed, one was hardly encouraged to keep one's bowels open, since the only aperients tolerated were castor oil or another almost equally horrible drink called liquorice powder. One was supposed to go into the plunge bath every morning, but some boys shirked it for days on end, simply making themselves scarce when the bell sounded, or else slipping along the edge of the bath among the crowd, and then wetting their hair with a little dirty water off the floor. A little boy of eight or nine will not necessarily keep himself clean unless there is someone to see that he does it. There was a new boy named Hazel, a pretty, mother's darling of a boy, who came a little while before I left. The first thing I noticed about him was the beautiful pearly whiteness of his teeth. By the end of that term his teeth were an extraordinary shade of green. During all that time, apparently, no one had taken sufficient interest in him to see that he brushed them.

But of course the differences between home and school were more than physical. That bump on the hard mattress, on the first night of term, used to give me a feeling of abrupt awakening, a feeling of: 'This is reality, this is what you are up against.' Your home might be far from perfect, but at least it was a place ruled by love rather than by fear, where you did not have to be perpetually on your guard against the people surrounding you. At eight years old you were suddenly taken out of this warm nest and flung into a world of force and fraud and secrecy, like a gold-fish into a tank full of pike. Against no matter what degree of bullying you had no redress. You could only have defended yourself by sneaking, which, except in a few rigidly defined circumstances, was the unforgivable sin. To write home and ask your parent to take you away would have been even less thinkable, since to do so would have been to admit yourself unhappy and unpopular, which a boy will never do. Boys are Erewhonians: they think that misfortune is disgraceful and must be concealed to all cost. It might perhaps have been considered permissible to complain to your parents about bad food, or an unjustified caning, or some other ill-treatment inflicted by masters and not by boys. The fact that Sambo never beat the richer boys suggests that such complaints were made occasionally. But in my own peculiar circumstances I could never have asked my parents to intervene on my behalf. Even before I understood about the reduced fees, I grasped that they were in some way under an obligation to Sambo, and therefore could not protect me against him. I have mentioned already that throughout my time at St Cyprian's I never had a cricket bat of my own. I had been told this was because 'your parents couldn't afford it'. One day in the holidays, by some casual remark, it came out that they had provided ten shillings to buy me one: yet no cricket bat appeared. I did not protest to my parents, let alone raise the subject with Sambo. How could I? I was dependent on him, and the ten shillings was merely a fragment of what I owed him. I realize now, of course, that it is immensely unlikely that Sambo had simply stuck to the money. No doubt the matter had slipped his memory. But the point is that I assumed that he had stuck to it, and that he had a right to do so if he chose.

How difficult it is for a child to have any real independence of attitude could be seen in our behaviour towards Flip. I think it would be true to say that every boy in the school hated and feared her. Yet we all fawned on her in the most abject way, and the top layer of our feelings towards her was a sort of guilt-stricken loyalty. Flip, although the discipline of the school depended more on her than on Sambo, hardly pretended to dispense strict justice. She was frankly capricious. An act which might get you a caning one day might next day be laughed off as a boyish prank, or even commended because it 'showed you had guts'. There were days when everyone cowered before those deep-set, accusing eyes, and there were days when she was like a flirtatious queen surrounded by courtier-lovers, laughing and joking, scattering largesse, or the promise of largesse ('And if you win the Harrow History Prize I'll give you a new case for your camera!'), and occasionally even packing three or four favoured boys into her Ford car and carrying them off to a teashop in town, where they were allowed to buy coffee and cakes. Flip was inextricably mixed up in my mind with Queen Elizabeth, whose relations with Leicester and Essex and Raleigh were intelligible to me from a very early age. A word we all constantly used in speaking of Flip was 'favour'. 'I'm in good favour;' we would say, or 'I'm in bad favour.' Except for the handful of wealthy or titled boys, no one was permanently in good favour, but on the other hand even the outcasts had patches of it from time to time. Thus, although my memories of Flip are mostly hostile, I also remember considerable periods when I basked under her smiles, when she called me 'old chap' and used my Christian name, and allowed me to frequent her private library, where I first made acquaintance with *Vanity Fair*. The high-water mark of good favour was to be invited to serve at table on Sunday nights when Flip and Sambo had guests to dinner. In clearing away, of course, one had a chance to finish off the scraps, but one also got a servile pleasure from standing behind the seated guests and darting deferentially forward when something was wanted. Whenever one had the chance to suck up, one did suck up, and at the first smile one's hatred turned into a sort of cringing love. I was always tremendously proud when I succeeded in making Flip laugh. I have even, at her command, written *vers d'occasion*, comic verses to celebrate memorable events in the life of the school.

I am anxious to make it clear that I was not a rebel, except by force of circumstances. I accepted the codes that I found in being. Once, towards the end of my time, I even sneaked to Brown about a suspected case of homosexuality. I did not know very well what homosexuality was, but I knew that it happened and was bad, and that this was one of the contexts in which it was proper to sneak. Brown told me I was 'a good fellow', which make me feel horribly ashamed. Before Flip one seemed as helpless as a snake before the snake-charmer. She had a hardly-varying vocabulary of praise and abuse, a whole series of set phrased, each of which promptly called forth the appropriate response. There was '*Buck* up, old chap!', which inspired one to paroxysms of energy; there was 'Don't *be* such a fool!' (or, 'It's path*et*ic, isn't it?'), which made one feel a born idiot; and there was 'It isn't very straight of you, is it?', which always brought one to the brink of tears. And yet all the while, at the middle of one's heart, there seemed to stand an incorruptible inner self who knew that whatever one did—whether one laughed or snivelled or went into frenzies of gratitude for small favours—one's only true feeling was hatred.

IV

I had learned early in my career that one can do wrong against one's will, and before long I also learned that one can do wrong without ever discovering what one has done or why it was wrong. There were sins that were too subtle to be explained, and there were others that were too terrible to be clearly mentioned. For example, there was sex, which was always smouldering just under the surface and which suddenly blew up into a tremendous row when I was about twelve.

At some preparatory schools homosexuality is not a problem but I think that St Cyprian's may have acquired a 'bad tone' thanks to the presence of the South American boys, who would perhaps mature a year or two earlier than an English boy. At that age I was not interested, so I do not actually know what went on, but I imagine it was group masturbation. At any rate, one day the storm suddenly burst over our heads. There were summonses, interrogations, confessions, floggings, repentances, solemn lectures of which one understood nothing except that some irredeemable sin known as 'swinishness' or 'beastliness' had been committed. One of the ringleaders, a boy named Horne, was flogged, according to eye-witnesses, for a quarter of an hour continuously before being expelled. His yells rang through the house. But we were all implicated, more or less, or felt ourselves to be implicated. Guilt seemed to hang in the air like a pall or smoke. A solemn, black-haired imbecile of an assistant master, who was later to be a Member of Parliament took the older boys to a secluded room and delivered a talk on the Temple of the Body.

'Don't you realize what a wonderful thing your body is?' he said gravely. 'You talk of your motor-car engines, your Rolls-Royces and Daimlers and so on. Don't you understand that no engine ever made is fit to be compared with your body? And then you go and wreck it, ruin it—for life!'

He turned his cavernous black eyes on me and added quite sadly:

'And you, whom I'd always believed to be quite a decent person after your fashion—you, I hear, are one of the very worst.'

A feeling of doom descended upon me. So I was guilty too. I too had done the dreadful thing, whatever it was, that wrecked you for life, body and soul, and ended in suicide or the lunatic asylum. Till then I had hoped that I was innocent, and the conviction of sin which now took possession of me was perhaps all the stronger because I did not know what I had done. I was not among those who were interrogated and flogged, and it was not until the row was well over that I even learned about the trivial accident that had connected my name with it. Even then I understood nothing. It was not till about two years later that I fully grasped what that lecture on the Temple of the Body had referred to.

At this time I was in an almost sexless state, which is normal, or at any rate common, in boys of that age; I was therefore in the position of simultaneously knowing and not knowing what used to be called the Facts of Life. At five or six, like many children, I had passed though a phase of sexuality. My friends were the plumber's children up the road, and we used sometimes to play games of a vaguely erotic kind. One was called 'playing at doctors', and I remember getting a faint but definitely pleasant thrill from holding a toy trumpet, which was supposed to be a stethoscope, against a little girl's belly. About the same time I fell deeply in love, a far more worshipping kind of love than I have ever felt for anyone since, with a girl named Elsie at the convent school which I attended. She seemed to me grown up, so I suppose she must have been fifteen. After that, as so often happens, all sexual feelings seemed to go out of me for many years. At twelve I knew more than I had known as a young child, but I understood less, because I no longer knew the essential fact that there is something pleasant in sexual activity. Between roughly seven and fourteen, the whole subject seemed to me uninteresting and, when for some reason I was forced to think of it, disgusting. My knowledge of the so-called Facts of Life was derived from animals, and was therefore distorted, and in any case was only intermittent. I knew that animals copulated and that human beings had bodies resembling those of animals: but that human beings also copulated I only knew as it were, reluctantly, when something, a phrase in the Bible, perhaps, compelled me to remember it. Not having desire, I had no curiosity, and was willing to leave many questions unanswered. Thus, I knew in principle how the baby gets into the woman, but I did not know how it gets out again, because I had never followed the subject up. I knew all the dirty words, and in my bad moments I would repeat them to myself, but I did not know what the worst of them meant, nor want to know. They were abstractly wicked, a sort of verbal charm. While I remained in this state, it was easy for me to remain ignorant of any sexual misdeeds that went on about me, and to be hardly wiser even when the row broke. At most, through the veiled and terrible warnings of Flip, Sambo and all the rest of them, I grasped that the crime of which we were all guilty was somehow connected with the sexual organs. I had noticed, without feeling much interest, that one's penis sometimes stands up of its own accord (this starts happening to a boy long before he has any conscious sexual desires), and I was inclined to believe, or half-believe, that that must be the crime. At any rate, it was something to do with the penis—so much I understood. Many other boys, I have no doubt, were equally in the dark.

After the talk on the Temple of the Body (days later, it seems in retrospect: the row seemed to continue for days), a dozen of us were seated at a long shiny table which Sambo used for the scholarship class, under Flip's lowering eye. A long desolate wail rang out from a room somewhere above. A very small boy named Ronalds, aged no more than about ten, who was implicated in some way, was being flogged, or was recovering from a flogging. At the sound, Flip's eyes searched our faces, and settled upon me.

'*You see*,' she said.

I will not swear that she said 'You see what you have done,' but that was the sense of it. We were all bowed down with shame. It was *our* fault. Somehow or other we had led poor Ronalds astray: *we* were responsible for his agony and his ruin. Then Flip turned upon another boy named Heath. It is thirty years ago, and I cannot remember for certain whether she merely quoted a verse from the Bible, or whether she actually brought out a Bible and made Heath read it; but at any rate the text indicated was: 'Who so shall offend one of these little ones that believe in me, it were better for him that a millstone were hanged about his neck, and that he were drowned in the depth of the sea.'

That, too, was terrible. Ronalds was one of these little ones, we had offended him; it were better that millstone were hanged about our necks and that we were drowned in the depth of the sea.

'Have you thought about that, Heath—have you thought what it means?' Flip said. And Heath broke down into snivelling tears.

Another boy, Beacham, whom I have mentioned already, was similarly overwhelmed with shame by the accusation that he 'had black rings round his eyes'.

'Have you looked in the glass lately, Beacham?' said Flip. 'Aren't you ashamed to go about with a face like that? Do you think everyone doesn't know what it means when a boy has black rings round his eyes?'

Once again the load of guilt and fear seemed to settle down upon me. Had *I* got black rings round my eyes? A couple of years later I realized that these were supposed to be a symptom by which masturbators could be detected. But already, without knowing this, I accepted the black rings as a sure sign of depravity, *some* kind of depravity. And many times, even before I grasped the supposed meaning, I have gazed anxiously into the glass, looking for the first hint of that dreaded stigma, the confession which the secret sinner writes upon his own face.

These terrors wore off, or became merely intermittent, without affecting what one might call my official beliefs. It was still true about the madhouse and the suicide's grave, but it was no longer acutely frightening. Some months later it happened that I once again saw Horne, the ringleader who had been flogged and expelled. Horne was one of the outcasts, the son of poor middle-class parents, which was no doubt part of the reason why Sambo had handled him so roughly. The term after his expulsion he went on to Eastbourne College, the small local public school, which was hideously despised at St Cyprian's and looked on as 'not really' a public school at all. Only a very few boys from St Cyprian's went there, and Sambo always spoke of them with a sort of contemptuous pity. You had no chance if you went to a school like that: at the best your destiny would be a clerkship. I thought of Horne as a person who at thirteen had already forfeited all hope of any decent future. Physically, morally and socially he was finished. Moreover I assumed that his parents had only sent him to Eastbourne College because after his disgrace no 'good' school would have him.

During the following term, when we were out for a walk, we passed Horne in the street. He looked completely normal. He was a strongly-built, rather good-looking boy with black hair. I immediately noticed that he looked better than when I had last seen him—his complexion, previously rather pale, was pinker—and that he did not seem embarrassed at meeting us. Apparently he was not ashamed either of having been expelled, or of being at Eastbourne College. If one could gather anything from the way he looked at us as we filed past, it was that he was glad to have escaped from St Cyprian's. But the encounter made very little impression on me. I drew no inference from the fact that Horne, ruined in body and soul, appeared to be happy and in good health. I still believed in the sexual mythology that had been taught me by Sambo and Flip. The mysterious, terrible dangers were still there. Any morning the black rings might appear round your eyes and you would know that you too were among the lost ones. Only it no longer seemed to matter very much. These contradictions can exist easily in the mind of a child, because of its own vitality. It accepts—how can it do otherwise?—the nonsense that its elders tell it, but its youthful body, and the sweetness of the physical world, tell it another story. It was the same with Hell, which up to the age of about fourteen I officially believed in. Almost certainly Hell existed, and there were occasions when a vivid sermon could scare you into fits. But somehow it never lasted. The fire that waited for you was real fire, it would hurt in the same way as when you burnt your finger, and for ever, but most of the time you could contemplate it without bothering.

V

The various codes which were presented to you at St Cyprian's—religious, moral, social and intellectual—contradicted one another if you worked out their implications. The essential conflict was between the tradition of nineteenth-century asceticism and the actually existing luxury and snobbery of the pre-1914 age. On the one side were low-church Bible Christianity, sex puritanism, insistence on hard work, respect for academic distinction, disapproval of self-indulgence: on the other, contempt for 'braininess', and worship of games, contempt for foreigners and the working class, an almost neurotic dread of poverty, and, above all, the assumption not only that money and privilege are the things that matter, but that it is better to inherit them than to have to work for them. Broadly, you were bidden to be at once a Christian and a social success, which is impossible. At the time I did not perceive that the various ideals which were set before us cancelled out. I merely saw that they were all, or nearly all, unattainable, so far as I was concerned, since they all depended not only on what you did but on what you *were*.

Very early, at the age of only ten or eleven, I reached the conclusion—no one told me this, but on the other hand I did not simply make it up out of my own head: somehow it was in the air I breathed—that you were no good unless you had £100,000. I had perhaps fixed on this particular sum as a result of reading Thackeray. The interest on £100,000 would be £4,000 a year (I was in favour of a safe 4 per cent), and this seemed to me the minimum income that you must possess if you were to belong to the real top crust, the people in the country houses. But it was clear that I could never find my way into that paradise, to which you did not really belong unless you were born into it. You could only make money, if at all by a mysterious operation called 'going to the city', and when you came out of the City, having won you £100,000, you were fat and old. But the truly enviable thing about the top-notchers was that they were rich while young. For people like me, the ambitious middle class, the examination-passers, only a bleak, laborious kind of success was possible. You clambered upwards on a ladder of scholarships into the Civil Service or the Indian Civil Service, or possibly you became a barrister. And if at any point you 'slacked' or 'went off' and missed one of the rungs in the ladder, you became 'a little office boy at forty pounds a year'. But even if you climbed to the highest niche that was open to you, you could still only be an underling, a hanger-on of the people who really counted.

Even if I had not learned this from Sambo and Flip, I would have learned it from other boys. Looking back, it is astonishing how intimately, intelligently snobbish we all were, how knowledgeable about names and addresses, how swift to detect small differences in accents and manners and the cut of clothes. There were some boys who seemed to drip money from their pores even in the bleak misery of the middle of a winter term. At the beginning and end of the term, especially, there was naively snobbish chatter about Switzerland, and Scotland with its ghillies and grouse moors, and 'my uncle's yacht', and 'our place in the country'. And 'my pony' and 'my pater's touring car'. There never was, I suppose, in the history of the world a time when the sheer vulgar fatness of wealth, without any kind of aristocratic elegance to redeem it, was so obtrusive as in those years before 1914. It was the age when crazy millionaires in curly top-hats and lavender waistcoats gave champagne parties in rococo house-boats on the Thames, the age of diabolo and hobble skirts, the age of the 'knut' in his grey bowler and cut-away coat, the age of *The Merry Widow*, Saki's novels, *Peter Pan* and *Where the Rainbow Ends*, the age when people talked about chocs and cigs and ripping and topping and heavenly, when they went for divvy week-ends at Brighton and had scrumptious teas at the Troc. From the whole decade before 1914 there seems to breathe forth a smell of the more vulgar, un-grown-up kind of luxury, a smell of brilliantine and crème-de-menthe and soft-centred chocolates—an atmosphere, as it were, of eating everlasting strawberry ices on green lawns to the tune of the Eton Boating Song. The extraordinary thing was the way in which everyone took it for granted that this oozing, bulging wealth of the English upper and upper-middle classes would last for ever, and was part of the order of things. After 1918 it was never quite the same again. Snobbishness and expensive habits came back, certainly, but they were self-conscious and on the defensive. Before the war the worship of money was entirely unreflecting and untroubled by any pang of conscience. The goodness of money was as unmistakable as the goodness of health or beauty, and a glittering car, a title or a horde of servants was mixed up in people's minds with the idea of actual moral virtue.

At St Cyprian's, in term-time, the general bareness of life enforced a certain democracy, but any mention of the holidays, and the consequent competitive swanking about cars and butlers and country houses, promptly called class distinctions into being. The school was pervaded by a curious cult of Scotland, which brought out the fundamental contradiction in our standard of values. Flip claimed Scottish ancestry, and she favoured the Scottish boys, encouraging them to wear kilts in their ancestral tartan instead of the school uniform, and even christened her youngest child by a Gaelic name. Ostensibly we were supposed to admire the Scots because they were 'grim' and 'dour' ('stern' was perhaps the key word), and irresistible on the field of battle. In the big schoolroom there was a steel engraving of the charge to the Scots Greys at Waterloo, all looking as though they enjoyed every moment of it. Our picture of Scotland was made up of burns, braes, kilts, sporrans, claymores, bagpipes and the like, all somehow mixed up with the invigorating effects of porridge, Protestantism and a cold climate. But underlying this was something quite different. The real reason for the cult of Scotland was that only very rich people could spend their summers there. And the pretended belief in Scottish superiority was a cover for the bad conscience of the occupying English, who had pushed the Highland peasantry off their farms to make way for the deer forests, and then compensated them by turning them into servants. Flip's face always beamed with innocent snobbishness when she spoke of Scotland. Occasionally she even attempted a trace of Scottish accent. Scotland was a private paradise which a few initiates could talk about and make outsiders feel small.

'You going to Scotland this hols?'

'Rather! We go every year.'

'My pater's got three miles of river.'

'My pater's giving me a new gun for the twelfth. There's jolly good black game where we go. Get out, Smith! What are listening for? You've never been to Scotland. I bet you don't know what a black-cock looks like.'

Following on this, imitations of the cry of a black-cock, of the roaring of a stag, of the accent of 'our ghillies', etc. etc.

And the questionings that new boys of doubtful social origin were sometimes put through—questionings quite surprising in their mean-minded particularity, when one reflects that the inquisitors were only twelve or thirteen!

'How much a year has your pater got? What part of London do you live in? Is that Knightsbridge or Kensington? How many bathrooms has you house got? How many servants do your people keep? Have you got a butler? Well, then, have you got a cook? Where do you get your clothes made? How many shows did you go to in the hols? How much money did you bring back with you?' etc. etc.

I have seen a little new boy, hardly older than eight, desperately lying his way through such a catechism:

'Have your people got a car?'

'Yes.'

'What sort of car?'

'Daimler.'

'How many horse-power?'

(Pause, and leap in the dark.) 'Fifteen.'

'What kind of lights?'

The little boy is bewildered.

'What kind of lights? Electric or acetylene?'

(A longer pause, and another leap in the dark.) 'Acetylene.'

'Coo! He says his pater's car's got acetylene lamps. They went out years ago. It must be as old as the hills.'

'Rot! He's making it up. He hasn't got a car. He's just a navvy. Your pater's a navvy.'

And so on.

By the social standards that prevailed about me, I was no good, and could not be any good. But all the different kinds of virtue seemed to be mysteriously interconnected and to belong to much the same people. It was not only money that mattered: there were also strength, beauty, charm, athleticism and something called 'guts' or 'character', which in reality meant the power to impose your will on others. I did not possess any of these qualities. At games, for instance, I was hopeless. I was a fairly good swimmer and not altogether contemptible at cricket, but these had no prestige value, because boys only attach importance to a game if it requires strength and courage. What counted was football, at which I was a funk. I loathed the game, and since I could see no pleasure or usefulness in it, it was very difficult for me to show courage at it. Football, it seemed to me, is not really played for the pleasure of kicking a ball about, but is a species of fighting. The lovers of football are large, boisterous, nobbly boys who are good at knocking down and trampling on slightly smaller boys. That was the pattern of school life—a continuous triumph of the strong over the weak. Virtue consisted in winning: it consisted in being bigger, stronger, handsomer, richer, more popular, more elegant, more unscrupulous than other people—in dominating them, bullying them, making them suffer pain, making them look foolish, getting the better of them in every way. Life was hierarchical and whatever happened was right. There were the strong, who deserved to win and always did win, and there were the weak, who deserved to lose and always did lose, everlastingly.

I did not question the prevailing standards, because so far as I could see there were no others. How could the rich, the strong, the elegant, the fashionable, the powerful, be in the wrong? It was their world, and the rules they made for it must be the right ones. And yet from a very early age I was aware of the impossibility of any *subjective* conformity. Always at the centre of my heart the inner self seemed to be awake, pointing out the difference between the moral obligation and the psychological *fact*. It was the same in all matters, worldly or other-worldly. Take religion, for instance. You were supposed to love God, and I did not question this. Till the age of about fourteen I believed in God, and believed that the accounts given of him were true. But I was well aware that I did not love him. On the contrary, I hated him, just as I hated Jesus and the Hebrew patriarchs. If I had sympathetic feelings towards any character in the Old Testament, it was towards such people as Cain, Jezebel, Haman, Agag, Sisera: in the New Testament my friends, if any, were Ananias, Caiaphas, Judas and Pontius Pilate. But the whole business of religion seemed to be strewn with psychological impossibilities. The Prayer Book told you, for example, to love God and fear him: but how could you love someone whom you feared? With your private affections it was the same. What you *ought* to feel was usually clear enough but the appropriate emotion could not be commanded. Obviously it was my duty to feel grateful towards Flip and Sambo; but I was not grateful. It was equally clear that one ought to love one's father, but I knew very well that I merely disliked my own father, whom I had barely seen before I was eight and who appeared to me simply as a gruff-voiced elderly man forever saying 'Don't'. It was not that one did not want to possess the right qualities or feel the correct emotions, but that one could not. The good and the possible never seemed to coincide.

There was a line of verse that I came across not actually while I was at St Cyprian's, but a year of two later, and which seemed to strike a sort of leaden echo in my heart. It was: 'The armies of unalterable law'. I understood to perfection what it meant to be Lucifer, defeated and justly defeated, with no possibility of revenge. The schoolmasters with their canes, the millionaires with their Scottish castles, the athletes with their curly hair—these were the armies of unalterable law. It was not easy, at that date, to realize that in fact it was alterable. And according to that law I was damned. I had no money, I was weak, I was ugly, I was unpopular, I had a chronic cough, I was cowardly, I smelt. This picture, I should add, was not altogether fanciful. I was an unattractive boy. St Cyprian's soon made me so, even if I had not been so before. But a child's belief in its own shortcomings is not much influenced by facts. I believed, for example, that I 'smelt'. But this was based simply on general probability. It was notorious that disagreeable people smelt, and therefore presumably I did so too. Again, until after I had left school for good I continued to believe that I was preternaturally ugly. It was what my schoolfellows had told me, and I had no other authority to refer to. The conviction that it was *not possible* for me to be a success went deep enough to influence my actions till far into adult life. Until I was about thirty I always planned my life on the assumption not only that any major undertaking was bound to fail, but that I could only expect to live a few years longer.

But this sense of guilt and inevitable failure was balanced by something else: that is, the instinct to survive. Even a creature that is weak, ugly, cowardly, smelly and in no way justifiable still wants to stay alive and be happy after its own fashion. I could not invert the existing scale of values, or turn myself into a success, but I could accept my failure and make the best of it. I could resign myself to being what I was, and then endeavour to survive on those terms.

To survive, or at least to preserve any kind of independence, was essentially criminal, since it meant breaking rules which you yourself recognized. There was a boy named Johnny Hale who for some months oppressed me horribly. He was a big, powerful, coarsely handsome boy with a very red face and curly black hair, who was forever twisting somebody's arm, wringing somebody's ear, flogging somebody with a riding-crop (he was a member of the Sixth Form), or performing prodigies of activity on the football field. Flip loved him (hence the fact he was habitually called by his Christian name) and Sambo commended him as a boy who 'had character' and 'could keep order'. He was followed about by a group of toadies who nicknamed him Strong Man.

One day, when we were taking off our overcoats in the changing-room, Hale picked on me for some reason. I 'answered him back'. Whereupon he gripped my wrist, twisted it round and bent my forearm back upon itself in a hideously painful way. I remember his handsome, jeering red face bearing down upon mine. He was, I think, older than I, besides being enormously stronger. As he let go of me a terrible, wicked resolve formed itself in my heart. I would get back on him by hitting him when he did not expect it. It was a strategic moment, for the master who had been 'taking' the walk would be coming back almost immediately, and then there could be no fight. I let perhaps a minute go by, walked up to Hale with the most harmless air I could assume, and then, getting the weight of my body behind it, smashed my fist into his face. He was flung backwards by the blow, and some blood ran out of his mouth. His always sanguine face turned almost black with rage. Then he turned away to rinse his mouth at the wash-basins.

'*All right!*' he said to me between his teeth as the master led us away.

For days after this he followed me about, challenging me to fight. Although terrified out of my wits, I steadily refused to fight. I said that the blow in the face had served him right, and there was an end of it. Curiously enough he did not simply fall upon me there and then, which public opinion would probably have supported him in doing. So gradually the matter tailed off, and there was no fight.

Now, I had behaved wrongly, by my own code no less than his. To hit him unawares was wrong. But to refuse afterwards to fight knowing that if we fought we would beat me—that was far worse: it was cowardly. If I had refused because I disapproved of fighting, or because I genuinely felt the matter to be closed, it would have been all right; but I had refused merely because I was afraid. Even my revenge was made empty by that fact. I had struck the blow in a moment of mindless violence, deliberately not looking far ahead and merely determined to get my own back for once and damn the consequences.

I had had time to realize that what I did was wrong, but it was the kind of crime from which you could get some satisfaction. Now all was nullified. There had been a sort of courage in the first act, but my subsequent cowardice had wiped it out.

The fact I hardly noticed was that though Hale formally challenged me to fight, he did not actually attack me. Indeed, after receiving that one blow he never oppressed me again. It was perhaps twenty years before I saw the significance of this. At the time I could not see beyond the moral dilemma that is presented to the weak in a world governed by the strong: Break the rules, or perish. I did not see that in that case the weak have the right to make a different set of rules for themselves; because, even if such an idea had occurred to me, there was no one in my environment who could have confirmed me in it. I lived in a world of boys, gregarious animals questioning nothing, accepting the law of the stronger and avenging their own humiliations by passing them down to someone smaller. My situation was that of countless other boys, and if potentially I was more of a rebel than most, it was only because, by boyish standards, I was a poorer specimen. But I never did rebel intellectually, only emotionally. I had nothing to help me except my dumb selfishness, my inability—not, indeed, to despise myself, but to *dislike* myself—my instinct to survive.

It was about a year after I hit Johnny Hale in the face that I left St Cyprian's for ever. It was the end of a winter term. With a sense of coming out from darkness into sunlight I put on my Old Boy's tie as we dressed for the journey. I well remember the feeling of emancipation, as though the tie had been at once a badge of manhood and an amulet against Flip's voice and Sambo's cane. I was escaping from bondage. It was not that I expected, or even intended, to be any more successful at a public school than I had been at St Cyprian's. But still, I was escaping. I knew that at a public school there would be more privacy, more neglect, more chance to be idle and self-indulgent and degenerate. For years I had been resolved—unconsciously at first, but consciously later on—that when once my scholarship was won I would 'slack off' and cram no longer. This resolve, by the way, was so fully carried out that between the ages of thirteen and twenty-two or three I hardly ever did a stroke of avoidable work.

Flip shook hands to say good-bye. She even gave me my Christian name for the occasion. But there was a sort of patronage, almost a sneer, in her face and in her voice. The tone in which she said good-bye was nearly the tone in which she had been used to say *little butterflies*. I had won two scholarships but I was a failure, because success was measured not by what you did but by what you *were*. I was 'not a good type of boy' and could bring no credit on the school. I did not possess character or courage or health or strength or money, or even good manners, the power to look like a gentlemen.

'Good-bye,' Flip's parting smile seemed to say; 'it's not worth quarrelling now. You haven't made much of a success of your time at St Cyprian's, have you? And I don't suppose you'll get on awfully well at a public school either. We make a mistake, really, in wasting our time and money on you. This kind of education hasn't much to offer to a boy with your background and your outlook. Oh, don't think we don't understand you! We know all about those ideas you have at the back of your head, we know you disbelieve in everything we've taught you, and we know you aren't in the least grateful for all we've done for you. But there's no use in bringing it all up now. We aren't responsible for you any longer, and we shan't be seeing you again. Let's just admit that you're one of our failures and part without ill-feeling. And so, good-bye.'

That at least was what I read into her face. And yet how happy I was, that winter morning, as the train bore me away with the gleaming new silk tie (dark green, pale blue and black, if I remember rightly) round my neck! The world was opening before me, just a little, like a grey sky which exhibits a narrow crack of blue. A public school would be better fun than St Cyprian's, but at bottom equally alien. In a world where the prime necessities were money, titled relatives, athleticism, tailor-made clothes, neatly-brushed hair, a charming smile, I was no good. All I had gained was a breathing-space. A little quietude, a little self-indulgence, a little respite from cramming—and then, ruin. What kind of ruin I did not know: perhaps the colonies or an office stool, perhaps prison or an early death. But first a year or two in which one could 'slack off' and get the benefit of one's sins, like Doctor Faustus. I believed firmly in my evil destiny, and yet I was acutely happy. It is the advantage of being thirteen that you can not only live in the moment, but do so with full consciousness, foreseeing the future and yet not caring about it. Next term I was going to Wellington. I had also won a scholarship at Eton, but it was uncertain whether there would be a vacancy, and I was going to Wellington first. At Eton you had a room to yourself—a room which might even have a fire in it. At Wellington you had your own cubicle, and could make yourself cocoa in the evenings. The privacy of it, the grown-upness! And there would be libraries to hang about in, and summer afternoons when you could shirk games and mooch about the countryside alone, with no master driving you along. Meanwhile there were the holidays. There was the .22 rifle that I had bought the previous holidays (the Crackshot, it was called, costing twenty-two and sixpence), and Christmas was coming next week. There were also the pleasures of overeating. I thought of some particularly voluptuous cream buns which could be bought for twopence each at a shop in our town. (This was 1916, and food-rationing had not yet started.) Even the detail that my journey-money had been slightly miscalculated, leaving about a shilling over—enough for an unforeseen cup of coffee and a cake or two somewhere on the way—was enough to fill me with bliss. There was time for a bit of happiness before the future closed in upon me. But I did know that the future was dark. Failure, failure, failure—failure behind me, failure ahead of me—that was by far the deepest conviction that I carried away.

VI

All this was thirty years ago and more. The question is: Does a child at school go through the same kind of experiences nowadays?

The only honest answer, I believe, is that we do not with certainty know. Of course it is obvious that the present-day *attitude* towards education is enormously more humane and sensible than that of the past. The snobbishness that was an integral part of my own education would be almost unthinkable today, because the society that nourished it is dead. I recall a conversation that must have taken place about a year before I left St Cyprian's. A Russian boy, large and fair-haired, a year older than myself, was questioning me.

'How much a year has your father got?'

I told him what I thought it was, adding a few hundreds to make it sound better. The Russian boy, neat in his habits, produced a pencil and a small note-book and made a calculation.

'My father has over two hundred times as much money as yours,' he announced with a sort of amused contempt.

That was in 1915. What happened to that money a couple of years later, I wonder? And still more I wonder, do conversations of that kind happen at preparatory schools now?

Clearly there has been a vast change of outlook, a general growth of 'enlightenment', even among ordinary, unthinking middle-class people. Religious belief, for instance, has largely vanished, dragging other kinds of nonsense after it. I imagine that very few people nowadays would tell a child that if it masturbates it will end in the lunatic asylum. Beating, too, has become discredited, and has even been abandoned at many schools. Nor is the underfeeding of children looked on as a normal, almost meritorious act. No one now would openly set out to give his pupils as little food as they could do with, or tell them that it is healthy to get up from a meal as hungry as you sat down. The whole status of children has improved, partly because they have grown relatively less numerous. And the diffusion of even a little psychological knowledge has made it harder for parents and schoolteachers to indulge their aberrations in the name of discipline. Here is a case, not known to me personally, but known to some one I can vouch for, and happening within my own lifetime. A small girl, daughter of a clergyman, continued wetting her bed at an age when she should have grown out of it. In order to punish her for this dreadful deed, her father took her to a large garden party and there introduced her to the whole company as a little girl who wetted her bed: and to underline her wickedness he had previously painted her face black. I do not suggest that Flip and Sambo would actually have done a thing like this, but I doubt whether it would have much surprised them. After all, things do change. And yet—!

The question is not whether boys are still buckled into Eton collars on Sunday, or told that babies are dug up under gooseberry bushes. That kind of thing is at an end, admittedly. The real question is whether it is still normal for a school child to live for years amid irrational terrors and lunatic misunderstandings. And here one is up against the very great difficulty of knowing what a child really feels and thinks. A child which appears reasonably happy may actually be suffering horrors which it cannot or will not reveal. It lives in a sort of alien under-water world which we can only penetrate by memory or divination. Our chief clue is the fact that we were once children ourselves, and many people appear to forget the atmosphere of their own childhood almost entirely. Think for instance of the unnecessary torments that people will inflict by sending a child back to school with clothes of the wrong pattern, and refusing to see that this matters! Over things of this kind a child will sometimes utter a protest, but a great deal of the time its attitude is one of simple concealment. Not to expose your true feelings to an adult seems to be instinctive from the age of seven or eight onwards. Even the affection that one feels for a child, the desire to protect and cherish it, is a cause of misunderstanding. One can love a child, perhaps, more deeply than one can love another adult, but it is rash to assume that the child feels any love in return. Looking back on my own childhood, after the infant years were over, I do not believe that I ever felt love for any mature person, except my mother, and even her I did not trust, in the sense that shyness made me conceal most of my real feelings from her. Love, the spontaneous, unqualified emotion of love, was something I could only feel for people who were young. Towards people who were old—and remember that 'old' to a child means over thirty, or even over twenty-five—I could feel reverence, respect, admiration or compunction, but I seemed cut off from them by a veil of fear and shyness mixed up with physical distaste. People are too ready to forget the child's *physical* shrinking from the adult. The enormous size of grown-ups, their ungainly, rigid bodies, their coarse, wrinkled skins, their great relaxed eyelids, their yellow teeth, and the whiffs of musty clothes and beer and sweat and tobacco that disengage from them at every movement! Part of the reason for the ugliness of adults, in a child's eyes, is that the child is usually looking upwards, and few faces are at their best when seen from below. Besides, being fresh and unmarked itself, the child has impossibly high standards in the matter of skin and teeth and complexion. But the greatest barrier of all is the child's misconception about age. A child can hardly envisage life beyond thirty, and in judging people's ages it will make fantastic mistakes. It will think that a person of twenty-five is forty, that a person of forty is sixty-five, and so on. Thus, when I fell in love with Elsie I took her to be grown-up. I met her again, when I was thirteen and she, I think, must have been twenty-three; she now seemed to me a middle-aged woman, somewhat past her best. And the child thinks of growing old as an almost obscene calamity, which for some mysterious reason will never happen to itself. All who have passed the age of thirty are joyless grotesques, endlessly fussing about things of no importance and staying alive without, so far as the child can see, having anything to live for. Only child life is real life. The schoolmaster who imagines that he is loved and trusted by his boys is in fact mimicked and laughed at behind his back. An adult who does not seem dangerous nearly always seems ridiculous.

I base these generalizations on what I can recall of my own childhood outlook. Treacherous though memory is, it seems to me the chief means we have of discovering how a child's mind works. Only by resurrecting our own memories can we realize how incredibly distorted is the child's vision of the world. Consider this, for example. How would St Cyprian's appear to me now, if I could go back, at my present age, and see it as it was in 1915? What should I think of Sambo and Flip, those terrible, all-powerful monsters? I should see them as a couple of silly, shallow, ineffectual people, eagerly clambering up a social ladder which any thinking person could see to be on the point of collapse. I would no more be frightened of them than I would be frightened of a dormouse. Moreover, in those days they seemed to me fantastically old, whereas—though of this I am not certain—I imagine they must have been somewhat younger than I am now. And how would Johnny Hale appear with his blacksmith's arms and his red, jeering face? Merely a scruffy little boy, barely distinguishable from hundreds of other scruffy little boys. The two sets of facts can lie side by side in my mind, because those happen to be my own memories. But it would be very difficult for me to see with the eyes of any other child, except by an effort of the imagination which might lead me completely astray. The child and the adult live in different worlds. If that is so, we cannot be certain that school, at any rate boarding school, is not still for many children as dreadful an experience as it used to be. Take away God, Latin, the cane, class distinctions and sexual taboos, and the fear, the hatred, the snobbery and the misunderstanding might still all be there. It will have been seen that my own main trouble was an utter lack of any sense of proportion or probability. This led me to accept outrages and believe absurdities, and to suffer torments over things which were in fact of no importance. It is not enough to say that I was 'silly' and 'ought to have known better'. Look back into your own childhood and think of the nonsense you used to believe and the trivialities which could make you suffer. Of course my own case had its individual variations, but essentially it was that of countless other boys. The weakness of the child is that it starts with a blank sheet. It neither understands nor questions the society in which it lives, and because of its credulity other people can work upon it, infecting it with the sense of inferiority and the dread of offending against mysterious, terrible laws. It may be that everything that happened to me at St Cyprian's could happen in the most 'enlightened' school, though perhaps in subtler forms. Of one thing, however, I do feel fairly sure, and that is that boarding schools are worse than day schools. A child has a better chance with the sanctuary of its home near at hand. And I think the characteristic faults of the English upper and middle classes may be partly due to the practice, general until recently, of sending children away from home as young as nine, eight or even seven.

I have never been back to St Cyprian's. Reunions, old boys'

dinners and such-like leave me something more than cold, even when my memories are friendly. I have never even been down to Eton, where I was relatively happy, though I did once pass through it in 1933 and noted with interest that nothing seemed to have changed, except that the shops now sold radios. As for St Cyprian's, for years I loathed its very name so deeply that I could not view it with enough detachment to see the significance of the things that happened to me there. In a way it is only within the last decade that I have really thought over my schooldays, vividly though their memory has always haunted me. Nowadays, I believe, it would make very little impression on me to see the place again, if it still exists. (I remember hearing a rumour some years ago that it had been burnt down.) If I had to pass through Eastbourn I would not make a detour to avoid the school: and if I happened to pass the school itself I might even stop for a moment by the low brick wall, with the steep bank running down from it, and look across the flat playing field at the ugly building with the square of asphalt in front of it. And if I went inside and smelt again the inky, dusty smell of the big schoolroom, the rosiny smell of the chapel, the stagnant smell of the swimming bath and the cold reek of the lavatories, I think I should only feel what one invariably feels in revisiting any scene of childhood: How small everything has grown, and how terrible is the deterioration in myself! But it is a fact that for many years I could hardly have borne to look at it again. Except upon dire necessity I would not have set foot in Eastbourne. I even conceived a prejudice against Sussex, as the country that contained St Cyprian's, and as an adult I have only once been in Sussex, on a short visit. Now, however, the place is out of my system for good. Its magic works no longer, and I have not even enough animosity left to make me hope that Flip and Sambo are dead or that the story of the school being burnt down was true.

9

HATEFUL THINGS

Sei Shonagon

One is in a hurry to leave, but one's visitor keeps chattering away. If it is someone of no importance, one can get rid of him by saying, 'You must tell me all about it next time'; but, should it be the sort of visitor whose presence commands one's best behaviour, the situation is hateful indeed.

One finds that a hair has got caught in the stone on which one is rubbing one's inkstick, or again that gravel is lodged in the inkstick, making a nasty, grating sound.

Someone has suddenly fallen ill and one summons the exorcist. Since he is not at home, one has to send messengers to look for him. After one has had a long, fretful wait, the exorcist finally arrives, and with a sigh of relief one asks him to start his incantations. But perhaps he has been exorcizing too many evil spirits lately, for hardly has he installed himself and begun praying when his voice becomes drowsy. Oh, how hateful!

A man who has nothing in particular to recommend him discusses all sorts of subjects at random as though he knew everything.

An elderly person warms the palms of his hands over a brazier and stretches out the wrinkles. No young man would dream of behaving in such a fashion; old people can really be quite shameless. I have seen some dreary old creatures actually resting their feet on the brazier and rubbing them against the edge while they speak. These are the kind of people who in visiting someone's house first use their fans to wipe away the dust from the mat and, when they finally sit on it, cannot stay still but are forever spreading out the front of their hunting costume or even tucking it up under their knees. One might suppose that such behaviour was restricted to people of humble station, but I have observed it in quite well-bred people, including a Senior Secretary of the Fifth Rank in the Ministry of Ceremonial and a former Governor of Suruga.

I hate the sight of men in their cups who shout, poke their fingers in their mouths, stroke their beards and pass on the wine to their neighbours with cries of 'Have some more! Drink up!' They tremble, shake their heads, twist their faces and gesticulate like children who are singing, 'We're off to see the governor!' I have seen really well-bred people behave like this and I find it most distasteful.

To envy others and complain about one's own lot; to speak badly about people; to be inquisitive about the most trivial matters and to resent and abuse people for not telling one, or, if one does manage to worm out some facts, to inform everyone in the most detailed fashion as if one had known all from the beginning—oh, how hateful!

One is just about to be told some interesting piece of news when a baby starts crying.

A flight of crows circle over with loud caws.

An admirer has come on a clandestine visit, but a dog catches sight of him and starts barking. One feels like killing the beast.

One has been foolish enough to invite a man to spend the night in an unsuitable place—and then he starts snoring.

A gentleman has visited one secretly. Though he is wearing a tall, lacquered hat, he nevertheless wants no one to see him. He is so flurried, in fact, that on leaving he bangs into something with his hat. Most hateful! It is annoying too when he lifts up the Iyo blind that hangs at the entrance of the room, then lets it fall with a great rattle. If it is a head-blind, things are still worse, for being more solid it makes a terrible noise when it is dropped. There is no excuse for such carelessness. Even a head-blind does not make any noise if one lifts it up gently when entering and leaving the room; the same applies to sliding-doors. If one's movements are rough, even a paper door will bend and resonate when opened; but, if one lifts the door a little when pushing it, there need be no sound.

One has gone to bed and is about to doze off when a mosquito appears, announcing himself in a reedy voice. One can actually feel the wind made by his wings, and, slight though it is, one finds it hateful in the extreme.

A carriage passes by with a nasty, creaking noise. Annoying to think that the passengers may not even be aware of this! If I am travelling in someone's carriage and I hear it creaking, I dislike not only the noise but the owner of the carriage.

One is in the middle of a story when someone butts in and tries to show that he is the only clever person in the room. Such a person is hateful, and so, indeed, is anyone, child or adult, who tries to push himself forward.

One is telling a story about old times when someone breaks in with a little detail that he happens to know, implying that one's own version is inaccurate—disgusting behaviour!

Very hateful is a mouse that scurries all over the place.

Some children have called at one's house. One makes a great fuss of them and gives them toys to play with. The children become accustomed to this treatment and start to come regularly, forcing their way into one's inner rooms and scattering one's furnishings and possessions. Hateful!

A certain gentleman whom one does not wish to see visits one at home or in the Palace, and one pretends to be asleep. But a maid comes to tell one and shakes one awake, with a look on her face that says, 'What a sleepyhead!' Very hateful.

A newcomer pushes ahead of the other members in a group; with a knowing look, this person starts laying down the law and forcing advice upon everyone—most hateful.

A man with whom one is having an affair keeps singing the praises of some woman he used to know. Even if it is a thing of the past, this can be very annoying. How much more so if he is still seeing the woman! (Yet sometimes I find it is not as unpleasant as all that.)

A person who recites a spell himself after sneezing. In fact I detest anyone who sneezes, except the master of the house.

Fleas too, are very hateful. When they dance about under

someone's clothes, they really seem to be lifting them up.

The sound of dogs when they bark for a long time in chorus is ominous and hateful.

I cannot stand people who leave without closing the panel behind them.

I hate people whose letters show that they lack respect for worldly civilities, whether by discourtesy in the phrasing or by extreme politeness to someone who does not deserve it. This sort of thing is, of course, most odious if the letter is for oneself, but it is bad enough even if it is addressed to someone else.

As a matter of fact, most people are too casual, not only in their letters but in their direct conversation. Sometimes I am quite disgusted at noting how little decorum people observe when talking to each other. It is particularly unpleasant to hear some foolish man or woman omit the proper marks of respect when addressing a person of quality; and, when servants fail to use honorific forms of speech in referring to their masters, it is very bad indeed. No less odious, however, are those masters who, in addressing their servants, use such phrases as 'When you were good enough to do such-and-such' or 'As you so kindly remarked.' No doubt there are some masters who, in describing their own actions to a servant, say, 'I presumed to do so-and-so'!

Sometimes a person who is utterly devoid of charm will try to create a good impression by using very elegant language; yet he succeeds only in being ridiculous. No doubt he believes this refined language to be just what the occasion demands, but, when it goes so far that everyone bursts out laughing, surely something must be wrong.

When speaking to young noblemen and courtiers of high rank, one should always (unless Their Majesties are present) refer to them by their official posts. Incidentally, I have been very shocked to hear important people use the word 'I' while conversing in Their Majesties' presence. Such a breach of etiquette is really distressing, and I fail to see why people cannot avoid it.

A man who has nothing in particular to recommend him, but who speaks in an affected tone and poses as being elegant.

An inkstone with such a hard, smooth surface that the stick glides over it without leaving any deposit of ink.

Ladies-in-waiting who want to know everything that is going on.

Sometimes one greatly dislikes a person for no particular reason—and then that person goes and does something hateful.

A gentleman who travels alone in his carriage to see a procession or some other spectacle. What sort of man is he? Even though he may not be a person of the greatest quality, surely he should have taken along a few of the many young men who are anxious to see the sights. But no, there he sits by himself (one can see his silhouette through the blinds) with a proud look on his face, keeping all his impressions to himself.

A lover who is leaving at dawn announces that he has to find his fan and his paper. 'I know I put them somewhere last night,' he says. Since it is pitch-dark, he gropes about the room, bumping into the furniture and muttering, 'Strange! Where can they be?' Finally he discovers the objects. He thrusts the paper into the breast of his robe with a great rustling sound; then he snaps open his fan and busily fans away with it. Only now is he ready to take his leave. What charmless behaviour! 'Hateful' is an understatement.

Equally disagreeable is the man who, when leaving in the middle of the night, takes care to fasten the cord of his headdress. This is quite unnecessary; he could perfectly well put it gently on his head without tying the cord. And why must he spend time adjusting his cloak or hunting costume? Does he really think that someone may see him at this time of night and criticize him for not being impeccably dressed?

A good lover will behave as elegantly at dawn as at any other time. He drags himself out of bed with a look of dismay on his face. The lady urges him on: 'Come, my friend, it's getting light. You don't want anyone to find you here.' He gives a deep sigh, as if to say that the night has not been nearly long enough and that it is agony to leave. Once up, he does not instantly pull on his trousers. Instead, he comes close to the lady and whispers whatever was left unsaid during the night. Even when he is dressed, he still lingers, vaguely pretending to be fastening his sash.

Presently he raises the lattice, and the two lovers stand together by the side door while he tells her how he dreads the coming day, which will keep them apart; then he slips away. The lady watches him go, and this moment of parting will remain among her most charming memories.

Indeed, one's attachment to a man depends largely on the elegance of his leave-taking. When he jumps out of bed, scurries about the room, tightly fastens his trouser-sash, rolls up the sleeves of his Court cloak, over-robe or hunting costume, stuffs his belongings into the breast of his robe and then briskly secures the outer sash—one really begins to hate him.

10

AREOPAGITICA

John Milton

This is true liberty, when free-born men,
Having to advise the public, may speak free,
Which he who can, and will, deserves high praise;
Who neither can, nor will, may hold his peace:
What can be juster in a state than this?

Euripid. Hicetid.

They, who to states and governors of the Commonwealth direct their speech, High Court of Parliament, or, wanting such access in a private condition, write that which they foresee may advance the public good; I suppose them, as at the beginning of no mean endeavour, not a little altered and moved inwardly in their minds: some with doubt of what will be the success, others with fear of what will be the censure; some with hope, others with confidence of what they have to speak. And me perhaps each of these dispositions, as the subject was whereon I entered, may have at other times variously affected; and likely might in these foremost expressions now also disclose which of them swayed most, but that the very attempt of this address thus made, and the thought of whom it hath recourse to, hath got the power within me to a passion, far more welcome than incidental to a preface.

Which though I stay not to confess ere any ask, I shall be blameless, if it be no other than the joy and gratulation which it brings to all who wish and promote their country's liberty; whereof this whole discourse proposed will be a certain testimony, if not a trophy. For this is not the liberty which we can hope, that no grievance ever should arise in the Commonwealth—that let no man in this world expect; but when complaints are freely heard, deeply considered and speedily reformed, then is the utmost bound of civil liberty attained that wise men look for. To which if I now manifest by the very sound of this which I shall utter, that we are already in good part arrived, and yet from such a steep disadvantage of tyranny and superstition grounded into our principles as was beyond the manhood of a Roman recovery, it will be attributed first, as is most due, to the strong assistance of God our deliverer, next to your faithful guidance and undaunted wisdom, Lords and Commons of England. Neither is it in God's esteem the diminution of his glory, when honourable things are spoken of good men and worthy magistrates; which if I now first should begin to do, after so fair a progress of your laudable deeds, and such a long obligement upon the whole realm to your indefatigable virtues, I might be justly reckoned among the tardiest, and the unwillingest of them that praise ye.

Nevertheless there being three principal things, without which all praising is but courtship and flattery: First, when that only is praised which is solidly worth praise: next, when greatest likelihoods are brought that such things are truly and really in those persons to whom they are ascribed: the other, when he who praises, by showing that such his actual persuasion is of whom he writes, can demonstrate that he flatters not; the former two of these I have heretofore endeavoured, rescuing the employment from him who went about to impair your merits with a trivial and malignant encomium; the latter as belonging chiefly to mine own acquittal, that whom I so extolled I did not flatter, hath been reserved opportunely to this occasion.

For he who freely magnifies what hath been nobly done, and fears not to declare as freely what might be done better, gives ye the best covenant of his fidelity; and that his loyalest affection and his hope waits on your proceedings. His highest praising is not flattery, and his plainest advice is a kind of praising. For though I should affirm and hold by argument, that it would fare better with truth, with learning and the Commonwealth, if one of your published Orders, which I should name, were called in; yet at the same time it could not but much redound to the lustre of your mild and equal government, whenas private persons are hereby animated to think ye better pleased with public advice, than other statists have been delighted heretofore with public flattery. And men will then see what difference there is between the magnanimity of a triennial Parliament, and that jealous haughtiness of prelates and cabin counsellors that usurped of late, whenas they shall observe ye in the midst of your victories and successes more gently brooking written exceptions against a voted Order than other courts, which had produced nothing worth memory but the weak ostentation of wealth, would have endured the least signified dislike at any sudden proclamation.

If I should thus far presume upon the meek demeanour of your civil and gentle greatness, Lords and Commons, as what your published Order hath directly said, that to gainsay, I might defend myself with ease, if any should accuse me of being new or insolent, did they but know how much better I find ye esteem it to imitate the old and elegant humanity of Greece, than the barbaric pride of a Hunnish and Norwegian stateliness. And out of those ages, to whose polite wisdom and letters we owe that we are not yet Goths and Jutlanders, I could name him who from his private house wrote that discourse to the Parliament of Athens, that persuades them to change the form of democracy which was then established. Such honour was done in those days to men who professed the study of wisdom and eloquence, not only in their own country, but in other lands, that cities and signiories heard them gladly, and with great respect, if they had aught in public to admonish the state. Thus did Dion Prusaeus, a stranger and a private orator, counsel the Rhodians against a former edict; and I abound with other like examples, which to set here would be superfluous.

But if from the industry of a life wholly dedicated to studious labours, and those natural endowments haply not the worst for two and fifty degrees of northern latitude, so much must be derogated, as to count me not equal to any of those who had this privilege, I would obtain to be thought not so inferior, as yourselves are superior to the most of them who received their counsel: and how far you excel them, be assured, Lords and Commons, there can no greater testimony appear, than when your prudent spirit acknowledges and obeys the voice of reason from what quarter soever it be heard speaking; and renders ye as willing to repeal any Act of your own setting forth, as any set forth by your predecessors.

If ye be thus resolved, as it were injury to think ye were not, I know not what should withhold me from presenting ye with a fit instance wherein to show both that love of truth which ye eminently profess, and that uprightness of your judgment which is not wont to be partial to yourselves; by judging over again that Order which ye have ordained to regulate printing:—that no book, pamphlet, or paper shall be henceforth printed, unless the same be first approved and licensed by such, or at least one of such, as shall be thereto appointed. For that part which preserves justly every man's copy to himself, or provides for the poor, I touch not, only wish they be not made pretences to abuse and persecute honest and painful men, who offend not in either of these particulars. But that other clause of licensing books, which we thought had died with his brother quadragesimal and matrimonial when the prelates expired, I shall now attend with such a homily, as shall lay before ye, first the inventors of it to be those whom ye will be loath to own; next what is to be thought in general of reading, whatever sort the books be; and that this Order avails nothing to the suppressing of scandalous, seditious, and libellous books, which were mainly intended to be suppressed. Last, that it will be primely to the discouragement of all learning, and the stop of truth, not only by disexercising and blunting our abilities in what we know already, but by hindering and cropping the discovery that might be yet further made both in religious and civil wisdom.

I deny not, but that it is of greatest concernment in the Church and Commonwealth, to have a vigilant eye how books demean themselves as well as men; and thereafter to confine, imprison, and do sharpest justice on them as malefactors. For books are not absolutely dead things, but do contain a potency of life in them to

be as active as that soul was whose progeny they are; nay, they do preserve as in a vial the purest efficacy and extraction of that living intellect that bred them. I know they are as lively, and as vigorously productive, as those fabulous dragon's teeth; and being sown up and down, may chance to spring up armed men. And yet, on the other hand, unless wariness be used, as good almost kill a man as kill a good book. Who kills a man kills a reasonable creature, God's image; but he who destroys a good book, kills reason itself, kills the image of God, as it were in the eye. Many a man lives a burden to the earth; but a good book is the precious life-blood of a master spirit, embalmed and treasured up on purpose to a life beyond life.
'Tis true, no age can restore a life, whereof perhaps there is no great loss; and revolutions of ages do not oft recover the loss of a rejected truth, for the want of which whole nations fare the worse.

We should be wary therefore what persecution we raise against the living labours of public men, how we spill that seasoned life of man, preserved and stored up in books; since we see a kind of homicide may be thus committed, sometimes a martyrdom, and if it extend to the whole impression, a kind of massacre; whereof the execution ends not in the slaying of an elemental life, but strikes at that ethereal and fifth essence, the breath of reason itself, slays an immortality rather than a life. But lest I should be condemned of introducing license, while I oppose licensing, I refuse not the pains to be so much historical, as will serve to show what hath been done by ancient and famous commonwealths against this disorder, till the very time that this project of licensing crept out of the Inquisition, was catched up by our prelates, and hath caught some of our presbyters.

In Athens, where books and wits were ever busier than in any other part of Greece, I find but only two sorts of writings which the magistrate cared to take notice of; those either blasphemous and atheistical, or libellous. Thus the books of Protagoras were by the judges of Areopagus commanded to be burnt, and himself banished the territory for a discourse begun with his confessing not to know WHETHER THERE WERE GODS, OR WHETHER NOT. And against defaming, it was decreed that none should be traduced by name, as was the manner of Vetus Comoedia, whereby we may guess how they censured libelling. And this course was quick enough, as Cicero writes, to quell both the desperate wits of other atheists, and the open way of defaming, as the event showed. Of other sects and opinions, though tending to voluptuousness, and the denying of divine Providence, they took no heed.

Therefore we do not read that either Epicurus, or that libertine school of Cyrene, or what the Cynic impudence uttered, was ever questioned by the laws. Neither is it recorded that the writings of those old comedians were suppressed, though the acting of them were forbid; and that Plato commended the reading of Aristophanes, the loosest of them all, to his royal scholar Dionysius, is commonly known, and may be excused, if holy Chrysostom, as is reported, nightly studied so much the same author and had the art to cleanse a scurrilous vehemence into the style of a rousing sermon.

That other leading city of Greece, Lacedaemon, considering that Lycurgus their lawgiver was so addicted to elegant learning, as to have been the first that brought out of Ionia the scattered works of Homer, and sent the poet Thales from Crete to prepare and mollify the Spartan surliness with his smooth songs and odes, the better to plant among them law and civility, it is to be wondered how museless and unbookish they were, minding nought but the feats of war. There needed no licensing of books among them, for they disliked all but their own laconic apophthegms, and took a slight occasion to chase Archilochus out of their city, perhaps for composing in a higher strain than their own soldierly ballads and roundels could reach to. Or if it were for his broad verses, they were not therein so cautious but they were as dissolute in their promiscuous conversing; whence Euripides affirms in *Andromache*, that their women were all unchaste. Thus much may give us light after what sort of books were prohibited among the Greeks.

The Romans also, for many ages trained up only to a military roughness resembling most the Lacedaemonian guise, knew of learning little but what their twelve Tables, and the Pontific College with their augurs and flamens taught them in religion and law; so unacquainted with other learning, that when Carneades and Critolaus, with the Stoic Diogenes, coming ambassadors to Rome, took thereby occasion to give the city a taste of their philosophy, they were suspected for seducers by no less a man than Cato the Censor, who moved it in the Senate to dismiss them speedily, and to banish all such Attic babblers out of Italy. But Scipio and others of the noblest senators withstood him and his old Sabine austerity; honoured and admired the men; and the censor himself at last, in his old age, fell to the study of that whereof before he was so scrupulous. And yet at the same time Naevius and Plautus, the first Latin comedians, had filled the city with all the borrowed scenes of Menander and Philemon. Then began to be considered there also what was to be done to libellous books and authors; for Naevius was quickly cast into prison for his unbridled pen, and released by the tribunes upon his recantation; we read also that libels were burnt, and the makers punished by Augustus. The like severity, no doubt, was used, if aught were impiously written against their esteemed gods. Except in these two points, how the world went in books, the magistrate kept no reckoning.

And therefore Lucretius without impeachment versifies his Epicurism to Memmius, and had the honour to be set forth the second time by Cicero, so great a father of the Commonwealth; although himself disputes against that opinion in his own writings. Nor was the satirical sharpness or naked plainness of Lucilius, or Catullus, or Flaccus, by any order prohibited. And for matters of state, the story of Titus Livius, though it extolled that part which Pompey held, was not therefore suppressed by Octavius Caesar of the other faction. But that Naso was by him banished in his old age, for the wanton poems of his youth, was but a mere covert of state over some secret cause: and besides, the books were neither banished nor called in. From hence we shall meet with little else but tyranny in the Roman empire, that we may not marvel, if not so often bad as good books were silenced. I shall therefore deem to have been large enough, in producing what among the ancients was punishable to write; save only which, all other arguments were free to treat on.

By this time the emperors were become Christians, whose

discipline in this point I do not find to have been more severe than what was formerly in practice. The books of those whom they took to be grand heretics were examined, refuted, and condemned in the general Councils; and not till then were prohibited, or burnt, by authority of the emperor. As for the writings of heathen authors, unless they were plain invectives against Christianity, as those of Porphyrius and Proclus, they met with no interdict that can be cited, till about the year 400, in a Carthaginian Council, wherein bishops themselves were forbid to read the books of Gentiles, but heresies they might read: while others long before them, on the contrary, scrupled more the books of heretics than of Gentiles. And that the primitive Councils and bishops were wont only to declare what books were not commendable, passing no further, but leaving it to each one's conscience to read or to lay by, till after the year 800, is observed already by Padre Paolo, the great unmasker of the Trentine Council.

After which time the Popes of Rome, engrossing what they pleased of political rule into their own hands, extended their dominion over men's eyes, as they had before over their judgments, burning and prohibiting to be read what they fancied not; yet sparing in their censures, and the books not many which they so dealt with: till Martin V, by his bull, not only prohibited, but was the first that excommunicated the reading of heretical books; for about that time Wickliffe and Huss, growing terrible, were they who first drove the Papal Court to a stricter policy of prohibiting. Which course Leo X and his successors followed, until the Council of Trent and the Spanish Inquisition engendering together brought forth, or perfected, those Catalogues and expurging Indexes, that rake through the entrails of many an old good author, with a violation worse than any could be offered to his tomb. Nor did they stay in matters heretical, but any subject that was not to their palate, they either condemned in a Prohibition, or had it straight into the new purgatory of an index.

To fill up the measure of encroachment, their last invention was to ordain that no book, pamphlet, or paper should be printed (as if St Peter had bequeathed them the keys of the press also out of Paradise) unless it were approved and licensed under the hands of two or three glutton friars. For example:

> Let the Chancellor Cini be pleased to see if in this present work be contained aught that may withstand the printing.

VINCENT RABBATTA, Vicar of Florence.

> I have seen this present work, and find nothing athwart the Catholic faith and good manners: in witness whereof I have given, etc.

NICOLO GINI, Chancellor of Florence.

> Attending the precedent relation, it is allowed that this present work of Davanzati may be printed.

VINCENT RABBATTA, etc.

> It may be printed, July 15.

FRIAR SIMON MOMPEI D'AMELIA,
Chancellor of the Holy Office in Florence.

Sure they have a conceit, if he of the bottomless pit had not long since broke prison, that this quadruple exorcism would bar him down. I fear their next design will be to get into their custody the licensing of that which they say Claudius intended, but went not through with. Vouchsafe to see another of their forms, the Roman stamp:

> Imprimatur, If it seem good to the reverend Master of the Holy Palace.

BELCASTRO, Vicegerent.

> Imprimatur, Friar Nicolo Rodolphi, Master of the Holy Palace.

Sometimes five Imprimaturs are seen together dialogue-wise in the piazza of one title-page, complimenting and ducking each to other with their shaven reverences, whether the author, who stands by in perplexity at the foot of his epistle, shall to the press or to the sponge. These are the pretty responsories, these are the dear antiphonies, that so bewitched of late our prelates and their chaplains with the goodly echo they made; and besotted us to the gay imitation of a lordly Imprimatur, one from Lambeth House, another from the west end of Paul's; so apishly Romanizing, that the word of command still was set down in Latin; as if the learned grammatical pen that wrote it would cast no ink without Latin; or perhaps, as they thought, because no vulgar tongue was worthy to express the pure conceit of an Imprimatur, but rather, as I hope, for that our English, the language of men ever famous and foremost in the achievements of liberty, will not easily find servile letters enow to spell such a dictatory presumption English.

And thus ye have the inventors and the original of book-licensing ripped up and drawn as lineally as any pedigree. We have it not, that can be heard of, from any ancient state, or polity or church; nor by any statute left us by our ancestors elder or later; nor from the modern custom of any reformed city or church abroad, but from the most antichristian council and the most tyrannous inquisition that ever inquired. Till then books were ever as freely admitted into the world as any other birth; the issue of the brain was no more stifled than the issue of the womb: no envious Juno sat cross-legged over the nativity of any man's intellectual offspring; but if it proved a monster, who denies, but that it was justly burnt, or sunk into the sea? But that a book, in worse condition than a peccant soul, should be to stand before a jury ere it be born to the world, and undergo yet in darkness the judgment of Radamanth and his colleagues, ere it can pass the ferry backward into light, was never heard before, till that mysterious iniquity, provoked and troubled at the first entrance of Reformation, sought out new limbos and new hells wherein they might include our books also within the number of their damned. And this was the rare morsel so officiously snatched up, and so ill-favouredly imitated by our inquisiturient bishops, and the attendant minorites their chaplains. That ye like not now these most certain authors of this licensing order, and that all sinister intention was far distant from your thoughts, when ye were importuned the passing it, all men who know the integrity of your actions, and how ye honour truth, will clear ye readily.

But some will say, what though the inventors were bad, the thing for all that may be good? It may so; yet if that thing be no such deep invention, but obvious, and easy for any man to light on, and yet best and wisest commonwealths through all ages and occasions have forborne to use it, and falsest seducers and oppressors of men were the first who took it up, and to no other purpose but to obstruct and hinder the first approach of Reformation; I am of those who believe it will be a harder alchemy than Lullius ever knew, to sublimate any good use out of such an invention. Yet this only is what I request to gain from this reason, that it may be held a dangerous and suspicious fruit, as certainly it deserves, for the tree that bore it, until I can dissect one by one the properties it has. But I have first to finish, as was propounded, what is to be thought in general of reading books, whatever sort they be, and whether be more the benefit or the harm that thence proceeds.

Not to insist upon the examples of Moses, Daniel, and Paul, who were skilful in all the learning of the Egyptians, Chaldeans, and Greeks, which could not probably be without reading their books of all sorts; in Paul especially, who thought it no defilement to insert into Holy Scripture the sentences of three Greek poets, and one of them a tragedian; the question was notwithstanding sometimes controverted among the primitive doctors, but with great odds on that side which affirmed it both lawful and profitable; as was then evidently perceived, when Julian the Apostate and subtlest enemy to our faith made a decree forbidding Christians the study of heathen learning: for, said he, they wound us with our own weapons, and with our own arts and sciences they overcome us. And indeed the Christians were put so to their shifts by this crafty means, and so much in danger to decline into all ignorance, that the two Apollinarii were fain, as a man may say, to coin all the seven liberal sciences out of the Bible, reducing it into divers forms of orations, poems, dialogues, even to the calculating of a new Christian grammar. But, saith the historian

Socrates, the providence of God provided better than the industry of Apollinarius and his son, by taking away that illiterate law with the life of him who devised it. So great an injury they then held it to be deprived of Hellenic learning; and thought it a persecution more undermining, and secretly decaying the Church, than the open cruelty of Decius or Diocletian.

And perhaps it was the same politic drift that the devil whipped St Jerome in a lenten dream, for reading Cicero; or else it was a phantasm bred by the fever which had then seized him. For had an angel been his discipliner, unless it were for dwelling too much upon Ciceronianisms, and had chastised the reading, not the vanity, it had been plainly partial; first to correct him for grave Cicero, and not for scurril Plautus, whom he confesses to have been reading, not long before; next to correct him only, and let so many more ancient fathers wax old in those pleasant and florid studies without the lash of such a tutoring apparition; insomuch that Basil teaches how some good use may be made of Margites, a sportful poem, not now extant, writ by Homer; and why not then of Morgante, an Italian romance much to the same purpose?

But if it be agreed we shall be tried by visions, there is a vision recorded by Eusebius, far ancienter than this tale of Jerome, to the nun Eustochium, and, besides, has nothing of a fever in it. Dionysius Alexandrinus was about the year 240 a person of great name in the Church for piety and learning, who had wont to avail himself much against heretics by being conversant in their books; until a certain presbyter laid it scrupulously to his conscience, how he durst venture himself among those defiling volumes. The worthy man, loath to give offence, fell into a new debate with himself what was to be thought; when suddenly a vision sent from God (it is his own epistle that so avers it) confirmed him in these words: READ ANY BOOKS WHATEVER COME TO THY HANDS, FOR THOU ART SUFFICIENT BOTH TO JUDGE ARIGHT AND TO EXAMINE EACH MATTER. To this revelation he assented the sooner, as he confesses, because it was answerable to that of the Apostle to the Thessalonians, PROVE ALL THINGS, HOLD FAST THAT

WHICH IS GOOD. And he might have added another remarkable saying of the same author: TO THE PURE, ALL THINGS ARE PURE; not only meats and drinks, but all kind of knowledge whether of good or evil; the knowledge cannot defile, nor consequently the books, if the will and conscience be not defiled.

For books are as meats and viands are; some of good, some of evil substance; and yet God, in that unapocryphal vision, said without exception, RISE, PETER, KILL AND EAT, leaving the choice to each man's discretion. Wholesome meats to a vitiated stomach differ little or nothing from unwholesome; and best books to a naughty mind are not unappliable to occasions of evil. Bad meats will scarce breed good nourishment in the healthiest concoction; but herein the difference is of bad books, that they to a discreet and judicious reader serve in many respects to discover, to confute, to forewarn, and to illustrate. Whereof what better witness can ye expect I should produce, than one of your own now sitting in Parliament, the chief of learned men reputed in this land, Mr Selden; whose volume of natural and national laws proves, not only by great authorities brought together, but by exquisite reasons and theorems almost mathematically demonstrative, that all opinions, yea errors, known, read, and collated, are of main service and assistance toward the speedy attainment of what is truest. I conceive, therefore, that when God did enlarge the universal diet of man's body, saving ever the rules of temperance, he then also, as before, left arbitrary the dieting and repasting of our minds; as wherein every mature man might have to exercise his own leading capacity.

How great a virtue is temperance, how much of moment through the whole life of man! Yet God commits the managing so great a trust, without particular law or prescription, wholly to the demeanour of every grown man. And therefore when he himself tabled the Jews from heaven, that omer, which was every man's daily portion of manna, is computed to have been more than might have well sufficed the heartiest feeder thrice as many meals. For those actions which enter into a man, rather than issue out of him, and therefore defile not, God uses not to captivate under a perpetual childhood of prescription, but trusts him with the gift of reason to be his own chooser; there were but little work left for preaching, if law and compulsion should grow so fast upon those things which heretofore were governed only by exhortation. Solomon informs us, that much reading is a weariness to the flesh; but neither he nor other inspired author tells us that such or such reading is unlawful: yet certainly had God thought good to limit us herein, it had been much more expedient to have told us what was unlawful than what was wearisome. As for the burning of those Ephesian books by St Paul's converts; 'tis replied the books were magic, the Syriac so renders them. It was a private act, a voluntary act, and leaves us to a voluntary imitation: the men in remorse burnt those books which were their own; the magistrate by this example is not appointed; these men practised the books, another might perhaps have read them in some sort usefully.

Good and evil we know in the field of this world grow up together almost inseparably; and the knowledge of good is so involved and interwoven with the knowledge of evil, and in so many cunning resemblances hardly to be discerned, that those confused seeds which were imposed upon Psyche as an incessant labour to cull out, and sort asunder, were not more intermixed. It was from out the rind of one apple tasted, that the knowledge of good and evil, as two twins cleaving together, leaped forth into the world. And perhaps this is that doom which Adam fell into of knowing good and evil, that is to say of knowing good by evil. As therefore the state of man now is; what wisdom can there be to choose, what continence to forbear without the knowledge of evil? He that can apprehend and consider vice with all her baits and seeming pleasures, and yet abstain, and yet distinguish, and yet prefer that which is truly better, he is the true warfaring Christian.

I cannot praise a fugitive and cloistered virtue, unexercised and unbreathed, that never sallies out and sees her adversary but slinks out of the race, where that immortal garland is to be run for, not without dust and heat. Assuredly we bring not innocence into the world, we bring impurity much rather; that which purifies us is trial, and trial is by what is contrary. That virtue therefore which is but a youngling in the contemplation of evil, and knows not the utmost that vice promises to her followers, and rejects it, is but a blank virtue, not a pure; her whiteness is but an excremental whiteness. Which was the reason why our sage and serious poet Spenser, whom I dare be known to think a better teacher than Scotus or Aquinas, describing true temperance under the person of Guion, brings him in with his palmer through the cave of Mammon, and the bower of earthly bliss, that he might see and know, and yet abstain. Since therefore the knowledge and survey of vice is in this world so necessary to the constituting of human virtue, and the scanning of error to the confirmation of truth, how can we more safely, and with less danger, scout into the regions of sin and falsity than by reading all manner of tractates and hearing all manner of reason? And this is the benefit which may be had of books promiscuously read.

But of the harm that may result hence three kinds are usually reckoned. First, is feared the infection that may spread; but then all human learning and controversy in religious points must remove out of the world, yea the Bible itself; for that ofttimes relates blasphemy not nicely, it describes the carnal sense of wicked men not unelegantly, it brings in holiest men passionately murmuring against Providence through all the arguments of Epicurus: in other great disputes it answers dubiously and darkly to the common reader. And ask a Talmudist what ails the modesty of his marginal Keri, that Moses and all the prophets cannot persuade him to pronounce the textual Chetiv. For these causes we all know the Bible itself put by the Papist put by the Papist into the first rank of prohibited books. The ancientest Fathers must be next removed, as Clement of Alexandria, and that Eusebian book of Evangelic preparation, transmitting our ears through a hoard of heathenish obscenities to receive the Gospel. Who finds not that Irenaeus, Epiphanius, Jerome, and others discover more heresies than they well confute, and that oft for heresy which is the truer opinion?

Nor boots it to say for these, and all the heathen writers of greatest infection, if it must be thought so, with whom is bound up the life of human learning, that they writ in an unknown tongue, so long as we are sure those languages are known as well to the worst of men, who are both most able and most diligent to instil the poison they suck, first into the courts of princes, acquainting them with the choicest delights and criticisms of sin. As perhaps did that Petronius whom Nero called his Arbiter, the master of his revels; and the notorious ribald of Arezzo, dreaded and yet dear to the Italian courtiers. I name not him for posterity's sake, whom Henry VIII named in merriment his vicar of hell. By which compendious way all the contagion that foreign books can infuse will find a passage to the people far easier and shorter than an Indian voyage, though it could be sailed either by the north of Cataio eastward, or of Canada westward, while our Spanish licensing gags the English press never so severely.

But on the other side that infection which is from books of controversy in religion is more doubtful and dangerous to the learned than to the ignorant; and yet those books must be permitted untouched by the licenser. It will be hard to instance where any ignorant man hath been ever seduced by papistical book in English, unless it were commended and expounded to him by some of that clergy: and indeed all such tractates, whether false or true, are as the prophecy of Isaiah was to the eunuch, not to be UNDERSTOOD WITHOUT A GUIDE. But of our priests and doctors how many have been corrupted by studying the comments of Jesuits and Sorbonists, and how fast they could transfuse that corruption into the people, our experience is both late and sad. It is not forgot, since the acute and distinct Arminius was perverted merely by the perusing of a nameless discourse written at Delft, which at first he took in hand to confute.

Seeing, therefore, that those books, and those in great abundance, which are likeliest to taint both life and doctrine, cannot be suppressed without the fall of learning and of all ability in disputation, and that these books of either sort are most and soonest catching to the learned, from whom to the common people whatever is heretical or dissolute may quickly be conveyed, and that evil manners are as perfectly learnt without books a thousand other ways which cannot be stopped, and evil doctrine not with books can propagate, except a teacher guide, which he might also do without writing, and so beyond prohibiting, I am not able to unfold, how this cautelous enterprise of licensing can be exempted from the number of vain and impossible attempts. And he who were pleasantly disposed could not well avoid to liken it to the exploit of that gallant man who thought to pound up the crows by shutting his park gate.

Besides another inconvenience, if learned men be the first receivers out of books and dispreaders both of vice and error, how shall the licensers themselves be confided in, unless we can confer upon them, or they assume to themselves above all others in the land, the grace of infallibility and uncorruptedness? And again, if it be true that a wise man, like a good refiner, can gather gold out of the drossiest volume, and that a fool will be a fool with the best book, yea or without book; there is no reason that we should deprive a wise man of any advantage to his wisdom, while we seek to restrain from a fool, that which being restrained will be no hindrance to his folly. For if there should be so much exactness always used to keep that from him which is unfit for his reading, we should in the judgment of Aristotle not only, but of Solomon and of our Saviour, not vouchsafe him good precepts, and by consequence not willingly admit him to good books; as being certain that a wise man will make better use of an idle pamphlet, than a fool will do of sacred Scripture.

'Tis next alleged we must not expose ourselves to temptations without necessity, and next to that, not employ our time in vain things. To both these objections one answer will serve, out of the grounds already laid, that to all men such books are not temptations, nor vanities, but useful drugs and materials wherewith to temper and compose effective and strong medicines, which man's life cannot want. The rest, as children and childish men, who have not the art to qualify and prepare these working minerals, well may be exhorted to forbear, but hindered forcibly they cannot be by all the licensing that Sainted Inquisition could ever yet contrive. Which is what I promised to deliver next: that this order of licensing conduces nothing to the end for which it was framed; and hath almost prevented me by being clear already while thus much hath been explaining. See the ingenuity of Truth, who, when she gets a free and willing hand, opens herself faster than the pace of method and discourse can overtake her.

It was the task which I began with, to show that no nation, or well-instituted state, if they valued books at all, did ever use this way of licensing; and it might be answered, that this is a piece of prudence lately discovered. To which I return, that as it was a thing slight and obvious to think on, so if it had been difficult to find out, there wanted not among them long since who suggested such a course; which they not following, leave us a pattern of their judgment that it was not the rest knowing, but the not approving, which was the cause of their not using it.

Plato, a man of high authority, indeed, but least of all for his Commonwealth, in the book of his Laws, which no city ever yet received, fed his fancy by making many edicts to his airy burgomasters, which they who otherwise admire him wish had been rather buried and excused in the genial cups of an Academic night sitting. By which laws he seems to tolerate no kind of learning but by unalterable decree, consisting most of practical traditions, to the attainment whereof a library of smaller bulk than his own Dialogues would be abundant. And there also enacts, that no poet should so much as read to any private man what he had written, until the judges and law-keepers had seen it, and allowed it. But that Plato meant this law peculiarly to that commonwealth which he had imagined, and to no other, is evident. Why was he not else a lawgiver to himself, but a transgressor, and to be expelled by his own magistrates; both for the wanton epigrams and dialogues which he made, and his perpetual reading of Sophron Mimus and Aristophanes, books of grossest infamy, and also for commending the latter of them, though he were the malicious libeller of his chief friends, to be read by the tyrant Dionysius, who had little need of such trash to spend his time on? But that he knew this licensing of poems had reference and dependence to many other provisos there set down in his fancied republic, which in this world could have no place: and so neither he himself, nor any magistrate or city, ever imitated that course, which, taken apart from those other collateral injunctions, must needs be vain and fruitless. For if they fell upon one kind of strictness, unless their care were equal to regulate all other things of like aptness to corrupt the mind, that single endeavour they knew would be but a fond labour; to shut and fortify one gate against corruption, and be necessitated to leave others round about wide open.

If we think to regulate printing, thereby to rectify manners, we must regulate all recreation and pastimes, all that is delightful to man. No music must be heard, no song be set or sung, but what is grave and Doric. There must be licensing dancers, that no gesture, motion, or deportment be taught our youth but what by their allowance shall be thought honest; for such Plato was provided of. It will ask more than the work of twenty licensers to examine all the lutes, the violins, and the guitars in every house; they must not be suffered to prattle as they do, but must be licensed what they may say. And who shall silence all the airs and madrigals that whisper softness in chambers? The windows also, and the balconies must be thought on; there are shrewd books, with dangerous frontispieces, set to sale; who shall prohibit them, shall twenty licensers? The villages also must have their visitors to inquire what lectures the bagpipe and the rebeck reads, even to the ballatry and the gamut of every municipal fiddler, for these are the countryman's Arcadias, and his Monte Mayors.

Next, what more national corruption, for which England hears ill abroad, than household gluttony: who shall be the rectors of our daily rioting? And what shall be done to inhibit the multitudes that frequent those houses where drunkenness is sold and harboured? Our garments also should be referred to the licensing of some more sober workmasters to see them cut into a less wanton garb. Who shall regulate all the mixed conversation of our youth, male and female together, as is the fashion of this country? Who shall still appoint what shall be discoursed, what presumed, and no further? Lastly, who shall forbid and separate all idle resort, all evil company? These things will be, and must be; but how they shall be least hurtful, how least enticing, herein consists the grave and governing wisdom of a state.

To sequester out of the world into Atlantic and Utopian polities, which never can be drawn into use, will not mend our condition; but to ordain wisely as in this world of evil, in the midst whereof God hath placed us unavoidably. Nor is it Plato's licensing of books will do this, which necessarily pulls along with it so many other kinds of licensing, as will make us all both ridiculous and weary, and yet frustrate; but those unwritten, or at least unconstraining, laws of virtuous education, religious and civil nurture, which Plato there mentions as the bonds and ligaments of the commonwealth, the pillars and the sustainers of every written statute; these they be which will bear chief sway in such matters as these, when all licensing will be easily eluded. Impunity and remissness, for certain, are the bane of a commonwealth; but here the great art lies, to discern in what the law is to bid restraint and punishment, and in what things persuasion only is to work.

If every action, which is good or evil in man at ripe years, were to be under pittance and prescription and compulsion, what were virtue but a name, what praise could be then due to well-doing, what gramercy to be sober, just, or continent? Many there be that complain of divine Providence for suffering Adam to transgress; foolish tongues! When God gave him reason, he gave him freedom to choose, for reason is but choosing; he had been else a mere artificial Adam, such an Adam as he is in the motions. We ourselves esteem not of that obedience, or love, or gift, which is of force: God therefore left him free, set before him a provoking object, ever almost in his eyes; herein consisted his merit, herein the right of his reward, the praise of his abstinence. Wherefore did he create passions within us, pleasures round about us, but that these rightly tempered are the very ingredients of virtue?

They are not skilful considerers of human things, who imagine to remove sin by removing the matter of sin; for, besides that it is a huge heap increasing under the very act of diminishing, though some part of it may for a time be withdrawn from some persons, it cannot from all, in such a universal thing as books are; and when this is done, yet the sin remains entire. Though ye take from a covetous man all his treasure, he has yet one jewel left, ye cannot bereave him of his covetousness. Banish all objects of lust, shut up all youth into the severest discipline that can be exercised in any hermitage, ye cannot make them chaste, that came not hither so; such great care and wisdom is required to the right managing of this point. Suppose we could expel sin by this means; look how much we thus expel of sin, so much we expel of virtue: for the matter of them both is the same; remove that, and ye remove them both alike.

This justifies the high providence of God, who, though he command us temperance, justice, continence, yet pours out before us, even to a profuseness, all desirable things, and gives us minds that can wander beyond all limit and satiety. Why should we then affect a rigour contrary to the manner of God and of nature, by abridging or scanting those means, which books freely permitted are, both to the trial of virtue and the exercise of truth? It would be better done, to learn that the law must needs be frivolous, which goes to restrain things, uncertainly and yet equally working to good and to evil. And were I the chooser, a dream of well-doing should be preferred before many times as much the forcible hindrance of evil-doing. For God sure esteems the growth and completing of one virtuous person more than the restraint of ten vicious.

And albeit whatever thing we hear or see, sitting, walking, travelling, or conversing, may be fitly called our book, and is of the same effect that writings are, yet grant the thing to be prohibited were only books, it appears that this Order hitherto is far insufficient to the end which it intends. Do we not see, not once or oftener, but weekly, that continued court-libel against the Parliament and City, printed, as the wet sheets can witness, and dispersed among us, for all that licensing can do? Yet this is the prime service a man would think, wherein this Order should give proof of itself. If it were executed, you'll say. But certain, if execution be remiss or blindfold now, and in this particular, what will it be hereafter and in other books? If then the Order shall not be vain and frustrate, behold a new labour, Lords and Commons, ye must repeal and proscribe all scandalous and unlicensed books already printed and divulged; after ye have drawn them up into a list, that all may know which are condemned, and which not; and ordain that no foreign books be delivered out of custody, till they have been read over. This office will require the whole time of not a few overseers, and those no vulgar men. There be also books which are partly useful and excellent, partly culpable and pernicious; this work will ask as many more officials, to make expurgations and expunctions, that the commonwealth of learning be not damnified. In fine, when the multitude of books increase upon their hands, ye must be fain to catalogue all those printers who are found frequently offending, and forbid the importation of their whole suspected typography. In a word, that this your Order may be exact and not deficient, ye must reform it perfectly according to the model of Trent and Seville, which I know ye abhor to do.

Yet though ye should condescend to this, which God forbid, the Order still would be but fruitless and defective to that end whereto ye meant it. If to prevent sects and schisms, who is so unread or so uncatechized in story, that hath not heard of many sects refusing books as a hindrance, and preserving their doctrine unmixed for many ages, only by unwritten traditions? The Christian faith, for that was once a schism, is not unknown to have spread all over Asia, ere any Gospel or Epistle was seen in writing. If the amendment of manners be aimed at, look into Italy and Spain, whether those places be one scruple the better, the honester, the wiser, the chaster, since all the inquisitional rigour that hath been executed upon books.

Another reason, whereby to make it plain that this Order will miss the end it seeks, consider by the quality which ought to be in every licenser. It cannot be denied but that he who is made judge to sit upon the birth or death of books, whether they may be wafted into this world or not, had need to be a man above the common measure, both studious, learned, and judicious; there may be else no mean mistakes in the censure of what is passable or not; which is also no mean injury. If he be of such worth as behooves him, there cannot be a more tedious and unpleasing journey-work, a greater loss of time levied upon his head, than to be made the perpetual reader of unchosen books and pamphlets, ofttimes huge volumes. There is no book that is acceptable unless at certain seasons; but to be enjoined the reading of that at all times, and in a hand scarce legible, whereof three pages would not down at any time in the fairest print, is an imposition which I cannot believe how he that values time and his own studies, or is but of a sensible nostril, should be able to endure. In this one thing I crave leave of the present licensers to be pardoned for so thinking; who doubtless took this office up, looking on it through their obedience to the Parliament, whose command perhaps made all things seem easy and unlaborious to them; but that this short trial hath wearied them out already, their own expressions and excuses to them who make so many journeys to solicit their licence are testimony enough. Seeing therefore those who now possess the employment by all evident signs wish themselves well rid of it; and that no man of worth, none that is not a plain unthrift of his own hours, is ever likely to succeed them, except he mean to put himself to the salary of a press corrector; we may easily foresee what kind of licensers we are to expect hereafter, either ignorant, imperious, and remiss, or basely pecuniary. This is what I had to show, wherein this Order cannot conduce to that end whereof it bears the intention.

I lastly proceed from the no good it can do, to the manifest hurt it causes, in being first the greatest discouragement and affront that can be offered to learning, and to learned men.

It was the complaint and lamentation of prelates, upon every least breath of a motion to remove pluralities, and distribute more equally Church revenues, that then all learning would be for ever dashed and discouraged. But as for that opinion, I never found cause to think that the tenth part of learning stood or fell with the clergy: nor could I ever but hold it for a sordid and unworthy speech of any churchman who had a competency left him. If therefore ye be loath to dishearten utterly and discontent, not the mercenary crew of false pretenders to learning, but the free and ingenuous sort of such as evidently were born to study, and love learning for itself, not for lucre or any other end but the service of God and of truth, and perhaps that lasting fame and perpetuity of praise which God and good men have consented shall be the reward of those whose published labours advance the good of mankind; then know that, so far to distrust the judgment and the honesty of one who hath but a common repute in learning, and never yet offended, as not to count him fit to print his mind without a tutor and examiner, lest he should drop a schism, or something of corruption, is the greatest displeasure and indignity to a free and knowing spirit that can be put upon him.

What advantage is it to be a man over it is to be a boy at school, if we have only escaped the ferula to come under the fescue of an Imprimatur; if serious and elaborate writings, as if they were no more than the theme of a grammar-lad under his pedagogue, must not be uttered without the cursory eyes of a temporizing and extemporizing licenser? He who is not trusted with his own actions, his drift not being known to be evil, and standing to the hazard of law and penalty, has no great argument to think himself reputed in the Commonwealth wherein he was born for other than a fool or a foreigner. When a man writes to the world, he summons up all his reason and deliberation to assist him; he searches, meditates, is industrious, and likely consults and confers with his judicious friends; after all which done he takes himself to be informed in what he writes, as well as any that writ before him. If, in this the most consummate act of his fidelity and ripeness, no years, no industry, no former proof of his abilities can bring him to that state of maturity, as not to be still mistrusted and suspected, unless he carry all his considerate diligence, all his midnight watchings and expense of Palladian oil, to the hasty view of an unleisured licenser, perhaps much his younger, perhaps his inferior in judgment, perhaps one who never knew the labour of book-writing, and if he be not repulsed or slighted, must appear in print like a puny with his guardian, and his censor's hand on the back of his title to be his bail and surety that he is no idiot or seducer, it cannot be but a dishonour and derogation to the author, to the book, to the privilege and dignity of learning.

And what if the author shall be one so copious of fancy, as to have many things well worth the adding come into his mind after licensing, while the book is yet under the press, which not seldom happens to the best and diligentest writers; and that perhaps a dozen times in one book? The printer dares not go beyond his licensed copy; so often then must the author trudge to his leave-giver, that those his new insertions may be viewed; and many a jaunt will be made, ere that licenser, for it must be the same man, can either be found, or found at leisure; meanwhile either the press must stand still, which is no small damage, or the author lose his accuratest thoughts, and send the book forth worse than he had made it, which to a diligent writer is the greatest melancholy and vexation that can befall.

And how can a man teach with authority, which is the life of teaching; how can he be a doctor in his book as he ought to be, or else had better be silent, whenas all he teaches, all he delivers, is but under the tuition, under the correction of his patriarchal licenser to blot or alter what precisely accords not with the hidebound humour which he calls his judgment? When every acute reader, upon the first sight of a pedantic licence, will be ready with these like words to ding the book a quoit's distance from him: I hate a pupil teacher, I endure not an instructor that comes to me under the wardship of an overseeing fist. I know nothing of the licenser, but that I have his own hand here for his arrogance; who shall warrant me his judgment? The State, sir, replies the stationer, but has a quick return: The State shall be my governors, but not my critics; they may be mistaken in the choice of a licenser, as easily as this licenser may be mistaken in an author; this is some common stuff; and he might add from Sir Francis Bacon, THAT SUCH AUTHORIZED BOOKS ARE BUT THE LANGUAGE OF THE TIMES. For though a licenser should happen to be judicious more than ordinary, which will be a great jeopardy of the next succession, yet his very office and his commission enjoins him to let pass nothing but what is vulgarly received already.

Nay, which is more lamentable, if the work of any deceased author, though never so famous in his lifetime and even to this day, come to their hands for licence to be printed, or reprinted, if there be found in his book one sentence of a venturous edge, uttered in the height of zeal (and who knows whether it might not be the dictate of a divine spirit?) yet not suiting with every low decrepit humour of their own, though it were Knox himself, the reformer of a kingdom, that spake it, they will not pardon him their dash: the sense of that great man shall to all posterity be lost, for the fearfulness or the presumptuous rashness of a perfunctory licenser. And to what an author this violence hath been lately done, and in what book of greatest consequence to be faithfully published, I could now instance, but shall forbear till a more convenient season.

Yet if these things be not resented seriously and timely by them who have the remedy in their power, but that such iron-moulds as these shall have authority to gnaw out the choicest periods of exquisitest books, and to commit such a treacherous fraud against the orphan remainders of worthiest men after death, the more sorrow will belong to that hapless race of men, whose misfortune it is to have understanding. Henceforth let no man care to learn, or care to be more than worldly-wise; for certainly in higher matters to be ignorant and slothful, to be a common steadfast dunce, will be the only pleasant life, and only in request.

And it is a particular disesteem of every knowing person alive, and most injurious to the written labours and monuments of the dead, so to me it seems an undervaluing and vilifying of the whole nation. I cannot set so light by all the invention, the art, the wit, the grave and solid judgment which is in England, as that it can be comprehended in any twenty capacities how good soever, much less that it should not pass except their superintendence be over it, except it be sifted and strained with their strainers, that it should be uncurrent without their manual stamp. Truth and understanding are not such wares as to be monopolized and traded in by tickets and statutes and standards. We must not think to make a staple commodity of all the knowledge in the land, to mark and licence it like our broadcloth and our woolpacks. What is it but a servitude like that imposed by the Philistines, not to be allowed the sharpening of our own axes and coulters, but we must repair from all quarters to twenty licensing forges? Had anyone written and divulged erroneous things and scandalous to honest life, misusing and forfeiting the esteem had of his reason among men, if after conviction this only censure were adjudged him that he should never henceforth write but what were first examined by an appointed officer, whose hand should be annexed to pass his credit for him that now he might be safely read; it could not be apprehended less than a disgraceful punishment. Whence to include the whole nation, and those that never yet thus offended, under such a diffident and suspectful prohibition, may plainly be understood what a disparagement it is. So much the more, whenas debtors and delinquents may walk abroad without a keeper, but unoffensive books must not stir forth without a visible jailer in their title.

Nor is it to the common people less than a reproach; for if we be so jealous over them, as that we dare not trust them with an English pamphlet, what do we but censure them for a giddy, vicious, and ungrounded people; in such a sick and weak state of faith and discretion, as to be able to take nothing down but through the pipe of a licenser? That this is care or love of them, we cannot pretend, whenas, in those popish places where the laity are most hated and despised, the same strictness is used over them. Wisdom we cannot call it, because it stops but one breach of licence, nor that neither: whenas those corruptions, which it seeks to prevent, break in faster at other doors which cannot be shut.

And in conclusion it reflects to the disrepute of our ministers also, of whose labours we should hope better, and of the proficiency which their flock reaps by them, than that after all this light of the Gospel which is, and is to be, and all this continual preaching, they should still be frequented with such an unprincipled, unedified and laic rabble, as that the whiff of every new pamphlet should stagger them out of their catechism and Christian walking. This may have much reason to discourage the ministers when such a low conceit is had of all their exhortations, and the benefiting of their hearers, as that they are not thought fit to be turned loose to three sheets of paper without a licenser; that all the sermons, all the lectures preached, printed, vented in such numbers, and such volumes, as have now well nigh made all other books unsaleable, should not be armour enough against one single Enchiridion, without the castle of St Angelo of an Imprimatur.

And lest some should persuade ye, Lords and Commons, that these arguments of learned men's discouragement at this your Order are mere flourishes, and not real, I could recount what I have seen and heard in other countries, where this kind of inquisition tyrannizes; when I have sat among their learned men, for that honour I had, and been counted happy to be born in such a place of philosophic freedom, as they supposed England was, while themselves did nothing but bemoan the servile condition into which learning amongst them was brought; that this was it which had damped the glory of Italian wits; that nothing had been there written now these many years but flattery and fustian. There it was that I found and visited the famous Galileo, grown old, a prisoner to the Inquisition, for thinking in astronomy otherwise than the Franciscan and Dominican licensers thought. And though I knew that England then was groaning loudest under the prelatical yoke, nevertheless I took it as a pledge of future happiness, that other nations were so persuaded of her liberty. Yet was it beyond my hope that those worthies were then breathing in her air, who should be her leaders to such a deliverance, as shall never be forgotten by any revolution of time that this world hath to finish. When that was once begun, it was as little in my fear that what words of complaint I heard among learned men of other parts uttered against the Inquisition, the same I should hear by as learned men at home, uttered in time of Parliament against an order of licensing; and that so generally that, when I had disclosed myself a companion of their discontent, I might say, if without envy, that he whom an honest quaestorship had endeared to the Sicilians was not more by them importuned against Verres, than the favourable opinion which I had among many who honour ye, and are known and respected by ye, loaded me with entreaties and persuasions, that I would not despair to lay together that which just reason should bring into my mind, toward the removal of an undeserved thraldom upon learning. That this is not therefore the disburdening of a particular fancy, but the common grievance of all those who had prepared their minds and studies above the vulgar pitch to advance truth in others, and from others to entertain it, thus much may satisfy.

And in their name I shall for neither friend nor foe conceal what the general murmur is; that if it come to inquisitioning again and licensing, and that we are so timorous of ourselves, and so suspicious of all men, as to fear each book and the shaking of every leaf, before we know what the contents are; if some who but of late were little better than silenced from preaching shall come now to silence us from reading, except what they please, it cannot be guessed what is intended by some but a second tyranny over learning: and will soon put it out of controversy, that bishops and presbyters are the same to us, both name and thing. That those evils of prelaty, which before from five or six and twenty sees were distributively charged upon the whole people, will now light wholly upon learning, is not obscure to us: whenas now the pastor of a small unlearned parish on the sudden shall be exalted archbishop over a large diocese of books, and yet not remove, but keep his other cure too, a mystical pluralist. He who but of late cried down the sole ordination of every novice Bachelor of Art, and denied sole jurisdiction over the simplest parishioner, shall now at home in his private chair assume both these over worthiest and excellentest books and ablest authors that write them.

This is not, ye Covenants and Protestations that we have made! this is not to put down prelaty; this is but to chop an episcopacy; this is but to translate the Palace Metropolitan from one kind of dominion into another; this is but an old canonical sleight of commuting our penance. To startle thus betimes at a mere unlicensed pamphlet will after a while be afraid of every conventicle, and a while after will make a conventicle of every Christian meeting. But I am certain that a State governed by the rules of justice and fortitude, or a Church built and founded upon the rock of faith and true knowledge, cannot be so pusillanimous. While things are yet not constituted in religion, that freedom of writing should be restrained by a discipline imitated from the prelates and learnt by them from the Inquisition, to shut us up all again into the breast of a licenser, must needs give cause of doubt and discouragement to all learned and religious men.

Who cannot but discern the fineness of this politic drift, and who are the contrivers; that while bishops were to be baited down, then all presses might be open; it was the people's birthright and privilege in time of Parliament, it was the breaking forth of light. But now, the bishops abrogated and voided out of the Church, as if our Reformation sought no more but to make room for others into their seats under another name, the episcopal arts begin to bud again, the cruse of truth must run no more oil, liberty of printing must be enthralled again under a prelatical commission of twenty, the privilege of the people nullified, and, which is worse, the freedom of learning must groan again, and to her old fetters: all this the Parliament yet sitting. Although their own late arguments and defences against the prelates might remember them, that this obstructing violence meets for the most part with an event utterly opposite to the end which it drives at: instead of suppressing sects and schisms, it raises them and invests them with a reputation. The punishing of wits enhances their authority, saith the Viscount St Albans; and a forbidden writing is thought to be a certain spark of truth that flies up in the faces of them who seek to tread it out. This Order, therefore, may prove a nursing-mother to sects, but I shall easily show how it will be a step-dame to Truth: and first by disenabling us to the maintenance of what is known already.

Well knows he who uses to consider, that our faith and knowledge thrives by exercise, as well as our limbs and complexion. Truth is compared in Scripture to a streaming fountain; if her waters flow not in a perpetual progression, they sicken into a muddy pool of conformity and tradition. A man may be a heretic in the truth; and if he believe things only because his pastor says so, or the Assembly so determines, without knowing other reason, though his belief be true, yet the very truth he holds becomes his heresy.

There is not any burden that some would gladlier post off to another than the charge and care of their religion. There be—who knows not that there be?—of Protestants and professors who live and die in as arrant an implicit faith as any lay Papist of Loretto. A wealthy man, addicted to his pleasure and to his profits, finds religion to be a traffic so entangled, and of so many piddling accounts, that of all mysteries he cannot skill to keep a stock going upon that trade. What should he do? fain he would have the name to be religious, fain he would bear up with his neighbours in that. What does he therefore, but resolves to give over toiling, and to find himself out some factor, to whose care and credit he may commit the whole managing of his religious affairs; some divine of note and estimation that must be.

To him he adheres, resigns the whole warehouse of his religion, with all the locks and keys, into his custody; and indeed makes the very person of that man his religion; esteems his associating with him a sufficient evidence and commendatory of his own piety. So that a man may say his religion is now no more within himself, but is become a dividual movable, and goes and comes near him, according as that good man frequents the house. He entertains him, gives him gifts, feasts him, lodges him; his religion comes home at night, prays, is liberally supped, and sumptuously laid to sleep; rises, is saluted, and after the malmsey, or some well-spiced brewage, and better breakfasted than he whose morning appetite would have gladly fed on green figs between Bethany and Jerusalem, his religion walks abroad at eight, and leaves his kind entertainer in the shop trading all day without his religion.

Another sort there be who, when they hear that all things shall be ordered, all things regulated and settled, nothing written but what passes through the custom-house of certain publicans that have the tonnaging and poundaging of all free-spoken truth, will straight give themselves up into your hands, make 'em and cut 'em out what religion ye please: there be delights, there be recreations and jolly pastimes that will fetch the day about from sun to sun, and rock the tedious year as in a delightful dream. What need they torture their heads with that which others have taken so strictly and so unalterably into their own purveying? These are the fruits which a dull ease and cessation of our knowledge will bring forth among the people. How goodly and how to be wished were such an obedient unanimity as this, what a fine conformity would it starch us all into! Doubtless a staunch and solid piece of framework, as any January could freeze together.

Nor much better will be the consequence even among the clergy themselves. It is no new thing never heard of before, for a parochial minister, who has his reward and is at his Hercules' pillars in a warm benefice, to be easily inclinable, if he have nothing else that may rouse up his studies, to finish his circuit in an English Concordance and a topic folio, the gatherings and savings of a sober graduateship, a Harmony and a Catena; treading the constant round of certain common doctrinal heads, attended with their uses, motives, marks, and means, out of which, as out of an alphabet, or sol-fa, by forming and transforming, joining and disjoining variously, a little book-craft, and two hours' meditation, might furnish him unspeakably to the performance of more than a weekly charge of sermoning: not to reckon up the infinite helps of interlinearies, breviaries, synopses, and other loitering gear. But as for the multitude of sermons ready printed and piled up, on every text that is not difficult, our London trading St Thomas in his vestry, and add to boot St Martin and St Hugh, have not within their hallowed limits more vendible ware of all sorts ready made: so that penury he never need fear of pulpit provision, having where so plenteously to refresh his magazine. But if his rear and flanks be not impaled, if his back door be not secured by the rigid licenser, but that a bold book may now and then issue forth and give the assault to some of his old collections in their trenches, it will concern him then to keep waking, to stand in watch, to set good guards and sentinels about his received opinions, to walk the round and counter-round with his fellow inspectors, fearing lest any of his flock be seduced, who also then would be better instructed, better exercised and disciplined. And God send that the fear of this diligence, which must then be used, do not make us affect the laziness of a licensing Church.

For if we be sure we are in the right, and do not hold the truth guiltily, which becomes not, if we ourselves condemn not our own weak and frivolous teaching, and the people for an untaught and irreligious gadding rout, what can be more fair than when a man judicious, learned, and of a conscience, for aught we know, as good as theirs that taught us what we know, shall not privily from house to house, which is more dangerous, but openly by writing publish to the world what his opinion is, what his reasons, and wherefore that which is now thought cannot be sound? Christ urged it as wherewith to justify himself, that he preached in public; yet writing is more public than preaching; and more easy to refutation, if need be, there being so many whose business and profession merely it is to be the champions of truth; which if they neglect, what can be imputed but their sloth, or unability?

Thus much we are hindered and disinured by this course of licensing, toward the true knowledge of what we seem to know. For how much it hurts and hinders the licensers themselves in the calling of their ministry, more than any secular employment, if they will discharge that office as they ought, so that of necessity they must neglect either the one duty or the other, I insist not, because it is a particular, but leave it to their own conscience, how they will decide it there.

There is yet behind of what I purposed to lay open, the incredible loss and detriment that this plot of licensing puts us to; more than if some enemy at sea should stop up all our havens and ports and creeks, it hinders and retards the importation of our richest merchandise, truth; nay, it was first established and put in practice by antichristian malice and mystery on set purpose to extinguish, if it were possible, the light of Reformation, and to settle falsehood; little differing from that policy wherewith the Turk upholds his Alcoran, by the prohibition of printing. 'Tis not denied, but gladly confessed, we are to send our thanks and vows to Heaven louder than most of nations, for that great measure of truth which we enjoy, especially in those main points between us and the Pope, with his appurtenances the prelates: but he who thinks we are to pitch our tent here, and have attained the utmost prospect of reformation that the mortal glass wherein we contemplate can show us, till we come to beatific vision, that man by this very opinion declares that he is yet far short of truth.

Truth indeed came once into the world with her divine Master, and was a perfect shape most glorious to look on: but when he ascended, and his Apostles after him were laid asleep, then straight arose a wicked race of deceivers, who, as that story goes of the Egyptian Typhon with his conspirators, how they dealt with the good Osiris, took the virgin Truth, hewed her lovely form into a thousand pieces, and scattered them to the four winds. From that time ever since, the sad friends of Truth, such as durst appear, imitating the careful search that Isis made for the mangled body of Osiris, went up and down gathering up limb by limb, still as they could find them. We have not yet found them all, Lords and Commons, nor ever shall do, till her Master's second coming; he shall bring together every joint and member, and shall mould them into an immortal feature of loveliness and perfection. Suffer not these licensing prohibitions to stand at every place of opportunity, forbidding and disturbing them that continue seeking, that continue to do our obsequies to the torn body of our martyred saint.

We boast our light; but if we look not wisely on the sun itself, it smites us into darkness. Who can discern those planets that are oft combust, and those stars of brightest magnitude that rise and set with the sun, until the opposite motion of their orbs bring them to such a place in the firmament, where they may be seen evening or morning? The light which we have gained was given us, not to be ever staring on, but by it to discover onward things more remote from our knowledge. It is not the unfrocking of a priest, the unmitring of a bishop, and the removing him from off the presbyterian shoulders, that will make us a happy nation. No, if other things as great in the Church, and in the rule of life both economical and political, be not looked into and reformed, we have looked so long upon the blaze that Zuinglius and Calvin hath beaconed up to us, that we are stark blind. There be who perpetually complain of schisms and sects, and make it such a calamity that any man dissents from their maxims. 'Tis their own pride and ignorance which causes the disturbing, who neither will hear with meekness, nor can convince; yet all must be suppressed which is not found in their Syntagma. They are the troublers, they are the dividers of unity, who neglect and permit not others to unite those dissevered pieces which are yet wanting to the body of Truth. To be still searching what we know not by what we know, still closing up truth to truth as we find it (for all her body is homogeneal and proportional), this is the golden rule in theology as well as in arithmetic, and makes up the best harmony in a Church; not the forced and outward union of cold, and neutral, and inwardly divided minds.

Lords and Commons of England! consider what nation it is whereof ye are, and whereof ye are the governors: a nation not slow and dull, but of a quick, ingenious and piercing spirit, acute to invent, subtle and sinewy to discourse, not beneath the reach of any point the highest that human capacity can soar to. Therefore the studies of learning in her deepest sciences have been so ancient and so eminent among us, that writers of good antiquity and ablest judgment have been persuaded that even the school of Pythagoras and the Persian wisdom took beginning from the old philosophy of this island. And that wise and civil Roman, Julius Agricola, who governed once here for Caesar, preferred the natural wits of Britain before the laboured studies of the French. Nor is it for nothing that the grave and frugal Transylvanian sends out yearly from as far as the mountainous borders of Russia, and beyond the Hercynian wilderness, not their youth, but their staid men, to learn our language and our theologic arts.

Yet that which is above all this, the favour and the love of Heaven, we have great argument to think in a peculiar manner propitious and propending towards us. Why else was this nation chosen before any other, that out of her, as out of Sion, should be proclaimed and sounded forth the first tidings and trumpet of Reformation to all Europe? And had it not been the obstinate perverseness of our prelates against the divine and admirable spirit of Wickliff, to suppress him as a schismatic and innovator, perhaps neither the Bohemian Huss and Jerome, no nor the name of Luther or of Calvin, had been ever known: the glory of reforming all our neighbours had been completely ours. But now, as our obdurate clergy have with violence demeaned the matter, we are become hitherto the latest and the backwardest scholars, of whom God offered to have made us the teachers. Now once again by all concurrence of signs, and by the general instinct of holy and devout men, as they daily and solemnly express their thoughts, God is decreeing to begin some new and great period in his Church, even to the reforming of Reformation itself: what does he then but reveal himself to his servants, and as his manner is, first to his Englishmen? I say, as his manner is, first to us, though we mark not the method of his counsels, and are unworthy.

Behold now this vast city: a city of refuge, the mansion house of liberty, encompassed and surrounded with his protection; the shop of war hath not there more anvils and hammers waking, to fashion out the plates and instruments of armed justice in defence of beleaguered truth, than there be pens and heads there, sitting by their studious lamps, musing, searching, revolving new notions and ideas wherewith to present, as with their homage and their fealty, the approaching Reformation: others as fast reading, trying all things, assenting to the force of reason and convincement. What could a man require more from a nation so pliant and so prone to seek after knowledge? What wants there to such a towardly and pregnant soil, but wise and faithful labourers, to make a knowing people, a nation of prophets, of sages, and of worthies? We reckon more than five months yet to harvest; there need not be five weeks; had we but eyes to lift up, the fields are white already.

Where there is much desire to learn, there of necessity will be much arguing, much writing, many opinions; for opinion in good men is but knowledge in the making. Under these fantastic terrors of sect and schism, we wrong the earnest and zealous thirst after knowledge and understanding which God hath stirred up in this city. What some lament of, we rather should rejoice at, should rather praise this pious forwardness among men, to reassume the ill-deputed care of their religion into their own hands again. A little generous prudence, a little forbearance of one another, and some grain of charity might win all these diligences to join, and unite in one general and brotherly search after truth; could we but forgo this prelatical tradition of crowding free consciences and Christian liberties into canons and precepts of men. I doubt not, if some great and worthy stranger should come among us, wise to discern the mould and temper of a people, and how to govern it, observing the high hopes and aims, the diligent alacrity of our extended thoughts and reasonings in the pursuance of truth and freedom, but that he would cry out as Pyrrhus did, admiring the Roman docility and courage: If such were my Epirots, I would not despair the greatest design that could be attempted, to make a Church or kingdom happy.

Yet these are the men cried out against for schismatics and sectaries; as if, while the temple of the Lord was building, some cutting, some squaring the marble, others hewing the cedars, there should be a sort of irrational men who could not consider there must be many schisms and many dissections made in the quarry and in the timber, ere the house of God can be built. And when every stone is laid artfully together, it cannot be united into a continuity, it can but be contiguous in this world; neither can every piece of the building be of one form; nay rather the perfection consists in this, that, out of many moderate varieties and brotherly dissimilitudes that are not vastly disproportional, arises the goodly and the graceful symmetry that commends the whole pile and structure.

Let us therefore be more considerate builders, more wise in spiritual architecture, when great reformation is expected. For now the time seems come, wherein Moses the great prophet may sit in heaven rejoicing to see that memorable and glorious wish of his fulfilled, when not only our seventy elders, but all the Lord's people, are become prophets. No marvel then though some men, and some good men too perhaps, but young in goodness, as Joshua then was, envy them. They fret, and out of their own weakness are in agony, lest these divisions and subdivisions will undo us. The adversary again applauds, and waits the hour: when they have branched themselves out, saith he, small enough into parties and partitions, then will be our time. Fool! he sees not the firm root, out of which we all grow, though into branches: nor will beware until he see our small divided maniples cutting through at every angle of his ill-united and unwieldy brigade. And that we are to hope better of all these supposed sects and schisms, and that we shall not need that solicitude, honest perhaps, though over-timorous, of them that vex in this behalf, but shall laugh in the end at those malicious applauders of our differences, I have these reasons to persuade me.

First, when a city shall be as it were besieged and blocked about, her navigable river infested, inroads and incursions round, defiance and battle oft rumoured to be marching up even to her walls and suburb trenches, that then the people, or the greater part, more than at other times, wholly taken up with the study of highest and most important matters to be reformed, should be disputing, reasoning, reading, inventing, discoursing, even to a rarity and admiration, things not before discoursed or written of, argues first a singular goodwill, contentedness and confidence in your prudent foresight and safe government, Lords and Commons; and from thence derives itself to a gallant bravery and well-grounded contempt of their enemies, as if there were no small number of as great spirits among us, as his was, who when Rome was nigh besieged by Hannibal, being in the city, bought that piece of ground at no cheap rate, whereon Hannibal himself encamped his own regiment.

Next, it is a lively and cheerful presage of our happy success and victory. For as in a body, when the blood is fresh, the spirits pure and vigorous, not only to vital but to rational faculties, and those in the acutest and the pertest operations of wit and subtlety, it argues in what good plight and constitution the body is; so when the cheerfulness of the people is so sprightly up, as that it has not only wherewith to guard well its own freedom and safety, but to spare, and to bestow upon the solidest and sublimest points of controversy and new invention, it betokens us not degenerated, nor drooping to a fatal decay, but casting off the old and wrinkled skin of corruption to outlive these pangs and wax young again, entering the glorious ways of truth and prosperous virtue, destined to become great and honourable in these latter ages. Methinks I see in my mind a noble and puissant nation rousing herself like a strong man after sleep, and shaking her invincible locks: methinks I see her as an eagle mewing her mighty youth, and kindling her undazzled eyes at the full midday beam; purging and unscaling her long-abused sight at the fountain itself of heavenly radiance; while the whole noise of timorous and flocking birds, with those also that love the twilight, flutter about, amazed at what she means, and in their envious gabble would prognosticate a year of sects and schisms.

What would ye do then? should ye suppress all this flowery crop of knowledge and new light sprung up and yet springing daily in this city? Should ye set an oligarchy of twenty engrossers over it, to bring a famine upon our minds again, when we shall know nothing but what is measured to us by their bushel? Believe it, Lords and Commons, they who counsel ye to such a suppressing do as good as bid ye suppress yourselves; and I will soon show how. If it be desired to know the immediate cause of all this free writing and free speaking, there cannot be assigned a truer than your own mild and free and humane government. It is the liberty, Lords and Commons, which your own valorous and happy counsels have purchased us, liberty which is the nurse of all great wits; this is that which hath rarefied and enlightened our spirits like the influence of heaven; this is that which hath enfranchised, enlarged and lifted up our apprehensions, degrees above themselves.

Ye cannot make us now less capable, less knowing, less eagerly pursuing of the truth, unless ye first make yourselves, that made us so, less the lovers, less the founders of our true liberty. We can grow ignorant again, brutish, formal and slavish, as ye found us; but you then must first become that which ye cannot be, oppressive, arbitrary and tyrannous, as they were from whom ye have freed us. That our hearts are now more capacious, our thoughts more erected to the search and expectation of greatest and exactest things, is the issue of your own virtue propagated in us; ye cannot suppress that, unless ye reinforce an abrogated and merciless law, that fathers may dispatch at will their own children. And who shall then stick closest to ye, and excite others? not he who takes up arms for coat and conduct, and his four nobles of Danegelt. Although I dispraise not the defence of just immunities, yet love my peace better, if that were all. Give me the liberty to know, to utter, and to argue freely according to conscience, above all liberties.

What would be best advised, then, if it be found so hurtful and so unequal to suppress opinions for the newness or the unsuitableness to a customary acceptance, will not be my task to say. I only shall repeat what I have learned from one of your own honourable number, a right noble and pious lord, who, had he not sacrificed his life and fortunes to the Church and Commonwealth, we had not now missed and bewailed a worthy and undoubted patron of this argument. Ye know him, I am sure; yet I for honour's sake, and may it be eternal to him, shall name him, the Lord Brook. He writing of episcopacy, and by the way treating of sects and schisms, left ye his vote, or rather now the last words of his dying charge, which I know will ever be of dear and honoured regard with ye, so full of meekness and breathing charity, that next to his last testament, who bequeathed love and peace to his disciples, I cannot call to mind where I have read or heard words more mild and peaceful. He there exhorts us to hear with patience and humility those, however they be miscalled, that desire to live purely, in such a use of God's ordinances, as the best guidance of their conscience gives them, and to tolerate them, though in some disconformity to ourselves. The book itself will tell us more at large, being published to the world, and dedicated to the Parliament by him who, both for his life and for his death, deserves that what advice he left be not laid by without perusal.

And now the time in special is, by privilege to write and speak what may help to the further discussing of matters in agitation. The temple of Janus with his two controversial faces might now not unsignificantly be set open. And though all the winds of doctrine were let loose to play upon the earth, so Truth be in the field, we do injuriously, by licensing and prohibiting, to misdoubt her strength. Let her and Falsehood grapple; who ever knew Truth put to the worse, in a free and open encounter? Her confuting is the best and surest suppressing. He who hears what praying there is for light and clearer knowledge to be sent down among us, would think of other matters to be constituted beyond the discipline of Geneva, framed and fabricked already to our hands. Yet when the new light which we beg for shines in upon us, there be who envy and oppose, if it come not first in at their casements. What a collusion is this, whenas we are exhorted by the wise man to use diligence, to seek for wisdom as for hidden treasures early and late, that another order shall enjoin us to know nothing but by statute? When a man hath been labouring the hardest labour in the deep mines of knowledge, hath furnished out his findings in all their equipage: drawn forth his reasons as it were a battle ranged: scattered and defeated all objections in his way; calls out his adversary into the plain, offers him the advantage of wind and sun, if he please, only that he may try the matter by dint of argument: for his opponents then to skulk, to lay ambushments, to keep a narrow bridge of licensing where the challenger should pass, though it be valour enough in soldiership, is but weakness and cowardice in the wars of Truth.

For who knows not that Truth is strong, next to the Almighty? She needs no policies, nor stratagems, nor licensings to make her victorious; those are the shifts and the defences that error uses against her power. Give her but room, and do not bind her when she sleeps, for then she speaks not true, as the old Proteus did, who spake oracles only when he was caught and bound, but then rather she turns herself into all shapes, except her own, and perhaps tunes her voice according to the time, as Micaiah did before Ahab, until she be adjured into her own likeness. Yet is it not impossible that she may have more shapes than one. What else is all that rank of things indifferent, wherein Truth may be on this side or on the other, without being unlike herself? What but a vain shadow else is the abolition of those ordinances, that hand-writing nailed to the cross? What great purchase is this Christian liberty which Paul so often boasts of? His doctrine is, that he who eats or eats not, regards a day or regards it not, may do either to the Lord. How many other things might be tolerated in peace, and left to conscience, had we but charity, and were it not the chief stronghold of our hypocrisy to be ever judging one another?

I fear yet this iron yoke of outward conformity hath left a slavish print upon our necks; the ghost of a linen decency yet haunts us. We stumble and are impatient at the least dividing of one visible congregation from another, though it be not in fundamentals; and through our forwardness to suppress, and our backwardness to recover any enthralled piece of truth out of the gripe of custom, we care not to keep truth separated from truth, which is the fiercest rent and disunion of all. We do not see that, while we still affect by all means a rigid external formality, we may as soon fall again into a gross conforming stupidity, a stark and dead congealment of wood and hay and stubble, forced and frozen together, which is more to the sudden degenerating of a Church than many subdichotomies of petty schisms.

Not that I can think well of every light separation, or that all in a Church is to be expected gold and silver and precious stones: it is not possible for man to sever the wheat from the tares, the good fish from the other fry; that must be the Angels' ministry at the end of mortal things. Yet if all cannot be of one mind—as who looks they should be?—this doubtless is more wholesome, more prudent, and more Christian, that many be tolerated, rather than all compelled. I mean not tolerated popery, and open superstition, which, as it extirpates all religions and civil supremacies, so itself should be extirpate, provided first that all charitable and compassionate means be used to win and regain the weak and the misled: that also which is impious or evil absolutely either against faith or manners no law can possibly permit, that intends not to unlaw itself: but those neighbouring differences, or rather indifferences, are what I speak of, whether in some point of doctrine or of discipline, which, though they may be many, yet need not interrupt THE UNITY OF SPIRIT, if we could but find among us THE BOND OF PEACE.

In the meanwhile if any one would write, and bring his helpful hand to the slow-moving Reformation which we labour under, if Truth have spoken to him before others, or but seemed at least to speak, who hath so bejesuited us that we should trouble that man with asking license to do so worthy a deed? and not consider this, that if it come to prohibiting, there is not aught more likely to be prohibited than truth itself; whose first appearance to our eyes, bleared and dimmed with prejudice and custom, is more unsightly and unplausible than many errors, even as the person is of many a great man slight and contemptuous to see to. And what do they tell us vainly of new opinions, when this very opinion of theirs, that none must be heard but whom they like, is the worst and newest opinion of all others; and is the chief cause why sects and schisms do so much abound, and true knowledge is kept at distance from us; besides yet a greater danger which is in it.

For when God shakes a kingdom with strong and healthful commotions to a general reforming, 'tis not untrue that many sectaries and false teachers are then busiest in seducing; but yet more true it is, that God then raises to his own work men of rare abilities, and more than common industry, not only to look back and revise what hath been taught heretofore, but to gain further and go on some new enlightened steps in the discovery of truth. For such is the order of God's enlightening his Church, to dispense and deal out by degrees his beam, so as our earthly eyes may best sustain it.

Neither is God appointed and confined, where and out of what place these his chosen shall be first heard to speak; for he sees not as man sees, chooses not as man chooses, lest we should devote ourselves again to set places, and assemblies, and outward callings of men; planting our faith one while in the old Convocation house, and another while in the Chapel at Westminster; when all the faith and religion that shall be there canonized is not sufficient without plain convincement, and the charity of patient instruction to supple the least bruise of conscience, to edify the meanest Christian, who desires to walk in the Spirit, and not in the letter of human trust, for all the number of voices that can be there made; no, though Harry VII himself there, with all his liege tombs about him, should lend them voices from the dead, to swell their number.

And if the men be erroneous who appear to be the leading schismatics, what withholds us but our sloth, our self-will, and distrust in the right cause, that we do not give them gentle meetings and gentle dismissions, that we debate not and examine the matter thoroughly with liberal and frequent audience; if not for their sakes, yet for our own? seeing no man who hath tasted learning, but will confess the many ways of profiting by those who, not contented with stale receipts, are able to manage and set forth new positions to the world. And were they but as the dust and cinders of our feet, so long as in that notion they may yet serve to polish and brighten the armoury of Truth, even for that respect they were not utterly to be cast away. But if they be of those whom God hath fitted for the special use of these times with eminent and ample gifts, and those perhaps neither among the priests nor among the Pharisees, and we in the haste of a precipitant zeal shall make no distinction, but resolve to stop their mouths, because we fear they come with new and dangerous opinions, as we commonly forejudge them ere we understand them; no less than woe to us, while, thinking thus to defend the Gospel, we are found the persecutors.

There have been not a few since the beginning of this Parliament, both of the presbytery and others, who by their unlicensed books, to the contempt of an Imprimatur, first broke that triple ice clung about our hearts, and taught the people to see day: I hope that none of those were the persuaders to renew upon us this bondage which they themselves have wrought so much good by contemning. But if neither the check that Moses gave to young Joshua, nor the countermand which our Saviour gave to young John, who was so ready to prohibit those whom he thought unlicensed, be not enough to admonish our elders how unacceptable to God their testy mood of prohibiting is; if neither their own remembrance what evil hath abounded in the Church by this set of licensing, and what good they themselves have begun by transgressing it, be not enough, but that they will persuade and execute the most Dominican part of the Inquisition over us, and are already with one foot in the stirrup so active at suppressing, it would be no unequal distribution in the first place to suppress the suppressors themselves: whom the change of their condition hath puffed up, more than their late experience of harder times hath made wise.

And as for regulating the press, let no man think to have the honour of advising ye better than yourselves have done in that Order published next before this, 'that no book be printed, unless the printer's and the author's name, or at least the printer's, be registered.' Those which otherwise come forth, if they be found mischievous and libellous, the fire and the executioner will be the timeliest and the most effectual remedy that man's prevention can use. For this authentic Spanish policy of licensing books, if I have said aught, will prove the most unlicensed book itself within a short while; and was the immediate image of a Star Chamber decree to that purpose made in those very times when that Court did the rest of those her pious works, for which she is now fallen from the stars with Lucifer. Whereby ye may guess what kind of state prudence, what love of the people, what care of religion or good manners there was at the contriving, although with singular hypocrisy it pretended to bind books to their good behaviour. And how it got the upper hand of your precedent

Order so well constituted before, if we may believe those men whose profession gives them cause to inquire most, it may be doubted there was in it the fraud of some old patentees and monopolizers in the trade of bookselling; who under pretence of the poor in their Company not to be defrauded, and the just retaining of each man his several copy, which God forbid should be gainsaid, brought divers glossing colours to the House, which were indeed but colours, and serving to no end except it be to exercise a superiority over their neighbours; men who do not therefore labour in an honest profession to which learning is indebted, that they should be made other men's vassals. Another end is thought was aimed at by some of them in procuring by petition this Order, that, having power in their hands, malignant books might the easier scape abroad, as the event shows.

But of these sophisms and elenchs of merchandise I skill not. This I know, that errors in a good government and in a bad are equally almost incident; for what magistrate may not be misinformed, and much the sooner, if liberty of printing be reduced into the power of a few? But to redress willingly and speedily what hath been erred, and in highest authority to esteem a plain advertisement more than others have done a sumptuous bride, is a virtue (honoured Lords and Commons) answerable to your highest actions, and whereof none can participate but greatest and wisest men.

11

COMPENSATION

Ralph Waldo Emerson

The wings of Time are black and white,
Pied with morning and with night.
Mountain tall and ocean deep
Trembling balance duly keep.
In changing moon, in tidal wave,
Glows the feud of Want and Have.
Gauge of more and less through space
Electric star and pencil plays.
The lonely Earth amid the balls
That hurry through the eternal halls,
A makeweight flying to the void,
Supplemental asteroid,
Or compensatory spark,
Shoots across the neutral Dark.

Man's the elm, and Wealth the vine;
Stanch and strong the tendrils twine:
Though the frail ringlets thee deceive,
None from its stock that vine can reave.
Fear not, then, thou child infirm,
There's no god dare wrong a worm.
Laurel crowns cleave to deserts,
And power to him who power exerts;
Hast not thy share? On winged feet,
Lo! it rushes thee to meet;

And all that Nature made thy own,
Floating in air or pent in stone,
Will rive the hills and swim the sea,
And, like thy shadow, follow thee.

Ever since I was a boy, I have wished to write a discourse on Compensation: for it seemed to me when very young, that on this subject life was ahead of theology, and the people knew more than the preachers taught. The documents, too, from which the doctrine is to be drawn, charmed my fancy by their endless variety, and lay always before me, even in sleep; for they are the tools in our hands, the bread in our basket, the transactions of the street, the farm, and the dwelling-house, greetings, relations, debts and credits, the influence of character, the nature and endowment of all men. It seemed to me, also, that in it might be shown men a ray of divinity, the present action of the soul of this world, clean from all vestige of tradition, and so the heart of man might be bathed by an inundation of eternal love, conversing with that which he knows was always and always must be, because it really is now. It appeared, moreover, that if this doctrine could be stated in terms with any resemblance to those bright intuitions in which this truth is sometimes revealed to us, it would be a star in many dark hours and crooked passages in our journey that would not suffer us to lose our way.

I was lately confirmed in these desires by hearing a sermon at church. The preacher, a man esteemed for his orthodoxy, unfolded in the ordinary manner the doctrine of the Last Judgment. He assumed, that judgment is not executed in this world; that the wicked are successful; that the good are miserable; and then urged from reason and from Scripture a compensation to be made to both parties in the next life. No offence appeared to be taken by the congregation at this doctrine. As far as I could observe, when the meeting broke up, they separated without remark on the sermon.

Yet what was the import of this teaching? What did the preacher mean by saying that the good are miserable in the present life? Was it that houses and lands, offices, wine, horses, dress, luxury, are had by unprincipled men, whilst the saints are poor and despised; and that a compensation is to be made to these last hereafter, by giving them the like gratifications another day,—bank-stock and doubloons, venison and champagne? This must be the compensation intended; for what else? Is it that they are to have leave to pray and praise? to love and serve men? Why, that they can do now. The legitimate inference the disciple would draw was,—'We are to have such a good time as the sinners have now;'—or, to push it to its extreme import,—'You sin now; we shall sin by and by; we would sin now, if we could; not being successful, we expect our revenge to-morrow.'

The fallacy lay in the immense concession, that the bad are successful; that justice is not done now. The blindness of the preacher consisted in deferring to the base estimate of the market of what constitutes a manly success, instead of confronting and convicting the world from the truth; announcing the presence of the soul; the omnipotence of the will: and so establishing the standard of good and ill, of success and falsehood.

I find a similar base tone in the popular religious works of the day, and the same doctrines assumed by the literary men when occasionally they treat the related topics. I think that our popular theology has gained in decorum, and not in principle, over the superstitions it has displaced. But men are better than this theology. Their daily life gives it the lie. Every ingenuous and aspiring soul leaves the doctrine behind him in his own experience; and all men feel sometimes the falsehood which they cannot demonstrate. For men are wiser than they know. That which they hear in schools and pulpits without after-thought, if said in conversation, would probably be questioned in silence. If a man dogmatize in a mixed company on Providence and the divine laws, he is answered by a silence which conveys well enough to an observer the dissatisfaction of the hearer, but his incapacity to make his own statement.

I shall attempt in this and the following chapter to record some facts that indicate the path of the law of Compensation; happy beyond my expectation, if I shall truly draw the smallest arc of this circle.

POLARITY, or action and reaction, we meet in every part of

nature; in darkness and light; in heat and cold; in the ebb and flow of waters; in male and female; in the inspiration and expiration of plants and animals; in the equation of quantity and quality in the fluids of the animal body; in the systole and diastole of the heart; in the undulations of fluids, and of sound; in the centrifugal and centripetal gravity; in electricity, galvanism, and chemical affinity. Superinduce magnetism at one end of a needle; the opposite magnetism takes place at the other end. If the south attracts, the north repels. To empty here, you must condense there. An inevitable dualism bisects nature, so that each thing is a half, and suggests another thing to make it whole; as, spirit, matter; man, woman; odd, even; subjective, objective; in, out; upper, under; motion, rest; yea, nay.

Whilst the world is thus dual, so is every one of its parts. The entire system of things gets represented in every particle. There is somewhat that resembles the ebb and flow of the sea, day and night, man and woman, in a single needle of the pine, in a kernel of corn, in each individual of every animal tribe. The reaction, so grand in the elements, is repeated within these small boundaries. For example, in the animal kingdom the physiologist has observed that no creatures are favorites, but a certain compensation balances every gift and every defect. A surplusage given to one part is paid out of a reduction from another part of the same creature. If the head and neck are enlarged, the trunk and extremities are cut short.

The theory of the mechanic forces is another example. What we gain in power is lost in time; and the converse. The periodic or compensating errors of the planets is another instance. The influences of climate and soil in political history are another. The cold climate invigorates. The barren soil does not breed fevers, crocodiles, tigers, or scorpions.

The same dualism underlies the nature and condition of man. Every excess causes a defect; every defect an excess. Every sweet hath its sour; every evil its good. Every faculty which is a receiver of pleasure has an equal penalty put on its abuse. It is to answer for its moderation with its life. For every grain of wit there is a grain of folly. For every thing you have missed, you have gained something else; and for every thing you gain, you lose something. If riches increase, they are increased that use them. If the gatherer gathers too much, nature takes out of the man what she puts into his chest; swells the estate, but kills the owner. Nature hates monopolies and exceptions. The waves of the sea do not more speedily seek a level from their loftiest tossing, than the varieties of condition tend to equalize themselves. There is always some levelling circumstance that puts down the overbearing, the strong, the rich, the fortunate, substantially on the same ground with all others. Is a man too strong and fierce for society, and by temper and position a bad citizen,—a morose ruffian, with a dash of the pirate in him;—nature sends him a troop of pretty sons and daughters, who are getting along in the dame's classes at the village school, and love and fear for them smooths his grim scowl to courtesy. Thus she contrives to intenerate the granite and felspar, takes the boar out and puts the lamb in, and keeps her balance true.

The farmer imagines power and place are fine things. But the President has paid dear for his White House. It has commonly cost him all his peace, and the best of his manly attributes. To preserve for a short time so conspicuous an appearance before the world, he is content to eat dust before the real masters who stand erect behind the throne. Or, do men desire the more substantial and permanent grandeur of genius? Neither has this an immunity. He who by force of will or of thought is great, and overlooks thousands, has the charges of that eminence. With every influx of light comes new danger. Has he light? he must bear witness to the light, and always outrun that sympathy which gives him such keen satisfaction, by his fidelity to new revelations of the incessant soul. He must hate father and mother, wife and child. Has he all that the world loves and admires and covets?—he must cast behind him their admiration, and afflict them by faithfulness to his truth, and become a by-word and a hissing.

This law writes the laws of cities and nations. It is in vain to build or plot or combine against it. Things refuse to be mismanaged long. *Res nolunt diu male administrari.* Though no checks to a new evil appear, the checks exist, and will appear. If the government is cruel, the governor's life is not safe. If you tax too high, the revenue will yield nothing. If you make the criminal code sanguinary, juries will not convict. If the law is too mild, private vengeance comes in. If the government is a terrific democracy, the pressure is resisted by an overcharge of energy in the citizen, and life glows with a fiercer flame. The true life and satisfactions of man seem to elude the utmost rigors or felicities of condition, and to establish themselves with great indifferency under all varieties of circumstances. Under all governments the influence of character remains the same,—in Turkey and in New England about alike. Under the primeval despots of Egypt, history honestly confesses that man must have been as free as culture could make him.

These appearances indicate the fact that the universe is represented in every one of its particles. Every thing in nature contains all the powers of nature. Every thing is made of one hidden stuff; as the naturalist sees one type under every metamorphosis, and regards a horse as a running man, a fish as a swimming man, a bird as a flying man, a tree as a rooted man. Each new form repeats not only the main character of the type, but part for part all the details, all the aims, furtherances, hindrances, energies, and whole system of every other. Every occupation, trade, art, transaction, is a compend of the world, and a correlative of every other. Each one is an entire emblem of human life; of its good and ill, its trials, its enemies, its course and its end. And each one must somehow accommodate the whole man, and recite all his destiny.

The world globes itself in a drop of dew. The microscope cannot find the animalcule which is less perfect for being little. Eyes, ears, taste, smell, motion, resistance, appetite, and organs of reproduction that take hold on eternity,—all find room to consist in the small creature. So do we put our life into every act. The true doctrine of omnipresence is, that God reappears with all his parts in every moss and cobweb. The value of the universe contrives to throw itself into every point. If the good is there, so is the evil; if the affinity, so the repulsion; if the force, so the limitation.

Thus is the universe alive. All things are moral. That soul, which within us is a sentiment, outside of us is a law. We feel its inspiration;

out there in history we can see its fatal strength. 'It is in the world, and the world was made by it.' Justice is not postponed. A perfect equity adjusts its balance in all parts of life. Οἱ κύβοι Διὸς ἀεὶ εὐπίπτουσι,—The dice of God are always loaded. The world looks like a multiplication-table, or a mathematical equation, which, turn it how you will, balances itself. Take what figure you will, its exact value, nor more nor less, still returns to you. Every secret is told, every crime is punished, every virtue rewarded, every wrong redressed, in silence and certainty. What we call retribution is the universal necessity by which the whole appears wherever a part appears. If you see smoke, there must be fire. If you see a hand or a limb, you know that the trunk to which it belongs is there behind.

Every act rewards itself, or, in other words, integrates itself, in a twofold manner; first, in the thing, or in real nature; and secondly, in the circumstance, or in apparent nature. Men call the circumstance the retribution. The causal retribution is in the thing, and is seen by the soul. The retribution in the circumstance is seen by the understanding; it is inseparable from the thing, but is often spread over a long time, and so does not become distinct until after many years. The specific stripes may follow late after the offence, but they follow because they accompany it. Crime and punishment grow out of one stem. Punishment is a fruit that unsuspected ripens within the flower of the pleasure which concealed it. Cause and effect, means and ends, seed and fruit, cannot be severed; for the effect already blooms in the cause, the end preexists in the means, the fruit in the seed.

Whilst thus the world will be whole, and refuses to be disparted, we seek to act partially, to sunder, to appropriate; for example,—to gratify the senses, we sever the pleasure of the senses from the needs of the character. The ingenuity of man has always been dedicated to the solution of one problem,—how to detach the sensual sweet, the sensual strong, the sensual bright, etc., from the moral sweet, the moral deep, the moral fair; that is, again, to contrive to cut clean off this upper surface so thin as to leave it bottomless; to get a *one end*, without an *other end*. The soul says, Eat; the body would feast. The soul says, The man and woman shall be one flesh and one soul; the body would join the flesh only. The soul says, Have dominion over all things to the ends of virtue; the body would have the power over things to its own ends.

The soul strives amain to live and work through all things. It would be the only fact. All things shall be added unto it,—power, pleasure, knowledge, beauty. The particular man aims to be somebody; to set up for himself; to truck and higgle for a private good; and, in particulars, to ride, that he may ride; to dress, that he may be dressed; to eat, that he may eat; and to govern, that he may be seen. Men seek to be great; they would have offices, wealth, power, and fame. They think that to be great is to possess one side of nature,—the sweet, without the other side,—the bitter.

This dividing and detaching is steadily counteracted. Up to this day, it must be owned, no projector has had the smallest success. The parted water reunites behind our hand. Pleasure is taken out of pleasant things, profit out of profitable things, power out of strong things, as soon as we seek to separate them from the whole. We can no more halve things and get the sensual good, by itself, than we can get an inside that shall have no outside, or a light without a shadow. 'Drive out nature with a fork, she comes running back.'

Life invests itself with inevitable conditions, which the unwise seek to dodge, which one and another brags that he does not know; that they do not touch him;—but the brag is on his lips, the conditions are in his soul. If he escapes them in one part, they attack him in another more vital part. If he has escaped them in form, and in the appearance, it is because he has resisted his life, and fled from himself, and the retribution is so much death. So signal is the failure of all attempts to make this separation of the good from the tax, that the experiment would not be tried,—since to try it is to be mad,—but for the circumstance, that when the disease began in the will, of rebellion and separation, the intellect is at once infected, so that the man ceases to see God whole in each object, but is able to see the sensual allurement of an object, and not see the sensual hurt; he sees the mermaid's head, but not the dragon's tail; and thinks he can cut off that which he would have, from that which he would not have.

'How secret art thou who dwellest in the highest heavens in silence, O thou only great God, sprinkling with an unwearied Providence certain penal blindnesses upon such as have unbridled desires!'

The human soul is true to these facts in the painting of fable, of history, of law, of proverbs, of conversation. It finds a tongue in literature unawares. Thus the Greeks called Jupiter, Supreme Mind; but having traditionally ascribed to him many base actions, they involuntarily made amends to reason, by tying up the hands of so bad a god. He is made as helpless as a king of England. Prometheus knows one secret which Jove must bargain for; Minerva, another. He cannot get his own thunders; Minerva keeps the key of them.

'Of all the gods, I only know the keys
That ope the solid doors within whose vaults
His thunders sleep.'

A plain confession of the in-working of the All, and of its moral aim. The Indian mythology ends in the same ethics; and it would seem impossible for any fable to be invented and get any currency which was not moral. Aurora forgot to ask youth for her lover, and though Tithonus is immortal, he is old. Achilles is not quite invulnerable; the sacred waters did not wash the heel by which Thetis held him. Siegfried, in the Nibelungen, is not quite immortal, for a leaf fell on his back whilst he was bathing in the dragon's blood, and that spot which it covered is mortal. And so it must be. There is a crack in every thing God has made. It would seem, there is always this vindictive circumstance stealing in at unawares, even into the wild poesy in which the human fancy attempted to make bold holiday, and to shake itself free of the old laws,—this back-stroke, this kick of the gun, certifying that the law is fatal; that in nature nothing can be given, all things are sold.

This is that ancient doctrine of Nemesis, who keeps watch in the universe, and lets no offence go unchastised. The Furies, they said, are attendants on justice, and if the sun in heaven should transgress his path, they would punish him. The poets related that stone walls, and iron swords, and leathern thongs had an occult sympathy with the wrongs of their owners; that the belt which Ajax gave Hector dragged the Trojan hero over the field at the wheels of the car of Achilles, and the sword which Hector gave Ajax was that on whose point Ajax fell. They recorded, that when the Thasians erected a statue to Theagenes, a victor in the games, one of his rivals went to it by night, and endeavored to throw it down by repeated blows, until at last he moved it from its pedestal, and was crushed to death beneath its fall.

This voice of fable has in it somewhat divine. It came from thought above the will of the writer. That is the best part of each writer, which has nothing private in it; that which he does not know; that which flowed out of his constitution, and not from his too active invention; that which in the study of a single artist you might not easily find, but in the study of many, you would abstract as the spirit of them all. Phidias it is not, but the work of man in that early Hellenic world, that I would know. The name and circumstance of Phidias, however convenient for history, embarrass when we come to the highest criticism. We are to see that which man was tending to do in a given period, and was hindered, or, if you will, modified in doing, by the interfering volitions of Phidias, of Dante, of Shakespeare, the organ whereby man at the moment wrought.

Still more striking is the expression of this fact in the proverbs of all nations, which are always the literature of reason, or the statements of an absolute truth, without qualification. Proverbs, like the sacred books of each nation, are the sanctuary of the intuitions. That which the droning world, chained to appearances, will not allow the realist to say in his own words, it will suffer him to say in proverbs without contradiction. And this law of laws which the pulpit, the senate, and the college deny, is hourly preached in all markets and workshops by flights of proverbs, whose teaching is as true and as omnipresent as that of birds and flies.

All things are double, one against another.—Tit for tat; an eye for an eye; a tooth for a tooth; blood for blood; measure for measure; love for love.—Give and it shall be given you.—He that watereth shall be watered himself.—What will you have? quoth God; pay for it and take it.—Nothing venture, nothing have.—Thou shalt be paid exactly for what thou hast done, no more, no less.—Who doth not work shall not eat.—Harm watch, harm catch.—Curses always recoil on the head of him who imprecates them.—If you put a chain around the neck of a slave, the other end fastens itself around your own.—Bad counsel confounds the adviser.—The Devil is an ass.

It is thus written, because it is thus in life. Our action is overmastered and characterized above our will by the law of nature. We aim at a petty end quite aside from the public good, but our act arranges itself by irresistible magnetism in a line with the poles of the world.

A man cannot speak but he judges himself. With his will, or against his will, he draws his portrait to the eye of his companions by every word. Every opinion reacts on him who utters it. It is a thread-ball thrown at a mark, but the other end remains in the thrower's bag. Or, rather, it is a harpoon hurled at the whale, unwinding, as it flies, a coil of cord in the boat, and if the harpoon is not good, or not well thrown, it will go nigh to cut the steersman in twain, or to sink the boat.

You cannot do wrong without suffering wrong. 'No man had ever a point of pride that was not injurious to him,' said Burke. The exclusive in fashionable life does not see that he excludes himself from enjoyment, in the attempt to appropriate it. The exclusionist in religion does not see that he shuts the door of heaven on himself, in striving to shut out others. Treat men as pawns and ninepins, and you shall suffer as well as they. If you leave out their heart, you shall lose your own. The senses would make things of all persons; of women, of children, of the poor. The vulgar proverb, 'I will get it from his purse or get it from his skin,' is sound philosophy.

All infractions of love and equity in our social relations are speedily punished. They are punished by fear. Whilst I stand in simple relations to my fellow-man, I have no displeasure in meeting him. We meet as water meets water, or as two currents of air mix, with perfect diffusion and interpenetration of nature. But as soon as there is any departure from simplicity, and attempt at halfness, or good for me that is not good for him, my neighbor feels the wrong; he shrinks from me as far as I have shrunk from him; his eyes no longer seek mine; there is war between us; there is hate in him and fear in me.

All the old abuses in society, universal and particular, all unjust accumulations of property and power, are avenged in the same manner. Fear is an instructor of great sagacity, and the herald of all revolutions. One thing he teaches, that there is rottenness where he appears. He is a carrion crow, and though you see not well what he hovers for, there is death somewhere. Our property is timid, our laws are timid, our cultivated classes are timid. Fear for ages has boded and mowed and gibbered over government and property. That obscene bird is not there for nothing. He indicates great wrongs which must be revised.

Of the like nature is that expectation of change which instantly follows the suspension of our voluntary activity. The terror of cloudless noon, the emerald of Polycrates, the awe of prosperity, the instinct which leads every generous soul to impose on itself tasks of a noble asceticism and vicarious virtue, are the tremblings of the balance of justice through the heart and mind of man.

Experienced men of the world know very well that it is best to pay scot and lot as they go along, and that a man often pays dear for a small frugality. The borrower runs in his own debt. Has a man gained any thing who has received a hundred favors and rendered none? Has he gained by borrowing, through indolence or cunning, his neighbor's wares, or horses, or money? There arises on the deed the instant acknowledgment of benefit on the one part, and of debt on the other; that is, of superiority and inferiority. The transaction remains in the memory of himself and his neighbor; and every new transaction alters, according to its nature, their relation to each other. He may soon come to see that he had better have broken his own bones than to have ridden in his neighbor's coach, and that 'the highest price he can pay for a thing is to ask for it.'

A wise man will extend this lesson to all parts of life, and know that it is the part of prudence to face every claimant, and pay every just demand on your time, your talents, or your heart. Always pay; for, first or last, you must pay your entire debt. Persons and events may stand for a time between you and justice, but it is only a postponement.

You must pay at last your own debt. If you are wise, you will dread a prosperity which only loads you with more. Benefit is the end of nature. But for every benefit which you receive, a tax is levied. He is great who confers the most benefits. He is base—and that is the one base thing in the universe—to receive favors and render none. In the order of nature we cannot render benefits to those from whom we receive them, or only seldom. But the benefit we receive must be rendered again, line for line, deed for deed, cent for cent, to somebody. Beware of too much good staying in your hand. It will fast corrupt and worm worms. Pay it away quickly in some sort.

Labor is watched over by the same pitiless laws. Cheapest, say the prudent, is the dearest labor. What we buy in a broom, a mat, a wagon, a knife, is some application of good sense to a common want. It is best to pay in your land a skillful gardener, or to buy good sense applied to gardening; in your sailor, good sense applied to navigation; in the house, good sense applied to cooking, sewing, serving; in your agent, good sense applied to accounts and affairs. So do you multiply your presence, or spread yourself throughout your estate. But because of the dual constitution of things, in labor as in life there can be no cheating. The thief steals from himself. The swindler swindles himself. For the real price of labor is knowledge and virtue, whereof wealth and credit are signs. These signs, like paper money, may be counterfeited or stolen, but that which they represent, namely, knowledge and virtue, cannot be counterfeited or stolen. These ends of labor cannot be answered but by real exertions of the mind, and in obedience to pure motives. The cheat, the defaulter, the gambler, cannot extort the knowledge of material and moral nature which his honest care and pains yield to the operative. The law of nature is, Do the thing, and you shall have the power: but they who do not the thing have not the power.

Human labor, through all its forms, from the sharpening of a stake to the construction of a city or an epic, is one immense illustration of the perfect compensation of the universe. The absolute balance of Give and Take, the doctrine that every thing has its price,—and if that price is not paid, not that thing but something else is obtained, and that it is impossible to get any thing without its price,—is not less sublime in the columns of a ledger than in the budgets of states, in the laws of light and darkness, in all the action and reaction of nature. I cannot doubt that the high laws which each man sees implicated in those processes with which he is conversant, the stern ethics which sparkle on his chisel-edge, which are measured out by his plumb and foot-rule, which stand as manifest in the footing of the shop-bill as in the history of a state,—do recommend to him his trade, and though seldom named, exalt his business to his imagination.

The league between virtue and nature engages all things to assume a hostile front to vice. The beautiful laws and substances of the world persecute and whip the traitor. He finds that things are arranged for truth and benefit, but there is no den in the wide world to hide a rogue. Commit a crime, and the earth is made of glass. Commit a crime, and it seems as if a coat of snow fell on the ground, such as reveals in the woods the track of every partridge and fox and squirrel and mole. You cannot recall the spoken word, you cannot wipe out the foot-track, you cannot draw up the ladder, so as to leave no inlet or clew. Some damning circumstance always transpires. The laws and substances of nature—water, snow, wind, gravitation—become penalties to the thief.

On the other hand, the law holds with equal sureness for all right action. Love, and you shall be loved. All love is mathematically just, as much as the two sides of an algebraic equation. The good man has absolute good, which like fire turns every thing to its own nature, so that you cannot do him any harm; but as the royal armies sent against Napoleon, when he approached, cast down their colors and from enemies became friends, so disasters of all kinds, as sickness, offence, poverty, prove benefactors:—

'Winds blow and waters roll
Strength to the brave, and power and deity,
Yet in themselves are nothing.'

The good are befriended even by weakness and defect. As no man had ever a point of pride that was not injurious to him, so no man had ever a defect that was not somewhere made useful to him. The stag in the fable admired his horns and blamed his feet, but when the hunter came, his feet saved him, and afterwards, caught in the thicket, his horns destroyed him. Every man in his lifetime needs to thank his faults. As no man thoroughly understands a truth until he has contended against it, so no man has a thorough acquaintance with the hindrances or talents of men, until he has suffered from the one, and seen the triumph of the other over his own want of the same. Has he a defect of temper that unfits him to live in society? Thereby he is driven to entertain himself alone, and acquire habits of self-help; and thus, like the wounded oyster, he mends his shell with pearl.

Our strength grows out of our weakness. The indignation which arms itself with secret forces does not awaken until we are pricked and stung and sorely assailed. A great man is always willing to be little. Whilst he sits on the cushion of advantages, he goes to sleep. When he is pushed, tormented, defeated, he has a chance to learn something; he has been put on his wits, on his manhood; he has gained facts; learns his ignorance; is cured of the insanity of conceit; has got moderation and real skill. The wise man throws himself on the side of his assailants. It is more his interest than it is theirs to find his weak point. The wound cicatrizes and falls off from him like a dead skin, and when they would triumph, lo! he has passed on invulnerable. Blame is safer than praise. I hate to be defended in a newspaper. As long as all that is said is said against me, I feel a certain assurance of success. But as soon as honeyed words of praise are spoken for me, I feel as one that lies unprotected before his enemies. In general, every evil to which we do not succumb is a benefactor. As the Sandwich Islander believes that the strength and valor of the enemy he kills passes into himself, so we gain the strength of the temptation we resist.

The same guards which protect us from disaster, defect, and enmity, defend us, if we will, from selfishness and fraud. Bolts and bars are not the best of our institutions, nor is shrewdness in trade a mark of wisdom. Men suffer all their life long, under the foolish superstition that they can be cheated. But it is as impossible for a man to be cheated by any one but himself, as for a thing to be and not to be at the same time. There is a third silent party to all our bargains. The nature and soul of things takes on itself the guaranty of the fulfillment of every contract, so that honest service cannot come to loss. If you serve an ungrateful master, serve him the more. Put God in your debt. Every stroke shall be repaid. The longer the payment is withholden, the better for you; for compound interest on compound interest is the rate and usage of this exchequer.

The history of persecution is a history of endeavors to cheat nature, to make water run up hill, to twist a rope of sand. It makes no difference whether the actors be many or one, a tyrant or a mob. A mob is a society of bodies voluntarily bereaving themselves of reason, and traversing its work. The mob is man voluntarily descending to the nature of the beast. Its fit hour of activity is night. Its actions are insane like its whole constitution. It persecutes a principle; it would whip a right; it would tar and feather justice, by inflicting fire and outrage upon the houses and persons of those who have these. It resembles the prank of boys, who run with fire-engines to put out the ruddy aurora streaming to the stars. The inviolate spirit turns their spite against the wrongdoers. The martyr cannot be dishonored. Every lash inflicted is a tongue of fame; every prison, a more illustrious abode; every burned book or house enlightens the world; every suppressed or expunged word reverberates through the earth from side to side. Hours of sanity and consideration are always arriving to communities, as to individuals, when the truth is seen, and the martyrs are justified.

Thus do all things preach the indifferency of circumstances. The man is all. Every thing has two sides, a good and an evil. Every advantage has its tax. I learn to be content. But the doctrine of compensation is not the doctrine of indifferency. The thoughtless say, on hearing these representations,—What boots it to do well? there is one event to good and evil; if I gain any good, I must pay for it; if I lose any good, I gain some other; all actions are indifferent.

There is a deeper fact in the soul than compensation, to wit, its own nature. The soul is not a compensation, but a life. The soul *is*. Under all this running sea of circumstance, whose waters ebb and flow with perfect balance, lies the aboriginal abyss of real Being. Essence, or God, is not a relation, or a part, but the whole. Being is the vast affirmative, excluding negation, self-balanced, and swallowing up all relations, parts, and times within itself. Nature, truth, virtue, are the influx from thence. Vice is the absence or departure of the same. Nothing, Falsehood, may indeed stand as the great Night or shade, on which, as a background, the living universe paints itself forth; but no fact is begotten by it; it cannot work; for it is not. It cannot work any good; it cannot work any harm. It is harm inasmuch as it is worse not to be than to be.

We feel defrauded of the retribution due to evil acts, because the criminal adheres to his vice and contumacy, and does not come to a crisis or judgment anywhere in visible nature. There is no stunning confutation of his nonsense before men and angels. Has he therefore outwitted the law? Inasmuch as he carries the malignity and the lie with him, he so far deceases from nature. In some manner there will be a demonstration of the wrong to the understanding also; but should we not see it, this deadly deduction makes square the eternal account.

Neither can it be said, on the other hand, that the gain of rectitude must be bought by any loss. There is no penalty to virtue; no penalty to wisdom; they are proper additions of being. In a virtuous action, I properly am; in a virtuous act, I add to the world; I plant into deserts conquered from Chaos and Nothing, and see the darkness receding on the limits of the horizon. There can be no excess to love; none to knowledge; none to beauty, when these attributes are considered in the purest sense. The soul refuses limits, and always affirms an Optimism, never a Pessimism.

Man's life is a progress, and not a station. His instinct is trust. Our instinct uses 'more' and 'less' in application to man, of the *presence of the soul*, and not of its absence; the brave man is greater than the coward; the true, the benevolent, the wise, is more a man, and not less, than the fool and knave. There is no tax on the good of virtue; for that is the incoming of God himself, or absolute existence, without any comparative. Material good has its tax, and if it came without desert or sweat, has no root in me, and the next wind will blow it away. But all the good of nature is the soul's, and may be had, if paid for in nature's lawful coin, that is, by labor which the heart and the head allow. I no longer wish to meet a good I do not earn, for example, to find a pot of buried gold, knowing that it brings with it new burdens. I do not wish more external goods,—neither possessions, nor honors, nor powers, nor persons. The gain is apparent; the tax is certain. But there is no tax on the knowledge that the compensation exists, and that it is not desirable to dig up treasure. Herein I rejoice with a serene eternal peace. I contract the boundaries of possible mischief. I learn the wisdom of St Bernard,—'Nothing can work me damage except myself; the harm that I sustain I carry about with me, and never am a real sufferer but by my own fault.'

In the nature of the soul is the compensation for the inequalities of condition. The radical tragedy of nature seems to be the distinction of More and Less. How can Less not feel the pain; how not feel indignation or malevolence towards More? Look at those who have less faculty, and one feels sad, and knows not well what to make of it. He almost shuns their eye; he fears they will upbraid God. What should they do? It seems a great injustice. But see the facts nearly, and these mountainous inequalities vanish. Love reduces them, as the sun melts the iceberg in the sea. The heart and soul of all men being one, this bitterness of *His* and *Mine* ceases. His is mine. I am my brother, and my brother is me. If I feel overshadowed and outdone by great neighbors, I can yet love; I can still receive; and he that loveth maketh his own the grandeur he loves. Thereby I make the discovery that my brother is my guardian, acting for me with the friendliest designs, and the estate I so admired and envied is my own. It is the nature of the soul to appropriate all things. Jesus and Shakespeare are fragments of the soul, and by love I conquer and incorporate them in my own conscious domain. His virtue,—is not that mine? His wit,—if it cannot be made mine, it is not wit.

Such, also, is the natural history of calamity. The changes which break up at short intervals the prosperity of men are advertisements of a nature whose law is growth. Every soul is by this intrinsic necessity quitting its whole system of things, its friends, and home, and laws, and faith, as the shell-fish crawls out of its beautiful but stony case, because it no longer admits of its growth, and slowly forms a new house. In proportion to the vigor of the individual, these revolutions are frequent, until in some happier mind they are incessant, and all worldly relations hang very loosely about him, becoming, as it were, a transparent fluid membrane through which the living form is seen, and not, as in most men, an indurated heterogeneous fabric of many dates, and of no settled character in which the man is imprisoned. Then there can be enlargement, and the man of to-day scarcely recognizes the man of yesterday. And such should be the outward biography of man in time, a putting off of dead circumstances day by day, as he renews his raiment day by day. But to us, in our lapsed estate, resting, not advancing, resisting, not cooperating with the divine expansion, this growth comes by shocks.

We cannot part with our friends. We cannot let our angels go. We do not see that they only go out, that archangels may come in. We are idolaters of the old. We do not believe in the riches of the soul, in its proper eternity and omnipresence. We do not believe there is any force in to-day to rival or recreate that beautiful yesterday. We linger in the ruins of the old tent, where once we had bread and shelter and organs, nor believe that the spirit can feed, cover, and nerve us again. We cannot again find aught so dear, so sweet, so graceful. But we sit and weep in vain. The voice of the Almighty saith, 'Up and onward forevermore!' We cannot stay amid the ruins. Neither will we rely on the new; and so we walk ever with reverted eyes, like those monsters who look backwards.

And yet the compensations of calamity are made apparent to the understanding also, after long intervals of time. A fever, a mutilation, a cruel disappointment, a loss of wealth, a loss of friends, seems at the moment unpaid loss, and unpayable. But the sure years reveal the deep remedial force that underlies all facts. The death of a dear friend, wife, brother, lover, which seemed nothing but privation, somewhat later assumes the aspect of a guide or genius; for it commonly operates revolutions in our way of life, terminates an epoch of infancy or of youth which was waiting to be closed, breaks up a wonted occupation, or a household, or style of living, and allows the formation of new ones more friendly to the growth of character. It permits or constrains the formation of new acquaintances, and the reception of new influences that prove of the first importance to the next years; and the man or woman who would have remained a sunny garden-flower, with no room for its roots and too much sunshine for its head, by the falling of the walls and the neglect of the gardener, is made the banyan of the forest, yielding shade and fruit to wide neighborhoods of men.

12

UPON SOME VERSES OF VIRGIL

Michel de Montaigne

By how much profitable thoughts are more full and solid, by so much are they also more cumbersome and heavy: vice, death, poverty, diseases, are grave and grievous subjects. A man should have his soul instructed in the means to sustain and to contend with evils, and in the rules of living and believing well: and often rouse it up, and exercise it in this noble study; but in an ordinary soul it must be by intervals and with moderation; it will otherwise grow besotted if continually intent upon it. I found it necessary, when I was young, to put myself in mind and solicit myself to keep me to my duty; gaiety and health do not, they say, so well agree with those grave and serious meditations: I am at present in another state: the conditions of age but too much put me in mind, urge me to wisdom, and preach to me. From the excess of sprightliness I am fallen into that of severity, which is much more troublesome; and for that reason I now and then suffer myself purposely a little to run into disorder, and occupy my mind in wanton and youthful thoughts, wherewith it diverts itself. am of late but too reserved, too heavy, and too ripe; years every day read to me lectures of coldness and temperance. This body of mine avoids disorder and dreads it; 'tis now my body's turn to guide my mind towards reformation; it governs, in turn, and more rudely and imperiously than the other; it lets me not an hour alone, sleeping or waking, but is always preaching to me death, patience, and repentance. I now defend myself from temperance, as I have formerly done from pleasure; it draws me too much back, and even to stupidity. Now I will be master of myself, to all intents and purposes; wisdom has its excesses, and has no less need of moderation than folly. Therefore, lest I should wither, dry up, and overcharge myself with prudence, in the intervals and truces my infirmities allow me:

> '*Mens intenta suis ne seit usque malis.*'
>
> ['That my mind may not eternally be intent upon my ills.' —Ovid., Trist., iv. i, 4.]

I gently turn aside, and avert my eyes from the stormy and cloudy sky I have before me, which, thanks be to God, I regard without fear, but not without meditation and study, and amuse myself in the remembrance of my better years:

> '*Animus quo perdidit, optat,*
> *Atque in praeterita se totus imagine versat.*'
>
> ['The mind wishes to have what it has lost, and throws itself wholly into memories of the past.' —Petronius, c. 128.]

Let childhood look forward and age backward; was not this the signification of Janus' double face? Let years draw me along if they will, but it shall be backward; as long as my eyes can discern the pleasant season expired, I shall now and then turn them that way; though it escape from my blood and veins, I shall not, however, root the image of it out of my memory:

> '*Hoc est*
> *Vivere bis, vita posse priore frui.*'
>
> [''Tis to live twice to be able to enjoy one's former life again.' —Martial, x. 23, 7.]

Plato ordains that old men should be present at the exercises, dances, and sports of young people, that they may rejoice in others for the activity and beauty of body which is no more in themselves, and call to mind the grace and comeliness of that flourishing age; and wills that in these recreations the honour of the prize should be given to that young man who has most diverted the company. I was formerly wont to mark cloudy and gloomy days as extraordinary; these are now my ordinary days; the extraordinary are the clear and bright; I am ready to leap for joy, as for an unwonted favour, when nothing happens me. Let me tickle myself, I cannot force a poor smile from this wretched body of mine; I am only merry in conceit and in dreaming, by artifice to divert the melancholy of age; but, in faith, it requires another remedy than a dream. A weak contest of art against nature. 'Tis great folly to lengthen and anticipate human incommodities, as every one does; I had rather be a less while old than be old before I am really so. I seize on even the least occasions of pleasure I can meet. I know very well, by hearsay, several sorts of prudent pleasures, effectually so, and glorious to boot; but opinion has not power enough over me to give me an appetite to them. I covet not so much to have them magnanimous, magnificent, and pompous, as I do to have them sweet, facile, and ready:

> '*A natura discedimus; populo nos damus,*
> *nullius rei bono auctori.*'

> ['We depart from nature and give ourselves to the people, who understand nothing.' —Seneca, Ep., 99.]

My philosophy is in action, in natural and present practice, very little in fancy: what if I should take pleasure in playing at cob-nut or to whip a top!

> '*Non ponebat enim rumores ante salutem.*'

> ['He did not sacrifice his health even to rumours.' Ennius, apud Cicero, De Offic., i. 24]

Pleasure is a quality of very little ambition; it thinks itself rich enough of itself without any addition of repute; and is best pleased where most retired. A young man should be whipped who pretends to a taste in wine and sauces; there was nothing which, at that age, I less valued or knew: now I begin to learn; I am very much ashamed on't; but what should I do? I am more ashamed and vexed at the occasions that put me upon't. 'Tis for us to dote and trifle away the time, and for young men to stand upon their reputation and nice punctilios; they are going towards the world and the world's opinion; we are retiring from it:

> '*Sibi arma, sibi equos, sibi hastas, sibi clavam, sibi pilam, sibi natationes, et cursus habeant: nobis senibus, ex lusionibus multis, talos relinquant et tesseras;*'
>
> ['Let them reserve to themselves arms, horses, spears, clubs, tennis, swimming, and races; and of all the sports leave to us old men cards and dice.' —Cicero, De Senec., c. 16.]

the laws themselves send us home. I can do no less in favour of this wretched condition into which my age has thrown me than furnish it with toys to play withal, as they do children; and, in truth, we become such. Both wisdom and folly will have enough to do to support and relieve me by alternate services in this calamity of age:

> '*Misce stultitiam consiliis brevem.*'
>
> ['Mingle with counsels a brief interval of folly.'
> —Horace, Od., iv. 12, 27.]

I accordingly avoid the lightest punctures; and those that formerly would not have rippled the skin, now pierce me through and through: my habit of body is now so naturally declining to ill:

> '*In fragili corpore odiosa omnis offensio est;*'
>
> ['In a fragile body every shock is obnoxious.'
> —Cicero, De Senec., c. 18.]
>
> '*Mensque pati durum sustinet aegra nihil.*'
>
> ['And the infirm mind can bear no difficult exertion.'
> —Ovid, De Ponto., i. 5, 18.]

I have ever been very susceptibly tender as to offences: I am much more tender now, and open throughout.

'*Et minimae vires frangere quassa valent.*'

['And little force suffices to break what was cracked before.' — Ovid, De Tris., iii. 11, 22.]

My judgment restrains me from kicking against and murmuring at the inconveniences that nature orders me to endure, but it does not take away my feeling them: I, who have no other thing in my aim but to live and be merry, would run from one end of the world to the other to seek out one good year of pleasant and jocund tranquillity. A melancholic and dull tranquillity may be enough for me, but it benumbs and stupefies me; I am not contented with it. If there be any person, any knot of good company in country or city, in France or elsewhere, resident or in motion, who can like my humour, and whose humours I can like, let them but whistle and I will run and furnish them with essays in flesh and bone:

Seeing it is the privilege of the mind to rescue itself from old age, I advise mine to it with all the power I have; let it meanwhile continue green, and flourish if it can, like mistletoe upon a dead tree. But I fear 'tis a traitor; it has contracted so strict a fraternity with the body that it leaves me at every turn, to follow that in its need. I wheedle and deal with it apart in vain; I try in vain to wean it from this correspondence, to no effect; quote to it Seneca and Catullus, and ladies and royal masques; if its companion have the stone, it seems to have it too; even the faculties that are most peculiarly and properly its own cannot then perform their functions, but manifestly appear stupefied and asleep; there is no sprightliness in its productions, if there be not at the same time an equal proportion in the body too.

Our masters are to blame, that in searching out the causes of the extraordinary emotions of the soul, besides attributing it to a divine ecstasy, love, martial fierceness, poesy, wine, they have not also attributed a part to health: a boiling, vigorous, full, and lazy health, such as formerly the verdure of youth and security, by fits, supplied me withal; that fire of sprightliness and gaiety darts into the mind flashes that are lively and bright beyond our natural light, and of all enthusiasms the most jovial, if not the most extravagant.

It is, then, no wonder if a contrary state stupefy and clog my spirit, and produce a contrary effect:

'*Ad nullum consurgit opus, cum corpore languet*;'

['When the mind is languishing, the body is good for nothing.'
(Or:) 'It rises to no effort; it languishes with the body.'
—Pseudo Gallus, i. 125.]

and yet would have me obliged to it for giving, as it wants to make out, much less consent to this stupidity than is the ordinary case with men of my age. Let us, at least, whilst we have truce, drive away incommodities and difficulties from our commerce:

'*Dum licet, obducta solvatur fronte senectus*:'

['Whilst we can, let us banish old age from the brow.'
—Herod., Ep., xiii. 7.]

'*Tetrica sunt amcenanda jocularibus*.'

['Sour things are to be sweetened with those that are pleasant.'
—Sidonius Apollin., Ep., i. 9.]

I love a gay and civil wisdom, and fly from all sourness and austerity of manners, all repellent, mien being suspected by me:

'*Tristemque vultus tetrici arrogantiam*:'

['The arrogant sadness of a crabbed face.' —Auctor Incert.]

'*Et habet tristis quoque turba cinaedos*.'

['And the dull crowd also has its voluptuaries.' (Or:) 'An austere countenance sometimes covers a debauched mind.' —Idem.]

I am very much of Plato's opinion, who says that facile or harsh humours are great indications of the good or ill disposition of the mind. Socrates had a constant countenance, but serene and smiling, not sourly austere, like the elder Crassus, whom no one ever saw laugh. Virtue is a pleasant and gay quality.

I know very well that few will quarrel with the licence of my writings, who have not more to quarrel with in the licence of their own thoughts: I conform myself well enough to their inclinations, but I offend their eyes. 'Tis a fine humour to strain the writings of Plato, to wrest his pretended intercourses with Phaedo, Dion, Stella, and Archeanassa:

> '*Non pudeat dicere, quod non pudet sentire.*'
>
> ['Let us not be ashamed to speak what we are not ashamed to think.']

I hate a froward and dismal spirit, that slips over all the pleasures of life and seizes and feeds upon misfortunes; like flies, that cannot stick to a smooth and polished body, but fix and repose themselves upon craggy and rough places, and like cupping-glasses, that only suck and attract bad blood.

As to the rest, I have enjoined myself to dare to say all that I dare to do; even thoughts that are not to be published, displease me; the worst of my actions and qualities do not appear to me so evil as I find it evil and base not to dare to own them. Every one is wary and discreet in confession, but men ought to be so in action; the boldness of doing ill is in some sort compensated and restrained by the boldness of confessing it. Whoever will oblige himself to tell all, should oblige himself to do nothing that he must be forced to conceal. I wish that this excessive licence of mine may draw men to freedom, above these timorous and mincing virtues sprung from our imperfections, and that at the expense of my immoderation I may reduce them to reason. A man must see and study his vice to correct it; they who conceal it from others, commonly conceal it from themselves; and do not think it close enough, if they themselves see it: they withdraw and disguise it from their own consciences:

> '*Quare vitia sua nemo confitetur? Quia etiam nunc in illia est; somnium narrare vigilantis est.*'
>
> ['Why does no man confess his vices? because he is yet in them; 'tis for a waking man to tell his dream.' —Seneca, Ep., 53.]

The diseases of the body explain themselves by their increase; we find that to be the gout which we called a rheum or a strain; the diseases of the soul, the greater they are, keep, themselves the most obscure; the most sick are the least sensible; therefore it is that with an unrelenting hand they most often, in full day, be taken to task, opened, and torn from the hollow of the heart. As in doing well, so in doing ill, the mere confession is sometimes satisfaction. Is there any deformity in doing amiss, that can excuse us from confessing ourselves? It is so great a pain to me to dissemble, that I evade the trust of another's secrets, wanting the courage to disavow my knowledge. I can keep silent, but deny I cannot without the greatest trouble and violence to myself imaginable to be very secret, a man must be so by nature, not by obligation. 'Tis little worth, in the service of a prince, to be secret, if a man be not a liar to boot. If he who asked Thales the Milesian whether he ought solemnly to deny that he had committed adultery, had applied himself to me, I should have told him that he ought not to do it; for I look upon lying as a worse fault than the other. Thales advised him quite contrary, bidding him swear to shield the greater fault by the less;

> [Montaigne's memory here serves him ill, for the question being put to Thales, his answer was: 'But is not perjury worse than adultery?' —Diogenes Laertius, in vita, i. 36.]

nevertheless, this counsel was not so much an election as a multiplication of vice. Upon which let us say this in passing, that we deal liberally with a man of conscience when we propose to him some difficulty in counterpoise of vice; but when we shut him up betwixt two vices, he is put to a hard choice as Origen was either to idolatrize or to suffer himself to be carnally abused by a great Ethiopian slave they brought to him. He submitted to the first condition, and wrongly, people say. Yet those women of our times are not much out, according to their error, who protest they had rather burden their consciences with ten men than one mass.

If it be indiscretion so to publish one's errors, yet there is no great danger that it pass into example and custom; for Ariston said, that the winds men most fear are those that lay them open. We must tuck up this ridiculous rag that hides our manners: they send their consciences to the stews, and keep a starched countenance: even traitors and assassins espouse the laws of ceremony, and there fix their duty. So that neither can injustice complain of incivility, nor malice of indiscretion. 'Tis pity but a bad man should be a fool to boot, and that outward decency should palliate his vice: this rough-cast only appertains to a good and sound wall, that deserves to be preserved and whited.

In favour of the Huguenots, who condemn our auricular and private confession, I confess myself in public, religiously and purely: St Augustin, Origeti, and Hippocrates have published the errors of their opinions; I, moreover, of my manners. I am greedy of making myself known, and I care not to how many, provided it be truly; or to say better, I hunger for nothing; but I mortally hate to be mistaken by those who happen to learn my name. He who does all things for honour and glory, what can he think to gain by shewing himself to the world in a vizor, and by concealing his true being from the people? Praise a humpback for his stature, he has reason to take it for an affront: if you are a coward, and men commend you for your valour, is it of you they speak? They take you for another. I should like him as well who glorifies himself in the compliments and congees that are made him as if he were master of the company, when he is one of the least of the train. Archelaus, king of Macedon, walking along the street, somebody threw water on his head, which they who were with him said he ought to punish: 'Aye, but,' said he, 'whoever it was, he did not throw the water upon me, but upon him whom he took me to be.' Socrates being told that people spoke ill of him, 'Not at all,' said he, 'there is nothing, in me of what they say.'

For my part, if any one should recommend me as a good pilot, as being very modest or very chaste, I should owe him no thanks; and so, whoever should call me traitor, robber, or drunkard, I should be as little concerned. They who do not rightly know themselves, may feed themselves with false approbations; not I, who see myself, and who examine myself even to my very bowels, and who very well know what is my due. I am content to be less commended, provided I am better known. I may be reputed a wise man in such a sort of wisdom as I take to be folly. I am vexed that my Essays only serve the ladies for a common piece of furniture, and a piece for the hall; this chapter will make me part of the water-closet. I love to traffic with them a little in private; public conversation is without favour and without savour. In farewells, we oftener than not heat our affections towards the things we take leave of; I take my last leave of the pleasures of this world: these are our last embraces.

But let us come to my subject: what has the act of generation, so natural, so necessary, and so just, done to men, to be a thing not to be spoken of without blushing, and to be excluded from all serious and moderate discourse? We boldly pronounce kill, rob, betray, and that we dare only to do betwixt the teeth. Is it to say, the less we expend in words, we may pay so much the more in thinking? For it is certain that the words least in use, most seldom written, and best kept in, are the best and most generally known: no age, no manners, are ignorant of them, no more than the word bread they imprint themselves in every one without being, expressed, without voice, and without figure; and the sex that most practises it is bound to say least of it. 'Tis an act that we have placed in the franchise of silence, from which to take it is a crime even to accuse and judge it; neither dare we reprehend it but by periphrasis and picture. A great favour to a criminal to be so execrable that justice thinks it unjust to touch and see him; free, and safe by the benefit of the severity of his condemnation. Is it not here as in matter of books, that sell better and become more public for being suppressed? For my part, I will take Aristotle at his word, who says, that 'bashfulness is an ornament to youth, but a reproach to old age.' These verses are preached in the ancient school, a school that I much more adhere to than the modern: its virtues appear to me to be greater, and the vices less:

> '*Ceux qui par trop fuyant Venus estrivent,*
> *Faillent autant que ceulx qui trop la suyvent.*'

> ['They err as much who too much forbear Venus, as they who are too frequent in her rites.' —A translation by Amyot from Plutarch, A philosopher should converse with princes.]

'*Tu, dea, rerum naturam sola gubernas,*
Nec sine to quicquam dias in luminis oras
Exoritur, neque fit laetum, nec amabile quidquam.'

['Goddess, still thou alone governest nature, nor without thee anything comes into light; nothing is pleasant, nothing joyful.' —Lucretius, i. 22.]

I know not who could set Pallas and the Muses at variance with Venus, and make them cold towards Love; but I see no deities so well met, or that are more indebted to one another. Who will deprive the Muses of amorous imaginations, will rob them of the best entertainment they have, and of the noblest matter of their work: and who will make Love lose the communication and service of poesy, will disarm him of his best weapons: by this means they charge the god of familiarity and good will, and the protecting goddesses of humanity and justice, with the vice of ingratitude and unthankfulness. I have not been so long cashiered from the state and service of this god, that my memory is not still perfect in his force and value:

'*Agnosco veteris vestigia flammae*;'

['I recognize vestiges of my old flame.' —Aeneid., iv. 23.]

There are yet some remains of heat and emotion after the fever:

'*Nec mihi deficiat calor hic, hiemantibus annis!*'

['Nor let this heat of youth fail me in my winter years.']

Withered and drooping as I am, I feel yet some remains of the past ardour:

'*Qual l'alto Egeo, per the Aquilone o Noto*
Cessi, the tutto prima il volse et scosse,
Non 's accheta ei pero; ma'l suono e'l moto
Ritien del l'onde anco agitate e grosse:'

['As Aegean seas, when storms be calmed again,
That rolled their tumbling waves with troublous blasts,

Do yet of tempests passed some show retain,
And here and there their swelling billows cast.' —Fairfax.]

but from what I understand of it, the force and power of this god are more lively and animated in the picture of poesy than in their own essence:

'*Et versus digitos habet*.'

['Verse has fingers.' —Altered from Juvenal, iv. 196.]

it has I know not what kind of air, more amorous than love itself. Venus is not so beautiful, naked, alive, and panting, as she is here in Virgil:

'*Dixerat; et niveis hinc atque hinc Diva lacertis*
Cunctantem amplexu molli fovet. Ille repente
Accepit solitam flammam; notusque medullas
Intravit calor, et labefacta per ossa cucurrit
Non secus atque olim tonitru, cum rupta corusco
Ignea rima micans percurrit lumine nimbos.
......Ea verba loquutus,
Optatos dedit amplexus; placidumque petivit
Conjugis infusus gremio per membra soporem.'

['The goddess spoke, and throwing round him her snowy arms in soft embraces, caresses him hesitating. Suddenly he caught the wonted flame, and the well-known warmth pierced his marrow, and ran thrilling through his shaken bones: just as when at times, with thunder, a stream of fire in lightning flashes shoots across the skies. Having spoken these words, he gave her the wished embrace, and in the bosom of his spouse sought placid sleep.' —Aeneid, viii. 387 and 392.]

All that I find fault with in considering it is, that he has represented her a little too passionate for a married Venus; in this discreet kind of coupling, the appetite is not usually so wanton, but more grave and dull. Love hates that people should hold of any but itself, and goes but faintly to work in familiarities derived from any other title, as marriage is: alliance, dowry, therein sway by reason, as much or more than grace and beauty. Men do not marry for themselves, let them say what they will; they marry as much or more for their posterity and family; the custom and interest of marriage concern our race much more than us; and therefore it is, that I like to have a match carried on by a third hand rather than a man's own, and by another man's liking than that of the party himself; and how much is all this opposite to the conventions of love? And also it is a kind of incest to employ in this venerable and sacred alliance the heat and extravagance of amorous licence, as I think I have said elsewhere. A man, says Aristotle, must approach his wife with prudence and temperance, lest in dealing too lasciviously with her, the extreme pleasure make her exceed the bounds of reason. What he says upon the account of conscience, the physicians say upon the account of health: 'that a pleasure excessively lascivious, voluptuous, and frequent, makes the seed too hot, and hinders conception': 'tis said, elsewhere, that to a languishing intercourse, as this naturally is, to supply it with a due and fruitful heat, a man must do it but seldom and at appreciable intervals:

> '*Quo rapiat sitiens Venerem, interiusque recondat.*'
>
> ['But let him thirstily snatch the joys of love and enclose them in his bosom.' —Virg., Georg., iii. 137.]

I see no marriages where the conjugal compatibility sooner fails than those that we contract upon the account of beauty and amorous desires; there should be more solid and constant foundation, and they should proceed with greater circumspection; this furious ardour is worth nothing.

They who think they honour marriage by joining love to it, do, methinks, like those who, to favour virtue, hold that nobility is nothing else but virtue. They are indeed things that have some relation to one another, but there is a great deal of difference; we should not so mix their names and titles; 'tis a wrong to them both so to confound them. Nobility is a brave quality, and with good reason introduced; but forasmuch as 'tis a quality depending upon others, and may happen in a vicious person, in himself nothing, 'tis in estimate infinitely below virtue';

> ['If nobility be virtue, it loses its quality in all things wherein not virtuous: and if it be not virtue, 'tis a small matter.' —La Byuyere.]

'tis a virtue, if it be one, that is artificial and apparent, depending upon time and fortune: various in form, according to the country; living and mortal; without birth, as the river Nile; genealogical and common; of succession and similitude; drawn by consequence, and a very weak one. Knowledge, strength, goodness, beauty, riches, and all other qualities, fall into communication and commerce, but this is consummated in itself, and of no use to the service of others. There was proposed to one of our kings the choice of two candidates for the same command, of whom one was a gentleman, the other not; he ordered that, without respect to quality, they should choose him who had the most merit; but where the worth of the competitors should appear to be entirely equal, they should have respect to birth: this was justly to give it its rank. A young man unknown, coming to Antigonus to make suit for his father's command, a valiant man lately dead: 'Friend,' said he, 'in such preferments as these, I have not so much regard to the nobility of my soldiers as to their prowess.' And, indeed, it ought not to go as it did with the officers of the kings of Sparta, trumpeters, fiddlers, cooks, the children of whom always succeeded to their places, how ignorant soever, and were preferred before the most experienced in the trade. They of Calicut make of nobles a sort of superhuman persons: they are interdicted marriage and all but warlike employments: they may have of concubines their fill, and the women as many lovers, without being jealous of one another; but 'tis a capital and irremissible crime to couple with a person of meaner conditions than themselves; and they think themselves polluted, if they have but touched one in walking along; and supposing their nobility to be marvellously interested and injured in it, kill such as only approach a little too near them: insomuch that the ignoble are obliged to cry out as they walk, like the gondoliers of Venice, at the turnings of streets for fear of jostling; and the nobles command them to step aside to what part they please: by that means these avoid what they repute a perpetual ignominy, those certain death. No time, no favour of the prince, no office, or virtue, or riches, can ever prevail to make a plebeian become noble: to which this custom contributes, that marriages are interdicted betwixt different trades; the daughter of one of the cordwainers' gild is not permitted to marry a carpenter; and parents are obliged to train up their children precisely in their own callings, and not put them to any other trade; by which means the distinction and continuance of their fortunes are maintained.

A good marriage, if there be any such, rejects the company and conditions of love, and tries to represent those of friendship. 'Tis a sweet society of life, full of constancy, trust, and an infinite number of useful and solid services and mutual obligations; which any woman who has a right taste:

'*Optato quam junxit lumine taeda*'—

['Whom the marriage torch has joined with the desired light.' — Catullus, lxiv. 79.]

would be loth to serve her husband in quality of a mistress. If she be lodged in his affection as a wife, she is more honourably and securely placed. When he purports to be in love with another, and works all he can to obtain his desire, let any one but ask him, on which he had rather a disgrace should fall, his wife or his mistress, which of their misfortunes would most afflict him, and to which of them he wishes the most grandeur, the answer to these questions is out of dispute in a sound marriage.

And that so few are observed to be happy, is a token of its price and value. If well formed and rightly taken, 'tis the best of all human societies; we cannot live without it, and yet we do nothing but decry it. It happens, as with cages, the birds without despair to get in, and those within despair of getting out. Socrates being asked, whether it was more commodious to take a wife or not, 'Let a man take which course he will,' said he; 'he will repent.' 'Tis a contract to which the common saying:

> '*Homo homini aut deus aut lupus,*'
>
> ['Man to man is either a god or a wolf.' —Erasmus, Adag.]

may very fitly be applied; there must be a concurrence of many qualities in the construction. It is found nowadays more convenient for simple and plebeian souls, where delights, curiosity, and idleness do not so much disturb it; but extravagant humours, such as mine, that hate all sorts of obligation and restraint, are not so proper for it:

> '*Et mihi dulce magis resoluto vivere collo.*'
>
> ['And it is sweet to me to live with a loosened neck.' —Pseudo Gallus, i. 61.]

Might I have had my own will, I would not have married Wisdom herself, if she would have had me. But 'tis to much purpose to evade it; the common custom and usance of life will have it so. The most of my actions are guided by example, not by choice, and yet I did not go to it of my own voluntary motion; I was led and drawn to it by extrinsic occasions; for not only things that are incommodious in themselves, but also things however ugly, vicious, and to be avoided, may be rendered acceptable by some condition or accident; so unsteady and vain is all human resolution! and I was persuaded to it, when worse prepared and less tractable than I am at present, that I have tried what it is: and as great a libertine as I am taken to be, I have in truth more strictly observed the laws of marriage, than I either promised or expected. 'Tis in vain to kick, when a man has once put on his fetters: a man must prudently manage his liberty; but having once submitted to obligation, he must confine himself within the laws of common duty, at least, do what he can towards it. They who engage in this contract, with a design to carry themselves in it with hatred and contempt, do an unjust and inconvenient thing; and the fine rule that I hear pass from hand to hand amongst the women, as a sacred oracle:

> ['Serve thy husband as thy master, but guard thyself against him as from a traitor.']

which is to say, comport thyself towards him with a dissembled, inimical, and distrustful reverence (a cry of war and defiance), is equally injurious and hard. I am too mild for such rugged designs: to say the truth, I am not arrived to that perfection of ability and refinement of wit, to confound reason with injustice, and to laugh at all rule and order that does not please my palate; because I hate superstition, I do not presently run into the contrary extreme of irreligion.

> [If a man hate superstition he cannot love religion. D.W.]

If a man does not always perform his duty, he ought at least to love and acknowledge it; 'tis treachery to marry without espousing.

Let us proceed.

Our poet represents a marriage happy in a good accord wherein nevertheless there is not much loyalty. Does he mean, that it is not impossible but a woman may give the reins to her own passion, and yield to the importunities of love, and yet reserve some duty toward marriage, and that it may be hurt, without being totally broken? A serving man may cheat his master, whom nevertheless he does not hate. Beauty, opportunity, and destiny (for destiny has also a hand in't),

> '*Fatum est in partibus illis*
> *Quas sinus abscondit; nam, si tibi sidera cessent,*
> *Nil faciet longi mensura incognita nervi;*'

> ['There is a fatality about the hidden parts: let nature have endowed you however liberally, 'tis of no use, if your good star fails you in the nick of time.' —Juvenal, ix. 32.]

have attached her to a stranger; though not so wholly, peradventure, but that she may have some remains of kindness for her husband. They are two designs, that have several paths leading to them, without being confounded with one another; a woman may yield to a man she would by no means have married, not only for the condition of his fortune, but for those also of his person. Few men have made a wife of a mistress, who have not repented it. And even in the other world, what an unhappy life does Jupiter lead with his, whom he had first enjoyed as a mistress! 'Tis, as the proverb runs, to befoul a basket and then put it upon one's head. I have in my time, in a good family, seen love shamefully and dishonestly cured by marriage: the considerations are widely different. We love at once, without any tie, two things contrary in themselves.

Socrates was wont to say, that the city of Athens pleased, as ladies do whom men court for love; every one loved to come thither to take a turn, and pass away his time; but no one liked it so well as to espouse it, that is, to inhabit there, and to make it his constant residence. I have been vexed to see husbands hate their wives only because they themselves do them wrong; we should not, at all events, methinks, love them the less for our own faults; they should at least, upon the account of repentance and compassion, be dearer to us.

They are different ends, he says, and yet in some sort compatible; marriage has utility, justice, honour, and constancy for its share; a flat, but more universal pleasure: love founds itself wholly upon pleasure, and, indeed, has it more full, lively, and sharp; a pleasure inflamed by difficulty; there must be in it sting and smart: 'tis no longer love, if without darts and fire. The bounty of ladies is too profuse in marriage, and dulls the point of affection and desire: to evade which inconvenience, do but observe what pains Lycurgus and Plato take in their laws.

Women are not to blame at all, when they refuse the rules of life that are introduced into the world, forasmuch as the men make them without their help. There is naturally contention and brawling betwixt them and us; and the strictest friendship we have with them is yet mixed with tumult and tempest. In the opinion of our author, we deal inconsiderately with them in this: after we have discovered that they are, without comparison, more able and ardent in the practice of love than we, and that the old priest testified as much, who had been one while a man, and then a woman:

'*Venus huic erat utraque nota*:'

['Both aspects of love were known to him,' —Tiresias. Ovid. Metam., iii. 323.]

and moreover, that we have learned from their own mouths the proof that, in several ages, was made by an Emperor and Empress of Rome,—[Proclus.]—both famous for ability in that affair! for he in one night deflowered ten Sarmatian virgins who were his captives: but she had five-and-twenty bouts in one night, changing her man according to her need and liking;

'*Adhuc ardens rigidae tentigine vulvae*
Et lassata viris, nondum satiata, recessit:'

['Ardent still, she retired, fatigued, but not satisfied.' —Juvenal, vi. 128.]

and that upon the dispute which happened in Cataluna, wherein a wife complaining of her husband's too frequent addresses to her, not so much, as I conceive, that she was incommodated by it (for I believe no miracles out of religion) as under this pretence, to curtail and curb in this, which is the fundamental act of marriage, the authority of husbands over their wives, and to shew that their frowardness and malignity go beyond the nuptial bed, and spurn under foot even the graces and sweets of Venus; the husband, a man truly brutish and unnatural, replied, that even on fasting days he could not subsist with less than ten courses: whereupon came out that notable sentence of the Queen of Arragon, by which, after mature deliberation of her council, this good queen, to give a rule and example to all succeeding ages of the moderation required in a just marriage, set down six times a day as a legitimate and necessary stint; surrendering and quitting a great deal of the needs and desires of her sex, that she might, she said, establish an easy, and consequently, a permanent and immutable rule. Hereupon the doctors cry out: what must the female appetite and concupiscence be, when their reason, their reformation and virtue, are taxed at such a rate, considering the divers judgments of our appetites?

for Solon, master of the law school, taxes us but at three a month,—that men may not fail in point of conjugal frequentation: after having, I say, believed and preached all this, we go and enjoin them continency for their particular share, and upon the last and extreme penalties.

There is no passion so hard to contend with as this, which we would have them only resist, not simply as an ordinary vice, but as an execrable abomination, worse than irreligion and parricide; whilst we, at the same time, go to't without offence or reproach. Even those amongst us who have tried the experiment have sufficiently confessed what difficulty, or rather impossibility, they have found by material remedies to subdue, weaken, and cool the body. We, on the contrary, would have them at once sound, vigorous plump, high-fed, and chaste; that is to say, both hot and cold; for the marriage, which we tell them is to keep them from burning, is but small refreshment to them, as we order the matter. If they take one whose vigorous age is yet boiling, he will be proud to make it known elsewhere;

'*Sit tandem pudor; aut eamus in jus;*
Multis mentula millibus redempta,
Non est haec tua, Basse; vendidisti;'

['Let there be some shame, or we shall go to law: your vigour, bought by your wife with many thousands, is no longer yours: thou hast sold it.' —Martial, xii. 90.]

Polemon the philosopher was justly by his wife brought before the judge for sowing in a barren field the seed that was due to one that was fruitful: if, on the other hand, they take a decayed fellow, they are in a worse condition in marriage than either maids or widows. We think them well provided for, because they have a man to lie with, as the Romans concluded Clodia Laeta, a vestal nun, violated, because Caligula had approached her, though it was declared he did no more but approach her: but, on the contrary, we by that increase their necessity, forasmuch as the touch and company of any man whatever rouses their desires, that in solitude would be more quiet. And to the end, 'tis likely, that they might render their chastity more meritorious by this circumstance and consideration, Boleslas and Kinge his wife, kings of Poland, vowed it by mutual consent, being in bed together, on their very wedding day, and kept their vow in spite of all matrimonial conveniences.

We train them up from their infancy to the traffic of love; their grace, dressing, knowledge, language, and whole instruction tend that way: their governesses imprint nothing in them but the idea of love, if for nothing else but by continually representing it to them, to give them a distaste for it. My daughter, the only child I have, is now of an age that forward young women are allowed to be married at; she is of a slow, thin, and tender complexion, and has accordingly been brought up by her mother after a retired and particular manner, so that she but now begins to be weaned from her childish simplicity. She was reading before me in a French book where the word 'fouteau', the name of a tree very well known, occurred;—[The beech-tree; the name resembles in sound an obscene French word.] —the woman, to whose conduct she is committed, stopped her short a little roughly, and made her skip over that dangerous step. I let her alone, not to trouble their rules, for I never concern myself in that sort of government; feminine polity has a mysterious procedure; we must leave it to them; but if I am not mistaken the commerce of twenty lacquies could not, in six months' time, have so imprinted in her memory the meaning, usage, and all the consequence of the sound of these wicked syllables, as this good old woman did by reprimand and interdiction.

'Motus doceri gaudet Ionicos
Matura virgo, et frangitur artibus;
Jam nunc et incestos amores
De tenero, meditatur ungui.'

['The maid ripe for marriage delights to learn Ionic dances, and to imitate those lascivious movements. Nay, already from her infancy she meditates criminal amours.' —Horace, Od., iii. 6, 21., the text has 'fingitur'.]

Let them but give themselves the rein a little, let them but enter into liberty of discourse, we are but children to them in this science. Hear them but describe our pursuits and conversation, they will very well make you understand that we bring them nothing they have not known before, and digested without our help.

> [This sentence refers to a conversation between some young women in his immediate neighbourhood, which the Essayist just below informs us that he overheard, and which was too shocking for him to repeat. It must have been tolerably bad. —Remark by the editor of a later edition.]

Is it, perhaps, as Plato says, that they have formerly been debauched young fellows? I happened one day to be in a place where I could hear some of their talk without suspicion; I am sorry I cannot repeat it. By'rlady, said I, we had need go study the phrases of Amadis, and the tales of Boccaccio and Aretin, to be able to discourse with them: we employ our time to much purpose indeed. There is neither word, example, nor step they are not more perfect in than our books; 'tis a discipline that springs with their blood,

> '*Et mentem ipsa Venus dedit,*'

> ['Venus herself made them what they are,' —Virg., Georg., iii. 267.]

which these good instructors, nature, youth, and health, are continually inspiring them with; they need not learn, they breed it:

> '*Nec tantum niveo gavisa est ulla columbo,*
> *Compar, vel si quid dicitur improbius,*
> *Oscula mordenti semper decerpere rostro,*
> *Quantum praecipue multivola est mulier.*'

> ['No milk-white dove, or if there be a thing more lascivious, takes so much delight in kissing as woman, wishful for every man she sees.' —Catullus, lxvi. 125.]

So that if the natural violence of their desire were not a little restrained by fear and honour, which were wisely contrived for them, we should be all shamed. All the motions in the world resolve into and tend to this conjunction; 'tis a matter infused throughout: 'tis a centre to which all things are directed. We yet see the edicts of the old and wise Rome made for the service of love, and the precepts of Socrates for the instruction of courtezans:

> '*Noncon libelli Stoici inter sericos*
> *Jacere pulvillos amant*.'

> ['There are writings of the Stoics which we find lying upon silken cushions.' —Horace, Epod., viii. 15.]

Zeno, amongst his laws, also regulated the motions to be observed in getting a maidenhead. What was the philosopher Strato's book Of Carnal Conjunction?—[Diogenes Laertius, v. 59.]—And what did Theophrastus treat of in those he intituled, the one 'The Lover', and the other 'Of Love?' Of what Aristippus in his 'Of Former Delights'? What do the so long and lively descriptions in Plato of the loves of his time pretend to? and the book called 'The Lover', of Demetrius Phalereus? and 'Clinias', or the 'Ravished Lover', of Heraclides; and that of Antisthenes, 'Of Getting Children', or, 'Of Weddings', and the other, 'Of the Master or the Lover'? And that of Aristo: 'Of Amorous Exercises' What those of Cleanthes: one, 'Of Love', the other, 'Of the Art of Loving'? The amorous dialogues of Sphaereus? and the fable of Jupiter and Juno, of Chrysippus, impudent beyond all toleration? And his fifty so lascivious epistles? I will let alone the writings of the philosophers of the Epicurean sect, protectress of voluptuousness. Fifty deities were, in time past, assigned to this office; and there have been nations where, to assuage the lust of those who came to their devotion, they kept men and women in their temples for the worshippers to lie with; and it was an act of ceremony to do this before they went to prayers:

> '*Nimirum propter continentiam incontinentia necessaria est; incendium ignibus extinguitur*.'

> ['Forsooth incontinency is necessary for continency's sake; a conflagration is extinguished by fire.']

In the greatest part of the world, that member of our body was deified; in the same province, some flayed off the skin to offer and consecrate a piece; others offered and consecrated their seed. In another, the young men publicly cut through betwixt the skin and the flesh of that part in several places, and thrust pieces of wood into the openings as long and thick as they would receive, and of these pieces of wood afterwards made a fire as an offering to their gods; and were reputed neither vigorous nor chaste, if by the force of that cruel pain they seemed to be at all dismayed. Elsewhere the most sacred magistrate was reverenced and acknowledged by that member and in several ceremonies the effigy of it was carried in pomp to the honour of various divinities. The Egyptian ladies, in their Bacchanalia, each carried one finely-carved of wood about their necks, as large and heavy as she could so carry it; besides which, the statue of their god presented one, which in greatness surpassed all the rest of his body.—[Herodotus, ii. 48, says 'nearly as large as the body itself.']—The married women, near the place where I live, make of their kerchiefs the figure of one upon their foreheads, to glorify themselves in the enjoyment they have of it; and coming to be widows, they throw it behind, and cover it with their headcloths. The most modest matrons of Rome thought it an honour to offer flowers and garlands to the god Priapus; and they made the virgins, at the time of their espousals, sit upon his shameful parts. And I know not whether I have not in my time seen some air of like devotion. What was the meaning of that ridiculous piece of the chaussuye of our forefathers, and that is still worn by our Swiss? ['Cod-pieces worn' —Cotton]—To what end do we make a show of our implements in figure under our breeches, and often, which is worse, above their natural size, by falsehood and imposture? I have half a mind to believe that this sort of vestment was invented in the better and more conscientious ages, that the world might not be deceived, and that every one should give a public account of his proportions: the simple nations wear them yet, and near about the real size. In those days, the tailor took measure of it, as the shoemaker does now of a man's foot. That good man, who, when I was young, gelded so many noble and ancient statues in his great city, that they might not corrupt the sight of the ladies, according to the advice of this other ancient worthy:

> '*Flagitii principium est, nudare inter gives corpora,*'
>
> [''Tis the beginning of wickedness to expose their persons among the citizens' —Ennius, ap. Cicero, Tusc. Quaes., iv. 33.]

should have called to mind, that, as in the mysteries of the Bona Dea, all masculine appearance was excluded, he did nothing, if he did not geld horses and asses, in short, all nature:

> '*Omne adeo genus in terris, hominumque, ferarumque,*
> *Et genus aequoreum, pecudes, pictaeque volucres,*
> *In furias ignemque ruunt.*'
>
> ['So that all living things, men and animals, wild or tame, and fish and gaudy fowl, rush to this flame of love.' —Virgil, Georg., iii. 244.]

The gods, says Plato, have given us one disobedient and unruly member that, like a furious animal, attempts, by the violence of its appetite, to subject all things to it; and so they have given to women one like a greedy and ravenous animal, which, if it be refused food in season, grows wild, impatient of delay, and infusing its rage into their bodies, stops the passages, and hinders respiration, causing a thousand ills, till, having imbibed the fruit of the common thirst, it has plentifully bedewed the bottom of their matrix. Now my legislator—[The Pope who, as Montaigne has told us, took it into his head to geld the statues.]— should also have considered that, peradventure, it were a chaster and more fruitful usage to let them know the fact as it is betimes, than permit them to guess according to the liberty and heat of their own fancy; instead of the real parts they substitute, through hope and desire, others that are three times more extravagant; and a certain friend of mine lost himself by producing his in place and time when the opportunity was not present to put them to their more serious use. What mischief do not those pictures of prodigious dimension do that the boys make upon the staircases and galleries of the royal houses? they give the ladies a cruel contempt of our natural furniture. And what do we know but that Plato, after other well-instituted republics, ordered that the men and women, old and young, should expose themselves naked to the view of one another, in his gymnastic exercises, upon that very account? The Indian women who see the men in their natural state, have at least cooled the sense of seeing. And let the women of the kingdom of Pegu say what they will, who below the waist have nothing to cover them but a cloth slit before, and so strait, that what decency and modesty soever they pretend by it, at every step all is to be seen, that it is an invention to allure the men to them, and to divert them from boys, to whom that nation is generally inclined; yet, peradventure they lose more by it than they get, and one may venture to say, that an entire appetite is more sharp than one already half-glutted by the eyes. Livia was wont to say, that to a virtuous woman a naked man was but a statue. The Lacedaemonian women, more virgins when wives than our daughters are, saw every day the young men of their city stripped naked in their exercises, themselves little heeding to cover their thighs in walking, believing themselves, says Plato, sufficiently covered by their virtue without any other robe. But those, of whom St Augustin speaks, have given nudity a wonderful power of temptation, who have made it a doubt, whether women at the day of judgment shall rise again in their own sex, and not rather in ours, for fear of tempting us again in that holy state. In brief, we allure and flesh them by all sorts of ways: we incessantly heat and stir up their imagination, and then we find fault. Let us confess the truth; there is scarce one of us who does not more apprehend the shame that accrues to him by the vices of his wife than by his own, and that is not more solicitous (a wonderful charity) of the conscience of his virtuous wife than of his own; who had not rather commit theft and sacrilege, and that his wife was a murderess and a heretic, than that she should not be more chaste than her husband: an unjust estimate of vices. Both we and they are capable of a thousand corruptions more prejudicial and unnatural than lust: but we weigh vices, not according to nature, but according to our interest; by which means they take so many unequal forms.

The austerity of our decrees renders the application of women to this vice more violent and vicious than its own condition needs, and engages it in consequences worse than their cause: they will readily offer to go to the law courts to seek for gain, and to the wars to get reputation, rather than in the midst of ease and delights, to have to keep so difficult a guard. Do not they very well see that there is neither merchant nor soldier who will not leave his business to run after this sport, or the porter or cobbler, toiled and tired out as they are with labour and hunger?

'Num tu, qux tenuit dives Achaemenes,
Aut pinguis Phrygiae Mygdonias opes,
Permutare velis crine Licymnim?
Plenas aut Arabum domos,
Dum fragrantia detorquet ad oscula
Cervicem, aut facili sxvitia negat,
Quae poscente magis gaudeat eripi,
Interdum rapere occupet?'

['Wouldst thou not exchange all that the wealthy Arhaemenes had, or the Mygdonian riches of fertile Phrygia, for one ringlet of Licymnia's hair? or the treasures of the Arabians, when she turns her head to you for fragrant kisses, or with easily assuaged anger denies them, which she would rather by far you took by force, and sometimes herself snatches one!' —Horace, Od., ii. 12, 21.]

I do not know whether the exploits of Alexander and Caesar really surpass the resolution of a beautiful young woman, bred up after our fashion, in the light and commerce of the world, assailed by so many contrary examples, and yet keeping herself entire in the midst of a thousand continual and powerful solicitations. There is no doing more difficult than that not doing, nor more active:

I hold it more easy to carry a suit of armour all the days of one's life than a maidenhead; and the vow of virginity of all others is the most noble, as being the hardest to keep:

'Diaboli virtus in lumbis est,'

says St Jerome. We have, doubtless, resigned to the ladies the most difficult and most vigorous of all human endeavours, and let us resign to them the glory too. This ought to encourage them to be obstinate in it; 'tis a brave thing for them to defy us, and to spurn under foot that vain pre-eminence of valour and virtue that we pretend to have over them; they will find if they do but observe it, that they will not only be much more esteemed for it, but also much more beloved. A gallant man does not give over his pursuit for being refused, provided it be a refusal of chastity, and not of choice; we may swear, threaten, and complain to much purpose; we therein do but lie, for we love them all the better: there is no allurement like modesty, if it be not rude and crabbed. 'Tis stupidity and meanness to be obstinate against hatred and disdain; but against a virtuous and constant resolution, mixed with goodwill, 'tis the exercise of a noble and generous soul. They may acknowledge our service to a certain degree, and give us civilly to understand that they disdain us not; for the law that enjoins them to abominate us because we adore them, and to hate us because we love them, is certainly very cruel, if but for the difficulty of it. Why should they not give ear to our offers and requests, so long as they are kept within the bounds of modesty? wherefore should we fancy them to have other thoughts within, and to be worse than they seem? A queen of our time said with spirit, 'that to refuse these courtesies is a testimony of weakness in women and a self-accusation of facility, and that a lady could not boast of her chastity who was never tempted.'

The limits of honour are not cut so short; they may give themselves a little rein, and relax a little without being faulty: there lies on the frontier some space free, indifferent, and neuter. He that has beaten and pursued her into her fort is a strange fellow if he be not satisfied with his fortune: the price of the conquest is considered by the difficulty. Would you know what impression your service and merit have made in her heart? Judge of it by her behaviour. Such an one may grant more, who does not grant so much. The obligation of a benefit wholly relates to the good will of those who confer it: the other coincident circumstances are dumb, dead, and casual; it costs her dearer to grant you that little, than it would do her companion to grant all. If in anything rarity give estimation, it ought especially in this: do not consider how little it is that is given, but how few have it to give; the value of money alters according to the coinage and stamp of the place. Whatever the spite and indiscretion of some may make them say in the excess of their discontent, virtue and truth will in time recover all the advantage. I have known some whose reputation has for a great while suffered under slander, who have afterwards been restored to the world's universal approbation by their mere constancy without care or artifice; every one repents, and gives himself the lie for what he has believed and said; and from girls a little suspected they have been afterward advanced to the first rank amongst the ladies of honour. Somebody told Plato that all the world spoke ill of him. 'Let them talk,' said he; 'I will live so as to make them change their note.' Besides the fear of God, and the value of so rare a glory, which ought to make them look to themselves, the corruption of the age we live in compels them to it; and if I were they, there is nothing I would not rather do than intrust my reputation in so dangerous hands. In my time the pleasure of telling (a pleasure little inferior to that of doing) was not permitted but to those who had some faithful and only friend; but now the ordinary discourse and common table-talk is nothing but boasts of favours received and the secret liberality of ladies. In earnest, 'tis too abject, too much meanness of spirit, in men to suffer such ungrateful, indiscreet, and giddy-headed people so to persecute, forage, and rifle those tender and charming favours.

This our immoderate and illegitimate exasperation against this vice springs from the most vain and turbulent disease that afflicts human minds, which is jealousy:

'*Quis vetat apposito lumen de lumine sumi?*
Dent licet assidue, nil tamen inde perit;'

['Who says that one light should not be lighted from another light? Let them give ever so much, as much ever remains to lose.' —Ovid, De Arte Amandi, iii. 93. The measure of the last line is not good; but the words are taken from the epigram in the Catalecta entitled Priapus.]

she, and envy, her sister, seem to me to be the most foolish of the whole troop. As to the last, I can say little about it; 'tis a passion that, though said to be so mighty and powerful, had never to do with me. As to the other, I know it by sight, and that's all. Beasts feel it; the shepherd Cratis, having fallen in love with a she-goat, the he-goat, out of jealousy, came, as he lay asleep, to butt the head of the female, and crushed it. We have raised this fever to a greater excess by the examples of some barbarous nations; the best disciplined have been touched with it, and 'tis reason, but not transported:

> '*Ense maritali nemo confossus adulter*
> *Purpureo Stygias sanguine tinxit aquas.*'

> ['Never did adulterer slain by a husband stain with purple blood the Stygian waters.']

Lucullus, Caesar, Pompey, Antony, Cato, and other brave men were cuckolds, and knew it, without making any bustle about it; there was in those days but one coxcomb, Lepidus, that died for grief that his wife had used him so.

> '*Ah! tum te miserum malique fati,*
> *Quem attractis pedibus, patente porta,*
> *Percurrent raphanique mugilesque:*'

> ['Wretched man! when, taken in the fact, thou wilt be dragged out of doors by the heels, and suffer the punishment of thy adultery.' —Catullus, xv. 17.]

and the god of our poet, when he surprised one of his companions with his wife, satisfied himself by putting them to shame only,

> '*Atque aliquis de dis non tristibus optat*
> *Sic fieri turpis:*'

> ['And one of the merry gods wishes that he should himself like to be so disgraced.' —Ovid, Metam., iv. 187.]

and nevertheless took anger at the lukewarm embraces she gave him;

complaining that upon that account she was grown jealous of his affection:

> '*Quid causas petis ex alto? fiducia cessit*
> *Quo tibi, diva, mei?*'
>
> ['Dost thou seek causes from above? Why, goddess, has your confidence in me ceased?' —Virgil, Aeneid, viii. 395.]

nay, she entreats arms for a bastard of hers,

> '*Arena rogo genitrix nato.*'
>
> ['I, a mother, ask armour for a son.' —Idem, ibid., 383.]

which are freely granted; and Vulcan speaks honourably of Aeneas,

> '*Arma acri facienda viro,*'
>
> ['Arms are to be made for a valiant hero.' —Aeneid, viii. 441.]

with, in truth, a more than human humanity. And I am willing to leave this excess of kindness to the gods:

> '*Nec divis homines componier aequum est.*'
>
> ['Nor is it fit to compare men with gods.' —Catullus, lxviii. 141.]

As to the confusion of children, besides that the gravest legislators ordain and affect it in their republics, it touches not the women, where this passion is, I know not how, much better seated:

> '*Saepe etiam Juno, maxima coelicolam,*
> *Conjugis in culpa flagravit quotidiana.*'
>
> ['Often was Juno, greatest of the heaven-dwellers, enraged by her husband's daily infidelities.' —Idem, ibid.]

When jealousy seizes these poor souls, weak and incapable of resistance, 'tis pity to see how miserably it torments and tyrannizes over them; it insinuates itself into them under the title of friendship, but after it has once possessed them, the same causes that served for a foundation of good-will serve them for a foundation of mortal hatred. 'Tis, of all the diseases of the mind, that which the most things serve for aliment and the fewest for remedy: the virtue, health, merit, reputation of the husband are incendiaries of their fury and ill-will:

> '*Nullae sunt inimicitiae, nisi amoris, acerbae.*'

> ['No enmities are bitter, save that of love.' (Or:) 'No hate is implacable except the hatred of love' —Propertius, ii. 8, 3.]

This fever defaces and corrupts all they have of beautiful and good besides; and there is no action of a jealous woman, let her be how chaste and how good a housewife soever, that does not relish of anger and wrangling; 'tis a furious agitation, that rebounds them to an extremity quite contrary to its cause. This held good with one Octavius at Rome. Having lain with Pontia Posthumia, he augmented love with fruition, and solicited with all importunity to marry her: unable to persuade her, this excessive affection precipitated him to the effects of the most cruel and mortal hatred: he killed her. In like manner, the ordinary symptoms of this other amorous disease are intestine hatreds, private conspiracies, and cabals:

> '*Notumque furens quid faemina possit,*'

> ['And it is known what an angry woman is capable of doing.' — Aeneid, v. 21.]

and a rage which so much the more frets itself, as it is compelled to excuse itself by a pretence of good-will.

Now, the duty of chastity is of a vast extent; is it the will that we would have them restrain? This is a very supple and active thing; a thing very nimble, to be stayed. How? if dreams sometimes engage them so far that they cannot deny them: it is not in them, nor, peradventure, in chastity itself, seeing that is a female, to defend itself from lust and desire. If we are only to trust to their will, what a case are we in, then? Do but imagine what crowding there would be amongst men in pursuance of the privilege to run full speed, without tongue or eyes, into every woman's arms who would accept them. The Scythian women put out the eyes of all their slaves and prisoners of war, that they might have their pleasure of them, and they never the wiser. O, the furious advantage of opportunity! Should any one ask me, what was the first thing to be considered in love matters, I should answer that it was how to take a fitting time; and so the second; and so the third—'tis a point that can do everything. I have sometimes wanted fortune, but I have also sometimes been wanting to myself in matters of attempt. God help him, who yet makes light of this! There is greater temerity required in this age of ours, which our young men excuse under the name of heat; but should women examine it more strictly, they would find that it rather proceeds from contempt. I was always superstitiously afraid of giving offence, and have ever had a great respect for her I loved: besides, he who in this traffic takes away the reverence, defaces at the same time the lustre. I would in this affair have a man a little play the child, the timorous, and the servant. If not this, I have in other bashfulness whereof altogether in things some air of the foolish Plutarch makes mention; and the course of my life has been divers ways hurt and blemished with it; a quality very ill suiting my universal form: and, indeed, what are we but sedition and discrepancy? I am as much out of countenance to be denied as I am to deny; and it so much troubles me to be troublesome to others that on occasion when duty compels me to try the good-will of any one in a thing that is doubtful and that will be chargeable to him, I do it very faintly, and very much against my will: but if it be for my own particular (whatever Homer truly says, that modesty is a foolish virtue in an indigent person), I commonly commit it to a third person to blush for me, and deny those who employ me with the same difficulty: so that it has sometimes befallen me to have had a mind to deny, when I had not the power to do it.

'Tis folly, then, to attempt to bridle in women a desire that is so powerful in them, and so natural to them. And when I hear them brag of having so maidenly and so temperate a will, I laugh at them: they retire too far back. If it be an old toothless trot, or a young dry consumptive thing, though it be not altogether to be believed, at least they say it with more similitude of truth. But they who still move and breathe, talk at that ridiculous rate to their own prejudice, by reason that inconsiderate excuses are a kind of self-accusation; like a gentleman, a neighbour of mine, suspected to be insufficient:

'*Languidior tenera cui pendens sicula beta,*
Numquam se mediam sustulit ad tunicam,'

[Catullus, lxvii. 2, i.—The sense is in the context.]

who three or four days after he was married, to justify himself, went about boldly swearing that he had ridden twenty stages the night before: an oath that was afterwards made use of to convict him of his ignorance in that affair, and to divorce him from his wife. Besides, it signifies nothing, for there is neither continency nor virtue where there are no opposing desires. It is true, they may say, but we will not yield; saints themselves speak after that manner. I mean those who boast in good gravity of their coldness and insensibility, and who expect to be believed with a serious countenance; for when 'tis spoken with an affected look, when their eyes give the lie to their tongue, and when they talk in the cant of their profession, which always goes against the hair, 'tis good sport. I am a great servant of liberty and plainness; but there is no remedy; if it be not wholly simple or childish, 'tis silly, and unbecoming ladies in this commerce, and presently runs into impudence. Their disguises and figures only serve to cosen fools; lying is there in its seat of honour; 'tis a by-way, that by a back-door leads us to truth. If we cannot curb their imagination, what would we have from them. Effects? There are enough of them that evade all foreign communication, by which chastity may be corrupted:

'*Illud saepe facit, quod sine teste facit;*'

['He often does that which he does without a witness.' — Martial, vii. 62, 6.]

and those which we fear the least are, peradventure, most to be feared; their sins that make the least noise are the worst:

> '*Offendor maecha simpliciore minus.*'
>
> ['I am less offended with a more professed strumpet.' —Idem, vi. 7,6.]

There are ways by which they may lose their virginity without prostitution, and, which is more, without their knowledge:

> '*Obsterix, virginis cujusdam integritatem manu velut explorans, sive malevolentia, sive inscitia, sive casu, dum inspicit, perdidit.*'
>
> ['By malevolence, or unskilfulness, or accident, the midwife, seeking with the hand to test some maiden's virginity, has sometimes destroyed it.' —St Augustine, De Civit. Dei, i. 18.]

Such a one, by seeking her maidenhead, has lost it; another by playing with it has destroyed it. We cannot precisely circumscribe the actions, we interdict them; they must guess at our meaning under general and doubtful terms; the very idea we invent for their chastity is ridiculous: for, amongst the greatest patterns that I have is Fatua, the wife of Faunus: who never, after her marriage, suffered herself to be seen by any man whatever; and the wife of Hiero, who never perceived her husband's stinking breath, imagining that it was common to all men. They must become insensible and invisible to satisfy us.

Now let us confess that the knot of this judgment of duty principally lies in the will; there have been husbands who have suffered cuckoldom, not only without reproach or taking offence at their wives, but with singular obligation to them and great commendation of their virtue. Such a woman has been, who prized her honour above her life, and yet has prostituted it to the furious lust of a mortal enemy, to save her husband's life, and who, in so doing, did that for him she would not have done for herself! This is not the place wherein we are to multiply these examples; they are too high and rich to be set off with so poor a foil as I can give them here; let us reserve them for a nobler place; but for examples of ordinary lustre, do we not every day see women amongst us who surrender themselves for their husbands sole benefit, and by their express order and mediation? and, of old,

Phaulius the Argian, who offered his to King Philip out of ambition; as Galba did it out of civility, who, having entertained Maecenas at supper, and observing that his wife and he began to cast glances at one another and to make eyes and signs, let himself sink down upon his cushion, like one in a profound sleep, to give opportunity to their desires: which he handsomely confessed, for thereupon a servant having made bold to lay hands on the plate upon the table, he frankly cried, 'What, you rogue? do you not see that I only sleep for Maecenas?' Such there may be, whose manners may be lewd enough, whose will may be more reformed than another, who outwardly carries herself after a more regular manner. As we see some who complain of having vowed chastity before they knew what they did; and I have also known others really, complain of having been given up to debauchery before they were of the years of discretion. The vice of the parents or the impulse of nature, which is a rough counsellor, may be the cause.

In the East Indies, though chastity is of singular reputation, yet custom permitted a married woman to prostitute herself to any one who presented her with an elephant, and that with glory, to have been valued at so high a rate. Phaedo the philosopher, a man of birth, after the taking of his country Elis, made it his trade to prostitute the beauty of his youth, so long as it lasted, to any one that would, for money thereby to gain his living: and Solon was the first in Greece, 'tis said, who by his laws gave liberty to women, at the expense of their chastity, to provide for the necessities of life; a custom that Herodotus says had been received in many governments before his time. And besides, what fruit is there of this painful solicitude? For what justice soever there is in this passion, we are yet to consider whether it turns to account or no: does any one think to curb them, with all his industry?

> '*Pone seram; cohibe: sed quis custodiet ipsos*
> *Custodes? cauta est, et ab illis incipit uxor.*'

> ['Put on a lock; shut them up under a guard; but who shall guard the guard? she knows what she is about, and begins with them.' —Juvenal, vi. 346.]

What commodity will not serve their turn, in so knowing an age?

Curiosity is vicious throughout; but 'tis pernicious here. 'Tis folly to examine into a disease for which there is no physic that does not inflame and make it worse; of which the shame grows still greater and more public by jealousy, and of which the revenge more wounds our children than it heals us. You wither and die in the search of so obscure a proof. How miserably have they of my time arrived at that knowledge who have been so unhappy as to have found it out? If the informer does not at the same time apply a remedy and bring relief, 'tis an injurious information, and that better deserves a stab than the lie. We no less laugh at him who takes pains to prevent it, than at him who is a cuckold and knows it not. The character of cuckold is indelible: who once has it carries it to his grave; the punishment proclaims it more than the fault. It is to much purpose to drag out of obscurity and doubt our private misfortunes, thence to expose them on tragic scaffolds; and misfortunes that only hurt us by being known; for we say a good wife or a happy marriage, not that they are really so, but because no one says to the contrary. Men should be so discreet as to evade this tormenting and unprofitable knowledge: and the Romans had a custom, when returning from any expedition, to send home before to acquaint their wives with their coming, that they might not surprise them; and to this purpose it is that a certain nation has introduced a custom, that the priest shall on the wedding-day open the way to the bride, to free the husband from the doubt and curiosity of examining in the first assault, whether she comes a virgin to his bed, or has been at the trade before.

But the world will be talking. I know, a hundred honest men cuckolds, honestly and not unbeseemingly; a worthy man is pitied, not disesteemed for it. Order it so that your virtue may conquer your misfortune; that good men may curse the occasion, and that he who wrongs you may tremble but to think on't. And, moreover, who escapes being talked of at the same rate, from the least even to the greatest?

> '*Tot qui legionibus imperitivit*
> *Et melior quam to multis fuit, improbe, rebus.*'
>
> ['Many who have commanded legions, many a man much better far than you, you rascal.' —Lucretius, iii. 1039, 1041.]

Seest thou how many honest men are reproached with this in thy presence; believe that thou art no more spared elsewhere. But, the very ladies will be laughing too; and what are they so apt to laugh at in this virtuous age of ours as at a peaceable and well-composed marriage? Each amongst you has made somebody cuckold; and nature runs much in parallel, in compensation, and turn for turn. The frequency of this accident ought long since to have made it more easy; 'tis now passed into custom.

Miserable passion! which has this also, that it is incommunicable,

> '*Fors etiam nostris invidit questibus aures;*'
>
> ['Fortune also refuses ear to our complaints.' —Catullus, lxvii.]

for to what friend dare you intrust your griefs, who, if he does not laugh at them, will not make use of the occasion to get a share of the quarry? The sharps, as well as the sweets of marriage, are kept secret by the wise; and amongst its other troublesome conditions this to a prating fellow, as I am, is one of the chief, that custom has rendered it indecent and prejudicial to communicate to any one all that a man knows and all that a man feels. To give women the same counsel against jealousy would be so much time lost; their very being is so made up of suspicion, vanity, and curiosity, that to cure them by any legitimate way is not to be hoped. They often recover of this infirmity by a form of health much more to be feared than the disease itself; for as there are enchantments that cannot take away the evil but by throwing it upon another, they also willingly transfer this ever to their husbands, when they shake it off themselves. And yet I know not, to speak truth, whether a man can suffer worse from them than their jealousy; 'tis the most dangerous of all their conditions, as the head is of all their members. Pittacus used to say,—[Plutarch, On Contentment, c. II.]—that every one had his trouble, and that his was the jealous head of his wife; but for which he should think himself perfectly happy. A mighty inconvenience, sure, which could poison the whole life of so just, so wise, and so valiant a man; what must we other little fellows do? The senate of Marseilles had reason to grant him his request who begged leave to kill himself that he might be delivered from the clamour of his wife; for 'tis a mischief that is never removed but by removing the whole piece; and that has no remedy but flight or patience, though both of them very hard. He was, methinks, an understanding fellow who said, 'twas a happy marriage betwixt a blind wife and a deaf husband.

Let us also consider whether the great and violent severity of obligation we enjoin them does not produce two effects contrary to our design namely, whether it does not render the pursuants more eager to attack, and the women more easy to yield. For as to the first, by raising the value of the place, we raise the value and the desire of the conquest. Might it not be Venus herself, who so cunningly enhanced the price of her merchandise, by making the laws her bawds; knowing how insipid a delight it would be that was not heightened by fancy and hardness to achieve? In short, 'tis all swine's flesh, varied by sauces, as Flaminius' host said. Cupid is a roguish god, who makes it his sport to contend with devotion and justice: 'tis his glory that his power mates all powers, and that all other rules give place to his:

> '*Materiam culpae prosequiturque suae.*'
>
> ['And seeks out a matter (motive) for his crimes.' —Ovid, Trist., iv. I. 34.]

As to the second point; should we not be less cuckolds, if we less feared to be so? according to the humour of women whom interdiction incites, and who are more eager, being forbidden:

> '*Ubi velis, nolunt; ubi nolis, volunt ultro;*
> *Concessa pudet ire via.*'
>
> ['Where thou wilt, they won't; where thou wilt not, they spontaneously agree; they are ashamed to go in the permitted path.' —Terence, Eunuchus, act iv., sc. 8, v 43]

What better interpretation can we make of Messalina's behaviour? She, at first, made her husband a cuckold in private, as is the common use; but, bringing her business about with too much ease, by reason of her husband's stupidity, she soon scorned that way, and presently fell to making open love, to own her lovers, and to favour and entertain them in the sight of all: she would make him know and see how she used him. This animal, not to be roused with all this, and rendering her pleasures dull and flat by his too stupid facility, by which he seemed to authorize and make them lawful; what does she? Being the wife of a living and healthful emperor, and at Rome, the theatre of the world, in the face of the sun, and with solemn ceremony, and to Silius, who had long before enjoyed her, she publicly marries herself one day that her husband was gone out of the city. Does it not seem as if she was going to become chaste by her husband's negligence? or that she sought another husband who might sharpen her appetite by his jealousy, and who by watching should incite her? But the first difficulty she met with was also the last: this beast suddenly roused these sleepy, sluggish sort of men are often the most dangerous: I have found by experience that this extreme toleration, when it comes to dissolve, produces the most severe revenge; for taking fire on a sudden, anger and fury being combined in one, discharge their utmost force at the first onset,

'*Irarumque omnes effundit habenas*:'

['He let loose his whole fury.' —Aeneid, xii. 499.]

he put her to death, and with her a great number of those with whom she had intelligence, and even one of them who could not help it, and whom she had caused to be forced to her bed with scourges.

What Virgil says of Venus and Vulcan, Lucretius had better expressed of a stolen enjoyment betwixt her and Mars:

'*Belli fera moenera Mavors*
Armipotens regit, ingremium qui saepe tuum se
Rejictt, aeterno devinctus vulnere amoris
...

Pascit amore avidos inhians in te, Dea, visus,
Eque tuo pendet resupini spiritus ore
Hunc tu, Diva, tuo recubantem corpore sancto
Circumfusa super, suaveis ex ore loquelas
Funde.'

['Mars, the god of wars, who controls the cruel tasks of war, often reclines on thy bosom, and greedily drinks love at both his eyes, vanquished by the eternal wound of love: and his breath, as he reclines, hangs on thy lips; bending thy head over him as he lies upon thy sacred person, pour forth sweet and persuasive words.' —Lucretius, i. 23.]

When I consider this *rejicit, fiascit, inhians, ynolli, fovet, medullas, labefacta, pendet, percurrit,* and that noble *circumfusa,* mother of the pretty *infusus*; I disdain those little quibbles and verbal allusions that have since sprung up. Those worthy people stood in need of no subtlety to disguise their meaning; their language is downright, and full of natural and continued vigour; they are all epigram; not only the tail, but the head, body, and feet. There is nothing forced, nothing languishing, but everything keeps the same pace:

'*Contextus totes virilis est; non sunt circa flosculos occupati.*'

['The whole contexture is manly; they don't occupy themselves with little flowers of rhetoric.' —Seneca, Ep., 33.]

'Tis not a soft eloquence, and without offence only; 'tis nervous and solid, that does not so much please, as it fills and ravishes the greatest minds. When I see these brave forms of expression, so lively, so profound, I do not say that 'tis well said, but well thought. 'Tis the sprightliness of the imagination that swells and elevates the words:

'*Pectus est quod disertum Tacit.*'

['The heart makes the man eloquent.' —Quintilian, x. 7.]

Our people call language, judgment, and fine words, full conceptions. This painting is not so much carried on by dexterity of hand as by having the object more vividly imprinted in the soul. Gallus speaks simply because he conceives simply: Horace does not content himself with a superficial expression; that would betray him; he sees farther and more clearly into things; his mind breaks into and rummages all the magazine of words and figures wherewith to express himself, and he must have them more than ordinary, because his conception is so. Plutarch says that he sees the Latin tongue by the things: 'tis here the same: the sense illuminates and produces the words, no more words of air, but of flesh and bone; they signify more than they say. Moreover, those who are not well skilled in a language present some image of this; for in Italy I said whatever I had a mind to in common discourse, but in more serious talk, I durst not have trusted myself with an idiom that I could not wind and turn out of its ordinary pace; I would have a power of introducing something of my own.

The handling and utterance of fine wits is that which sets off language; not so much by innovating it, as by putting it to more vigorous and various services, and by straining, bending, and adapting it to them. They do not create words, but they enrich their own, and give them weight and signification by the uses they put them to, and teach them unwonted motions, but withal ingeniously and discreetly. And how little this talent is given to all is manifest by the many French scribblers of this age: they are bold and proud enough not to follow the common road, but want of invention and discretion ruins them; there is nothing seen in their writings but a wretched affectation of a strange new style, with cold and absurd disguises, which, instead of elevating, depress the matter: provided they can but trick themselves out with new words, they care not what they signify; and to bring in a new word by the head and shoulders, they leave the old one, very often more sinewy and significant than the other.

There is stuff enough in our language, but there is a defect in cutting out: for there is nothing that might not be made out of our terms of hunting and war, which is a fruitful soil to borrow from; and forms of speaking, like herbs, improve and grow stronger by being transplanted. I find it sufficiently abundant, but not sufficiently pliable and vigorous; it commonly quails under a powerful conception; if you would maintain the dignity of your style, you will often perceive it to flag and languish under you, and there Latin steps in to its relief, as Greek does to others. Of some of these words I have just picked out we do not so easily discern the energy, by reason that the frequent use of them has in some sort abased their beauty, and rendered it common; as in our ordinary language there are many excellent phrases and metaphors to be met with, of which the beauty is withered by age, and the colour is sullied by too common handling; but that nothing lessens the relish to an understanding man, nor does it derogate from the glory of those ancient authors who, 'tis likely, first brought those words into that lustre.

The sciences treat of things too refinedly, after an artificial, very different from the common and natural, way. My page makes love, and understands it; but read to him Leo Hebraeus—[Leo the Jew, Ficinus, Cardinal Bembo, and Mario Equicola all wrote Treatises on Love.]—and Ficinus, where they speak of love, its thoughts and actions, he understands it not. I do not find in Aristotle most of my ordinary motions; they are there covered and disguised in another robe for the use of the schools. Good speed them! were I of the trade, I would as much naturalize art as they artificialize nature. Let us let Bembo and Equicola alone.

When I write, I can very well spare both the company and the remembrance of books, lest they should interrupt my progress; and also, in truth, the best authors too much humble and discourage me: I am very much of the painter's mind, who, having represented cocks most wretchedly ill, charged all his boys not to suffer any natural cock to come into his shop; and had rather need to give myself a little lustre, of the invention of Antigenides the musician, who, when he was asked to sing or play, took care beforehand that the auditory should, either before or after, be satiated with some other ill musicians. But I can hardly be without Plutarch; he is so universal and so full, that upon all occasions, and what extravagant subject soever you take in hand, he will still be at your elbow, and hold out to you a liberal and not to be exhausted hand of riches and embellishments. It vexes me that he is so exposed to be the spoil of those who are conversant with him: I can scarce cast an eye upon him but I purloin either a leg or a wing.

And also for this design of mine 'tis convenient for me for me to write at home, in a wild country, where I have nobody to assist or relieve me; where I hardly see a man who understands the Latin of his Paternoster, and of French a little less. I might have made it better elsewhere, but then the work would have been less my own; and its principal end and perfection is to be exactly mine. I readily correct an accidental error, of which I am full, as I run carelessly on; but for my ordinary and constant imperfections, it were a kind of treason to put them out. When another tells me, or that I say to myself, 'Thou art too thick of figures: this is a word of rough Gascon: that is a dangerous phrase (I do not reject any of those that are used in the common streets of France; they who would fight custom with grammar are triflers): this is an ignorant discourse: this is a paradoxical discourse: that is going too far: thou makest thyself too merry at times: men will think thou sayest a thing in good earnest which thou only speakest in jest.'—'Yes, I know, but I correct the faults of inadvertence, not those of custom. Do I not talk at the same rate throughout? Do I not represent myself to the life? 'Tis enough that I have done what I designed; all the world knows me in my book, and my book in me.'

Now I have an apish, imitative quality: when I used to write verses (and I never made any but Latin), they evidently discovered the poet I had last read, and some of my first essays have a little exotic taste: I speak something another kind of language at Paris than I do at Montaigne. Whoever I steadfastly look upon easily leaves some impression of his upon me; whatever I consider I usurp, whether a foolish countenance, a disagreeable look, or a ridiculous way of speaking; and vices most of all, because they seize and stick to me, and will not leave hold without shaking. I swear more by imitation than by complexion: a murderous imitation, like that of the apes so terrible both in stature and strength, that Alexander met with in a certain country of the Indies, and which he would have had much ado any other way to have subdued; but they afforded him the means by that inclination of theirs to imitate whatever they saw done; for by that the hunters were taught to put on shoes in their sight, and to tie them fast with many knots, and to muffle up their heads in caps all composed of running nooses, and to seem to anoint their eyes with glue; so did those poor beasts employ their imitation to their own ruin they glued up their own eyes, haltered and bound themselves. The other faculty of playing the mimic, and ingeniously acting the words and gestures of another, purposely to make people merry and to raise their admiration, is no more in me than in a stock. When I swear my own oath, 'tis only, by God! of all oaths the most direct. They say that Socrates swore by the dog; Zeno had for his oath the same interjection at this time in use amongst the Italians, Cappari! Pythagoras swore By water and air. I am so apt, without thinking of it, to receive these superficial impressions, that if I have Majesty or Highness in my mouth three days together, they come out instead of Excellency and Lordship eight days after; and what I say to-day in sport and fooling I shall say the same to-morrow seriously. Wherefore, in writing, I more unwillingly undertake beaten arguments, lest I should handle them at another's expense. Every subject is equally fertile to me: a fly will serve the purpose, and 'tis well if this I have in hand has not been undertaken at the recommendation of as flighty a will. I may begin, with that which pleases me best, for the subjects are all linked to one another.

But my soul displeases me, in that it ordinarily produces its deepest and most airy conceits and which please me best, when I least expect or study for them, and which suddenly vanish, having at the instant, nothing to apply them to; on horseback, at table, and in bed: but most on horseback, where I am most given to think. My speaking is a little nicely jealous of silence and attention: if I am talking my best, whoever interrupts me, stops me. In travelling, the necessity of the way will often put a stop to discourse; besides which I, for the most part, travel without company fit for regular discourses, by which means I have all the leisure I would to entertain myself. It falls out as it does in my dreams; whilst dreaming I recommend them to my memory (for I am apt to dream that I dream), but, the next morning, I may represent to myself of what complexion they were, whether gay, or sad, or strange, but what they were, as to the rest, the more I endeavour to retrieve them, the deeper I plunge them in oblivion. So of thoughts that come accidentally into my head, I have no more but a vain image remaining in my memory; only enough to make me torment myself in their quest to no purpose.

Well, then, laying books aside, and more simply and materially speaking, I find, after all, that Love is nothing else but the thirst of enjoying the object desired, or Venus any other thing than the pleasure of discharging one's vessels, just as the pleasure nature gives in discharging other parts, that either by immoderation or indiscretion become vicious. According to Socrates, love is the appetite of generation by the mediation of beauty. And when I consider the ridiculous titillation of this pleasure, the absurd, crack-brained, wild motions with which it inspires Zeno and Cratippus, the indiscreet rage, the countenance inflamed with fury and cruelty in the sweetest effects of love, and then that austere air, so grave, severe, ecstatic, in so wanton an action; that our delights and our excrements are promiscuously shuffled together; and that the supreme pleasure brings along with it, as in pain, fainting and complaining; I believe it to be true, as Plato says, that the gods made man for their sport:

> '*Quaenam ista jocandi*
> *Saevitia!*'
>
> ['With a sportive cruelty' (Or:) 'What an unkindness there is in jesting!' —Claudian in Eutrop. i. 24.]

and that it was in mockery that nature has ordered the most agitative of actions and the most common, to make us equal, and to put fools and wise men, beasts and us, on a level. Even the most contemplative and prudent man, when I imagine him in this posture, I hold him an impudent fellow to pretend to be prudent and contemplative; they are the peacocks' feet that abate his pride:

> '*Ridentem dicere verum*
> *Quid vetat?*'

['What prevents us from speaking truth with a smile?' —Horace, Sat., i. I, 24.]

They who banish serious imaginations from their sports, do, says one, like him who dares not adore the statue of a saint, if not covered with a veil. We eat and drink, indeed, as beasts do; but these are not actions that obstruct the functions of the soul, in these we maintain our advantage over them; this other action subjects all other thought, and by its imperious authority makes an ass of all Plato's divinity and philosophy; and yet there is no complaint of it. In everything else a man may keep some decorum, all other operations submit to the rules of decency; this cannot so much as in imagination appear other than vicious or ridiculous: find out, if you can, therein any serious and discreet procedure. Alexander said, that he chiefly knew himself to be mortal by this act and sleeping; sleep suffocates and suppresses the faculties of the soul; the familiarity with women likewise dissipates and exhausts them: doubtless 'tis a mark, not only of our original corruption, but also of our vanity and deformity.

On the one side, nature pushes us on to it, having fixed the most noble, useful, and pleasant of all her functions to this desire: and, on the other side, leaves us to accuse and avoid it, as insolent and indecent, to blush at it, and to recommend abstinence. Are we not brutes to call that work brutish which begets us? People of so many differing religions have concurred in several proprieties, as sacrifices, lamps, burning incense, fasts, and offerings; and amongst others, in the condemning this act: all opinions tend that way, besides the widespread custom of circumcision, which may be regarded as a punishment. We have, peradventure, reason to blame ourselves for being guilty of so foolish a production as man, and to call the act, and the parts that are employed in the act, shameful (mine, truly, are now shameful and pitiful). The Essenians, of whom Pliny speaks, kept up their country for several ages without either nurse or baby-clouts, by the arrival of strangers who, following this pretty humour, came continually to them: a whole nation being resolute, rather to hazard a total extermination, than to engage themselves in female embraces, and rather to lose the succession of men, than to beget one. 'Tis said, that Zeno never had to do with a woman but once in his life, and then out of civility, that he might not seem too obstinately to disdain the sex.

> [Diogenes Laertius, vii. 13.—What is there said, however, is that Zeno seldom had commerce with boys, lest he should be deemed a very misogynist.]

Every one avoids seeing a man born, every one runs to see him die; to destroy him a spacious field is sought out in the face of the sun, but, to make him, we creep into as dark and private a corner as we can: 'tis a man's duty to withdraw himself bashfully from the light to create; but 'tis glory and the fountain of many virtues to know how to destroy what we have made: the one is injury, the other favour: for Aristotle says that to do any one a kindness, in a certain phrase of his country, is to kill him. The Athenians, to couple the disgrace of these two actions, having to purge the Isle of Delos, and to justify themselves to Apollo, interdicted at once all births and burials in the precincts thereof:

> '*Nostri nosmet paenitet.*'

> ['We are ashamed of ourselves.' —Terence, Phoymio, i. 3, 20.]

There are some nations that will not be seen to eat. I know a lady, and of the best quality, who has the same opinion, that chewing disfigures the face, and takes away much from the ladies' grace and beauty; and therefore unwillingly appears at a public table with an appetite; and I know a man also, who cannot endure to see another eat, nor himself to be seen eating, and who is more shy of company when putting in than when putting out. In the Turkish empire, there are a great number of men who, to excel others, never suffer themselves to be seen when they make their repast: who never have any more than one a week; who cut and mangle their faces and limbs; who never speak to any one: fanatic people who think to honour their nature by disnaturing themselves; who value themselves upon their contempt of themselves, and purport to grow better by being worse. What monstrous animal is this, that is a horror to himself, to whom his delights are grievous, and who weds himself to misfortune? There are people who conceal their life:

> '*Exilioque domos et dulcia limina mutant,*'
>
> ['And change for exile their homes and pleasant abodes.' —Virgil, Georg., ii. 511.]

and withdraw them from the sight of other men; who avoid health and cheerfulness, as dangerous and prejudicial qualities. Not only many sects, but many peoples, curse their birth, and bless their death; and there is a place where the sun is abominated and darkness adored. We are only ingenious in using ourselves ill: 'tis the real quarry our intellects fly at; and intellect, when misapplied, is a dangerous tool!

> '*O miseri! quorum gaudia crimen habent!*'
>
> ['O wretched men, whose pleasures are a crime!' —Pseudo Gallus, i. 180.]

Alas, poor man! thou hast enough inconveniences that are inevitable, without increasing them by thine own invention; and art miserable enough by nature, without being so by art; thou hast real and essential deformities enough, without forging those that are imaginary. Dost thou think thou art too much at ease unless half thy ease is uneasy? dost thou find that thou hast not performed all the necessary offices that nature has enjoined thee, and that she is idle in thee, if thou dost not oblige thyself to other and new offices? Thou dost not stick to infringe her universal and undoubted laws; but stickest to thy own special and fantastic rules, and by how much more particular, uncertain, and contradictory they are, by so much thou employest thy whole endeavour in them: the laws of thy parish occupy and bind thee: those of God and the world concern thee not. Run but a little over the examples of this kind; thy life is full of them.

Whilst the verses of these two poets, treat so reservedly and discreetly of wantonness as they do, methinks they discover it much more openly. Ladies cover their necks with network, priests cover several sacred things, and painters shadow their pictures to give them greater lustre: and 'tis said that the sun and wind strike more violently by reflection than in a direct line. The Egyptian wisely answered him who asked him what he had under his cloak, 'It is hid under my cloak,' said he, 'that thou mayest not know what it is:' but there are certain other things that people hide only to show them. Hear that one, who speaks plainer,

> '*Et nudum pressi corpus ad usque meum*:'
>
> ['And pressed her naked body to mine' (Or:) 'My body I applied even to her naked side' —Ovid, Amor., i. 5, 24.]

methinks that he emasculates me. Let Martial turn up Venus as high as he may, he cannot shew her so naked: he who says all that is to be said gluts and disgusts us. He who is afraid to express himself, draws us on to guess at more than is meant; there is treachery in this sort of modesty, and specially when they half open, as these do, so fair a path to imagination. Both the action and description should relish of theft.

The more respectful, more timorous, more coy, and secret love of the Spaniards and Italians pleases me. I know not who of old wished his throat as long as that of a crane, that he might the longer taste what he swallowed; it had been better wished as to this quick and precipitous pleasure, especially in such natures as mine that have the fault of being too prompt. To stay its flight and delay it with preambles: all things—a glance, a bow, a word, a sign, stand for favour and recompense betwixt them. Were it not an excellent piece of thrift in him who could dine on the steam of the roast? 'Tis a passion that mixes with very little solid essence, far more vanity and feverish raving; and we should serve and pay it accordingly. Let us teach the ladies to set a better value and esteem upon themselves, to amuse and fool us: we give the last charge at the first onset; the French impetuosity will still show itself; by spinning out their favours, and exposing them in small parcels, even miserable old age itself will find some little share of reward, according to its worth and merit. He who has no fruition but in fruition, who wins nothing unless he sweeps the stakes, who takes no pleasure in the chase but in the quarry, ought not to introduce himself in our school: the more steps and degrees there are, so much higher and more honourable is the uppermost seat: we should take a pleasure in being conducted to it, as in magnificent palaces, by various porticoes and passages, long and pleasant galleries, and many windings. This disposition of things would turn to our advantage; we should there longer stay and longer love; without hope and without desire we proceed not worth a pin. Our conquest and entire possession is what they ought infinitely to dread: when they wholly surrender themselves up to the mercy of our fidelity and constancy they run a mighty hazard; they are virtues very rare and hard to be found; the ladies are no sooner ours, than we are no more theirs:

> '*Postquam cupidae mentis satiata libido est,*
> *Verba nihil metuere, nihil perjuria curant;*'

> ['When our desires are once satisfied, we care little for oaths and promises.' —Catullus, lxiv. 147.]

And Thrasonides, a young man of Greece, was so in love with his passion that, having, gained a mistress's consent, he refused to enjoy her, that he might not by fruition quench and stupefy the unquiet ardour of which he was so proud, and with which he so fed himself. Dearness is a good sauce to meat: do but observe how much the manner of salutation, particular to our nation, has, by its facilities, made kisses, which Socrates says are so powerful and dangerous for the stealing of hearts, of no esteem. It is a displeasing custom and injurious for the ladies, that they must be obliged to lend their lips to every fellow who has three footmen at his heels, however ill-favoured he may be in himself:

> '*Cujus livida naribus caninis*
> *Dependet glacies, rigetque barba ...*
> *Centum occurrere malo culilingis:*'

Martial, vii. 94.

and we ourselves barely gain by it; for as the world is divided, for three beautiful women we must kiss fifty ugly ones; and to a tender stomach, like those of my age, an ill kiss overpays a good one.

In Italy they passionately court even their common women who sell themselves for money, and justify the doing so by saying, 'that there are degrees of fruition, and that by such service they would procure for themselves that which is most entire; the women sell nothing but their bodies; the will is too free and too much of its own to be exposed to sale.' So that these say, 'tis the will they undertake and they have reason. 'Tis indeed the will that we are to serve and gain by wooing. I abhor to imagine mine, a body without affection: and this madness is, methinks, cousin-german to that of the boy who would needs pollute the beautiful statue of Venus made by Praxiteles; or that of the furious Egyptian, who violated the dead carcase of a woman he was embalming: which was the occasion of the law then made in Egypt, that the corpses of beautiful young women, of those of good quality, should be kept three days before they should be delivered to those whose office it was to take care for the interment. Periander did more wonderfully, who extended his conjugal affection (more regular and legitimate) to the enjoyment of his wife Melissa after she was dead. Does it not seem a lunatic humour in the Moon, seeing she could no otherwise enjoy her darling Endymion, to lay-him for several months asleep, and to please herself with the fruition of a boy who stirred not but in his sleep? I likewise say that we love a body without a soul or sentiment when we love a body without its consent and desire. All enjoyments are not alike: there are some that are hectic and languishing: a thousand other causes besides good-will may procure us this favour from the ladies; this is not a sufficient testimony of affection: treachery may lurk there, as well as elsewhere: they sometimes go to't by halves:

'*Tanquam thura merumque parent*
Absentem marmoreamve putes:'

['As if they are preparing frankincense and wine … you might think her absent or marble.' —Martial, xi. 103, 12, and 59, 8.]

I know some who had rather lend that than their coach, and who only impart themselves that way. You are to examine whether your company pleases them upon any other account, or, as some strong-chined groom, for that only; in what degree of favour and esteem you are with them:

> '*Tibi si datur uni,*
> *Quem lapide illa diem candidiore notat.*'
>
> ['Wherefore that is enough, if that day alone is given us which she marks with a whiter stone.' —Catullus, lxviii. 147.]

What if they eat your bread with the sauce of a more pleasing imagination.

> '*Te tenet, absentes alios suspirat amores.*'
>
> ['She has you in her arms; her thoughts are with other absent lovers.' —Tibullus, i. 6, 35.]

What? have we not seen one in these days of ours who made use of this act for the purpose of a most horrid revenge, by that means to kill and poison, as he did, a worthy lady?

Such as know Italy will not think it strange if, for this subject, I seek not elsewhere for examples; for that nation may be called the regent of the world in this. They have more generally handsome and fewer ugly women than we; but for rare and excellent beauties we have as many as they. I think the same of their intellects: of those of the common sort, they have evidently far more: brutishness is immeasurably rarer there; but in individual characters of the highest form, we are nothing indebted to them. If I should carry on the comparison, I might say, as touching valour, that, on the contrary, it is, to what it is with them, common and natural with us; but sometimes we see them possessed of it to such a degree as surpasses the greatest examples we can produce: The marriages of that country are defective in this; their custom commonly imposes so rude and so slavish a law upon the women, that the most distant acquaintance with a stranger is as capital an offence as the most intimate; so that all approaches being rendered necessarily substantial, and seeing that all comes to one account, they have no hard choice to make; and when they have broken down the fence, we may safely presume they get on fire:

> '*Luxuria ipsis vinculis, sicut fera bestia, irritata, deinde emissa.*'

> ['Lust, like a wild beast, being more excited by being bound, breaks from his chains with greater wildness.' —Livy, xxxiv. 4.]

They must give them a little more rein:

> '*Vidi ego nuper equum, contra sua frena tenacem,*
> *Ore reluctanti fulminis ire modo*':

> ['I saw, the other day, a horse struggling against his bit, rush like a thunderbolt.' —Ovid, Amor., iii. 4, 13.]

the desire of company is allayed by giving it a little liberty. We are pretty much in the same case they are extreme in constraint, we in licence. 'Tis a good custom we have in France that our sons are received into the best families, there to be entertained and bred up pages, as in a school of nobility; and 'tis looked upon as a discourtesy and an affront to refuse this to a gentleman. I have taken notice (for, so many families, so many differing forms) that the ladies who have been strictest with their maids have had no better luck than those who allowed them a greater liberty. There should be moderation in these things; one must leave a great deal of their conduct to their own discretion; for, when all comes to all, no discipline can curb them throughout. But it is true withal that she who comes off with flying colours from a school of liberty, brings with her whereon to repose more confidence than she who comes away sound from a severe and strict school.

Our fathers dressed up their daughters' looks in bashfulness and fear (their courage and desires being the same); we ours in confidence and assurance; we understand nothing of the matter; we must leave it to the Sarmatian women, who may not lie with a man till with their own hands they have first killed another in battle. For me, who have no other title left me to these things but by the ears, 'tis sufficient if, according to the privilege of my age, they retain me for one of their counsel. I advise them then, and us men too, to abstinence; but if the age we live in will not endure it, at least modesty and discretion. For, as in the story of Aristippus, who, speaking to some young men who blushed to see him go into a scandalous house, said 'the vice is in not coming out, not in going in,' let her who has no care of her conscience have yet some regard to her reputation; and though she be rotten within, let her carry a fair outside at least.

I commend a gradation and delay in bestowing their favours: Plato declares that, in all sorts of love, facility and promptness are forbidden to the defendant. 'Tis a sign of eagerness which they ought to disguise with all the art they have, so rashly, wholly, and hand-over-hand to surrender themselves. In carrying themselves orderly and measuredly in the granting their last favours, they much more allure our desires and hide their own. Let them still fly before us, even those who have most mind to be overtaken: they better conquer us by flying, as the Scythians did. To say the truth, according to the law that nature has imposed upon them, it is not properly for them either to will or desire; their part is to suffer, obey, and consent and for this it is that nature has given them a perpetual capacity, which in us is but at times and uncertain; they are always fit for the encounter, that they may be always ready when we are so 'Pati natee.'—['Born to suffer.' —Seneca, Ep., 95.]—And whereas she has ordered that our appetites shall be manifest by a prominent demonstration, she would have theirs to be hidden and concealed within, and has furnished them with parts improper for ostentation, and simply defensive. Such proceedings as this that follows must be left to the Amazonian licence: Alexander marching his army through Hyrcania, Thalestris, Queen of the Amazons, came with three hundred light horse of her own sex, well mounted, and armed, having left the remainder of a very great army that followed her behind the neighbouring mountains to give him a visit; where she publicly and in plain terms told him that the fame of his valour and victories had brought her thither to see him, and to make him an offer of her forces to assist him in the pursuit of his enterprises; and that, finding him so handsome, young, and vigorous, she, who was also perfect in all those qualities, advised that they might lie together, to the end that from the most valiant woman of the world and the bravest man then living, there might spring some great and wonderful issue for the time to come. Alexander returned her thanks for all the rest; but, to give leisure for the accomplishment of her last demand, he detained her thirteen days in that place, which were spent in royal feasting and jollity, for the welcome of so courageous a princess.

We are, almost throughout, unjust judges of their actions, as they are of ours. I confess the truth when it makes against me, as well as when 'tis on my side. 'Tis an abominable intemperance that pushes them on so often to change, and that will not let them limit their affection to any one person whatever; as is evident in that goddess to whom are attributed so many changes and so many lovers. But 'tis true withal that 'tis contrary to the nature of love if it be, not violent; and contrary to the nature of violence if it be constant. And they who wonder, exclaim, and keep such a clutter to find out the causes of this frailty of theirs, as unnatural and not to be believed, how comes it to pass they do not discern how often they are themselves guilty of the same, without any astonishment or miracle at all? It would, peradventure, be more strange to see the passion fixed; 'tis not a simply corporeal passion. If there be no end to avarice and ambition, there is doubtless no more in desire; it still lives after satiety; and 'tis impossible to prescribe either constant satisfaction or end; it ever goes beyond its possession. And by that means inconstancy, peradventure, is in some sort more pardonable in them than in us: they may plead, as well as we, the inclination to variety and novelty common to us both; and secondly, without us, that they buy a cat in a sack: Joanna, queen of Naples, caused her first husband, Andrews, to be hanged at the bars of her window in a halter of gold and silk woven with her own hand, because in matrimonial performances she neither found his parts nor abilities answer the expectation she had conceived from his stature, beauty, youth, and activity, by which she had been caught and deceived. They may say there is more pains required in doing than in suffering; and so they are on their part always at least provided for necessity, whereas on our part it may fall out otherwise. For this reason it was, that Plato wisely made a law that before marriage, to determine of the fitness of persons, the judges should see the young men who pretended to it stripped stark naked, and the women but to the girdle only. When they come to try us they do not, perhaps, find us worthy of their choice:

> '*Experta latus, madidoque simillima loro*
> *Inguina, nec lassa stare coacta manu,*
> *Deserit imbelles thalamos.*'
>
> ['After using every endeavour to arouse him to action, she quits the barren couch.' —Martial, vii. 58.]

'Tis not enough that a man's will be good; weakness and insufficiency lawfully break a marriage,

> '*Et quaerendum aliunde foret nervosius illud,*
> *Quod posset zonam solvere virgineam:*'
>
> ['And seeks a more vigorous lover to undo her virgin zone.' —Catullus, lxvii. 27.]

why not? and according to her own standard, an amorous intelligence, more licentious and active,

> '*Si blando nequeat superesse labori.*'
>
> ['If his strength be unequal to the pleasant task.' —Virgil, Georg., iii. 127.]

But is it not great impudence to offer our imperfections and imbecilities, where we desire to please and leave a good opinion and esteem of ourselves? For the little that I am able to do now:

> '*Ad unum*
> *Mollis opus.*'
>
> ['Fit but for once.' —Horace, Epod., xii. 15.]

I would not trouble a woman, that I am to reverence and fear:

'Fuge suspicari,
Cujus undenum trepidavit aetas
Claudere lustrum.'

['Fear not him whose eleventh lustrum is closed.' —Horace, Od., ii. 4, 12, limits it to the eighth.]

Nature should satisfy herself in having rendered this age miserable, without rendering it ridiculous too. I hate to see it, for one poor inch of pitiful vigour which comes upon it but thrice a week, to strut and set itself out with as much eagerness as if it could do mighty feats; a true flame of flax; and laugh to see it so boil and bubble and then in a moment so congealed and extinguished. This appetite ought to appertain only to the flower of beautiful youth: trust not to its seconding that indefatigable, full, constant, magnanimous ardour you think in you, for it will certainly leave you in a pretty corner; but rather transfer it to some tender, bashful, and ignorant boy, who yet trembles at the rod, and blushes:

'Indum sanguineo veluti violaverit ostro
Si quis ebur, vel mista rubent ubi lilia multa
Alba rosa.'

['As Indian ivory streaked with crimson, or white lilies mixed with the damask rose.' —Aeneid, xii. 67.]

Who can stay till the morning without dying for shame to behold the disdain of the fair eyes of her who knows so well his fumbling impertinence,

'Et taciti fecere tamen convicia vultus,'

['Though she nothing say, her looks betray her anger.' —Ovid, Amor., i. 7, 21.]

has never had the satisfaction and the glory of having cudgelled them till they were weary, with the vigorous performance of one heroic night. When I have observed any one to be vexed with me, I have not presently accused her levity, but have been in doubt, if I had not reason rather to complain of nature; she has doubtless used me very uncivilly and unkindly:

> '*Si non longa satis, si non bene mentula crassa*
> *Nimirum apient, videntque parvam*
> *Matronae quoque mentulam illibenter*.'

> [The first of these verses is the commencement of an epigram of the Veterum Poetayurra Catalecta, and the two others are from an epigram in the same collection (Ad Matrones). They describe untranslatably Montaigne's charge against nature, indicated in the previous passage.]

and done me a most enormous injury. Every member I have, as much one as another, is equally my own, and no other more properly makes me a man than this.

I universally owe my entire picture to the public. The wisdom of my instruction consists in liberty, in truth, in essence: disdaining to introduce those little, feigned, common, and provincial rules into the catalogue of its real duties; all natural, general, and constant, of which civility and ceremony are daughters indeed, but illegitimate. We are sure to have the vices of appearance, when we shall have had those of essence: when we have done with these, we run full drive upon the others, if we find it must be so; for there is danger that we shall fancy new offices, to excuse our negligence towards the natural ones, and to confound them: and to manifest this, is it not seen that in places where faults are crimes, crimes are but faults; that in nations where the laws of decency are most rare and most remiss, the primitive laws of common reason are better observed: the innumerable multitude of so many duties stifling and dissipating our care. The application of ourselves to light and trivial things diverts us from those that are necessary and just. Oh, how these superficial men take an easy and plausible way in comparison of ours! These are shadows wherewith we palliate and pay one another; but we do not pay, but inflame the reckoning towards that great judge, who tucks up our rags and tatters above our shameful parts, and suckles not to view us all over, even to our inmost and most secret ordures: it were a useful decency of our maidenly modesty, could it keep him from this discovery. In fine, whoever could reclaim man from so scrupulous a verbal superstition, would do the world no great disservice. Our life is divided betwixt folly and prudence: whoever will write of it but what is reverend and canonical, will leave above the one-half behind. I do not excuse myself to myself; and if I did, it should rather be for my excuses that I would excuse myself than for any other fault; I excuse myself of certain humours, which I think more strong in number than those that are on my side. In consideration of which, I will further say this (for I desire to please every one, though it will be hard to do):

> '*Esse unum hominem accommodatum ad tantam morum ac sermonum et voluntatum varietatem,*'
>
> ['For a man to conform to such a variety of manners, discourses, and will.' —Q. Cicero, De Pet. Consul, c. 14.]

that they ought not to condemn me for what I make authorities, received and approved by so many ages, to utter: and that there is no reason that for want of rhyme they should refuse me the liberty they allow even to churchmen of our nation and time, and these amongst the most notable, of which here are two of their brisk verses:

> '*Rimula, dispeream, ni monogramma tua est.*'
>
> '*Un vit d'amy la contente et bien traicte:*'
>
> [St Gelais, (Euvres Poetiques), p. 99, ed. of Lyons, 1574.]

besides how many others. I love modesty; and 'tis not out of judgment that I have chosen this scandalous way of speaking; 'tis nature that has chosen it for me. I commend it not, no more than other forms that are contrary to common use: but I excuse it, and by circumstances both general and particular, alleviate its accusation.

But to proceed. Whence, too, can proceed that usurpation of sovereign authority you take upon you over the women, who favour you at their own expense,

'Si furtiva dedit mira munuscula nocte,'

['If, in the stealthy night, she has made strange gifts.'
—Catullus, lxviii. 145.]

so that you presently assume the interest, coldness, and authority of a husband? 'Tis a free contract why do you not then keep to it, as you would have them do? there is no prescription upon voluntary things. 'Tis against the form, but it is true withal, that I in my time have conducted this bargain as much as the nature of it would permit, as conscientiously and with as much colour of justice, as any other contract; and that I never pretended other affection than what I really had, and have truly acquainted them with its birth, vigour, and declination, its fits and intermissions: a man does not always hold on at the same rate. I have been so sparing of my promises, that I think I have been better than my word. They have found me faithful even to service of their inconstancy, a confessed and sometimes multiplied inconstancy. I never broke with them, whilst I had any hold at all, and what occasion soever they have given me, never broke with them to hatred or contempt; for such privacies, though obtained upon never so scandalous terms, do yet oblige to some good will: I have sometimes, upon their tricks and evasions, discovered a little indiscreet anger and impatience; for I am naturally subject to rash emotions, which, though light and short, often spoil my market. At any time they have consulted my judgment, I never stuck to give them sharp and paternal counsels, and to pinch them to the quick. If I have left them any cause to complain of me, 'tis rather to have found in me, in comparison of the modern use, a love foolishly conscientious than anything else. I have kept my, word in things wherein I might easily have been dispensed; they sometimes surrendered themselves with reputation, and upon articles that they were willing enough should be broken by the conqueror: I have, more than once, made pleasure in its greatest effort strike to the interest of their honour; and where reason importuned me, have armed them against myself; so that they ordered themselves more decorously and securely by my rules, when they frankly referred themselves to them, than they would have done by their own. I have ever, as much as I could, wholly taken upon myself alone the hazard of our assignations, to acquit them; and have always contrived our meetings after the hardest and most unusual manner, as less suspected, and, moreover, in my opinion, more accessible. They are chiefly more open, where they think they are most securely shut; things least feared are least interdicted and observed; one may more boldly dare what nobody thinks you dare, which by its difficulty becomes easy. Never had any man his approaches more impertinently generative; this way of loving is more according to discipline but how ridiculous it is to our people, and how ineffectual, who better knows than I? yet I shall not repent me of it; I have nothing there more to lose:

'*Me tabula sacer*
Votiva paries, indicat uvida
Suspendisse potenti
Vestimenta maris deo:'

['The holy wall, by my votive table, shows that I have hanged up my wet clothes in honour of the powerful god of the sea.' — Horace, Od., i. 5, 13.]

'tis now time to speak out. But as I might, per adventure, say to another, 'Thou talkest idly, my friend; the love of thy time has little commerce with faith and integrity;'

'*Haec si tu postules*
Ratione certa facere, nihilo plus agas,
Quam si des operam, ut cum ratione insanias:'

['If you seek to make these things certain by reason, you will do no more than if you should seek to be mad in your senses.' — Terence, Eun., act i., sc. i, v. 16.]

on the contrary, also, if it were for me to begin again, certainly it should be by the same method and the same progress, how fruitless soever it might be to me; folly and insufficiency are commendable in an incommendable action: the farther I go from their humour in this,

I approach so much nearer to my own. As to the rest, in this traffic, I did not suffer myself to be totally carried away; I pleased myself in it, but did not forget myself. I retained the little sense and discretion that nature has given me, entire for their service and my own: a little emotion, but no dotage. My conscience, also, was engaged in it, even to debauch and licentiousness; but, as to ingratitude, treachery, malice, and cruelty, never. I would not purchase the pleasure of this vice at any price, but content myself with its proper and simple cost:

'*Nullum intra se vitium est.*'

['Nothing is a vice in itself.' —Seneca, Ep., 95.]

I almost equally hate a stupid and slothful laziness, as I do a toilsome and painful employment; this pinches, the other lays me asleep. I like wounds as well as bruises, and cuts as well as dry blows. I found in this commerce, when I was the most able for it, a just moderation betwixt these extremes. Love is a sprightly, lively, and gay agitation; I was neither troubled nor afflicted with it, but heated, and moreover, disordered; a man must stop there; it hurts nobody but fools. A young man asked the philosopher Panetius if it were becoming a wise man to be in love? 'Let the wise man look to that,' answered he, 'but let not thou and I, who are not so, engage ourselves in so stirring and violent an affair, that enslaves us to others, and renders us contemptible to ourselves.' He said true that we are not to intrust a thing so precipitous in itself to a soul that has not wherewithal to withstand its assaults and disprove practically the saying of Agesilaus, that prudence and love cannot live together. 'Tis a vain employment, 'tis true, unbecoming, shameful, and illegitimate; but carried on after this manner, I look upon it as wholesome, and proper to enliven a drowsy soul and to rouse up a heavy body; and, as an experienced physician, I would prescribe it to a man of my form and condition, as soon as any other recipe whatever, to rouse and keep him in vigour till well advanced in years, and to defer the approaches of age. Whilst we are but in the suburbs, and that the pulse yet beats:

> *'Dum nova canities, dum prima et recta senectus,*
> *Dum superest lachesi quod torqueat, et pedibus me*
> *Porto meis, nullo dextram subeunte bacillo,'*

> ['Whilst the white hair is new, whilst old age is still straight shouldered, whilst there still remains something for Lachesis to spin, whilst I walk on my own legs, and need no staff to lean upon.' —Juvenal, iii. 26.]

we have need to be solicited and tickled by some such nipping incitation as this. Do but observe what youth, vigour, and gaiety it inspired the good Anacreon withal: and Socrates, who was then older than I, speaking of an amorous object:

'Leaning,' said he, 'my shoulder to her shoulder, and my head to hers, as we were reading together in a book, I felt, without dissembling, a sudden sting in my shoulder like the biting of an insect, which I still felt above five days after, and a continual itching crept into my heart.' So that merely the accidental touch, and of a shoulder, heated and altered a soul cooled and enerved by age, and the strictest liver of all mankind. And, pray, why not? Socrates was a man, and would neither be, nor seem, any other thing. Philosophy does not contend against natural pleasures, provided they be moderate, and only preaches moderation, not a total abstinence; the power of its resistance is employed against those that are adulterate and strange. Philosophy says that the appetites of the body ought not to be augmented by the mind, and ingeniously warns us not to stir up hunger by saturity; not to stuff, instead of merely filling, the belly; to avoid all enjoyments that may bring us to want; and all meats and drinks that bring thirst and hunger: as, in the service of love, she prescribes us to take such an object as may simply satisfy the body's need, and does not stir the soul, which ought only barely to follow and assist the body, without mixing in the affair. But have I not reason to hold that these precepts, which, indeed, in my opinion, are somewhat over strict, only concern a body in its best plight; and that in a body broken with age, as in a weak stomach, 'tis excusable to warm and support it by art, and by the mediation of the fancy to restore the appetite and cheerfulness it has lost of itself.

May we not say that there is nothing in us, during this earthly prison, that is purely either corporeal or spiritual; and that we injuriously break up a man alive; and that it seems but reasonable that we should carry ourselves as favourably, at least, towards the use of pleasure as we do towards that of pain! Pain was (for example) vehement even to perfection in the souls of the saints by penitence: the body had there naturally a sham by the right of union, and yet might have but little part in the cause; and yet are they not contented that it should barely follow and assist the afflicted soul: they have afflicted itself with grievous and special torments, to the end that by emulation of one another the soul and body might plunge man into misery by so much more salutiferous as it is more severe. In like manner, is it not injustice, in bodily pleasures, to subdue and keep under the soul, and say that it must therein be dragged along as to some enforced and servile obligation and necessity? 'Tis rather her part to hatch and cherish them, there to present herself, and to invite them, the authority of ruling belonging to her; as it is also her part, in my opinion, in pleasures that are proper to her, to inspire and infuse into the body all the sentiment it is capable of, and to study how to make them sweet and useful to it. For it is good reason, as they say, that the body should not pursue its appetites to the prejudice of the mind; but why is it not also the reason that the mind should not pursue hers to the prejudice of the body?

I have no other passion to keep me in breath. What avarice, ambition, quarrels, lawsuits do for others who, like me, have no particular vocation, love would much more commodiously do; it would restore to me vigilance, sobriety, grace, and the care of my person; it would reassure my countenance, so that the grimaces of old age, those deformed and dismal looks, might not come to disgrace it; would again put me upon sound and wise studies, by which I might render myself more loved and esteemed, clearing my mind of the despair of itself and of its use, and redintegrating it to itself; would divert me from a thousand troublesome thoughts, a thousand melancholic humours that idleness and the ill posture of our health loads us withal at such an age; would warm again, in dreams at least, the blood that nature is abandoning; would hold up the chin, and a little stretch out the nerves, the vigour and gaiety of life of that poor man who is going full drive towards his ruin. But Ivery well understand that it is a commodity hard to recover: by weakness and long experience our taste is become more delicate and nice; we ask most when we bring least, and are harder to choose when we least deserve to be accepted: and knowing ourselves for what we are, we are less confident and more distrustful; nothing can assure us of being beloved, considering our condition and theirs. I am out of countenance to see myself in company with those young wanton creatures:

> '*Cujus in indomito constantior inguine nervus,*
> *Quam nova collibus arbor inhaeret.*'

> ['In whose unbridled reins the vigour is more inherent than in the young tree on the hills.' —Horace, Epod., xii. 19.]

To what end should we go insinuate our misery amid their gay and sprightly humour?

> '*Possint ut juvenes visere fervidi.*
> *Multo non sine risu,*
> *Dilapsam in cineres facem.*'

> ['As the fervid youths may behold, not without laughter, a burning worn to ashes.' —Horace, Od., iv. 13, 21.]

They have strength and reason on their side; let us give way; we have nothing to do there: and these blossoms of springing beauty suffer not themselves to be handled by such benumbed hands nor dealt with by mere material means, for, as the old philosopher answered one who jeered him because he could not gain the favour of a young girl he made love to: 'Friend, the hook will not stick in such soft cheese.' It is a commerce that requires relation and correspondence: the other pleasures we receive may be acknowledged by recompenses of another nature, but this is not to be paid but with the same kind of coin. In earnest, in this sport, the pleasure I give more tickles my imagination than that they give me; now, he has nothing of generosity in him who can receive pleasure where he confers none—it must needs be a mean soul that will owe all, and can be content to maintain relations with persons to whom he is a continual charge; there is no beauty, grace, nor privacy so exquisite that a gentleman ought to desire at this rate. If they can only be kind to us out of pity, I had much rather die than live upon charity. I would have right to ask, in the style wherein I heard them beg in Italy: 'Fate ben per voi,'—['Do good for yourself.']—or after the manner that Cyrus exhorted his soldiers, 'Who loves himself let him follow me.'—'Consort yourself,' some one will say to me, 'with women of your own condition, whom like fortune will render more easy to your desire.' O ridiculous and insipid composition!

'*Nolo*
Barbam vellere mortuo leoni.'

['I would not pluck the beard from a dead lion.' —Martial]

Xenophon lays it for an objection and an accusation against Menon, that he never made love to any but old women. For my part, I take more pleasure in but seeing the just and sweet mixture of two young beauties, or only in meditating on it in my fancy, than myself in acting second in a pitiful and imperfect conjunction;

[Which Cotton renders, 'Than to be myself an actor in the second with a deformed creature.']

I leave that fantastic appetite to the Emperor Galba, who was only for old curried flesh: and to this poor wretch:

'*O ego Di faciant talem to cernere possim,*
Caraque mutatis oscula ferre comis,
Amplectique meis corpus non pingue lacertis!'

[Ovid, who (Ex. Ponto, i. 4, 49) writes to his wife, 'O would the gods arrange that such I might see thee, and bring dear kisses to thy changed locks, and embrace thy withered body with my arms']

Amongst chief deformities I reckon forced and artificial beauties:

Hemon, a young boy of Chios, thinking by fine dressing to acquire the beauty that nature had denied him, came to the philosopher Arcesilaus and asked him if it was possible for a wise man to be in love—'Yes,' replied he, 'provided it be not with a farded and adulterated beauty like thine.'

> [Diogenes Laertius, iv. 36. The question was whether a wise man could love him. Cotton has 'Emonez, a young courtezan of Chios.']

Ugliness of a confessed antiquity is to me less old and less ugly than another that is polished and plastered up. Shall I speak it, without the danger of having my throat cut? love, in my opinion, is not properly and naturally in its season, but in the age next to childhood,

> '*Quem si puellarum insereres choro,*
> *Mille sagaces falleret hospites,*
> *Discrimen obscurum, solutis*
> *Crinibus ambiguoque vultu:*'

> ['Whom if thou shouldst place in a company of girls, it would require a thousand experts to distinguish him, with his loose locks and ambiguous countenance.' —Horace, Od., ii. 5, 21.]

nor beauty neither; for whereas Homer extends it so far as to the budding of the beard, Plato himself has remarked this as rare: and the reason why the sophist Bion so pleasantly called the first appearing hairs of adolescence 'Aristogitons' and 'Harmodiuses'—[Plutarch, On Love, c.34.]—is sufficiently known. I find it in virility already in some sort a little out of date, though not so much as in old age;

> '*Importunus enim transvolat aridas*
> *Quercus.*'

> ['For it uncivilly passes over withered oaks.'
> —Horace, Od., iv. 13, 9.]

and Marguerite, Queen of Navarre, like a woman, very far extends the advantage of women, ordaining that it is time, at thirty years old, to convert the title of fair into that of good. The shorter authority we give to love over our lives, 'tis so much the better for us. Do but observe his port; 'tis a beardless boy. Who knows not how, in his school they proceed contrary to all order; study, exercise, and usage are their ways for insufficiency: there novices rule:—

> '*Amor ordinem nescit.*'
>
> ['Love ignores rules.' (Or:) 'Love knows no rule.' —St Jerome, Letter to Chyomatius.]

Doubtless his conduct is much more graceful when mixed with inadvertency and trouble; miscarriages and ill successes give him point and grace; provided it be sharp and eager, 'tis no great matter whether it be prudent or no: do but observe how he goes reeling, tripping, and playing: you put him in the stocks when you guide him by art and wisdom; and he is restrained of his divine liberty when put into those hairy and callous clutches.

As to the rest, I often hear the women set out this intelligence as entirely spiritual, and disdain to put the interest the senses there have into consideration; everything there serves; but I can say that I have often seen that we have excused the weakness of their understandings in favour of their outward beauty, but have never yet seen that in favour of mind, how mature and full soever, any of them would hold out a hand to a body that was never so little in decadence. Why does not some one of them take it into her head to make that noble Socratical bargain between body and soul, purchasing a philosophical and spiritual intelligence and generation at the price of her thighs, which is the highest price she can get for them? Plato ordains in his Laws that he who has performed any signal and advantageous exploit in war may not be refused during the whole expedition, his age or ugliness notwithstanding, a kiss or any other amorous favour from any woman whatever. What he thinks to be so just in recommendation of military valour, why may it not be the same in recommendation of any other good quality? and why does not some woman take a fancy to possess over her companions the glory of this chaste love? I may well say chaste;

'Nam si quando ad praelia ventum est,
Ut quondam in stipulis magnus sine viribus ignis,
Incassum furit:'

['For when they sometimes engage in love's battle, his sterile ardour lights up but as the flame of a straw.' —Virgil, Georg., iii. 98.]

the vices that are stifled in the thought are not the worst.

To conclude this notable commentary, which has escaped from me in a torrent of babble, a torrent sometimes impetuous and hurtful,

'Ut missum sponsi furtivo munere malum
Procurrit casto virginis a gremio,
Quod miserae oblitae molli sub veste locatuat,
Dum adventu matris prosilit, excutitur,
Atque illud prono praeceps agitur decursu
Huic manat tristi conscius ore rubor.'

['As when an apple, sent by a lover secretly to his mistress, falls from the chaste virgin's bosom, where she had quite forgotten it; when, starting at her mother's coming in, it is shaken out and rolls over the floor before her eyes, a conscious blush covers her face.' —Catullus, lxv. 19.]

I say that males and females are cast in the same mould, and that, education and usage excepted, the difference is not great. Plato indifferently invites both the one and the other to the society of all studies, exercises, and vocations, both military and civil, in his Commonwealth; and the philosopher Antisthenes rejected all distinction betwixt their virtue and ours. It is much more easy to accuse one sex than to excuse the other; 'tis according to the saying,

'Le fourgon se moque de la paele.'

['The Pot and the Kettle.']

13

CIVIL DISOBEDIENCE

Henry David Thoreau

I heartily accept the motto, 'That government is best which governs least'; and I should like to see it acted up to more rapidly and systematically. Carried out, it finally amounts to this, which also I believe—'That government is best which governs not at all'; and when men are prepared for it, that will be the kind of government which they will have. Government is at best but an expedient; but most governments are usually, and all governments are sometimes, inexpedient. The objections which have been brought against a standing army, and they are many and weighty, and deserve to prevail, may also at last be brought against a standing government. The standing army is only an arm of the standing government. The government itself, which is only the mode which the people have chosen to execute their will, is equally liable to be abused and perverted before the people can act through it. Witness the present Mexican war, the work of comparatively a few individuals using the standing government as their tool; for, in the outset, the people would not have consented to this measure.

This American government—what is it but a tradition, though a recent one, endeavoring to transmit itself unimpaired to posterity, but each instant losing some of its integrity? It has not the vitality and force of a single living man; for a single man can bend it to his will. It is a sort of wooden gun to the people themselves. But it is not the less necessary for this; for the people must have some complicated machinery or other, and hear its din, to satisfy that idea of government which they have. Governments show thus how successfully men can be imposed on, even impose on themselves, for their own advantage. It is excellent, we must all allow. Yet this government never of itself furthered any enterprise, but by the alacrity with which it got out of its way. *It* does not keep the country free. *It* does not settle the West. *It* does not educate. The character inherent in the American people has done all that has been accomplished; and it would have done somewhat more, if the government had not sometimes got in its way. For government is an expedient by which men would fain succeed in letting one another alone; and, as has been said, when it is most expedient, the governed are most let alone by it. Trade and commerce, if they were not made of India-rubber, would never manage to bounce over the obstacles which legislators are continually putting in their way; and, if one were to judge these men wholly by the effects of their actions and not partly by their intentions, they would deserve to be classed and punished with those mischievous persons who put obstructions on the railroads.

But, to speak practically and as a citizen, unlike those who call themselves no-government men, I ask for, not at once no government, but *at once* a better government. Let every man make known what kind of government would command his respect, and that will be one step toward obtaining it.

After all, the practical reason why, when the power is once in the hands of the people, a majority are permitted, and for a long period continue, to rule is not because they are most likely to be in the right, nor because this seems fairest to the minority, but because they are physically the strongest. But a government in which the majority rule in all cases cannot be based on justice, even as far as men understand it. Can there not be a government in which majorities do not virtually decide right and wrong, but conscience?—in which majorities decide only those questions to which the rule of expediency is applicable? Must the citizen ever for a moment, or in the least degree, resign his conscience to the legislator? Why has every man a conscience, then? I think that we should be men first, and subjects afterward. It is not desirable to cultivate a respect for the law, so much as for the right. The only obligation which I have a right to assume is to do at any time what I think right. It is truly enough said that a corporation has no conscience; but a corporation of conscientious men is a corporation *with* a conscience. Law never made men a whit more just; and, by means of their respect for it, even the well-disposed are daily made the agents of injustice. A common and natural result of an undue respect for law is, that you may see a file of soldiers, colonel, captain, corporal, privates, powder-monkeys, and all, marching in admirable order over hill and dale to the wars, against their wills, ay, against their common sense and consciences, which makes it very steep marching indeed, and produces a palpitation of the heart. They have no doubt that it is a damnable business in which they are concerned; they are all peaceably inclined. Now, what are they? Men at all? or small movable forts and magazines, at the service of some unscrupulous man in power? Visit the Navy-Yard, and behold a marine, such a man as an American government can make, or such as it can make a man with its black arts,—a mere shadow and reminiscence of humanity, a man laid out alive and standing, and already, as one may say, buried under arms with funeral accompaniments, though it may be,

> 'Not a drum was heard, not a funeral note,
> As his corse to the rampart we hurried;
> Not a soldier discharged his farewell shot
> O'er the grave where our hero we buried.'

The mass of men serve the state thus, not as men mainly, but as machines, with their bodies. They are the standing army, and the militia, jailers, constables, *posse comitatus*, etc. In most cases there is no free exercise whatever of the judgment or of the moral sense; but they put themselves on a level with wood and earth and stones; and wooden men can perhaps be manufactured that will serve the purpose as well. Such command no more respect than men of straw or a lump of dirt. They have the same sort of worth only as horses and dogs. Yet such as these even are commonly esteemed good citizens. Others—as most legislators, politicians, lawyers, ministers, and office-holders—serve the state chiefly with their heads; and, as they rarely make any moral distinctions, they are as likely to serve the devil, without *intending* it, as God. A very few—as heroes, patriots, martyrs, reformers in the great sense, and *men*—serve the state with their consciences also, and so necessarily resist it for the most part; and they are commonly treated as enemies by it. A wise man will only be useful as a man, and will not submit to be 'clay,' and 'stop a hole to keep the wind away,' but leave that office to his dust at least:

> 'I am too high-born to be propertied,
> To be a secondary at control,
> Or useful serving-man and instrument
> To any sovereign state throughout the world.'

He who gives himself entirely to his fellow-men appears to them useless and selfish; but he who gives himself partially to them is pronounced a benefactor and philanthropist.

How does it become a man to behave toward this American government today? I answer, that he cannot without disgrace be associated with it. I cannot for an instant recognize that political organization as *my* government which is the *slave's* government also.

All men recognize the right of revolution; that is, the right to refuse allegiance to, and to resist, the government, when its tyranny or its inefficiency are great and unendurable. But almost all say that such is not the case now. But such was the case, they think, in the Revolution of '75. If one were to tell me that this was a bad government because it taxed certain foreign commodities brought to its ports, it is most probable that I should not make an ado about it, for I can do without them. All machines have their friction; and possibly this does enough good to counterbalance the evil. At any rate, it is a great evil to make a stir about it. But when the friction comes to have its machine, and oppression and robbery are organized, I say, let us not have such a machine any longer. In other words, when a sixth of the population of a nation which has undertaken to be the refuge of liberty are slaves, and a whole country is unjustly overrun and conquered by a foreign army, and subjected to military law, I think that it is not too soon for honest men to rebel and revolutionize. What makes this duty the more urgent is the fact that the country so overrun is not our own, but ours is the invading army.

Paley, a common authority with many on moral questions, in his chapter on the 'Duty of Submission to Civil Government,' resolves all civil obligation into expediency; and he proceeds to say that 'so long as the interest of the whole society requires it, that is, so long as the established government cannot be resisted or changed without public inconveniency, it is the will of God that the established government be obeyed, and no longer… This principle being admitted, the justice of every particular case of resistance is reduced to a computation of the quantity of the danger and grievance on the one side, and of the probability and expense of redressing it on the other.' Of this, he says, every man shall judge for himself. But Paley appears never to have contemplated those cases to which the rule of expediency does not apply, in which a people, as well as an individual, must do justice, cost what it may. If I have unjustly wrested a plank from a drowning man, I must restore it to him though I drown myself. This, according to Paley, would be inconvenient. But he that would save his life, in such a case, shall lose it. This people must cease to hold slaves, and to make war on Mexico, though it cost them their existence as a people.

In their practice, nations agree with Paley; but does any one think that Massachusetts does exactly what is right at the present crisis?

> 'A drab of state, a cloth-o'-silver slut,
> To have her train borne up, and her soul trail in the dirt.'

Practically speaking, the opponents to a reform in Massachusetts are not a hundred thousand politicians at the South, but a hundred thousand merchants and farmers here, who are more interested in commerce and agriculture than they are in humanity, and are not prepared to do justice to the slave and to Mexico, *cost what it may*. I quarrel not with far-off foes, but with those who, near at home, cooperate with, and do the bidding of those far away, and without whom the latter would be harmless. We are accustomed to say, that the mass of men are unprepared; but improvement is slow, because the few are not materially wiser or better than the many. It is not so important that many should be as good as you, as that there be some absolute goodness somewhere; for that will leaven the whole lump. There are thousands who are *in opinion* opposed to slavery and to the war, who yet in effect do nothing to put an end to them; who, esteeming themselves children of Washington and Franklin, sit down with their hands in their pockets, and say that they know not what to do, and do nothing; who even postpone the question of freedom to the question of free trade, and quietly read the prices-current along with the latest advices from Mexico, after dinner, and, it may be, fall asleep over them both. What is the price-current of an honest man and patriot today? They hesitate, and they regret, and sometimes they petition; but they do nothing in earnest and with effect. They will wait, well disposed, for others to remedy the evil, that they may no longer have it to regret. At most, they give only a cheap vote, and a feeble countenance and God-speed, to the right, as it goes by them. There are nine hundred and ninety-nine patrons of virtue to one virtuous man. But it is easier to deal with the real possessor of a thing than with the temporary guardian of it.

All voting is a sort of gaming, like checkers or backgammon, with a slight moral tinge to it, a playing with right and wrong, with moral questions; and betting naturally accompanies it. The character of the voters is not staked. I cast my vote, perchance, as I think right; but I am not vitally concerned that that right should prevail. I am willing to leave it to the majority. Its obligation, therefore, never exceeds that of expediency. Even voting *for the right* is *doing* nothing for it. It is only expressing to men feebly your desire that it should prevail. A wise man will not leave the right to the mercy of chance, nor wish it to prevail through the power of the majority. There is but little virtue in the action of masses of men. When the majority shall at length vote for the abolition of slavery, it will be because they are indifferent to slavery, or because there is but little slavery left to be abolished by their vote. *They* will then be the only slaves. Only *his* vote can hasten the abolition of slavery who asserts his own freedom by his vote.

I hear of a convention to be held at Baltimore, or elsewhere, for the selection of a candidate for the Presidency, made up chiefly of editors, and men who are politicians by profession; but I think, what is it to any independent, intelligent, and respectable man what decision they may come to? Shall we not have the advantage of his wisdom and honesty, nevertheless? Can we not count upon some independent votes? Are there not many individuals in the country who do not attend conventions? But no: I find that the respectable man, so called, has immediately drifted from his position, and despairs of his country, when his country has more reason to despair of him. He forthwith adopts one of the candidates thus selected as the only *available* one, thus proving that he is himself *available* for any purposes of the demagogue. His vote is of no more worth than that of any unprincipled foreigner or hireling native, who may have been bought. O for a man who is a *man*, and, as my neighbor says, has a bone in his back which you cannot pass your hand through! Our statistics are at fault: the population has been returned too large. How many *men* are there to a square thousand miles in this country? Hardly one. Does not America offer any inducement for men to settle here? The American has dwindled into an Odd Fellow—one who may be known by the development of his organ of gregariousness, and a manifest lack of intellect and cheerful self-reliance; whose first and chief concern, on coming into the world, is to see that the almshouses are in good repair; and, before yet he has lawfully donned the virile garb, to collect a fund for the support of the widows and orphans that may be; who, in short, ventures to live only by the aid of the Mutual Insurance company, which has promised to bury him decently.

It is not a man's duty, as a matter of course, to devote himself to the eradication of any, even the most enormous, wrong; he may still properly have other concerns to engage him; but it is his duty, at least, to wash his hands of it, and, if he gives it no thought longer, not to give it practically his support. If I devote myself to other pursuits and contemplations, I must first see, at least, that I do not pursue them sitting upon another man's shoulders. I must get off him first, that he may pursue his contemplations too. See what gross inconsistency is tolerated. I have heard some of my townsmen say, 'I should like to have them order me out to help put down an insurrection of the slaves, or to march to Mexico;—see if I would go;' and yet these very men have each, directly by their allegiance, and so indirectly, at least, by their money, furnished a substitute. The soldier is applauded who refuses to serve in an unjust war by those who do not refuse to sustain the unjust government which makes the war; is applauded by those whose own act and authority he disregards and sets at naught; as if the state were penitent to that degree that it hired one to scourge it while it sinned, but not to that degree that it left off sinning for a moment. Thus, under the name of Order and Civil Government, we are all made at last to pay homage to and support our own meanness. After the first blush of sin comes its indifference; and from immoral it becomes, as it were, *un*moral, and not quite unnecessary to that life which we have made.

The broadest and most prevalent error requires the most disinterested virtue to sustain it. The slight reproach to which the virtue of patriotism is commonly liable, the noble are most likely to incur. Those who, while they disapprove of the character and measures of a government, yield to it their allegiance and support are undoubtedly its most conscientious supporters, and so frequently the most serious obstacles to reform. Some are petitioning the State to dissolve the Union, to disregard the requisitions of the President. Why do they not dissolve it themselves—the union between themselves and the State—and refuse to pay their quota into its treasury? Do not they stand in the same relation to the State that the State does to the Union? And have not the same reasons prevented the State from resisting the Union which have prevented them from resisting the State?

How can a man be satisfied to entertain an opinion merely, and enjoy *it*? Is there any enjoyment in it, if his opinion is that he is aggrieved? If you are cheated out of a single dollar by your neighbor, you do not rest satisfied with knowing that you are cheated, or with saying that you are cheated, or even with petitioning him to pay you your due; but you take effectual steps at once to obtain the full amount, and see that you are never cheated again. Action from principle, the perception and the performance of right, changes things and relations; it is essentially revolutionary, and does not consist wholly with anything which was. It not only divides states and churches, it divides families; ay, it divides the *individual*, separating the diabolical in him from the divine.

Unjust laws exist: shall we be content to obey them, or shall we endeavor to amend them, and obey them until we have succeeded, or shall we transgress them at once? Men generally, under such a government as this, think that they ought to wait until they have persuaded the majority to alter them. They think that, if they should resist, the remedy would be worse than the evil. But it is the fault of the government itself that the remedy *is* worse than the evil. *It* makes it worse. Why is it not more apt to anticipate and provide for reform? Why does it not cherish its wise minority? Why does it cry and resist before it is hurt? Why does it not encourage its citizens to be on the alert to point out its faults, and *do* better than it would have them? Why does it always crucify Christ, and excommunicate Copernicus and Luther, and pronounce Washington and Franklin rebels?

One would think, that a deliberate and practical denial of its authority was the only offence never contemplated by government; else, why has it not assigned its definite, its suitable and proportionate penalty? If a man who has no property refuses but once to earn nine shillings for the State, he is put in prison for a period unlimited by any law that I know, and determined only by the discretion of those who placed him there; but if he should steal ninety times nine shillings from the State, he is soon permitted to go at large again.

If the injustice is part of the necessary friction of the machine of government, let it go, let it go: perchance it will wear smooth—certainly the machine will wear out. If the injustice has a spring, or a pulley, or a rope, or a crank, exclusively for itself, then perhaps you may consider whether the remedy will not be worse than the evil; but if it is of such a nature that it requires you to be the agent of injustice to another, then, I say, break the law. Let your life be a counter-friction to stop the machine. What I have to do is to see, at any rate, that I do not lend myself to the wrong which I condemn.

As for adopting the ways which the State has provided for remedying the evil, I know not of such ways. They take too much time, and a man's life will be gone. I have other affairs to attend to. I came into this world, not chiefly to make this a good place to live in, but to live in it, be it good or bad. A man has not everything to do, but something; and because he cannot do *everything*, it is not necessary that he should do *something* wrong. It is not my business to be petitioning the Governor or the Legislature any more than it is theirs to petition me; and if they should not bear my petition, what should I do then? But in this case the state has provided no way: its very Constitution is the evil. This may seem to be harsh and stubborn and unconciliatory; but it is to treat with the utmost kindness and consideration the only spirit that can appreciate or deserves it. So is all change for the better, like birth and death, which convulse the body.

I do not hesitate to say, that those who call themselves Abolitionists should at once effectually withdraw their support, both in person and property, from the government of Massachusetts, and not wait till they constitute a majority of one, before they suffer the right to prevail through them. I think that it is enough if they have God on their side, without waiting for that other one. Moreover, any man more right than his neighbors constitutes a majority of one already.

I meet this American government, or its representative, the state government, directly, and face to face, once a year—no more—in the person of its tax-gatherer; this is the only mode in which a man situated as I am necessarily meets it; and it then says distinctly, Recognize me; and the simplest, the most effectual, and, in the present posture of affairs, the indispensablest mode of treating with it on this head, of expressing your little satisfaction with and love for it, is to deny it then. My civil neighbor, the tax-gatherer, is the very man I have to deal with—for it is, after all, with men and not with parchment that I quarrel—and he has voluntarily chosen to be an agent of the government. How shall he ever know well what he is and does as an officer of the government, or as a man, until he is obliged to consider whether he shall treat me, his neighbor, for whom he has respect, as a neighbor and well-disposed man, or as a maniac and disturber of the peace, and see if he can get over this obstruction to his neighborliness without a ruder and more impetuous thought or speech corresponding with his action. I know this well, that if one thousand, if one hundred, if ten men whom I could name—if ten *honest* men only—ay, if *one* HONEST man, in this state of Massachusetts, *ceasing to hold slaves*, were actually to withdraw from this copartnership, and be locked up in the county jail therefor, it would be the abolition of slavery in America. For it matters not how small the beginning may seem to be: what is once well done is done forever. But we love better to talk about it: that we say is our mission, Reform keeps many scores of newspapers in its service, but not one man. If my esteemed neighbor, the State's ambassador, who will devote his days to the settlement of the question of human rights in the Council Chamber, instead of being threatened with the prisons of Carolina, were to sit down the prisoner of Massachusetts, that state which is so anxious to foist the sin of slavery upon her sister—though at present she can discover only an act of inhospitality to be the ground of a quarrel with her—the Legislature would not wholly waive the subject the following winter.

Under a government which imprisons any unjustly, the true place for a just man is also a prison. The proper place today, the only place which Massachusetts has provided for her freer and less desponding spirits, is in her prisons, to be put out and locked out of the State by her own act, as they have already put themselves out by their principles. It is there that the fugitive slave, and the Mexican prisoner on parole, and the Indian come to plead the wrongs of his race should find them; on that separate, but more free and honorable, ground, where the State places those who are not *with* her, but *against* her—the only house in a slave state in which a free man can abide with honor. If any think that their influence would be lost there, and their voices no longer afflict the ear of the State, that they would not be as an enemy within its walls, they do not know by how much truth is stronger than error, nor how much more eloquently and effectively he can combat injustice who has experienced a little in his own person. Cast your whole vote, not a strip of paper merely, but your whole influence. A minority is powerless while it conforms to the majority; it is not even a minority then; but it is irresistible when it clogs by its whole weight. If the alternative is to keep all just men in prison, or give up war and slavery, the State will not hesitate which to choose. If a thousand men were not to pay their tax-bills this year, that would not be a violent and bloody measure, as it would be to pay them, and enable the State to commit violence and shed innocent blood. This is, in fact, the definition of a peaceable revolution, if any such is possible. If the tax-gatherer, or any other public officer, asks me, as one has done, 'But what shall I do?' my answer is, 'If you really wish to do anything, resign your office.' When the subject has refused allegiance, and the officer has resigned his office, then the revolution is accomplished. But even suppose blood should flow. Is there not a sort of blood shed when the conscience is wounded? Through this wound a man's real manhood and immortality flow out, and he bleeds to an everlasting death. I see this blood flowing now.

I have contemplated the imprisonment of the offender, rather than the seizure of his goods—though both will serve the same purpose—because they who assert the purest right, and consequently are most dangerous to a corrupt State, commonly have not spent much time in accumulating property. To such the State renders comparatively small service, and a slight tax is wont to appear exorbitant, particularly if they are obliged to earn it by special labor with their hands. If there were one who lived wholly without the use of money, the State itself would hesitate to demand it of him. But the rich man—not to make any invidious comparison—is always sold to the institution which makes him rich. Absolutely speaking, the more money, the less virtue; for money comes between a man and his objects, and obtains them for him; and it was certainly no great virtue to obtain it. It puts to rest many questions which he would otherwise be taxed to answer; while the only new question which it puts is the hard but superfluous one, how to spend it. Thus his moral ground is taken from under his feet. The opportunities of living are diminished in proportion as what are called the 'means'are increased. The best thing a man can do for his culture when he is rich is to endeavor to carry out those schemes which he entertained when he was poor. Christ answered the Herodians according to their condition. 'Show me the tribute-money,' said he;—and one took a penny out of his pocket;—if you use money which has the image of Caesar on it, and which he has made current and valuable, that is, if you are men of the State, and gladly enjoy the advantages of Caesar's government, then pay him back some of his own when he demands it. 'Render therefore to Caesar that which is Caesar's, and to God those things which are God's'—leaving them no wiser than before as to which was which; for they did not wish to know.

When I converse with the freest of my neighbors, I perceive that, whatever they may say about the magnitude and seriousness of the question, and their regard for the public tranquillity, the long and the short of the matter is, that they cannot spare the protection of the existing government, and they dread the consequences to their property and families of disobedience to it. For my own part, I should not like to think that I ever rely on the protection of the State. But, if I deny the authority of the State when it presents its tax-bill, it will soon take and waste all my property, and so harass me and my children without end. This is hard. This makes it impossible for a man to live honestly, and at the same time comfortably, in outward respects. It will not be worth the while to accumulate property; that would be sure to go again. You must hire or squat somewhere, and raise but a small crop, and eat that soon. You must live within yourself, and depend upon yourself always tucked up and ready for a start, and not have many affairs. A man may grow rich in Turkey even, if he will be in all respects a good subject of the Turkish government. Confucius said: 'If a state is governed by the principles of reason, poverty and misery are subjects of shame; if a state is not governed by the principles of reason, riches and honors are the subjects of shame.' No: until I want the protection of Massachusetts to be extended to me in some distant Southern port, where my liberty is endangered, or until I am bent solely on building up an estate at home by peaceful enterprise, I can afford to refuse allegiance to Massachusetts, and her right to my property and life. It costs me less in every sense to incur the penalty of disobedience to the State than it would to obey. I should feel as if I were worth less in that case.

Some years ago, the State met me in behalf of the Church,

and commanded me to pay a certain sum toward the support of a clergyman whose preaching my father attended, but never I myself. 'Pay,' it said, 'or be locked up in the jail.' I declined to pay. But, unfortunately, another man saw fit to pay it. I did not see why the schoolmaster should be taxed to support the priest, and not the priest the schoolmaster; for I was not the State's schoolmaster, but I supported myself by voluntary subscription. I did not see why the lyceum should not present its tax-bill, and have the State to back its demand, as well as the Church. However, at the request of the selectmen, I condescended to make some such statement as this in writing:—'Know all men by these presents, that I, Henry Thoreau, do not wish to be regarded as a member of any incorporated society which I have not joined.' This I gave to the town clerk; and he has it. The State, having thus learned that I did not wish to be regarded as a member of that church, has never made a like demand on me since; though it said that it must adhere to its original presumption that time. If I had known how to name them, I should then have signed off in detail from all the societies which I never signed on to; but I did not know where to find a complete list.

I have paid no poll-tax for six years. I was put into a jail once on this account, for one night; and, as I stood considering the walls of solid stone, two or three feet thick, the door of wood and iron, a foot thick, and the iron grating which strained the light, I could not help being struck with the foolishness of that institution which treated me as if I were mere flesh and blood and bones, to be locked up. I wondered that it should have concluded at length that this was the best use it could put me to, and had never thought to avail itself of my services in some way. I saw that, if there was a wall of stone between me and my townsmen, there was a still more difficult one to climb or break through before they could get to be as free as I was. I did not for a moment feel confined, and the walls seemed a great waste of stone and mortar. I felt as if I alone of all my townsmen had paid my tax. They plainly did not know how to treat me, but behaved like persons who are underbred. In every threat and in every compliment there was a blunder; for they thought that my chief desire was to stand the other side of that stone wall. I could not but smile to see how industriously they locked the door on my meditations, which followed them out again without let or hindrance, and *they* were really all that was dangerous. As they could not reach me, they had resolved to punish my body; just as boys, if they cannot come at some person against whom they have a spite, will abuse his dog. I saw that the State was half-witted, that it was timid as a lone woman with her silver spoons, and that it did not know its friends from its foes, and I lost all my remaining respect for it, and pitied it.

Thus the State never intentionally confronts a man's sense, intellectual or moral, but only his body, his senses. It is not armed with superior wit or honesty, but with superior physical strength. I was not born to be forced. I will breathe after my own fashion. Let us see who is the strongest. What force has a multitude? They only can force me who obey a higher law than I. They force me to become like themselves. I do not hear of *men* being *forced* to live this way or that by masses of men. What sort of life were that to live? When I meet a government which says to me, 'Your money or your life,' why should I be in haste to give it my money? It may be in a great strait, and not know what to do: I cannot help that. It must help itself; do as I do. It is not worth the while to snivel about it. I am not responsible for the successful working of the machinery of society. I am not the son of the engineer. I perceive that, when an acorn and a chestnut fall side by side, the one does not remain inert to make way for the other, but both obey their own laws, and spring and grow and flourish as best they can, till one, perchance, overshadows and destroys the other. If a plant cannot live according to its nature, it dies; and so a man.

The night in prison was novel and interesting enough. The prisoners in their shirt-sleeves were enjoying a chat and the evening air in the doorway, when I entered. But the jailer said, 'Come, boys, it is time to lock up;' and so they dispersed, and I heard the sound of their steps returning into the hollow apartments. My room-mate was introduced to me by the jailer as 'a first-rate fellow and a clever man.' When the door was locked, he showed me where to hang my hat, and how he managed matters there. The rooms were whitewashed once a month; and this one, at least, was the whitest, most simply furnished, and probably the neatest apartment in the town. He naturally wanted to know where I came from, and what brought me there; and, when I had told him, I asked him in my turn how he came there, presuming him to be an honest man, of course; and, as the world goes, I believe he was. 'Why,' said he, 'they accuse me of burning a barn; but I never did it.' As near as I could discover, he had probably gone to bed in a barn when drunk, and smoked his pipe there; and so a barn was burnt. He had the reputation of being a clever man, had been there some three months waiting for his trial to come on, and would have to wait as much longer; but he was quite domesticated and contented, since he got his board for nothing, and thought that he was well treated.

He occupied one window, and I the other; and I saw that if one stayed there long, his principal business would be to look out the window. I had soon read all the tracts that were left there, and examined where former prisoners had broken out, and where a grate had been sawed off, and heard the history of the various occupants of that room; for I found that even here there was a history and a gossip which never circulated beyond the walls of the jail. Probably this is the only house in the town where verses are composed, which are afterward printed in a circular form, but not published. I was shown quite a long list of verses which were composed by some young men who had been detected in an attempt to escape, who avenged themselves by singing them.

I pumped my fellow-prisoner as dry as I could, for fear I should never see him again; but at length he showed me which was my bed, and left me to blow out the lamp.

It was like travelling into a far country, such as I had never expected to behold, to lie there for one night. It seemed to me that I never had heard the town-clock strike before, nor the evening sounds of the village; for we slept with the windows open, which were inside the grating. It was to see my native village in the light of the Middle Ages, and our Concord was turned into a Rhine stream, and visions of knights and castles passed before me. They were the voices of old burghers that I heard in the streets. I was an involuntary spectator and auditor of whatever was done and said in the kitchen of the adjacent village inn—a wholly new and rare experience to me. It was a closer view of my native town. I was fairly inside of it. I never had seen its institutions before. This is one of its peculiar institutions; for it is a shire town. I began to comprehend what its inhabitants were about.

In the morning, our breakfasts were put through the hole in the door, in small oblong-square tin pans, made to fit, and holding a pint of chocolate, with brown bread, and an iron spoon. When they called for the vessels again, I was green enough to return what bread I had left; but my comrade seized it, and said that I should lay that up for lunch or dinner. Soon after he was let out to work at haying in a neighboring field, whither he went every day, and would not be back till noon; so he bade me good-day, saying that he doubted if he should see me again.

When I came out of prison—for some one interfered, and paid that tax—I did not perceive that great changes had taken place on the common, such as he observed who went in a youth and emerged a tottering and gray-headed man; and yet a change had to my eyes come over the scene—the town, and State, and country—greater than any that mere time could effect. I saw yet more distinctly the State in which I lived. I saw to what extent the people among whom I lived could be trusted as good neighbors and friends; that their friendship was for summer weather only; that they did not greatly propose to do right; that they were a distinct race from me by their prejudices and superstitions, as the Chinamen and Malays are; that in their sacrifices to humanity they ran no risks, not even to their property; that after all they were not so noble but they treated the thief as he had treated them, and hoped, by a certain outward observance and a few prayers, and by walking in a particular straight though useless path from time to time, to save their souls. This may be to judge my neighbors harshly; for I believe that many of them are not aware that they have such an institution as the jail in their village.

It was formerly the custom in our village, when a poor debtor came out of jail, for his acquaintances to salute him, looking through their fingers, which were crossed to represent the grating of a jail window, 'How do ye do?' My neighbors did not thus salute me, but first looked at me, and then at one another, as if I had returned from a long journey. I was put into jail as I was going to the shoemaker's to get a shoe which was mended. When I was let out the next morning, I proceeded to finish my errand, and, having put on my mended shoe, joined a huckleberry party, who were impatient to put themselves under my conduct; and in half an hour—for the horse was soon tackled—was in the midst of a huckleberry field, on one of our highest hills, two miles off, and then the State was nowhere to be seen.

This is the whole history of 'My Prisons.'

I have never declined paying the highway tax, because I am as desirous of being a good neighbor as I am of being a bad subject; and as for supporting schools, I am doing my part to educate my fellow-countrymen now. It is for no particular item in the tax-bill that I refuse to pay it. I simply wish to refuse allegiance to the State, to withdraw and stand aloof from it effectually. I do not care to trace the course of my dollar, if I could, till it buys a man or a musket to shoot one with—the dollar is innocent—but I am concerned to trace the effects of my allegiance. In fact, I quietly declare war with the State, after my fashion, though I will still make what use and get what advantage of her I can, as is usual in such cases.

If others pay the tax which is demanded of me, from a sympathy with the State, they do but what they have already done in their own case, or rather they abet injustice to a greater extent than the State requires. If they pay the tax from a mistaken interest in the individual taxed, to save his property, or prevent his going to jail, it is because they have not considered wisely how far they let their private feelings interfere with the public good.

This, then, is my position at present. But one cannot be too much on his guard in such a case, lest his action be biased by obstinacy or an undue regard for the opinions of men. Let him see that he does only what belongs to himself and to the hour.

I think sometimes, Why, this people mean well, they are only ignorant; they would do better if they knew how: why give your neighbors this pain to treat you as they are not inclined to? But I think again, This is no reason why I should do as they do, or permit others to suffer much greater pain of a different kind. Again, I sometimes say to myself, When many millions of men, without heat, without ill will, without personal feeling of any kind, demand of you a few shillings only, without the possibility, such is their constitution, of retracting or altering their present demand, and without the possibility, on your side, of appeal to any other millions, why expose yourself to this overwhelming brute force? You do not resist cold and hunger, the winds and the waves, thus obstinately; you quietly submit to a thousand similar necessities. You do not put your head into the fire. But just in proportion as I regard this as not wholly a brute force, but partly a human force, and consider that I have relations to those millions as to so many millions of men, and not of mere brute or inanimate things, I see that appeal is possible, first and instantaneously, from them to the Maker of them, and, secondly, from them to themselves. But if I put my head deliberately into the fire, there is no appeal to fire or to the Maker of fire, and I have only myself to blame. If I could convince myself that I have any right to be satisfied with men as they are, and to treat them accordingly, and not according, in some respects, to my requisitions and expectations of what they and I ought to be, then, like a good Mussulman and fatalist, I should endeavor to be satisfied with things as they are, and say it is the will of God. And, above all, there is this difference between resisting this and a purely brute or natural force, that I can resist this with some effect; but I cannot expect, like Orpheus, to change the nature of the rocks and trees and beasts.

I do not wish to quarrel with any man or nation. I do not wish to split hairs, to make fine distinctions, or set myself up as better than my neighbors. I seek rather, I may say, even an excuse for conforming to the laws of the land. I am but too ready to conform to them. Indeed, I have reason to suspect myself on this head; and each year, as the tax-gatherer comes round, I find myself disposed to review the acts and position of the general and State governments, and the spirit of the people, to discover a pretext for conformity.

> 'We must affect our country as our parents,
> And if at any time we alienate
> Our love or industry from doing it honor,
> We must respect effects and teach the soul
> Matter of conscience and religion,
> And not desire of rule or benefit.'

I believe that the State will soon be able to take all my work of this sort out of my hands, and then I shall be no better a patriot than my fellow-countrymen. Seen from a lower point of view, the Constitution, with all its faults, is very good; the law and the courts are very respectable; even this State and this American government are, in many respects, very admirable, and rare things, to be thankful for, such as a great many have described them; but seen from a point of view a little higher, they are what I have described them; seen from a higher still, and the highest, who shall say what they are, or that they are worth looking at or thinking of at all?

However, the government does not concern me much, and I shall bestow the fewest possible thoughts on it. It is not many moments that I live under a government, even in this world. If a man is thought-free, fancy-free, imagination-free, that which *is not* never for a long time appearing *to be* to him, unwise rulers or reformers cannot fatally interrupt him.

I know that most men think differently from myself; but those whose lives are by profession devoted to the study of these or kindred subjects content me as little as any. Statesmen and legislators, standing so completely within the institution, never distinctly and nakedly behold it. They speak of moving society, but have no resting-place without it. They may be men of a certain experience and discrimination, and have no doubt invented ingenious and even useful systems, for which we sincerely thank them; but all their wit and usefulness lie within certain not very wide limits. They are wont to forget that the world is not governed by policy and expediency. Webster never goes behind government, and so cannot speak with authority about it. His words are wisdom to those legislators who contemplate no essential reform in the existing government; but for thinkers, and those who legislate for all time, he never once glances at the subject. I know of those whose serene and wise speculations on this theme would soon reveal the limits of his mind's range and hospitality. Yet, compared with the cheap professions of most reformers, and the still cheaper wisdom and eloquence of politicians in general, his are almost the only sensible and valuable words, and we thank Heaven for him. Comparatively, he is always strong, original, and, above all, practical. Still, his quality is not wisdom, but prudence. The lawyer's truth is not Truth, but consistency or a consistent expediency. Truth is always in harmony with herself, and is not concerned chiefly to reveal the justice that may consist with wrong-doing. He well deserves to be called, as he has been called, the Defender of the Constitution. There are really no blows to be given by him but defensive ones. He is not a leader, but a follower. His leaders are the men of '87—'I have never made an effort,' he says, 'and never propose to make an effort; I have never countenanced an effort, and never mean to countenance an effort, to disturb the arrangement as originally made, by which the various States came into the Union.' Still thinking of the sanction which the Constitution gives to slavery, he says, 'Because it was a part of the original compact—let it stand.' Notwithstanding his special acuteness and ability, he is unable to take a fact out of its merely political relations, and behold it as it lies absolutely to be disposed of by the intellect—what, for instance, it behooves a man to do here in America today with regard to slavery—but ventures, or is driven, to make some such desperate answer as the following, while professing to speak absolutely, and as a private man—from which what new and singular code of social duties might be inferred? 'The manner,' says he, 'in which the governments of those States where slavery exists are to regulate it is for their own consideration, under their responsibility to their constituents, to the general laws of propriety, humanity, and justice, and to God. Associations formed elsewhere, springing from a feeling of humanity, or any other cause, have nothing whatever to do with it. They have never received any encouragement from me, and they never will.'

They who know of no purer sources of truth, who have traced up its stream no higher, stand, and wisely stand, by the Bible and the Constitution, and drink at it there with reverence and humility; but they who behold where it comes trickling into this lake or that pool, gird up their loins once more, and continue their pilgrimage toward its fountain-head.

No man with a genius for legislation has appeared in America. They are rare in the history of the world. There are orators, politicians, and eloquent men, by the thousand; but the speaker has not yet opened his mouth to speak who is capable of settling the much-vexed questions of the day. We love eloquence for its own sake, and not for any truth which it may utter, or any heroism it may inspire. Our legislators have not yet learned the comparative value of free trade and of freedom, of union, and of rectitude, to a nation. They have no genius or talent for comparatively humble questions of taxation and finance, commerce and manufactures and agriculture. If we were left solely to the wordy wit of legislators in Congress for our guidance, uncorrected by the seasonable experience and the effectual complaints of the people, America would not long retain her rank among the nations. For eighteen hundred years, though perchance I have no right to say it, the New Testament has been written; yet where is the legislator who has wisdom and practical talent enough to avail himself of the light which it sheds on the science of legislation?

The authority of government, even such as I am willing to submit to—for I will cheerfully obey those who know and can do better than I, and in many things even those who neither know nor can do so well—is still an impure one: to be strictly just, it must have the sanction and consent of the governed. It can have no pure right over my person and property but what I concede to it. The progress from an absolute to a limited monarchy, from a limited monarchy to a democracy, is a progress toward a true respect for the individual. Even the Chinese philosopher was wise enough to regard the individual as the basis of the empire. Is a democracy, such as we know it, the last improvement possible in government? Is it not possible to take a step further towards recognizing and organizing the rights of man? There will never be a really free and enlightened State until the State comes to recognize the individual as a higher and independent power, from which all its own power and authority are derived, and treats him accordingly. I please myself with imagining a State at least which can afford to be just to all men, and to treat the individual with respect as a neighbor; which even would not think it inconsistent with its own repose if a few were to live aloof from it, not meddling with it, nor embraced by it, who fulfilled all the duties of neighbors and fellow-men. A State which bore this kind of fruit, and suffered it to drop off as fast as it ripened, would prepare the way for a still more perfect and glorious State, which also I have imagined, but not yet anywhere seen.

14

THE LANTERN BEARERS

Robert Louis Stevenson

I

These boys congregated every autumn about a certain easterly fisher-village, where they tasted in a high degree the glory of existence. The place was created seemingly on purpose for the diversion of young gentlemen. A street or two of houses, mostly red and many of, them tiled; a number of fine trees clustered about the manse and the kirkyard, and turning the chief street into a shady alley; many little gardens more than usually bright with flowers; nets a-drying, and fisher-wives scolding in the backward parts; a smell of fish, a genial smell of seaweed; whiffs of blowing sand at the street-corners; shops with golf-balls and bottled lollipops; another shop with penny pickwicks (that remarkable cigar) and the *London Journal*, dear to me for its startling pictures, and a few novels, dear for their suggestive names: such, as well as memory serves me, were the ingredients of the town. These, you are to conceive posted on a spit between two sandy bays, and sparsely flanked with villas—enough for the boys to lodge in with their subsidiary parents, not enough (not yet enough) to cocknify the scene: a haven in the rocks in front: in front of that, a file of gray islets: to the left, endless links and sand wreaths, a wilderness of hiding-holes, alive with popping rabbits and soaring gulls: to the right, a range of seaward crags, one rugged brow beyond another; the ruins of a mighty and ancient fortress on the brink of one; coves between—now charmed into sunshine quiet, now whistling with wind and clamorous with bursting surges; the dens and sheltered hollows redolent of thyme and southernwood, the air at the cliff's edge brisk and clean and pungent of the sea—in front of all, the Bass Rock, tilted seaward like a doubtful bather, the surf ringing it with white, the solan-geese hanging round its summit like a great and glittering smoke. This choice piece of seaboard was sacred, besides, to the wrecker; and the Bass, in the eye of fancy, still flew the colours of King James; and in the ear of fancy the arches of Tantallon still rang with horse-shoe iron, and echoed to the commands of Bell-the-Cat.

There was nothing to mar your days, if you were a boy summering in that part, but the embarrassment of pleasure. You might golf if you wanted; but I seem to have been better employed. You might secrete yourself in the Lady's Walk, a certain sunless dingle of elders, all mossed over by the damp as green as grass, and dotted here and there by the stream-side with roofless walls, the cold homes of anchorites. To fit themselves for life, and with a special eye to acquire the art of smoking, it was even common for the boys to harbour there; and you might have seen a single penny pickwick, honestly shared in lengths with a blunt knife, bestrew the glen with these apprentices. Again, you might join our fishing parties, where we sat perched as thick as solan-geese, a covey of little anglers, boy and girl, angling over each other's heads, to the much entanglement of lines and loss of podleys and consequent shrill recrimination—shrill as the geese themselves. Indeed, had that been all, you might have done this often; but though fishing be a fine pastime, the podley is scarce to be regarded as a dainty for the table; and it was a point of honour that a boy should eat all that he had taken. Or again, you might climb the Law, where the whale's jawbone stood landmark in the buzzing wind, and behold the face of many counties, and the smoke and spires of many towns, and the sails of distant ships. You might bathe, now in the flaws of fine weather, that we pathetically call our summer, now in a gale of wind, with the sand scourging your bare hide, your clothes thrashing abroad from underneath their guardian stone, the froth of the great breakers casting you headlong ere it had drowned your knees. Or you might explore the tidal rocks, above all in the ebb of springs, when the very roots of the hills were for the nonce discovered; following my leader from one group to another, groping in slippery tangle for the wreck of ships, wading in pools after the abominable creatures of the sea, and ever with an eye cast backward on the march off the tide and the menaced line of your retreat. And then you might go Crusoeing, a word that covers all extempore eating in the open air: digging perhaps a house under the margin of the links, kindling a fire of the sea-ware, and cooking apples there—if they were truly apples, for I sometimes suppose the merchant must have played us off with some inferior and quite local fruit capable of resolving, in the neighbourhood of fire, into mere sand and smoke and iodine; or perhaps pushing to Tantallon, you might lunch on sandwiches and visions in the grassy court, while the wind hummed in the crumbling turrets; or clambering along the coast, eat geans (the worst, I must suppose, in Christendom) from an adventurous gean tree that had taken root under a cliff, where it was shaken with an ague of east wind, and silvered after gales with salt, and grew so foreign among its bleak surroundings that to eat of its produce was an adventure in itself.

There are mingled some dismal memories with so many that were joyous. Of the fisher-wife, for instance, who had cut her throat at Canty Bay; and of how I ran with the other children to the top of the Quadrant, and beheld a posse of silent people escorting a cart, and on the cart, bound in a chair, her throat bandaged, and the bandage all bloody—horror!—the fisher-wife herself, who continued thenceforth to hag-ride my thoughts, and even to-day (as I recall the scene) darkens daylight. She was lodged in the little old jail in the chief street; but whether or no she died there, with a wise terror of the worst, I never inquired. She had been tippling; it was but a dingy tragedy; and it seems strange and hard that, after all these years, the poor crazy sinner should be still pilloried on her cart in the scrap-book of my memory. Nor shall I readily forget a certain house in the Quadrant where a visitor died, and a dark old woman continued to dwell alone with the dead body; nor how this old woman conceived a hatred to myself and one of my cousins, and in the dread hour of the dusk, as we were clambering on the garden-walls, opened a window in that house of mortality and cursed us in a shrill voice and with a marrowy choice of language. It was a pair of very colourless urchins that fled down the lane from this remarkable experience! But I recall with a more doubtful sentiment, compounded out of fear and exultation, the coil of equinoctial tempests; trumpeting squalls, scouring flaws of rain; the boats with their reefed lugsails scudding for the harbour mouth, where danger lay, for it was hard to make when the wind had any east in it; the wives clustered with blowing shawls at the pier-head, where (if fate was against them) they might see boat and husband and sons—their whole wealth and their whole family—engulfed under their eyes; and (what I saw but once) a troop of neighbours forcing such an unfortunate homeward, and she squalling and battling in their midst, a figure scarcely human, a tragic Mænad.

These are things that I recall with interest; but what my memory dwells upon the most, I have been all this while withholding. It was a sport peculiar to the place, and indeed to a week or so of our two months' holiday there. Maybe it still flourishes in its native spot; for boys and their pastimes are swayed by periodic forces inscrutable to man; so that tops and marbles reappear in their due season, regular like the sun and moon; and the harmless art of knucklebones has seen the fall of the Roman empire and the rise of the United States. It may still flourish in its native spot, but nowhere else, I am persuaded; for I tried myself to introduce it on Tweedside, and was defeated lamentably; its charm being quite local, like a country wine that cannot be exported.

The idle manner of it was this:—

Toward the end of September, when school-time was drawing near and the nights were already black, we would begin to sally from our-respective villas, each equipped with a tin bull's-eye lantern. The thing was so well known that it had worn a rut in the commerce of Great Britain; and the grocers, about the due time, began to garnish their windows with our particular brand of luminary. We wore them buckled to the waist upon a cricket belt, and over them, such was the rigour of the game, a buttoned top-coat. They smelled noisomely of blistered tin; they never burned aright, though they would always burn our fingers; their use was naught; the pleasure of them merely fanciful; and yet a boy with a bull's-eye under his top-coat asked for nothing more. The fishermen used lanterns about their boats, and it was from them, I suppose, that we had got the hint; but theirs were not bull's-eyes, nor did we ever play at being fishermen. The police carried them at their belts, and we had plainly copied them in that; yet we did not pretend to be policemen. Burglars, indeed, we may have had some haunting thoughts of; and we had certainly an eye to past ages when lanterns were more common, and to certain story-books in which we had found them to figure very largely. But take it for all in all, the pleasure of the thing was substantive; and to be a boy with a bull's-eye under his top-coat was good enough for us.

When two of these asses met, there would be an anxious 'Have you got your lantern?' and a gratified 'Yes!' That was the shibboleth, and very needful too; for, as it was the rule to keep our glory contained, none could recognize a lantern-bearer, unless (like the polecat) by the smell. Four or five would sometimes climb into the belly of a ten-man lugger, with nothing but the thwarts above them—for the cabin was usually locked, or choose out some hollow of the links where the wind might whistle overhead. There the coats would be unbuttoned and the bull's-eyes discovered; and in the chequering glimmer, under the huge windy hall of the night, and cheered by a rich steam of toasting tinware, these fortunate young gentlemen would crouch together in the cold sand of the links or on the scaly bilges of the fishing-boat, and delight themselves with inappropriate talk. Woe is me that I may not give some specimens—some of their foresights of life, or deep inquiries into the rudiments of man and nature, these were so fiery and so innocent, they were so richly silly, so romantically young. But the talk, at any rate, was but a condiment; and these gatherings themselves only accidents in the career of the lantern-bearer. The essence of this bliss was to walk by yourself in the black night; the slide shut, the top-coat buttoned; not a ray escaping, whether to conduct your footsteps or to make your glory public: a mere pillar of darkness in the dark; and all the while, deep down in the privacy of your fool's heart, to know you had a bull's-eye at your belt, and to exult and sing over the knowledge.

II

It is said that a poet has died young in the breast of the most stolid. It may be contended, rather, that this (somewhat minor) bard in almost every case survives, and is the spice of life to his possessor. Justice is not done to the versatility and the unplumbed childishness of man's imagination. His life from without may seem but a rude mound of mud; there will be some golden chamber at the heart of it, in which he dwells delighted; and for as dark as his pathway seems to the observer, he will have some kind of a bull's-eye at his belt.

It would be hard to pick out a career more cheerless than that of Dancer, the miser, as he figures in the 'Old Bailey Reports,' a prey to the most sordid persecutions, the butt of his neighbourhood, betrayed by his hired man, his house beleaguered by the impish schoolboy, and he himself grinding and fuming and impotently fleeing to the law against these pin-pricks. You marvel at first that any one should willingly prolong a life so destitute of charm and dignity; and then you call to memory that had he chosen, had he ceased to be a miser, he could have been freed at once from these trials, and might have built himself a castle and gone escorted by a squadron. For the love of more recondite joys, which we cannot estimate, which, it may be, we should envy, the man had willingly forgone both comfort and consideration. 'His mind to him a kingdom was'; and sure enough, digging into that mind, which seems at first a dust-heap, we unearth some priceless jewels. For Dancer must have had the love of power and the disdain of using it, a noble character in itself; disdain of many pleasures, a chief part of what is commonly called wisdom; disdain of the inevitable end, that finest trait of mankind; scorn of men's opinions, another element of virtue; and at the back of all, a conscience just like yours and mine, whining like a cur, swindling like a thimble-rigger, but still pointing (there or there-about) to some conventional standard. Here were a cabinet portrait to which Hawthorne perhaps had done justice; and yet not Hawthorne either, for he was mildly minded, and it lay not in him to create for us that throb of the miser's pulse, his fretful energy of gusto, his vast arms of ambition clutching in he knows not what: insatiable, insane, a god with a muck-rake. Thus, at least, looking in the bosom of the miser, consideration detects the poet in the full tide of life, with more, indeed, of the poetic fire than usually goes to epics; and tracing that mean man about his cold hearth, and to and fro in his discomfortable house, spies within him a blazing bonfire of delight. And so with others, who do not live by bread alone, but by some cherished and perhaps fantastic pleasure; who are meat salesmen to the external eye, and possibly to themselves are Shakespeares, Napoleons, or Beethovens; who have not one virtue to rub against another in the field of active life, and yet perhaps, in the life of contemplation, sit with the saints. We see them on the street, and we can count their buttons; but heaven knows in what they pride themselves! heaven knows where they have set their treasure!

There is one fable that touches very near the quick of life: the fable of the monk who passed into the woods, heard a bird break into song, hearkened for a trill or two, and found himself on his return a stranger at his convent gates; for he had been absent fifty years, and of all his comrades there survived but one to recognize him. It is not only in the woods that this enchanter carols, though perhaps he is native there. He sings in the most doleful places. The miser hears him and chuckles, and the days are moments. With no more apparatus than an ill-smelling lantern I have evoked him on the naked links. All life that is not merely mechanical is spun out of two strands: seeking for that bird and hearing him. And it is just this that makes life so hard to value, and the delight of each so incommunicable. And just a knowledge of this, and a remembrance of those fortunate hours in which the bird has sung to us, that fills us with such wonder when we turn the pages of the realist. There, to be sure, we find a picture of life in so far as it consists of mud and of old iron, cheap desires and cheap fears, that which we are ashamed to remember and that which we are careless whether we forget; but of the note of that time-devouring nightingale we hear no news.

The case of these writers of romance is most obscure. They have been boys and youths; they have lingered outside the window of the beloved, who was then most probably writing to some one else; they have sat before a sheet of paper, and felt themselves mere continents of congested poetry, not one line of which would flow; they have walked alone in the woods, they have walked in cities under the countless lamps; they have been to sea, they have hated, they have feared, they have longed to knife a man, and maybe done it; the wild taste of life has stung their palate. Or, if you deny them all the rest, one pleasure at least they have tasted to the full—their books are there to prove it—the keen pleasure of successful literary composition. And yet they fill the globe with volumes, whose cleverness inspires me with despairing admiration, and whose consistent falsity to all I care to call existence, with despairing wrath. If I had no better hope than to continue to revolve among the dreary and petty businesses, and to be moved by the paltry hopes and fears with which they surround and animate their heroes, I declare I would die now. But there has never an hour of mine gone quite so dully yet; if it were spent waiting at a railway junction, I would have some scattering thoughts, I could count some grains of memory, compared to which the whole of one of these romances seems but dross.

These writers would retort (if I take them properly) that this was very true; that it was the same with themselves and other persons of (what they call) the artistic temperament; that in this we were exceptional, and should apparently be ashamed of ourselves; but that our works must deal exclusively with (what they call) the average man, who was a prodigious dull fellow, and quite dead to all but the paltriest considerations. I accept the issue. We can only know others by ourselves. The artistic temperament (a plague on the expression!) does not make us different from our fellowmen, or it would make us incapable of writing novels; and the average man (a murrain on the word!) is just like you and me, or he would not be average. It was Whitman who stamped a kind of Birmingham sacredness upon the latter phrase; but Whitman knew very well, and showed very nobly, that the average man was full of joys and full of a poetry of his own. And this harping on life's dulness and man's meanness is a loud profession of incompetence; it is one of two things: the cry of the blind eye, *I cannot see*, or the complaint of the dumb tongue, *I cannot utter*. To draw a life without delights is to prove I have not realized it. To picture a man without some sort of poetry—well, it goes near to prove my case, for it shows an author may have little enough. To see Dancer only as a dirty, old, small-minded, impotently fuming man, in a dirty house, besieged by Harrow boys, and probably beset by small attorneys, is to show myself as keen an observer as... the Harrow boys. But these young gentlemen (with a more becoming modesty) were content to pluck Dancer by the coat-tails; they did not suppose they had surprised his secret or could put him living in a book: and it is there my error would have lain. Or say that in the same romance—I continue to call these books romances, in the hope of giving pain—say that in the same romance, which now begins really to take shape, I should leave to speak of Dancer, and follow instead the Harrow boys; and say that I came on some such business as that of my lantern-bearers on the links; and described the boys as very cold, spat upon by flurries of rain, and drearily surrounded, all of which they were; and their talk as silly and indecent, which it certainly was. I might upon these lines, and had I Zola's genius, turn out, in a page or so, a gem of literary art, render the lantern-light with the touches of a master, and lay on the indecency with the ungrudging hand of love; and when all was done, what a triumph would my picture be of shallowness and dulness! how it would have missed the point! how it would have belied the boys! To the ear of the stenographer, the talk is merely silly and indecent; but ask the boys themselves, and they are discussing (as it is highly proper they should) the possibilities of existence. To the eye of the observer they are wet and cold and drearily surrounded; but ask themselves, and they are in the heaven of a recondite pleasure, the ground of which is an ill-smelling lantern.

III

For, to repeat, the ground of a man's joy is often hard to hit. It may hinge at times upon a mere accessory, like the lantern; it may reside, like Dancer's, in the mysterious inwards of psychology. It may consist with perpetual failure, and find exercise in the continued chase.

It has so little bond with externals (such as the observer scribbles in his note-book) that it may even touch them not; and the man's true life, for which he consents to live, lie altogether in the field of fancy. The clergyman, in his spare hours, may be winning battles, the farmer sailing ships, the banker reaping triumph in the arts: all leading another life, plying another trade from that they chose; like the poet's housebuilder, who, after all, is cased in stone,

> 'By his fireside, as impotent fancy prompts.
> Rebuilds it to his liking.'

In such a case the poetry runs underground. The observer (poor soul, with his documents!) is all abroad. For to look at the man is but to court deception. We shall see the trunk from which he draws his nourishment; but he himself is above and abroad in the green dome of foliage, hummed through by winds and nested in by nightingales. And the true realism were that of the poets, to climb up after him like a squirrel, and catch some glimpse of the heaven for which he lives.

And, the true realism, always and everywhere, is that of the poets: to find out where joy resides, and give it a voice far beyond singing.

For to miss the joy is to miss all. In the joy of the actors lies the sense of any action. That is the explanation, that the excuse. To one who has not the secret of the lanterns, the scene upon the links is meaningless. And hence the haunting and truly spectral unreality of realistic books. Hence, when we read the English realists, the incredulous wonder with which we observe the hero's constancy under the submerging tide of dulness, and how he bears up with his jibbing sweetheart, and endures the chatter of idiot girls, and stands by his whole unfeatured wilderness of an existence, instead of seeking relief in drink or foreign travel. Hence in the French, in that meat-market of middle-aged sensuality, the disgusted surprise with which we see the hero drift sidelong, and practically quite untempted, into every description of misconduct and dishonour. In each, we miss the personal poetry, the enchanted atmosphere, that rainbow work of fancy that clothes what is naked and seems to ennoble what is base; in each, life falls dead like dough, instead of soaring away like a balloon into the colours of the sunset; each is true, each inconceivable; for no man lives in the external truth, among salts and acids, but in the warm, phantasmagoric chamber of his brain, with the painted windows and the storied walls.

Of this falsity we have had a recent example from a man who knows far better—Tolstoi's *Powers of Darkness.* Here is a piece full of force and truth, yet quite untrue. For before Mikita was led into so dire a situation he was tempted, and temptations are beautiful at least in part; and a work which dwells on the ugliness of crime and gives no hint of any loveliness in the temptation, sins against the modesty of life, and even when a Tolstoi writes it, sinks to melodrama. The peasants are not understood; they saw their life in fairer colours; even the deaf girl was clothed in poetry for Mikita, or he had never fallen. And so, once again, even an Old Bailey melodrama, without some brightness of poetry and lustre of existence, falls into the inconceivable and ranks with fairy tales.

IV

In nobler books we are moved with something like the emotions of life; and this emotion is very variously provoked. We are so moved when Levine labours in the field, when André sinks beyond emotion, when Richard Feverel and Lucy Desborough meet beside the river, when Antony, 'not cowardly, puts off his helmet,' when Kent has infinite pity on the dying Lear, when, in Dostoieffky's *Despised and Rejected,* the uncomplaining hero drains his cup of suffering and virtue. These are notes that please the great heart of man. Not only love, and the fields, and the bright face of danger, but sacrifice and death and unmerited suffering humbly supported, touch in us the vein of the poetic. We love to think of them, we long to try them, we are humbly hopeful that we may prove heroes also.

We have heard, perhaps, too much of lesser matters. Here is the door, here is the open air. *Itur in antiquam silvam.*

15

HOW TO TELL A STORY

Mark Twain

The Humorous Story an American Development.—Its Difference from Comic and Witty Stories

I do not claim that I can tell a story as it ought to be told. I only claim to know how a story ought to be told, for I have been almost daily in the company of the most expert story-tellers for many years.

There are several kinds of stories, but only one difficult kind—the humorous. I will talk mainly about that one. The humorous story is American, the comic story is English, the witty story is French. The humorous story depends for its effect upon the *manner* of the telling; the comic story and the witty story upon the *matter*.

The humorous story may be spun out to great length, and may wander around as much as it pleases, and arrive nowhere in particular; but the comic and witty stories must be brief and end with a point. The humorous story bubbles gently along, the others burst.

The humorous story is strictly a work of art—high and delicate art—and only an artist can tell it; but no art is necessary in telling the comic and the witty story; anybody can do it. The art of telling a humorous story—understand, I mean by word of mouth, not print—was created in America, and has remained at home.

The humorous story is told gravely; the teller does his best to conceal the fact that he even dimly suspects that there is anything funny about it; but the teller of the comic story tells you beforehand that it is one of the funniest things he has ever heard, then tells it with eager delight, and is the first person to laugh when he gets through. And sometimes, if he has had good success, he is so glad and happy that he will repeat the 'nub' of it and glance around from face to face, collecting applause, and then repeat it again. It is a pathetic thing to see.

Very often, of course, the rambling and disjointed humorous story finishes with a nub, point, snapper, or whatever you like to call it. Then the listener must be alert, for in many cases the teller will divert attention from that nub by dropping it in a carefully casual and indifferent way, with the pretence that he does not know it is a nub.

Artemus Ward used that trick a good deal; then when the belated audience presently caught the joke he would look up with innocent surprise, as if wondering what they had found to laugh at. Dan Setchell used it before him, Nye and Riley and others use it to-day.

But the teller of the comic story does not slur the nub; he shouts it at you—every time. And when he prints it, in England, France, Germany, and Italy, he italicizes it, puts some whooping exclamation-points after it, and sometimes explains it in a parenthesis. All of which is very depressing, and makes one want to renounce joking and lead a better life.

Let me set down an instance of the comic method, using an anecdote which has been popular all over the world for twelve or fifteen hundred years. The teller tells it in this way:

The Wounded Soldier.

In the course of a certain battle a soldier whose leg had been shot off appealed to another soldier who was hurrying by to carry him to the rear, informing him at the same time of the loss which he had sustained; whereupon the generous son of Mars, shouldering the unfortunate, proceeded to carry out his desire. The bullets and cannon-balls were flying in all directions, and presently one of the latter took the wounded man's head off—without, however, his deliverer being aware of it. In no long time he was hailed by an officer, who said:

'Where are you going with that carcass?'

'To the rear, sir—he's lost his leg!'

'His leg, forsooth?' responded the astonished officer; 'you mean his head, you booby.'

Whereupon the soldier dispossessed himself of his burden, and stood looking down upon it in great perplexity. At length he said:

'It is true, sir, just as you have said.' Then after a pause he added, 'But he TOLD me IT WAS HIS LEG—'

Here the narrator bursts into explosion after explosion of thunderous horse-laughter, repeating that nub from time to time through his gaspings and shriekings and suffocatings.

It takes only a minute and a half to tell that in its comic-story form; and isn't worth the telling, after all. Put into the humorous-story form it takes ten minutes, and is about the funniest thing I have ever listened to—as James Whitcomb Riley tells it.

He tells it in the character of a dull-witted old farmer who has just heard it for the first time, thinks it is unspeakably funny, and is trying to repeat it to a neighbor. But he can't remember it; so he gets all mixed up and wanders helplessly round and round, putting in tedious details that don't belong in the tale and only retard it; taking them out conscientiously and putting in others that are just as useless; making minor mistakes now and then and stopping to correct them and explain how he came to make them; remembering things which he forgot to put in in their proper place and going back to put them in there; stopping his narrative a good while in order to try to recall the name of the soldier that was hurt, and finally remembering that the soldier's name was not mentioned, and remarking placidly that the name is of no real importance, anyway—better, of course, if one knew it, but not essential, after all—and so on, and so on, and so on.

The teller is innocent and happy and pleased with himself, and has to stop every little while to hold himself in and keep from laughing outright; and does hold in, but his body quakes in a jelly-like way with interior chuckles; and at the end of the ten minutes the audience have laughed until they are exhausted, and the tears are running down their faces.

The simplicity and innocence and sincerity and unconsciousness of the old farmer are perfectly simulated, and the result is a performance which is thoroughly charming and delicious. This is art and fine and beautiful, and only a master can compass it; but a machine could tell the other story.

To string incongruities and absurdities together in a wandering and sometimes purposeless way, and seem innocently unaware that they are absurdities, is the basis of the American art, if my position is correct. Another feature is the slurring of the point. A third is the dropping of a studied remark apparently without knowing it, as if one were thinking aloud. The fourth and last is the pause.

Artemus Ward dealt in numbers three and four a good deal. He would begin to tell with great animation something which he seemed to think was wonderful; then lose confidence, and after an apparently absent-minded pause add an incongruous remark in a soliloquizing way; and that was the remark intended to explode the mine—and it did.

For instance, he would say eagerly, excitedly, 'I once knew a man in New Zealand who hadn't a tooth in his head'—here his animation would die out; a silent, reflective pause would follow, then he would say dreamily, and as if to himself, 'and yet that man could beat a drum better than any man I ever saw.'

The pause is an exceedingly important feature in any kind of story, and a frequently recurring feature, too. It is a dainty thing, and delicate, and also uncertain and treacherous; for it must be exactly the right length—no more and no less—or it fails of its purpose and makes trouble. If the pause is too short the impressive point is passed, and [and if too long] the audience have had time to divine that a surprise is intended—and then you can't surprise them, of course.

On the platform I used to tell a negro ghost story that had a pause in front of the snapper on the end, and that pause was the most important thing in the whole story. If I got it the right length precisely, I could spring the finishing ejaculation with effect enough to make some impressible girl deliver a startled little yelp and jump out of her seat—and that was what I was after. This story was called

'The Golden Arm,' and was told in this fashion. You can practise with it yourself—and mind you look out for the pause and get it right.

The Golden Arm.

Once 'pon a time dey wuz a monsus mean man, en he live 'way out in de prairie all 'lone by hisself, 'cep'n he had a wife. En bimeby she died, en he tuck en toted her way out dah in de prairie en buried her. Well, she had a golden arm—all solid gold, fum de shoulder down. He wuz pow'ful mean—pow'ful; en dat night he couldn't sleep, caze he want dat golden arm so bad.

When it come midnight he couldn't stan' it no mo'; so he git up, he did, en tuck his lantern en shoved out thoo de storm en dug her up en got de golden arm; en he bent his head down 'gin de win', en plowed en plowed en plowed thoo de snow. Den all on a sudden he stop (make a considerable pause here, and look startled, and take a listening attitude) en say: 'My *lan'*, what's dat!'

En he listen—en listen—en de win' say (set your teeth together and imitate the wailing and wheezing singsong of the wind), 'Bzzz-z-zzz'—en den, way back yonder whah de grave is, he hear a *voice*! he hear a voice all mix' up in de win' can't hardly tell 'em 'part—'Bzzz-zzz—W-h-o—g-o-t—m-y—g-o-l-d-e-n *arm*?—zzz—zzz—W-h-o g-o-t m-y g-o-l-d-e-n *arm*!" (You must begin to shiver violently now.)

En he begin to shiver en shake, en say, 'Oh, my! *Oh*, my lan'!' en de win' blow de lantern out, en de snow en sleet blow in his face en mos' choke him, en he start a-plowin' knee-deep towards home mos' dead, he so sk'yerd—en pooty soon he hear de voice agin, en (pause) it 'us comin' *after* him! 'Bzzz—zzz—zzz—W-h-o—g-o-t m-y—g-o-l-d-e-n—*arm*?'

When he git to de pasture he hear it agin closter now, en a-*comin'*!—a-comin' back dah in de dark en de storm—(repeat the wind and the voice). When he git to de house he rush up-stairs en jump in de bed en kiver up, head and years, en lay dah shiverin' en shakin'—en den way out dah he hear it *agin*!—en a-*comin'*! En bimeby he hear (pause—awed, listening attitude)—pat—pat—pat—

hit's a-comin' up-stairs! Den he hear de latch, en he *know* it's in de room!

Den pooty soon he know it's a-*stannin' by de bed*! (Pause.) Den—he know it's a-*bendin' down over him*—en he cain't skasely git his breath! Den—den—he seem to feel someth'n *c-o-l-d*, right down 'most agin his head! (Pause.)

Den de voice say, *right at his year*—'W-h-o g-o-t—m-y—g-o-l-d-e-n *arm*?' (You must wail it out very plaintively and accusingly; then you stare steadily and impressively into the face of the farthest-gone auditor—a girl, preferably—and let that awe-inspiring pause begin to build itself in the deep hush. When it has reached exactly the right length, jump suddenly at that girl and yell, '*You've* got it!')

If you've got the pause right, she'll fetch a dear little yelp and spring right out of her shoes. But you must get the pause right; and you will find it the most troublesome and aggravating and uncertain thing you ever undertook.

16

OF TRUTH

Francis Bacon

'What is truth?' said jesting Pilate, and would not stay for an answer. Certainly, there be that delight in giddiness, and count it a bondage to fix a belief, affecting free-will in thinking as well as in acting. And though the sects of philosophers of that kind be gone, yet there remain certain discoursing wits which are of the same veins, though there be not so much blood in them as was in those of the ancients. But it is not only the difficulty and labor which men take in finding out of truth, nor again that when it is found it imposeth upon men's thoughts, that doth bring lies in favor, but a natural though corrupt love of the lie itself. One of the later school of the Grecians examineth the matter, and is at a stand to think what should be in it, that men should love lies where neither they make for pleasure, as with poets, nor for advantage, as with the merchant; but for the lie's sake. But I cannot tell: this same truth is a naked and open daylight that doth not show the masques and mummeries and triumphs of the world half so stately and daintily as candle-lights. Truth may perhaps come to the price of a pearl that showeth best by day; but it will not rise to the price of a diamond or carbuncle, that showeth best in varied lights. A mixture of a lie doth ever add pleasure. Doth any man doubt that if there were taken out of men's minds vain opinions, flattering hopes, false valuations, imaginations as one would, and the like, but it would leave the minds of a number of men poor shrunken things, full of melancholy and indisposition, and unpleasing to themselves? One of the fathers, in great severity, called poesy *vinum daemonum* [the wine of devils] because it filleth the imagination, and yet it is but with the shadow of a lie. But it is not the lie that passeth through the mind, but the lie that sinketh in and settleth in it that doth the hurt, such as we spake of before. But howsoever these things are thus in men's depraved judgments and affections, yet truth, which only doth judge itself, teacheth that the inquiry of truth, which is the love-making or wooing of it; the knowledge of truth, which is the presence of it; and the belief of truth, which is the enjoying of it, is the sovereign good of human nature.

The first creature of God, in the works of the days, was the light of the sense; the last was the light of reason; and his Sabbath work ever since is the illumination of his spirit. First he breathed light upon the face of the matter, or chaos; then he breathed light into the face of man; and still he breatheth and inspireth light into the face of his chosen. The poet that beautified the sect that was otherwise inferior to the rest, saith yet excellently well, 'It is a pleasure to stand upon the shore, and to see ships tossed upon the sea; a pleasure to stand in the window of a castle, and to see a battle and the adventures thereof below; but no pleasure is comparable to the standing upon the vantage ground of truth (a hill not to be commanded, and where the air is always clear and serene), and to see the errors and wanderings and mists and tempests in the vale below;' so always that this prospect be with pity, and not with swelling or pride. Certainly it is heaven upon earth to have a man's mind move in charity, rest in providence, and turn upon the poles of truth.

To pass from theological and philosophical truth to the truth of civil business: it will be acknowledged, even by those that practise it not, that clear and round dealing is the honor of man's nature, and that mixture of falsehood is like alloy in coin of gold and silver, which may make the metal work the better, but it embaseth it. For these winding and crooked courses are the goings of the serpent, which goeth basely upon the belly and not upon the feet. There is no vice that doth so cover a man with shame as to be found false and perfidious; and therefore Montaigne saith prettily, when he inquired the reason why the word of the lie should be such a disgrace and such an odious charge. Saith he, 'If it be well weighed, to say that a man lieth, is as much as to say that he is brave towards God, and a coward towards man.' For a lie faces God, and shrinks from man. Surely the wickedness of falsehood and breach of faith cannot possibly be so highly expressed as in that it shall be the last peal to call the judgments of God upon the generations of men: it being foretold that when Christ cometh, 'He shall not find faith upon the earth.'

17

THE LONG VOYAGE

Charles Dickens

When the wind is blowing and the sleet or rain is driving against the dark windows, I love to sit by the fire, thinking of what I have read in books of voyage and travel. Such books have had a strong fascination for my mind from my earliest childhood; and I wonder it should have come to pass that I never have been round the world, never have been shipwrecked, ice-environed, tomahawked, or eaten.

Sitting on my ruddy hearth in the twilight of New Year's Eve, I find incidents of travel rise around me from all the latitudes and longitudes of the globe. They observe no order or sequence, but appear and vanish as they will—'come like shadows, so depart.' Columbus, alone upon the sea with his disaffected crew, looks over the waste of waters from his high station on the poop of his ship, and sees the first uncertain glimmer of the light, 'rising and falling with the waves, like a torch in the bark of some fisherman,' which is the shining star of a new world. Bruce is caged in Abyssinia, surrounded by the gory horrors which shall often startle him out of his sleep at home when years have passed away. Franklin, come to the end of his unhappy overland journey—would that it had been his last!—lies perishing of hunger with his brave companions: each emaciated figure stretched upon its miserable bed without the power to rise: all, dividing the weary days between their prayers, their remembrances of the dear ones at home, and conversation on the pleasures of eating; the last-named topic being ever present to them, likewise, in their dreams. All the African travellers, wayworn, solitary and sad, submit themselves again to drunken, murderous, man-selling despots, of the lowest order of humanity; and Mungo Park, fainting under a tree and succoured by a woman, gratefully remembers how his Good Samaritan has always come to him in woman's shape, the wide world over.

A shadow on the wall in which my mind's eye can discern some traces of a rocky sea-coast, recalls to me a fearful story of travel derived from that unpromising narrator of such stories, a parliamentary blue-book. A convict is its chief figure, and this man escapes with other prisoners from a penal settlement. It is an island, and they seize a boat, and get to the main land. Their way is by a rugged and precipitous sea-shore, and they have no earthly hope of ultimate escape, for the party of soldiers despatched by an easier course to cut them off, must inevitably arrive at their distant bourne long before them, and retake them if by any hazard they survive the horrors of the way. Famine, as they all must have foreseen, besets them early in their course. Some of the party die and are eaten; some are murdered by the rest and eaten. This one awful creature eats his fill, and sustains his strength, and lives on to be recaptured and taken back. The unrelateable experiences through which he has passed have been so tremendous, that he is not hanged as he might be, but goes back to his old chained-gang work. A little time, and he tempts one other prisoner away, seizes another boat, and flies once more—necessarily in the old hopeless direction, for he can take no other. He is soon cut off, and met by the pursuing party face to face, upon the beach. He is alone. In his former journey he acquired an inappeasable relish for his dreadful food. He urged the new man away, expressly to kill him and eat him. In the pockets on one side of his coarse convict-dress, are portions of the man's body, on which he is regaling; in the pockets on the other side is an untouched store of salted pork (stolen before he left the island) for which he has no appetite. He is taken back, and he is hanged. But I shall never see that sea-beach on the wall or in the fire, without him, solitary monster, eating as he prowls along, while the sea rages and rises at him.

Captain Bligh (a worse man to be entrusted with arbitrary power there could scarcely be) is handed over the side of the Bounty, and turned adrift on the wide ocean in an open boat, by order of Fletcher

Christian, one of his officers, at this very minute. Another flash of my fire, and 'Thursday October Christian,' five-and-twenty years of age, son of the dead and gone Fletcher by a savage mother, leaps aboard His Majesty's ship Briton, hove-to off Pitcairn's Island; says his simple grace before eating, in good English; and knows that a pretty little animal on board is called a dog, because in his childhood he had heard of such strange creatures from his father and the other mutineers, grown grey under the shade of the bread-fruit trees, speaking of their lost country far away.

See the Halsewell, East Indiaman outward bound, driving madly on a January night towards the rocks near Seacombe, on the island of Purbeck! The captain's two dear daughters are aboard, and five other ladies. The ship has been driving many hours, has seven feet water in her hold, and her mainmast has been cut away. The description of her loss, familiar to me from my early boyhood, seems to be read aloud as she rushes to her destiny.

'About two in the morning of Friday the sixth of January, the ship still driving, and approaching very fast to the shore, Mr Henry Meriton, the second mate, went again into the cuddy, where the captain then was. Another conversation taking place, Captain Pierce expressed extreme anxiety for the preservation of his beloved daughters, and earnestly asked the officer if he could devise any method of saving them. On his answering with great concern, that he feared it would be impossible, but that their only chance would be to wait for morning, the captain lifted up his hands in silent and distressful ejaculation.

'At this dreadful moment, the ship struck, with such violence as to dash the heads of those standing in the cuddy against the deck above them, and the shock was accompanied by a shriek of horror that burst at one instant from every quarter of the ship.

'Many of the seamen, who had been remarkably inattentive and remiss in their duty during great part of the storm, now poured upon deck, where no exertions of the officers could keep them, while their assistance might have been useful. They had actually skulked in their hammocks, leaving the working of the pumps and other necessary labours to the officers of the ship, and the soldiers, who had made uncommon exertions. Roused by a sense of their danger, the same seamen, at this moment, in frantic exclamations, demanded of heaven and their fellow-sufferers that succour which their own efforts, timely made, might possibly have procured.

'The ship continued to beat on the rocks; and soon bilging, fell with her broadside towards the shore. When she struck, a number of the men climbed up the ensign-staff, under an apprehension of her immediately going to pieces.

'Mr Meriton, at this crisis, offered to these unhappy beings the best advice which could be given; he recommended that all should come to the side of the ship lying lowest on the rocks, and singly to take the opportunities which might then offer, of escaping to the shore.

'Having thus provided, to the utmost of his power, for the safety of the desponding crew, he returned to the round-house, where, by this time, all the passengers and most of the officers had assembled. The latter were employed in offering consolation to the unfortunate ladies; and, with unparalleled magnanimity, suffering their compassion for the fair and amiable companions of their misfortunes to prevail over the sense of their own danger.

'In this charitable work of comfort, Mr Meriton now joined, by assurances of his opinion, that, the ship would hold together till the morning, when all would be safe. Captain Pierce, observing one of the young gentlemen loud in his exclamations of terror, and frequently cry that the ship was parting, cheerfully bid him be quiet, remarking that though the ship should go to pieces, he would not, but would be safe enough.

'It is difficult to convey a correct idea of the scene of this deplorable catastrophe, without describing the place where it happened. The Haleswell struck on the rocks at a part of the shore where the cliff is of vast height, and rises almost perpendicular from its base. But at this particular spot, the foot of the cliff is excavated into a cavern of ten or twelve yards in depth, and of breadth equal to the length of a large ship. The sides of the cavern are so nearly upright, as to be of extremely difficult access; and the bottom is strewed with sharp and uneven rocks, which seem, by some convulsion of the earth, to have been detached from its roof.

'The ship lay with her broadside opposite to the mouth of this cavern, with her whole length stretched almost from side to side of it. But when she struck, it was too dark for the unfortunate persons on board to discover the real magnitude of the danger, and the extreme horror of such a situation.

'In addition to the company already in the round-house, they had admitted three black women and two soldiers' wives; who, with the husband of one of them, had been allowed to come in, though the seamen, who had tumultuously demanded entrance to get the lights, had been opposed and kept out by Mr Rogers and Mr Brimer, the third and fifth mates. The numbers there were, therefore, now increased to near fifty. Captain Pierce sat on a chair, a cot, or some other moveable, with a daughter on each side, whom he alternately pressed to his affectionate breast. The rest of the melancholy assembly were seated on the deck, which was strewed with musical instruments, and the wreck of furniture and other articles.

'Here also Mr Meriton, after having cut several wax-candles in pieces, and stuck them up in various parts of the round-house, and lighted up all the glass lanthorns he could find, took his seat, intending to wait the approach of dawn; and then assist the partners of his dangers to escape. But, observing that the poor ladies appeared parched and exhausted, he brought a basket of oranges and prevailed on some of them to refresh themselves by sucking a little of the juice. At this time they were all tolerably composed, except Miss Mansel, who was in hysteric fits on the floor of the deck of the round-house.

'But on Mr Meriton's return to the company, he perceived a considerable alteration in the appearance of the ship; the sides were visibly giving way; the deck seemed to be lifting, and he discovered other strong indications that she could not hold much longer together. On this account, he attempted to go forward to look out, but immediately saw that the ship had separated in the middle, and that the forepart having changed its position, lay rather further out towards the sea. In such an emergency, when the next moment might plunge him into eternity, he determined to seize the present opportunity, and follow the example of the crew and the soldiers, who were now quitting the ship in numbers, and making their way to the shore, though quite ignorant of its nature and description.

'Among other expedients, the ensign-staff had been unshipped, and attempted to be laid between the ship's side and some of the rocks, but without success, for it snapped asunder before it reached them. However, by the light of a lanthorn, which a seaman handed through the skylight of the round-house to the deck, Mr Meriton discovered a spar which appeared to be laid from the ship's side to the rocks, and on this spar he resolved to attempt his escape.

'Accordingly, lying down upon it, he thrust himself forward; however, he soon found that it had no communication with the rock; he reached the end of it, and then slipped off, receiving a very violent bruise in his fall, and before he could recover his legs, he was washed off by the surge. He now supported himself by swimming, until a returning wave dashed him against the back part of the cavern. Here he laid hold of a small projection in the rock, but was so much benumbed that he was on the point of quitting it, when a seaman, who had already gained a footing, extended his hand, and assisted him until he could secure himself a little on the rock; from which he clambered on a shelf still higher, and out of the reach of the surf.

'Mr Rogers, the third mate, remained with the captain and the unfortunate ladies and their companions nearly twenty minutes after Mr Meriton had quitted the ship. Soon after the latter left the round-house, the captain asked what was become of him, to which Mr Rogers replied, that he was gone on deck to see what could be done. After this, a heavy sea breaking over the ship, the ladies exclaimed, 'Oh, poor Meriton! he is drowned; had he stayed with us he would have been safe!' and they all, particularly Miss Mary Pierce, expressed great concern at the apprehension of his loss.

'The sea was now breaking in at the fore part of the ship, and reached as far as the mainmast. Captain Pierce gave Mr Rogers a nod, and they took a lamp and went together into the stern-gallery, where, after viewing the rocks for some time, Captain Pierce asked Mr Rogers if he thought there was any possibility of saving the girls; to which he replied, he feared there was none; for they could only discover the black face of the perpendicular rock, and not the cavern which afforded shelter to those who escaped. They then returned to the round-house, where Mr Rogers hung up the lamp, and Captain Pierce sat down between his two daughters.

'The sea continuing to break in very fast, Mr Macmanus, a midshipman, and Mr Schutz, a passenger, asked Mr Rogers what they could do to escape. 'Follow me,' he replied, and they all went into the stern-gallery, and from thence to the upper-quarter-gallery on the poop. While there, a very heavy sea fell on board, and the round-house gave way; Mr Rogers heard the ladies shriek at intervals, as if the water reached them; the noise of the sea at other times drowning their voices.

'Mr Brimer had followed him to the poop, where they remained together about five minutes, when on the breaking of this heavy sea, they jointly seized a hen-coop. The same wave which proved fatal to some of those below, carried him and his companion to the rock, on which they were violently dashed and miserably bruised.

'Here on the rock were twenty-seven men; but it now being low water, and as they were convinced that on the flowing of the tide all must be washed off, many attempted to get to the back or the sides of the cavern, beyond the reach of the returning sea. Scarcely more than six, besides Mr Rogers and Mr Brimer, succeeded.

'Mr Rogers, on gaining this station, was so nearly exhausted, that had his exertions been protracted only a few minutes longer, he must have sunk under them. He was now prevented from joining Mr Meriton, by at least twenty men between them, none of whom could move, without the imminent peril of his life.

'They found that a very considerable number of the crew, seamen and soldiers, and some petty officers, were in the same situation as themselves, though many who had reached the rocks below, perished in attempting to ascend. They could yet discern some part of the ship, and in their dreary station solaced themselves with the hopes of its remaining entire until day-break; for, in the midst of their own distress, the sufferings of the females on board affected them with the most poignant anguish; and every sea that broke inspired them with terror for their safety.

'But, alas, their apprehensions were too soon realised! Within a very few minutes of the time that Mr Rogers gained the rock, an universal shriek, which long vibrated in their ears, in which the voice of female distress was lamentably distinguished, announced the dreadful catastrophe. In a few moments all was hushed, except the roaring of the winds and the dashing of the waves; the wreck was buried in the deep, and not an atom of it was ever afterwards seen.'

The most beautiful and affecting incident I know, associated with a shipwreck, succeeds this dismal story for a winter night. The Grosvenor, East Indiaman, homeward bound, goes ashore on the coast of Caffraria. It is resolved that the officers, passengers, and crew, in number one hundred and thirty-five souls, shall endeavour to penetrate on foot, across trackless deserts, infested by wild beasts and cruel savages, to the Dutch settlements at the Cape of Good Hope. With this forlorn object before them, they finally separate into two parties—never more to meet on earth.

There is a solitary child among the passengers—a little boy of seven years old who has no relation there; and when the first party is moving away he cries after some member of it who has been kind to him. The crying of a child might be supposed to be a little thing to men in such great extremity; but it touches them, and he is immediately taken into that detachment.

From which time forth, this child is sublimely made a sacred charge. He is pushed, on a little raft, across broad rivers by the swimming sailors; they carry him by turns through the deep sand and long grass (he patiently walking at all other times); they share with him such putrid fish as they find to eat; they lie down and wait for him when the rough carpenter, who becomes his especial friend, lags behind. Beset by lions and tigers, by savages, by thirst, by hunger, by death in a crowd of ghastly shapes, they never—O Father of all mankind, thy name be blessed for it!—forget this child. The captain stops exhausted, and his faithful coxswain goes back and is seen to sit down by his side, and neither of the two shall be any more beheld until the great last day; but, as the rest go on for their lives, they take the child with them. The carpenter dies of poisonous berries eaten in starvation; and the steward, succeeding to the command of the party, succeeds to the sacred guardianship of the child.

God knows all he does for the poor baby; how he cheerfully carries him in his arms when he himself is weak and ill; how he feeds him when he himself is griped with want; how he folds his ragged jacket round him, lays his little worn face with a woman's tenderness upon his sunburnt breast, soothes him in his sufferings, sings to him as he limps along, unmindful of his own parched and bleeding feet. Divided for a few days from the rest, they dig a grave in the sand and bury their good friend the cooper—these two companions alone in the wilderness—and then the time comes when they both are ill, and beg their wretched partners in despair, reduced and few in number now, to wait by them one day. They wait by them one day, they wait by them two days. On the morning of the third, they move very softly about, in making their preparations for the resumption of their journey; for, the child is sleeping by the fire, and it is agreed with one consent that he shall not be disturbed until the last moment. The moment comes, the fire is dying—and the child is dead.

His faithful friend, the steward, lingers but a little while behind him. His grief is great, he staggers on for a few days, lies down in the desert, and dies. But he shall be re-united in his immortal spirit—who can doubt it!—with the child, when he and the poor carpenter shall be raised up with the words, 'Inasmuch as ye have done it unto the least of these, ye have done it unto Me.'

As I recall the dispersal and disappearance of nearly all the participators in this once famous shipwreck (a mere handful being recovered at last), and the legends that were long afterwards revived from time to time among the English officers at the Cape, of a white woman with an infant, said to have been seen weeping outside a savage hut far in the interior, who was whisperingly associated with the remembrance of the missing ladies saved from the wrecked vessel, and who was often sought but never found, thoughts of another kind of travel came into my mind.

Thoughts of a voyager unexpectedly summoned from home, who travelled a vast distance, and could never return. Thoughts of this unhappy wayfarer in the depths of his sorrow, in the bitterness of his anguish, in the helplessness of his self-reproach, in the desperation of his desire to set right what he had left wrong, and do what he had left undone.

For, there were many, many things he had neglected. Little matters while he was at home and surrounded by them, but things of mighty moment when he was at an immeasurable distance. There were many many blessings that he had inadequately felt, there were many trivial injuries that he had not forgiven, there was love that he had but poorly returned, there was friendship that he had too lightly prized: there were a million kind words that he might have spoken, a million kind looks that he might have given, uncountable slight easy deeds in which he might have been most truly great and good. O for a day (he would exclaim), for but one day to make amends! But the sun never shone upon that happy day, and out of his remote captivity he never came.

Why does this traveller's fate obscure, on New Year's Eve, the other histories of travellers with which my mind was filled but now, and cast a solemn shadow over me! Must I one day make his journey? Even so. Who shall say, that I may not then be tortured by such late regrets: that I may not then look from my exile on my empty place and undone work? I stand upon a sea-shore, where the waves are years. They break and fall, and I may little heed them; but, with every wave the sea is rising, and I know that it will float me on this traveller's voyage at last.

18

A MEDITATION UPON A BROOMSTICK

Jonathan Swift

This single Stick, which you now behold Ingloriously lying in that neglected Corner, I once knew in a Flourishing State in a Forest, it was full of Sap, full of Leaves, and full of Boughs; but now, in vain does the busie Art of Man pretend to Vye with Nature, by tying that withered Bundle of Twigs to its sapless Trunk; It's now at best but the Reverse of what it was, a Tree turned upside down, the Branches on the Earth, and the Root in the Air; 'tis now handled by every Dirty Wench, condemned to doe her Drudgery, and by a Capricious kind of Fate, destined to make other Things Clean, and be Nasty it self: At Length, worn to the Stumps in the Service of the Maids, 'tis either thrown out of Doors, or condemned to its last use of kindling a Fire. When I beheld this, I sigh'd and said within my self, Surely Mortal Man is a Broom Stick; Nature sent him into the World Strong and Lusty, in a Thriving Condition, wearing his own Hair on his Head, the proper Branches of this Reasoning Vegetable, till the Axe of Intemperance has lopt off his Green Boughs, and left him a withered Trunk: He then flies to Art, and puts on a Perewig, valuing himself upon an Unnatural Bundle of Hairs all covered with Powder, that never grew on his Head; but now should this our Broom-Stick pretend to enter the Scene, proud of those Birchen Spoils it never bore, and all covered with Dust, though the Sweepings of the Finest Lady's Chamber, we should be apt to Ridicule and Despise its Vanity; Partial Judges that we are of Our own Excellencies, and other Men's Defaults!

BUT a Broom-Stick, perhaps you will say, is an Emblem of a Tree standing on its Head; and pray what is Man, but a Topsy-turvey

Creature, his Animal Faculties perpetually mounted on his Rational; His Head where his Heels should be, groveling on the Earth, and yet with all his Faults, he sets up to be an universal Reformer and Corrector of Abuses, a Remover of Grievances, rakes into every Sluts Corner of Nature, bringing hidden Corruptions to the Light, and raises a mighty Dust where there was none before, sharing deeply all the while, in the very same Pollutions he pretends to sweep away: His last Days are spent in Slavery to Women, and generally the least deserving; till worn to the Stumps, like his Brother Bezom, he is either kickt out of Doors, or made use of to kindle Flames, for others to warm themselves by.

19

ON AUTHORSHIP

Arthur Schopenhauer

There are, first of all, two kinds of authors: those who write for the subject's sake, and those who write for writing's sake. While the one have had thoughts or experiences which seem to them worth communicating, the others want money; and so they write, for money. Their thinking is part of the business of writing. They may be recognized by the way in which they spin out their thoughts to the greatest possible length; then, too, by the very nature of their thoughts, which are only half-true, perverse, forced, vacillating; again, by the aversion they generally show to saying anything straight out, so that they may seem other than they are. Hence their writing is deficient in clearness and definiteness, and it is not long before they betray that their only object in writing at all is to cover paper. This sometimes happens with the best authors; now and then, for example, with Lessing in his *Dramaturgie*, and even in many of Jean Paul's romances. As soon as the reader perceives this, let him throw the book away; for time is precious. The truth is that when an author begins to write for the sake of covering paper, he is cheating the reader; because he writes under the pretext that he has something to say.

Writing for money and reservation of copyright are, at bottom, the ruin of literature. No one writes anything that is worth writing, unless he writes entirely for the sake of his subject. What an inestimable boon it would be, if in every branch of literature there were only a few books, but those excellent! This can never happen, as long as money is to be made by writing. It seems as though the money lay under a curse; for every author degenerates as soon as he begins to put pen to paper in any way for the sake of gain. The best works of the greatest men all come from the time when they had to write for nothing or for very little. And here, too, that Spanish proverb holds good, which declares that honor and money are not to be found in the same purse—*honora y provecho no caben en un saco*. The reason why Literature is in such a bad plight nowadays is simply and solely that people write books to make money. A man who is in want sits down and writes a book, and the public is stupid enough to buy it. The secondary effect of this is the ruin of language.

A great many bad writers make their whole living by that foolish mania of the public for reading nothing but what has just been printed,—journalists, I mean. Truly, a most appropriate name. In plain language it is *journeymen, day-labourers*!

Again, it may be said that there are three kinds of authors. First come those who write without thinking. They write from a full memory, from reminiscences; it may be, even straight out of other people's books. This class is the most numerous. Then come those who do their thinking whilst they are writing. They think in order to write; and there is no lack of them. Last of all come those authors who think before they begin to write. They are rare.

Authors of the second class, who put off their thinking until they come to write, are like a sportsman who goes forth at random and is not likely to bring very much home. On the other hand, when an author of the third or rare class writes, it is like a battue. Here the game has been previously captured and shut up within a very small space; from which it is afterwards let out, so many at a time, into another space, also confined. The game cannot possibly escape the sportsman; he has nothing to do but aim and fire—in other words, write down his thoughts. This is a kind of sport from which a man has something to show.

But even though the number of those who really think seriously before they begin to write is small, extremely few of them think about *the subject itself*: the remainder think only about the books that have been written on the subject, and what has been said by others. In order to think at all, such writers need the more direct and powerful stimulus of having other people's thoughts before them. These become their immediate theme; and the result is that they are always under their influence, and so never, in any real sense of the word, are original. But the former are roused to thought by the subject itself, to which their thinking is thus immediately directed. This is the only class that produces writers of abiding fame.

It must, of course, be understood that I am speaking here of writers who treat of great subjects; not of writers on the art of making brandy.

Unless an author takes the material on which he writes out of his own head, that is to say, from his own observation, he is not worth reading. Book-manufacturers, compilers, the common run of history-writers, and many others of the same class, take their material immediately out of books; and the material goes straight to their finger-tips without even paying freight or undergoing examination as it passes through their heads, to say nothing of elaboration or revision. How very learned many a man would be if he knew everything that was in his own books! The consequence of this is that these writers talk in such a loose and vague manner, that the reader puzzles his brain in vain to understand what it is of which they are really thinking. They are thinking of nothing. It may now and then be the case that the book from which they copy has been composed exactly in the same way: so that writing of this sort is like a plaster cast of a cast; and in the end, the bare outline of the face, and that, too, hardly recognizable, is all that is left to your Antinous. Let compilations be read as seldom as possible. It is difficult to avoid them altogether; since compilations also include those text-books which contain in a small space the accumulated knowledge of centuries.

There is no greater mistake than to suppose that the last work is always the more correct; that what is written later on is in every case an improvement on what was written before; and that change always means progress. Real thinkers, men of right judgment, people who are in earnest with their subject,—these are all exceptions only. Vermin is the rule everywhere in the world: it is always on the alert, taking the mature opinions of the thinkers, and industriously seeking to improve upon them (save the mark!) in its own peculiar way.

If the reader wishes to study any subject, let him beware of rushing to the newest books upon it, and confining his attention to them alone, under the notion that science is always advancing, and that the old books have been drawn upon in the writing of the new. They have been drawn upon, it is true; but how? The writer of the new book often does not understand the old books thoroughly, and yet he is unwilling to take their exact words; so he bungles them, and says in his own bad way that which has been said very much better and more clearly by the old writers, who wrote from their own lively knowledge of the subject. The new writer frequently omits the best things they say, their most striking illustrations, their happiest remarks; because he does not see their value or feel how pregnant they are. The only thing that appeals to him is what is shallow and insipid.

It often happens that an old and excellent book is ousted by new and bad ones, which, written for money, appear with an air of great pretension and much puffing on the part of friends. In science a man tries to make his mark by bringing out something fresh. This often means nothing more than that he attacks some received theory which is quite correct, in order to make room for his own false notions. Sometimes the effort is successful for a time; and then a return is made to the old and true theory. These innovators are serious about nothing but their own precious self: it is this that they want to put forward, and the quick way of doing so, as they think, is to start a paradox. Their sterile heads take naturally to the path of negation; so they begin to deny truths that have long been admitted—the vital power, for example, the sympathetic nervous system, *generatio equivoca*, Bichat's distinction between the working of the passions and the working of intelligence; or else they want us to return to crass atomism, and the like. Hence it frequently happens that *the course of science is retrogressive.*

To this class of writers belong those translators who not only translate their author but also correct and revise him; a proceeding which always seems to me impertinent. To such writers I say: Write books yourself which are worth translating, and leave other people's works as they are!

The reader should study, if he can, the real authors, the men who have founded and discovered things; or, at any rate, those who are recognized as the great masters in every branch of knowledge. Let him buy second-hand books rather than read their contents in new ones. To be sure, it is easy to add to any new discovery—*inventis aliquid addere facile est*; and, therefore, the student, after well mastering the rudiments of his subject, will have to make himself acquainted with the more recent additions to the knowledge of it. And, in general, the following rule may be laid down here as elsewhere: if a thing is new, it is seldom good; because if it is good, it is only for a short time new.

What the address is to a letter, the title should be to a book; in other words, its main object should be to bring the book to those amongst the public who will take an interest in its contents. It should, therefore, be expressive; and since by its very nature it must be short, it should be concise, laconic, pregnant, and if possible give the contents in one word. A prolix title is bad; and so is one that says nothing, or is obscure and ambiguous, or even, it may be, false and misleading; this last may possibly involve the book in the same fate as overtakes a wrongly addressed letter. The worst titles of all are those which have been stolen, those, I mean, which have already been borne by other books; for they are in the first place a plagiarism, and secondly the most convincing proof of a total lack of originality in the author. A man who has not enough originality to invent a new title for his book, will be still less able to give it new contents. Akin to these stolen titles are those which have been imitated, that is to say, stolen to the extent of one half; for instance, long after I had produced my treatise *On Will in Nature*, Oersted wrote a book entitled *On Mind in Nature*.

A book can never be anything more than the impress of its author's thoughts; and the value of these will lie either in *the matter about which he has thought*, or in the *form* which his thoughts take, in other words, *what it is that he has thought about it*.

The matter of books is most various; and various also are the several excellences attaching to books on the score of their matter. By matter I mean everything that comes within the domain of actual experience; that is to say, the facts of history and the facts of nature, taken in and by themselves and in their widest sense. Here it is the *thing* treated of, which gives its peculiar character to the book; so that a book can be important, whoever it was that wrote it.

But in regard to the form, the peculiar character of a book depends upon the *person* who wrote it. It may treat of matters which are accessible to everyone and well known; but it is the way in which they are treated, what it is that is thought about them, that gives the book its value; and this comes from its author. If, then, from this point of view a book is excellent and beyond comparison, so is its author. It follows that if a writer is worth reading, his merit rises just in proportion as he owes little to his matter; therefore, the better known and the more hackneyed this is, the greater he will be. The three great tragedians of Greece, for example, all worked at the same subject-matter.

So when a book is celebrated, care should be taken to note whether it is so on account of its matter or its form; and a distinction should be made accordingly.

Books of great importance on account of their matter may proceed from very ordinary and shallow people, by the fact that they alone have had access to this matter; books, for instance, which describe journeys in distant lands, rare natural phenomena, or experiments; or historical occurrences of which the writers were witnesses, or in connection with which they have spent much time and trouble in the research and special study of original documents.

On the other hand, where the matter is accessible to everyone or very well known, everything will depend upon the form; and what it is that is thought about the matter will give the book all the value it possesses. Here only a really distinguished man will be able to produce anything worth reading; for the others will think nothing but what anyone else can think. They will just produce an impress of their own minds; but this is a print of which everyone possesses the original.

However, the public is very much more concerned to have matter than form; and for this very reason it is deficient in any high degree of culture. The public shows its preference in this respect in the most laughable way when it comes to deal with poetry; for there it devotes much trouble to the task of tracking out the actual events or personal circumstances in the life of the poet which served as the occasion of his various works; nay, these events and circumstances come in the end to be of greater importance than the works themselves; and rather than read Goethe himself, people prefer to read what has been written about him, and to study the legend of Faust more industriously than the drama of that name. And when Bürger declared that 'people would write learned disquisitions on the question, Who Leonora really was,' we find this literally fulfilled in Goethe's case; for we now possess a great many learned disquisitions on Faust and the legend attaching to him. Study of this kind is, and remains, devoted to the material of the drama alone. To give such preference to the matter over the form, is as though a man were to take a fine Etruscan vase, not to admire its shape or coloring, but to make a chemical analysis of the clay and paint of which it is composed.

The attempt to produce an effect by means of the material employed—an attempt which panders to this evil tendency of the public—is most to be condemned in branches of literature where any merit there may be lies expressly in the form; I mean, in poetical work. For all that, it is not rare to find bad dramatists trying to fill the house by means of the matter about which they write. For example, authors of this kind do not shrink from putting on the stage any man who is in any way celebrated, no matter whether his life may have been entirely devoid of dramatic incident; and sometimes, even, they do not wait until the persons immediately connected with him are dead.

The distinction between matter and form to which I am here alluding also holds good of conversation. The chief qualities which enable a man to converse well are intelligence, discernment, wit and vivacity: these supply the form of conversation. But it is not long before attention has to be paid to the matter of which he speaks; in other words, the subjects about which it is possible to converse with him—his knowledge. If this is very small, his conversation will not be worth anything, unless he possesses the above-named formal qualities in a very exceptional degree; for he will have nothing to talk about but those facts of life and nature which everybody knows. It will be just the opposite, however, if a man is deficient in these formal qualities, but has an amount of knowledge which lends value to what he says. This value will then depend entirely upon the matter of his conversation; for, as the Spanish proverb has it, *mas sabe el necio en su casa, que el sabio en la agena*—a fool knows more of his own business than a wise man does of others.

20

ON STYLE

Arthur Schopenhauer

Style is the physiognomy of the mind, and a safer index to character than the face. To imitate another man's style is like wearing a mask, which, be it never so fine, is not long in arousing disgust and abhorrence, because it is lifeless; so that even the ugliest living face is better. Hence those who write in Latin and copy the manner of ancient authors, may be said to speak through a mask; the reader, it is true, hears what they say, but he cannot observe their physiognomy too; he cannot see their *style*. With the Latin works of writers who think for themselves, the case is different, and their style is visible; writers, I mean, who have not condescended to any sort of imitation, such as Scotus Erigena, Petrarch, Bacon, Descartes, Spinoza, and many others. An affectation in style is like making grimaces. Further, the language in which a man writes is the physiognomy of the nation to which he belongs; and here there are many hard and fast differences, beginning from the language of the Greeks, down to that of the Caribbean islanders.

To form a provincial estimate of the value of a writer's productions, it is not directly necessary to know the subject on which he has thought, or what it is that he has said about it; that would imply a perusal of all his works. It will be enough, in the main, to know *how* he has thought. This, which means the essential temper or general quality of his mind, may be precisely determined by his style. A man's style shows the *formal* nature of all his thoughts—the formal nature which can never change, be the subject or the character of his thoughts what it may: it is, as it were, the dough out of which all the contents of his mind are kneaded. When Eulenspiegel was asked how long it would take to walk to the next village, he gave the seemingly incongruous answer: *Walk*. He wanted to find out by the man's pace the distance he would cover in a given time. In the same way, when I have read a few pages of an author, I know fairly well how far he can bring me.

Every mediocre writer tries to mask his own natural style, because in his heart he knows the truth of what I am saying. He is thus forced, at the outset, to give up any attempt at being frank or naïve—a privilege which is thereby reserved for superior minds, conscious of their own worth, and therefore sure of themselves. What I mean is that these everyday writers are absolutely unable to resolve upon writing just as they think; because they have a notion that, were they to do so, their work might possibly look very childish and simple. For all that, it would not be without its value. If they would only go honestly to work, and say, quite simply, the things they have really thought, and just as they have thought them, these writers would be readable and, within their own proper sphere, even instructive.

But instead of that, they try to make the reader believe that their thoughts have gone much further and deeper than is really the case. They say what they have to say in long sentences that wind about in a forced and unnatural way; they coin new words and write prolix periods which go round and round the thought and wrap it up in a sort of disguise. They tremble between the two separate aims of communicating what they want to say and of concealing it. Their object is to dress it up so that it may look learned or deep, in order to give people the impression that there is very much more in it than for the moment meets the eye. They either jot down their thoughts bit by bit, in short, ambiguous, and paradoxical sentences, which apparently mean much more than they say,—of this kind of writing Schelling's treatises on natural philosophy are a splendid instance; or else they hold forth with a deluge of words and the most intolerable diffusiveness, as though no end of fuss were necessary to make the reader understand the deep meaning of their sentences, whereas it is some quite simple if not actually trivial idea,—examples of which may be found in plenty in the popular works of Fichte, and the philosophical manuals of a hundred other miserable dunces not worth mentioning; or, again, they try to write in some particular style which they have been pleased to take up and think very grand, a style, for example, *par excellence* profound and scientific, where the reader is tormented to death by the narcotic effect of longspun periods without a single idea in them,—such as are furnished in a special measure by those most impudent of all mortals, the Hegelians; or it may be that it is an intellectual style they have striven after, where it seems as though their object were to go crazy altogether; and so on in many other cases. All these endeavors to put off the *nascetur ridiculus mus*—to avoid showing the funny little creature that is born after such mighty throes—often make it difficult to know what it is that they really mean. And then, too, they write down words, nay, even whole sentences, without attaching any meaning to them themselves, but in the hope that someone else will get sense out of them.

And what is at the bottom of all this? Nothing but the untiring effort to sell words for thoughts; a mode of merchandise that is always trying to make fresh openings for itself, and by means of odd expressions, turns of phrase, and combinations of every sort, whether new or used in a new sense, to produce the appearence of intellect in order to make up for the very painfully felt lack of it.

It is amusing to see how writers with this object in view will attempt first one mannerism and then another, as though they were putting on the mask of intellect! This mask may possibly deceive the inexperienced for a while, until it is seen to be a dead thing, with no life in it at all; it is then laughed at and exchanged for another. Such an author will at one moment write in a dithyrambic vein, as though he were tipsy; at another, nay, on the very next page, he will be pompous, severe, profoundly learned and prolix, stumbling on in the most cumbrous way and chopping up everything very small; like the late Christian Wolf, only in a modern dress. Longest of all lasts the mask of unintelligibility; but this is only in Germany, whither it was introduced by Fichte, perfected by Schelling, and carried to its highest pitch in Hegel—always with the best results.

And yet nothing is easier than to write so that no one can

understand; just as contrarily, nothing is more difficult than to express deep things in such a way that every one must necessarily grasp them. All the arts and tricks I have been mentioning are rendered superfluous if the author really has any brains; for that allows him to show himself as he is, and confirms to all time Horace's maxim that good sense is the source and origin of good style:

Scribendi recte sapere est et principium et fons.

But those authors I have named are like certain workers in metal, who try a hundred different compounds to take the place of gold—the only metal which can never have any substitute. Rather than do that, there is nothing against which a writer should be more upon his guard than the manifest endeavour to exhibit more intellect than he really has; because this makes the reader suspect that he possesses very little; since it is always the case that if a man affects anything, whatever it may be, it is just there that he is deficient.

That is why it is praise to an author to say that he is *naïve*; it means that he need not shrink from showing himself as he is. Generally speaking, to be *naïve* is to be attractive; while lack of naturalness is everywhere repulsive. As a matter of fact we find that every really great writer tries to express his thoughts as purely, clearly, definitely and shortly as possible. Simplicity has always been held to be a mark of truth; it is also a mark of genius. Style receives its beauty from the thought it expresses; but with sham-thinkers the thoughts are supposed to be fine because of the style. Style is nothing but the mere silhouette of thought; and an obscure or bad style means a dull or confused brain.

The first rule, then, for a good style is that *the author should have something to say*; nay, this is in itself almost all that is necessary. Ah, how much it means! The neglect of this rule is a fundamental trait in the philosophical writing, and, in fact, in all the reflective literature, of my country, more especially since Fichte. These writers all let it be seen that they want to appear as though they had something to say; whereas they have nothing to say. Writing of this kind was brought in by the pseudo-philosophers at the universities, and now it is current everywhere, even among the first literary notabilities of the age. It is the mother of that strained and vague style, where there seem to be two or even more meanings in the sentence; also of that prolix and cumbrous manner of expression, called *le stile empesé*; again, of that mere waste of words which consists in pouring them out like a flood; finally, of that trick of concealing the direst poverty of thought under a farrago of never-ending chatter, which clacks away like a windmill and quite stupefies one—stuff which a man may read for hours together without getting hold of a single clearly expressed and definite idea. However, people are easy-going, and they have formed the habit of reading page upon page of all sorts of such verbiage, without having any particular idea of what the author really means. They fancy it is all as it should be, and fail to discover that he is writing simply for writing's sake.

On the other hand, a good author, fertile in ideas, soon wins his reader's confidence that, when he writes, he has really and truly *something to say*; and this gives the intelligent reader patience to follow him with attention. Such an author, just because he really has something to say, will never fail to express himself in the simplest and most straightforward manner; because his object is to awake the very same thought in the reader that he has in himself, and no other. So he will be able to affirm with Boileau that his thoughts are everywhere open to the light of the day, and that his verse always says something, whether it says it well or ill:

Ma pensée au grand jour partout s'offre et s'expose,
Et mon vers, bien ou mal, dit toujours quelque chose:

while of the writers previously described it may be asserted, in the words of the same poet, that they talk much and never say anything at all—*quiparlant beaucoup ne disent jamais rien.*

Another characteristic of such writers is that they always avoid a positive assertion wherever they can possibly do so, in order to leave a loophole for escape in case of need. Hence they never fail to choose the more *abstract* way of expressing themselves; whereas intelligent people use the more *concrete*; because the latter brings things more within the range of actual demonstration, which is the source of all evidence.

There are many examples proving this preference for abstract expression; and a particularly ridiculous one is afforded by the use of the verb *to condition* in the sense of *to cause* or *to produce*. People say *to condition something* instead of *to cause it*, because being abstract and indefinite it says less; it affirms that *A* cannot happen without *B*, instead of that *A* is caused by *B*. A back door is always left open; and this suits people whose secret knowledge of their own incapacity inspires them with a perpetual terror of all positive assertion; while with other people it is merely the effect of that tendency by which everything that is stupid in literature or bad in life is immediately imitated—a fact proved in either case by the rapid way in which it spreads. The Englishman uses his own judgment in what he writes as well as in what he does; but there is no nation of which this eulogy is less true than of the Germans. The consequence of this state of things is that the word *cause* has of late almost disappeared from the language of literature, and people talk only of *condition*. The fact is worth mentioning because it is so characteristically ridiculous.

The very fact that these commonplace authors are never more than half-conscious when they write, would be enough to account for their dullness of mind and the tedious things they produce. I say they are only half-conscious, because they really do not themselves understand the meaning of the words they use: they take words ready-made and commit them to memory. Hence when they write, it is not so much words as whole phrases that they put together—*phrases banales*. This is the explanation of that palpable lack of clearly-expressed thought in what they say. The fact is that they do not possess the die to give this stamp to their writing; clear thought of their own is just what they have not got. And what do we find in its place?—a vague, enigmatical intermixture of words, current phrases, hackneyed terms, and fashionable expressions. The result is that the foggy stuff they write is like a page printed with very old type.

On the other hand, an intelligent author really speaks to us when he writes, and that is why he is able to rouse our interest and commune with us. It is the intelligent author alone who puts individual words together with a full consciousness of their meaning, and chooses them with deliberate design. Consequently, his discourse stands to that of the writer described above, much as a picture that has been really painted, to one that has been produced by the use of a stencil. In the one case, every word, every touch of the brush, has a special purpose; in the other, all is done mechanically. The same distinction may be observed in music. For just as Lichtenberg says that Garrick's soul seemed to be in every muscle in his body, so it is the omnipresence of intellect that always and everywhere characterizes the work of genius.

I have alluded to the tediousness which marks the works of these writers; and in this connection it is to be observed, generally, that tediousness is of two kinds; objective and subjective. A work is objectively tedious when it contains the defect in question; that is to say, when its author has no perfectly clear thought or knowledge to communicate. For if a man has any clear thought or knowledge in him, his aim will be to communicate it, and he will direct his energies to this end; so that the ideas he furnishes are everywhere clearly expressed. The result is that he is neither diffuse, nor unmeaning, nor confused, and consequently not tedious. In such a case, even though the author is at bottom in error, the error is at any rate clearly worked out and well thought over, so that it is at least formally correct; and thus some value always attaches to the work. But for the same reason a work that is objectively tedious is at all times devoid of any value whatever.

The other kind of tediousness is only relative: a reader may find a work dull because he has no interest in the question treated of in it, and this means that his intellect is restricted. The best work may, therefore, be tedious subjectively, tedious, I mean, to this or that particular person; just as, contrarily, the worst work may be subjectively engrossing to this or that particular person who has an interest in the question treated of, or in the writer of the book.

It would generally serve writers in good stead if they would see that, whilst a man should, if possible, think like a great genius, he should talk the same language as everyone else. Authors should use common words to say uncommon things. But they do just the opposite. We find them trying to wrap up trivial ideas in grand words, and to clothe their very ordinary thoughts in the most extraordinary phrases, the most far-fetched, unnatural, and out-of-the-way expressions. Their sentences perpetually stalk about on stilts. They take so much pleasure in bombast, and write in such a high-flown, bloated, affected, hyperbolical and acrobatic style that their prototype is Ancient Pistol, whom his friend Falstaff once impatiently told to say what he had to say *like a man of this world.*

There is no expression in any other language exactly answering to the French *stile empesé*; but the thing itself exists all the more often. When associated with affectation, it is in literature what assumption of dignity, grand airs and primeness are in society; and equally intolerable. Dullness of mind is fond of donning this dress; just as an ordinary life it is stupid people who like being demure and formal.

An author who writes in the prim style resembles a man who dresses himself up in order to avoid being confounded or put on the same level with a mob—a risk never run by the *gentleman*, even in his worst clothes. The plebeian may be known by a certain showiness of attire and a wish to have everything spick and span; and in the same way, the commonplace person is betrayed by his style.

Nevertheless, an author follows a false aim if he tries to write exactly as he speaks. There is no style of writing but should have a certain trace of kinship with the *epigraphic* or *monumental* style, which is, indeed, the ancestor of all styles. For an author to write as he speaks is just as reprehensible as the opposite fault, to speak as he writes; for this gives a pedantic effect to what he says, and at the same time makes him hardly intelligible.

An obscure and vague manner of expression is always and everywhere a very bad sign. In ninety-nine cases out of a hundred it comes from vagueness of thought; and this again almost always means that there is something radically wrong and incongruous about the thought itself—in a word, that it is incorrect. When a right thought springs up in the mind, it strives after expression and is not long in reaching it; for clear thought easily finds words to fit it. If a man is capable of thinking anything at all, he is also always able to express it in clear, intelligible, and unambiguous terms. Those writers who construct difficult, obscure, involved, and equivocal sentences, most certainly do not know aright what it is that they want to say: they have only a dull consciousness of it, which is still in the stage of struggle to shape itself as thought. Often, indeed, their desire is to conceal from themselves and others that they really have nothing at all to say. They wish to appear to know what they do not know, to think what they do not think, to say what they do not say. If a man has some real communication to make, which will he choose—an indistinct or a clear way of expressing himself? Even Quintilian remarks that things which are said by a highly educated man are often easier to understand and much clearer; and that the less educated a man is, the more obscurely he will write—*plerumque accidit ut faciliora sint ad intelligendum et lucidiora multo que a doctissimo quoque dicuntur... Erit ergo etiam obscurior quo quisque deterior.*

An author should avoid enigmatical phrases; he should know whether he wants to say a thing or does not want to say it. It is this indecision of style that makes so many writers insipid. The only case that offers an exception to this rule arises when it is necessary to make a remark that is in some way improper.

As exaggeration generally produces an effect the opposite of that aimed at; so words, it is true, serve to make thought intelligible—but only up to a certain point. If words are heaped up beyond it, the thought becomes more and more obscure again. To find where the point lies is the problem of style, and the business of the critical faculty; for a word too much always defeats its purpose. This is what Voltaire means when he says that *the adjective is the enemy of the substantive.* But, as we have seen, many people try to conceal their poverty of thought under a flood of verbiage.

Accordingly let all redundancy be avoided, all stringing together of remarks which have no meaning and are not worth perusal. A writer must make a sparing use of the reader's time, patience and attention; so as to lead him to believe that his author writes what is worth careful study, and will reward the time spent upon it. It is always better to omit something good than to add that which is not worth saying at all. This is the right application of Hesiod's maxim, [Greek: pleon aemisu pantos]—the half is more than the whole. *Le secret pour être ennuyeux, c'est de tout dire.* Therefore, if possible, the quintessence only! mere leading thoughts! nothing that the reader would think for himself. To use many words to communicate few thoughts is everywhere the unmistakable sign of mediocrity. To gather much thought into few words stamps the man of genius.

Truth is most beautiful undraped; and the impression it makes is deep in proportion as its expression has been simple. This is so, partly because it then takes unobstructed possession of the hearer's whole soul, and leaves him no by-thought to distract him; partly, also, because he feels that here he is not being corrupted or cheated by the arts of rhetoric, but that all the effect of what is said comes from the thing itself. For instance, what declamation on the vanity of human existence could ever be more telling than the words of Job? *Man that is born of a woman hath but a short time to live and is full of misery. He cometh up, and is cut down, like a flower; he fleeth as it were a shadow, and never continueth in one stay.*

For the same reason Goethe's naïve poetry is incomparably greater than Schiller's rhetoric. It is this, again, that makes many popular songs so affecting. As in architecture an excess of decoration is to be avoided, so in the art of literature a writer must guard against all rhetorical finery, all useless amplification, and all superfluity of expression in general; in a word, he must strive after *chastity* of style. Every word that can be spared is hurtful if it remains. The law of simplicity and naïveté holds good of all fine art; for it is quite possible to be at once simple and sublime.

True brevity of expression consists in everywhere saying only what is worth saying, and in avoiding tedious detail about things which everyone can supply for himself. This involves correct discrimination between what it necessary and what is superfluous. A writer should never be brief at the expense of being clear, to say nothing of being grammatical. It shows lamentable want of judgment to weaken the expression of a thought, or to stunt the meaning of a period for the sake of using a few words less. But this is the precise endeavour of that false brevity nowadays so much in vogue, which proceeds by leaving out useful words and even by sacrificing grammar and logic. It is not only that such writers spare a word by making a single verb or adjective do duty for several different periods, so that the reader, as it were, has to grope his way through them in the dark; they also practice, in many other respects, an unseemingly economy of speech, in the effort to effect what they foolishly take to be brevity of expression and conciseness of style. By omitting something that might have thrown a light over the whole sentence, they turn it into a conundrum, which the reader tries to solve by going over it again and again.

It is wealth and weight of thought, and nothing else, that gives brevity to style, and makes it concise and pregnant. If a writer's ideas are important, luminous, and generally worth communicating, they will necessarily furnish matter and substance enough to fill out the periods which give them expression, and make these in all their parts both grammatically and verbally complete; and so much will this be the case that no one will ever find them hollow, empty or feeble. The diction will everywhere be brief and pregnant, and allow the thought to find intelligible and easy expression, and even unfold and move about with grace.

Therefore instead of contracting his words and forms of speech, let a writer enlarge his thoughts. If a man has been thinned by illness and finds his clothes too big, it is not by cutting them down, but by recovering his usual bodily condition, that he ought to make them fit him again.

Let me here mention an error of style, very prevalent nowadays, and, in the degraded state of literature and the neglect of ancient languages, always on the increase; I mean *subjectivity*. A writer commits this error when he thinks it enough if he himself knows what he means and wants to say, and takes no thought for the reader, who is left to get at the bottom of it as best he can. This is as though the author were holding a monologue; whereas, it ought to be a dialogue; and a dialogue, too, in which he must express himself all the more clearly inasmuch as he cannot hear the questions of his interlocutor.

Style should for this very reason never be subjective, but *objective*;

and it will not be objective unless the words are so set down that they directly force the reader to think precisely the same thing as the author thought when he wrote them. Nor will this result be obtained unless the author has always been careful to remember that thought so far follows the law of gravity that it travels from head to paper much more easily than from paper to head; so that he must assist the latter passage by every means in his power. If he does this, a writer's words will have a purely objective effect, like that of a finished picture in oils; whilst the subjective style is not much more certain in its working than spots on the wall, which look like figures only to one whose phantasy has been accidentally aroused by them; other people see nothing but spots and blurs. The difference in question applies to literary method as a whole; but it is often established also in particular instances. For example, in a recently published work I found the following sentence: *I have not written in order to increase the number of existing books.* This means just the opposite of what the writer wanted to say, and is nonsense as well.

He who writes carelessly confesses thereby at the very outset that he does not attach much importance to his own thoughts. For it is only where a man is convinced of the truth and importance of his thoughts, that he feels the enthusiasm necessary for an untiring and assiduous effort to find the clearest, finest, and strongest expression for them,—just as for sacred relics or priceless works of art there are provided silvern or golden receptacles. It was this feeling that led ancient authors, whose thoughts, expressed in their own words, have lived thousands of years, and therefore bear the honored title of *classics*, always to write with care. Plato, indeed, is said to have written the introduction to his *Republic* seven times over in different ways.

As neglect of dress betrays want of respect for the company a man meets, so a hasty, careless, bad style shows an outrageous lack of regard for the reader, who then rightly punishes it by refusing to read the book. It is especially amusing to see reviewers criticizing the works of others in their own most careless style—the style of a hireling. It is as though a judge were to come into court in dressing-gown and slippers! If I see a man badly and dirtily dressed, I feel some hesitation, at first, in entering into conversation with him: and when, on taking up a book, I am struck at once by the negligence of its style, I put it away.

Good writing should be governed by the rule that a man can think only one thing clearly at a time; and, therefore, that he should not be expected to think two or even more things in one and the same moment. But this is what is done when a writer breaks up his principal sentence into little pieces, for the purpose of pushing into the gaps thus made two or three other thoughts by way of parenthesis; thereby unnecessarily and wantonly confusing the reader. And here it is again my own countrymen who are chiefly in fault. That German lends itself to this way of writing, makes the thing possible, but does not justify it. No prose reads more easily or pleasantly than French, because, as a rule, it is free from the error in question. The Frenchman strings his thoughts together, as far as he can, in the most logical and natural order, and so lays them before his reader one after the other for convenient deliberation, so that every one of them may receive undivided attention. The German, on the other hand, weaves them together into a sentence which he twists and crosses, and crosses and twists again; because he wants to say six things all at once, instead of advancing them one by one. His aim should be to attract and hold the reader's attention; but, above and beyond neglect of this aim, he demands from the reader that he shall set the above mentioned rule at defiance, and think three or four different thoughts at one and the same time; or since that is impossible, that his thoughts shall succeed each other as quickly as the vibrations of a cord. In this way an author lays the foundation of his *stile empesé*, which is then carried to perfection by the use of high-flown, pompous expressions to communicate the simplest things, and other artifices of the same kind.

In those long sentences rich in involved parenthesis, like a box of boxes one within another, and padded out like roast geese stuffed with apples, it is really the *memory* that is chiefly taxed; while it is the understanding and the judgment which should be called into play, instead of having their activity thereby actually hindered and weakened. This kind of sentence furnishes the reader with mere half-phrases, which he is then called upon to collect carefully and store up in his memory, as though they were the pieces of a torn letter, afterwards to be completed and made sense of by the other halves to which they respectively belong. He is expected to go on reading for a little without exercising any thought, nay, exerting only his memory, in the hope that, when he comes to the end of the sentence, he may see its meaning and so receive something to think about; and he is thus given a great deal to learn by heart before obtaining anything to understand. This is manifestly wrong and an abuse of the reader's patience.

The ordinary writer has an unmistakable preference for this style, because it causes the reader to spend time and trouble in understanding that which he would have understood in a moment without it; and this makes it look as though the writer had more depth and intelligence than the reader. This is, indeed, one of those artifices referred to above, by means of which mediocre authors unconsciously, and as it were by instinct, strive to conceal their poverty of thought and give an appearance of the opposite. Their ingenuity in this respect is really astounding.

It is manifestly against all sound reason to put one thought obliquely on top of another, as though both together formed a wooden cross. But this is what is done where a writer interrupts what he has begun to say, for the purpose of inserting some quite alien matter; thus depositing with the reader a meaningless half-sentence, and bidding him keep it until the completion comes. It is much as though a man were to treat his guests by handing them an empty plate, in the hope of something appearing upon it. And commas used for a similar purpose belong to the same family as notes at the foot of the page and parenthesis in the middle of the text; nay, all three differ only in degree. If Demosthenes and Cicero occasionally inserted words by ways of parenthesis, they would have done better to have refrained.

But this style of writing becomes the height of absurdity when the parenthesis are not even fitted into the frame of the sentence, but wedged in so as directly to shatter it. If, for instance, it is an impertinent thing to interrupt another person when he is speaking, it is no less impertinent to interrupt oneself. But all bad, careless, and hasty authors, who scribble with the bread actually before their eyes, use this style of writing six times on a page, and rejoice in it. It consists in—it is advisable to give rule and example together, wherever it is possible—breaking up one phrase in order to glue in another. Nor is it merely out of laziness that they write thus. They do it out of stupidity; they think there is a charming *légèreté* about it; that it gives life to what they say. No doubt there are a few rare cases where such a form of sentence may be pardonable.

Few write in the way in which an architect builds; who, before he sets to work, sketches out his plan, and thinks it over down to its smallest details. Nay, most people write only as though they were playing dominoes; and, as in this game, the pieces are arranged half by design, half by chance, so it is with the sequence and connection of their sentences. They only have an idea of what the general shape of their work will be, and of the aim they set before themselves. Many are ignorant even of this, and write as the coral-insects build; period joins to period, and the Lord only knows what the author means.

Life now-a-days goes at a gallop; and the way in which this affects literature is to make it extremely superficial and slovenly.

21

THE PHILOSOPHY OF COMPOSITION

Edgar Allan Poe

Charles Dickens, in a note now lying before me, alluding to an examination I once made of the mechanism of *Barnaby Rudge*, says—'By the way, are you aware that Godwin wrote his *Caleb Williams* backwards? He first involved his hero in a web of difficulties, forming the second volume, and then, for the first, cast about him for some mode of accounting for what had been done.'

I cannot think this the *precise* mode of procedure on the part of Godwin—and indeed what he himself acknowledges, is not altogether in accordance with Mr Dickens' idea—but the author of *Caleb Williams* was too good an artist not to perceive the advantage derivable from at least a somewhat similar process. Nothing is more clear than that every plot, worth the name, must be elaborated to its *dénouement* before any thing be attempted with the pen. It is only with the *dénouement* constantly in view that we can give a plot its indispensable air of consequence, or causation, by making the incidents, and especially the tone at all points, tend to the development of the intention.

There is a radical error, I think, in the usual mode of constructing a story. Either history affords a thesis—or one is suggested by an incident of the day—or, at best, the author sets himself to work in the combination of striking events to form merely the basis of his narrative—designing, generally, to fill in with description, dialogue, or autorial comment, whatever crevices of fact, or action, may, from page to page, render themselves apparent.

I prefer commencing with the consideration of an *effect*. Keeping originality *always* in view—for he is false to himself who ventures to dispense with so obvious and so easily attainable a source of interest—I say to myself, in the first place, 'Of the innumerable effects, or impressions, of which the heart, the intellect, or (more generally) the soul is susceptible, what one shall I, on the present occasion, select?' Having chosen a novel, first, and secondly a vivid effect, I consider whether it can best be wrought by incident or tone—whether by ordinary incidents and peculiar tone, or the converse, or by peculiarity both of incident and tone—afterward looking about me (or rather within) for such combinations of event, or tone, as shall best aid me in the construction of the effect.

I have often thought how interesting a magazine paper might be written by any author who would—that is to say, who could—detail, step by step, the processes by which any one of his compositions attained its ultimate point of completion. Why such a paper has never been given to the world, I am much at a loss to say—but, perhaps, the autorial vanity has had more to do with the omission than any one other cause. Most writers—poets in especial—prefer having it understood that they compose by a species of fine frenzy—an ecstatic intuition—and would positively shudder at letting the public take a peep behind the scenes, at the elaborate and vacillating crudities of thought—at the true purposes seized only at the last moment—at the innumerable glimpses of idea that arrived not at the maturity of full view—at the fully matured fancies discarded in despair as unmanageable—at the cautious selections and rejections—at the painful erasures and interpolations—in a word, at the wheels and pinions—the tackle for scene-shifting—the step-ladders and demon-traps—the cock's feathers, the red paint and the black patches, which, in ninety-nine cases out of the hundred, constitute the properties of the literary *histrio*.

I am aware, on the other hand, that the case is by no means common, in which an author is at all in condition to retrace the steps by which his conclusions have been attained. In general, suggestions, having arisen pell-mell, are pursued and forgotten in a similar manner.

For my own part, I have neither sympathy with the repugnance alluded to, nor, at any time, the least difficulty in recalling to mind the progressive steps of any of my compositions; and, since the interest of an analysis, or reconstruction, such as I have considered a *desideratum*, is quite independent of any real or fancied interest in the thing analyzed, it will not be regarded as a breach of decorum on my part to show the *modus operandi* by which some one of my own works was put together. I select 'The Raven,' as the most generally known. It is my design to render it manifest that no one point in its composition is referable either to accident or intuition—that the work proceeded, step by step, to its completion with the precision and rigid consequence of a mathematical problem.

Let us dismiss, as irrelevant to the poem *per se*, the circumstance—or say the necessity—which, in the first place, gave rise to the intention of composing *a* poem that should suit at once the popular and the critical taste.

We commence, then, with this intention.

The initial consideration was that of extent. If any literary work is too long to be read at one sitting, we must be content to dispense with the immensely important effect derivable from unity of impression—for, if two sittings be required, the affairs of the world interfere, and every thing like totality is at once destroyed. But since, *ceteris paribus*, no poet can afford to dispense with *any thing* that may advance his design, it but remains to be seen whether there is, in extent, any advantage to counterbalance the loss of unity which attends it. Here I say no, at once. What we term a long poem is, in fact, merely a succession of brief ones—that is to say, of brief poetical effects. It is needless to demonstrate that a poem is such, only inasmuch as it intensely excites, by elevating, the soul; and all intense excitements are, through a psychal necessity, brief. For this reason, at least one half of the *Paradise Lost* is essentially prose—a succession of poetical excitements interspersed, *inevitably*, with corresponding depressions—the whole being deprived, through the extremeness of its length, of the vastly important artistic element, totality, or unity, of effect.

It appears evident, then, that there is a distinct limit, as regards length, to all works of literary art—the limit of a single sitting—and that, although in certain classes of prose composition, such as *Robinson*

Crusoe, (demanding no unity,) this limit may be advantageously overpassed, it can never properly be overpassed in a poem. Within this limit, the extent of a poem may be made to bear mathematical relation to its merit—in other words, to the excitement or elevation—again in other words, to the degree of the true poetical effect which it is capable of inducing; for it is clear that the brevity must be in direct ratio to the intensity of the intended effect:—this, with one proviso—that a certain degree of duration is absolutely requisite for the production of any effect at all.

Holding in view these considerations, as well as that degree of excitement which I deemed not above the popular, while not below the critical, taste, I reached at once what I conceived the proper *length* for my intended poem—a length of about one hundred lines. It is, in fact, a hundred and eight.

My next thought concerned the choice of an impression, or effect, to be conveyed: and here I may as well observe that, throughout the construction, I kept steadily in view the design of rendering the work *universally* appreciable. I should be carried too far out of my immediate topic were I to demonstrate a point upon which I have repeatedly insisted, and which, with the poetical, stands not in the slightest need of demonstration—the point, I mean, that Beauty is the sole legitimate province of the poem. A few words, however, in elucidation of my real meaning, which some of my friends have evinced a disposition to misrepresent. That pleasure which is at once the most intense, the most elevating, and the most pure, is, I believe, found in the contemplation of the beautiful. When, indeed, men speak of Beauty, they mean, precisely, not a quality, as is supposed, but an effect—they refer, in short, just to that intense and pure elevation of *soul*—*not* of intellect, or of heart—upon which I have commented, and which is experienced in consequence of contemplating 'the beautiful.' Now I designate Beauty as the province of the poem, merely because it is an obvious rule of Art that effects should be made to spring from direct causes—that objects should be attained through means best adapted for their attainment—no one as yet having been weak enough to deny that the peculiar elevation alluded to, is *most readily* attained in the poem. Now the object, Truth, or the satisfaction of the intellect, and the object, Passion, or the excitement of the heart, are, although attainable, to a certain extent, in poetry, far more readily attainable in prose. Truth, in fact, demands a precision, and Passion, a *homeliness* (the truly passionate will comprehend me) which are absolutely antagonistic to that Beauty which, I maintain, is the excitement, or pleasurable elevation, of the soul. It by no means follows from any thing here said, that passion, or even truth, may not be introduced, and even profitably introduced, into a poem—for they may serve in elucidation, or aid the general effect, as do discords in music, by contrast—but the true artist will always contrive, first, to tone them into proper subservience to the predominant aim, and, secondly, to enveil them, as far as possible, in that Beauty which is the atmosphere and the essence of the poem.

Regarding, then, Beauty as my province, my next question referred to the *tone* of its highest manifestation—and all experience has shown that this tone is one of *sadness*. Beauty of whatever kind, in its supreme development, invariably excites the sensitive soul to tears. Melancholy is thus the most legitimate of all the poetical tones.

The length, the province, and the tone, being thus determined, I betook myself to ordinary induction, with the view of obtaining some artistic piquancy which might serve me as a key-note in the construction of the poem—some pivot upon which the whole structure might turn. In carefully thinking over all the usual artistic effects—or more properly *points*, in the theatrical sense—I did not fail to perceive immediately that no one had been so universally employed as that of the *refrain*. The universality of its employment sufficed to assure me of its intrinsic value, and spared me the necessity of submitting it to analysis. I considered it, however, with regard to its susceptibility of improvement, and soon saw it to be in a primitive condition. As commonly used, the *refrain*, or burden, not only is limited to lyric verse, but depends for its impression upon the force of monotone—both in sound and thought. The pleasure is deduced solely from the sense of identity—of repetition. I resolved to diversify, and so vastly heighten, the effect, by adhering, in general, to the monotone of sound, while I continually varied that of thought: that is to say, I determined to produce continuously novel effects, by the variation *of the application* of the *refrain*—the *refrain* itself remaining, for the most part, unvaried.

These points being settled, I next bethought me of the *nature* of my *refrain*. Since its application was to be repeatedly varied, it was clear that the *refrain* itself must be brief, for there would have been an insurmountable difficulty in frequent variations of application in any sentence of length. In proportion to the brevity of the sentence, would, of course, be the facility of the variation. This led me at once to a single word as the best *refrain*.

The question now arose as to the *character* of the word. Having made up my mind to a *refrain*, the division of the poem into stanzas was, of course, a corollary: the *refrain* forming the close to each stanza. That such a close, to have force, must be sonorous and susceptible of protracted emphasis, admitted no doubt: and these considerations inevitably led me to the long *o* as the most sonorous vowel, in connection with *r* as the most producible consonant.

The sound of the *refrain* being thus determined, it became necessary to select a word embodying this sound, and at the same time in the fullest possible keeping with that melancholy which I had predetermined as the tone of the poem. In such a search it would have been absolutely impossible to overlook the word 'Nevermore.' In fact, it was the very first which presented itself.

The next *desideratum* was a pretext for the continuous use of the one word 'nevermore.' In observing the difficulty which I at once found in inventing a sufficiently plausible reason for its continuous repetition, I did not fail to perceive that this difficulty arose solely from the pre-assumption that the word was to be so continuously or monotonously spoken by *a human* being—I did not fail to perceive, in short, that the difficulty lay in the reconciliation of this monotony with the exercise of reason on the part of the creature repeating the word. Here, then, immediately arose the idea of a *non*-reasoning creature capable of speech; and, very naturally, a parrot, in the first instance, suggested itself, but was superseded forthwith by a Raven, as equally capable of speech, and infinitely more in keeping with the intended *tone.*

I had now gone so far as the conception of a Raven—the bird of ill omen—monotonously repeating the one word, 'Nevermore,' at the conclusion of each stanza, in a poem of melancholy tone, and in length about one hundred lines. Now, never losing sight of the object *supremeness*, or perfection, at all points, I asked myself—'Of all melancholy topics, what, according to the *universal* understanding of mankind, is the *most* melancholy?' Death—was the obvious reply. 'And when,' I said, 'is this most melancholy of topics most poetical?' From what I have already explained at some length, the answer, here also, is obvious—'When it most closely allies itself to *Beauty:* the death, then, of a beautiful woman is, unquestionably, the most poetical topic in the world—and equally is it beyond doubt that the lips best suited for such topic are those of a bereaved lover.'

I had now to combine the two ideas, of a lover lamenting his deceased mistress and a Raven continuously repeating the word 'Nevermore'—I had to combine these, bearing in mind my design of varying, at every turn, the *application* of the word repeated; but the only intelligible mode of such combination is that of imagining the Raven employing the word in answer to the queries of the lover. And here it was that I saw at once the opportunity afforded for the effect on which I had been depending—that is to say, the effect of the *variation of application.* I saw that I could make the first query propounded by the lover—the first query to which the Raven should reply 'Nevermore'—that I could make this first query a commonplace one—the second less so—the third still less, and so on—until at length the lover, startled from his original *nonchalance* by the melancholy character of the word itself—by its frequent repetition—and by a consideration of the ominous reputation of the fowl that uttered it—is at length excited to superstition, and wildly propounds queries of a far different character—queries whose solution he has passionately at heart—propounds them half in superstition and half in that species of despair which delights in self-torture—propounds them not altogether because he believes in the prophetic or demoniac character of the bird (which, reason assures him, is merely repeating a lesson learned by rote) but because he experiences a phrenzied pleasure in so modeling his questions as to receive from the *expected* 'Nevermore' the most delicious because the most intolerable of sorrow. Perceiving the opportunity thus afforded me—or, more strictly, thus forced upon me in the progress of the construction—I first established in mind the climax, or concluding query—that to which 'Nevermore' should be in the last place an answer—that in reply to which this word 'Nevermore' should involve the utmost conceivable amount of sorrow and despair.

Here then the poem may be said to have its beginning—at the end, where all works of art should begin—for it was here, at this point of my preconsiderations, that I first put pen to paper in the composition of the stanza:

> 'Prophet,' said I, 'thing of evil! prophet still if bird or devil!
> By that heaven that bends above us—by that God we both adore—
> Tell this soul with sorrow laden if, within the distant Aidenn,
> It shall clasp a sainted maiden whom the angels name Lenore—
> Clasp a rare and radiant maiden whom the angels name Lenore.'
> Quoth the Raven 'Nevermore.'

I composed this stanza, at this point, first that, by establishing the climax, I might the better vary and graduate, as regards seriousness and importance, the preceding queries of the lover—and, secondly, that I might definitely settle the rhythm, the metre, and the length and general arrangement of the stanza—as well as graduate the stanzas which were to precede, so that none of them might surpass this in rhythmical effect. Had I been able, in the subsequent composition, to construct more vigorous stanzas, I should, without scruple, have purposely enfeebled them, so as not to interfere with the climacteric effect.

And here I may as well say a few words of the versification. My first object (as usual) was originality. The extent to which this has been neglected, in versification, is one of the most unaccountable things in the world. Admitting that there is little possibility of variety in mere *rhythm*, it is still clear that the possible varieties of metre and stanza are absolutely infinite—and yet, *for centuries, no man, in verse, has ever done, or ever seemed to think of doing, an original thing*. The fact is, originality (unless in minds of very unusual force) is by no means a matter, as some suppose, of impulse or intuition. In general, to be found, it must be elaborately sought, and although a positive merit of the highest class, demands in its attainment less of invention than negation.

Of course, I pretend to no originality in either the rhythm or metre of 'The Raven.' The former is trochaic—the latter is octameter acatalectic, alternating with heptameter catalectic repeated in the *refrain* of the fifth verse, and terminating with tetrameter catalectic. Less pedantically—the feet employed throughout (trochees) consist of a long syllable followed by a short: the first line of the stanza consists of eight of these feet—the second of seven and a half (in effect two-thirds)—the third of eight—the fourth of seven and a half—the fifth the same—the sixth three and a half. Now, each of these lines, taken individually, has been employed before, and what originality 'The Raven' has, is in their *combination into stanza;* nothing even remotely approaching this combination has ever been attempted. The effect of this originality of combination is aided by other unusual, and some altogether novel effects, arising from an extension of the application of the principles of rhyme and alliteration.

The next point to be considered was the mode of bringing together the lover and the Raven—and the first branch of this consideration was the *locale*. For this the most natural suggestion might seem to be a forest, or the fields—but it has always appeared to me that a close *circumscription of space* is absolutely necessary to the effect of insulated incident:—it has the force of a frame to a picture. It has an indisputable moral power in keeping concentrated the attention, and, of course, must not be confounded with mere unity of place.

I determined, then, to place the lover in his chamber—in a chamber rendered sacred to him by memories of her who had frequented it. The room is represented as richly furnished—this in mere pursuance of the ideas I have already explained on the subject of Beauty, as the sole true poetical thesis.

The *locale* being thus determined, I had now to introduce the bird—and the thought of introducing him through the window, was inevitable. The idea of making the lover suppose, in the first instance, that the flapping of the wings of the bird against the shutter, is a 'tapping' at the door, originated in a wish to increase, by prolonging, the reader's curiosity, and in a desire to admit the incidental effect arising from the lover's throwing open the door, finding all dark, and thence adopting the half-fancy that it was the spirit of his mistress that knocked.

I made the night tempestuous, first, to account for the Raven's seeking admission, and secondly, for the effect of contrast with the (physical) serenity within the chamber.

I made the bird alight on the bust of Pallas, also for the effect of contrast between the marble and the plumage—it being understood that the bust was absolutely *suggested* by the bird—the bust of *Pallas* being chosen, first, as most in keeping with the scholarship of the lover, and, secondly, for the sonorousness of the word, Pallas, itself.

About the middle of the poem, also, I have availed myself of the force of contrast, with a view of deepening the ultimate impression. For example, an air of the fantastic—approaching as nearly to the ludicrous as was admissible—is given to the Raven's entrance. He comes in 'with many a flirt and flutter.'

> Not the least obeisance made he; not a moment stopped or
> stayed he;
> But, with mien of lord or lady, perched above my chamber door.

In the two stanzas which follow, the design is more obviously carried out:—

> Then this ebony bird beguiling my sad fancy into smiling,
> By the grave and stern decorum of the countenance it wore,
> 'Though thy crest be shorn and shaven thou,' I said, 'art sure no
> craven,
> Ghastly grim and ancient Raven wandering from the nightly shore—
> Tell me what thy lordly name is on the Night's Plutonian shore!'
> Quoth the Raven 'Nevermore.'

Much I marvelled this ungainly fowl to hear discourse so plainly,
Though its answer little meaning—little relevancy bore;
For we cannot help agreeing that no living human being
Ever yet was blessed with seeing bird above his chamber door—
Bird or beast upon the sculptured bust above his chamber door,
With such name as 'Nevermore.'

The effect of the *dénouement* being thus provided for, I immediately drop the fantastic for a tone of the most profound seriousness:—this tone commencing in the stanza directly following the one last quoted, with the line,

But the Raven, sitting lonely on that placid bust, spoke only, etc.

From this epoch the lover no longer jests—no longer sees any thing even of the fantastic in the Raven's demeanor. He speaks of him as a 'grim, ungainly, ghastly, gaunt, and ominous bird of yore,' and feels the 'fiery eyes' burning into his 'bosom's core.' This revolution of thought, or fancy, on the lover's part, is intended to induce a similar one on the part of the reader—to bring the mind into a proper frame for the *dénouement*—which is now brought about as rapidly and as *directly* as possible.

With the *dénouement* proper—with the Raven's reply, 'Nevermore,' to the lover's final demand if he shall meet his mistress in another world—the poem, in its obvious phase, that of a simple narrative, may be said to have its completion. So far, every thing is within the limits of the accountable—of the real. A raven, having learned by rote the single word 'Nevermore,' and having escaped from the custody of its owner, is driven, at midnight, through the violence of a storm, to seek admission at a window from which a light still gleams—the chamber-window of a student, occupied half in poring over a volume, half in dreaming of a beloved mistress deceased. The casement being thrown open at the fluttering of the bird's wings, the bird itself perches on the most convenient seat out of the immediate reach of the student, who, amused by the incident and the oddity of the visitor's demeanor, demands of it, in jest and without looking for a reply, its name. The raven addressed, answers with its customary word, 'Nevermore'—a word which finds immediate echo in the melancholy heart of the student, who, giving utterance aloud to certain thoughts suggested by the occasion, is again startled by the fowl's repetition of 'Nevermore.' The student now guesses the state of the case, but is impelled, as I have before explained, by the human thirst for self-torture, and in part by superstition, to propound such queries to the bird as will bring him, the lover, the most of the luxury of sorrow, through the anticipated answer 'Nevermore.' With the indulgence, to the utmost extreme, of this self-torture, the narration, in what I have termed its first or obvious phase, has a natural termination, and so far there has been no overstepping of the limits of the real.

But in subjects so handled, however skilfully, or with however vivid an array of incident, there is always a certain hardness or nakedness, which repels the artistical eye. Two things are invariably required—first, some amount of complexity, or more properly, adaptation; and, secondly, some amount of suggestiveness—some under-current, however indefinite of meaning. It is this latter, in especial, which imparts to a work of art so much of that *richness* (to borrow from colloquy a forcible term) which we are too fond of confounding with *the ideal.* It is the *excess* of the suggested meaning—it is the rendering this the upper instead of the under-current of the theme—which turns into prose (and that of the very flattest kind) the so-called poetry of the so-called transcendentalists.

Holding these opinions, I added the two concluding stanzas of the poem—their suggestiveness being thus made to pervade all the narrative which has preceded them. The under-current of meaning is rendered first apparent in the lines—

> 'Take thy beak from out my heart, and take thy form from off
> my door!'
> Quoth the Raven 'Nevermore!'

It will be observed that the words, 'from out my heart,' involve the first metaphorical expression in the poem. They, with the answer, 'Nevermore,' dispose the mind to seek a moral in all that has been previously narrated. The reader begins now to regard the Raven as emblematical—but it is not until the very last line of the very last stanza, that the intention of making him emblematical of *Mournful and Never-ending Remembrance* is permitted distinctly to be seen:

And the Raven, never flitting, still is sitting, still is sitting
On the pallid bust of Pallas just above my chamber door;
And his eyes have all the seeming of a demon's that is dreaming,
And the lamplight o'er him streaming throws his shadow on the
  floor;
And my soul from out that shadow that lies floating on the floor
    Shall be lifted—nevermore!

22

JOHN BULL

Washington Irving

'An old song, made by an aged old pate,
Of an old worshipful gentleman who had a great estate,
That kept a brave old house at a bountiful rate,
And an old porter to relieve the poor at his gate.
With an old study fill'd full of learned old books,
With an old reverend chaplain, you might know him by his looks,
With an old buttery hatch worn quite off the hooks,
And an old kitchen that maintained half-a-dozen old cooks.
Like an old courtier, etc.'

—OLD SONG.

There is no species of humor in which the English more excel, than that which consists in caricaturing and giving ludicrous appellations, or nicknames. In this way they have whimsically designated, not merely individuals, but nations; and, in their fondness for pushing a joke, they have not spared even themselves. One would think that, in personifying itself, a nation would be apt to picture something grand, heroic and imposing, but it is characteristic of the peculiar humor of the English, and of their love for what is blunt, comic, and familiar, that they have embodied their national oddities in the figure of a sturdy, corpulent old fellow, with a three-cornered hat, red waistcoat, leather breeches, and stout oaken cudgel. Thus they have taken a singular delight in exhibiting their most private foibles in a laughable point of view; and have been so successful in their delineations, that there is scarcely a being in actual existence more absolutely present to the public mind than that eccentric personage, John Bull.

Perhaps the continual contemplation of the character thus drawn of them has contributed to fix it upon the nation; and thus to give reality to what at first may have been painted in a great measure from the imagination. Men are apt to acquire peculiarities that are continually ascribed to them. The common orders of English seem wonderfully captivated with the beau ideal which they have formed of John Bull, and endeavor to act up to the broad caricature that is perpetually before their eyes. Unluckily, they sometimes make their boasted Bull-ism an apology for their prejudice or grossness; and this I have especially noticed among those truly homebred and genuine sons of the soil who have never migrated beyond the sound of Bow-bells. If one of these should be a little uncouth in speech, and apt to utter impertinent truths, he confesses that he is a real John Bull, and always speaks his mind. If he now and then flies into an unreasonable burst of passion about trifles, he observes, that John Bull is a choleric old blade, but then his passion is over in a moment, and he bears no malice. If he betrays a coarseness of taste, and an insensibility to foreign refinements, he thanks heaven for his ignorance—he is a plain John Bull, and has no relish for frippery and knick-knacks. His very proneness to be gulled by strangers, and to pay extravagantly for absurdities, is excused under the plea of munificence—for John is always more generous than wise.

Thus, under the name of John Bull, he will contrive to argue every fault into a merit, and will frankly convict himself of being the honestest fellow in existence.

However little, therefore, the character may have suited in the first instance, it has gradually adapted itself to the nation, or rather they have adapted themselves to each other; and a stranger who wishes to study English peculiarities, may gather much valuable information from the innumerable portraits of John Bull, as exhibited in the windows of the caricature-shops. Still, however, he is one of those fertile humorists, that are continually throwing out new portraits, and presenting different aspects from different points of view; and, often as he has been described, I cannot resist the temptation to give a slight sketch of him, such as he has met my eye.

John Bull, to all appearance, is a plain downright matter-of-fact fellow, with much less of poetry about him than rich prose. There is little of romance in his nature, but a vast deal of strong natural feeling. He excels in humor more than in wit; is jolly rather than gay; melancholy rather than morose; can easily be moved to a sudden tear, or surprised into a broad laugh; but he loathes sentiment, and has no turn for light pleasantry. He is a boon companion, if you allow him to have his humor, and to talk about himself; and he will stand by a friend in a quarrel, with life and purse, however soundly he may be cudgeled.

In this last respect, to tell the truth, he has a propensity to be somewhat too ready. He is a busy-minded personage, who thinks not merely for himself and family, but for all the country round, and is most generously disposed to be everybody's champion. He is continually volunteering his services to settle his neighbors' affairs, and takes it in great dudgeon if they engage in any matter of consequence without asking his advice; though he seldom engages in any friendly office of the kind without finishing by getting into a squabble with all parties, and then railing bitterly at their ingratitude. He unluckily took lessons in his youth in the noble science of defense, and having accomplished himself in the use of his limbs and his weapons, and become a perfect master at boxing and cudgel-play, he has had a troublesome life of it ever since. He cannot hear of a quarrel between the most distant of his neighbors, but he begins incontinently to fumble with the head of his cudgel, and consider whether his interest or honor does not require that he should meddle in the broil. Indeed he has extended his relations of pride and policy so completely over the whole country, that no event can take place, without infringing some of his finely-spun rights and dignities. Couched in his little domain, with these filaments stretching forth in every direction, he is like some choleric, bottle-bellied old spider, who has woven his web over a whole chamber, so that a fly cannot buzz, nor a breeze blow, without startling his repose, and causing him to sally forth wrathfully from his den.

Though really a good-hearted, good-tempered old fellow at bottom, yet he is singularly fond of being in the midst of contention. It is one of his peculiarities, however, that he only relishes the beginning of an affray; he always goes into a fight with alacrity, but comes out of it grumbling even when victorious; and though no one fights with more obstinacy to carry a contested point, yet, when the battle is over, and he comes to the reconciliation, he is so much taken up with the mere shaking of hands, that he is apt to let his antagonist pocket all that they have been quarreling about. It is not, therefore, fighting that he ought so much to be on his guard against, as making friends. It is difficult to cudgel him out of a farthing; but put him in a good humor, and you may bargain him out of all the money in his pocket. He is like a stout ship, which will weather the roughest storm uninjured, but roll its masts overboard in the succeeding calm.

He is a little fond of playing the magnifico abroad; of pulling out a long purse; flinging his money bravely about at boxing matches, horse races, cock fights, and carrying a high head among 'gentlemen of the fancy:' but immediately after one of these fits of extravagance, he will be taken with violent qualms of economy; stop short at the most trivial expenditure; talk desperately of being ruined and brought upon the parish; and, in such moods, will not pay the smallest tradesman's bill, without violent altercation. He is in fact the most punctual and discontented paymaster in the world; drawing his coin out of his breeches pocket with infinite reluctance; paying to the uttermost farthing, but accompanying every guinea with a growl.

With all his talk of economy, however, he is a bountiful provider, and a hospitable housekeeper. His economy is of a whimsical kind, its chief object being to devise how he may afford to be extravagant; for he will begrudge himself a beefsteak and pint of port one day, that he may roast an ox whole, broach a hogshead of ale, and treat all his neighbors on the next.

His domestic establishment is enormously expensive: not so much from any great outward parade, as from the great consumption of solid beef and pudding; the vast number of followers he feeds and clothes; and his singular disposition to pay hugely for small services.

He is a most kind and indulgent master, and, provided his servants humor his peculiarities, flatter his vanity a little now and then, and do not peculate grossly on him before his face, they may manage him to perfection. Everything that lives on him seems to thrive and grow fat. His house-servants are well paid, and pampered, and have little to do. His horses are sleek and lazy, and prance slowly before his state carriage; and his house-dogs sleep quietly about the door, and will hardly bark at a housebreaker.

His family mansion is an old castellated manor-house, gray with age, and of a most venerable, though weather-beaten appearance. It has been built upon no regular plan, but is a vast accumulation of parts, erected in various tastes and ages. The center bears evident traces of Saxon architecture, and is as solid as ponderous stone and old English oak can make it. Like all the relics of that style, it is full of obscure passages, intricate mazes, and dusky chambers; and though these have been partially lighted up in modern days, yet there are many places where you must still grope in the dark. Additions have been made to the original edifice from time to time, and great alterations have taken place; towers and battlements have been erected during wars and tumults: wings built in time of peace; and out-houses, lodges, and offices, run up according to the whim or convenience of different generations, until it has become one of the most spacious, rambling tenements imaginable. An entire wing is taken up with the family chapel, a reverend pile, that must have been exceedingly sumptuous, and, indeed, in spite of having been altered and simplified at various periods, has still a look of solemn religious pomp. Its walls within are stored with the monuments of John's ancestors; and it is snugly fitted up with soft cushions and well-lined chairs, where such of his family as are inclined to church services, may doze comfortably in the discharge of their duties.

To keep up this chapel has cost John much money; but he is stanch in his religion, and piqued in his zeal, from the circumstance that many dissenting chapels have been erected in his vicinity, and several of his neighbors, with whom he has had quarrels, are strong papists.

To do the duties of the chapel he maintains, at a large expense, a pious and portly family chaplain. He is a most learned and decorous personage, and a truly well-bred Christian, who always backs the old gentleman in his opinions, winks discreetly at his little peccadilloes, rebukes the children when refractory, and is of great use in exhorting the tenants to read their Bibles, say their prayers, and, above all, to pay their rents punctually, and without grumbling.

The family apartments are in a very antiquated taste, somewhat heavy, and often inconvenient, but full of the solemn magnificence of former times; fitted up with rich, though faded tapestry, unwieldy furniture, and loads of massy gorgeous old plate. The vast fireplaces, ample kitchens, extensive cellars, and sumptuous banqueting halls, all speak of the roaring hospitality of days of yore, of which the modern festivity at the manor-house is but a shadow. There are, however, complete suites of rooms apparently deserted and time-worn; and towers and turrets that are tottering to decay; so that in high winds there is danger of their tumbling about the ears of the household.

John has frequently been advised to have the old edifice thoroughly overhauled; and to have some of the useless parts pulled down, and the others strengthened with their materials; but the old gentleman always grows testy on this subject. He swears the house is an excellent house—that it is tight and weather-proof, and not to be shaken by tempests—that it has stood for several hundred years, and, therefore, is not likely to tumble down now—that as to its being inconvenient, his family is accustomed to the inconveniences, and would not be comfortable without them—that as to its unwieldy size and irregular construction, these result from its being the growth of centuries, and being improved by the wisdom of every generation—that an old family, like his, requires a large house to dwell in; new, upstart families may live in modern cottages and snug boxes; but an old English family should inhabit an old English manor-house. If you point out any part of the building as superfluous, he insists that it is material to the strength or decoration of the rest, and the harmony of the whole; and swears that the parts are so built into each other, that if you pull down one, you run the risk of having the whole about your ears.

The secret of the matter is, that John has a great disposition to protect and patronize. He thinks it indispensable to the dignity of an ancient and honorable family, to be bounteous in its appointments, and to be eaten up by dependents; and so, partly from pride, and partly from kind-heartedness, he makes it a rule always to give shelter and maintenance to his superannuated servants.

The consequence is, that, like many other venerable family establishments, his manor is encumbered by old retainers whom he cannot turn off, and an old style which he cannot lay down. His mansion is like a great hospital of invalids, and, with all its magnitude, is not a whit too large for its inhabitants. Not a nook or corner but is of use in housing some useless personage. Groups of veteran beef-eaters, gouty pensioners, and retired heroes of the buttery and the larder, are seen lolling about its walls, crawling over its lawns, dozing under its trees, or sunning themselves upon the benches at its doors. Every office and out-house is garrisoned by these supernumeraries and their families; for they are amazingly prolific, and when they die off, are sure to leave John a legacy of hungry mouths to be provided for. A mattock cannot be struck against the most mouldering tumble-down tower, but out pops, from some cranny or loop-hole, the gray pate of some superannuated hanger-on, who has lived at John's expense all his life, and makes the most grievous outcry at their pulling down the roof from over the head of a worn-out servant of the family. This is an appeal that John's honest heart never can withstand; so that a man, who has faithfully eaten his beef and pudding all his life, is sure to be rewarded with a pipe and tankard in his old days.

A great part of his park, also, is turned into paddocks, where his broken-down chargers are turned loose to graze undisturbed for the remainder of their existence—a worthy example of grateful recollection, which if some of his neighbors were to imitate, would not be to their discredit. Indeed, it is one of his great pleasures to point out these old steeds to his visitors, to dwell on their good qualities, extol their past services, and boast, with some little vainglory, of the perilous adventures and hardy exploits through which they have carried him.

He is given, however, to indulge his veneration for family usages, and family encumbrances, to a whimsical extent. His manor is infested by gangs of gypsies; yet he will not suffer them to be driven off, because they have infested the place time out of mind, and been regular poachers upon every generation of the family. He will scarcely permit a dry branch to be lopped from the great trees that surround the house, lest it should molest the rooks, that have bred there for centuries. Owls have taken possession of the dovecote; but they are hereditary owls, and must not be disturbed. Swallows have nearly choked up every chimney with their nests; martins build in every frieze and cornice; crows flutter about the towers, and perch on every weathercock; and old gray-headed rats may be seen in every quarter of the house, running in and out of their holes undauntedly in broad daylight. In short, John has such a reverence for everything that has been long in the family, that he will not hear even of abuses being reformed, because they are good old family abuses.

All those whims and habits have concurred woefully to drain the old gentleman's purse; and as he prides himself on punctuality in money matters, and wishes to maintain his credit in the neighborhood, they have caused him great perplexity in meeting his engagements. This, too, has been increased by the altercations and heart-burnings which are continually taking place in his family. His children have been brought up to different callings, and are of different ways of thinking; and as they have always been allowed to speak their minds freely, they do not fail to exercise the privilege most clamorously in the present posture of his affairs. Some stand up for the honor of the race, and are clear that the old establishment should be kept up in all its state, whatever may be the cost; others, who are more prudent and considerate, entreat the old gentleman to retrench his expenses, and to put his whole system of housekeeping on a more moderate footing. He has, indeed, at times, seemed inclined to listen to their opinions, but their wholesome advice has been completely defeated by the obstreperous conduct of one of his sons. This is a noisy, rattle-pated fellow, of rather low habits, who neglects his business to frequent ale-houses—is the orator of village clubs, and a complete oracle among the poorest of his father's tenants. No sooner does he hear any of his brothers mention reform or retrenchment, than up he jumps, takes the words out of their mouths, and roars out for an overturn. When his tongue is once going nothing can stop it. He rants about the room; hectors the old man about his spendthrift practices; ridicules his tastes and pursuits; insists that he shall turn the old servants out of doors; give the broken-down horses to the hounds; send the fat chaplain packing, and take a field-preacher in his place—nay, that the whole family mansion shall be leveled with the ground, and a plain one of brick and mortar built in its place. He rails at every social entertainment and family festivity, and skulks away growling to the ale-house whenever an equipage drives up to the door. Though constantly complaining of the emptiness of his purse, yet he scruples not to spend all his pocket-money in these tavern convocations, and even runs up scores for the liquor over which he preaches about his father's extravagance.

It may readily be imagined how little such thwarting agrees with the old cavalier's fiery temperament. He has become so irritable, from repeated crossings, that the mere mention of retrenchment or reform is a signal for a brawl between him and the tavern oracle. As the latter is too sturdy and refractory for paternal discipline, having grown out of all fear of the cudgel, they have frequent scenes of wordy warfare, which at times run so high, that John is fain to call in the aid of his son Tom, an officer who has served abroad, but is at present living at home, on half-pay. This last is sure to stand by the old gentleman, right or wrong; likes nothing so much as a racketing, roistering life; and is ready at a wink or nod, to out saber, and flourish it over the orator's head, if he dares to array himself against paternal authority.

These family dissensions, as usual, have got abroad, and are rare food for scandal in John's neighborhood. People begin to look wise, and shake their heads, whenever his affairs are mentioned. They all 'hope that matters are not so bad with him as represented; but when a man's own children begin to rail at his extravagance, things must be badly managed. They understand he is mortgaged over head and ears, and is continually dabbling with money-lenders. He is certainly an open-handed old gentleman, but they fear he has lived too fast;

indeed, they never knew any good come of this fondness for hunting, racing, reveling and prize-fighting. In short, Mr Bull's estate is a very fine one, and has been in the family a long time; but, for all that, they have known many finer estates come to the hammer.'

What is worst of all, is the effect which these pecuniary embarrassments and domestic feuds have had on the poor man himself. Instead of that jolly round corporation, and smug rosy face, which he used to present, he has of late become as shriveled and shrunk as a frost-bitten apple. His scarlet gold-laced waistcoat, which bellied out so bravely in those prosperous days when he sailed before the wind, now hangs loosely about him like a mainsail in a calm. His leather breeches are all in folds and wrinkles, and apparently have much ado to hold up the boots that yawn on both sides of his once sturdy legs.

Instead of strutting about as formerly, with his three-cornered hat on one side; flourishing his cudgel, and bringing it down every moment with a hearty thump upon the ground; looking everyone sturdily in the face, and trolling out a stave of a catch or a drinking-song; he now goes about whistling thoughtfully to himself, with his head drooping down, his cudgel tucked under his arm, and his hands thrust to the bottom of his breeches pockets, which are evidently empty.

Such is the plight of honest John Bull at present; yet for all this the old fellow's spirit is as tall and as gallant as ever. If you drop the least expression of sympathy or concern, he takes fire in an instant; swears that he is the richest and stoutest fellow in the country; talks of laying out large sums to adorn his house or buy another estate; and with a valiant swagger and grasping of his cudgel, longs exceedingly to have another bout at quarter-staff.

Though there may be something rather whimsical in all this, yet I confess I cannot look upon John's situation without strong feelings of interest. With all his odd humors and obstinate prejudices, he is a sterling-hearted old blade. He may not be so wonderfully fine a fellow as he thinks himself, but he is at least twice as good as his neighbors represent him. His virtues are all his own; all plain, homebred, and unaffected. His very faults smack of the raciness of his good qualities.

His extravagance savors of his generosity; his quarrelsomeness of his courage; his credulity of his open faith; his vanity of his pride; and his bluntness of his sincerity. They are all the redundancies of a rich and liberal character. He is like his own oak, rough without, but sound and solid within; whose bark abounds with excrescences in proportion to the growth and grandeur of the timber; and whose branches make a fearful groaning and murmuring in the least storm, from their very magnitude and luxuriance. There is something, too, in the appearance of his old family mansion that is extremely poetical and picturesque; and, as long as it can be rendered comfortably habitable, I should almost tremble to see it meddled with, during the present conflict of tastes and opinions. Some of his advisers are no doubt good architects, that might be of service; but many, I fear, are mere levelers, who, when they had once got to work with their mattocks on this venerable edifice, would never stop until they had brought it to the ground, and perhaps buried themselves among the ruins. All that I wish is, that John's present troubles may teach him more prudence in future. That he may cease to distress his mind about other people's affairs; that he may give up the fruitless attempt to promote the good of his neighbors, and the peace and happiness of the world, by dint of the cudgel; that he may remain quietly at home; gradually get his house into repair; cultivate his rich estate according to his fancy; husband his income—if he thinks proper; bring his unruly children into order—if he can; renew the jovial scenes of ancient prosperity; and long enjoy, on his paternal lands, a green, an honorable, and a merry old age.

23

SHAKESPEARE, OR THE POET

Ralph Waldo Emerson

Great men are more distinguished by range and extent than by originality. If we require the originality which consists in weaving, like a spider, their web from their own bowels; in finding clay and making bricks and building the house; no great men are original. Nor does valuable originality consist in unlikeness to other men. The hero is in the press of knights and the thick of events; and seeing what men want and sharing their desire, he adds the needful length of sight and of arm, to come at the desired point. The greatest genius is the most indebted man. A poet is no rattle-brain, saying what comes uppermost, and, because he says every thing, saying at last something good; but a heart in unison with his time and country. There is nothing whimsical and fantastic in his production, but sweet and sad earnest, freighted with the weightiest convictions and pointed with the most determined aim which any man or class knows of in his times.

The Genius of our life is jealous of individuals, and will not have any individual great, except through the general. There is no choice to genius. A great man does not wake up on some fine morning and say, 'I am full of life, I will go to sea and find an Antarctic continent: to-day I will square the circle: I will ransack botany and find a new food for man: I have a new architecture in my mind: I foresee a new mechanic power': no, but he finds himself in the river of the thoughts and events, forced onward by the ideas and necessities of his contemporaries. He stands where all the eyes of men look one way, and their hands all point in the direction in which he should go. The

Church has reared him amidst rites and pomps, and he carries out the advice which her music gave him, and builds a cathedral needed by her chants and processions. He finds a war raging: it educates him, by trumpet, in barracks, and he betters the instruction. He finds two counties groping to bring coal, or flour, or fish, from the place of production to the place of consumption, and he hits on a railroad. Every master has found his materials collected, and his power lay in his sympathy with his people and in his love of the materials he wrought in. What an economy of power! and what a compensation for the shortness of life! All is done to his hand. The world has brought him thus far on his way. The human race has gone out before him, sunk the hills, filled the hollows and bridged the rivers. Men, nations, poets, artisans, women, all have worked for him, and he enters into their labors. Choose any other thing, out of the line of tendency, out of the national feeling and history, and he would have all to do for himself: his powers would be expended in the first preparations. Great genial power, one would almost say, consists in not being original at all; in being altogether receptive; in letting the world do all, and suffering the spirit of the hour to pass unobstructed through the mind.

Shakespeare's youth fell in a time when the English people were importunate for dramatic entertainments. The court took offence easily at political allusions and attempted to suppress them. The Puritans, a growing and energetic party, and the religious among the Anglican church, would suppress them. But the people wanted them. Inn-yards, houses without roofs, and extemporaneous enclosures at country fairs were the ready theatres of strolling players. The people had tasted this new joy; and, as we could not hope to suppress newspapers now,—no, not by the strongest party,—neither then could king, prelate, or puritan, alone or united, suppress an organ which was ballad, epic, newspaper, caucus, lecture, Punch and library, at the same time. Probably king, prelate and puritan, all found their own account in it. It had become, by all causes, a national interest,—by no means conspicuous, so that some great scholar would have thought of treating it in an English history,—but not a whit less considerable because it was cheap and of no account, like a baker's-shop. The best proof of its vitality is the crowd of writers which suddenly broke into this field; Kyd, Marlow, Greene, Jonson, Chapman, Dekker, Webster, Heywood, Middleton, Peele, Ford, Massinger, Beaumont and Fletcher.

The secure possession, by the stage, of the public mind, is of the first importance to the poet who works for it. He loses no time in idle experiments. Here is audience and expectation prepared. In the case of Shakespeare there is much more. At the time when he left Stratford and went up to London, a great body of stage-plays of all dates and writers existed in manuscript and were in turn produced on the boards. Here is the Tale of Troy, which the audience will bear hearing some part of, every week; the Death of Julius Caesar, and other stories out of Plutarch, which they never tire of; a shelf full of English history, from the chronicles of Brut and Arthur, down to the royal Henries, which men hear eagerly; and a string of doleful tragedies, merry Italian tales and Spanish voyages, which all the London 'prentices know. All the mass has been treated, with more or less skill, by every playwright, and the prompter has the soiled and tattered manuscripts. It is now no longer possible to say who wrote them first. They have been the property of the Theatre so long, and so many rising geniuses have enlarged or altered them, inserting a speech or a whole scene, or adding a song, that no man can any longer claim copyright in this work of numbers. Happily, no man wishes to. They are not yet desired in that way. We have few readers, many spectators and hearers. They had best lie where they are.

Shakespeare, in common with his comrades, esteemed the mass of old plays waste stock, in which any experiment could be freely tried. Had the prestige which hedges about a modern tragedy existed, nothing could have been done. The rude warm blood of the living England circulated in the play, as in street-ballads, and gave body which he wanted to his airy and majestic fancy. The poet needs a ground in popular tradition on which he may work, and which, again, may restrain his art within the due temperance. It holds him to the people, supplies a foundation for his edifice, and in furnishing so much work done to his hand, leaves him at leisure and in full strength for the audacities of his imagination. In short, the poet owes to his legend what sculpture owed to the temple. Sculpture in Egypt and in Greece grew up in subordination to architecture. It was the ornament of the temple wall: at first a rude relief carved on pediments, then the relief became bolder and a head or arm was projected from the wall; the groups being still arranged with reference to the building, which serves also as a frame to hold the figures; and when at last the greatest freedom of style and treatment was reached, the prevailing genius of architecture still enforced a certain calmness and continence in the statue. As soon as the statue was begun for itself, and with no reference to the temple or palace, the art began to decline: freak, extravagance and exhibition took the place of the old temperance. This balance-wheel, which the sculptor found in architecture, the perilous irritability of poetic talent found in the accumulated dramatic materials to which the people were already wonted, and which had a certain excellence which no single genius, however extraordinary, could hope to create.

In point of fact it appears that Shakespeare did owe debts in all directions, and was able to use whatever he found; and the amount of indebtedness may be inferred from Malone's laborious computations in regard to the First, Second and Third parts of Henry VI, in which, 'out of 6043 lines, 1771 were written by some author preceding Shakespeare, 2373 by him, on the foundation laid by his predecessors, and 1899 were entirely his own.' And the proceeding investigation hardly leaves a single drama of his absolute invention. Malone's sentence is an important piece of external history. In Henry VIII I think I see plainly the cropping out of the original rock on which his own finer stratum was laid. The first play was written by a superior, thoughtful man, with a vicious ear. I can mark his lines, and know well their cadence. See Wolsey's soliloquy, and the following scene with Cromwell, where instead of the metre of Shakespeare, whose secret is that the thought constructs the tune, so that reading for the sense will best bring out the rhythm,—here the lines are constructed on a given tune, and the verse has even a trace of pulpit eloquence. But the play contains through all its length unmistakable traits of Shakespeare's hand, and some passages, as the account of the coronation, are like autographs. What is odd, the compliment to Queen Elizabeth is in the bad rhythm.

Shakespeare knew that tradition supplies a better fable than any invention can. If he lost any credit of design, he augmented his resources; and, at that day, our petulant demand for originality was not so much pressed. There was no literature for the million. The universal reading, the cheap press, were unknown. A great poet who appears in illiterate times, absorbs into his sphere all the light which is any where radiating. Every intellectual jewel, every flower of sentiment it is his fine office to bring to his people; and he comes to value his memory equally with his invention. He is therefore little solicitous whence his thoughts have been derived; whether through translation, whether through tradition, whether by travel in distant countries, whether by inspiration; from whatever source, they are equally welcome to his uncritical audience. Nay, he borrows very near home. Other men say wise things as well as he; only they say a good many foolish things, and do not know when they have spoken wisely. He knows the sparkle of the true stone, and puts it in high place, wherever he finds it. Such is the happy position of Homer perhaps; of Chaucer, of Saadi. They felt that all wit was their wit. And they are librarians and historiographers, as well as poets. Each romancer was heir and dispenser of all the hundred tales of the world,—

> 'Presenting Thebes' and Pelops' line
> And the tale of Troy divine.'

The influence of Chaucer is conspicuous in all our early literature; and more recently not only Pope and Dryden have been beholden to him, but, in the whole society of English writers, a large unacknowledged debt is easily traced. One is charmed with the opulence which feeds so many pensioners. But Chaucer is a huge borrower. Chaucer, it seems, drew continually, through Lydgate and Caxton, from Guido di Colonna, whose Latin romance of the Trojan war was in turn a compilation from Dares Phrygius, Ovid and Statius. Then Petrarch, Boccaccio and the Provencal poets are his benefactors: the Romaunt of the Rose is only judicious translation from William of Lorris and John of Meung: Troilus and Creseide, from Lollius of Urbino: The Cock and the Fox, from the *Lais* of Marie: The House of Fame, from the French or Italian: and poor Gower he uses as if he were only a brick-kiln or stone-quarry out of which to build his house. He steals by this apology,—that what he takes has no worth where he finds it and the greatest where he leaves it. It has come to be practically a sort of rule in literature, that a man having once shown himself capable of original writing, is entitled thenceforth to steal from the writings of others at discretion. Thought is the property of him who can entertain it and of him who can adequately place it. A certain awkwardness marks the use of borrowed thoughts; but as soon as we have learned what to do with them they become our own.

Thus all originality is relative. Every thinker is retrospective. The learned member of the legislature, at Westminster or at Washington, speaks and votes for thousands. Show us the constituency, and the now invisible channels by which the senator is made aware of their wishes; the crowd of practical and knowing men, who, by correspondence or conversation, are feeding him with evidence, anecdotes and estimates, and it will bereave his fine attitude and resistance of something of their impressiveness. As Sir Robert Peel and Mr Webster vote, so Locke and Rousseau think, for thousands; and so there were fountains all around Homer, Menu, Saadi, or Milton, from which they drew; friends, lovers, books, traditions, proverbs,—all perished,—which, if seen, would go to reduce the wonder. Did the bard speak with authority? Did he feel himself overmatched by any companion? The appeal is to the consciousness of the writer. Is there at last in his breast a Delphi whereof to ask concerning any thought or thing, whether it be verily so, yea or nay? and to have answer, and to rely on that? All the debts which such a man could contract to other wit would never disturb his consciousness of originality; for the ministrations of books and of other minds are a whiff of smoke to that most private reality with which he has conversed.

It is easy to see that what is best written or done by genius in the world, was no man's work, but came by wide social labor, when a thousand wrought like one, sharing the same impulse. Our

English Bible is a wonderful specimen of the strength and music of the English language. But it was not made by one man, or at one time; but centuries and churches brought it to perfection. There never was a time when there was not some translation existing. The Liturgy, admired for its energy and pathos, is an anthology of the piety of ages and nations, a translation of the prayers and forms of the Catholic church,—these collected, too, in long periods, from the prayers and meditations of every saint and sacred writer all over the world. Grotius makes the like remark in respect to the Lord's Prayer, that the single clauses of which it is composed were already in use in the time of Christ, in the Rabbinical forms. He picked out the grains of gold. The nervous language of the Common Law, the impressive forms of our courts and the precision and substantial truth of the legal distinctions, are the contribution of all the sharp-sighted, strong-minded men who have lived in the countries where these laws govern. The translation of Plutarch gets its excellence by being translation on translation. There never was a time when there was none. All the truly idiomatic and national phrases are kept, and all others successively picked out and thrown away. Something like the same process had gone on, long before, with the originals of these books. The world takes liberties with world-books. Vedas, Aesop's Fables, Pilpay, Arabian Nights, Cid, Iliad, Robin Hood, Scottish Minstrelsy, are not the work of single men. In the composition of such works the time thinks, the market thinks, the mason, the carpenter, the merchant, the farmer, the fop, all think for us. Every book supplies its time with one good word; every municipal law, every trade, every folly of the day; and the generic catholic genius who is not afraid or ashamed to owe his originality to the originality of all, stands with the next age as the recorder and embodiment of his own.

We have to thank the researches of antiquaries, and the Shakespeare Society, for ascertaining the steps of the English drama, from the Mysteries celebrated in churches and by churchmen, and the final detachment from the church, and the completion of secular plays, from Ferrex and Porrex, and Gammer Gurton's Needle, down to the possession of the stage by the very pieces which Shakespeare altered, remodelled and finally made his own. Elated with success and piqued by the growing interest of the problem, they have left no book-stall unsearched, no chest in a garret unopened, no file of old yellow accounts to decompose in damp and worms, so keen was the hope to discover whether the boy Shakespeare poached or not, whether he held horses at the theatre door, whether he kept school, and why he left in his will only his second-best bed to Ann Hathaway, his wife.

There is somewhat touching in the madness with which the passing age mischooses the object on which all candles shine and all eyes are turned; the care with which it registers every trifle touching Queen Elizabeth and King James, and the Essexes, Leicesters, Burleighs and Buckinghams; and lets pass without a single valuable note the founder of another dynasty, which alone will cause the Tudor dynasty to be remembered,—the man who carries the Saxon race in him by the inspiration which feeds him, and on whose thoughts the foremost people of the world are now for some ages to be nourished, and minds to receive this and not another bias. A popular player;—nobody suspected he was the poet of the human race; and the secret was kept as faithfully from poets and intellectual men as from courtiers and frivolous people. Bacon, who took the inventory of the human understanding for his times, never mentioned his name. Ben Jonson, though we have strained his few words of regard and panegyric, had no suspicion of the elastic fame whose first vibrations he was attempting. He no doubt thought the praise he has conceded to him generous, and esteemed himself, out of all question, the better poet of the two.

If it need wit to know wit, according to the proverb, Shakespeare's time should be capable of recognizing it. Sir Henry Wotton was born four years after Shakespeare, and died twenty-three years after him; and I find, among his correspondents and acquaintances, the following persons: Theodore Beza, Isaac Casaubon, Sir Philip Sidney, the Earl of Essex, Lord Bacon, Sir Walter Raleigh, John Milton, Sir Henry Vane, Isaac Walton, Dr Donne, Abraham Cowley, Bellarmine, Charles Cotton, John Pym, John Hales, Kepler, Vieta, Albericus Gentilis, Paul Sarpi, Arminius; with all of whom exists some token of his having communicated, without enumerating many others whom doubtless he saw,—Shakespeare, Spenser, Jonson, Beaumont, Massinger, the two Herberts, Marlow, Chapman and the rest. Since the constellation of great men who appeared in Greece in the time of Pericles, there was never any such society;—yet their genius failed them to find out the best head in the universe. Our poet's mask was impenetrable. You cannot see the mountain near. It took a century to make it suspected; and not until two centuries had passed, after his death, did any criticism which we think adequate begin to appear. It was not possible to write the history of Shakespeare till now; for he is the father of German literature: it was with the introduction of Shakespeare into German, by Lessing, and the translation of his works by Wieland and Schlegel, that the rapid burst of German literature was most intimately connected. It was not until the nineteenth century, whose speculative genius is a sort of living Hamlet, that the tragedy of Hamlet could find such wondering readers. Now, literature, philosophy and thought are Shakespearized. His mind is the horizon beyond which, at present, we do not see. Our ears are educated to music by his rhythm. Coleridge and Goethe are the only critics who have expressed our convictions with any adequate fidelity: but there is in all cultivated minds a silent appreciation of his superlative power and beauty, which, like Christianity, qualifies the period.

The Shakespeare Society have inquired in all directions, advertised the missing facts, offered money for any information that will lead to proof,—and with what result? Beside some important illustration of the history of the English stage, to which I have adverted, they have gleaned a few facts touching the property, and dealings in regard to property, of the poet. It appears that from year to year he owned a larger share in the Blackfriars' Theatre: its wardrobe and other appurtenances were his: that he bought an estate in his native village with his earnings as writer and shareholder; that he lived in the best house in Stratford; was intrusted by his neighbors with their commissions in London, as of borrowing money, and the like; that he was a veritable farmer. About the time when he was writing *Macbeth*, he sues Philip Rogers, in the borough-court of Stratford, for thirty-five shillings, ten pence, for corn delivered to him at different times;

and in all respects appears as a good husband, with no reputation for eccentricity or excess. He was a good-natured sort of man, an actor and shareholder in the theatre, not in any striking manner distinguished from other actors and managers. I admit the importance of this information. It was well worth the pains that have been taken to procure it.

But whatever scraps of information concerning his condition these researches may have rescued, they can shed no light upon that infinite invention which is the concealed magnet of his attraction for us. We are very clumsy writers of history. We tell the chronicle of parentage, birth, birth-place, schooling, school-mates, earning of money, marriage, publication of books, celebrity, death; and when we have come to an end of this gossip, no ray of relation appears between it and the goddess-born; and it seems as if, had we dipped at random into the 'Modern Plutarch,' and read any other life there, it would have fitted the poems as well. It is the essence of poetry to spring, like the rainbow daughter of Wonder, from the invisible, to abolish the past and refuse all history. Malone, Warburton, Dyce and Collier have wasted their oil. The famed theatres, Covent Garden, Drury Lane, the Park and Tremont have vainly assisted. Betterton, Garrick, Kemble, Kean and Macready dedicate their lives to this genius; him they crown, elucidate, obey and express. The genius knows them not. The recitation begins; one golden word leaps out immortal from all this painted pedantry and sweetly torments us with invitations to its own inaccessible homes. I remember I went once to see the Hamlet of a famed performer, the pride of the English stage; and all I then heard and all I now remember of the tragedian was that in which the tragedian had no part; simply Hamlet's question to the ghost:—

> 'What may this mean,
> That thou, dead corse, again in complete steel
> Revisit'st thus the glimpses of the moon?'

That imagination which dilates the closet he writes in to the world's dimension, crowds it with agents in rank and order, as quickly reduces the big reality to be the glimpses of the moon. These tricks of his magic spoil for us the illusions of the greenroom. Can any biography shed light on the localities into which *The Midsummer Night's Dream* admits me? Did Shakespeare confide to any notary or parish recorder, sacristan, or surrogate in Stratford, the genesis of that delicate creation? The forest of Arden, the nimble air of Scone Castle, the moonlight of Portia's villa, 'the antres vast and desarts idle' of Othello's captivity,—where is the third cousin, or grand-nephew, the chancellor's file of accounts, or private letter, that has kept one word of those transcendent secrets? In fine, in this drama, as in all great works of art,—in the Cyclopean architecture of Egypt and India, in the Phidian sculpture, the Gothic minsters, the Italian painting, the Ballads of Spain and Scotland,—the Genius draws up the ladder after him, when the creative age goes up to heaven, and gives way to a new age, which sees the works and asks in vain for a history.

Shakespeare is the only biographer of Shakespeare; and even he can tell nothing, except to the Shakespeare in us, that is, to our most apprehensive and sympathetic hour. He cannot step from off his tripod and give us anecdotes of his inspirations. Read the antique documents extricated, analyzed and compared by the assiduous Dyce and Collier, and now read one of these skyey sentences,—aerolites,—which seem to have fallen out of heaven, and which not your experience but the man within the breast has accepted as words of fate, and tell me if they match; if the former account in any manner for the latter; or which gives the most historical insight into the man.

Hence, though our external history is so meagre, yet, with Shakespeare for biographer, instead of Aubrey and Rowe, we have really the information which is material; that which describes character and fortune, that which, if we were about to meet the man and deal with him, would most import us to know. We have his recorded convictions on those questions which knock for answer at every heart,—on life and death, on love, on wealth and poverty, on the prizes of life and the ways whereby we come at them; on the characters of men, and the influences, occult and open, which affect their fortunes; and on those mysterious and demoniacal powers which defy our science and which yet interweave their malice and their gift in our brightest hours. Who ever read the volume of the Sonnets without finding that the poet had there revealed, under masks that are no masks to the intelligent, the lore of friendship and of love; the confusion of sentiments in the most susceptible, and, at the same time, the most intellectual of men? What trait of his private mind has he hidden in his dramas? One can discern, in his ample pictures of the gentleman and the king, what forms and humanities pleased him; his delight in troops of friends, in large hospitality, in cheerful giving. Let Timon, let Warwick, let Antonio the merchant answer for his great heart. So far from Shakespeare's being the least known, he is the one person, in all modern history, known to us. What point of morals, of manners, of economy, of philosophy, of religion, of taste, of the conduct of life, has he not settled? What mystery has he not signified his knowledge of? What office, or function, or district of man's work, has he not remembered? What king has he not taught state, as Talma taught Napoleon? What maiden has not found him finer than her delicacy? What lover has he not outloved? What sage has he not outseen? What gentleman has he not instructed in the rudeness of his behavior?

Some able and appreciating critics think no criticism on Shakespeare valuable that does not rest purely on the dramatic merit; that he is falsely judged as poet and philosopher. I think as highly as these critics of his dramatic merit, but still think it secondary. He was a full man, who liked to talk; a brain exhaling thoughts and images, which, seeking vent, found the drama next at hand. Had he been less, we should have had to consider how well he filled his place, how good a dramatist he was,—and he is the best in the world. But it turns out that what he has to say is of that weight as to withdraw some attention from the vehicle; and he is like some saint whose history is to be rendered into all languages, into verse and prose, into songs and pictures, and cut up into proverbs; so that the occasion which gave the saint's meaning the form of a conversation, or of a prayer, or of a code of laws, is immaterial compared with the universality of its application. So it fares with the wise Shakespeare and his book of life. He wrote the airs for all our modern music: he wrote the text of modern life; the text of manners: he drew the man of England

and Europe; the father of the man in America; he drew the man, and described the day, and what is done in it: he read the hearts of men and women, their probity, and their second thought and wiles; the wiles of innocence, and the transitions by which virtues and vices slide into their contraries: he could divide the mother's part from the father's part in the face of the child, or draw the fine demarcations of freedom and of fate: he knew the laws of repression which make the police of nature: and all the sweets and all the terrors of human lot lay in his mind as truly but as softly as the landscape lies on the eye. And the importance of this wisdom of life sinks the form, as of Drama or Epic, out of notice 'Tis like making a question concerning the paper on which a king's message is written.

Shakespeare is as much out of the category of eminent authors, as he is out of the crowd. He is inconceivably wise; the others, conceivably. A good reader can, in a sort, nestle into Plato's brain and think from thence; but not into Shakespeare's. We are still out of doors. For executive faculty, for creation, Shakespeare is unique. No man can imagine it better. He was the farthest reach of subtlety compatible with an individual self,—the subtilest of authors, and only just within the possibility of authorship. With this wisdom of life is the equal endowment of imaginative and of lyric power. He clothed the creatures of his legend with form and sentiments as if they were people who had lived under his roof; and few real men have left such distinct characters as these fictions. And they spoke in language as sweet as it was fit. Yet his talents never seduced him into an ostentation, nor did he harp on one string. An omnipresent humanity coordinates all his faculties. Give a man of talents a story to tell, and his partiality will presently appear. He has certain observations, opinions, topics, which have some accidental prominence, and which he disposes all to exhibit. He crams this part and starves that other part, consulting not the fitness of the thing, but his fitness and strength. But Shakespeare has no peculiarity, no importunate topic; but all is duly given; no veins, no curiosities; no cow-painter, no bird-fancier, no mannerist is he: he has no discoverable egotism: the great he tells greatly; the small subordinately. He is wise without emphasis or assertion; he is strong, as nature is strong, who lifts the land into mountain slopes without effort and by the same rule as she floats a bubble in the air, and likes as well to do the one as the other. This makes that equality of power in farce, tragedy, narrative, and love-songs; a merit so incessant that each reader is incredulous of the perception of other readers.

This power of expression, or of transferring the inmost truth of things into music and verse, makes him the type of the poet and has added a new problem to metaphysics. This is that which throws him into natural history, as a main production of the globe, and as announcing new eras and ameliorations. Things were mirrored in his poetry without loss or blur: he could paint the fine with precision, the great with compass, the tragic and the comic indifferently and without any distortion or favor. He carried his powerful execution into minute details, to a hair point; finishes an eyelash or a dimple as firmly as he draws a mountain; and yet these, like nature's, will bear the scrutiny of the solar microscope.

In short, he is the chief example to prove that more or less of production, more or fewer pictures, is a thing indifferent. He had the power to make one picture. Daguerre learned how to let one flower etch its image on his plate of iodine, and then proceeds at leisure to etch a million. There are always objects; but there was never representation. Here is perfect representation, at last; and now let the world of figures sit for their portraits. No recipe can be given for the making of a Shakespeare; but the possibility of the translation of things into song is demonstrated.

His lyric power lies in the genius of the piece. The sonnets, though their excellence is lost in the splendor of the dramas, are as inimitable as they; and it is not a merit of lines, but a total merit of the piece; like the tone of voice of some incomparable person, so is this a speech of poetic beings, and any clause as unproducible now as a whole poem.

Though the speeches in the plays, and single lines, have a beauty which tempts the ear to pause on them for their euphuism, yet the sentence is so loaded with meaning and so linked with its foregoers and followers, that the logician is satisfied. His means are as admirable as his ends; every subordinate invention, by which he helps himself to connect some irreconcilable opposites, is a poem too. He is not reduced to dismount and walk because his horses are running off with him in some distant direction: he always rides.

The finest poetry was first experience; but the thought has suffered a transformation since it was an experience. Cultivated men often attain a good degree of skill in writing verses; but it is easy to read, through their poems, their personal history: any one acquainted with the parties can name every figure; this is Andrew and that is Rachel. The sense thus remains prosaic. It is a caterpillar with wings, and not yet a butterfly. In the poet's mind the fact has gone quite over into the new element of thought, and has lost all that is exuvial. This generosity abides with Shakespeare. We say, from the truth and closeness of his pictures, that he knows the lesson by heart. Yet there is not a trace of egotism.

One more royal trait properly belongs to the poet. I mean his cheerfulness, without which no man can be a poet,—for beauty is his aim. He loves virtue, not for its obligation but for its grace: he delights in the world, in man, in woman, for the lovely light that sparkles from them. Beauty, the spirit of joy and hilarity, he sheds over the universe. Epicurus relates that poetry hath such charms that a lover might forsake his mistress to partake of them. And the true bards have been noted for their firm and cheerful temper. Homer lies in sunshine; Chaucer is glad and erect; and Saadi says, 'It was rumored abroad that I was penitent; but what had I to do with repentance?' Not less sovereign and cheerful,—much more sovereign and cheerful, is the tone of Shakespeare. His name suggests joy and emancipation to the heart of men. If he should appear in any company of human souls, who would not march in his troop? He touches nothing that does not borrow health and longevity from his festal style.

And now, how stands the account of man with this bard and benefactor, when, in solitude, shutting our ears to the reverberations of his fame, we seek to strike the balance? Solitude has austere lessons; it can teach us to spare both heroes and poets; and it weighs Shakespeare also, and finds him to share the halfness and imperfection of humanity.

Shakespeare, Homer, Dante, Chaucer, saw the splendor of meaning that plays over the visible world; knew that a tree had another use than for apples, and corn another than for meal, and the ball of the earth, than for tillage and roads: that these things bore a second and finer harvest to the mind, being emblems of its thoughts, and conveying in all their natural history a certain mute commentary on human life. Shakespeare employed them as colors to compose his picture. He rested in their beauty; and never took the step which seemed inevitable to such genius, namely to explore the virtue which resides in these symbols and imparts this power:—what is that which they themselves say? He converted the elements which waited on his command, into entertainments. He was master of the revels to mankind. Is it not as if one should have, through majestic powers of science, the comets given into his hand, or the planets and their moons, and should draw them from their orbits to glare with the municipal fireworks on a holiday night, and advertise in all towns, 'Very superior pyrotechny this evening!' Are the agents of nature, and the power to understand them, worth no more than a street serenade, or the breath of a cigar? One remembers again the trumpet-text in the Koran,—'The heavens and the earth and all that is between them, think ye we have created them in jest?'As long as the question is of talent and mental power, the world of men has not his equal to show. But when the question is, to life and its materials and its auxiliaries, how does he profit me? What does it signify? It is but a *Twelfth Night*, or *Midsummer-Night's Dream*, or *Winter Evening's Tale*: what signifies another picture more or less? The Egyptian verdict of the Shakespeare Societies comes to mind; that he was a jovial actor and manager. I can not marry this fact to his verse. Other admirable men have led lives in some sort of keeping with their thought; but this man, in wide contrast. Had he been less, had he reached only the common measure of great authors, of Bacon, Milton, Tasso, Cervantes, we might leave the fact in the twilight of human fate: but that this man of men, he who gave to the science of mind a new and larger subject than had ever existed, and planted the standard of humanity some furlongs forward into Chaos,—that he should not be wise for himself;—it must even go into the world's history that the best poet led an obscure and profane life, using his genius for the public amusement.

Well, other men, priest and prophet, Israelite, German and Swede, beheld the same objects: they also saw through them that which was contained. And to what purpose? The beauty straightway vanished; they read commandments, all-excluding mountainous duty; an obligation, a sadness, as of piled mountains, fell on them, and life became ghastly, joyless, a pilgrim's progress, a probation, beleaguered round with doleful histories of Adam's fall and curse behind us; with doomsdays and purgatorial and penal fires before us; and the heart of the seer and the heart of the listener sank in them.

It must be conceded that these are half-views of half-men. The world still wants its poet-priest, a reconciler, who shall not trifle, with Shakespeare the player, nor shall grope in graves, with Swedenborg the mourner; but who shall see, speak, and act, with equal inspiration. For knowledge will brighten the sunshine; right is more beautiful than private affection; and love is compatible with universal wisdom.

24

NIAGARA FALLS

Rupert Brooke

Samuel Butler has a lot to answer for. But for him, a modern traveller could spend his time peacefully admiring the scenery instead of feeling himself bound to dog the simple and grotesque of the world for the sake of their too-human comments. It is his fault if a peasant's naïveté has come to outweigh the beauty of rivers, and the remarks of clergymen are more than mountains. It is very restful to give up all effort at observing human nature and drawing social and political deductions from trifles, and to let oneself relapse into wide-mouthed worship of the wonders of nature. And this is very easy at Niagara. Niagara means nothing. It is not leading anywhere. It does not result from anything. It throws no light on the effects of Protection, nor on the Facility for Divorce in America, nor on Corruption in Public Life, nor on Canadian character, nor even on the Navy Bill. It is merely a great deal of water falling over some cliffs. But it is very remarkably that. The human race, apt as a child to destroy what it admires, has done its best to surround the Falls with every distraction, incongruity, and vulgarity. Hotels, powerhouses, bridges, trams, picture post-cards, sham legends, stalls, booths, rifle-galleries, and side-shows frame them about. And there are Touts. Niagara is the central home and breeding-place for all the touts of earth. There are touts insinuating, and touts raucous, greasy touts, brazen touts, and upper-class, refined, gentlemanly, take-you-by-the-arm touts; touts who intimidate and touts who wheedle; professionals, amateurs, and dilettanti, male and female; touts who would photograph you with your arm round a young lady against a faked background of the sublimest cataract, touts who would bully you into cars, char-à-bancs, elevators, or tunnels, or deceive you into a carriage and pair, touts who would sell you picture post-cards, moccasins, sham Indian beadwork, blankets, tee-pees, and crockery, and touts, finally, who have no apparent object in the world, but just purely, simply, merely, incessantly, indefatigably, and ineffugibly to tout. And in the midst of all this, overwhelming it all, are the Falls. He who sees them instantly forgets humanity. They are not very high, but they are overpowering. They are divided by an island into two parts, the Canadian and the American.

Half a mile or so above the Falls, on either side, the water of the great stream begins to run more swiftly and in confusion. It descends with ever-growing speed. It begins chattering and leaping, breaking into a thousand ripples, throwing up joyful fingers of spray. Sometimes it is divided by islands and rocks, sometimes the eye can see nothing but a waste of laughing, springing, foamy waves, turning, crossing, even seeming to stand for an instant erect, but always borne impetuously forward like a crowd of triumphant feasters. Sit close down by it, and you see a fragment of the torrent against the sky, mottled, steely, and foaming, leaping onward in far-flung criss-cross strands of water. Perpetually the eye is on the point of descrying a pattern in this weaving, and perpetually it is cheated by change. In one place part of the flood plunges over a ledge a few feet high and a quarter of a mile or so long, in a uniform and stable curve. It gives an impression of almost military concerted movement, grown suddenly out of confusion. But it is swiftly lost again in the multitudinous tossing merriment. Here and there a rock close to the surface is marked by a white wave that faces backwards and seems to be rushing madly up-stream, but is really stationary in the headlong charge. But for these signs of reluctance, the waters seem to fling themselves on with some foreknowledge of their fate, in an ever wilder frenzy. But it is no Maeterlinckian prescience. They prove, rather, that Greek belief that the great crashes are preceded by a louder merriment and a wilder gaiety. Leaping in the sunlight, careless, entwining, clamorously joyful, the waves riot on towards the verge.

But there they change. As they turn to the sheer descent, the white and blue and slate color, in the heart of the Canadian Falls at least, blend and deepen to a rich, wonderful, luminous green. On the edge of disaster the river seems to gather herself, to pause, to lift a head noble in ruin, and then, with a slow grandeur, to plunge into the eternal thunder and white chaos below. Where the stream runs shallower it is a kind of violet color, but both violet and green fray and frill to white as they fall. The mass of water, striking some ever-hidden base of rock, leaps up the whole two hundred feet again in pinnacles and domes of spray. The spray falls back into the lower river once more; all but a little that fines to foam and white mist, which drifts in layers along the air, graining it, and wanders out on the wind over the trees and gardens and houses, and so vanishes.

The manager of one of the great power-stations on the banks of the river above the Falls told me that the centre of the riverbed at the Canadian Falls is deep and of a saucer shape. So it may be possible to fill this up to a uniform depth, and divert a lot of water for the power-houses. And this, he said, would supply the need for more power, which will certainly soon arise, without taking away from the beauty of Niagara. This is a handsome concession of the utilitarians to the ordinary sight-seers. Yet, I doubt if we shall be satisfied. The real secret of the beauty and terror of the Falls is not their height or width, but the feeling of colossal power and of unintelligible disaster caused by the plunge of that vast body of water. If that were taken away, there would be little visible change, but the heart would be gone.

The American Falls do not inspire this feeling in the same way as the Canadian. It is because they are less in volume, and because the water does not fall so much into one place. By comparison their beauty is almost delicate and fragile. They are extraordinarily level, one long curtain of lacework and woven foam. Seen from opposite, when the sun is on them, they are blindingly white, and the clouds of spray show dark against them. With both Falls the color of the water is the ever-altering wonder. Greens and blues, purples and whites, melt into one another, fade, and come again, and change with the changing sun. Sometimes they are as richly diaphanous as a precious stone, and glow from within with a deep, inexplicable light. Sometimes the white intricacies of dropping foam become opaque and creamy. And always there are the rainbows. If you come suddenly upon the Falls from above, a great double rainbow, very vivid, spanning the extent of spray from top to bottom, is the first thing you see. If you wander along the cliff opposite, a bow springs into being in the American Falls, accompanies you courteously on your walk, dwindles and dies as the mist ends, and awakens again as you reach the Canadian tumult. And the bold traveler who attempts the trip under the American Falls sees, when he dare open his eyes to anything, tiny baby rainbows, some four or five yards in span, leaping from rock to rock among the foam, and gamboling beside him, barely out of hand's reach, as he goes. One I saw in that place was a complete circle, such as I have never seen before, and so near that I could put my foot on it. It is a terrifying journey, beneath and behind the Falls. The senses are battered and bewildered by the thunder of the water and the assault of wind and spray; or rather, the sound is not of falling water, but merely of falling; a noise of unspecified ruin. So, if you are close behind the endless clamor, the sight cannot recognize liquid in the masses that hurl past. You are dimly and pitifully aware that sheets of light and darkness are falling in great curves in front of you. Dull omnipresent foam washes the face. Farther away, in the roar and hissing, clouds of spray seem literally to slide down some invisible plane of air.

Beyond the foot of the Falls the river is like a slipping floor of marble, green with veins of dirty white, made by the scum that was foam. It slides very quietly and slowly down for a mile or two, sullenly exhausted. Then it turns to a dull sage green, and hurries more swiftly, smooth and ominous. As the walls of the ravine close in, trouble stirs, and the waters boil and eddy. These are the lower rapids, a sight more terrifying than the Falls, because less intelligible. Close in its bands of rock the river surges tumultuously forward, writhing and leaping as if inspired by a demon. It is pressed by the straits into a visibly convex form. Great planes of water slide past. Sometimes it is thrown up into a pinnacle of foam higher than a house, or leaps with incredible speed from the crest of one vast wave to another, along the shining curve between, like the spring of a wild beast. Its motion continually suggests muscular action. The power manifest in these rapids moves one with a different sense of awe and terror from that of the Falls. Here the inhuman life and strength are spontaneous, active, almost resolute; masculine vigor compared with the passive gigantic power, female, helpless and overwhelming, of the Falls. A place of fear.

One is drawn back, strangely, to a contemplation of the Falls, at every hour, and especially by night, when the cloud of spray becomes an immense visible ghost, straining and wavering high above the river, white and pathetic and translucent. The Victorian lies very close below the surface in every man. There one can sit and let great cloudy thoughts of destiny and the passage of empires drift through the mind; for such dreams are at home by Niagara. I could not get out of my mind the thought of a friend, who said that the rainbows over the Falls were like the arts and beauty and goodness, with regard to the stream of life—caused by it, thrown upon its spray, but unable to stay or direct or affect it, and ceasing when it ceased. In all comparisons that rise in the heart, the river, with its multitudinous waves and its single current, likens itself to a life, whether of an individual or of a community. A man's life is of many flashing moments, and yet one stream; a nation's flows through all its citizens, and yet is more than they. In such places, one is aware, with an almost insupportable and yet comforting certitude, that both men and nations are hurried onwards to their ruin or ending as inevitably as this dark flood. Some go down to it unreluctant, and meet it, like the river, not without nobility. And as incessant, as inevitable, and as unavailing as the spray that hangs over the Falls, is the white cloud of human crying... With some such thoughts does the platitudinous heart win from the confusion and thunder of a Niagara peace that the quietest plains or most stable hills can never give.

25

THE ALMOST PERFECT STATE

Don Marquis

I

No matter how nearly perfect an Almost Perfect State may be, it is not nearly enough perfect unless the individuals who compose it can, somewhere between death and birth, have a perfectly corking time for a few years. The most wonderful governmental system in the world does not attract us, as a system; we are after a system that scarcely knows it is a system; the great thing is to have the largest number of individuals as happy as may be, for a little while at least, some time before they die.

Infancy is not what it is cracked up to be. The child seems happy all the time to the adult, because the adult knows that the child is untouched by the real problems of life; if the adult were similarly untouched he is sure that he would be happy. But children, not knowing that they are having an easy time, have a good many hard times. Growing and learning and obeying the rules of their elders, of fighting against them, are not easy things to do. Adolescence is certainly far from a uniformly pleasant period. Early manhood might be the most glorious time of all were it not that the sheer excess of life and vigor gets a fellow into continual scrapes. Of middle age the best that can be said is that a middle aged person has likely learned how to have a little fun in spite of his troubles.

It is to old age that we look for reimbursement, the most of us. And most of us look in vain. For the most of us have been wrenched and racked, in one way or another, until old age is the most trying time of all.

In the Almost Perfect State every person shall have at least ten years before he dies of easy, carefree, happy living...things will be so arranged economically that this will be possible for each individual.

Personally we look forward to an old age of dissipation and indolence and unreverend disrepute. In fifty years we shall be ninety-two years old. We intend to work rather hard during those fifty years and accumulate enough to live on without working any more for the next ten years, for we have determined to die at the age of one hundred two.

During the last ten years we shall indulge ourself in many things that we have been forced by circumstances to forego. We have always been compelled, and we shall be compelled for many years to come, to be prudent, cautious, staid, sober, conservative, industrious, respectful of established institutions, a model citizen. We have not liked it, but we have been unable to escape it. Our mind, our logical faculties, our observation, inform us that the conservatives have the right side of the argument in all human affairs. But the people whom we really prefer as associates, though we do not approve their ideas, are the rebels, the radicals, the wastrels, the vicious, the poets, the Bolshevists, the idealists, the nuts, the Lucifers, the agreeable good-for-nothings, the sentimentalists, the prophets, the freaks. We have never dared to know any of them, far less become intimate with them.

Between the years of ninety-two and a hundred and two, however, we shall be the ribald, useless, drunken outcast person we have always wished to be. We shall have a long white beard and long white hair; we shall not walk at all, but recline in a wheel chair and bellow for alcoholic beverages; in the winter we shall sit before the fire with our feet in a bucket of hot water, with a decanter of corn whiskey near at hand, and write ribald songs against organized society; strapped to one arm of our chair will be a forty-five caliber revolver, and we shall shoot out the lights when we want to go to sleep, instead of turning them off; when we want air we shall throw a silver candlestick through the front window and be damned to it; we shall address public meetings to which we have been invited because of our wisdom in a vein of jocund malice. We shall...but we don't wish to make any one envious of the good time that is coming to us...we look forward to a disreputable, vigorous, unhonored and disorderly old age.

(In the meantime, of course, you understand you can't have us pinched and deported for our yearnings.)

We shall know that the Almost Perfect State is here when the kind of old age each person wants is possible to him. Of course, all of you may not want the kind we want...some of you may prefer prunes and morality to the bitter end. Some of you may be dissolute now and may look forward to becoming like one of the nice old fellows in a Wordsworth poem. But for our part we have always been a hypocrite and we shall have to continue being a hypocrite for a good many years yet, and we yearn to come out in our true colors at last. The point is, that no matter what you want to be, during those last ten years, that you may be, in the Almost Perfect State.

Any system of government under which the individual does all the sacrificing for the sake of the general good, for the sake of the community, the State, gets off on its wrong foot. We don't want things that cost us too much. We don't want too much strain all the time.

The best good that you can possibly achieve is not good enough if you have to strain yourself all the time to reach it. A thing is only worth doing, and doing again and again, if you can do it rather easily, and get some joy out of it.

Do the best you can, without straining yourself too much and too continuously, and leave the rest to God. If you strain yourself too much you'll have to ask God to patch you up. And for all you know, patching you up may take time that it was planned to use some other way.

BUT...overstrain yourself *now and then*. For this reason: The things you create easily and joyously will not continue to come easily and joyously unless you yourself are getting bigger all the time. And when you overstrain yourself you are assisting in the creation of a new self—if you get what we mean. And if you should ask us suddenly just what this has to do with the picture of the old guy in the wheel chair we should answer: Hanged if we know, but we seemed to sort o' run into it, somehow.

II

Interplanetary communication is one of the persistent dreams of the inhabitants of this oblate spheroid on which we move, breathe and suffer for lack of beer. There seems to be a feeling in many quarters that if we could get speech with the Martians, let us say, we might learn from them something to our advantage. There is a disposition to concede the superiority of the fellows Out There... just as some Americans capitulate without a struggle to poets from England, rugs from Constantinople, song and sausage from Germany, religious enthusiasts from Hindustan and cheese from Switzerland, although they have not tested the goods offered and really lack the discrimination to determine their quality. Almost the only foreign importations that were ever sneezed at in this country were Swedish matches and Spanish influenza.

But are the Martians...if Martians there be...any more capable than the persons dwelling between the Woolworth Building and the Golden Horn, between Shwe Dagon and the First Church, Scientist, in Boston, Mass.? Perhaps the Martians yearn toward earth, romantically, poetically, the Romeos swearing by its light to the Juliets; the idealists and philosophers fabling that already there exists upon it an ALMOST PERFECT STATE—and now and then a wan prophet lifting his heart to its gleams, as a cup to be filled from Heaven with fresh waters of hope and courage. For this earth, it is also a star.

We know they are wrong about us, the lovers in the far stars, the philosophers, poets, the prophets...or are they wrong?

They are both right and wrong, as we are probably both right and wrong about them. If we tumbled into Mars or Arcturus of Sirius this evening we should find the people there discussing the shimmy, the jazz, the inconstancy of cooks and the iniquity of retail butchers, no doubt...and they would be equally disappointed by the way we flitter, frivol, flutter and flivver.

And yet, that other thing would be there too...that thing that made them look at our star as a symbol of grace and beauty.

Men could not think of THE ALMOST PERFECT STATE if they did not have it in them ultimately to create THE ALMOST PERFECT STATE.

We used sometimes to walk over the Brooklyn Bridge, that song in stone and steel of an engineer who was also a great artist, at dusk, when the tides of shadow flood in from the lower bay to break in a surf of glory and mystery and illusion against the tall towers of Manhattan. Seen from the middle arch of the bridge at twilight, New York with its girdle of shifting waters and its drift of purple cloud and its quick pulsations of unstable light is a miracle of splendor and beauty that lights up the heart like the laughter of a god.

But, descend. Go down into the city. Mingle with the details. The dirty old shed from which the 'L' trains and trolleys put out with their jammed and mangled thousands for flattest Flatbush and the unknown bourne of ulterior Brooklyn is still the same dirty old shed; on a hot, damp night the pasty streets stink like a paperhanger's overalls; you are trodden and over-ridden by greasy little profiteers and their hopping victims; you are encompassed round about by the ugly and the sordid, and the objectionable is exuded upon you from a myriad candid pores; your elation and your illusion vanish like ingenuous snowflakes that have kissed a hot dog sandwich on its fiery brow, and you say: 'Beauty? Aw, h—l! What's the use?'

And yet you have seen beauty. And beauty that was created by these people and people like these...You have seen the tall towers of Manhattan, wonderful under the stars. How did it come about that such growths came from such soil—that a breed lawless and sordid and prosaic has written such a mighty hieroglyphic against the sky? This glamor out of a pigsty...how come? How is it that this hideous, half-brute city is also beautiful and a fit habitation for demi-gods? How come?

It comes about because the wise and subtle deities permit nothing worthy to be lost. It was with no thought of beauty that the builders labored; no conscious thought; they were masters or slaves in the bitter wars of commerce, and they never saw as a whole what they were making; no one of them did. But each one had had his dream. And the baffled dreams and the broken visions and the ruined hopes and the secret desires of each one labored with him as he labored; the things that were lost and beaten and trampled down went into the stone and steel and gave it soul; the aspiration denied and the hope abandoned and the vision defeated were the things that lived, and not the apparent purpose for which each one of all the millions sweat and toiled or cheated; the hidden things, the silent things, the winged things, so weak they are easily killed, the unacknowledged things, the rejected beauty, the strangled appreciation, the inchoate art, the submerged spirit—these groped and found each other and gathered themselves together and worked themselves into the tiles and mortar of the edifice and made a town that is a worthy fellow of the sunrise and the sea winds.

Humanity triumphs over its details.

The individual aspiration is always defeated of its perfect fruition and expression, but it is never lost; it passes into the conglomerate being of the race.

The way to encourage yourself about the human race is to look at it first from a distance; look at the lights on the high spots. Coming closer, you will be profoundly discouraged at the number of low spots, not to say two-spots. Coming still closer, you will become discouraged once more by the reflection that the same stuff that is in the high spots is also in the two-spots.

26

THE RUSSIAN QUARTER

Thomas Burke

I had known the quarter for many years before it interested me. It was not until I was prowling around on a Fleet Street assignment that I learned to hate it. A murder had been committed over a café in Lupin Street; a popular murder, fruity, cleverly done, and with a sex interest. Of course every newspaper and agency developed a virtuous anxiety to track the culprit, and all resources were directed to that end. Journalism is perhaps the only profession in which so fine a public spirit may be found. So it was that the North Country paper of which I was a hanger-on flung every available man into the fighting line, and the editor told me that I might, in place of the casual paragraphs for the London Letter, do something good on the Vassiloff murder.

It was a night of cold rain, and the pavements were dashed with smears of light from the shop windows. Through the streaming streets my hansom leaped; and as I looked from the window, and noted the despondent biliousness of Bethanal Green, I realized that the grass withereth, the flower fadeth.

I dismissed the cab at Brick Lane, and, continuing the tradition which had been instilled into me by my predecessor on the London Letter, I turned into one of the hostelries and had a vodka to keep the cold out. Little Russia was shutting up. The old shawled women, who sit at every corner with huge baskets of black bread and sweet cakes, were departing beneath umbrellas. The stalls of Osborn Street, usually dressed with foreign-looking confectionery, were also retiring. Indeed, everybody seemed to be slinking away, and as I sipped my vodka, and felt it burn me with raw fire, I cursed news editors and all publics which desired to read about murders. I was perfectly sure that I shouldn't do the least good; so I had another, and gazed through the kaleidoscopic window, rushing with rain, at the cheerful world that held me.

Oh, so sad it is, this quarter! By day the streets are a depression, with their frowzy doss-houses and their vapo-baths. Gray and sickly is the light. Gray and sickly, too, are the leering shops, and gray and sickly are the people and the children. Everything has followed the grass and the flowers. Childhood has no place; so above the roofs you may see the surly points of a Council School. Such games as happen are played but listlessly, and each little face is smirched. The gaunt warehouses hardly support their lopping heads, and the low, beetling, gabled houses of the alleys seem for ever to brood on nights of bitter adventure. Fit objects for contempt by day they may be, but when night creeps upon London, the hideous darkness that can almost be touched, then their faces become very powers of terror, and the cautious soul, wandered from the comfort of the main streets, walks and walks in a frenzy, seeking outlet and finding none. Sometimes a hoarse laugh will break sharp on his ear. Then he runs.

Well, I finished my second, and then sauntered out. As I was passing a cruel-looking passage, a girl stepped forward. She looked at me. I looked at her. She had the haunting melancholy of Russia in her face, but her voice was as the voice of Cockaigne. For she spoke and said:—

'Funny-looking little guy, ain't you?'

I suppose I was. So I smiled and said: 'We are as God made us, old girl.'

She giggled…

I said I felt sure I should do no good on the Vassiloff murder. I didn't. For just then two of her friends came out of the court, each with a boy. It was apparent that she had no boy. I had no idea what the occasion might be, but the other four marched ahead, crying, 'Come on!' And, surprised, yet knowing of no good reason for being surprised, I felt the girl's arm slip into mine, and we joined the main column…

That is one of London's greatest charms: it is always ready to toss you little encounters of this sort, if you are out for them.

Across the road we went, through mire and puddle, and down a long, winding court. At about midway our friends disappeared, and, suddenly drawn to the right, I was pushed from behind up a steep, fusty stair. Then I knew where we were going. We were going to the tenements where most of the Russians meet of an evening. The atmosphere in these places is a little more cheerful than that of the café—if you can imagine a Russian ever rising to cheerfulness. Most of the girls lodge over the milliners' shops, and thither their friends resort. Every establishment here has a piano, for music, with them, is a somber passion rather than a diversion. You will not hear comic opera, but if you want to climb the lost heights of melody, stand in Bell Yard, and listen to a piano, lost in the high glooms, wailing the heart of Chopin, or Rubinstein or Glazounoff through the fingers of pale, moist girls, while the ghost of Peter the Painter parades the naphtha'd highways.

At the top of the stair I was pushed into a dark, fusty room, and guided to a low, fusty sofa or bed. Then some one struck a match, and a lamp was lit and set on the mantelshelf. It flung a soft, caressing radiance on its shabby home, and on its mistress, and on the other girls and boys. The boys were tough youngsters of the district, evidently very much at home, smoking Russian cigarettes and settling themselves on the bed in a manner that seemed curiously continental in Cockney toughs. I doubt if you would have loved the girls at that moment; and yet...you know...their black or brassy hair, their untidiness, and the cotton blouses half-dropped from their tumultuous breasts...

The girl who had collared me disappeared for a moment, and then brought a tray of Russian tea. 'Help 'selves, boys!' We did so, and, watching the others, I discovered that it was the correct thing to lemon the ladies' tea for them and stir it well and light their cigarettes. I did so for Katarina—that was her name—while she watched me with little truant locks of hair running everywhere, and a slow, alluring smile that seemed to hold all the agony and mystery of the steppes.

The room, on which the wallpaper hung in dank strips, contained a full-sized bed and a chair bedstead, a washstand, a samovar, a potpourri of a carpet, and certain mysteries of feminine toilet. A rickety three-legged table stood by the window, and Katarina's robes hung in a dainty riot of frill and color behind the door, which only shut when you thrust a peg of wood through a wired catch.

One of the boys sprawled himself, in clumsy luxury, on the bed, and his girl arranged herself at his side, and when she was settled her hair tumbled in a shower of hairpins, and everybody laughed like children. The other girl went to the piano, and her boy squatted on the floor at her feet.

She began to play... You would not understand, I suppose, the intellectual emotion of the situation. It is more than curious to sit in these rooms, in the filthiest spot in London, and listen to Moszkowsky, Tchaikowsky, and Sibelius, played by a factory girl. It is...something indefinable. I had visited similar places in Stepney before, but then I had not had a couple of vodkas, and I had not been taken in tow by an unknown girl. They play and play, while tea and cigarettes, and sometimes vodka or whisky, go round; and as the room gets warmer. So does one's sense of smell get sharper; so do the pale faces get moister; and so does one lone more and more for a breath of cold air from the Ural Mountains. The best you can do is to ascend to the flat roof, and take a deep breath of Spitalifields ozone. Then back to the room for more tea and more music.

Sanya played... Despite the unventilated room, the greasy appointments, and other details that would have turned the stomach of Kensington, that girl at the piano, her dress cunningly disarranged, playing, as no one would have dreamed she could play, the finer intensities of Wieniawski and Moussorgsky, shook all sense of responsibility from me. The burdens of life vanished. News editors and their assignments be damned. Enjoy yourself, was what the cold, insidious music said. Take your moments when the fates send them; that was life's best lesson. Snatch the joy of the fleeting moment. Why ponder on time and tears?

Devilish little fingers they were, Sanya's. Her technique was not perhaps all that it might have been; she might not have won the

Gold Medal of our whiteshirted academies, but she had enough temperament to make half a dozen Bechstein Hall virtuosi. From valse to nocturne, from sonata to prelude, her fancy ran. With crashing chords she dropped from 'L'Automne Bacchanale' to the Nocturne in E flat; scarcely murmured of that, then tripped elvishly into Moszkowsky's Waltz, and from that she dropped to a song of Tchaikowsky, almost heartbreaking in its childish beauty, and then to the lecherous music of the second act of 'Tristan.' Mazurka, polonaise, and nocturne wailed in the stuffy chamber; her little hands lit up the enchanted gloom of the place with bright thrills, until the bed and the dingy surroundings faded into phantoms and left only two startled souls in colloquy: Katarina's and mine.

Katarina had settled, I forget how, on the sofa, and was reclining very comfortably with her head on my shoulder and both arms about me. We did not talk. No questions passed as to why we had picked one another up. There we were, warmed with vodka and tea, at eleven o'clock at night, five stories above the clamorous world, while her friend shook the silly souls out of us. With the shy boldness of my native country, I stretched a hand and inclosed her fingers. She smiled; a curious smile that no other girl in London could have given; not a flushed smile, or a startled smile, or a satisfied smile, or a coy smile; but a smile of companionship, which seemed to have realized the tragedy of our living. So it was that she had, by slow stages, reached her comfortable position, for as my hand wandered from finger to wrist, from wrist to soft, rounded arm, and so inclosed her neck, she slipped and buried me in an avalanche of flaming, scented tresses.

Sanya at the piano shot a glance over her shoulder, a very sad-gay glance; she laughed, curiously, I almost said foreignly. I felt somehow as though I had been taken complete possession of by these people. I hardly belonged to myself. Fleet Street was but a street of dream. I seemed now to be awake and in an adorable captivity.

With a final volley of chords, the pianist slid from the chair, and sat by her boy on the carpet, smoothing his face with tobacco-stained fingers, and languishing while her thick, over-ripe lips took his kisses as a baby bird takes food from its mother.

We talked—all of us—in jerks and snatches. Then the oil in the lamp began to give out, and the room grew dim. Some one said: 'Play something!' And some one said: 'Too tired!' The girl reclining on the bed grew snappy. She did not lean for caresses. She seemed morose, preoccupied, almost impatient. Twice she snapped up her boy on a casual remark. I believe I talked vodka'd nonsense…

But suddenly there came a whisper of soft feet on the landing, and a secret tap at the door. Some one opened it, and slipped out. One heard the lazy hum of voices in busy conversation. Then silence; and some one entered the room and shut the door. One of the boys asked, casually, 'What's up?' His question was not answered, but the girl who had gone to the door snapped something in a sharp tone which might have been either Russian or Yiddish. Katarina loosened herself from me, and sat up. The girl on the bed sat up. The three of them spat angry phrases about, I called over to one of the boys: 'What's the joke? Anything Wrong?' and received a reply: 'Ownshdiknow? I ain't a ruddy Russian, am I?'

Katarina suddenly drew back her flaming face. 'Here,' she said, 'you better go.'

'Go?'

'Yes—fathead! Go's what I said.'

'But—' I began, looking and feeling like a flabbergasted cat.

'Don't I speak plain? Go!'

I suppose a man never feels a finer idiot than when a woman tells him she doesn't want him. If he ever does, it is when a woman tells him that she loves him. Katarina had given me the bullet, and, of course, I felt a fool; but I derived some consolation from the fact that the other boys were being told off. Clearly, big things were in the air, about to happen. Something, evidently, had already happened. I wondered… Then I sat down on the sofa, and flatly told Katarina that I was not going unless I had a reason.

'Oh,' she said, blithely, 'ain't you? This is my room, ain't it? I brought you here, and you stay here just as long as I choose, and no longer. Who d'you think you are, saying you won't go? This is my room. I let you come here for a drink, and you just got to go when I say. See?'

I was about to make a second stand, when again there came a stealthy tap at the door, and the whispering of slippered feet. Sanya glided to the door, opened it, and disappeared. In a moment she came back, and called, "Rina!' Katarina slipped from my embrace, went to the door, and disappeared too. One girl and three boys remained—in silence.

Next moment Katarina reappeared, and said something to Sanya. Sanya pulled her boy by the arm, and went out. The other girl pushed her boy at the neck and literally threw him out. Katarina came over to me, and said: 'Go, little fool!'

I said: 'Shan't unless I know what the game is.'

She stood over me; glared; searched for words to meet the occasion; found none. She gestured. I sat as rigid as an immobile comedian. Finally, she flung her arms, and swept away. At the door she turned; 'Blasted little fool! He'll do us both in if y'ain't careful. You don't know him. Both of us he'll have. Serveyeh right.'

She disappeared. I was alone. I heard the sup-sup of her slippered feet down the stair.

I got up, and moved to the door. I heard nothing. I stood by the window, my thoughts dancing a ragtime. I wondered what to do, and how, and whether. I wondered what was up exactly. I wondered...well, I just wondered. My thoughts got into a tangle, sank, and swam, and sank again. Then there was a sudden struggle and spurt from the lamp, and it went black out. From a room across the landing a clock ticked menacingly. I saw, by the thin light from the window, the smoke of a discarded cigarette curling up and up to the ceiling like a snake.

I went again to the door, peered down the steep stair and over the crazy balustrade. Nobody was about; no voices. I slipped swiftly down the five flights, met nobody. I stood in the slobbered vestibule. From afar I heard the sluck of the waters against the staples of the wharves, and the wicked hoot of the tugs.

It was then that a sudden nameless fear seized me; it was that simple terror that comes from nothing but ourselves. I am not usually afraid of any man or thing. I am normally nervous, and there are three or four things that have power to terrify me. But I am not, I think, afraid. At that moment, however, I was afraid of everything: of the room I had left, of the house, of the people, of the inviting lights of the warehouses and the threatening shoals of the alleys.

I stood a moment longer. Then I raced into Brick Lane, and out into the brilliance of Commercial Street.

27

THE STUDENT LIFE

William Osler

I

Except it be a lover, no one is more interesting as an object of study than a student. Shakespeare might have made him a fourth in his immortal group. The lunatic with his fixed idea, the poet with his fine frenzy, the lover with his frantic idolatry, and the student aflame with the desire for knowledge are of 'imagination all compact.' To an absorbing passion, a wholesouled devotion, must be joined an enduring energy, if the student is to become a devotee of the grey-eyed goddess to whose law his services are bound. Like the quest of the Holy Grail, the quest of Minerva is not for all. For the one, the pure life; for the other, what Milton calls 'a strong propensity of nature.' Here again the student often resembles the poet—he is born, not made. While the resultant of two moulding forces, the accidental, external conditions, and the hidden germinal energies, which produce in each one of us national, family, and individual traits, the true student possesses in some measure a divine spark which sets at naught their laws. Like the Snark, he defies definition, but there are three unmistakable signs by which you may recognize the genuine article from a Boojum—an absorbing desire to know the truth, an unswerving steadfastness in its pursuit, and an open, honest heart, free from suspicion, guile, and jealousy.

At the outset do not be worried about this big question—Truth. It is a very simple matter if each one of you starts with the desire to get as much as possible. No human being is constituted to know the truth, the whole truth, and nothing but the truth; and even the best of men must be content with fragments, with partial glimpses, never the full fruition. In this unsatisfied quest the attitude of mind, the desire, the thirst—a thirst that from the soul must rise!—the fervent longing, are the be-all and the end-all. What is the student but a lover courting a fickle mistress who ever eludes his grasp? In this very elusiveness is brought out his second great characteristic—steadfastness of purpose. Unless from the start the limitations incident to our frail human faculties are frankly accepted, nothing but disappointment awaits you. The truth is the best you can get with your best endeavour, the best that the best men accept—with this you must learn to be satisfied, retaining at the same time with due humility an earnest desire for an ever larger portion. Only by keeping the mind plastic and receptive does the student escape perdition. It is not, as Charles Lamb remarks, that some people do not know what to do with truth when it is offered to them, but the tragic fate is to reach, after years of patient search, a condition of mind-blindness in which the truth is not recognized, though it stares you in the face. This can never happen to a man who has followed step by step the growth of a truth, and who knows the painful phases of its evolution. It is one of the great tragedies of life that every truth has to struggle to acceptance against honest but mind-blind students. Harvey knew his contemporaries well, and for twelve successive years demonstrated the circulation of the blood before daring to publish the facts on which the truth was based. Only steadfastness of purpose and humility enable the student to shift his position to meet the new conditions in which new truths are born, or old ones modified beyond recognition.

And, thirdly, the honest heart will keep him in touch with his fellow students, and furnish that sense of comradeship without which he travels an arid waste alone. I say advisedly an honest *heart*—the honest head is prone to be cold and stern, given to judgment, not mercy, and not always able to entertain that true charity which, while it thinketh no evil, is anxious to put the best possible interpretation upon the motives of a fellow worker. It will foster, too, an attitude of generous, friendly rivalry untinged by the green peril, jealousy, that is the best preventive of the growth of a bastard scientific spirit, loving seclusion and working in a lock-and-key laboratory, as timorous of light as is a thief.

You have all become brothers in a great society, not apprentices, since that implies a master, and nothing should be further from the attitude of the teacher than much that is meant in that word, used though it be in another sense, particularly by our French brethren in a most delightful way, signifying a bond of intellectual filiation. A fraternal attitude is not easy to cultivate the chasm between the chair and the bench is difficult to bridge. Two things have helped to put up a cantilever across the gulf. The successful teacher is no longer on a height, pumping knowledge at high pressure into passive receptacles. The new methods have changed all this. He is no longer *Sir Oracle*, perhaps unconsciously by his very manner antagonizing minds to whose level he cannot possibly descend, but he is a senior student anxious to help his juniors. When a simple, earnest spirit animates a college, there is no appreciable interval between the teacher and the taught—both are in the same class, the one a little more advanced than the other. So animated, the student feels that he has joined a family whose honour is his honour, whose welfare is his own, and whose interests should be his first consideration.

The hardest conviction to get into the mind of a beginner is that the education upon which he is engaged is not a college course, not a medical course, but a life course, for which the work of a few years under teachers is but a preparation. Whether you will falter and fail in the race or whether you will be faithful to the end depends on the training before the start, and on your staying powers, points upon which I need not enlarge. You can all become good students, a few may become great students, and now and again one of you will be found who does easily and well what others cannot do at all, or very badly, which is John Ferriar's excellent definition of a genius.

In the hurry and bustle of a business world, which is the life of this continent, it is not easy to train first-class students. Under present conditions it is hard to get the needful seclusion, on which account it is that our educational market is so full of wayside fruit. I have always been much impressed by the advice of St Chrysostom: 'Depart from the highway and transplant thyself in some enclosed ground, for it is hard for a tree which stands…by the wayside to keep her fruit till it be ripe.' The dilettante is abroad in the land, the man who is always venturing on tasks for which he is imperfectly equipped, a habit of mind fostered by the multiplicity of subjects of the curriculum; and while many things are studied, few are studied thoroughly. Men will not take time to get to the heart of a matter. After all, concentration is the price the modern student pays for success. Thoroughness is the most difficult habit to acquire, but it is the pearl of great price, worth all the worry and trouble of the search. The dilettante lives an easy, butterfly life, knowing nothing of the toil and labour with which the treasures of knowledge are dug out of the past, or wrung by patient research in the laboratories. Take, for example, the early history of this country—how easy for the student of the one type to get a smattering, even a fairly full acquaintance with the events of the French and Spanish settlements. Put an original document before him, and it might as well be Arabic. What we need is the other type, the man who knows the records, who, with a broad outlook and drilled in what may be called the embryology of history, has yet a powerful vision for the minutiae of life. It is these kitchen and backstair men who are to be encouraged, the men who know the subject in hand in all possible relationships. Concentration has its drawbacks. It is possible to become so absorbed in the problem of the 'enclitic δε:' or the structure of the flagella of the Trichomonas, or of the toes of the prehistoric horse, that the student loses the sense of proportion in his work, and even wastes a lifetime in researches which are valueless because not in touch with current knowledge. You remember poor Casaubon, in *Middlemarch*, whose painful scholarship was lost on this account. The best preventive to this is to get denationalized early. The true student is a citizen of the world, the allegiance of whose soul, at any rate, is too precious to be restricted to a single country. The great minds, the great works transcend all limitations of time, of language, and of race, and the scholar can never feel initiated into the company of the elect until he can approach all of life's problems from the cosmopolitan standpoint. I care not in what subject he may work, the full knowledge cannot be reached without drawing on supplies from lands other than his own—French, English, German, American, Japanese, Russian, Italian—there must be no discrimination by the loyal student, who should willingly draw from any and every source with an open mind and a stern resolve to render unto all their dues. I care not on what stream of knowledge he may embark, follow up its course, and the rivulets that feed it flow from many lands. If the work is to be effective he must keep in touch with scholars in other countries. How often has it happened that years of precious time have been given to a problem already solved or shown to be insoluble, because of the ignorance of what had been done elsewhere. And it is not only book knowledge and journal knowledge, but a knowledge of men that is needed. The student will, if possible, see the men in other lands. Travel not only widens the vision and gives certainties in place of vague surmises, but the personal contact with foreign workers enables him to appreciate better the failings or successes in his own line of work, perhaps to look with more charitable eyes on the work of some brother whose limitations and opportunities have been more restricted than his own. Or, in contact with a mastermind, he may take fire, and the glow of the enthusiasm may be the inspiration of his life. Concentration must then be associated with large views on the relation of the problem, and a knowledge of its status elsewhere; otherwise it may land him in the slough of a specialism so narrow that is has depth and no breadth, or he may be led to make what he believes to be important discoveries, but which have long been current coin in other lands. It is sad to think that the day of the great polymathic student is at an end; that we may, perhaps, never again see a Scaliger, a Haller, or a Humboldt—men who took the whole field of knowledge for their domain and viewed it as from a pinnacle. And yet a great specializing generalist may arise, who can tell? Some twentieth-century Aristotle may be now tugging at his bottle, as little dreaming as are his parents or his friends of a conquest of the mind, beside which the wonderful victories of the Stagirite will look pale. The value of a really great student to the country is equal to half a dozen grain elevators or a new transcontinental railway. He is a commodity singularly fickle and variable, and not to be grown to order. So far as his advent is concerned there is no telling when or where he may arise. The conditions seem to be present even under the most unlikely externals. Some of the greatest students this country has produced have come from small villages and country places. It is impossible to predict from a study of the environment, which a 'strong propensity of nature,' to quote Milton's phrase again, will easily bend or break.

The student must be allowed full freedom in his work, undisturbed by the utilitarian spirit of the Philistine, who cries, *Cui bono?* and distrusts pure science. The present remarkable position in applied science and in industrial trades of all sorts has been made possible by men who did pioneer work in chemistry, in physics, in biology, and in physiology, without a thought in their researches of any practical application. The members of this higher group of productive students are rarely understood by the common spirits, who appreciate as little their unselfish devotion as their unworldly neglect of the practical side of the problems.

Everywhere now the medical student is welcomed as an honoured member of the guild. There was a time, I confess, and it is within memory of some of us, when, like Falstaff, he was given to 'taverns and sack and wine and metheglins, and to drinkings and swearings and starings, pribbles and prabbles'; but all that has changed with the curriculum, and the 'Meds' now roar you as gently as the 'Theologs.' On account of the peculiar character of the subject-matter of your studies, what I have said upon the general life and mental attitude of the student applies with tenfold force to you. Man, with all his mental and bodily anomalies and diseases—the machine in order, the machine in disorder, and the business yours to put it to rights. Through all the phases of its career this most complicated mechanism of this wonderful world will be the subject of our study and of your care—the naked, new-born infant, the artless child, the lad and the lassie just aware of the tree of knowledge overhead, the strong man in the pride of life, the woman with the benediction of maternity on her brow, and the aged, peaceful in the contemplation of the past. Almost everything has been renewed in the science and in the art of medicine, but all through the long centuries there has been no variableness or shadow of change in the essential features of the life which is our contemplation and our care. The sick love-child of Israel's sweet singer, the plague-stricken hopes of the great Athenian statesman, Elpenor bereft of his beloved Artemidora, and 'Tully's daughter mourned so tenderly:' are not of any age or any race—they are here with us today, with the Hamlets, the Ophelias, and the Lears. Amid an eternal heritage of sorrow and suffering our work is laid, and this eternal note of sadness would be insupportable if the daily tragedies were not relieved by the spectacle of the heroism and devotion displayed by the actors. Nothing will sustain you more potently than the power to recognize in your humdrum routine, as perhaps it may be thought, the true poetry of life—the poetry of the commonplace, of the ordinary man, of the plain, toil-worn woman, with their loves and their joys, their sorrows and their griefs. The comedy, too, of life will be spread before you, and nobody laughs more often than the doctor at the pranks Puck plays upon the Titanias and the Bottoms among his patients. The humorous side is really almost as frequently turned towards him as the tragic. Lift up one hand to heaven and thank your stars if they have given you the proper sense to enable you to appreciate the inconceivably droll situations in which we catch our fellow creatures. Unhappily, this is one of the free gifts of the gods, unevenly distributed, not bestowed on all, or on all in equal portions. In undue measure it is not without risk, and in any case in the doctor it is better appreciated by the eye than expressed on the tongue. Hilarity and good humour, a breezy cheerfulness, a nature 'sloping toward the southern side;' as Lowell has it, help enormously both in the study and in the practice of medicine. To many of a sombre and sour disposition it is hard to maintain good spirits amid the trials and tribulations of the day, and yet it is an unpardonable mistake to go about among patients with a long face.

Divide your attentions equally between books and men. The strength of the student of books is to sit still—two or three hours at a stretch—eating the heart out of a subject with pencil and notebook in hand, determined to master the details and intricacies, focussing all your energies on its difficulties. Get accustomed to test all sorts of book problems and statements for yourself, and take as little as possible on trust. The Hunterian 'Do not think, but try' attitude of mind is the important one to cultivate. The question came up one day, when discussing the grooves left on the nails after fever, how long it took for the nail to grow out, from root to edge. A majority of the class had no further interest; a few looked it up in books; two men marked their nails at the root with nitrate of silver, and a few months later had positive knowledge on the subject. They showed the proper spirit. The little points that come up in your reading try to test for yourselves. With one fundamental difficulty many of you will have to contend from the outset—a lack of proper preparation for really hard study. No one can have watched successive groups of young men pass through the special schools without profoundly regretting the haphazard, fragmentary character of their preliminary education. It does seem too bad that we cannot have a student in his eighteenth year sufficiently grounded in the humanities and in the sciences preliminary to medicine—but this is an educational problem upon which only a Milton or a Locke could discourse with profit. With pertinacity you can overcome the preliminary defects and once thoroughly interested, the work in books becomes a pastime. A serious drawback in the student life is the self-consciousness, bred of too close devotion to books. A man gets shy, 'dysopic;' as old Timothy Bright calls it, and shuns the looks of men, and blushes like a girl.

The strength of a student of men is to travel—to study men, their habits, character, mode of life, their behaviour under varied conditions, their vices, virtues, and peculiarities. Begin with a careful observation of your fellow students and of your teachers; then, every patient you see is a lesson in much more than the malady from which he suffers. Mix as much as you possibly can with the outside world, and learn its ways. Cultivated systematically, the student societies, the students' union, the gymnasium, and the outside social circle will enable you to conquer the diffidence so apt to go with bookishness and which may prove a very serious drawback in after-life. I cannot too strongly impress upon the earnest and attentive men among you the necessity of overcoming this unfortunate failing in your student days. It is not easy for everyone to reach a happy medium, and the distinction between a proper self-confidence and 'cheek' particularly in junior students, is not always to be made. The latter is met with chiefly among the student pilgrims who, in travelling down the Delectable Mountains, have gone astray and have passed to the left hand, where lieth the country of Conceit, the country in which you remember the brisk lad Ignorance met Christian.

I wish we could encourage on this continent among our best students the habit of wandering. I do not know that we are quite prepared for it, as there is still great diversity in the curricula, even among the leading schools, but it is undoubtedly a great advantage to study under different teachers, as the mental horizon is widened and the sympathies enlarged. The practice would do much to lessen that narrow 'I am of Paul and I am of Apollos' spirit which is hostile to the best interests of the profession.

There is much that I would like to say on the question of work, but I can spare only a few moments for a word or two. Who will venture to settle upon so simple a matter as the best time for work? One will tell us there is no best time; all are equally good; and truly, all times are the same to a man whose soul is absorbed in some great problem. The other day I asked Edward Martin, the well-known story-writer, what time he found best for work. 'Not in the evening, and never between meals!' was his answer, which may appeal to some of my hearers. One works best at night; another, in the morning; a majority of the students of the past favour the latter. Erasmus, the great exemplar, says, 'Never work at night; it dulls the brain and hurts the health.' One day, going with George Ross through Bedlam, Dr Savage, at that time the physician in charge, remarked upon two great groups of patients—those who were depressed in the morning and those who were cheerful, and he suggested that the spirits rose and fell with the bodily temperature—those with very low morning temperatures were depressed, and vice versa. This, I believe, expresses a truth which may explain the extraordinary difference in the habits of students in this matter of the time at which the best work can be done. Outside of the asylum there are also the two great types, the student-lark who loves to see the sun rise, who comes to breakfast with a cheerful morning face, never so 'fit' as at 6 a.m. We all know the type. What a contrast to the student-owl with his saturnine morning face, thoroughly unhappy, cheated by the wretched breakfast bell of the two best hours of the day for sleep, no appetite, and permeated with an unspeakable hostility to his vis-a-vis, whose morning garrulity and good humour are equally offensive. Only gradually, as the day wears on and his temperature rises, does he become endurable to himself and to others. But see him really awake at 10 p.m. while our blithe lark is in hopeless coma over his books, from which it is hard to rouse him sufficiently to get his boots off for bed, our lean owl-friend, Saturn no longer in the ascendant, with bright eyes and cheery face, is ready for four hours of anything you wish: deep study, or

> Heart-affluence in discursive talk,

and by 2 a.m. he will undertake to unsphere the spirit of Plato. In neither a virtue, in neither a fault we must recognize these two types of students, differently constituted, owing possibly—though I have but little evidence for the belief—to thermal peculiarities.

II

In the days of probation the student's life may be lived by each one of you in its fullness and in its joys, but the difficulties arise in the break which follows departure from college and the entrance upon new duties. Much will now depend on the attitude of mind which has been encouraged. If the work has been for your degree, if the diploma has been its sole aim and object, you will rejoice in a freedom from exacting and possibly unpleasant studies, and with your books you will throw away all thoughts of further systematic work. On the other hand, with good habits of observation you may have got deep enough into the subject to feel that there is still much to be learned, and if you have had ground into you the lesson that the collegiate period is only the beginning of the student life, there is a hope that you may enter upon the useful career of the *student-practitioner.* Five years, at least, of trial await the man after parting from his teachers, and entering upon an independent course—years upon which his future depends, and from which his horoscope may be cast with certainty. It is all the same whether he settles in a country village or goes on with hospital and laboratory work; whether he takes a prolonged trip abroad; or whether he settles down in practice with a father or a friend—these five waiting years fix his fate so far as the student life is concerned. Without any strong natural propensity to study, he may feel such a relief after graduation that the effort to take to books is beyond his mental strength, and a weekly journal with an occasional textbook furnish pabulum enough, at least to keep his mind hibernating. But ten years later he is dead mentally, past any possible hope of galvanizing into life as a student, fit to do a routine practice, often a capable, resourceful man, but without any deep convictions, and probably more interested in stocks or in horses than in diagnosis or therapeutics. But this is not always the fate of the student who finishes his work on Commencement Day. There are men full of zeal in practice who give good service to their fellow creatures, who have not the capacity or the energy to keep up with the times. While they have lost interest in science, they are loyal members of the profession, and appreciate their responsibilities as such. That fateful first lustrum ruins some of our most likely material. Nothing is more trying to the soldier than inaction, to mark time while the battle is raging all about him; and waiting for practice is a serious strain under which many yield. In the cities it is not so hard to keep up: there is work in the dispensaries and colleges, and the stimulus of the medical societies; but in smaller towns and in the country it takes a strong man to live through the years of waiting without some deterioration. I wish the custom of taking junior men as partners and assistants would grow on this continent. It has become a necessity, and no man in large general practice can do his work efficiently without skilled help. How incalculably better for the seniors, how beneficial to the patients, how helpful in every way if each one of you, for the first five or ten years, was associated with an older practitioner, doing his night work, his laboratory work, his chores of all sorts. You would, in this way, escape the chilling and killing isolation of the early years, and amid congenial surroundings you could, in time, develop into that flower of our calling—the cultivated general practitioner. May this be the destiny of a large majority of you! Have no higher ambition! You cannot reach any better position in a community; the family doctor is the man behind the gun, who does our effective work. That his life is hard and exacting; that he is underpaid and overworked; that he has but little time for study and less for recreation—these are the blows that may give finer temper to his steel, and bring out the nobler elements in his character. What lot or portion has the general practitioner in the student life? Not, perhaps, the fruitful heritage of Judah or Benjamin but he may make of it the goodly portion of Ephraim. A man with powers of observation, well trained in the wards, and with the strong natural propensity to which I have so often referred, may live the ideal student life, and even reach the higher levels of scholarship. Adams, of Banchory (a little Aberdeenshire village), was not only a good practitioner and a skilful operator, but he was an excellent naturalist. This is by no means an unusual or remarkable combination, but Adams became, in addition, one of the great scholars of the profession. He had a perfect passion for the classics, and amid a very exacting practice found time to read 'almost every Greek work which has come down to us from antiquity, except the ecclesiastical writers.' He translated the works of Paulus Aegineta, the works of Hippocrates, and the works of Aretaeus, all of which are in the Sydenham Society's publications, monuments of the patient skill and erudition of a Scottish village doctor, an incentive to every one of us to make better use of our precious time.

Given the sacred hunger and proper preliminary training, the student-practitioner requires at least three things with which to stimulate and maintain his education, a notebook, a library, and a quinquennial brain-dusting. I wish I had time to speak of the value of note-taking. You can do nothing as a student in practice without it. Carry a small notebook which will fit into your waistcoat pocket, and never ask a new patient a question without notebook and pencil in hand. After the examination of a pneumonia case two minutes will suffice to record the essentials in the daily progress. Routine and system when once made a habit, facilitate work, and the busier you are the more time you will have to make observations after examining a patient. Jot a comment at the end of the notes: 'clear case;' 'case illustrating obscurity of symptoms;' 'error in diagnosis;' etc. The making of observations, may become the exercise of a jackdaw trick, like the craze which so many of us have to collect articles of all sorts. The study of the cases, the relation they bear to each other and to the cases in literature—here comes in the difficulty. Begin early to make a threefold category—clear cases, doubtful cases, mistakes. And learn to play the game fair, no self-deception, no shrinking from the truth; mercy and consideration for the other man, but none for yourself, upon whom you have to keep an incessant watch. You remember Lincoln's famous *mot* about the impossibility of fooling all of the people all the time. It does not hold good for the individual who can fool himself to his heart's content all of the time. If necessary, be cruel; use the knife and the cautery to cure the intumescence and moral necrosis which you will feel in the posterior parietal region, in Gall and Spurzheim's centre of self-esteem, where you will find a sore spot after you have made a mistake in diagnosis. It is only by getting your cases grouped in this way that you can make any real progress in your post-collegiate education; only in this way can you gain wisdom with experience. It is a common error to think that the more a doctor sees the greater his experience and the more he knows. No one ever drew a more skilful distinction than Cowper in his oft-quoted lines, which I am never tired of repeating in a medical audience:

> Knowledge and wisdom, far from being one,
> Have oft-times no connexion. Knowledge dwells
> In heads replete with thoughts of other men;
> Wisdom in minds attentive to their own.
> Knowledge is proud that he has learned so much;
> Wisdom is humble that he knows no more.

What we call sense or wisdom is knowledge, ready for use, made effective, and bears the same relation to knowledge itself that bread does to wheat. The full knowledge of the parts of a steam engine and the theory of its action may be possessed by a man who could not be trusted to pull the lever to its throttle. It is only by collecting data and using them that you can get sense. One of the most delightful sayings of antiquity is the remark of Heraclitus upon his predecessors—that they had much knowledge but no sense—which indicates that the noble old Ephesian had a keen appreciation of their difference; and the distinction, too, is well drawn by Tennyson in the oft-quoted line:

> Knowledge comes but wisdom lingers.

Of the three well-stocked rooms which it should be the ambition of every young doctor to have in his house, the library, the laboratory, and the nursery—books, balances, and bairns—as he may not achieve all three, I would urge him to start at any rate with the books and the balances. A good weekly and a good monthly journal to begin with, and read them. Then, for a systematic course of study, supplement your college textbooks with the larger systems—Allbutt or Nothnagel—a system of surgery, and, as your practice increases, make a habit of buying a few special monographs every year. Read with two objects: first, to acquaint yourself with the current knowledge on the subject and the steps by which it has been reached; and secondly, and more important, read to understand and analyse your cases. To this line of work we should direct the attention of the student before he leaves the medical school, pointing in specific cases just where the best articles are to be found, sending him to the Index Catalogue—that marvellous storehouse, every page of which is interesting and the very titles instructive. Early learn to appreciate the differences between the descriptions of disease and the manifestations of that disease in an individual—the difference between the composite portrait and one of the component pictures. By exercise of a little judgment you can collect at moderate cost a good working library. Try, in the waiting years, to get a clear idea of the history of medicine. Read Foster's *Lectures on the History of Physiology* and Baas's *History of Medicine.*

Get the 'Masters of Medicine' Series, and subscribe to the *Library and Historical Journal.*

Every day do some reading or work apart from your profession. I fully realize, no one more so, how absorbing is the profession of medicine; how applicable to it is what Michelangelo says: 'There are sciences which demand the whole of a man, without leaving the least portion of his spirit free for other distractions'; but you will be a better man and not a worse practitioner for an avocation. I care not what it may be; gardening or farming, literature or history or bibliography, anyone of which will bring you into contact with books. (I wish that time permitted me to speak of the other two rooms which are really of equal importance with the library, but which are more difficult to equip, though of coordinate value in the education of the head, the heart, and the hand.) The third essential for the practitioner as a student is the quinquennial brain-dusting, and this will often seem to him the hardest task to carry out. Every fifth year, back to the hospital, back to the laboratory, for renovation, rehabilitation, rejuvenation, reintegration, resuscitation, etc. Do not forget to take the notebooks with you, or the sheets, in three separate bundles, to work over. From the very start begin to save for the trip. Deny yourself all luxuries for it; shut up the room you meant for the nursery—have the definite determination to get your education thoroughly well started; if you are successful you may, perhaps, have enough saved at the end of three years to spend six weeks in special study; or in five years you may be able to spend six months. Hearken not to the voice of old 'Dr Hayseed,' who tells you it will ruin your prospects, and that he 'never heard of such a thing' as a young man, not yet five years in practice, taking three months' holiday. To him it seems preposterous. Watch him wince when you say it is a speculation in the only gold mine in which the physician should invest—*Grey Cortex*! What about the wife and babies, if you have them? Leave them! Heavy as are your responsibilities to those nearest and dearest, they are outweighed by the responsibilities to yourself, to the profession, and to the public. Like Isaphaena, the story of whose husband—ardent, earnest soul, peace to his ashes!—I have told in the little sketch of *An Alabama Student*, your wife will be glad to bear her share in the sacrifice you make.

With good health and good habits the end of the second lustrum should find you thoroughly established—all three rooms well furnished, a good stable, a good garden, no mining stock, but a life insurance, and, perhaps, a mortgage or two on neighbouring farms. Year by year you have dealt honestly with yourself; you have put faithfully the notes of each case into their proper places, and you will be gratified to find that, though the doubtful cases, and mistakes still make a rather formidable pile, it has grown relatively smaller. You literally 'own' the countryside, as the expression is. All the serious and dubious cases come to you, and you have been so honest in the frank acknowledgement of your own mistakes, and so charitable in the contemplation of theirs, that neighbouring doctors, old and young, are glad to seek your advice. The work, which has been very heavy, is now lightened by a good assistant, one of your own students, who becomes in a year or so your partner. This is not an overdrawn picture, and it is one which may be seen in many places except, I am sorry to say, in the particular as to the partner. This is the type of man we need in the country districts and the smaller towns. He is not a whit too good to look after the sick, not a whit too highly-educated—impossible! And with an optimistic temperament and a good digestion he is the very best product of our profession, and may do more to stop quackery and humbuggery, inside and outside of the ranks, than could a dozen prosecuting county attorneys. Nay, more! such a doctor may be a daily benediction in the community—a strong, sensible, whole-souled man, often living a life of great self-denial, and always of tender sympathy, worried neither by the vagaries of the well nor by the testy waywardness of the sick, and to him, if to any, may come (even when he knows it not) the true spiritual blessing—that 'blessing which maketh rich and addeth no sorrow.'

The danger in such a man's life comes with prosperity. He is safe in the hard-working day, when he is climbing the hill, but once success is reached, with it come the temptations to which many succumb. Politics has been the ruin of many country doctors, and often of the very best, of just such a good fellow as he of whom I have been speaking. He is popular; he has a little money; and he, if anybody, can save the seat for the party! When the committee leaves you, take the offer under consideration, and if in the ten or twelve years you have kept on intimate terms with those friends of your student days, Montaigne and Plutarch, you will know what answer to return. If you live in a large town, resist the temptation to open a sanatorium. It is not the work for a general practitioner, and there are risks that you may sacrifice your independence and much else besides. And, thirdly, resist the temptation to move into a larger place. In a good agricultural district, or in a small town, if you handle your resources aright, taking good care of your education, of your habits, and of your money, and devoting part of your energies to the support of the societies, etc., you may reach a position in the community of which any man may be proud. There are country practitioners among my friends with whom I would rather change places than with any in our ranks, men whose stability of character and devotion to duty make one proud of the profession.

Curiously enough, the student-practitioner may find studiousness to be a stumbling-block in his career. A bookish man may never succeed; deep-versed in books, he may not be able to use his knowledge to practical effect; or, more likely, his failure is not because he has studied books much, but because he has not studied men more. He has never got over that shyness, that diffidence, against which I have warned you. I have known instances in which this malady was incurable; in others I have known a cure effected not by the public, but by the man's professional brethren, who, appreciating his work, have insisted upon utilizing his mental treasures. It is very hard to carry student habits into a large city practice; only zeal, a fiery passion, keeps the flame alive, smothered as it is so apt to be by the dust and ashes of the daily routine. A man may be a good student who reads only the book of nature. Such a one I remember in the early days of my residence in Montreal—a man whose devotion to patients and whose kindness and skill quickly brought him an enormous practice. Reading in his carriage and by lamplight at Lucina's bedside, he was able to keep well informed; but he had an insatiable desire to know the true inwardness of a disease, and it was in this way I came into contact with him. Hard pushed day and night, yet he was never too busy to spend a couple of hours with me searching for data which had not been forthcoming during life, or helping to unravel the mysteries of a new disease, such as pernicious anaemia.

III

The *student-specialist* has to walk warily, as with two advantages there are two great dangers against which he has constantly to be on guard. In the bewildering complexity of modern medicine it is a relief to limit the work of a life to a comparatively narrow field which can be thoroughly tilled. To many men there is a feeling of great satisfaction in the mastery of a small department, particularly one in which technical skill is required. How much we have benefited from this concentration of effort in dermatology, laryngology, opthalmology, and in gynecology! Then, as a rule, the specialist is a free man, with leisure or, at any rate, with some leisure; not the slave of the public, with the incessant demands upon him of the general practitioner. He may live a more rational life, and has time to cultivate his mind, and he is able to devote himself to public interests and to the welfare of his professional brethren, on whose suffrages he so largely depends. How much we are indebted in the larger cities to the disinterested labours of this favoured class the records of our libraries and medical societies bear witness. The dangers do not come to the strong man in a speciality, but to the weak brother who seeks in it an easier field in which specious garrulity and mechanical dexterity may take the place of solid knowledge. All goes well when the man is larger than his speciality and controls it, but when the speciality runs away with the man there is disaster, and a topsy-turvy condition which, in every branch, has done incalculable injury. Next to the danger from small men is the serious risk of the loss of perspective in prolonged and concentrated effort in a narrow field. Against this there is but one safeguard—the cultivation of the sciences upon which the speciality is based. The student-specialist may have a wide vision—no student wider—if he gets away from the mechanical side of the art, and keeps in touch with the physiology and pathology upon which his art depends. More than any other of us, he needs the lessons of the laboratory, and wide contact with men in other departments may serve to correct the inevitable tendency to a narrow and perverted vision, in which the life of the anthill is mistaken for the world at large.

Of the *student-teacher* every faculty affords examples in varying degrees. It goes without saying that no man can teach successfully who is not at the same time a student. Routine, killing routine, saps the vitality of many who start with high aims, and who, for years, strive with all their energies against the degeneration which it is so prone to entail. In the smaller schools isolation, the absence of congenial spirits working at the same subject, favours stagnation, and after a few years the fires of early enthusiasm no longer glow in the perfunctory lectures. In many teachers the ever-increasing demands of practice leave less and less time for study, and a first-class man may lose touch with his subject through no fault of his own, but through an entanglement in outside affairs which he deeply regrets yet cannot control. To his five natural senses the student-teacher must add two more—the sense of responsibility and the sense of proportion. Most of us start with a highly developed sense of the importance of the work, and with a desire to live up to the responsibilities entrusted to us. Punctuality, the class first, always and at all times; the best that a man has in him, nothing less; the best the profession has on the subject, nothing less; fresh energies and enthusiasm in dealing with dry details; animated, unselfish devotion to all alike; tender consideration for his assistants—these are some of the fruits of a keen sense of responsibility in a good teacher. The sense of proportion is not so easy to acquire, and much depends on the training and on the natural disposition. There are men who never possess it; to others it seems to come naturally. In the most careful ones it needs constant cultivation—nothing over-much should be the motto of every teacher. In my early days I came under the influence of an ideal student-teacher, the late Palmer Howard, of Montreal. If you ask what manner of man he was, read Matthew Arnold's noble tribute to his father in his well-known poem, *Rugby*

Chapel. When young, Dr Howard had chosen a path—'path to a clear-purposed goal;' and he pursued it with unswerving devotion. With him the study and the teaching of medicine were an absorbing passion, the ardour of which neither the incessant and ever-increasing demands upon his time nor the growing years could quench. When I first, as a senior student, came into intimate contact with him in the summer of 1871, the problem of tuberculosis was under discussion, stirred up by the epoch-making work of Villemin and the radical views of Niemeyer. Every lung lesion at the Montreal General Hospital had to be shown to him, and I got my first-hand introduction to Laennec, to Graves, and to Stokes, and became familiar with their works. No matter what the hour, and it usually was after 10 p.m., I was welcome with my bag, and if Wilks and Moxon, Virchow, or Rokitanski gave us no help, there were the *Transactions of the Pathological Society* and the big *Dictionnaire* of Dechambre. An ideal teacher because a student, ever alert to the new problems, an indomitable energy enabled him in the midst of an exacting practice to maintain an ardent enthusiasm, still to keep bright the fires which he had lighted in his youth. Since those days I have seen many teachers, and I have had many colleagues, but I have never known one in whom was more happily combined a stern sense of duty with the mental freshness of youth.

But as I speak, from out the memory of the past there rises before me a shadowy group, a long line of students whom I have taught and loved, and who have died prematurely—mentally, morally, or bodily. To the successful we are willing and anxious to bring the tribute of praise, but none so poor to give recognition to the failures. From one cause or another, perhaps because when not absorbed in the present, my thoughts are chiefly in the past, I have cherished the memory of many young men whom I have loved and lost. Io victis: let us sometimes sing of the vanquished. Let us sometimes think of those who have fallen in the battle of life, who have striven and failed, who have failed even without the strife. How many have I lost from the student band by mental death, and from so many causes—some stillborn from college, others dead within the first year of infantile marasmus, while mental rickets, teething, tabes, and fits have carried off many of the most promising minds! Due to improper feeding within the first five fateful years, scurvy and rickets head the mental mortality bills of students. To the teacher-nurse it is a sore disappointment to find at the end of ten years so few minds with the full stature, of which the early days gave promise. Still, so widespread is mental death that we scarcely comment upon it in our friends. The real tragedy is the moral death which, in different forms, overtakes so many good fellows who fall away from the pure, honourable, and righteous service of Minerva into the idolatry of Bacchus, of Venus, or of Circe. Against the background of the past these tragedies stand out, lurid and dark, and as the names and faces of my old boys recur (some of them my special pride), I shudder to think of the blighted hopes and wrecked lives, and I force my memory back to those happy days when they were as you are now, joyous and free from care, and I think of them on the benches, in the laboratories, and in the wards—and there I leave them. Less painful to dwell upon, though associated with a more poignant grief, is the fate of those whom physical death has snatched away in the bud or blossom of the student life. These are among the tender memories of the teacher's life, of which he does not often care to speak, feeling with Longfellow that the surest pledge of their remembrance is 'the silent homage of thoughts unspoken.' As I look back it seems now as if the best of us had died, that the brightest and the keenest had been taken and the more commonplace among us had been spared. An old mother, a devoted sister, a loving brother, in some cases a brokenhearted wife, still pay the tribute of tears for the untimely ending of their high hopes, and in loving remembrance I would mingle mine with theirs. What a loss to our profession have been the deaths of such true disciples as Zimmerman, of Toronto; of Jack Cline and of R. L. MacDonnell, of Montreal; of Fred Packard and of Kirkbride, of Philadelphia; of Livingood, of Lazear, of Oppenheimer, and of Oechsner, in Baltimore—cut off with their leaves still in the green, to the inconsolable grief of their friends! To each one of you the practice of medicine will be very much as you make it—to one a worry, a care, a perpetual annoyance; to another, a daily joy and a life of as much happiness and usefulness as can well fall to the lot of man. In the student spirit you can best fulfil the high mission of our noble calling—in his humility, conscious of weakness, while seeking strength; in his confidence, knowing the power, while recognizing the limitations of his art, in his pride in the glorious heritage from which the greatest gifts to man have been derived; and in his sure and certain hope that the future holds for us richer blessings than the past.

28

ON LYING AWAKE AT NIGHT

Stewart Edward White

'Who hath lain alone to hear the wild goose cry?'

About once in so often you are due to lie awake at night. Why this is so I have never been able to discover. It apparently comes from no predisposing uneasiness of indigestion, no rashness in the matter of too much tea or tobacco, no excitation of unusual incident or stimulating conversation. In fact, you turn in with the expectation of rather a good night's rest. Almost at once the little noises of the forest grow larger, blend in the hollow bigness of the first drowse; your thoughts drift idly back and forth between reality and dream; when—snap!—you are broad awake!

Perhaps the reservoir of your vital forces is full to the overflow of a little waste; or perhaps, more subtly, the great Mother insists thus that you enter the temple of her larger mysteries.

For, unlike mere insomnia, lying awake at night in the woods is pleasant. The eager, nervous straining for sleep gives way to a delicious indifference. You do not care. Your mind is cradled in an exquisite poppy-suspension of judgment and of thought. Impressions slip vaguely into your consciousness and as vaguely out again. Sometimes they stand stark and naked for your inspection; sometimes they lose themselves in the mist of half-sleep. Always they lay soft velvet fingers on the drowsy imagination, so that in their caressing you feel the vaster spaces from which they have come. Peaceful-brooding your faculties receive. Hearing, sight, smell—all are preternaturally keen to whatever of sound and sight and woods perfume is abroad through the night;

and yet at the same time active appreciation dozes, so these things lie on it sweet and cloying like fallen rose-leaves.

In such circumstance you will hear what the *voyageurs* call the voices of the rapids. Many people never hear them at all. They speak very soft and low and distinct beneath the steady roar and dashing, beneath even the lesser tinklings and gurglings whose quality superimposes them over the louder sounds. They are like the tear-forms swimming across the field of vision, which disappear so quickly when you concentrate your sight to look at them, and which reappear so magically when again your gaze turns vacant. In the stillness of your hazy half-consciousness they speak; when you bend your attention to listen, they are gone, and only the tumults and the tinklings remain.

But in the moments of their audibility they are very distinct. Just as often an odor will wake all a vanished memory, so these voices, by the force of a large impressionism, suggest whole scenes. Far off are the cling-clang-cling of chimes and the swell-and-fall murmur of a multitude *en fête*, so that subtly you feel the gray old town, with its walls, the crowded market-place, the decent peasant crowd, the booths, the mellow church building with its bells, the warm, dust-moted sun. Or, in the pauses between the swish-dash-dashings of the waters, sound faint and clear voices singing intermittently, calls, distant notes of laughter, as though many canoes were working against the current—only the flotilla never gets any nearer, nor the voices louder. The *voyageurs* call these mist people the Huntsmen; and look frightened. To each is his vision, according to his experience. The nations of the earth whisper to their exiled sons through the voices of the rapids. Curiously enough, by all reports, they suggest always peaceful scenes—a harvest-field, a street fair, a Sunday morning in a cathedral town, careless travelers—never the turmoils and struggles. Perhaps this is the great Mother's compensation in a harsh mode of life.

Nothing is more fantastically unreal to tell about, nothing more concretely real to experience, than this undernote of the quick water. And when you do lie awake at night, it is always making its unobtrusive appeal. Gradually its hypnotic spell works. The distant chimes ring louder and nearer as you cross the borderland of sleep. And then outside the tent some little woods noise snaps the thread. An owl hoots, a whippoorwill cries, a twig cracks beneath the cautious prowl of some night creature—at once the yellow sunlit French meadows puff away—you are staring at the blurred image of the moon spraying through the texture of your tent.

The voices of the rapids have dropped into the background, as have the dashing noises of the stream. Through the forest is a great silence, but no stillness at all. The whippoorwill swings down and up the short curve of his regular song; over and over an owl says his rapid *whoo, whoo, whoo*. These, with the ceaseless dash of the rapids, are the web on which the night traces her more delicate embroideries of the unexpected. Distant crashes, single and impressive; stealthy footsteps near at hand; the subdued scratching of claws; a faint *sniff! sniff! sniff!* of inquiry; the sudden clear tin-horn *ko-ko-ko-óh* of the little owl; the mournful, long-drawn-out cry of the loon, instinct with the spirit of loneliness; the ethereal call-note of the birds of passage high in the air; a *patter, patter, patter*, among the dead leaves, immediately stilled; and then at the last, from the thicket close at hand, the beautiful silver purity of the white-throated sparrow—the nightingale of the North—trembling with the ecstasy of beauty, as though a shimmering moonbeam had turned to sound; and all the while the blurred figure of the moon mounting to the ridge-line of your tent—these things combine subtly, until at last the great Silence of which they are a part overarches the night and draws you forth to contemplation.

No beverage is more grateful than the cup of spring water you drink at such a time; no moment more refreshing than that in which you look about you at the darkened forest. You have cast from you with the warm blanket the drowsiness of dreams. A coolness, physical and spiritual, bathes you from head to foot. All your senses are keyed to the last vibrations. You hear the littler night prowlers; you glimpse the greater. A faint, searching woods perfume of dampness greets your nostrils. And somehow, mysteriously, in a manner not to be understood, the forces of the world seem in suspense, as though a touch might crystallize infinite possibilities into infinite power and motion. But the touch lacks. The forces hover on the edge of action, unheeding the little noises. In all humbleness and awe, you are a dweller of the Silent Places.

At such a time you will meet with adventures. One night we put fourteen inquisitive porcupines out of camp. Near McGregor's Bay I discovered in the large grass park of my camp-site nine deer, cropping the herbage like so many beautiful ghosts. A friend tells me of a fawn that every night used to sleep outside his tent and within a foot of his head, probably by way of protection against wolves. Its mother had in all likelihood been killed. The instant my friend moved toward the tent opening the little creature would disappear, and it was always gone by earliest daylight. Nocturnal bears in search of pork are not uncommon. But even though your interest meets nothing but the bats and the woods shadows and the stars, that few moments of the sleeping world forces is a psychical experience to be gained in no other way. You cannot know the night by sitting up; she will sit up with you. Only by coming into her presence from the borders of sleep can you meet her face to face in her intimate mood.

The night wind from the river, or from the open spaces of the wilds, chills you after a time. You begin to think of your blankets. In a few moments you roll yourself in their soft wool. Instantly it is morning.

And, strange to say, you have not to pay by going through the day unrefreshed. You may feel like turning in at eight instead of nine, and you may fall asleep with unusual promptitude, but your journey will begin clear-headedly, proceed springily, and end with much in reserve. No languor, no dull headache, no exhaustion, follows your experience. For this once your two hours of sleep have been as effective as nine.

29

A WOODLAND VALENTINE

Marian Storm

Forces astir in the deepest roots grow restless beneath the lock of frost. Bulbs try the door. February's stillness is charged with a faint anxiety, as if the powers of light, pressing up from the earth's center and streaming down from the stronger sun, had troubled the buried seeds, who strive to answer their liberator, so that the guarding mother must whisper over and over, 'Not yet, not yet!' Better to stay behind the frozen gate than to come too early up into realms where the wolves of cold are still aprowl. Wisely the snow places a white hand over eager—life unseen, but perceived in February's woods as a swimmer feels the changing moods of water in a lake fed by springs. Only the thick stars, closer and more companionable than in months of foliage, burn alert and serene. In February the Milky Way is revealed divinely lucent to lonely peoples—herdsmen, mountaineers, fishermen, trappers—who are abroad in the starlight hours of this grave and silent time of year. It is in the long, frozen nights that the sky has most red flowers.

February knows the beat of twilight wings. Drifting north again come birds who only pretended to forsake us—adventurers, not so fond of safety but that they dare risk finding how snow bunting and pine finch have plundered the cones of the evergreens, while chickadees, sparrows, and crows are supervising from established stations all the more domestic supplies available; a sparrow often making it possible to annoy even a duck out of her share of cracked corn. Ranged along a brown-draped oak branch in the waxing light, crows show a lordly glistening of feathers. (Sun on a sweeping wing in flight has the quality of sun on a ripple.) Where hemlocks gather, deep in somber woods, the great horned owl has thus soon, perhaps working amid snows at her task, built a nest wherein March will find sturdy balls of fluff. The thunderous love song of her mate sounds through the timber. By the time the wren has nested these winter babies will be solemn with the wisdom of their famous race.

There is no season like the end of February for cleaning out brooks. Hastening yellow waters toss a dreary wreckage of torn or ashen leaves, twigs, acorn cups, stranded rafts of bark, and buttonballs from the sycamore, never to come to seed. Standing on one bank or both, according to the sundering flood's ambition, the knight with staff and bold forefinger sets the water princess free. She goes then curtsying and dimpling over the shining gravel, sliding from beneath the ice that roofs her on the uplands down to the softer valleys, where her quickened step will be heard by the frogs in their mansions of mud, and the fish, recluses in rayless pools, will rise to the light she brings.

Down from the frozen mountains, in summer, birds and winds must bear the seed of alpine flowers—lilies that lean against unmelting snows, poppies, bright-colored herbs, and the palely gleaming, fringed beauties that change names with countries. How just and reasonable it would seem to be that flowers which edge the ice in July should consent to bloom in lowlands no colder in February! The pageant of blue, magenta, and scarlet on the austere upper slopes of the Rockies, where nights are bitter to the summer wanderer—why should it not flourish to leeward of a valley barn in months when icicles hang from the eaves in this tamer setting? But no. Mountain tempests are endurable to the silken-petaled. The treacherous lowland winter, with its coaxing suns followed by roaring desolation, is for blooms bred in a different tradition.

The light is clear but hesitant, a delicate wine, by no means the mighty vintage of April. February has no intoxication; the vague eagerness that gives the air a pulse where fields lie voiceless comes from the secret stirring of imprisoned life. Spring and sunrise are forever miracles, but the early hour of the wonder hardly hints the exuberance of its fulfillment. Even the forest dwellers move gravely, thankful for any promise of kindness from the lord of day as he hangs above a sea-gray landscape, but knowing well that their long duress is not yet to end. Deer pathetically haunt the outskirts of farms, gazing upon cattle feeding in winter pasture from the stack, and often, after dark, clearing the fences and robbing the same disheveled storehouse. Not a chipmunk winks from the top rail. The woodchuck, after his single expeditionary effort on Candlemas, which he is obliged to make for mankind's enlightenment, has retired without being seen, in sunshine or shadow, and has not the slightest intention of disturbing himself just yet. Though snowdrops may feel uneasy, he knows too much about the Ides of March! Quietest of all Northern woods creatures, the otter slides from one ice-hung waterfall to the next. The solitary scamperer left is the cottontail, appealing because he is the most pursued and politest of the furry; faithfully trying to give no offense, except when starvation points to winter cabbage, he is none the less fey. So is the mink, though he moves like a phantom.

Mosses, whereon March in coming treads first, show one hue brighter in the swamps. Pussy willows have made a gray dawn in viny caverns where the day's own dawn looks in but faintly, and the flushing of the red willow betrays reveries of a not impossible cowslip upon the bank beneath. The blue jay has mentioned it in the course of his voluble recollections. He is unwilling to prophesy arbutus, but he will just hint that when the leaves in the wood lot show through snow as early as this… Once he found a hepatica bud the last day of February… Speaking with his old friend, the muskrat, last week… And when you can see red pebbles in the creek at five o'clock in the afternoon… But it is no use to expect yellow orchids on the west knoll this spring, for some people found them there last year, and after that you might as well… Of course cowslips beside red willows are remarkably pretty, just as blue jays in a cedar with blue berries… He is interminable, but then he has seen a great deal of life. And February needs her blue jays' unwearied and conquering faith.

30

NOCTURNE

Simeon Strunsky

Once every three months, with fair regularity, she was brought into the Night Court, found guilty, and fined. She came in between eleven o'clock and midnight, when the traffic of the court is at its heaviest, and it would be an hour, perhaps, before she was called to the bar. When her turn came she would rise from her seat at one end of the prisoners' bench and confront the magistrate.

Her eyes did not reach to the level of the magistrate's desk. A policeman in citizen's clothes would mount the witness stand, take oath with a seriousness of mien which was surprising, in view of the frequency with which he was called upon to repeat the formula, and testify in an illiterate drone to a definite infraction of the law of the State, committed in his presence and with his encouragement. While he spoke the magistrate would look at the ceiling. When she was called upon to answer she defended herself with an obvious lie or two, while the magistrate looked over her head. He would then condemn her to pay the sum of ten dollars to the State and let her go.

She came to look forward to her visits at the Night Court.

The Night Court is no longer a center of general interest. During the first few months after it was established, two or three years ago, it was one of the great sights of a great city. For the newspapers it was a rich source of human-interest stories. It replaced Chinatown in its appeal to visitors from out-of-town. It stirred even the languid pulses of the native inhabitant with its offerings of something new in the way of 'life.' The sociologists, sincere and amateur, crowded the benches and took notes.

To-day the novelty is worn off. The newspapers long ago abandoned the Night Court, clergymen go to it rarely for their texts, and the tango has taken its place. But the sociologists and the casual visitor have not disappeared. Serious people, anxious for an immediate vision of the pity of life, continue to fill the benches comfortably. No session of the court is without its little group of social investigators, among whom the women are in the majority. Many of them are young women, exceedingly sympathetic, handsomely gowned, and very well taken care of.

As she sat at one end of the prisoners' bench waiting her turn before the magistrate's desk, she would cast a sidelong glance over the railing that separated her from the handsomely gowned, gently bred, sympathetic young women in the audience. She observed with extraordinary admiration and delight those charming faces softened in pity, the graceful bearing, the admirably constructed yet simple coiffures, the elegance of dress, which she compared with the best that the windows in Sixth Avenue could show. She was amazed to find such gowns actually being worn instead of remaining as an unattainable ideal on smiling lay figures in the shop windows.

Occupants of the prisoners' bench are not supposed to stare at the spectators. She had to steal a glance now and then. Her visits to the Night Court had become so much a matter of routine that she would venture a peep over the railing while the case immediately preceding her own was being tried. Once or twice she was surprised by the clerk who called her name. She stood up mechanically and faced the magistrate as Officer Smith, in civilian clothes, mounted the witness stand.

She had no grudge against Officer Smith. She did not visualize him either as a person or as a part of a system. He was merely an incident of her trade. She had neither the training nor the imagination to look behind Officer Smith and see a communal policy which has not the power to suppress, nor the courage to acknowledge, nor the skill to regulate, and so contents itself with sending out full-fed policemen in civilian clothes to work up the evidence that defends society against her kind through the imposition of a ten-dollar fine.

To some of the women on the visitors' benches the cruelty of the process came home: this business of setting a two-hundred-pound policeman in citizen's clothes, backed up by magistrates, clerks, court criers, interpreters, and court attendants, to worrying a ten-dollar fine out of a half-grown woman under an enormous imitation ostrich plume. The professional sociologists were chiefly interested in the money cost of this process to the tax-payer, and they took notes on the proportion of first offenders. Yet the Night Court is a remarkable advance in civilization. Formerly, in addition to her fine, the prisoner would pay a commission to the professional purveyor of bail.

Sometimes, if the magistrate was young or new to the business, she would be given a chance against Officer Smith. She would be called to the witness chair and under oath be allowed to elaborate on the obvious lies which constituted her usual defense. This would give her the opportunity, between the magistrate's questions, of sweeping the courtroom with a full, hungry look for as much as half a minute at a time. She saw the women in the audience only, and their clothes. The pity in their eyes did not move her, because she was not in the least interested in what they thought, but in how they looked and what they wore. They were part of a world which she would read about—she read very little—in the society columns of the Sunday newspaper. They were the women around whom headlines were written and whose pictures were printed frequently on the first page.

She could study them with comparative leisure in the Night Court. Outside in the course of her daily routine she might catch an occasional glimpse of these same women, through the windows of a passing taxi, or in the matinée crowds, or going in and out of the fashionable shops. But her work took her seldom into the region of taxicabs and fashionable shops. The nature of her occupation kept her to furtive corners and the dark side of streets. Nor was she at such times in the mood for just appreciation of the beautiful things in life. More than any other walk of life, hers was of an exacting nature, calling for intense powers of concentration both as regards the public and the police. It was different in the Night Court. Here, having nothing to fear and nothing out of the usual to hope for, she might give herself up to the aesthetic contemplation of a beautiful world of which, at any other time, she could catch mere fugitive aspects.

Sometimes I wonder why people think that life is only what they see and hear, and not what they read of. Take the Night Court. The visitor really sees nothing and hears nothing that he has not read a thousand times in his newspaper and had it described in greater detail and with better-trained powers of observation than he can bring to bear in person. What new phase of life is revealed by seeing in the body, say, a dozen practitioners of a trade of whom we know there are several tens of thousands in New York? They have been described by the human-interest reporters, analyzed by the statisticians, defended by the social revolutionaries, and explained away by the optimists. For that matter, to the faithful reader of the newspapers, daily and Sunday, what can there be new in this world from the Pyramids by moonlight to the habits of the night prowler? Can the upper classes really acquire for themselves, through slumming parties and visits to the Night Court, anything like the knowledge that books and newspapers can furnish them? Can the lower classes ever hope to obtain that complete view of the Fifth Avenue set which the Sunday columns offer them? And yet there the case stands: only by seeing and hearing for ourselves, however imperfectly, do we get the sense of reality.

That is why our criminal courts are probably our most influential schools of democracy. More than our settlement houses, more than our subsidized dancing-schools for shopgirls, they encourage the get-together process through which one-half the world learns how the other half lives. On either side of the railing of the prisoners' cage is an audience and a stage.

That is why she would look forward to her regular visits at the Night Court. She saw life there.

31

BEER AND CIDER

George Saintsbury

There is no beverage which I have liked 'to live with' more than Beer; but I have never had a cellar large enough to accommodate much of it, or an establishment numerous enough to justify the accommodation. In the good days when servants expected beer, but did not expect to be treated otherwise than as servants, a cask or two was necessary; and persons who were 'quite' generally took care that the small beer they drank should be the same as that which they gave to their domestics, though they might have other sorts as well. For these better sorts at least the good old rule was, when you began on one cask always to have in another. Even Cobbett, whose belief in beer was the noblest feature in his character, allowed that it required some keeping. The curious 'white ale,' or lober agol—which, within the memory of man, used to exist in Devonshire and Cornwall, but which, even half a century ago, I have vainly sought there—was, I believe, drunk quite new; but then it was not pure malt and not hopped at all, but had eggs ('pullet-sperm in the brewage') and other foreign bodies in it.

I did once drink, at St David's, ale so new that it frothed from the cask as creamily as if it had been bottled: and I wondered whether the famous beer of Bala, which Borrow found so good at his first visit and so bad at his second, had been like it.

On the other hand, the very best Bass I ever drank had had an exactly contrary experience. In the year 1875, when I was resident at Elgin, I and a friend now dead, the Procurator-Fiscal of the district, devoted the May 'Sacrament holidays,' which were then still kept in those remote parts, to a walking tour up the Findhorn and across to Loch Ness and Glen Urquhart. At the Freeburn Inn on the first-named river we found some beer of singular excellence: and, asking the damsel who waited on us about it, were informed that a cask of Bass had been put in during the previous October, but, owing to a sudden break in the weather and the departure of all visitors, had never been tapped till our arrival.

Beer of ordinary strength left too long in the cask gets 'hard' of course; but no one who deserves to drink it would drink it from anything but the cask if he could help it. Jars are makeshifts, though useful makeshifts: and small beer will not keep in them for much more than a week. Nor are the very small barrels, known by various affectionate diminutives ('pin,' etc.) in the country districts, much to be recommended. 'We'll drink it in the firkin, my boy!' is the lowest admission in point of volume that should be allowed. Of one such firkin I have a pleasant memory and memorial, though it never reposed in my home cellar. It was just before the present century opened, and some years before we Professors in Scotland had, of our own motion and against considerable opposition, given up half of the old six months' holiday without asking for or receiving a penny more salary. (I have since chuckled at the horror and wrath with which Mr Smillie and Mr Thomas would hear of such profligate conduct.) One could therefore move about with fairly long halts: and I had taken from a friend a house at Abingdon for some time. So, though I could not even then drink quite as much beer as I could thirty years earlier a little higher up the Thames, it became necessary to procure a cask. It came—one of Bass's minor mildnesses—affectionately labeled 'Mr George Saintsbury. Full to the bung.' I detached the card, and I believe I have it to this day as my choicest (because quite unsolicited) testimonial.

Very strong beer permits itself, of course, to be bottled and kept in bottles: but I rather doubt whether it also is not best from the wood; though it is equally of course, much easier to cellar it and keep it bottled. Its kinds are various and curious. 'Scotch ale' is famous, and at its best (I never drank better than Younger's) excellent: but its tendency, I think, is to be too sweet. I once invested in some—not Younger's—which I kept for nearly sixteen years, and which was still treacle at the end. Bass's No. 1 requires no praises. Once when living in the Cambridgeshire village mentioned earlier I had some, bottled in Cambridge itself, of great age and excellence. Indeed, two guests, though both of them were Cambridge men, and should have had what Mr Lang once called the 'robust' habits of that university, fell into one ditch after partaking of it. (I own that the lanes thereabouts are very dark.) In former days, though probably not at present, you could often find rather choice specimens of strong beer produced at small breweries in the country. I remember such even in the Channel Islands. And I suspect the universities themselves have been subject to 'declensions and fallings off.' I know that in my undergraduate days at Merton we always had proper beer-glasses, like the old 'flute' champagnes, served regularly at cheese-time with a most noble beer called 'Archdeacon,' which was then actually brewed in the sacristy of the College chapel. I have since—a slight sorrow to season the joy of reinstatement there—been told that it is now obtained from outside. And All Souls is the only other college in which, from actual recent experience, I can imagine the possibility of the exorcism,

> Strongbeerum! discede a lay-fratre Petro,

if lay-brother Peter were so silly as to abuse, or play tricks with, the good gift.

I have never had many experiences of real 'home-brewed,' but two which I had were pleasing. There was much home-brewing in East Anglia at the time I lived there, and I once got the village carpenter to give me some of his own manufacture. It was as good light ale as I ever wish to drink (many times better than the wretched stuff that Dora has foisted on us), and he told me that, counting in every expense for material, cost and wear of plant, etc., it came to about a penny a quart. The other was very different. The late Lord de Tabley—better or at least longer known as Mr Leicester Warren—once gave a dinner at the Athenæum at which I was present, and had up from his Cheshire cellars some of the old ale for which that county is said to be famous, to make flip after dinner. It was shunned by most of the pusillanimous guests, but not by me, and it was excellent. But I should like to have tried it unflipped.

I never drank mum, which all know from The Antiquary, some from 'The Ryme of Sir Lancelot Bogle,' and some again from the notice which Mr Gladstone's love of Scott (may it plead for him!) gave it once in some Budget debate, I think. It is said to be brewed of wheat, which is not in its favor (wheat was meant to be eaten, not drunk) and very bitter, which is. Nearly all bitter drinks are good. The only time I ever drank 'spruce' beer I did not like it. The comeliest of black malts is, of course, that noble liquor called of Guinness. Here at least I think England cannot match Ireland, for our stouts are, as a rule, too sweet and 'clammy.' But there used to be in the country districts a sort of light porter which was one of the most refreshing liquids conceivable for hot weather. I have drunk it in Yorkshire at the foot of Roseberry Topping, out of big stone bottles like champagne magnums. But that was nearly sixty years ago. Genuine lager beer is no more to be boycotted than genuine hock, though, by the way, the best that I ever drank (it was at the good town of King's Lynn) was Low not High Dutch in origin. It was so good that I wrote to the shippers at Rotterdam to see if I could get some sent to Leith, but the usual difficulties in establishing connection between wholesale dealers and individual buyers prevented this. It was, however, something of a consolation to read the delightful name, 'our top-and-bottom-fermentation beer,' in which the manufacturer's letter, in very sound English for the most part, spoke of it. English lager I must say I have never liked; perhaps I have been unlucky in my specimens. And good as Scotch strong beer is, I cannot say that the lighter and medium kinds are very good in Scotland. In fact, in Edinburgh I used to import beer of this kind from Lincolnshire, where there is no mistake about it. My own private opinion is that John Barleycorn, north of Tweed, says: 'I am for whisky, and not for ale.'

'Cider and perry,' says Burton, 'are windy drinks'; yet he observes that the inhabitants of certain shires in England (he does not, I am sorry to say, mention Devon) of Normandy in France, and of

Guipuzcoa in Spain, 'are no whit offended by them.' I have never liked perry on the few occasions on which I have tasted it; perhaps because its taste has always reminded me of the smell of some stuff that my nurse used to put on my hair when I was small. But I certainly have been no whit offended by cider, either in divers English shires, including very specially those which Burton does not include, Devon, Dorset, and Somerset, or in Normandy. The Guipuzcoan variety I have, unfortunately, had no opportunity of tasting. Besides, perry seems to me to be an abuse of that excellent creature the pear, whereas cider-apples furnish one of the most cogent arguments to prove that Providence had the production of alcoholic liquors directly in its eye. They are good for nothing else whatever, and they are excellent good for that. I think I like the weak ciders, such as those of the west and the Normandy, better than the stronger ones, and draught cider much better than bottled. That of Norfolk, which has been much commended of late, I have never tasted; but I have had both Western and West-Midland cider in my cellar, often in bottle and once or twice in cask. It is a pity that the liquor—extremely agreeable to the taste, one of the most thirst-quenching to be anywhere found, of no overpowering alcoholic strength as a rule, and almost sovereign for gout—is not to be drunk without caution, and sometimes has to be given up altogether from other medical aspects. Qualified with brandy—a mixture which was first imparted to me at a roadside inn by a very amiable Dorsetshire farmer whom I met while walking from Sherborne to Blandford in my first Oxford 'long'—it is capital: and cider-cup who knoweth not? If there be any such, let him not wait longer than to-morrow before establishing knowledge. As for the pure juice of the apple, four gallons a day per man used to be the harvest allowance in Somerset when I was a boy. It is refreshing only to think of it now.

Of mead or metheglin, the third indigenous liquor of Southern Britain, I know little. Indeed, I should have known nothing at all of it had it not been that the parish-clerk and sexton of the Cambridgeshire village where I lived, and the caretaker of a vinery which I rented, was a bee-keeper and mead-maker. He gave me some once. I did not care much for it. It was like a sweet weak beer, with, of course, the special honey flavor. But I should imagine that it was susceptible of a great many different modes of preparation, and it is obvious, considering what it is made of, that it could be brewed of almost any strength. Old literary notices generally speak of it as strong.

32

SILLY NOVELS BY LADY NOVELISTS

George Eliot

Silly Novels by Lady Novelists are a genus with many species, determined by the particular quality of silliness that predominates in them—the frothy, the prosy, the pious, or the pedantic. But it is a mixture of all these—a composite order of feminine fatuity—that produces the largest class of such novels, which we shall distinguish as the *mind-and-millinery* species. The heroine is usually an heiress, probably a peeress in her own right, with perhaps a vicious baronet, an amiable duke, and an irresistible younger son of a marquis as lovers in the foreground, a clergyman and a poet sighing for her in the middle distance, and a crowd of undefined adorers dimly indicated beyond. Her eyes and her wit are both dazzling; her nose and her morals are alike free from any tendency to irregularity; she has a superb *contralto* and a superb intellect; she is perfectly well dressed and perfectly religious; she dances like a sylph, and reads the Bible in the original tongues. Or it may be that the heroine is not an heiress—that rank and wealth are the only things in which she is deficient; but she infallibly gets into high society, she has the triumph of refusing many matches and securing the best, and she wears some family jewels or other as a sort of crown of righteousness at the end. Rakish men either bite their lips in impotent confusion at her repartees, or are touched to penitence by her reproofs, which, on appropriate occasions, rise to a lofty strain of rhetoric; indeed, there is a general propensity in her to make speeches, and to rhapsodize at some length when she retires to her bedroom. In her recorded conversations she is amazingly eloquent, and in her unrecorded conversations amazingly witty. She is understood to have a depth of insight that looks through and through the shallow theories of philosophers, and her superior instincts are a sort of dial by which men have only to set their clocks and watches, and all will go well. The men play a very subordinate part by her side. You are consoled now and then by a hint that they have affairs, which keeps you in mind that the working-day business of the world is somehow being carried on, but ostensibly the final cause of their existence is that they may accompany the heroine on her 'starring' expedition through life. They see her at a ball, and they are dazzled; at a flower-show, and they are fascinated; on a riding excursion, and they are witched by her noble horsemanship; at church, and they are awed by the sweet solemnity of her demeanor. She is the ideal woman in feelings, faculties, and flounces. For all this she as often as not marries the wrong person to begin with, and she suffers terribly from the plots and intrigues of the vicious baronet; but even death has a soft place in his heart for such a paragon, and remedies all mistakes for her just at the right moment. The vicious baronet is sure to be killed in a duel, and the tedious husband dies in his bed requesting his wife, as a particular favor to him, to marry the man she loves best, and having already dispatched a note to the lover informing him of the comfortable arrangement. Before matters arrive at this desirable issue our feelings are tried by seeing the noble, lovely, and gifted heroine pass through many *mauvais moments*, but we have the satisfaction of knowing that her sorrows are wept into embroidered pocket-handkerchiefs, that her fainting form reclines on the very best upholstery, and that whatever vicissitudes she may undergo, from being dashed out of her carriage to having her head shaved in a fever, she comes out of them all with a complexion more blooming and locks more redundant than ever.

We may remark, by the way, that we have been relieved from a serious scruple by discovering that silly novels by lady novelists rarely introduce us into any other than very lofty and fashionable society. We had imagined that destitute women turned novelists, as they turned governesses, because they had no other 'ladylike' means of getting their bread. On this supposition, vacillating syntax, and improbable incident had a certain pathos for us, like the extremely supererogatory pincushions and ill-devised nightcaps that are offered for sale by a blind man. We felt the commodity to be a nuisance, but we were glad to think that the money went to relieve the necessitous, and we pictured to ourselves lonely women struggling for a maintenance, or wives and daughters devoting themselves to the production of 'copy' out of pure heroism—perhaps to pay their husband's debts or to purchase luxuries for a sick father. Under these impressions we shrank from criticizing a lady's novel: her English might be faulty, but we said to ourselves her motives are irreproachable; her imagination may be uninventive, but her patience is untiring. Empty writing was excused by an empty stomach, and twaddle was consecrated by tears. But no! This theory of ours, like many other pretty theories, has had to give way before observation. Women's silly novels, we are now convinced, are written under totally different circumstances. The fair writers have evidently never talked to a tradesman except from a carriage window; they have no notion of the working-classes except as 'dependents;' they think five hundred a year a miserable pittance; Belgravia and 'baronial halls' are their primary truths; and they have no idea of feeling interest in any man who is not at least a great landed proprietor, if not a prime minister. It is clear that they write in elegant boudoirs, with violet-colored ink and a ruby pen; that they must be entirely indifferent to publishers' accounts, and inexperienced in every form of poverty except poverty of brains. It is true that we are constantly struck with the want of verisimilitude in their representations of the high society in which they seem to live; but then they betray no closer acquaintance with any other form of life. If their peers and peeresses are improbable, their literary men, tradespeople, and cottagers are impossible; and their intellect seems to have the peculiar impartiality of reproducing both what they have seen and heard, and what they have not seen and heard, with equal unfaithfulness.

There are few women, we suppose, who have not seen something of children under five years of age, yet in *Compensation*, a recent novel of the mind-and-millinery species, which calls itself a 'story of real life,' we have a child of four and a half years old talking in this Ossianic fashion:

> '"Oh, I am so happy, dear grand mamma;—I have seen—I have seen such a delightful person; he is like everything beautiful—like the smell of sweet flowers, and the view from Ben Lemond;—or no, *better than that*—he is like what I think of and see when I am very, very happy; and he is really like mamma, too, when she sings; and his forehead is like *that distant sea*," she continued, pointing to the blue Mediterranean; "there seems no end—no end; or like the clusters of stars I like best to look at on a warm fine night... Don't look so...your forehead is like Loch Lomond, when the wind is blowing and the sun is gone in; I like the sunshine best when the lake is smooth... So now—I like it better than ever... It is more beautiful still from the dark cloud that has gone over it, *when the sun suddenly lights up all the colors of the forests and shining purple rocks, and it is all reflected in the waters below*."'

We are not surprised to learn that the mother of this infant phenomenon, who exhibits symptoms so alarmingly like those of adolescence repressed by gin, is herself a phœnix. We are assured, again and again, that she had a remarkably original in mind, that she was a genius, and 'conscious of her originality,' and she was fortunate enough to have a lover who was also a genius and a man of 'most original mind.'

This lover, we read, though 'wonderfully similar' to her 'in powers and capacity,' was 'infinitely superior to her in faith and development,' and she saw in him '"Agape"—so rare to find—of which she had read and admired the meaning in her Greek Testament; having, *from her great facility in learning languages*, read the Scriptures in their original *tongues*.' Of course! Greek and Hebrew are mere play to a heroine; Sanscrit is no more than *a b c* to her; and she can talk with perfect correctness in any language, except English. She is a polking polyglot, a Creuzer in crinoline. Poor men. There are so few of you who know even Hebrew; you think it something to boast of if, like Bolingbroke, you only 'understand that sort of learning and what is writ about it;' and you are perhaps adoring women who can think slightingly of you in all the Semitic languages successively. But, then, as we are almost invariably told that a heroine has a 'beautifully small head,' and as her intellect has probably been early invigorated by an attention to costume and deportment, we may conclude that she can pick up the Oriental tongues, to say nothing of their dialects, with the same aërial facility that the butterfly sips nectar. Besides, there can be no difficulty in conceiving the depth of the heroine's erudition when that of the authoress is so evident.

In *Laura Gay*, another novel of the same school, the heroine seems less at home in Greek and Hebrew but she makes up for the deficiency by a quite playful familiarity with the Latin classics—with the 'dear old Virgil,' 'the graceful Horace, the humane Cicero, and the pleasant Livy;' indeed, it is such a matter of course with her to quote Latin that she does it at a picnic in a very mixed company of ladies and gentlemen, having, we are told, 'no conception that the nobler sex were capable of jealousy on this subject. And if, indeed,' continues the biographer of Laura Gray, 'the wisest and noblest portion of that sex were in the majority, no such sentiment would exist; but while Miss Wyndhams and Mr Redfords abound, great sacrifices must be made to their existence.' Such sacrifices, we presume, as abstaining from Latin quotations, of extremely moderate interest and applicability, which the wise and noble minority of the other sex would be quite as willing to dispense with as the foolish and ignoble majority. It is as little the custom of well-bred men as of well-bred women to quote Latin in mixed parties; they can contain their familiarity with 'the humane Cicero' without allowing it to boil over in ordinary conversation, and even references to 'the pleasant Livy' are not absolutely irrepressible. But Ciceronian Latin is the mildest form of Miss Gay's conversational power. Being on the Palatine with a party of sight-seers, she falls into the following vein of well-rounded remark: 'Truth can only be pure objectively, for even in the creeds where it predominates, being subjective, and parcelled out into portions, each of these necessarily receives a hue of idiosyncrasy, that is, a taint of superstition more or less strong; while in such creeds as the Roman Catholic, ignorance, interest, the basis of ancient idolatries, and the force of authority, have gradually accumulated on the pure truth, and transformed it, at last, into a mass of superstition for the majority of its votaries; and how few are there, alas! whose zeal, courage, and intellectual energy are equal to the analysis of this accumulation, and to the discovery of the pearl of great price which lies hidden beneath this heap of rubbish.' We have often met with women much more novel and profound in their observations than Laura Gay, but rarely with any so inopportunely long-winded. A clerical lord, who is half in love with her, is alarmed by the daring remarks just quoted, and begins to suspect that she is inclined to free-thinking. But he is mistaken; when in a moment of sorrow he delicately begs leave to 'recall to her memory, a *depôt* of strength and consolation under affliction, which, until we are hard pressed by the trials of life, we are too apt to forget,' we learn that she really has 'recurrence to that sacred depôt,' together with the tea-pot. There is a certain flavor of orthodoxy mixed with the parade of fortunes and fine carriages in *Laura Gay*, but it is an orthodoxy mitigated by study of 'the humane Cicero,' and by an 'intellectual disposition to analyze.'

Compensation is much more heavily dosed with doctrine, but then it has a treble amount of snobbish worldliness and absurd incident to tickle the palate of pious frivolity. Linda, the heroine, is still more speculative and spiritual than Laura Gay, but she has been 'presented,' and has more and far grander lovers; very wicked and fascinating women are introduced—even a French *lionne*; and no expense is spared to get up as exciting a story as you will find in the most immoral novels. In fact, it is a wonderful *pot pourri* of Almack's, Scotch second-sight, Mr Rogers's breakfasts, Italian brigands, death-bed conversions, superior authoresses, Italian mistresses, and attempts at poisoning old ladies, the whole served up with a garnish of talk about 'faith and development' and 'most original minds.' Even Miss Susan Barton, the superior authoress, whose pen moves in a 'quick, decided manner when she is composing,' declines the finest opportunities of marriage; and though old enough to be Linda's mother (since we are told that she refused Linda's father), has her hand sought by a young earl, the heroine's rejected lover. Of course, genius and morality must be backed by eligible offers, or they would seem rather a dull affair; and piety, like other things, in order to be *comme il faut*, must be in 'society,' and have admittance to the best circles.

Rank and Beauty is a more frothy and less religious variety of the mind-and-millinery species. The heroine, we are told, 'if she inherited her father's pride of birth and her mother's beauty of person, had in herself a tone of enthusiastic feeling that, perhaps, belongs to her age even in the lowly born, but which is refined into the high spirit of wild romance only in the far descended, who feel that it is their best inheritance.' This enthusiastic young lady, by dint of reading the newspaper to her father, falls in love with the *prime minister*, who, through the medium of leading articles and 'the *resumé* of the debates,' shines upon her imagination as a bright particular star, which has no parallax for her living in the country as simple Miss Wyndham. But she forthwith becomes Baroness Umfraville in her own right, astonishes the world with her beauty and accomplishments when she bursts upon it from her mansion in Spring Gardens, and, as you foresee, will presently come into contact with the unseen *objet aimé*. Perhaps the words 'prime minister' suggest to you a wrinkled or obese sexagenarian; but pray dismiss the image. Lord Rupert Conway has been 'called while still almost a youth to the first situation which a subject can hold in the *universe*,' and even leading articles and a *resumé* of the debates have not conjured up a dream that surpasses the fact.

> 'The door opened again, and Lord Rupert Conway entered. Evelyn gave one glance. It was enough; she was not disappointed. It seemed as if a picture on which she had long gazed was suddenly instinct with life, and had stepped from its frame before her. His tall figure, the distinguished simplicity of his air—it was a living Vandyke, a cavalier, one of his noble cavalier ancestors, or one to whom her fancy had always likened him, who long of yore had with an Umfraville fought the Paynim far beyond the sea. Was this reality?'

Very little like it, certainly.

By and by it becomes evident that the ministerial heart is touched. Lady Umfraville is on a visit to the Queen at Windsor, and—

> 'The last evening of her stay, when they returned from riding, Mr Wyndham took her and a large party to the top of the Keep, to see the view. She was leaning on the battlements, gazing from that "stately height" at the prospect beneath her, when Lord Rupert was by her side. "What an unrivalled view!" exclaimed she.
>
> '"Yes, it would have been wrong to go without having been up here. You are pleased with your visit?"
>
> '"Enchanted! A Queen to live and die under, to live and die for!"
>
> '"Ha!" cried he, with sudden emotion, and with a *eureka* expression of countenance, as if he had *indeed found a heart in unison with his own.*'

The 'eureka expression of countenance' you see at once to be prophetic of marriage at the end of the third volume; but before that desirable consummation there are very complicated misunderstandings, arising chiefly from the vindictive plotting of Sir Luttrel Wycherley, who is a genius, a poet, and in every way a most remarkable character indeed. He is not only a romantic poet, but a hardened rake and a cynical wit; yet his deep passion for Lady Umfraville has so impoverished his epigrammatic talent that he cuts an extremely poor figure in conversation. When she rejects him, he rushes into the shrubbery and rolls himself in the dirt; and on recovering, devotes himself to the most diabolical and laborious schemes of vengeance, in the course of which he disguises himself as a quack physician and enters into general practice, foreseeing that Evelyn will fall ill, and that he shall be called in to attend her. At last, when all his schemes are frustrated, he takes leave of her in a long letter, written, as you will perceive from the following passage, entirely in the style of an eminent literary man:

> 'Oh, lady, nursed in pomp and pleasure, will you ever cast one thought upon the miserable being who addresses you? Will you

> ever, as your gilded galley is floating down the unruffled stream of prosperity, will you ever, while lulled by the sweetest music—thine own praises—hear the far-off sigh from that world to which I am going?'

On the whole, however, frothy as it is, we rather prefer *Rank and Beauty* to the two other novels we have mentioned. The dialogue is more natural and spirited; there is some frank ignorance and no pedantry; and you are allowed to take the heroine's astounding intellect upon trust, without being called on to read her conversational refutations of sceptics and philosophers, or her rhetorical solutions of the mysteries of the universe.

Writers of the mind-and-millinery school are remarkably unanimous in their choice of diction. In their novels there is usually a lady or gentleman who is more or less of a upas tree; the lover has a manly breast; minds are redolent of various things; hearts are hollow; events are utilized; friends are consigned to the tomb; infancy is an engaging period; the sun is a luminary that goes to his western couch, or gathers the rain-drops into his refulgent bosom; life is a melancholy boon; Albion and Scotia are conversational epithets. There is a striking resemblance, too, in the character of their moral comments, such, for instance, as that 'It is a fact, no less true than melancholy, that all people, more or less, richer or poorer, are swayed by bad example;' that 'Books, however trivial, contain some subjects from which useful information may be drawn;' that 'Vice can too often borrow the language of virtue;' that 'Merit and nobility of nature must exist, to be accepted, for clamor and pretension cannot impose upon those too well read in human nature to be easily deceived;' and that 'In order to forgive, we must have been injured.' There is doubtless a class of readers to whom these remarks appear peculiarly pointed and pungent; for we often find them doubly and trebly scored with the pencil, and delicate hands giving in their determined adhesion to these hardy novelties by a distinct *très vrai*, emphasized by many notes of exclamation. The colloquial style of these novels is often marked by much ingenious inversion, and a careful avoidance of such cheap phraseology as can be heard every day. Angry young gentlemen exclaim, "'Tis ever thus, methinks;' and in the half hour before dinner a young lady informs her next neighbor that the first day she read Shakespeare she 'stole away into the park, and beneath the shadow of the greenwood tree, devoured with rapture the inspired page of the great magician.' But the most remarkable efforts of the mind-and-millinery writers lie in their philosophic reflections. The authoress of *Laura Gay*, for example, having married her hero and heroine, improves the event by observing that 'if those sceptics, whose eyes have so long gazed on matter that they can no longer see aught else in man, could once enter with heart and soul, into such bliss as this, they would come to say that the soul of man and the polypus are not of common origin, or of the same texture.' Lady novelists, it appears, can see something else besides matter; they are not limited to phenomena, but can relieve their eyesight by occasional glimpses of the *noumenon*, and are, therefore, naturally better able than any one else to confound sceptics, even of that remarkable but to us unknown school which maintains that the soul of man is of the same texture as the polypus.

The most pitiable of all silly novels by lady novelists are what we may call the *oracular* species—novels intended to expound the writer's religious, philosophical, or moral theories. There seems to be a notion abroad among women, rather akin to the superstition that the speech and actions of idiots are inspired, and that the human being most entirely exhausted of common-sense is the fittest vehicle of revelation. To judge from their writings, there are certain ladies who think that an amazing ignorance, both of science and of life, is the best possible qualification for forming an opinion on the knottiest moral and speculative questions. Apparently, their recipe for solving all such difficulties is something like this: Take a woman's head, stuff it with a smattering of philosophy and literature chopped small, and with false notions of society baked hard, let it hang over a desk a few hours every day, and serve up hot in feeble English when not required. You will rarely meet with a lady novelist of the oracular class who is diffident of her ability to decide on theological questions—who has any suspicion that she is not capable of discriminating with the nicest accuracy between the good and evil in all church parties—who does not see precisely how it is that men have gone wrong hitherto—and pity philosophers in general that they have not had the opportunity of consulting her. Great writers, who have modestly contented themselves with putting their experience into fiction, and have thought it quite a sufficient task to exhibit men and things as they are, she sighs over as deplorably deficient in the application of their powers. 'They have solved no great questions'—and she is ready to remedy their omission by setting before you a complete theory of life and manual of divinity in a love story, where ladies and gentlemen of good family go through genteel vicissitudes, to the utter confusion of Deists, Puseyites, and ultra-Protestants, and to the perfect establishment of that peculiar view of Christianity which either condenses itself into a sentence of small caps, or explodes into a cluster of stars on the three hundred and thirtieth page. It is true, the ladies and gentlemen will probably seem to you remarkably little like any you have had the fortune or misfortune to meet with, for, as a general rule, the ability of a lady novelist to describe actual life and her fellow-men is in inverse proportion to her confident eloquence about God and the other world, and the means by which she usually chooses to conduct you to true ideas of the invisible is a totally false picture of the visible.

As typical a novel of the oracular kind as we can hope to meet with, is *The Enigma: a Leaf from the Chronicles of the Wolchorley House.* The 'enigma' which this novel is to solve is certainly one that demands powers no less gigantic than those of a lady novelist, being neither more nor less than the existence of evil. The problem is stated and the answer dimly foreshadowed on the very first page. The spirited young lady, with raven hair, says, 'All life is an inextricable confusion;' and the meek young lady, with auburn hair, looks at the picture of the Madonna which she is copying, and—'*There* seemed the solution of that mighty enigma.' The style of this novel is quite as lofty as its purpose; indeed, some passages on which we have spent much patient study are quite beyond our reach, in spite of the illustrative aid of italics and small caps; and we must await further 'development' in order to understand them. Of Ernest, the model young clergyman, who sets every one right on all occasions, we read that 'he held not of marriage in the marketable kind, after a social desecration;' that, on one eventful night, 'sleep had not visited his divided heart, where tumultuated, in varied type and combination, the aggregate feelings of grief and joy;' and that, 'for the *marketable* human article he had no toleration, be it of what sort, or set for what value it might, whether for worship or class, his upright soul abhorred it, whose ultimatum, the self-deceiver, was to him THE *great spiritual lie*, "living in a vain show, deceiving and being deceived;" since he did not suppose the phylactery and enlarged border on the garment to be *merely* a social trick.' (The italics and small caps are the author's, and we hope they assist the reader's comprehension.) Of Sir Lionel, the model old gentleman, we are told that 'the simple ideal of the middle age, apart from its anarchy and decadence, in him most truly seemed to live again, when the ties which knit men together were of heroic cast. The first-born colors of pristine faith and truth engraven on the common soul of man, and blent into the wide arch of brotherhood, where the primæval law of *order* grew and multiplied each perfect after his kind, and mutually interdependent.' You see clearly, of course, how colors are first engraven on the soul, and then blent into a wide arch, on which arch of colors—apparently a rainbow—the law of order grew and multiplied, each—apparently the arch and the law—perfect after his kind? If, after this, you can possibly want any further aid toward knowing what Sir Lionel was, we can tell you that in his soul 'the scientific combinations of thought could educe no fuller harmonies of the good and the true than lay in the primæval pulses which floated as an atmosphere around it!' and that, when he was sealing a letter, 'Lo! the responsive throb in that good man's bosom echoed back in simple truth the honest witness of a heart that condemned him not, as his eye, bedewed with love, rested, too, with something of ancestral pride, on the undimmed motto of the family—"LOIAUTE."'

The slightest matters have their vulgarity fumigated out of them by the same elevated style. Commonplace people would say that a copy of Shakespeare lay on a drawing-room table; but the authoress of *The Enigma*, bent on edifying periphrasis, tells you that there lay on the table, 'that fund of human thought and feeling, which teaches the heart through the little name, "Shakespeare."' A watchman sees a light burning in an upper window rather longer than usual, and thinks that people are foolish to sit up late when they have an opportunity of going to bed; but, lest this fact should seem too low and common, it is presented to us in the following striking and metaphysical manner: 'He marvelled—as a man *will* think for others in a necessarily separate personality, consequently (though disallowing it) in false mental premise—how differently *he* should act, how gladly *he* should prize the rest so lightly held of within.' A footman—an ordinary Jeames, with large calves and aspirated vowels—answers the door-bell, and the opportunity is seized to tell you that he was a 'type of the large class of pampered menials, who follow the curse of Cain—"vagabonds" on the face of the earth, and whose estimate of the human class varies in the graduated scale of money and expenditure… These, and such as these, O England, be the false lights of thy morbid civilization!' We have heard of various 'false lights,' from Dr Cumming to Robert Owen, from Dr Pusey to the Spirit-rappers, but we never before heard of the false light that emanates from plush and powder.

In the same way very ordinary events of civilized life are exalted into the most awful crises, and ladies in full skirts and *manches à la Chinoise*, conduct themselves not unlike the heroines of sanguinary melodramas. Mrs Percy, a shallow woman of the world, wishes her son Horace to marry the auburn-haired Grace, she being an heiress; but he, after the manner of sons, falls in love with the raven-haired Kate, the heiress's portionless cousin; and, moreover, Grace herself shows every symptom of perfect indifference to Horace. In such cases sons are often sulky or fiery, mothers are alternately manœuvring and waspish, and the portionless young lady often lies awake at night and cries a good deal. We are getting used to these things now, just as we are used to eclipses of the moon, which no longer set us howling and beating tin kettles. We never heard of a lady in a fashionable 'front' behaving like Mrs Percy under these circumstances. Happening one day to see Horace talking to Grace at a window, without in the least knowing what they are talking about, or having the least reason to believe that Grace, who is mistress of the house and a person of dignity, would accept her son if he were to offer himself, she suddenly rushes up to them and clasps them both, saying, 'with a flushed countenance and in an excited manner'—'This is indeed happiness; for, may I not call you so, Grace?—my Grace—my Horace's Grace!—my dear children!' Her son tells her she is mistaken, and that he is engaged to Kate, whereupon we have the following scene and tableau:

> 'Gathering herself up to an unprecedented height (!) her eyes lightening forth the fire of her anger:
>
> '"Wretched boy!" she said, hoarsely and scornfully, and clenching her hand, "Take then the doom of your own choice! Bow down your miserable head and let a mother's—"
>
> '"Curse not!" spake a deep low voice from behind, and Mrs Percy started, scared, as though she had seen a heavenly visitant appear, to break upon her in the midst of her sin.
>
> 'Meantime Horace had fallen on his knees, at her feet, and hid his face in his hands.
>
> 'Who then, is she—who! Truly his "guardian spirit" hath stepped between him and the fearful words, which, however unmerited, must have hung as a pall over his future existence;—a spell which could not be unbound—which could not be unsaid.
>
> 'Of an earthly paleness, but calm with the still, iron-bound calmness of death—the only calm one there—Katherine stood; and her words smote on the ear in tones whose appallingly slow and separate intonation rung on the heart like a chill, isolated tolling of some fatal knell.
>
> '"He would have plighted me his faith, but I did not accept it; you cannot, therefore—you *dare* not curse him. And here," she continued, raising her hand to heaven, whither her large dark eyes also rose with a chastened glow, which, for the first time, *suffering* had lighted in those passionate orbs—"here I promise, come weal, come woe, that Horace Wolchorley and I do never interchange vows without his mother's sanction—without his mother's blessing!"'

Here, and throughout the story, we see that confusion of purpose which is so characteristic of silly novels written by women. It is a story of quite modern drawing-room society—a society in which polkas are played and Puseyism discussed; yet we have characters, and incidents, and traits of manner introduced, which are mere shreds from the most heterogeneous romances. We have a blind Irish harper, 'relic of the picturesque bards of yore,' startling us at a Sunday-school festival of tea and cake in an English village; we have a crazy gypsy, in a scarlet cloak, singing snatches of romantic song, and revealing a secret on her death-bed which, with the testimony of a dwarfish miserly merchant, who salutes strangers with a curse and a devilish laugh, goes to prove that Ernest, the model young clergyman, is Kate's brother; and we have an ultra-virtuous Irish Barney, discovering that a document is forged, by comparing the date of the paper with the date of the alleged signature, although the same document has passed through a court of law and occasioned a fatal decision. The 'Hall' in which Sir Lionel lives is the venerable country-seat of an old family, and this, we suppose, sets the imagination of the authoress flying to donjons and battlements, where 'lo! the warder blows his horn;' for, as the inhabitants are in their bedrooms on a night certainly within the recollection of Pleaceman X. and a breeze springs up, which we are at first told was faint, and then that it made the old cedars bow their branches to the greensward, she falls into this mediæval vein of description (the italics are ours): 'The banner *unfurled it* at the sound, and shook its guardian wing above, while the startled owl *flapped her* in the ivy; the firmament looking down through her "argus eyes"—

"Ministers of heaven's mute melodies."

And lo! two strokes tolled from out the warder tower, and "Two o'clock" re-echoed its interpreter below.'

Such stories as this of *The Enigma* remind us of the pictures clever children sometimes draw 'out of their own head,' where you will see a modern villa on the right, two knights in helmets fighting in the foreground, and a tiger grinning in a jungle on the left, the several objects being brought together because the artist thinks each pretty, and perhaps still more because he remembers seeing them in other pictures.

But we like the authoress much better on her mediæval stilts than on her oracular ones—when she talks of the *Ich* and of 'subjective' and 'objective,' and lays down the exact line of Christian verity, between 'right-hand excesses and left-hand declensions.' Persons who deviate from this line are introduced with a patronizing air of charity. Of a certain Miss Inshquine she informs us, with all the lucidity of italics and small caps, that '*function*, not *form*, AS *the inevitable outer expression of the spirit in this tabernacle age*, weakly engrossed her.' And *à propos* of Miss Mayjar, an evangelical lady who is a little too apt to talk of her visits to sick women and the state of their souls, we are told that the model clergyman is 'not one to disallow, through the *super* crust, the undercurrent toward good in the *subject*, or the positive benefits, nevertheless, to the *object*.' We imagine the double-refined accent and protrusion of chin which are feebly represented by the italics in this lady's sentences! We abstain from quoting any of her oracular doctrinal passages, because they refer to matters too serious for our pages just now.

The epithet 'silly' may seem impertinent, applied to a novel which indicates so much reading and intellectual activity as *The Enigma*, but we use this epithet advisedly. If, as the world has long agreed, a very great amount of instruction will not make a wise man, still less will a very mediocre amount of instruction make a wise woman. And the most mischievous form of feminine silliness is the literary form, because it tends to confirm the popular prejudice against the more solid education of women.

When men see girls wasting their time in consultations about bonnets and ball dresses, and in giggling or sentimental love-confidences, or middle-aged women mismanaging their children, and solacing themselves with acrid gossip, they can hardly help saying, 'For Heaven's sake, let girls be better educated; let them have some better objects of thought—some more solid occupations.' But after a few hours' conversation with an oracular literary woman, or a few hours' reading of her books, they are likely enough to say, 'After all, when a woman gets some knowledge, see what use she makes of it! Her knowledge remains acquisition instead of passing into culture; instead of being subdued into modesty and simplicity by a larger acquaintance with thought and fact, she has a feverish consciousness of her attainments; she keeps a sort of mental pocket-mirror, and is continually looking in it at her own "intellectuality;" she spoils the taste of one's muffin by questions of metaphysics; "puts down" men at a dinner-table with her superior information; and seizes the opportunity of a *soirée* to catechize us on the vital question of the relation between mind and matter. And then, look at her writings! She mistakes vagueness for depth, bombast for eloquence, and affectation for originality; she struts on one page, rolls her eyes on another, grimaces in a third, and is hysterical in a fourth. She may have read many writings of great men, and a few writings of great women; but she is as unable to discern the difference between her own style and theirs as a Yorkshireman is to discern the difference between his own English and a Londoner's: rhodomontade is the native accent of her intellect. No—the average nature of women is too shallow and feeble a soil to bear much tillage; it is only fit for the very lightest crops.'

It is true that the men who come to such a decision on such very superficial and imperfect observation may not be among the wisest in the world; but we have not now to contest their opinion—we are only pointing out how it is unconsciously encouraged by many women who have volunteered themselves as representatives of the feminine intellect. We do not believe that a man was ever strengthened in such an opinion by associating with a woman of true culture, whose mind had absorbed her knowledge instead of being absorbed by it. A really cultured woman, like a really cultured man, is all the simpler and the less obtrusive for her knowledge; it has made her see herself and her opinions in something like just proportions; she does not make it a pedestal from which she flatters herself that she commands a complete view of men and things, but makes it a point of observation from which to form a right estimate of herself. She neither spouts poetry nor quotes Cicero on slight provocation; not because she thinks that a sacrifice must be made to the prejudices of men, but because that mode of exhibiting her memory and Latinity does not present itself to her as edifying or graceful. She does not write books to confound philosophers, perhaps because she is able to write books that delight them. In conversation she is the least formidable of women, because she understands you, without wanting to make you aware that you *can't* understand her. She does not give you information, which is the raw material of culture—she gives you sympathy, which is its subtlest essence.

A more numerous class of silly novels than the oracular (which are generally inspired by some form of High Church or transcendental Christianity) is what we may call the *white neck-cloth* species, which represent the tone of thought and feeling in the Evangelical party. This species is a kind of genteel tract on a large scale, intended as a sort of medicinal sweetmeat for Low Church young ladies; an Evangelical substitute for the fashionable novel, as the May Meetings are a substitute for the Opera. Even Quaker children, one would think, can hardly have been denied the indulgence of a doll; but it must be a doll dressed in a drab gown and a coal-scuttle-bonnet—not a worldly doll, in gauze and spangles. And there are no young ladies, we imagine—unless they belong to the Church of the United Brethren, in which people are married without any love-making—who can dispense with love stories. Thus, for Evangelical young ladies there are Evangelical love stories, in which the vicissitudes of the tender passion are sanctified by saving views of Regeneration and the Atonement. These novels differ from the oracular ones, as a Low Churchwoman often differs from a High Churchwoman: they are a little less supercilious and a great deal more ignorant, a little less correct in their syntax and a great deal more vulgar.

The Orlando of Evangelical literature is the young curate, looked at from the point of view of the middle class, where cambric bands are understood to have as thrilling an effect on the hearts of young ladies as epaulettes have in the classes above and below it. In the ordinary type of these novels the hero is almost sure to be a young curate, frowned upon, perhaps by worldly mammas, but carrying captive the hearts of their daughters, who can 'never forget *that* sermon;' tender glances are seized from the pulpit stairs instead of the opera-box; *tête-à-têtes* are seasoned with quotations from Scripture instead of quotations from the poets; and questions as to the state of the heroine's affections are mingled with anxieties as to the state of her soul. The young curate always has a background of well-dressed and wealthy if not fashionable society—for Evangelical silliness is as snobbish as any other kind of silliness—and the Evangelical lady novelist, while she explains to you the type of the scapegoat on one page, is ambitious on another to represent the manners and conversations of aristocratic people. Her pictures of fashionable society are often curious studies, considered as efforts of the Evangelical imagination; but in one particular the novels of the White Neck-cloth School are meritoriously realistic—their favorite hero, the Evangelical young curate, is always rather an insipid personage.

The most recent novel of this species that we happen to have before us is *The Old Grey Church*. It is utterly tame and feeble; there is no one set of objects on which the writer seems to have a stronger grasp than on any other; and we should be entirely at a loss to conjecture among what phases of life her experience has been gained, but for certain vulgarisms of style which sufficiently indicate that she has had the advantage, though she has been unable to use it, of mingling chiefly with men and women whose manners and characters have not had all their bosses and angles rubbed down by refined conventionalism. It is less excusable in an Evangelical novelist than in any other, gratuitously to seek her subjects among titles and carriages. The real drama of Evangelicalism—and it has abundance of fine drama for any one who has genius enough to discern and reproduce it—lies among the middle and lower classes; and are not Evangelical opinions understood to give an especial interest in the weak things of the earth, rather than in the mighty? Why, then, cannot our Evangelical lady novelists show us the operation of their religious views among people (there really are many such in the world) who keep no carriage, 'not so much as a brass-bound gig,' who even manage to eat their dinner without a silver fork, and in whose mouths the authoress's questionable English would be strictly consistent? Why can we not have pictures of religious life among the industrial classes in England, as interesting as Mrs Stowe's pictures of religious life among the negroes? Instead of this pious ladies nauseate us with novels which remind us of what we sometimes see in a worldly woman recently 'converted;'—she is as fond of a fine dinner-table as before, but she invites clergymen instead of beaux; she thinks as much of her dress as before, but she adopts a more sober choice of colors and patterns; her conversation is as trivial as before, but the triviality is flavored with gospel instead of gossip. In *The Old Grey Church* we have the same sort of Evangelical travesty of the fashionable novel, and of course the vicious, intriguing baronet is not wanting. It is worth while to give a sample of the style of conversation attributed to this high-born rake—a style that, in its profuse italics and palpable innuendoes, is worthy of Miss Squeers. In an evening visit to the ruins of the Colosseum, Eustace, the young clergyman, has been withdrawing the heroine, Miss Lushington, from the rest of the party, for the sake of a *tête-à-tête*. The baronet is jealous, and vents his pique in this way:

> 'There they are, and Miss Lushington, no doubt, quite safe; for she is under the holy guidance of Pope Eustace the First, who has, of course, been delivering to her an edifying homily on the wickedness of the heathens of yore, who, as tradition tells us, in this very place let loose the wild *beastises* on poor St Paul!—Oh, no! by the bye, I believe I am wrong, and betraying my want of clergy, and that it was not at all St Paul, nor was it here. But no matter, it would equally serve as a text to preach from, and from which to diverge to the degenerate *heathen* Christians of the present day, and all their naughty practices, and so end with an exhortation to "come but from among them, and be separate;"—and I am sure, Miss Lushington, you have most scrupulously conformed to that injunction this evening, for we have seen nothing of you since our arrival. But every one seems agreed it has been a *charming party of pleasure*, and I am sure we all feel *much indebted* to Mr Gray for having *suggested* it; and as he seems so capital a cicerone, I hope he will think of something else equally agreeable to *all*.'

This drivelling kind of dialogue, and equally drivelling narrative, which, like a bad drawing, represents nothing, and barely indicates what is meant to be represented, runs through the book; and we have no doubt is considered by the amiable authoress to constitute an improving novel, which Christian mothers will do well to put into the hands of their daughters. But everything is relative; we have met with American vegetarians whose normal diet was dry meal, and who, when their appetite wanted stimulating, tickled it with wet meal; and so, we can imagine that there are Evangelical circles in which *The Old Grey Church* is devoured as a powerful and interesting fiction.

But perhaps the least readable of silly women's novels are the *modern-antique* species, which unfold to us the domestic life of Jannes and Jambres, the private love affairs of Sennacherib, or the mental struggles and ultimate conversion of Demetrius the silversmith. From most silly novels we can at least extract a laugh; but those of the modern-antique school have a ponderous, a leaden kind of fatuity, under which we groan. What can be more demonstrative of the inability of literary women to measure their own powers than their frequent assumption of a task which can only be justified by the rarest concurrence of acquirement with genius? The finest effort to reanimate the past is of course only approximative—is always more or less an infusion of the modern spirit into the ancient form—

> Was ihr den Geist der Zeiten heisst,
> Das ist im Grund der Herren eigner Geist,
> In dem die Zeiten sich bespiegeln.

Admitting that genius which has familiarized itself with all the relics of an ancient period can sometimes, by the force of its sympathetic divination, restore the missing notes in the 'music of humanity,' and reconstruct the fragments into a whole which will really bring the remote past nearer to us, and interpret it to our duller apprehension—this form of imaginative power must always be among the very rarest, because it demands as much accurate and minute knowledge as creative vigor. Yet we find ladies constantly choosing to make their mental mediocrity more conspicuous by clothing it in a masquerade of ancient names; by putting their feeble sentimentality into the mouths of Roman vestals or Egyptian princesses, and attributing their rhetorical arguments to Jewish high-priests and Greek philosophers. A recent example of this heavy imbecility is *Adonijah, a Tale of the Jewish Dispersion*, which forms part of a series, 'uniting,' we are told, 'taste, humor, and sound principles.' 'Adonijah,' we presume, exemplifies the tale of 'sound principles;' the taste and humor are to be found in other members of the series. We are told on the cover that the incidents of this tale are 'fraught with unusual interest,' and the preface winds up thus: 'To those who feel interested in the dispersed of Israel and Judea, these pages may afford, perhaps, information on an important subject, as well as amusement.' Since the 'important subject' on which this book is to afford information is not specified, it may possibly lie in some esoteric meaning to which we have no key; but if it has relation to the dispersed of Israel and Judea at any period of their history, we believe a tolerably well-informed school-girl already knows much more of it than she will find in this 'Tale of the Jewish Dispersion.' *Adonijah* is simply the feeblest kind of love story, supposed to be instructive, we presume, because the hero is a Jewish captive and the heroine a Roman vestal; because they and their friends are converted to Christianity after the shortest and easiest method approved by the 'Society for Promoting the Conversion of the Jews;' and because, instead of being written in plain language, it is adorned with that peculiar style of grandiloquence which is held by some lady novelists to give an antique coloring, and which we recognize at once in such phrases as these:—'the splendid regnal talent, undoubtedly, possessed by the Emperor Nero'—'the expiring scion of a lofty stem'—'the virtuous partner of his couch'—'ah, by Vesta!'—and 'I tell thee, Roman.' Among the quotations which serve at once for instruction and ornament on the cover of this volume, there is one from Miss Sinclair, which informs us that 'Works of imagination are *avowedly* read by men of science, wisdom, and piety;' from which we suppose the reader is to gather the cheering inference that Dr Daubeny, Mr Mill, or Mr Maurice may openly indulge himself with the perusal of *Adonijah*, without being obliged to secrete it among the sofa cushions, or read it by snatches under the dinner-table.

'Be not a baker if your head be made of butter,' says a homely proverb, which, being interpreted, may mean, let no woman rush into print who is not prepared for the consequences. We are aware that our remarks are in a very different tone from that of the reviewers who, with perennial recurrence of precisely similar emotions, only paralleled, we imagine, in the experience of monthly nurses, tell one lady novelist after another that they 'hail' her productions 'with delight.' We are aware that the ladies at whom our criticism is pointed are accustomed to be told, in the choicest phraseology of puffery, that their pictures of life are brilliant, their characters well drawn, their style fascinating, and their sentiments lofty. But if they are inclined to resent our plainness of speech, we ask them to reflect for a moment on the chary praise, and often captious blame, which their panegyrists give to writers whose works are on the way to become classics. No sooner does a woman show that she has genius or effective talent, than she receives the tribute of being moderately praised and severely criticized. By a peculiar thermometric adjustment, when a woman's talent is at zero, journalistic approbation is at the boiling pitch; when she attains mediocrity, it is already at no more than summer heat; and if ever she reaches excellence, critical enthusiasm drops to the freezing point. Harriet Martineau, Currer Bell, and Mrs Gaskell have been treated as cavalierly as if they had been men. And every critic who forms a high estimate of the share women may ultimately take in literature, will on principle abstain from any exceptional indulgence toward the productions of literary women. For it must be plain to every one who looks impartially and extensively into feminine literature that its greatest deficiencies are due hardly more to the want of intellectual power than to the want of those moral qualities that contribute to literary excellence—patient diligence, a sense of the responsibility involved in publication, and an appreciation of the sacredness of the writer's art. In the majority of women's books you see that kind of facility which springs from the absence of any high standard; that fertility in imbecile combination or feeble imitation which a little self-criticism would check and reduce to barrenness; just as with a total want of musical ear people will sing out of tune, while a degree more melodic sensibility would suffice to render them silent. The foolish vanity of wishing to appear in print, instead of being counterbalanced by any consciousness of the intellectual or moral derogation implied in futile authorship, seems to be encouraged by the extremely false impression that to write *at all* is a proof of superiority in a woman. On this ground we believe that the average intellect of women is unfairly represented by the mass of feminine literature, and that while the few women who write well are very far above the ordinary intellectual level of their sex, the many women who write ill are very far below it. So that, after all, the severer critics are fulfilling a chivalrous duty in depriving the mere fact of feminine authorship of any false prestige which may give it a delusive attraction, and in recommending women of mediocre faculties—as at least a negative service they can render their sex—to abstain from writing.

The standing apology for women who become writers without any special qualification is that society shuts them out from other spheres of occupation. Society is a very culpable entity, and has to answer for the manufacture of many unwholesome commodities, from bad pickles to bad poetry. But society, like 'matter,' and Her Majesty's Government, and other lofty abstractions, has its share of excessive blame as well as excessive praise. Where there is one woman who writes from necessity, we believe there are three women who write from vanity; and besides, there is something so antiseptic in the mere healthy fact of working for one's bread, that the most trashy and rotten kind of feminine literature is not likely to have been produced under such circumstances. 'In all labor there is profit;' but ladies' silly novels, we imagine, are less the result of labor than of busy idleness.

Happily, we are not dependent on argument to prove that Fiction is a department of literature in which women can, after their kind, fully equal men. A cluster of great names, both living and dead, rush to our memories in evidence that women can produce novels not only fine, but among the very finest—novels, too, that have a precious speciality, lying quite apart from masculine aptitudes and experience. No educational restrictions can shut women out from the materials of fiction, and there is no species of art which is so free from rigid requirements. Like crystalline masses, it may take any form, and yet be beautiful; we have only to pour in the right elements—genuine observation, humor, and passion. But it is precisely this absence of rigid requirement which constitutes the fatal seduction of novel-writing to incompetent women. Ladies are not wont to be very grossly deceived as to their power of playing on the piano; here certain positive difficulties of execution have to be conquered, and incompetence inevitably breaks down. Every art which had its absolute technique is, to a certain extent, guarded from the intrusions of mere left-handed imbecility. But in novel-writing there are no barriers for incapacity to stumble against, no external criteria to prevent a writer from mistaking foolish facility for mastery. And so we have again and again the old story of La Fontaine's ass, who pats his nose to the flute, and, finding that he elicits some sound, exclaims, 'Moi, aussie, je joue de la flute'—a fable which we commend, at parting, to the consideration of any feminine reader who is in danger of adding to the number of 'silly novels by lady novelists.'

33

FRIENDSHIP

Joseph Addison

Nos duo turba sumus.
Ovid, *Met.* i. 355.

[We two are a multitude.]

One would think that the larger the company is in which we are engaged, the greater variety of thoughts and subjects would be started in discourse; but instead of this, we find that conversation is never so much straitened and confined as in numerous assemblies. When a multitude meet together upon any subject of discourse, their debates are taken up chiefly with forms and general positions; nay, if we come into a more contracted assembly of men and women, the talk generally runs upon the weather, fashions, news, and the like public topics. In proportion as conversation gets into clubs and knots of friends, it descends into particulars, and grows more free and communicative; but the most open, instructive, and unreserved discourse, is that which passes between two persons who are familiar and intimate friends. On these occasions, a man gives a loose to every passion and every thought that is uppermost, discovers his most retired opinions of persons and timings, tries the beauty and strength of his sentiments, and exposes his whole soul to the examination of his friend.

Tully was the first who observed, that friendship improves happiness and abates misery, by the doubling of our joy and dividing of our grief; a thought in which he hath been followed by all the essayers upon friendship, that have written since his time. Sir Francis Bacon has finely described other advantages, or, as he calls them, fruits of friendship; and indeed there is no subject of morality which has been better handled and more exhausted than this. Among the several fine things which have been spoken of it, I shall beg leave to quote some out of a very ancient author, whose book would be regarded by our modern wits as one of the most shining tracts of morality that is extant, if it appeared under the name of a Confucius, or of any celebrated Grecian philosopher I mean the little apocryphal treatise entitled, '*The Wisdom of the Son of Sirach*.' How finely has he described the art of making friends, by an obliging and affable behaviour! and laid down that precept which a late excellent author has delivered as his own, 'That we should have many well-wishers, but few friends.' 'Sweet language will multiply friends: and a fair-speaking tongue will increase kind greetings. Be in peace with many; nevertheless, have but one counsellor of a thousand.' With what prudence does he caution us in the choice of our friends; and with what strokes of nature (I could almost say of humour) has he described the behaviour of a treacherous and self-interested friend!

> 'If thou wouldest get a friend, prove him first, and be not hasty to credit him for some man is a friend for his own occasion, and will not abide in the day of thy trouble. And there is a friend who, being turned to enmity and strife, will discover thy reproach.'

Again,

> 'Some friend is a companion at the table, and will not continue in the day of thy affliction: but in thy prosperity he will be as thyself, and will be bold over thy servants. If thou be brought low, he will be against thee, and hide himself from thy face.'

What can be more strong and pointed than the following verse? 'Separate thyself from thine enemies, and take heed of thy friends.' In the next words he particularizes one of those fruits of friendship which is described at length by the two famous authors above-mentioned, and falls into a general eulogium of friendship, which is very just as well as very sublime.

> 'A faithful friend is a strong defence; and he that hath found such an one, hath found a treasure. Nothing doth countervail a faithful friend, and his excellency is unvaluable. A faithful friend is the medicine of life; and they that fear the Lord shall find him. Whoso feareth the Lord shall direct his friendship aright; for as he is, so shall his neighbour (that is, his friend) be also.'

I do not remember to have met with any saying that has pleased me more than that of a friend's being the medicine of life, to express the efficacy of friendship in healing the pains and anguish which naturally cleave to our existence in this world; and am wonderfully pleased with the turn in the last sentence; That a virtuous man shall as a blessing meet with a friend who is as virtuous as himself. There is another saying in the same author, which would have been very much admired in an heathen writer;

> 'Forsake not an old friend, for the new is not comparable to him: a new friend is as new wine; when it is old thou shalt drink it with pleasure.'

With what strength of allusion, and force of thought, has he described the breaches and violations of friendship!

> 'Whoso casteth a stone at the birds, frayeth them away; and he that upbraideth his friend, breaketh friendship. Though thou drawest a sword at a friend, yet despair not, for there may be a returning to favour. If thou hast opened thy mouth against thy friend, fear not, for there may be a reconciliation; except for upbraiding, or pride, or disclosing of secrets, or a treacherous wound; for, for these things every friend will depart.'

We may observe in this and several other precepts in this author, those little familiar instances and illustrations which are so much admired in the moral writings of Horace and Epicetus. There are very beautiful instances of this nature in the following passages, which are likewise written upon the same subject:

> 'Whoso discovereth secrets, loseth his credit, and shall never find a friend to his mind. Love thy friend and be faithful unto him; but if thou bewrayeth his secrets, follow no more after him: for as a man hath destroyed his enemy, so hast thou lost the love of thy friend; as one that letteth a bird go out of his hand, so hast thou let thy friend go, and shall not get him again. Follow after him no more, for he is too far off; he is as a roe escaped out of the snare. As for a wound, it may be bound up, and after reviling there may be reconciliation; but he that bewrayeth secrets is without hope.'

Among the several qualifications of a good friend, this wise man has very justly singled out constancy and faithfulness as the principal: to these others have added virtue, knowledge, discretion, equality in age and fortune, and as Cicero calls it, *morum comitas*, 'a pleasantness of temper.' If I were to give my opinion upon such an exhausted subject, I should join to these other qualifications a certain equability or evenness of behaviour. A man often contracts a friendship with one whom perhaps he does not find out till after a year's conversation; when on a sudden some latent ill-humour breaks out upon him, which he never discovered or suspected at his first entering into an intimacy with him. There are several persons who in some certain periods of their lives are inexpressibly agreeable, and at others as odious and detestable. Martial has given us a very pretty picture of one of this species in the following epigram:

> *Difficilis, facilis, jucundus, acerbus es idem,*
> *Nec tecum possum vivere, nec sine te*
>
> *Ep.* xii. 47
>
> [In all thy humours, whether grave or mellow,
> Thou'rt such a touchy, testy, pleasant fellow;
> Hast so much wit, and mirth, and spleen about thee,
> There is no living with thee, nor without thee.]

It is very unlucky for a man to be entangled in a friendship with one, who by these changes and vicissitudes of humour is sometimes amiable and sometimes odious: and as most men are at some times in an admirable frame and disposition of mind, it should be one of the greatest tasks of wisdom to keep ourselves well when we are so, and never to go out of that which is the agreeable part of our character.

34

OF LIARS

Michel de Montaigne

There is not a man living whom it would so little become to speak from memory as myself, for I have scarcely any at all, and do not think that the world has another so marvellously treacherous as mine. My other faculties are all sufficiently ordinary and mean; but in this I think myself very rare and singular, and deserving to be thought famous. Besides the natural inconvenience I suffer by it (for, certes, the necessary use of memory considered, Plato had reason when he called it a great and powerful goddess), in my country, when they would say a man has no sense, they say, such an one has no memory; and when I complain of the defect of mine, they do not believe me, and reprove me, as though I accused myself for a fool: not discerning the difference betwixt memory and understanding, which is to make matters still worse for me. But they do me wrong; for experience, rather, daily shows us, on the contrary, that a strong memory is commonly coupled with infirm judgment. They do, me, moreover (who am so perfect in nothing as in friendship), a great wrong in this, that they make the same words which accuse my infirmity, represent me for an ungrateful person; they bring my affections into question upon the account of my memory, and from a natural imperfection, make out a defect of conscience. 'He has forgot,' says one, 'this request, or that promise; he no more remembers his friends; he has forgot to say or do, or conceal such and such a thing, for my sake.' And, truly, I am apt enough to forget many things, but to neglect anything my friend has given me in charge, I never do it. And it should be enough, methinks, that I feel the misery and inconvenience of it, without branding me with malice, a vice so contrary to my humour.

However, I derive these comforts from my infirmity: first, that it is an evil from which principally I have found reason to correct a worse, that would easily enough have grown upon me, namely, ambition; the defect being intolerable in those who take upon them public affairs. That, like examples in the progress of nature demonstrate to us, she has fortified me in my other faculties proportionably as she has left me unfurnished in this; I should otherwise have been apt implicitly to have reposed my mind and judgment upon the bare report of other men, without ever setting them to work upon their own force, had the inventions and opinions of others been ever been present with me by the benefit of memory. That by this means I am not so talkative, for the magazine of the memory is ever better furnished with matter than that of the invention. Had mine been faithful to me, I had ere this deafened all my friends with my babble, the subjects themselves arousing and stirring up the little faculty I have of handling and employing them, heating and distending my discourse, which were a pity: as I have observed in several of my intimate friends, who, as their memories supply them with an entire and full view of things, begin their narrative so far back, and crowd it with so many impertinent circumstances, that though the story be good in itself, they make a shift to spoil it; and if otherwise, you are either to curse the strength of their memory or the weakness of their judgment: and it is a hard thing to close up a discourse, and to cut it short, when you have once started; there is nothing wherein the force of a horse is so much seen as in a round and sudden stop. I see even those who are pertinent enough, who would, but cannot stop short in their career; for whilst they are seeking out a handsome period to conclude with, they go on at random, straggling about upon impertinent trivialities, as men staggering upon weak legs. But, above all, old men who retain the memory of things past, and forget how often they have told them, are dangerous company; and I have known stories from the mouth of a man of very great quality, otherwise very pleasant in themselves, become very wearisome by being repeated a hundred times over and over again to the same people.

Secondly, that, by this means, I the less remember the injuries I have received; insomuch that, as the ancient said,—[Cicero, Pro Ligar. c. 12.]—I should have a register of injuries, or a prompter, as Darius, who, that he might not forget the offence he had received from those of Athens, so oft as he sat down to dinner, ordered one of his pages three times to repeat in his ear, 'Sir, remember the Athenians';—[Herod., v. 105.]—and then, again, the places which I revisit, and the books I read over again, still smile upon me with a fresh novelty.

It is not without good reason said 'that he who has not a good memory should never take upon him the trade of lying.' I know very well that the grammarians—[Nigidius, Aulus Gellius, xi. ii; Nonius, v. 80.]— distinguish betwixt an untruth and a lie, and say that to tell an untruth is to tell a thing that is false, but that we ourselves believe to be true; and that the definition of the word to lie in Latin, from which our French is taken, is to tell a thing which we know in our conscience to be untrue; and it is of this last sort of liars only that I now speak. Now, these do either wholly contrive and invent the untruths they utter, or so alter and disguise a true story that it ends in a lie. When they disguise and often alter the same story, according to their own fancy, 'tis very hard for them, at one time or another, to escape being trapped, by reason that the real truth of the thing, having first taken possession of the memory, and being there lodged impressed by the medium of knowledge and science, it will be difficult that it should not represent itself to the imagination, and shoulder out falsehood, which cannot there have so sure and settled footing as the other; and the circumstances of the first true knowledge evermore running in their minds, will be apt to make them forget those that are illegitimate, and only, forged by their own fancy. In what they, wholly invent, forasmuch as there is no contrary impression to jostle their invention there seems to be less danger of tripping; and yet even this by reason it is a vain body and without any hold, is very apt to escape the memory, if it be not well assured. Of which I had very pleasant experience, at the expense of such as profess only to form and accommodate their speech to the affair they have in hand, or to humour of the great folks to whom they are speaking; for the circumstances to which these men stick not to enslave their faith and conscience being subject to several changes, their language must vary accordingly: whence it happens that of the same thing they tell one man that it is this, and another that it is that, giving it several colours; which men, if they once come to confer notes, and find out the cheat, what becomes of this fine art? To which may be added, that they must of necessity very often ridiculously trap themselves; for what memory can be sufficient to retain so many different shapes as they have forged upon one and the same subject? I have known many in my time very ambitious of the repute of this fine wit; but they do not see that if they have the reputation of it, the effect can no longer be.

In plain truth, lying is an accursed vice. We are not men, nor have other tie upon one another, but by our word. If we did but discover the horror and gravity of it, we should pursue it with fire and sword, and more justly than other crimes. I see that parents commonly, and with indiscretion enough, correct their children for little innocent faults, and torment them for wanton tricks, that have neither impression nor consequence; whereas, in my opinion, lying only, and, which is of something a lower form, obstinacy, are the faults which are to be severely whipped out of them, both in their infancy and in their progress, otherwise they grow up and increase with them; and after a tongue has once got the knack of lying, 'tis not to be imagined how impossible it is to reclaim it whence it comes to pass that we see some, who are otherwise very honest men, so subject and enslaved to this vice. I have an honest lad to my tailor, whom I never knew guilty of one truth, no, not when it had been to his advantage. If falsehood had, like truth, but one face only, we should be upon better terms; for we should then take for certain the contrary to what the liar says: but the reverse of truth has a hundred thousand forms, and a field indefinite, without bound or limit. The Pythagoreans make good to be certain and finite, and evil, infinite and uncertain. There are a thousand ways to miss the white, there is only one to hit it. For my own part, I have this vice in so great horror, that I am not sure I could prevail with my conscience to secure myself from the most manifest and extreme danger by an impudent and solemn lie.

An ancient father says 'that a dog we know is better company than a man whose language we do not understand.'

> *'Ut externus alieno pene non sit hominis vice.'*

> ['As a foreigner cannot be said to supply us the place of a man.' —Pliny, *Nat. Hist.* vii. I]

And how much less sociable is false speaking than silence?

King Francis I vaunted that he had by this means nonplussed Francesco Taverna, ambassador of Francesco Sforza, Duke of Milan, a man very famous for his science in talking in those days. This gentleman had been sent to excuse his master to his Majesty about a thing of very great consequence, which was this: the King, still to maintain some intelligence with Italy, out of which he had lately been driven, and particularly with the duchy of Milan, had thought it convenient to have a gentleman on his behalf to be with that Duke: an ambassador in effect, but in outward appearance a private person who pretended to reside there upon his own particular affairs; for the Duke, much more depending upon the Emperor, especially at a time when he was in a treaty of marriage with his niece, daughter to the King of Denmark, who is now dowager of Lorraine, could not manifest any practice and conference with us without his great interest. For this commission one Merveille, a Milanese gentleman, and an equerry to the King, being thought very fit, was accordingly despatched thither with private credentials, and instructions as ambassador, and with other letters of recommendation to the Duke about his own private concerns, the better to mask and colour the business; and was so long in that court, that the Emperor at last had some inkling of his real employment there; which was the occasion of what followed after, as we suppose; which was, that under pretence of some murder, his trial was in two days despatched, and his head in the night struck off in prison. Messire Francesco being come, and prepared with a long counterfeit history of the affair (for the King had applied himself to all the princes of Christendom, as well as to the Duke himself, to demand satisfaction), had his audience at the morning council; where, after he had for the support of his cause laid open several plausible justifications of the fact, that his master had never looked upon this Merveille for other than a private gentleman and his own subject, who was there only in order to his own business, neither had he ever lived under any other aspect; absolutely disowning that he had ever heard he was one of the King's household or that his Majesty so much as knew him, so far was he from taking him for an ambassador: the King, in his turn, pressing him with several objections and demands, and challenging him on all sides, tripped him up at last by asking, why, then, the execution was performed by night, and as it were by stealth? At which the poor confounded ambassador, the more handsomely to disengage himself, made answer, that the Duke would have been very loth, out of respect to his Majesty, that such an execution should have been performed by day. Any one may guess if he was not well rated when he came home, for having so grossly tripped in the presence of a prince of so delicate a nostril as King Francis.

Pope Julius II having sent an ambassador to the King of England to animate him against King Francis, the ambassador having had his audience, and the King, before he would give an answer, insisting upon the difficulties he should find in setting on foot so great a preparation as would be necessary to attack so potent a King, and urging some reasons to that effect, the ambassador very unseasonably replied that he had also himself considered the same difficulties, and had represented them to the Pope. From which saying of his, so directly opposite to the thing propounded and the business he came about, which was immediately to incite him to war, the King of England first derived the argument (which he afterward found to be true), that this ambassador, in his own mind, was on the side of the French; of which having advertised his master, his estate at his return home was confiscated, and he himself very narrowly escaped the losing of his head.

35

CRISIS IN CIVILIZATION

Rabindranath Tagore

Today I complete eighty years of my life. As I look back on the vast stretch of years that lie behind me and see in clear perspective the history of my early development, I am struck by the change that has taken place both in my own attitude and in the psychology of my countrymen—a change that carries within it a cause of profound tragedy.

Our direct contact with the larger world of men was linked up with the contemporary history of the English people whom we came to know in those earlier days. It was mainly through their mighty literature that we formed our ideas with regard to these newcomers to our Indian shores. In those days the type of learning that was served out to us was neither plentiful nor diverse, nor was the spirit of scientific enquiry very much in evidence. Thus their scope being strictly limited, the educated of those days had recourse to English language and literature. Their days and nights were eloquent with the stately declamations of Burke, with Macaulay's long-rolling sentences; discussions centred upon Shakespeare's drama and Byron's poetry and above all upon the large-hearted liberalism of the nineteenth-century English politics.

At the time though tentative attempts were being made to gain our national independence, at heart we had not lost faith in the generosity of the English race. This belief was so firmly rooted in the sentiments of our leaders as to lead them to hope that the victor would of his own grace pave the path of freedom for the vanquished. This belief was based upon the fact that England at the time provided a shelter to all those who had to flee from persecution in their own country. Political martyrs who had suffered for the honour of their people were accorded unreserved welcome at the hands of the English. I was impressed by this evidence of liberal humanity in the character of the English and thus Iwas led to set them on the pedestal of my highest respect. This generosity in their national character had not yet been vitiated by imperialist pride. About this time, as a boy in England, I had the opportunity of listening to the speeches of John Bright, both in and outside Parliament. The large-hearted, radical liberalism of those speeches, overflowing all narrow national bounds, had made so deep an impression on my mind that something of it lingers even today, even in these days of graceless disillusionment.

Certainly that spirit of abject dependence upon the charity of our rulers was no matter for pride. What was remarkable, however, was the wholehearted way in which we gave our recognition to human greatness even when it revealed itself in the foreigner. The best and noblest gifts of humanity cannot be the monopoly of a particular race or country; its scope may not be limited nor may it be regarded as the miser's hoard buried underground. That is why English literature which nourished our minds in the past, does even now convey its deep resonance to the recesses of our heart.

It is difficult to find a suitable Bengali equivalent for the English word 'civilization'. That phase of civilization with which we were familiar in this country has been called by Manu 'Sadachar'(literally, proper conduct), that is, the conduct prescribed by the tradition of the race. Narrow in themselves these time-honoured social conventions originated and held good in a circumscribed geographical area, in that strip of land, Brahmavarta by name, bound on either side by the rivers Saraswati and Drisadvati. That is how a pharisaic formalism gradually got the upper hand of free thought and the ideal of 'proper conduct' which Manu found established in Brahmavarta steadily degenerated into socialized tyranny.

During my boyhood days the attitude towards the cultured and educated section of Bengal, nurtured on English learning, was charged with a feeling of revolt against these rigid regulations of society. A perusal of what Rajnarain Bose has written describing the ways of the educated gentry of those days will amply bear out what I have said just now. In place of these set codes of conduct we accepted the ideal of 'civilization' as represented by the English term.

In our own family this change of spirit was welcomed for the sake of its sheer rational and moral force and its influence was felt in every sphere of our life. Born in that atmosphere, which was moreover coloured by our intuitive bias for literature, I naturally set the English on the throne of my heart. Thus passed the first chapters of my life. Then came the parting of ways accompanied with a painful feeling of disillusion when I began increasingly to discover how easily those who accepted the highest truths of civilization disowned them with impunity whenever questions of national self-interest were involved.

There came a time when perforce I had to snatch myself away from the mere appreciation of literature. As I emerged into the stark light of bare facts, the sight of the dire poverty of the Indian masses rent my heart. Rudely shaken out of my dreams, I began to realize that perhaps in no other modern state was there such hopeless dearth of the most elementary needs of existence. And yet it was this country whose resources had fed for so long the wealth and magnificence of the British people. While I was lost in the contemplation of the great world of civilization, I could never have remotely imagined that the great ideals of humanity would end in such ruthless travesty. But today a glaring example of it stares me in the face in the utter and contemptuous indifference of a so-called civilized race to the wellbeing of crores of Indian people.

That mastery over the machine, by which the British have consolidated their sovereignty over their vast Empire, has been kept a sealed book, to which due access has been denied to this helpless country. And all the time before our very eyes Japan has been transforming herself into a mighty and prosperous nation. I have seen with my own eyes the admirable use to which Japan has put in her own country the fruits of this progress. I have also been privileged to witness, while in Moscow, the unsparing energy with which Russia has tried to fight disease and illiteracy, and has succeeded in steadily liquidating ignorance and poverty, wiping off the humiliation from the face of a vast continent. Her civilization is free from all invidious distinction between one class and another, between one sect and another. The rapid and astounding progress achieved by her made me happy and jealous at the same time. One aspect of the Soviet administration which particularly pleased me was that it provided no scope for unseemly conflict of religious differences, nor set one community against another by unbalanced distribution of political favours. That I consider a truly civilized administration which impartially serves the common interests of the people.

While other imperialist powers sacrifice the welfare of the subject races to their own national greed, in the USSR I found a genuine attempt being made to harmonize the interests of the various nationalities that are scattered over its vast area. I saw peoples and tribes, who, only the other day, were nomadic savages being encouraged and indeed trained, to avail themselves freely of the benefits of civilization. Enormous sums are being spent on their education to expedite the process. When I see elsewhere some two hundred nationalities—which only a few years ago were at vastly different stages of development—marching ahead in peaceful progress and amity, and when I look about my own country and see a very highly evolved and intellectual people drifting into the disorder of barbarism, I cannot help contrasting the two systems of governments, one based on cooperation, the other on exploitation, which have made such contrary conditions possible.

I have also seen Iran, newly awakened to a sense of national self-sufficiency, attempting to fulfil her own destiny freed from the deadly grinding-stones of two European powers. During my recent visit to that country I discovered to my delight that Zoroastrians who once suffered from the fanatical hatred of the major community and whose rights had been curtailed by the ruling power were now free from this age-long repression, and that civilized life had established itself in the happy land. It is significant that Iran's good fortune dates from the day when she finally disentangled herself from the meshes of European diplomacy. With all my heart I wish Iran well.

Turning to the neighbouring kingdom of Afghanistan I find that though there is much room for improvement in the field of education and social development, yet she is fortunate in that she can look forward to unending progress; for none of the European powers, boastful of their civilization, has yet succeeded in overwhelming and crushing her possibilities.

Thus while these other countries were marching ahead, India, smothered under the dead weight of British administration, lay static in her utter helplessness. Another great and ancient civilization for whose recent tragic history the British cannot disclaim responsibility, is China. To serve their own national profit the British first doped her people with opium and then appropriated a portion of her territory. As the world was about to forget the memory of this outrage, we were painfully surprised by another event. While Japan was quietly devouring North China, her act of wanton aggression was ignored as a minor incident by the veterans of British diplomacy. We have also witnessed from this distance how actively the British statesmen acquiesced in the destruction of the Spanish Republic.

On the other hand, we also noted with admiration how a band of valiant Englishmen laid down their lives for Spain. Even though the English had not aroused themselves sufficiently to their sense of responsibility towards China in the Far East, in their own immediate neighbourhood they did not hesitate to sacrifice themselves to the cause of freedom. Such acts of heroism reminded me over again of the true English spirit to which in those early days I had given my full faith, and made me wonder how imperialist greed could bring about so ugly a transformation in the character of so great a race.

Such is the tragic tale of the gradual loss of my faith in the claims of the European nations to civilization. In India the misfortune of being governed by a foreign race is daily brought home to us not only in the callous neglect of such minimum necessities of life as adequate provision for food, clothing, education and medical facilities for the people, but in an even unhappier form in the way people have divided themselves. The pity of it is that the blame is laid at the door of our own society. So frightful a culmination of the history of our people would never have been possible, but for the encouragement it has received from secret influences emanating from high places.

One cannot believe that Indians are in any way inferior to the Japanese in intellectual capacity. The most effective difference between these two eastern peoples is that whereas India lies at the mercy of the British, Japan has been spared the shadow of alien domination. We know what we have been deprived of. That which was truly best in their own civilizations, the upholding of the dignity of human relationships, has no place in the British administration of this country. If in its place they have established, with baton in hand, a reign of 'law and order', in other words a policeman's rule, such mockery of civilization can claim no respect from us. It is the mission of civilization to bring unity among people and establish peace and harmony. But in unfortunate India the social fabric is being rent into shreds by unseemly outbursts of hooliganism daily growing in intensity, right under the very aegis of 'law and order'. In India, so long as no personal injury is inflicted upon any member of the ruling race, this barbarism seems to be assured of perpetuity, making us ashamed to live under such an administration.

And yet my good fortune has often brought me into close contact with really large-hearted Englishmen. Without the slightest hesitation I may say that the nobility of their character was without parallel—in no country or community have I come across such greatness of soul. Such examples would not allow me to wholly lose faith in the race which produced them. I had the rare blessing of having Andrews—a real Englishman, a real Christian and a true man—for a very close friend. Today in the perspective of death his unselfish and courageous magnanimity shines all the brighter. The whole of India remains indebted to him for innumerable acts of love and devotion. But personally speaking, I am especially beholden to him because he helped me to retain in my old age that feeling of respect for the English race with which in the past I was inspired by their literature and which I was about to lose completely. I count such Englishmen as Andrews not only as my personal and intimate friends but as friends of the whole human race. To have known them has been to me a treasured privilege. It is my belief that such Englishmen will save

British honour from shipwreck. At any rate if I had not known them, my despair at the prospect of western civilization would be unrelieved.

In the meanwhile the demon of barbarity has given up all pretence and has emerged with unconcealed fangs, ready to tear up humanity in an orgy of devastation. From one end of the world to the other the poisonous fumes of hatred darken the atmosphere. The spirit of violence which perhaps lay dormant in the psychology of the West, has at last roused itself and desecrates the spirit of Man.

The wheels of Fate will some day compel the English to give up their Indian empire. But what kind of India will they leave behind, what stark misery? When the stream of their centuries' administration runs dry at last, what a waste of mud and filth they will leave behind them! I had at one time believed that the springs of civilization would issue out of the heart of Europe. But today when I am about to quit the world that faith has gone bankrupt altogether.

As I look around I see the crumbling ruins of a proud civilization strewn like a vast heap of futility. And yet I shall not commit the grievous sin of losing faith in Man. I would rather look forward to the opening of a new chapter in his history after the cataclysm is over and the atmosphere rendered clean with the spirit of service and sacrifice. Perhaps that dawn will come from this horizon, from the East where the sun rises. A day will come when unvanquished Man will retrace his path of conquest, despite all barriers, to win back his lost human heritage.

Today we witness the perils which attend on the insolence of might; one day shall be borne out the full truth of what the sages have proclaimed: 'By unrighteousness man prospers, gains what appears desirable, conquers enemies, but perishes at the root.'

36

THE ELEMENTS OF POETRY

George Santayana

If poetry in its higher reaches is more philosophical than history, because it presents the memorable types of men and things apart from unmeaning circumstances, so in its primary substance and texture poetry is more philosophical than prose because it is nearer to our immediate experience. Poetry breaks up the trite conceptions designated by current words into the sensuous qualities out of which those conceptions were originally put together. We name what we conceive and believe in, not what we see; things, not images; souls, not voices and silhouettes. This naming, with the whole education of the senses which it accompanies, subserves the uses of life; in order to thread our way through the labyrinth of objects which assault us, we must make a great selection in our sensuous experience; half of what we see and hear we must pass over as insignificant, while we piece out the other half with such an ideal complement as is necessary to turn it into a fixed and well-ordered conception of the world. This labor of perception and understanding, this spelling of the material meaning of experience, is enshrined in our workaday language and ideas; ideas which are literally poetic in the sense that they are 'made' (for every conception in an adult mind is a fiction), but which are at the same time prosaic because they are made economically, by abstraction, and for use.

When the child of poetic genius, who has learned this intellectual and utilitarian language in the cradle, goes afield and gathers for himself the aspects of nature, he begins to encumber his mind with the many living impressions which the intellect rejected, and which the language of the intellect can hardly convey; he labors with his nameless burden of perception, and wastes himself in aimless impulses of emotion and reverie, until finally the method of some art offers a vent to his inspiration, or to such part of it as can survive the test of time and the discipline of expression.

The poet retains by nature the innocence of the eye, or recovers it easily; he disintegrates the fictions of common perception into their sensuous elements, gathers these together again into chance groups as the accidents of his environment or the affinities of his temperament may conjoin them; and this wealth of sensation and this freedom of fancy, which make an extraordinary ferment in his ignorant heart, presently bubble over into some kind of utterance.

The fullness and sensuousness of such effusions bring them nearer to our actual perceptions than common discourse could come; yet they may easily seem remote, overloaded, and obscure to those accustomed to think entirely in symbols, and never to be interrupted in the algebraic rapidity of their thinking by a moment's pause and examination of heart, nor ever to plunge for a moment into that torrent of sensation and imagery over which the bridge of prosaic associations habitually carries us safe and dry to some conventional act. How slight that bridge commonly is, how much an affair of trestles and wire, we can hardly conceive until we have trained ourselves to an extreme sharpness of introspection. But psychologists have discovered, what laymen generally will confess, that we hurry by the procession of our mental images as we do by the traffic of the street, intent on business, gladly forgetting the noise and movement of the scene, and looking only for the corner we would turn or the door we would enter. Yet in our alertest moment the depths of the soul are still dreaming; the real world stands drawn in bare outline against a background of chaos and unrest. Our logical thoughts dominate experience only as the parallels and meridians make a checkerboard of the sea. They guide our voyage without controlling the waves, which toss forever in spite of our ability to ride over them to our chosen ends. Sanity is a madness put to good uses; waking life is a dream controlled.

Out of the neglected riches of this dream the poet fetches his wares. He dips into the chaos that underlies the rational shell of the world and brings up some superfluous image, some emotion dropped by the way, and reattaches it to the present object; he reinstates things unnecessary, he emphasizes things ignored, he paints in again into the landscape the tints which the intellect has allowed to fade from it. If he seems sometimes to obscure a fact, it is only because he is restoring an experience. The first element which the intellect rejects in forming its ideas of things is the emotion which accompanies the perception; and this emotion is the first thing the poet restores. He stops at the image, because he stops to enjoy. He wanders into the bypaths of association because the bypaths are delightful. The love of beauty which made him give measure and cadence to his words, the love of harmony which made him rhyme them, reappear in his imagination and make him select there also the material that is itself beautiful, or capable of assuming beautiful forms. The link that binds together the ideas, sometimes so wide apart, which his wit assimilates, is most often the link of emotion; they have in common some element of beauty or of horror.

37

MY FIRST ACQUAINTANCE WITH POETS

William Hazlitt

My father was a Dissenting Minister at Wem in Shropshire; and in the year 1798 (the figures that compose the date are to me like the 'dreaded name of Demogorgon') Mr Coleridge came to Shrewsbury, to succeed Mr Rowe in the spiritual charge of a Unitarian congregation there. He did not come till late on the Saturday afternoon before he was to preach; and Mr Rowe, who himself went down to the coach in a state of anxiety and expectation to look for the arrival of his successor, could find no one at all answering the description but a round-faced man in a short black coat (like a shooting-jacket) which hardly seemed to have been made for him, but who seemed to be talking at a great rate to his fellow-passengers. Mr Rowe had scarce returned to give an account of his disappointment, when the round-faced man in black entered, and dissipated all doubts on the subject, by beginning to talk. He did not cease while he stayed; nor has he since, that I know of. He held the good town of Shrewsbury in delightful suspense for three weeks that he remained there, 'fluttering the proud Salopians like an eagle in a dove-cote'; and the Welsh mountains that skirt the horizon with their tempestuous confusion, agree to have heard no such mystic sounds since the days of

> High-born Hoel's harp or soft Llewelyn's lay!

As we passed along between Wem and Shrewsbury, and I eyed their blue tops seen through the wintry branches, or the red rustling leaves of the sturdy oak-trees by the road-side, a sound was in my ears as of a Siren's song; I was stunned, startled with it, as from deep sleep;

but I had no notion then that I should ever be able to express my admiration to others in motley imagery or quaint allusion, till the light of his genius shone into my soul, like the sun's rays glittering in the puddles of the road. I was at that time dumb, inarticulate, helpless, like a worm by the way-side, crushed, bleeding, lifeless; but now, bursting from the deadly bands that bound them,

With Styx nine times round them,

my ideas float on winged words, and as they expand their plumes, catch the golden light of other years. My soul has indeed remained in its original bondage, dark, obscure, with longings infinite and unsatisfied; my heart, shut up in the prison-house of this rude clay, has never found, nor will it ever find, a heart to speak to; but that my understanding also did not remain dumb and brutish, or at length found a language to express itself, I owe to Coleridge. But this is not to my purpose.

My father lived ten miles from Shrewsbury, and was in the habit of exchanging visits with Mr Rowe, and with Mr Jenkins of Whitchurch (nine miles farther on) according to the custom of Dissenting Ministers in each other's neighbourhood. A line of communication is thus established, by which the flame of civil and religious liberty is kept alive, and nourishes its smouldering fire unquenchable, like the fires in the Agamemnon of Aeschylus, placed at different stations, that waited for ten long years to announce with their blazing pyramids the destruction of Troy. Coleridge had agreed to come over to see my father, according to the courtesy of the country, as Mr Rowe's probable successor; but in the meantime I had gone to hear him preach the Sunday after his arrival. A poet and a philosopher getting up into a Unitarian pulpit to preach the Gospel, was a romance in these degenerate days, a sort of revival of the primitive spirit of Christianity, which was not to be resisted.

It was in January, 1798, that I rose one morning before daylight, to walk ten miles in the mud, to hear this celebrated person preach. Never, the longest day I have to live, shall I have such another walk as this cold, raw, comfortless one, in the winter of the year 1798. *Il y a des impressions que ni le temps ni les circonstances peuvent effacer. Dussé-je vivre des siècles entiers, le doux temps de ma jeunesse ne peut renaitre pour moi, ni s'effacer jamais dans ma mémoire.* When I got there, the organ was playing the Hundredth Psalm, and, when it was done, Mr Coleridge rose and gave out his text, 'And he went up into the mountain to pray, HIMSELF, ALONE.' As he gave out this text, his voice 'rose like a steam of rich distilled perfumes,' and when he came to the two last words, which he pronounced loud, deep, and distinct, it seemed to me, who was then young, as if the sounds had echoed from the bottom of the human heart, and as if that prayer might have floated in solemn silence through the universe. The idea of St John came into mind, 'of one crying in the wilderness, who had his loins girt about, and whose food was locusts and wild honey.' The preacher then launched into his subject, like an eagle dallying with the wind. The sermon was upon peace and war; upon church and state—not their alliance, but their separation—on the spirit of the world and the spirit of Christianity, not as the same, but as opposed to one another. He talked of those who had 'inscribed the cross of Christ on banners dripping with human gore.' He made a poetical and pastoral excursion,—and to show the fatal effects of war, drew a striking contrast between the simple shepherd boy, driving his team afield, or sitting under the hawthorn, piping to his flock, 'as though he should never be old,' and the same poor country-lad, crimped, kidnapped, brought into town, made drunk at an alehouse, turned into a wretched drummer-boy, with his hair sticking on end with powder and pomatum, a long cue at his back, and tricked out in the loathsome finery of the profession of blood:

> Such were the notes our once-lov'd poet sung.

And for myself, I could not have been more delighted if I had heard the music of the spheres. Poetry and Philosophy had met together, Truth and Genius had embraced, under the eye and with the sanction of Religion. This was even beyond my hopes. I returned home well satisfied. The sun that was still labouring pale and wan through the sky, obscured by thick mists, seemed an emblem of the good cause;

and the cold dank drops of dew that hung half-melted on the beard of the thistle, had something genial and refreshing in them; for there was a spirit of hope and youth in all nature, that turned everything into good. The face of nature had not then the brand of Jus Divinum on it:

> Like to that sanguine flower inscrib'd with woe.

On the Tuesday following, the half-inspired speaker came. I was called down into the room where he was, and went half-hoping, half-afraid. He received me very graciously, and I listened for a long time without uttering a word. I did not suffer in his opinion by my silence. 'For those two hours,' he afterwards was pleased to say, 'he was conversing with W. H.'s forehead!' His appearance was different from what I had anticipated from seeing him before. At a distance, and in the dim light of the chapel, there was to me a strange wildness in his aspect, a dusky obscurity, and I thought him pitted with the small-pox. His complexion was at that time clear, and even bright—

> As are the children of yon azure sheen.

His forehead was broad and high, light as if built of ivory, with large projecting eyebrows, and his eyes rolling beneath them like a sea with darkened lustre. 'A certain tender bloom his face o'erspread,' a purple tinge as we see it in the pale thoughtful complexions of the Spanish portrait-painters, Murillo and Velasquez. His mouth was gross, voluptuous, open, eloquent; his chin good-humoured and round; but his nose, the rudder of the face, the index of the will, was small, feeble, nothing—like what he has done. It might seem that the genius of his face as from a height surveyed and projected him (with sufficient capacity and huge aspiration) into the world unknown of thought and imagination, with nothing to support or guide his veering purpose, as if Columbus had launched his adventurous course for the New World in a scallop, without oars or compass. So at least I comment on it after the event. Coleridge in his person was rather above the common size, inclining to the corpulent, or like Lord Hamlet, 'somewhat fat and pursy.' His hair (now, alas! grey) was then black and glossy as the raven's, and fell in smooth masses over his forehead. This long pendulous hair is peculiar to enthusiasts, to those whose minds tend heavenward; and is traditionally inseparable (though of a different colour) from the pictures of Christ. It ought to belong, as a character to all who preach *Christ crucified*, and Coleridge was at that time one of those!

It was curious to observe the contrast between him and my father, who was a veteran in the cause, and then declining into the vale of years. He had been a poor Irish lad, carefully brought up by his parents, and sent to the University of Glasgow (where he studied under Adam Smith) to prepare him for his future destination. It was his mother's proudest wish to see her son a Dissenting Minister. So if we look back to past generations (as far as eye can reach) we see the same hopes, fears, wishes, followed by the same disappointments, throbbing in the human heart; and so we may see them (if we look forward) rising up for ever, and disappearing, like vapourish bubbles, in the human breast! After being tossed about from congregation to congregation in the heats of the Unitarian controversy, and squabbles about the American war, he had been relegated to an obscure village, where he was to spend the last thirty years of his life, far from the only converse that he loved, the talk about disputed texts of Scripture and the cause of civil and religious liberty. Here he passed his days, repining but resigned, in the study of the Bible, and the perusal of the Commentators—huge folios, not easily got through, one of which would outlast a winter! Why did he pore on these from morn to night (with the exception of a walk in the fields or a turn in the garden to gather broccoli-plants or kidney-beans of his own rearing, with no small degree of pride and pleasure)?—Here were 'no figures nor no fantasies,'—neither poetry nor philosophy—nothing to dazzle, nothing to excite modern curiosity; but to his lack-lustre eyes there appeared, within the pages of the ponderous, unwieldy, neglected tomes, the sacred name of JEHOVAH in Hebrew capitals: pressed down by the weight of the style, worn to the last fading thinness of the understanding, there were glimpses, glimmering notions of the patriarchal wanderings, with palm-trees hovering in the horizon, and processions of camels at the distance of three thousand years; there was

Moses with the Burning Bush, the number of the Twelve Tribes, types, shadows, glosses on the law and the prophets; there were discussions (dull enough) on the age of Methuselah, a mighty speculation! there were outlines, rude guesses at the shape of Noah's Ark and at the riches of Solomon's Temple; questions as to the date of the creation, predictions of the end of all things; the great lapses of time, the strange mutations of the globe were unfolded with the voluminous leaf, as it turned over; and though the soul might slumber with an hieroglyphic veil of inscrutable mysteries drawn over it, yet it was in a slumber ill-exchanged for all the sharpened realities of sense, wit, fancy, or reason. My father's life was comparatively a dream; but it was a dream of infinity and eternity, of death, the resurrection, and a judgement to come!

No two individuals were ever more unlike than were the host and his guest. A poet was to my father a sort of nondescript: yet whatever added grace to the Unitarian cause was to him welcome. He could hardly have been more surprised or pleased, if our visitor had worn wings. Indeed, his thoughts had wings; and as the silken sounds rustled round our little wainscoted parlour, my father threw back his spectacles over his forehead, his white hairs mixing with its sanguine hue; and a smile of delight beamed across his rugged cordial face, to think that Truth had found a new ally in Fancy! Besides, Coleridge seemed to take considerable notice of me, and that of itself was enough. He talked very familiarly, but agreeably, and glanced over a variety of subjects. At dinner-time he grew more animated, and dilated in a very edifying manner on Mary Wollstonecraft and Mackintosh. The last, he said, he considered (on my father's speaking of his *Vindiciae Gallicae* as a capital performance) as a clever scholastic man—a master of the topics,—or as the ready warehouseman of letters, who knew exactly where to lay his hand on what he wanted, though the goods were not his own. He thought him no match for Burke, either in style or matter. Burke was a metaphysician, Mackintosh a mere logician. Burke was an orator (almost a poet) who reasoned in figures, because he had an eye for nature: Mackintosh, on the other hand, was a rhetorician, who had only an eye to commonplaces. On this I ventured to say that I had always entertained a great opinion of Burke, and that (as far as I could find) the speaking of him with contempt might be made the test of a vulgar democratical mind. This was the first observation I ever made to Coleridge, and he said it was a very just and striking one. I remember the leg of Welsh mutton and the turnips on the table that day had the finest flavour imaginable. Coleridge added that Mackintosh and Tom Wedgwood (of whom, however, he spoke highly) had expressed a very indifferent opinion of his friend Mr Wordsworth, on which he remarked to them—'He strides on so far before you, that he dwindles in the distance!' Godwin had once boasted to him of having carried on an argument with Mackintosh for three hours with dubious success; Coleridge told him—'If there had been a man of genius in the room he would have settled the question in five minutes.' He asked me if I had ever seen Mary Wollstonecraft, and I said, I had once for a few moments, and that she seemed to me to turn off Godwin's objections to something she advanced with quite a playful, easy air. He replied, that 'this was only one instance of the ascendancy which people of imagination exercised over those of mere intellect.' He did not rate Godwin very high (this was caprice or prejudice, real or affected) but he had a great idea of Mrs Wollstonecraft's powers of conversation, none at all of her talent for book-making. We talked a little about Holcroft. He had been asked if he was not much struck *with* him, and he said, he thought himself in more danger of being struck *by* him. I complained that he would not let me get on at all, for he required a definition of every the commonest word, exclaiming, 'What do you mean by a *sensation*, Sir? What do you mean by an *idea*?' This, Coleridge said, was barricadoing the road to truth:—it was setting up a turnpike-gate at every step we took. I forget a great number of things, many more than I remember; but the day passed off pleasantly, and the next morning Mr Coleridge was to return to Shrewsbury. When I came down to breakfast, I found that he had just received a letter from his friend, T. Wedgwood, making him an offer of 150*l.* a year if he chose to waive his present pursuit, and devote himself entirely to the study of poetry and philosophy. Coleridge seemed to make up his mind to close with this proposal in the act of tying on one of his shoes. It threw an additional damp on his departure. It took the wayward enthusiast quite from us to cast him into Deva's winding vales, or by the shores of old romance. Instead of living at ten miles' distance, of being the pastor of a Dissenting congregation at Shrewsbury, he was henceforth to inhabit the Hill of Parnassus, to be a Shepherd on the Delectable Mountains. Alas! I knew not the way thither, and felt very little gratitude for Mr Wedgwood's bounty. I was presently relieved from this dilemma; for Mr Coleridge, asking for a pen and ink, and going to a table to write something on a bit of card, advanced towards me with undulating step, and giving me the precious document, said that that was his address, *Mr Coleridge, Nether-Stowey, Somersetshire*; and that he should be glad to see me there in a few weeks' time, and, if I chose, would come half-way to meet me. I was not less surprised than the shepherd-boy (this simile is to be found in *Cassandra*) when he sees a thunderbolt fall close at his feet. I stammered out my acknowledgements and acceptance of this offer (I thought Mr Wedgwood's annuity a trifle to it) as well as I could; and this mighty business being settled, the poet-preacher took leave, and I accompanied him six miles on the road. It was a fine morning in the middle of winter, and he talked the whole way. The scholar in Chaucer is described as going

—Sounding on his way.

So Coleridge went on his. In digressing, in dilating, in passing from subject to subject, he appeared to me to float in air, to slide on ice. He told me in confidence (going along) that he should have preached two sermons before he accepted the situation at Shrewsbury, one on Infant Baptism, the other on the Lord's Supper, showing that he could not administer either, which would have effectually disqualified him for the object in view. I observed that he continually crossed me on the way by shifting from one side of the footpath to the other. This struck me as an odd movement; but I did not at that time connect it with any instability of purpose or involuntary change of principle, as I have done since. He seemed unable to keep on in a straight line. He spoke slightingly of Hume (whose *Essay on Miracles* he said was stolen from an objection started in one of South's Sermons—*Credat Judaeus Apella*!). I was not very much pleased at this account of Hume, for I had just been reading, with infinite relish, that completest of all metaphysical *choke-pears*, his *Treatise on Human Nature*, to which the *Essays*, in point of scholastic subtlety and close reasoning, are mere elegant trifling, light summer-reading. Coleridge even denied the excellence of Hume's general style, which I think betrayed a want of taste or candour. He however made me amends by the manner in which he spoke of Berkeley. He dwelt particularly on his *Essay on Vision* as a masterpiece of analytical reasoning. So it undoubtedly is. He was exceedingly angry with Dr Johnson for striking the stone with his foot, in allusion to this author's *Theory of Matter and Spirit*, and saying, 'Thus I confute him, Sir.' Coleridge drew a parallel (I don't know how he brought about the connexion) between Bishop Berkeley and Tom Paine. He said the one was an instance of a subtle, the other of an acute mind, than which no two things could be more distinct. The one was a shop-boy's quality, the other the characteristic of a philosopher. He considered Bishop Butler as a true philosopher, a profound and conscientious thinker, a genuine reader of nature and his own mind. He did not speak of his *Analogy*, but of his *Sermons at the Rolls' Chapel*, of which I had never heard. Coleridge somehow always contrived to prefer the *unknown* to the *known*. In this instance he was right. The *Analogy* is a tissue of sophistry, of wire-drawn, theological special-pleading; the *Sermons* (with the Preface to them) are in a fine vein of deep, matured reflection, a candid appeal to our observation of human nature, without pedantry and without bias. I told Coleridge I had written a few remarks, and was sometimes foolish enough to believe that I had made a discovery on the same subject (the *Natural Disinterestedness of the Human Mind*)—and I tried to explain my view of it to Coleridge, who listened with great willingness, but I did not succeed in making myself understood. I sat down to the task shortly afterwards for the twentieth time, got new pens and paper, determined to make clear work of it, wrote a few meagre sentences in the skeleton style of a mathematical demonstration, stopped half-way down the second page; and, after trying in vain to pump up any words, images, notions, apprehensions, facts, or observations, from that gulf of abstraction in which I had plunged myself for four or five years preceding, gave up the attempt as labour in vain, and shed tears of helpless despondency on the blank unfinished paper. I can write fast enough now. Am I better than I was then? Oh no! One truth discovered, one pang of regret at not being able to express it, is better than all the fluency and flippancy in the world. Would that I could go back to what I then was! Why can we not revive past times as we can revisit old places? If I had the quaint Muse of Sir Philip Sidney to assist me, I would write a *Sonnet to the Road between Wem and Shrewsbury*, and immortalize every step of it by some fond enigmatical conceit. I would swear that the very milestones had ears, and that Harmer-hill stooped with all its pines, to listen to a poet, as he passed! I remember but one other topic of discourse in this walk. He mentioned Paley, praised the naturalness and clearness of his style, but condemned his sentiments, thought him a mere time-serving casuist, and said that 'the fact of his work on Moral and Political Philosophy being made a text-book in our Universities was a disgrace to the national character.' We parted at the six-mile stone; and I returned homeward pensive but much pleased. I had met with unexpected notice from a person whom I believed to have been prejudiced against me. 'Kind and affable to me had been his condescension, and should be honoured ever with suitable regard.' He was the first poet I had known, and he certainly answered to that inspired name. I had heard a great deal of his powers of conversation, and was not disappointed. In fact, I never met with any thing at all like them, either before or since. I could easily credit the accounts which were circulated of his holding forth to a large party of ladies and gentlemen, an evening or two before, on the Berkeleian Theory, when he made the whole material universe look like a transparency of fine words; and another story (which I believe he has somewhere told himself) of his being asked to a party at Birmingham, of his smoking tobacco and going to sleep after dinner on a sofa, where the company found him to their no small surprise, which was increased to wonder when he started up of a sudden, and rubbing his eyes, looked about him, and launched into a three hours' description of the third heaven, of which he had had a dream, very different from Mr Southey's *Vision of Judgement*, and also from that other *Vision of Judgement*, which Mr Murray, the Secretary of the Bridge Street Junto, has taken into his especial keeping.

On my way back, I had a sound in my ears, it was the voice of Fancy: I had a light before me, it was the face of Poetry. The one still lingers there, the other has not quitted my side! Coleridge in truth met me half-way on the ground of philosophy, or I should not have been won over to his imaginative creed. I had an uneasy, pleasurable sensation all the time, till I was to visit him. During those months the chill breath of winter gave me a welcoming; the vernal air was balm and inspiration to me. The golden sunsets, the silver star of evening, lighted me on my way to new hopes and prospects. *I was to visit Coleridge in the Spring.* This circumstance was never absent from my thoughts, and mingled with all my feelings. I wrote to him at the time proposed, and received an answer postponing my intended visit for a week or two, but very cordially urging me to complete my promise then. This delay did not damp, but rather increase my ardour. In the meantime I went to Llangollen Vale, by way of initiating myself in the mysteries of natural scenery; and I must say I was enchanted with it. I had been reading Coleridge's description of England, in his fine *Ode on the Departing Year*, and I applied it, *con amore*, to the objects before me. That valley was to me (in a manner) the cradle of a new existence: in the river that winds through it, my spirit was baptized in the waters of Helicon!

I returned home, and soon after set out on my journey with unworn heart and untried feet. My way lay through Worcester and Gloucester, and by Upton, where I thought of Tom Jones and the adventure of the muff. I remember getting completely wet through one day, and stopping at an inn (I think it was at Tewkesbury) where I sat up all night to read *Paul and Virginia*. Sweet were the showers in early youth that drenched my body, and sweet the drops of pity that fell upon the books I read! I recollect a remark of Coleridge's upon this very book, that nothing could show the gross indelicacy of French manners and the entire corruption of their imagination more strongly than the behaviour of the heroine in the last fatal scene, who turns away from a person on board the sinking vessel, that offers to save her life, because he has thrown off his clothes to assist him in swimming. Was this a time to think of such a circumstance? I once hinted to Wordsworth, as we were sailing in his boat on Grasmere lake, that I thought he had borrowed the idea of his *Poems on the Naming of Places* from the local inscriptions of the same kind in *Paul and Virginia*. He did not own the obligation, and stated some distinction without a difference, in defence of his claim to originality. And the slightest variation would be sufficient for this purpose in his mind; for whatever *he* added or omitted would inevitably be worth all that any one else had done, and contain the marrow of the sentiment.—I was still two days before the time fixed for my arrival, for I had taken care to set out early enough. I stopped these two days at Bridgewater, and when I was tired of sauntering on the banks of its muddy river, returned to the inn, and read *Camilla*. So have I loitered my life away, reading books, looking at pictures, going to plays, hearing, thinking, writing on what pleased me best. I have wanted only one thing to make me happy; but wanting that, have wanted everything!

I arrived, and was well received. The country about Nether Stowey is beautiful, green and hilly, and near the sea-shore. I saw it but the other day, after an interval of twenty years, from a hill near Taunton. How was the map of my life spread out before me, as the map of the country lay at my feet! In the afternoon, Coleridge took me over to All-Foxden, a romantic old family mansion of the St Aubins, where Wordsworth lived. It was then in the possession of a friend of the poet's, who gave him the free use of it. Somehow that period (the time just after the French Revolution) was not a time when *nothing was given for nothing*. The mind opened, and a softness might be perceived coming over the heart of individuals, beneath 'the scales that fence' our self-interest. Wordsworth himself was from home, but his sister kept house, and set before us a frugal repast; and we had free access to her brother's poems, the *Lyrical Ballads*, which were still in manuscript, or in the form of *Sibylline Leaves*. I dipped into a few of these with great satisfaction, and with the faith of a novice.

I slept that night in an old room with blue hangings, and covered with the round-faced family-portraits of the age of George I and II, and from the wooded declivity of the adjoining park that overlooked my window, at the dawn of day, could

—hear the loud stag speak.

In the outset of life (and particularly at this time I felt it so) our imagination has a body to it. We are in a state between sleeping and waking, and have indistinct but glorious glimpses of strange shapes, and there is always something to come better than what we see. As in our dreams the fullness of the blood gives warmth and reality to the coinage of the brain, so in youth our ideas are clothed, and fed, and pampered with our good spirits; we breathe thick with thoughtless happiness, the weight of future years presses on the strong pulses of the heart, and we repose with undisturbed faith in truth and good. As we advance, we exhaust our fund of enjoyment and of hope. We are no longer wrapped in *lamb's-wool*, lulled in Elysium. As we taste the pleasures of life, their spirit evaporates, the sense palls; and nothing is left but the phantoms, the lifeless shadows of what *has been*!

That morning, as soon as breakfast was over, we strolled out into the park, and seating ourselves on the trunk of an old ash-tree that stretched along the ground, Coleridge read aloud with a sonorous and musical voice, the ballad of *Betty Foy*. I was not critically or sceptically inclined. I saw touches of truth and nature, and took the rest for granted. But in the *Thorn*, the *Mad Mother*, and the *Complaint of a Poor Indian Woman*, I felt that deeper power and pathos which have been since acknowledged,

In spite of pride, in erring reason's spite,

as the characteristics of this author; and the sense of a new style and a new spirit in poetry came over me. It had to me something of the effect that arises from the turning up of the fresh soil, or of the first welcome breath of Spring,

While yet the trembling year is unconfirmed.

Coleridge and myself walked back to Stowey that evening, and his voice sounded high

> Of Providence, foreknowledge, will, and fate,
> Fix'd fate, free-will, foreknowledge absolute,

as we passed through echoing grove, by fairy stream or waterfall, gleaming in the summer moonlight! He lamented that Wordsworth was not prone enough to believe in the traditional superstitions of the place, and that there was a something corporeal, a *matter-of-fact-ness*, a clinging to the palpable, or often to the petty, in his poetry, in consequence. His genius was not a spirit that descended to him through the air; it sprung out of the ground like a flower, or unfolded itself from a green spray, on which the goldfinch sang. He said, however (if I remember right), that this objection must be confined to his descriptive pieces, that his philosophic poetry had a grand and comprehensive spirit in it, so that his soul seemed to inhabit the universe like a palace, and to discover truth by intuition, rather than by deduction. The next day Wordsworth arrived from Bristol at Coleridge's cottage. I think I see him now. He answered in some degree to his friend's description of him, but was more gaunt and Don Quixote-like. He was quaintly dressed (according to the *costume* of that unconstrained period) in a brown fustian jacket and striped pantaloons. There was something of a roll, a lounge in his gait, not unlike his own *Peter Bell*. There was a severe, worn pressure of thought about his temples, a fire in his eye (as if he saw something in objects more than the outward appearance), an intense high narrow forehead, a Roman nose, cheeks furrowed by strong purpose and feeling, and a convulsive inclination to laughter about the mouth, a good deal at variance with the solemn, stately expression of the rest of his face. Chantrey's bust wants the marking traits; but he was teased into making it regular and heavy: Haydon's head of him, introduced into the *Entrance of Christ into Jerusalem*, is the most like his drooping weight of thought and expression. He sat down and talked very naturally and freely, with a mixture of clear gushing accents in his voice, a deep guttural intonation, and a strong tincture of the northern *burr*, like the crust on wine. He instantly began to make havoc of the half of a Cheshire cheese on the table, and said triumphantly that 'his marriage with experience had not been so productive as Mr Southey's in teaching him a knowledge of the good things of this life.' He had been to see the *Castle Spectre* by Monk Lewis, while at Bristol, and described it very well. He said 'it fitted the taste of the audience like a glove.' This *ad captandum* merit was, however, by no means a recommendation of it, according to the severe principles of the new school, which reject rather than court popular effect. Wordsworth, looking out of the low, latticed window, said, 'How beautifully the sun sets on that yellow bank!' I thought within myself, 'With what eyes these poets see nature!' and ever after, when I saw the sunset stream upon the objects facing it, conceived I had made a discovery, or thanked Mr Wordsworth for having made one for me! We went over to All-Foxden again the day following, and Wordsworth read us the story of *Peter Bell* in the open air; and the comment made upon it by his face and voice was very different from that of some later critics! Whatever might be thought of the poem, 'his face was as a book where men might read strange matters,' and he announced the fate of his hero in prophetic tones. There is a *chaunt* in the recitation both of Coleridge and Wordsworth, which acts as a spell upon the hearer, and disarms the judgement. Perhaps they have deceived themselves by making habitual use of this ambiguous accompaniment. Coleridge's manner is more full, animated, and varied; Wordsworth's more equable, sustained, and internal. The one might be termed more *dramatic*, the other more *lyrical*. Coleridge has told me that he himself liked to compose in walking over uneven ground, or breaking through the straggling branches of a copse wood; whereas Wordsworth always wrote (if he could) walking up and down a straight gravel-walk, or in some spot where the continuity of his verse met with no collateral interruption. Returning that same evening, I got into a metaphysical argument with Wordsworth, while Coleridge was explaining the different notes of the nightingale to his sister, in which we neither of us succeeded in making ourselves perfectly clear and intelligible. Thus I passed three weeks at Nether Stowey and in the neighbourhood, generally devoting the afternoons to a delightful chat in an arbour made of bark by the poet's friend Tom Poole, sitting under two fine elm-trees, and listening to the bees humming round us, while we quaffed our *flip*. It was agreed, among other things, that we should make a jaunt down the Bristol Channel, as far as Lynton. We set off together on foot, Coleridge, John Chester, and I. This Chester was a native of Nether Stowey, one of those who were attracted to Coleridge's discourse as flies are to honey, or bees in swarming-time to the sound of a brass pan. He 'followed in the chase, like a dog who hunts, not like one that made up the cry.' He had on a brown cloth coat, boots, and corduroy breeches, was low in stature, bow-legged, had a drag in his walk like a drover, which he assisted by a hazel switch, and kept on a sort of trot by the side of Coleridge, like a running footman by a state coach, that he might not lose a syllable or sound, that fell from Coleridge's lips. He told me his private opinion, that Coleridge was a wonderful man. He scarcely opened his lips, much less offered an opinion the whole way: yet of the three, had I to choose during that journey, I would be John Chester. He afterwards followed Coleridge into Germany, where the Kantean philosophers were puzzled how to bring him under any of their categories. When he sat down at table with his idol, John's felicity was complete; Sir Walter Scott's, or Mr Blackwood's, when they sat down at the same table with the King, was not more so. We passed Dunster on our right, a small town between the brow of a hill and the sea. I remember eyeing it wistfully as it lay below us: contrasted with the woody scene around, it looked as clear, as pure, as *embrowned* and ideal as any landscape I have seen since, of Gaspar Poussin's or Domenichino's. We had a long day's march—(our feet kept time to the echoes of Coleridge's tongue)—through Minehead and by the Blue Anchor, and on to Lynton, which we did not reach till near midnight, and where we had some difficulty in making a lodgment. We, however, knocked the people of the house up at last, and we were repaid for our apprehensions and fatigue by some excellent rashers of fried bacon and eggs. The view in coming along had been splendid. We walked for miles and miles on dark brown heaths overlooking the channel, with the Welsh hills beyond, and at times descended into little sheltered valleys close by the sea-side, with a smuggler's face scowling by us, and then had to ascend conical hills with a path winding up through a coppice to a barren top, like a monk's shaven crown, from one of which I pointed out to Coleridge's notice the bare masts of a vessel on the very edge of the horizon, and within the red-orbed disk of the setting sun, like his own spectre-ship in the *Ancient Mariner*. At Lynton the character of the sea-coast becomes more marked and rugged. There is a place called the '*Valley of Rocks*' (I suspect this was only the poetical name for it) bedded among precipices overhanging the sea, with rocky caverns beneath, into which the waves dash, and where the sea-gull for ever wheels its screaming flight. On the tops of these are huge stones thrown transverse, as if an earthquake had tossed them there, and behind these is a fretwork of perpendicular rocks, something like the '*Giant's Causeway*'. A thunder-storm came on while we were at the inn, and Coleridge was running out bareheaded to enjoy the commotion of the elements in the '*Valley of Rocks*', but as if in spite, the clouds only muttered a few angry sounds, and let fall a few refreshing drops. Coleridge told me that he and Wordsworth were to have made this place the scene of a prose-tale, which was to have been in the manner of, but far superior to, the *Death of Abel*, but they had relinquished the design. In the morning of the second day, we breakfasted luxuriously in an old-fashioned parlour on tea, toast, eggs, and honey, in the very sight of the bee-hives from which it had been taken, and a garden full of thyme and wild flowers that had produced it. On this occasion Coleridge spoke of Virgil's *Georgics*, but not well. I do not think he had much feeling for the classical or elegant. It was in this room that we found a little worn-out copy of the *Seasons*, lying in a window-seat, on which Coleridge exclaimed, '*That* is true fame!' He said Thomson was a great poet, rather than a good one; his style was as meretricious as his thoughts were natural. He spoke of Cowper as the best modern poet. He said the *Lyrical Ballads* were an experiment about to be tried by him and Wordsworth, to see how far the public taste would endure poetry written in a more natural and simple style than had hitherto been attempted; totally discarding the artifices of poetical diction, and making use only of such words as had probably been common in the most ordinary language since the days of Henry II. Some comparison was introduced between Shakespeare and Milton. He said 'he hardly knew which to prefer. Shakespeare appeared to him a mere stripling in the art; he was as tall and as strong, with infinitely more activity than Milton, but he never appeared to have come to man's estate; or if he had, he would not have been a man, but a monster.' He spoke with contempt of Gray, and with intolerance of Pope. He did not like the versification of the latter. He observed that 'the ears of these couplet-writers might be charged with having short memories, that could not retain the harmony of whole passages.' He thought little of Junius as a writer; he had a dislike of Dr Johnson; and a much higher opinion of Burke as an orator and politician, than of Fox or Pitt. He however thought him very inferior in richness of style and imagery to some of our elder prose-writers, particularly Jeremy Taylor. He liked Richardson, but not Fielding; nor could I get him to enter into the merits of *Caleb Williams*. In short, he was profound and discriminating with respect to those authors whom he liked, and where he gave his judgement fair play; capricious, perverse, and prejudiced in his antipathies and distastes. We loitered on the 'ribbed sea-sands', in such talk as this, a whole morning, and I recollect met with a curious sea-weed, of which John Chester told us the country name! A fisherman gave Coleridge an account of a boy that had been drowned the day before, and that they had tried to save him at the risk of their own lives. He said 'he did not know how it was that they ventured, but, Sir, we have a *nature* towards one another.' This expression, Coleridge remarked to me, was a fine illustration of that theory of disinterestedness which I (in common with Butler) had adopted. I broached to him an argument of mine to prove that *likeness* was not mere association of ideas. I said that the mark in the sand put one in mind of a man's foot, not because it was part of a former impression of a man's foot (for it was quite new) but because it was like the shape of a man's foot. He assented to the justness of this distinction (which I have explained at length elsewhere, for the benefit of the curious) and John Chester listened; not from any interest in the subject, but because he was astonished that I should be able to suggest anything to Coleridge that he did not already know. We returned on the third morning, and Coleridge remarked the silent cottage-smoke curling up the valleys where, a few evenings before, we had seen the lights gleaming through the dark.

In a day or two after we arrived at Stowey, we set out, I on my return home, and he for Germany. It was a Sunday morning, and he was to preach that day for Dr Toulmin of Taunton. I asked him if he had prepared anything for the occasion? He said he had not even thought of the text, but should as soon as we parted. I did not go to hear him,—this was a fault,—but we met in the evening at Bridgewater. The next day we had a long day's walk to Bristol, and sat down, I recollect, by a well-side on the road, to cool ourselves and satisfy our thirst, when Coleridge repeated to me some descriptive lines of his tragedy of *Remorse*; which I must say became his mouth and that occasion better than they, some years after, did Mr Elliston's and the Drury Lane boards,—

> Oh memory! shield me from the world's poor strife,
> And give those scenes thine everlasting life.

I saw no more of him for a year or two, during which period he had been wandering in the Hartz Forest in Germany; and his return was cometary, meteorous, unlike his setting out. It was not till some time after that I knew his friends Lamb and Southey. The last always appears to me (as I first saw him) with a commonplace book under his arm, and the first with a *bon-mot* in his mouth. It was at Godwin's that I met him with Holcroft and Coleridge, where they were disputing fiercely which was the best—*Man as he was, or man as he is to be*. 'Give me', says Lamb, 'man as he is *not* to be.' This saying was the beginning of a friendship between us, which I believe still continues.—Enough of this for the present.

> But there is matter for another rhyme,
> And I to this may add a second tale.

38

IN PRAISE OF OLD LADIES

Lucy Martin Donnelly

It is everywhere the custom, in life, in literature, to celebrate the young girl; to praise her pink cheeks, her shining hair, her innocence, her gayeties—her muslins, even, and blue ribbons. She has become in these latter days a proverb, a type—la jeune fille. Yet, to the discreet observer how gaudy is her charm, how showy and unsubstantial, and of the day only, when matched with graces like those of the truly incomparable old lady! It is an antique convention that hurries off old age with decrepitude and care and quavering palsy. And it may be that the old gentleman is unamiable; that, his days of strenuousness fairly over, he becomes crabbed, a lover of snuff, and unpoetical. But the old lady is a creature of another quality. The refinements of age only enhance the femininity of her charm; to her, whimsicalities, delicate occupations, the fine lines that etch themselves expressively across her brow and about her mouth, are all vastly becoming. With what ineffable grace, moreover, she pronounces certain words in the elegant fashion of an age ago! How softly the old Indian shawls she wears fall about her shoulders! What strange, unlikely stories she tells of the beginning of the century!

I am indeed no novice to her charms. I have been victim to the enchantments of a long line of old ladies from my earliest years upward. When my frocks were still short and I still suffered under the ignominy of pinafores, I remember very well following a friend of my grandmother's about, and fetching big books for her. She was an exceedingly learned old lady, I take it; indeed, my grandmother always spoke of her as strong-minded, wherefore I am sometimes led to doubt whether she would so unreservedly have pleased my maturer taste. But in those early days my devotion impelled me even to the point of learning the alphabets of the curious languages she read. What constituted her peculiar, her romantic charm, however, was the fact that she had traveled in many far-away countries. I always understood it was their strange suns that had turned her skin the yellow color of old parchment, and stopped the whitening of her hair at a grizzly gray. This particular ugly gray I admired along with the rest: it suggested worldly sophistication and a cosmopolitan experience, as did no less her deep voice and blue-veined hands, and her habit of taking a vigorous walk in the morning, before breakfast. Her daughter, she told me, was named Aurore. How I wished that I myself had been favored with such a name!

My grandmother was very different—much prettier and gentler, no doubt; but her daughters bore such stiff, old-fashioned names as Anne and Emeline, and she herself had seldom left New England, and took only a short walk in the sun at noonday, under a tiny black silk parasol. At other times she sat beside her work-table, which had legs of twisted mahogany, and a crimson silk bag hanging down from the middle in a way I never understood. Out of this she occasionally brought scraps of faded old brocades—pink and green they would be, with a rare yellow, or a blue still a little gay; and now and then, when the winter evenings until my bedtime were long, she even found bright-colored beads in a small drawer at the side. Although she had been 'a proficient' in music as a girl, I think she knew no language save English. Emerson she read chiefly; the prayers of Theodore Parker; black volumes of sermons by William Ellery Channing; and sometimes, to me, in a very soft voice, Whittier's poems. In the late afternoons she was accustomed to play at solitaire, letting me sit at a corner of the table to look on. Not infrequently, when excited by the odds against which we were fighting, I forgot to hold up my head, and my long brown curls, falling down among the cards, threw them into disarray, and obliged me to sit at a penitential distance. My grandmother did not choose to be interrupted. But all the games in turn she invariably won by a deft rearrangement of the cards when she saw them going wrong. 'With one's self, you know, my dear,' she would say, judiciously distributing diamonds among the spades—'with one's self it is quite understood.'

Since the days of my grandmother and her friends I have known a hundred other old ladies, if none more charming. There are, I dare say, persons who, in going about the world, meet people of other sorts: actors, perhaps, or ladies of fashion, or diplomatists—first of all, I fancy, to be desired—or spiritualists, or musicians. Personally, I never fall in with anyone except old ladies. In a railway train, for example, I am sure to find myself opposite or beside one, and of late years they have generally had birds with them.

The first I remember—with a bird, that is—was in a German railway carriage going from Berlin to Hanover. At least, my destination was Hanover; the old lady herself was on her way home to Düsseldorf. She had been visiting her nephews and nieces in Berlin; she had a great many of them, she told me. From her fingers, covered with old pearl and diamond rings, I gathered that she was very rich; and from the bouquets of many colors, ranged in the luggage-rack above her head, that the nephews and nieces were trying to persuade her to leave them her fortune. She wore, nevertheless, an air of extreme detachment, holding her long netted silk purse—through whose meshes the Prussian gold gleamed—tightly clasped between two fat fingers. Altogether she was a very portly and regal-looking person, and gave you the impression of being dressed in black velvet, though in point of fact I do not think that she was. But her mantle was fringed heavily several times about, and her hat—for she wore a hat with a brim that dropped slightly, discreetly, all around—was also bordered by a black fringe that just cleared her faded eyebrows and her black beady eyes. She had a gouty foot, too—she was quite complete—that rested on a little folding stool she had brought with her; and she rang imperiously for the guard. When he came she ordered coffee, bullying the cream-faced Teuton into bringing a double portion of sugar to feed her bird, a little green creature, disposed among the flowers above her head. It was with a good deal of difficulty that she struggled up to reach him, but to have him handed down would, she said, excite him unnecessarily. 'Mein Männchen, mein Männchen,' she murmured in a deep, tender tone, as she fed him each successive crumb. After feasting the bird she turned her attention to me, and asking to see the book that I was absorbed in, she kept it until we arrived at Hanover. I had evidently read too much in trains, she remarked, alluding to my eye-glasses. Americans, she knew, were very foolish. Then she asked me the price of everything in the States, and of my traveling bag in particular, and quarreled with me as to the number of marks in a dollar. 'You'll find that I am right,' she assured me, as I was squeezing myself and the brown leather bag she admired out of the narrow door of the German coupé. 'You'll find there are six marks in every dollar. Auf wiedersehen, Fräulein.'

The last of my old ladies with birds I met only a month or two ago, on the way from London down to Southsea—the one place in all the world, I suppose, whither a thin spinster, accompanied by a ragged-tailed bird named Tip, should be traveling. She was, of course, very different from the German dowager; not so far on in years, and, as I indicated, exaggeratedly thin; shy, furthermore, and dressed in a worn black-silk gown, with a lace collar at her throat drawn together by a hair brooch. And she spoke only from time to time, to inquire if we must change carriages at Woking; meanwhile looking a little greedily from Tip to the seedcakes in the hands of three English schoolgirls, who, with shortish frocks and longish hair hanging over their shoulders, sat in a row on my side of the carriage, and scattered crumbs enough to have fattened a family of partridges.

Old ladies at sea, though there without the embellishments of flowers and birds, I have found no less attractive than on land. I fell in with a party of them in the early summer, on their way to Carlsbad to drink the waters; with the exception, that is, of two or three whose destination was Kissingen, and who disbelieved altogether, I learned when we were a few days out from New York, in the rheumatism of the Carlsbad-bound ladies. Carlsbad, they assured me—punctuating their remarks with sniffs of their smelling-bottles as I tucked cushions behind their poor backs—Carlsbad was all fine clothes and frivolity and band music (than which surely nothing has a more wicked sound), and was by no means the place a person really ill would dream of retiring to for her health's sake.

But it matters very little whether I travel in trains or in ships, or whether I rest quietly at home, my companions are rarely of my own age. If I am asked out to luncheon to meet the wife of a melancholy doubtful poet who died young, and on my way to the house in question dwell, not unnaturally, on her youthful tragic grief, on my arrival I find myself confronted by a fat, kindly old lady, crowned with a large black-beaded bonnet that shows a bunch of purple flowers above either ear. If I go to visit some beautiful house secluded in the country, it is an old lady who stands on the threshold. I remember such a mansion, built in Tudor times, and topped with chimneys calculated to make you sigh your soul away in longing; it had once been the dower house of an English queen, and in front of it two peacocks paraded proudly all day long. Others, I knew, went to admire it, and were entertained by the granddaughter, or at least by the middle-aged daughter, of its mistress. Not so on the sunny morning of my visit. Lady W—— herself was working among the flowers in her garden, and herself showed me back to the cascade and the tulip tree, stepping over the lawn with the spirit of a girl, and apologizing with a girl's vanity, too, for her garden hat and gloves.

She was the very flower and mirror of all the old ladies I have ever known; conscious, if you will, of her charm, and all the more charming for that. She led me into the drawing room—she knew she held my heart in her hand—to see her portrait, which, though painted by a celebrated artist, made her look very like any other old lady in velvet and a bonnet and furs. Her great gayety, her beautiful eyes, the sweet curving lines about her mouth, were all forgotten. 'I don't know,' she said to me a little stiffly, as she paused before it, and for a moment glanced across to her maternal grandmother done by Reynolds, with pink cheeks, and with a pink rose in her hand instead of a muff, 'I don't know, my dear, whether it is like or not, but certainly it is a very odd picture.'

More delightful though each one be than the last, it is but reasonable that the wealth of my experience among old ladies should have led me to certain discriminations. Old ladies, I am prepared to say, divide themselves into two classes: the thin, namely, and the fat. Nor is this discrimination so artificial as it may appear. Another equally expressive, equally conclusive, could not be made. And of the two—but this is a matter of prejudice—I prefer the thin, as having commonly more wit, more liveliness, brighter eyes, and a taste for anecdote generally wanting, I think it only right to say, in the fatter, kindlier class. My point of view is possibly ultra-modern, but what will you? La grande dame, so called, vanished with the days and ideals of Louis XIV. At the end of two centuries or so she is rarely to be met with. I have known her only once in all her traditional fairness, but then she was of the essence of perfection. She gave one the impression of having never for a moment been out of the great world; of having lived, though in New York, perpetually with princes—'les princes du sang, les princes étrangers, les grands-seigneurs façon de princes'. But what is my ungraceful pen that it should hazard a description of her, or attempt the splendor of her white hair and her white hands! Her graciousness, her elegance, her worldliness, are not to be compassed by a sentence.

Among modern old ladies, of whom I speak somewhat less diffidently, I affect the more frivolous sort. My own feeling is, very strictly, that in old age the world of affairs should be left behind, and one's hours passed pleasantly among pleasant things. Age should be impulsive, light-hearted—brilliant, if you will; it should fill its days with flowers and music and embroidery; it should drive in low carriages behind plump ponies; it should write a pretty, pointed, epistolary hand, and read nothing heavier than memoirs. Intellectuality may be all very well in youth, but in an old lady anything beyond a delicate pedantry is unlovely. I like old ladies with decided opinions, with a gift for repartee and some skill in the passions. Curiosities, strange modesties—I knew of an old lady who brought her grandsons up never to look into a butcher's shop, deeming it indecorous, even indecent—fantastic economies, eccentricities of various sorts, are delightful. And of all these things the insipidity and jejuneness of youth perforce know nothing. The very pattern of young girls is bound by a strait-lacing conventionality. Formalities, anxieties, uncertainties, sit upon her sleeve. She has no alternative, innocent creature, save to order her days and lay her plans in behalf of a charming old ladyhood.

39

DOGS AND MEN

Henry C. Merwin

There are men and women in the world who, of their own free will, live a dogless life, not knowing what they miss; and for them this essay, securely placed in the dignified *Atlantic*, there to remain so long as libraries and books shall endure, is chiefly written. Let them not pass it by in scorn, but rather stop to consider what can be said of the animal as a fellow being entitled to their sympathy, and having, perhaps, a like destiny with themselves.

As to those few persons who are not only dogless but dog-haters, they should excite pity rather than resentment. The man who hates a good dog is abnormal, and cannot help it. I once knew such a man, a money-lender long since passed away, whose life was largely a crusade against dogs, carried on through newspapers, pamphlets, and in conversation.

He used to declare that he had often been bitten by these animals, and that, on one occasion, a terrier actually jumped on the street-car in which he was riding, took a small piece out of his leg (a mere soupçon, no doubt), and then jumped off—all without apparent provocation, and in a moment of time. Probably this story, strange as it may sound, was substantially true. The perceptions of the dog are wonderfully acute. A recent occurrence may serve as the converse of the money-lender's story. A lost collie, lame and nearly starved, was taken in, fed, and cared for by a household of charitable persons, who, however, did not like or understand dogs, and were anxious to get rid of this one, provided that a good home could be found for him. In the course of a week there came to call upon them in her buggy an old lady who is extremely fond of dogs, and who possesses that combination of a masterful spirit with deep affection which acts like witchcraft upon the lower animals. The collie was brought out, and the story of his arrival was related at length. Meanwhile the old lady and the dog looked each other steadfastly in the eye. 'Do you want to come with me, doggie?' she said at last, not really meaning to take him. Up jumped the dog, and sat down beside her, and could not be dislodged by any entreaties or commands—and all parties were loath to use force. She took him home, but brought him back the next day, intending to leave him behind her. Again, however, the dog refused to be parted from his new and real friend. He bestowed a perfunctory wag of the tail upon his benefactors—he was not ungrateful; but, like all dogs, he sought not chiefly meat and bones and a comfortable place by the fire, but affection and caresses. The dog does not live that would refuse to forsake his dinner for the companionship of his master.

The mission of the dog—I say it with all reverence—is the same as the mission of Christianity, namely, to teach mankind that the universe is ruled by love. Ownership of a dog tends to soften the hard hearts of men. There are two great mysteries about the lower animals: one, the suffering which they have to endure at the hands of man; the other, the wealth of affection which they possess, and which for the most part is unexpended. All animals have this capacity for loving other creatures, man included. Crows, for example, show it to a remarkable degree. 'As much latent affection goes to waste in every flock of crows that flies overhead as would fit a human household for heaven.' A crow and a dog, if kept together, will become almost as fond of each other as of their master.

Surely this fact, this capacity of the lower animals to love, not only man, but one another, is the most significant, the most deserving to be pondered, the most important in respect to their place in the universe, of all the facts that can be learned about them. Compared with it, how trivial is anything that the zoölogist or biologist or the physiologist can tell us about the nature of the lower animals!

The most beautiful sight in the world, I once heard it said (by myself, to be honest), is the expression in the eyes of an intelligent, sweet-tempered pup—a pup old enough to take an interest in things about him, and yet so young as to imagine that everybody will be good to him; so young as not to fear that any man or boy will kick him, or that any dog will take away his bone. In the eyes of such a pup there is a look of confiding innocence, a consciousness of his own weakness and inexperience, a desire to love and to be loved, which are irresistible. In older dogs one is more apt to notice an eager, anxious, inquiring look, as if they were striving to understand things which the Almighty had placed beyond their mental grasp; and the nearest approach to a really human expression is seen in dogs suffering from illness. Heine, who, as the reader well knows, served a long apprenticeship to pain, somewhere says that pain refines even the lower animals; and all who are familiar with dogs in health and in disease will see the truth of this statement. I have seen in the face of an intelligent dog, suffering acutely from distemper, a look so human as to be almost terrifying; as if I had accidentally caught a glimpse of some deep-lying trait in the animal which nature had intended to conceal from mortal gaze.

The dog, in fact, makes a continual appeal to the sympathies of his human friends, and thus tends to prevent them from becoming hard or narrow. There are certain families, especially perhaps in New England, and most of all, no doubt, in Boston, who need to be regenerated, and might be regenerated by keeping a dog, provided that they went about it in the proper spirit. A distinguished preacher and author, himself a Unitarian, remarked recently in an address to Unitarians that they were usually the most self-satisfied people that he ever met. It was a casual remark, and perhaps neither he nor those who heard it appreciated its full significance. However, the preacher was probably thinking, not so much of Unitarians as of a certain kind of person often found in this neighborhood, and not necessarily professing any particular form of religion. We all know the type. When a man *invariably* has money in the bank, and is respectable and respected, was graduated at Harvard, has a decorous wife and children, has never been carried away by any passion or enthusiasm, knows the right people, and conforms strictly to the customs of good society; and when this sort of thing has been going on for, perhaps, two or three generations, then there is apt to creep into the blood a coldness that would chill the heart of a bronze statue. Such persons are really degenerates of their peculiar kind, and need to be saved, perhaps by desperate measures. Let them elope with the cook; let them get religion of a violent Methodistic, or of an intense Ritualistic, kind (the two forms have much in common); or if they cannot get religion, let them get a dog, give him the run of the house, love him and spoil him, and so, by the blessing of Providence, their salvation may be effected.

Reformers and philanthropists should always keep dogs, in order that the spontaneous element may not wholly die out of them. Their tendency is to regard the human race as a problem, and particular persons as 'cases' to be dealt with, not according to one's impulses, but according to certain rules approved by good authority, and supposed to be consistent with sound economic principles. To my old friend ——, who once liked me for myself, without asking why, I have long ceased to be an individual, and am now simply an item of humanity to whom he owes such duty as my particular wants or vices would seem to indicate. But if he had a dog he could not regard him in that impersonal way, or worry about the dog's morals: he would simply take pleasure in his society, and love him for what he was, without considering what he might have been.

I know and honor one philanthropist who, in middle life or thereabout, became for the first time the possessor of a dog; and thenceforth there was disclosed in him a genuine vein of sentiment and affection which many years of doing good and virtuous living had failed to eradicate. Often had I heard of his civic deeds and of his well-directed charities, but my heart never quite warmed toward him until I learned that, with spectacles on nose and comb in hand, he had spent three laborious hours in painfully going over his spaniel, and eliminating those parasitic guests which sometimes infest the coat of the cleanest and most aristocratic dog. I am not ashamed to say that I have a confidence in his wisdom now which I did not have before, knowing that his head will never be allowed to tyrannize over his heart. His name should be recorded here, were it not that his modesty might be offended by the act. (Three letters would suffice to print it.)

In speaking of the dog as a kind of missionary in the household, I mean, it need hardly be said, something more than mere ownership of the animal. It will not suffice to pay a large sum for a dog of fashionable breed, equip him with a costly collar, and then relegate him to the stable or the kitchen. He should be one of the family, living on equal terms with the others, and their constant companion. The dog's life is short at the best, and every moment of it will be needed for his development. It is wonderful how, year by year, the household pet grows in intelligence, how many words he learns the meaning of, how quick he becomes in interpreting the look, the tone of voice, the mood of the person whom he loves. He is old at ten or eleven, and seldom lives beyond thirteen or fourteen. If he lived to be fifty, he would know so much that we should be uneasy, perhaps terrified, in his presence.

A certain amount of discipline is necessary for a dog. If left to his own devices, he is apt to become somewhat dissipated, to spend his evenings out, to scatter among many the affection which should be reserved for a few. But, on the other hand, a dog may easily receive too much discipline; he becomes like the child of a despotic father. A dog perfectly trained, from the martinet point of view,—one who never 'jumps up' on you, never lays an entreating paw on your arm, never gets into a chair, or enters the drawing-room,—such a dog is a sad sight to one who really knows and loves the animal. It is against his nature to be so repressed. Over-careful housewives, and persons who are burdened with costly surroundings, talk of injury to carpets and other furniture if the dog has a right of entry everywhere in the house. But what is furniture for? Is it for display, is it a guaranty of the wealth of the owners, or is it for use? Blessed are they whose furniture is so inexpensive or so shabby that children and dogs are not excluded from its sacred precincts. Perhaps the happiest household to which I ever had the honor of being admitted was one where it was sometimes a little difficult to find a comfortable vacant chair: the dogs always took the arm-chairs. Alas, where are those hospitable chairs now? Where the dogs that used to sit up in them, and wink and yawn, and give their paws in humorous embarrassment?

'The drawing-room was made for dogs, and not dogs for the drawing-room,' would be Lady Barnes's thesis, did she formulate it. It was this same Lady Barnes—Rhoda Broughton's—who once said, 'I have no belief in Eliza, the housemaid I leave in charge here. When last I came down from London the dogs were so unnaturally good that I felt sure she bullied them. I spoke very seriously to her, and this time, I am glad to say, they are as disobedient as ever, and have done even more mischief than when I am at home.' And she laughed with a delicate relish of her own folly.

Of all writers of fiction, by the way, is there any whose dogs quite equal those of Rhoda Broughton? Even the beloved author of *Rab and His Friends*, even Sir Walter himself, with his immortal Dandie Dinmonts, has not, it seems to me, given us such life-like and home-like pictures of dogs as those which occur in her novels. They seem to be there, not of set purpose, but as if dogs were such an essential part of her own existence that they crept into her books almost without her knowing it. No room in her novels is complete without a dog or two; and every remark that she makes about them has the quality of a caress. Even in a tragic moment, the heroine cannot help observing, that 'Mink is lying on his small hairy side in a sunpatch, with his little paws crossed like the hands of a dying saint.' 'Mr Brown,' that dear, faithful mongrel, is forever associated with the unfortunate Joan; and Brenda's 'wouff' will go resounding down the halls of time so long as novels are read.

Perhaps the final test of anybody's love of dogs is willingness to permit them to make a camping-ground of the bed. There is no other place in the world that suits the dog quite so well. On the bed he is safe from being stepped upon; he is out of the way of draughts; he has a commanding position from which to survey what goes on in the world; and, above all, the surface is soft and yielding to his outstretched limbs. No mere man can ever be so comfortable as a dog looks.

Some persons object to having a dog on the bed at night; and it must be admitted that he lies a little heavily upon one's limbs; but why be so base as to prefer comfort to companionship! To wake up in the dark night, and put your hand on that warm soft body, to feel the beating of that faithful heart—is not this better than undisturbed sloth? The best night's rest I ever had was once when a cocker spaniel puppy, who had just recovered from stomach-ache (dose one to two soda-mints), and was a little frightened by the strange experience, curled up on my shoulder like a fur tippet, gently pushed his cold, soft nose into my neck, and there slept sweetly and soundly until morning.

Companionship with his master is the dog's remedy for every ill, and only an extreme case will justify sending him away or boarding him out. To put a dog in a hospital, unless there is some surgical or other like necessity for doing so, is an act of doubtful kindness. Many and many a dog has died from homesickness. If he is ill, keep him warm and quiet, give him such simple remedies as you would give to a child: pour beef tea or malted milk down his throat, or even a little whiskey, if he is weak from want of food; and let him live or die, as did our fathers and our fathers' dogs—at home.

Many dogs are sensitive to an excessive degree, so sensitive indeed that any correction of them, beyond such as can be conveyed by a word, amounts to positive cruelty. A dog of that kind may easily be thrown by harsh treatment into a state of nervous disorder, and will be really unable to do what is required of him. In that state he often presents an appearance of obstinacy, whereas in fact he is suffering from a sort of nervous atrophy or paralysis, closely resembling that of a 'balky' horse.

This nervous temperament makes the dog susceptible to misery in many forms, but the worst evil that can befall is to be lost. The very words 'lost dog' call up such pictures of canine misery as can never be forgotten by those who have witnessed them. I have seen a lost dog, lame, emaciated, wounded, footsore, hungry, and thirsty, yet suffering so intensely from fear, and loneliness, and despair,—from the mere sense of being lost,—as to be absolutely unconscious of his bodily condition. The mental agony was so much greater that it swallowed up the physical pain.

A little Boston terrier, who was lost in a large city for two or three days, became so wrecked in his nervous system that no amount of care or petting could restore him to equanimity, and it was found necessary to kill him. Oh, reader, pass not by the lost dog! Succor him if you can; preserve him from what is worse than death. It is easy to recognize him by the look of nervous terror in his eye, by his drooping tail, by his uncertain movements.

There is a remorseful experience of my own, of which I should be glad to unburden myself to the reader. It once became my duty to kill a dog afflicted with some incurable disease. Instead of doing it myself, as I should have done, I took him to a place where lost dogs are received, and where those for whom no home can be found are mercifully destroyed. There, instead of myself leading him to the death-chamber, as, again, I should have done, I handed him over to the executioner. The dog was an abnormally nervous and timid one; and as he was dragged most unwillingly away, he turned around, as nearly as he could, and cast back at me a look of horror, of fear, of agonized appeal—a look that has haunted me for years.

Whether he had any inkling of what was in store for him, I do not know, but it is highly probable that he had. Dogs and other animals are wonderful mind-readers. I have known three cases in which some discussion about the necessity of killing an old dog, held in his presence, was quickly followed by the sudden, unaccountable disappearance of the animal; and no tidings of him could ever be obtained, although the greatest pains were taken to obtain them. Horses are inferior only to dogs in this capacity. Often, especially in the case of vicious or half-broken horses, an intention will flash from the mind of the horse to the mind of the rider or driver, and *vice versa*, without the slightest indication being given by horse or man. Men who ride race-horses have told me that a sudden conviction in their own minds, in the course of a race, that they could not win has passed immediately to the horse, and caused him to slacken his speed, although they had not ceased to urge him. It is notorious in the trotting world that faint-hearted and pessimistic drivers often lose races which they ought to win.

As to remarkable stories about this or that animal, perhaps it might be said that they are probably true when they illustrate the animal's perceptive abilities, and are probably false when they depend upon his power to originate. There appeared lately an account of a race between loons in the wild state: how the loons got together and arranged the preliminaries (whether they made books on the event or adopted the pool system of betting was not stated), how the race was run, or rather flown, amid intense loon excitement, and how the victor was greeted with screams of applause!

Some power of origination animals, and dogs especially, certainly have. There is the familiar trick which dogs play when one, to get a bone away from another, rushes off a little space, gives the bark which signifies the presence of an intruder, then comes back and quietly runs away with the bone which the other dog, in his curiosity to see who is coming, has impulsively dropped. This is an example, not of reasoning only, but of origination.

In general, however, when dogs surprise us, as they frequently do, it is by the delicacy and acuteness of their perceptive powers. How unerringly do they distinguish between different classes of persons, as, for example, between the members of the family and the servants; and again, between the servants and the friends of the household! Unquestionably the dog has three sets of manners for these three classes of persons. He will take liberties in the kitchen that he would never dream of taking in the dining-room. We have known our cook to fly in terror from the kitchen because Figaro, a masterful cocker spaniel, threatened to bite her if she did not give him a piece of meat forthwith. Figaro reasoned that the cook was partly *his* cook, and that he had a right to bully her if he could.

As for the different members of the family, the dog will 'size them up' with an unerring instinct. It is impossible to conceal any weakness of character from him; and if you are strong, he will know that, too. As I write these lines, the vision of 'Mr Guppy' rises before me. Mr Guppy was a very small Boston terrier with a white head, but otherwise of a brindle color. He had a beautiful 'mug,' much like that of a bull dog, with a short nose, wide jaws, and plenty of loose skin hanging about his stout little neck. It must be admitted that he was somewhat self-indulgent, being continually on the watch for a chance to lie close by the fire—a situation considered by his friends to be unwholesome for him. Mr Guppy understood me very well. He knew that I was a poor, weak, easy-going, absent-minded creature, with whom he could take liberties; accordingly, when we were alone together, the rogue would lie sleeping with his head on the hearth, while I was absorbed in my book. But hark! there is a step on the stairs, of one whom Mr Guppy both loved and feared more than any dog ever loved or feared me; and forthwith the little impostor would rise and crawl softly back to his place on a rug in the corner; and there he would be found lying and winking, with an expression of perfect innocence, when the disciplinarian entered the room.

Dogs have the same sensitiveness that we associate with well-bred men and women. Their politeness is remarkable. Offer a dog water when he is not thirsty, and he will almost always take a lap or two, just out of civility, and to show his gratitude. I know a group of dogs that never forget to come and tell their mistress when they have had their dinner, feeling sure that she will sympathize with them; and if they have failed to get it, they will notify her immediately of the omission. If you happen to step on a dog's tail or paw, how eagerly—after one irrepressible yelp of pain—will he tell you by his caresses that he knows you did not mean to hurt him and forgives you!

In their relations with one another, also, dogs have a keen sense of etiquette. A well-known traveler makes this unexpected remark about a tribe of naked black men, living on one of the South Sea Islands: 'In their everyday intercourse there is much that is stiff, formal, and precise.' Almost the same remark might be made about dogs. Unless they are on very intimate terms, they take great pains never to brush against or even to touch one another. For one dog to step over another is a dangerous breach of etiquette unless they are special friends. It is no uncommon thing for two dogs to belong to the same person, and live in the same house, and yet never take the slightest notice of each other. We have a spaniel so dignified that he will never permit another member of the dog family to pillow his head on him; but, with the egotism of a true aristocrat, he does not hesitate to make use of the other dogs for that purpose.

Often canine etiquette is so subtle that one has much difficulty in following it out. In our household are two uncongenial dogs, who, in ordinary circumstances, completely ignore each other, and between whom any familiarity would be resented fiercely. And yet, when we are all out walking, if I am obliged to scold or punish one of these two, the other will run up to the offender, bark at him, and even jostle him, as if he were saying, 'Well, old man, you got it that time; aren't you ashamed of yourself?' And the other dog, feeling that he is in the wrong, I suppose, submits meekly to the insult.

A family of six dogs used to pair off in couples, each couple being on terms of special intimacy and affection; and besides these relationships, there were many others among them. For example, they all deferred to the oldest dog, although he was smaller and weaker than the rest. If a fight began, he would jump in between the contestants and stop it; if a dog misbehaved, he would rush at the offender with a warning growl; and this exercise of authority was never resented. The other dogs seemed to respect his weight of years, his character, which was of the highest, and his moral courage, which was undoubted. This same dog—his name was Pedro—had many human traits. He and his companions slept together on a sofa upstairs, where, of a cold night, they would curl up together in an indistinguishable heap. Sometimes the old dog would put himself to bed before the others, and then, finding that he needed the warmth and companionship of their presence, he would go into the hall, put his head between the balusters, and whine softly until they came upstairs to join him.

That animals reason is a fact of everyday experience. That they can communicate their wants and feelings to one another and to man is equally plain. 'When a cat or a dog,' wrote the late Mr Romanes, 'pulls one's dress to lead one to the kittens or puppies in need of assistance, the animal is behaving in the same manner as a deaf mute might behave when invoking assistance from a friend. That is to say, the animal is translating the logic of feelings into the logic of signs; and so far as this particular action is concerned, it is psychologically indistinguishable from that which is performed by the deaf mute.'

Mentally, we are not so many epochs removed from the other animals, and emotionally the connection is closer yet. I will not discuss the question whether dumb animals have any sense of right and wrong. I believe that they have this sense in a rudimentary degree; or at least that it is latent in them, and may be developed. The popular instinctive notions about animals, the result of the experience of the race, seem to justify this view. 'If we say a *vicious* horse,' remarked Dr Arnold, 'why not a *virtuous* horse?' And we do speak of a 'kind' horse.

Moreover, it is obvious that dogs have a sense of humor; and they have also a sense of shame, perfectly distinct from the fear of punishment. Of this sense of shame let me give one example. The dog's eyesight, so far at least as stationary objects are concerned, is very poor, his real reliance being on his sense of smell; and I have often seen a dog mistake one of his own family for a strange animal, run toward him, with every sign of hostility, and then, when he came within a few feet of the other dog, suddenly drop his tail between his legs and slink away, as if he feared that somebody had noticed his absurd mistake.

Can it be that an animal should possess a sense of humor and a sense of shame, without having also some elementary sense of right and wrong? But even if it be thought that he is devoid of that sense, it is certain that he has those kindly impulses from which it has been developed. All that is best in man springs from something which is practically the same in the dog that it is in him, namely, the instinct of pity or benevolence. To that instinct, as it exists in the lower animals, Darwin attributed the origin of conscience in man; and there are now few, if any, philosophers who would give a different account of it.

I have seen a pup not six months old run to comfort another pup that cried out from pain; and the impulse that prompted this act was essentially the same as that which impels the noblest of mankind when they befriend the poor or the afflicted. We are akin to the lower animals morally, as well as physically and mentally.

But this is a modern discovery. It is astonishing and confusing to realize how little organized Christianity has done for the lower animals. The ecclesiastical conception of them was simply that they were creatures without souls, and therefore had no rights as against, or at the hands of, mankind. To this day that conception remains, although it is qualified, of course, by other and more humane considerations. Even Cardinal Newman said,—

'We have no duties toward the brute creation; there is no relation of justice between them and us. Of course, we are bound not to treat them ill, for cruelty is an offense against the holy law which our Maker has written on our hearts, and it is displeasing to Him. But they can claim nothing at our hand; into our hand they are absolutely delivered. We may use them, we may destroy them at our pleasure: not our wanton pleasure, but still for our own ends, for our own benefit and satisfaction, provided that we can give a rational account of what we do.'

This position, although not perhaps cruel in itself, inevitably results in immeasurable cruelties. When an English traveler remonstrated with a Spanish lady for throwing a sick kitten out of the second-story window, she justified herself by saying that the kitten had no soul; and that is the national point of view.

Protestantism has been almost as indifferent as Catholicism to the lower animals. In fact, the conscience which exists outside of the church, Catholic or Protestant, has in this matter, outstripped the conscience of the church. 'Cruelty,' said Du Maurier, 'is the only unpardonable sin'; and the world is slowly but surely coming to that opinion. The long-deferred awakening of mankind to the sufferings of dumb animals was not due to a decline of the ecclesiastical conception of them, although it has declined; nor even to the new knowledge concerning the common origin of man and beast—indeed, it slightly preceded that knowledge; but it was due to the gradual enlightenment and moral improvement of the race, especially of the English-speaking race.

The nineteenth century, as we are often told, saw more discoveries and inventions than had been made in the preceding six thousand years; but I believe that in future ages not one of those discoveries and inventions, nor all together, will bulk so large as factors in the development and uplifting of man, as will those humane laws and societies which first came into existence in that century.

We overvalue intellectual as compared with moral and emotional gifts. The material civilization upon which we pride ourselves is almost wholly the achievement of the intellect. Fame and wealth, luxury, cultivation, and leisure,—all the big prizes of the world, in fact,—are obtained by the successful exercise of the intellect. The moral qualities, of themselves, can procure us nothing but a clear conscience, and the approval, perhaps mixed with contempt, of our neighbors.

And yet, when the intellectual qualities are brought to the test of reality; when one's view of them is not clouded by pride, avarice, or passion, then how amazingly does their value shrink and shrivel! When a man lies on his deathbed, for example, his intellectual achievements, though of the highest order, will seem as nothing to him—he will ask himself simply whether he has lived a good or a bad life; and after his death his family and his friends will look at the matter in precisely the same way.

Even the progress of mankind is far more moral than intellectual. Competent authorities tell us that the Anglo-Saxon of to-day is mentally inferior to the Greek who lived two thousand years ago: and if the human race has improved during that time, it is not so much because man has advanced in knowledge as because he has acquired more sympathy with his inferiors, be they brute or human, more generosity, more mercy toward them. Not Stevenson, nor Faraday, nor Morse, nor Fulton, nor Bell, did so much for the human race, to say nothing of the other animals, as did that dueling Irishman who, in the year 1822, proposed in the English Parliament, amid shrieks and howls of derision, what afterward became the first law for the protection of dumb animals ever placed on the statute-book of any country. Every movement for the relief of the brute creation has originated in England; and when we damn, as we righteously may, John Bull for one thing and another, let us remember this fact to his eternal honor!

It is hard to part from an old dog-friend with no hope of ever meeting him again, hard to believe that the spirit of love which burned so steadfastly in him is quenched forever. But for those who hold what I have called the ecclesiastical conception of the lower animals, no other view is possible. That devout Catholic and exquisite poet, Dr Parsons, has beautifully expressed this fact:

> When parents die there's many a word to say—
> Kind words, consoling—one can always pray;
> When children die 't is natural to tell
> Their mother, 'Certainly with them 't is well!'
> But for a dog, 't was all the life he had,
> Since death is end of dogs, or good or bad.
> This was his world, he was contented here;
> Imagined nothing better, naught more dear,
> Than his young mistress; sought no higher sphere;
> Having no sin, asked not to be forgiven;
> Ne'er guessed at God nor ever dreamed of heaven.
> Now he has passed away, so much of love
> Goes from our life, without one hope above!

But is there no hope? Is there not as much—or, if the reader prefers, as little—hope for the dog as there is for man? I remember reading years ago in a prominent magazine the statement that doubtless a few men, the very wickedest, will become extinct at death, whereas the rest of mankind will be immortal. This view had some adherents then, but would now be regarded by almost everybody as irrational. Who can believe that between the best and the worst man there is any such gulf as would justify so diverse a fate!

Moreover we have learned that there are no chasms or jumps in nature. One thing slides into another; every creature is a link between two other creatures; and man himself can be traced back physically, mentally, and morally, to the lower animals. Is it not then reasonable to suppose that immortality belongs to all forms of life or to none? that if man is immortal, the dog is immortal, too? Even to speculate upon this subject seems almost ridiculous, our knowledge is so limited; and yet it is hard to refrain from speculation. The transmigration of souls may be a fact, or men and dogs and all other forms of life may be simply forms, temporary phases, proceeding from one source, and returning thereto. But alas, every supposition that we can make is rendered almost, if not quite, untenable by the mere fact that the human intellect has conceived it—it is so unlikely that we should hit upon the right solution!

In this situation, what we seem bound to do is to refrain from hasty, and especially from egotistic conclusions, to keep our minds open, to regard the lower animals, not only with pity, but with a certain reverence. We do not know what or whence they are; but we do know that their nature resembles ours; that they have Individuality, as we have it; that they feel pain, both physical and mental; that they are capable of affection; that, although innocent, as we believe, their sufferings have been, and are, unspeakable. Is there no mystery here?

To many men, to most men, perhaps, a dog is simply an animated machine, developed or created for the convenience of the human race. It may be so; and yet again it may be that the dog has his own rightful place in the universe, irrespective and independent of man, and that an injury done to him is an insult to the Creator.

40

THE FIFTY-FIRST DRAGON

Heywood Broun

Of all the pupils at the knight school Gawaine le Cœur-Hardy was among the least promising. He was tall and sturdy, but his instructors soon discovered that he lacked spirit. He would hide in the woods when the jousting class was called, although his companions and members of the faculty sought to appeal to his better nature by shouting to him to come out and break his neck like a man. Even when they told him that the lances were padded, the horses no more than ponies and the field unusually soft for late autumn, Gawaine refused to grow enthusiastic. The Headmaster and the Assistant Professor of Pleasaunce were discussing the case one spring afternoon and the Assistant Professor could see no remedy but expulsion.

'No,' said the Headmaster, as he looked out at the purple hills which ringed the school, 'I think I'll train him to slay dragons.'

'He might be killed,' objected the Assistant Professor.

'So he might,' replied the Headmaster brightly, but he added, more soberly, 'we must consider the greater good. We are responsible for the formation of this lad's character.'

'Are the dragons particularly bad this year?' interrupted the Assistant Professor. This was characteristic. He always seemed restive when the head of the school began to talk ethics and the ideals of the institution.

'I've never known them worse,' replied the Headmaster. 'Up in the hills to the south last week they killed a number of peasants, two cows and a prize pig. And if this dry spell holds there's no telling when they may start a forest fire simply by breathing around indiscriminately.'

'Would any refund on the tuition fee be necessary in case of an accident to young Cœur-Hardy?'

'No,' the principal answered, judicially, 'that's all covered in the contract. But as a matter of fact he won't be killed. Before I send him up in the hills I'm going to give him a magic word.'

'That's a good idea,' said the Professor. 'Sometimes they work wonders.'

From that day on Gawaine specialized in dragons. His course included both theory and practice. In the morning there were long lectures on the history, anatomy, manners and customs of dragons. Gawaine did not distinguish himself in these studies. He had a marvelously versatile gift for forgetting things. In the afternoon he showed to better advantage, for then he would go down to the South Meadow and practice with a battle-ax. In this exercise he was truly impressive, for he had enormous strength as well as speed and grace. He even developed a deceptive display of ferocity. Old alumni say that it was a thrilling sight to see Gawaine charging across the field toward the dummy paper dragon which had been set up for his practice. As he ran he would brandish his ax and shout 'A murrain on thee!' or some other vivid bit of campus slang. It never took him more than one stroke to behead the dummy dragon.

Gradually his task was made more difficult. Paper gave way to papier-mâché and finally to wood, but even the toughest of these dummy dragons had no terrors for Gawaine. One sweep of the ax always did the business. There were those who said that when the practice was protracted until dusk and the dragons threw long, fantastic shadows across the meadow Gawaine did not charge so impetuously nor shout so loudly. It is possible there was malice in this charge. At any rate, the Headmaster decided by the end of June that it was time for the test. Only the night before a dragon had come close to the school grounds and had eaten some of the lettuce from the garden. The faculty decided that Gawaine was ready. They gave him a diploma and a new battle-ax and the Headmaster summoned him to a private conference.

'Sit down,' said the Headmaster. 'Have a cigarette.'

Gawaine hesitated.

'Oh, I know it's against the rules,' said the Headmaster. 'But after all, you have received your preliminary degree. You are no longer a boy. You are a man. To-morrow you will go out into the world, the great world of achievement.'

Gawaine took a cigarette. The Headmaster offered him a match, but he produced one of his own and began to puff away with a dexterity which quite amazed the principal.

'Here you have learned the theories of life,' continued the Headmaster, resuming the thread of his discourse, 'but after all, life is not a matter of theories. Life is a matter of facts. It calls on the young and the old alike to face these facts, even though they are hard and sometimes unpleasant. Your problem, for example, is to slay dragons.'

'They say that those dragons down in the south wood are five hundred feet long,' ventured Gawaine, timorously.

'Stuff and nonsense!' said the Headmaster. 'The curate saw one last week from the top of Arthur's Hill. The dragon was sunning himself down in the valley. The curate didn't have an opportunity to look at him very long because he felt it was his duty to hurry back to make a report to me. He said the monster, or shall I say, the big lizard?—wasn't an inch over two hundred feet. But the size has nothing at all to do with it. You'll find the big ones even easier than the little ones. They're far slower on their feet and less aggressive, I'm told. Besides, before you go I'm going to equip you in such fashion that you need have no fear of all the dragons in the world.'

'I'd like an enchanted cap,' said Gawaine.

'What's that?' answered the Headmaster, testily.

'A cap to make me disappear,' explained Gawaine.

The Headmaster laughed indulgently. 'You mustn't believe all those old wives' stories,' he said. 'There isn't any such thing. A cap to make you disappear, indeed! What would you do with it? You haven't even appeared yet. Why, my boy, you could walk from here to London, and nobody would so much as look at you. You're nobody. You couldn't be more invisible than that.'

Gawaine seemed dangerously close to a relapse into his old habit of whimpering. The Headmaster reassured him: 'Don't worry; I'll give you something much better than an enchanted cap. I'm going to give you a magic word. All you have to do is to repeat this magic charm once and no dragon can possibly harm a hair of your head. You can cut off his head at your leisure.'

He took a heavy book from the shelf behind his desk and began to run through it. 'Sometimes,' he said, 'the charm is a whole phrase or even a sentence. I might, for instance, give you "To make the"—No, that might not do. I think a single word would be best for dragons.'

'A short word,' suggested Gawaine.

'It can't be too short or it wouldn't be potent. There isn't so much hurry as all that. Here's a splendid magic word: "Rumplesnitz." Do you think you can learn that?'

Gawaine tried and in an hour or so he seemed to have the word well in hand. Again and again he interrupted the lesson to inquire, 'And if I say "Rumplesnitz" the dragon can't possibly hurt me?' And always the Headmaster replied, 'If you only say "Rumplesnitz," you are perfectly safe.'

Toward morning Gawaine seemed resigned to his career. At daybreak the Headmaster saw him to the edge of the forest and pointed him to the direction in which he should proceed. About a mile away to the southwest a cloud of steam hovered over an open meadow in the woods and the Headmaster assured Gawaine that under the steam he would find a dragon. Gawaine went forward slowly. He wondered whether it would be best to approach the dragon on the run as he did in his practice in the South Meadow or to walk slowly toward him, shouting 'Rumplesnitz' all the way.

The problem was decided for him. No sooner had he come to the fringe of the meadow than the dragon spied him and began to charge. It was a large dragon and yet it seemed decidedly aggressive in spite of the Headmaster's statement to the contrary. As the dragon charged it released huge clouds of hissing steam through its nostrils. It was almost as if a gigantic teapot had gone mad. The dragon came forward so fast and Gawaine was so frightened that he had time to say 'Rumplesnitz' only once. As he said it, he swung his battle-ax and off popped the head of the dragon. Gawaine had to admit that it was even easier to kill a real dragon than a wooden one if only you said 'Rumplesnitz.'

Gawaine brought the ears home and a small section of the tail. His school mates and the faculty made much of him, but the Headmaster wisely kept him from being spoiled by insisting that he go on with his work. Every clear day Gawaine rose at dawn and went out to kill dragons. The Headmaster kept him at home when it rained, because he said the woods were damp and unhealthy at such times and that he didn't want the boy to run needless risks. Few good days passed in which Gawaine failed to get a dragon. On one particularly fortunate day he killed three, a husband and wife and a visiting relative. Gradually he developed a technique. Pupils who sometimes watched him from the hill-tops a long way off said that he often allowed the dragon to come within a few feet before he said 'Rumplesnitz.' He came to say it with a mocking sneer. Occasionally he did stunts. Once when an excursion party from London was watching him he went into action with his right hand tied behind his back. The dragon's head came off just as easily.

As Gawaine's record of killings mounted higher the Headmaster found it impossible to keep him completely in hand. He fell into the habit of stealing out at night and engaging in long drinking bouts at the village tavern. It was after such a debauch that he rose a little before dawn one fine August morning and started out after his fiftieth dragon. His head was heavy and his mind sluggish. He was heavy in other respects as well, for he had adopted the somewhat vulgar practice of wearing his medals, ribbons and all, when he went out dragon hunting. The decorations began on his chest and ran all the way down to his abdomen. They must have weighed at least eight pounds.

Gawaine found a dragon in the same meadow where he had killed the first one. It was a fair-sized dragon, but evidently an old one. Its face was wrinkled and Gawaine thought he had never seen so hideous a countenance. Much to the lad's disgust, the monster refused to charge and Gawaine was obliged to walk toward him. He whistled as he went. The dragon regarded him hopelessly, but craftily. Of course it had heard of Gawaine. Even when the lad raised his battle-ax the dragon made no move. It knew that there was no salvation in the quickest thrust of the head, for it had been informed that this hunter was protected by an enchantment. It merely waited, hoping something would turn up. Gawaine raised the battle-ax and suddenly lowered it again. He had grown very pale and he trembled violently. The dragon suspected a trick. 'What's the matter?' it asked, with false solicitude.

'I've forgotten the magic word,' stammered Gawaine.

'What a pity,' said the dragon. 'So that was the secret. It doesn't seem quite sporting to me, all this magic stuff, you know. Not cricket, as we used to say when I was a little dragon; but after all, that's a matter of opinion.'

Gawaine was so helpless with terror that the dragon's confidence rose immeasurably and it could not resist the temptation to show off a bit.

'Could I possibly be of any assistance?' it asked. 'What's the first letter of the magic word?'

'It begins with an "r,"' said Gawaine weakly.

'Let's see,' mused the dragon, 'that doesn't tell us much, does it? What sort of a word is this? Is it an epithet, do you think?'

Gawaine could do no more than nod.

'Why, of course,' exclaimed the dragon, 'reactionary Republican.'

Gawaine shook his head.

'Well, then,' said the dragon, 'we'd better get down to business. Will you surrender?'

With the suggestion of a compromise Gawaine mustered up enough courage to speak.

'What will you do if I surrender?' he asked.

'Why, I'll eat you,' said the dragon.

'And if I don't surrender?'

'I'll eat you just the same.'

'Then it doesn't mean any difference, does it?' moaned Gawaine.

'It does to me,' said the dragon with a smile. 'I'd rather you didn't surrender. You'd taste much better if you didn't.'

The dragon waited for a long time for Gawaine to ask 'Why?' but the boy was too frightened to speak. At last the dragon had to give the explanation without his cue line. 'You see,' he said, 'if you don't surrender you'll taste better because you'll die game.'

This was an old and ancient trick of the dragon's. By means of some such quip he was accustomed to paralyze his victims with laughter and then to destroy them. Gawaine was sufficiently paralyzed as it was, but laughter had no part in his helplessness. With the last word of the joke the dragon drew back his head and struck. In that second there flashed into the mind of Gawaine the magic word 'Rumplesnitz,' but there was no time to say it. There was time only to strike and, without a word, Gawaine met the onrush of the dragon with a full swing. He put all his back and shoulders into it. The impact was terrific and the head of the dragon flew away almost a hundred yards and landed in a thicket.

Gawaine did not remain frightened very long after the death of the dragon. His mood was one of wonder. He was enormously puzzled. He cut off the ears of the monster almost in a trance. Again and again he thought to himself, 'I didn't say "Rumplesnitz"!' He was sure of that and yet there was no question that he had killed the dragon. In fact, he had never killed one so utterly. Never before had he driven a head for anything like the same distance. Twenty-five yards was perhaps his best previous record. All the way back to the knight school he kept rumbling about in his mind seeking an explanation for what had occurred. He went to the Headmaster immediately and after closing the door told him what had happened. 'I didn't say "Rumplesnitz,"' he explained with great earnestness.

The Headmaster laughed. 'I'm glad you've found out,' he said. 'It makes you ever so much more of a hero. Don't you see that? Now you know that it was you who killed all these dragons and not that foolish little word "Rumplesnitz."'

Gawaine frowned. 'Then it wasn't a magic word after all?' he asked.

'Of course not,' said the Headmaster, 'you ought to be too old for such foolishness. There isn't any such thing as a magic word.'

'But you told me it was magic,' protested Gawaine. 'You said it was magic and now you say it isn't.'

'It wasn't magic in a literal sense,' answered the Headmaster, 'but it was much more wonderful than that. The word gave you confidence. It took away your fears. If I hadn't told you that you might have been killed the very first time. It was your battle-ax did the trick.'

Gawaine surprised the Headmaster by his attitude. He was obviously distressed by the explanation. He interrupted a long philosophic and ethical discourse by the Headmaster with, 'If I hadn't of hit 'em all mighty hard and fast any one of 'em might have crushed me like a, like a—' He fumbled for a word.

'Egg shell,' suggested the Headmaster.

'Like a egg shell,' assented Gawaine, and he said it many times. All through the evening meal people who sat near him heard him muttering, 'Like a egg shell, like a egg shell.'

The next day was clear, but Gawaine did not get up at dawn. Indeed, it was almost noon when the Headmaster found him cowering in bed, with the clothes pulled over his head. The principal called the Assistant Professor of Pleasaunce, and together they dragged the boy toward the forest.

'He'll be all right as soon as he gets a couple more dragons under his belt,' explained the Headmaster.

The Assistant Professor of Pleasaunce agreed. 'It would be a shame to stop such a fine run,' he said. 'Why, counting that one yesterday, he's killed fifty dragons.'

They pushed the boy into a thicket above which hung a meager cloud of steam. It was obviously quite a small dragon. But Gawaine did not come back that night or the next. In fact, he never came back. Some weeks afterward brave spirits from the school explored the thicket, but they could find nothing to remind them of Gawaine except the metal parts of his medals. Even the ribbons had been devoured.

The Headmaster and the Assistant Professor of Pleasaunce agreed that it would be just as well not to tell the school how Gawaine had achieved his record and still less how he came to die. They held that it might have a bad effect on school spirit. Accordingly, Gawaine has lived in the memory of the school as its greatest hero. No visitor succeeds in leaving the building to-day without seeing a great shield which hangs on the wall of the dining hall. Fifty pairs of dragons' ears are mounted upon the shield and underneath in gilt letters is 'Gawaine le Cœur-Hardy,' followed by the simple inscription, 'He killed fifty dragons.' The record has never been equaled.

41

O. HENRY

O. W. Firkins

There are two opinions concerning O. Henry. The middle class views him as the impersonation of vigor and brilliancy; part of the higher criticism sees in him little but sensation and persiflage. Between these views there is a natural relation; the gods of the heathens are *ipso facto* the demons of Christianity. Unmixed assertions, however, are commonly mixtures of truth and falsehood; there is room to-day for an estimate which shall respect both opinions and adopt neither.

There is one literary trait in which I am unable to name any writer of tales in any literature who surpasses O. Henry. It is not primary or even secondary among literary merits; it is less a value *per se* than the condition or foundation of values. But its utility is manifest, and it is rare among men: Chaucer and Shakespeare prove the possibility of its absence in masters of that very branch of art in which its presence would seem to be imperative. I refer to the designing of stories—not to the primary intuition or to skill in development, in both of which finer phases of invention O. Henry has been largely and frequently surpassed, but to the disposition of masses, to the blocking-out of plots. That a half-educated American provincial should have been original in a field in which original men have been copyists is enough of itself to make his personality observable.

Illustration, even of conceded truths, is rarely superfluous. I supply two instances. Two lads, parting in New York, agree to meet 'After Twenty Years' at a specified hour, date, and corner. Both are faithful; but the years in which their relation has slept in mutual silence and ignorance have turned the one into a dashing criminal, the other into a sober officer of the law. Behind the picturesque and captivating rendezvous lurks a powerful dramatic situation and a moral problem of arresting gravity. This is dealt with in six pages of the 'Four Million.' The 'Furnished Room,' two stories further on, occupies twelve pages. Through the wilderness of apartments on the lower West Side a man trails a woman. Chance leads him to the very room in which the woman ended her life the week before. Between him and the truth the avarice of a sordid landlady interposes the curtain of a lie. In the bed in which the girl slept and died, the man sleeps and dies, and the entrance of the deadly fumes into his nostrils shuts the sinister and mournful coincidence forever from the knowledge of mankind. O. Henry gave these tales neither extension nor prominence; so far as I know, they were received without bravos or salvos. The distinction of a body of work in which such specimens are undistinguished hardly requires comment.

A few types among these stories may be specified. There are the Sydney Cartonisms, defined in the name; love-stories in which divided hearts, or simply divided persons, are brought together by the strategy of chance; hoax stories—deft pictures of smiling roguery; 'prince and pauper' stories, in which wealth and poverty face each other, sometimes enact each other; disguise stories, in which the wrong clothes often draw the wrong bullets; complemental stories, in which Jim sacrifices his beloved watch to buy combs for Della, who, meanwhile, has sacrificed her beloved hair to buy a chain for Jim.

This imperfect list is eloquent in its way; it smooths our path to the assertion that O. Henry's specialty is the enlistment of original method in the service of traditional appeals. The ends are the ends of fifty years ago; O. Henry transports us by aeroplane to the old homestead.

Criticism of O. Henry falls into those superlatives and antitheses in which his own faculty delighted. In mechanical invention he is almost the leader of his race. In a related quality—a defect—his leadership is even more conspicuous. I doubt if the sense of the probable, or, more precisely, of the available in the improbable, ever became equally weakened or deadened in a man who made his living by its exercise. The improbable, even the impossible, has its place in art, though that place is relatively low; and it is curious that works such as the *Arabian Nights* and Grimm's fairy tales, whose stock-in-trade is the incredible, are the works which give almost no trouble on the score of verisimilitude. The truth is that we reject not what it is impossible to prove, or even what it is possible to disprove, but what it is impossible to imagine. O. Henry asks us to imagine the unimaginable—that is his crime.

The right and wrong improbabilities may be illustrated from two burglar stories. 'Sixes and Sevens' contains an excellent tale of a burglar and a citizen who fraternize, in a comic midnight interview, on the score of their common sufferings from rheumatism. This feeling in practice would not triumph over fear and greed; but the feeling is natural, and everybody with a grain of nature in him can imagine its triumph. Nature *tends* towards that impossibility, and art, lifting, so to speak, the lid which fact drops upon nature, reveals nature in belying fact. In another story, in 'Whirligigs,' a nocturnal interview takes place in which a burglar and a small boy discuss the etiquette of their mutual relation by formulas derived from short stories with which both are amazingly conversant. This is the wrong use of the improbable. Even an imagination inured to the virtues of burglars and the maturity of small boys will have naught to do with this insanity.

But O. Henry can go further yet. There are inventions in his tales the very utterance of which—not the mere substance but the utterance—on the part of a man not writing from Bedlam or for Bedlam impresses the reader as incredible. In a 'Comedy in Rubber,' two persons become so used to spectatorship at transactions in the street that they drift into the part of spectators when the transaction is their own wedding. Can human daring or human folly go further? O. Henry is on the spot to prove that they can. In the 'Romance of a Busy Broker,' a busy and forgetful man, in a freak of absent-mindedness, offers his hand to the stenographer *whom he had married the night before.*

The other day, in the journal of the Goncourts, I came upon the following sentence: 'Never will the imagination approach the improbabilities and the antitheses of truth' (II, 9). This is dated February 21, 1862. Truth had still the advantage. O. Henry was not born till September of the same year.

Passing on to style, we are still in the land of antithesis. The style is gross—and fine. Of the plenitude of its stimulus, there can be no question. In 'Sixes and Sevens,' a young man sinking under accidental morphia, is kept awake and alive by shouts, kicks, and blows. O. Henry's public seems imaged in that young man. But I draw a sharp distinction between the *tone* of the style and its *pattern*. The tone is brazen, or, better perhaps, brassy; its self-advertisement is incorrigible; it reeks with that air of *performance* which is opposed to real efficiency. But the pattern is another matter. The South rounds its periods like its vowels; O. Henry has read, not widely, but wisely, in his boyhood. His sentences are *built*—a rare thing in the best writers of to-day. In conciseness, that Spartan virtue, he was strong, though it must be confessed that the tale-teller was now and then hustled from the rostrum by his rival and enemy, the talker. He can introduce a felicity with a noiselessness that numbers him for a flying second among the sovereigns of English. 'In one of the second-floor front windows Mrs McCaskey awaited her husband. Supper was cooling on the table. Its heat went into Mrs McCaskey.'

I regret the tomfoolery; I wince at the slang. Yet even for these levities with which his pages are so liberally besprinkled or bedaubed, some half-apology may be circumspectly urged. In nonsense his ease is consummate. A horseman who should dismount to pick up a bauble would be childish; O. Henry picks it up without dismounting. Slang, again, is most pardonable in the man with whom its use is least exclusive and least necessary. There are men who, going for a walk, take their dogs with them; there are other men who give a walk to their dogs. Substitute slang for the dog, and the superiority of the first class to the second will exactly illustrate the superiority of O. Henry to the abject traffickers in slang.

In the 'Pendulum' Katy has a new patch in her crazy quilt which the ice man cut from the end of his four-in-hand. In the 'Day We Celebrate,' threading the mazes of a banana grove is compared to 'paging the palm room of a New York hotel for a man named Smith.' O. Henry's is the type of mind to which images like this four-in-hand and this palm room are presented in exhaustless abundance and unflagging continuity. There was hardly an object in the merry-go-round of civilized life that had not offered at least an end or an edge to the avidity of his consuming eyes. Nothing escapes from the besom of his allusiveness, and the style is streaked and pied, almost to monotony, by the accumulation of lively details.

If O. Henry's style was crude, it was also rare; but it is part of the grimness of the bargain that destiny drives with us that the mixture of the crude and the rare should be a crude mixture, as the sons of whites and negroes are numbered with the blacks. In the kingdom of style O. Henry's estates were princely, but, to pay his debts, he must have sold them all.

Thus far in our inquiry extraordinary merits have been offset by extraordinary defects. To lift our author out of the class of brilliant and skilful entertainers, more is needed. Is more forthcoming? I should answer, yes. In O. Henry, above the knowledge of setting, which is clear and first-hand, but subsidiary, above the order of events, which is, generally speaking, fantastic, above the emotions, which are sound and warm, but almost purely derivative, there is a rather small, but impressive body of first-hand perspicacities and reactions. On these his endurance may hinge.

I name, first of all, O. Henry's feeling for New York. With the exception of his New Orleans, I care little for his South and West, which are a boyish South and West, and as little, or even less, for his Spanish-American communities. My objection to his opera-bouffe republics is, not that they are inadequate as republics (for that we were entirely prepared), but that they are inadequate as opera. He lets us see his show from the coulisses. The pretense lacks standing even among pretenses, and a faith must be induced before its removal can enliven us. But his New York has quality. It is of the family of Dickens's London and Hugo's Paris, though it is plainly a cadet in the family. Mr Howells, in his profound and valuable study of the metropolis in a 'Hazard of New Fortunes,' is penetrating; O. Henry, on the other hand, is *penetrated.* His New York is intimate and clinging; it is caught in the mesh of the imagination.

O. Henry had rare but precious insights into human destiny and human nature. In these pictures he is not formally accurate; he could never or seldom set his truth before us in that moderation and proportion which truths acquire in the stringencies of actuality. He was apt to present his insight in a sort of parable or allegory, to upraise it before the eyes of mankind on the mast or flagpole of some vehement exaggeration. Epigram shows us truth in the embrace of a lie, and tales which are dramatized epigrams are subject to a like constraint. The force, however, is real. I could scarcely name anywhere a more powerful exposition of fatality than 'Roads of Destiny,' the initial story in the volume which appropriates its title. It wanted only the skilled romantic touch of a Gautier or Stevenson to enroll this tale among the masterpieces of its kind in contemporary letters.

Now and then the ingredient of parable is hardly perceptible; we draw close to the bare fact. O. Henry, fortunate in plots, is peculiarly fortunate in his renunciation of plot. If contrivance is lucrative, it is also costly. There is an admirable little story called the 'Pendulum' (in the 'Trimmed Lamp'), the simplicity of whose fable would have satisfied Coppée or Hawthorne. A man in a flat, by force of custom, has come to regard his wife as a piece of furniture. She departs for a few hours, and, by the break in usage, is restored, in his consciousness, to womanhood. She comes back, and relapses into furniture. That is all. O. Henry could not have given us less—or more. Farcical, clownish, if you will, the story resembles those clowns who carry daggers under their motley. When John Perkins takes up that inauspicious hat, the reader smiles, and quails. I will mention a few other examples of insights with the proviso that they are not specially commended to the man whose quest in the short story is the electrifying or the calorific. They include the 'Social Triangle,' the 'Making of a New Yorker,' and the 'Foreign Policy of Company 99,' all in the 'Trimmed Lamp,' the 'Brief Début of Tildy' in the 'Four Million,' and the 'Complete Life of John Hopkins' in the 'Voice of the City.' I cannot close this summary of good points without a passing reference to the not unsuggestive portrayal of humane and cheerful scoundrels in the 'Gentle Grafter.' The picture, if false to species, is faithful to genus.

O. Henry's egregiousness, on the superficial side, both in merits and defects, reminds us of those park benches so characteristic of his tales which are occupied by a millionaire at one end and a mendicant at the other. But, to complete the image, we must add as a casual visitor to that bench a seer or a student, who, sitting down between the previous comers and suspending the flamboyancies of their dialogue, should gaze with the pensive eye of Goldsmith or Addison upon the passing crowd.

In O. Henry American journalism and the Victorian tradition meet. His mind, quick to don the guise of modernity, was impervious to its spirit. The specifically modern movements, the scientific awakening, the religious upheaval and subsidence, the socialistic gospel, the enfranchisement of women—these never interfered with his artless and joyous pursuit of the old romantic motives of love, hate, wealth, poverty, gentility, disguise, and crime. On two points a moral record which, in his literature, is everywhere sound and stainless, rises almost to nobility. In an age when sexual excitement had become available and permissible, this worshiper of stimulus never touched with so much as a fingertip that insidious and meretricious fruit. The second point is his feeling for underpaid working-girls. His passionate concern for this wrong derives a peculiar emphasis from the general refusal of his books to bestow countenance or notice on philanthropy in its collective forms. When, in his dream of Heaven, he is asked: 'Are you one of the bunch?' (meaning one of the bunch of grasping and grinding employers), the response, through all its slang, is soul-stirring. '"Not on your immortality," said I. "I'm only the fellow that set fire to an orphan asylum and murdered a blind man for his pennies."' The author of that retort may have some difficulty with the sentries that watch the entrance of Parnassus; he will have none with the gatekeeper of the New Jerusalem.

42

A DEFENSE OF POETRY

Percy Bysshe Shelley

I

According to one mode of regarding those two classes of mental action, which are called reason and imagination, the former may be considered as mind contemplating the relations borne by one thought to another, however produced, and the latter, as mind acting upon those thoughts so as to colour them with its own light, and composing from them, as from elements, other thoughts, each containing within itself the principle of its own integrity. The one is the το ποιειν, or the principle of synthesis, and has for its objects those forms which are common to universal nature and existence itself; the other is the το λογιςειν, or principle of analysis, and its action regards the relations of things simply as relations; considering thoughts, not in their integral unity, but as the algebraical representations which conduct to certain general results. Reason is the enumeration of qualities already known; imagination is the perception of the value of those qualities, both separately and as a whole. Reason respects the differences, and imagination the similitudes of things. Reason is to imagination as the instrument to the agent, as the body to the spirit, as the shadow to the substance.

Poetry, in a general sense, may be defined to be 'the expression of the imagination': and poetry is connate with the origin of man. Man is an instrument over which a series of external and internal impressions are driven, like the alternations of an ever-changing wind over an Æolian lyre, which move it by their motion to ever-changing melody. But there is a principle within the human being, and perhaps within all sentient beings, which acts otherwise than in the lyre, and produces not melody alone, but harmony, by an internal adjustment of the sounds or motions thus excited to the impressions which excite them. It is as if the lyre could accommodate its chords to the motions of that which strikes them, in a determined proportion of sound; even as the musician can accommodate his voice to the sound of the lyre. A child at play by itself will express its delight by its voice and motions; and every inflexion of tone and every gesture will bear exact relation to a corresponding antitype in the pleasurable impressions which awakened it; it will be the reflected image of that impression; and as the lyre trembles and sounds after the wind has died away; so the child seeks, by prolonging in its voice and motions the duration of the effect, to prolong also a consciousness of the cause. In relation to the objects which delight a child these expressions are what poetry is to higher objects. The savage (for the savage is to ages what the child is to years) expresses the emotions produced in him by surrounding objects in a similar manner; and language and gesture, together with plastic or pictorial imitation, become the image of the combined effect of those objects, and of his apprehension of them. Man in society, with all his passions and his pleasures, next becomes the object of the passions and pleasures of man; an additional class of emotions produces an augmented treasure of expressions; and language, gesture, and the imitative arts, become at once the representation and the medium, the pencil and the picture, the chisel and the statute, the chord and the harmony. The social sympathies, or those laws from which, as from its elements, society results, begin to develop themselves from the moment that two human beings coexist; the future is contained within the present, as the plant within the seed; and equality, diversity, unity, contrast, mutual dependence, become the principles alone capable of affording the motives according to which the will of a social being is determined to action, inasmuch as he is social; and constitute pleasure in sensation, virtue in sentiment, beauty in art, truth in reasoning, and love in the intercourse of kind. Hence men, even in the infancy of society, observe a certain order in their words and actions, distinct from that of the objects and the impressions represented by them, all expression being subject to the laws of that from which it proceeds. But let us dismiss those more general considerations which might involve an inquiry into the principles of society itself, and restrict our view to the manner in which the imagination is expressed upon its forms.

In the youth of the world, men dance and sing and imitate natural objects observing in these actions, as in all others, a certain rhythm or order. And, although all men observe a similar, they observe not the same order, in the motions of the dance, in the melody of the song, in the combinations of language, in the series of their imitations of natural objects. For there is a certain order or rhythm belonging to each of these classes of mimetic representation, from which the hearer and the spectator receive an intenser and purer pleasure than from any other: the sense of an approximation to this order has been called taste by modern writers. Every man in the infancy of art observes an order which approximates more or less closely to that from which this highest delight results: but the diversity is not sufficiently marked, as that its gradations should be sensible, except in those instances where the predominance of this faculty of approximation to the beautiful (for so we may be permitted to name the relation between this highest pleasure and its cause) is very great. Those in whom it exists in excess are poets, in the most universal sense of the word; and the pleasure resulting from the manner in which they express the influence of society or nature upon their own minds, communicates itself to others, and gathers a sort of reduplication from that community. Their language is vitally metaphorical; that is, it marks the before unapprehended relations of things and perpetuates their apprehension, until the words which represent them, become, through time, signs for portions or classes of thoughts instead of pictures of integral thoughts; and then if no new poets should arise to create afresh the associations which have been thus disorganized, language will be dead to all the nobler purposes of human intercourse. These similitudes or relations are finely said by Lord Bacon to be 'the same footsteps of nature impressed upon the various subjects of the world' [De Augment. Scient., cap. i, lib. iii]—and he considers the faculty which perceives them as the store-house of axioms common to all knowledge. In the infancy of society every author is necessarily a poet, because language itself is poetry; and to be a poet is to apprehend the true and the beautiful, in a word, the good which exists in the relation, subsisting, first between existence and perception, and secondly between perception and expression. Every original language near to its source is in itself the chaos of a cyclic poem: the copiousness of lexicography and the distinctions of grammar are the works of a later age, and are merely the catalogue and the form of the creations of poetry.

But poets, or those who imagine and express this indestructible order, are not only the authors of language and of music, of the dance, and architecture, and statuary, and painting: they are the institutors of laws, and the founders of civil society, and the inventors of the arts of life, and the teachers, who draw into a certain propinquity with the beautiful and the true that partial apprehension of the agencies of the invisible world which is called religion. Hence all original religions are allegorical, or susceptible of allegory, and, like Janus, have a double face of false and true. Poets, according to the circumstances of the age and nation in which they appeared, were called, in the earlier epochs of the world, legislators, or prophets: a poet essentially comprises and unites both these characters. For he not only beholds intensely the present as it is, and discovers those laws according to which present things ought to be ordered, but he beholds the future in the present, and his thoughts are the germs of the flower and the fruit of latest time. Not that I assert poets to be prophets in the gross sense of the word, or that they can foretell the form as surely as they foreknow the spirit of events: such is the pretence of superstition, which would make poetry an attribute of prophecy, rather than prophecy an attribute of poetry. A poet participates in the eternal, the infinite, and the one; as far as relates to his conceptions, time and place and number are not. The grammatical forms which express the moods of time, and the difference of persons, and the distinction of place, are convertible with respect to the highest poetry without injuring it as poetry; and the choruses of Aeschylus, and the book of Job, and Dante's 'Paradise' would afford, more than any other writings, examples of this fact, if the limits of this essay did not forbid citation. The creations of sculpture, painting, and music are illustrations still more decisive.

Language, colour, form, and religious and civil habits of action, are all the instruments and materials of poetry; they may be called poetry by that figure of speech which considers the effect as a synonym of the cause. But poetry in a more restricted sense expresses those arrangements of language, and especially metrical language, which are created by that imperial faculty, whose throne is curtained within the invisible nature of man. And this springs from the nature itself of language, which is a more direct representation of the actions and passions of our internal being, and is susceptible of more various and delicate combinations, than colour, form, or motion, and is more plastic and obedient to the control of that faculty of which it is the creation. For language is arbitrarily produced by the imagination, and has relation to thoughts alone; but all other materials, instruments, and conditions of art have relations among each other, which limit and interpose between conception and expression. The former is as a mirror which reflects, the latter as a cloud which enfeebles, the light of which both are mediums of communication. Hence the fame of sculptors, painters, and musicians, although the intrinsic powers of the great masters of these arts may yield in no degree to that of those who have employed language as the hieroglyphic of their thoughts, has never equalled that of poets in the restricted sense of the term; as two performers of equal skill will produce unequal effects from a guitar and a harp. The fame of legislators and founders of religions, so long as their institutions last, alone seems to exceed that of poets in the restricted sense; but it can scarcely be a question, whether, if we deduct the celebrity which their flattery of the gross opinions of the vulgar usually conciliates, together with that which belonged to them in their higher character of poets, any excess will remain.

We have thus circumscribed the word poetry within the limits of that art which is the most familiar and the most perfect expression of the faculty itself. It is necessary, however, to make the circle still narrower, and to determine the distinction between measured and unmeasured language; for the popular division into prose and verse is inadmissible in accurate philosophy.

Sounds as well as thoughts have relation both between each other and towards that which they represent, and a perception of the order of those relations has always been found connected with a perception of the order of the relations of thoughts. Hence the language of poets has ever affected a certain uniform and harmonious recurrence of sound, without which it were not poetry, and which is scarcely less indispensable to the communication of its influence, than the words themselves, without reference to that peculiar order. Hence the vanity of translation; it were as wise to cast a violet into a crucible that you might discover the formal principle of its colour and odour, as seek to transfuse from one language into another the creations of a poet. The plant must spring again from its seed, or it will bear no flower—and this is the burden of the curse of Babel.

An observation of the regular mode of the recurrence of harmony in the language of poetical minds, together with its relation to music, produced metre, or a certain system of traditional forms of harmony and language. Yet it is by no means essential that a poet should accommodate his language to this traditional form, so that the harmony, which is its spirit, be observed. The practice is indeed convenient and popular, and to be preferred, especially in such composition as includes much action: but every great poet must inevitably innovate upon the example of his predecessors in the exact structure of his peculiar versification. The distinction between poets and prose writers is a vulgar error. The distinction between philosophers and poets has been anticipated. Plato was essentially a poet—the truth and splendour of his imagery, and the melody of his language, are the most intense that it is possible to conceive. He rejected the measure of the epic, dramatic, and lyrical forms, because he sought to kindle a harmony in thoughts divested of shape and action, and he forebore to invent any regular plan of rhythm which would include, under determinate forms, the varied pauses of his style. Cicero sought to imitate the cadence of his periods, but with little success. Lord Bacon was a poet.

[See the 'Filum Labyrinthi,' and the 'Essay on Death' particularly.] His language has a sweet and majestic rhythm, which satisfies the sense, no less than the almost superhuman wisdom of his philosophy satisfies the intellect; it is a strain which distends, and then bursts the circumference of the reader's mind, and pours itself forth together with it into the universal element with which it has perpetual sympathy. All the authors of revolutions in opinion are not only necessarily poets as they are inventors, nor even as their words unveil the permanent analogy of things by images which participate in the life of truth; but as their periods are harmonious and rhythmical, and contain in themselves the elements of verse; being the echo of the eternal music. Nor are those supreme poets, who have employed traditional forms of rhythm on account of the form and action of their subjects, less capable of perceiving and teaching the truth of things, than those who have omitted that form. Shakespeare, Dante, and Milton (to confine ourselves to modern writers) are philosophers of the very loftiest power.

A poem is the very image of life expressed in its eternal truth. There is this difference between a story and a poem, that a story is a catalogue of detached facts, which have no other connection than time, place, circumstance, cause and effect; the other is the creation of actions according to the unchangeable forms of human nature, as existing in the mind of the Creator, which is itself the image of all other minds. The one is partial, and applies only to a definite period of time, and a certain combination of events which can never again recur; the other is universal, and contains within itself the germ of a relation to whatever motives or actions have place in the possible varieties of human nature. Time, which destroys the beauty and the use of the story of particular facts, stripped of the poetry which should invest them, augments that of poetry, and forever develops new and wonderful applications of the eternal truth which it contains. Hence epitomes have been called the moths of just history; they eat out the poetry of it. A story of particular facts is as a mirror which obscures and distorts that which should be beautiful; poetry is a mirror which makes beautiful that which is distorted.

The parts of a composition may be poetical, without the composition as a whole being a poem. A single sentence may be considered as a whole, though it may be found in the midst of a series of unassimilated portions; a single word even may be a spark of inextinguishable thought. And thus all the great historians, Herodotus, Plutarch, Livy, were poets; and although the plan of these writers, especially that of Livy, restrained them from developing this faculty in its highest degree, they made copious and ample amends for their subjection, by filling all the interstices of their subjects with living images.

Having determined what is poetry, and who are poets, let us proceed to estimate its effects upon society.

Poetry is ever accompanied with pleasure: all spirits on which it falls open themselves to receive the wisdom which is mingled with its delight. In the infancy of the world, neither poets themselves nor their auditors are fully aware of the excellence of poetry: for it acts in a divine and unapprehended manner, beyond and above consciousness; and it is reserved for future generations to contemplate and measure the mighty cause and effect in all the strength and splendour of their union. Even in modern times, no living poet ever arrived at the fulness of his fame; the jury which sits in judgment upon a poet, belonging as he does to all time, must be composed of his peers: it must be impanelled by Time from the selectest of the wise of many generations. A poet is a nightingale, who sits in darkness and sings to cheer its own solitude with sweet sounds; his auditors are as men entranced by the melody of an unseen musician, who feel that they are moved and softened, yet know not whence or why. The poems of Homer and his contemporaries were the delight of infant Greece; they were the elements of that social system which is the column upon which all succeeding civilization has reposed. Homer embodied the ideal perfection of his age in human character; nor can we doubt that those who read his verses were awakened to an ambition of becoming like to Achilles, Hector, and Ulysses: the truth and beauty of friendship, patriotism, and persevering devotion to an object, were unveiled to the depths in these immortal creations: the sentiments of the auditors must have been refined and enlarged by a sympathy with such great and lovely impersonations, until from admiring they imitated, and from imitation they identified themselves with the objects of their admiration. Nor let it be objected that these characters are remote from moral perfection, and that they can by no means be considered as edifying patterns for general imitation. Every epoch, under names more or less specious, has deified its peculiar errors; Revenge is the naked idol of the worship of a semi-barbarous age: and Self-deceit is the veiled image of unknown evil, before which luxury and satiety lie prostrate. But a poet considers the vices of his contemporaries as the temporary dress in which his creations must be arrayed, and which cover without concealing the eternal proportions of their beauty. An epic or dramatic personage is understood to wear them around his soul, as he may the ancient armour or the modern uniform around his body; whilst it is easy to conceive a dress more graceful than either. The beauty of the internal nature cannot be so far concealed by its accidental vesture, but that the spirit of its form shall communicate itself to the very disguise, and indicate the shape it hides from the manner in which it is worn. A majestic form and graceful motions will express themselves through the most barbarous and tasteless costume. Few poets of the highest class have chosen to exhibit the beauty of their conceptions in its naked truth and splendour; and it is doubtful whether the alloy of costume, habit, etc., be not necessary to temper this planetary music for mortal ears.

The whole objection, however, of the immorality of poetry rests upon a misconception of the manner in which poetry acts to produce the moral improvement of man. Ethical science arranges the elements which poetry has created, and propounds schemes and proposes examples of civil and domestic life: nor is it for want of admirable doctrines that men hate, and despise, and censure, and deceive, and subjugate one another. But poetry acts in another and diviner manner. It awakens and enlarges the mind itself by rendering it the receptacle of a thousand unapprehended combinations of thought. Poetry lifts the veil from the hidden beauty of the world, and makes familiar objects be as if they were not familiar; it reproduces all that it represents, and the impersonations clothed in its Elysian light stand thenceforward in the minds of those who have once contemplated them, as memorials of that gentle and exalted content which extends itself over all thoughts and actions with which it coexists. The great secret of morals is love; or a going out of our nature, and an identification of ourselves with the beautiful which exists in thought, action, or person, not our own. A man, to be greatly good, must imagine intensely and comprehensively; he must put himself in the place of another and of many others; the pains and pleasure of his species must become his own. The great instrument of moral good is the imagination; and poetry administers to the effect by acting upon the cause. Poetry enlarges the circumference of the imagination by replenishing it with thoughts of ever new delight, which have the power of attracting and assimilating to their own nature all other thoughts, and which form new intervals and interstices whose void forever craves fresh food. Poetry strengthens the faculty which is the organ of the moral nature of man, in the same manner as exercise strengthens a limb. A poet therefore would do ill to embody his own conceptions of right and wrong, which are usually those of his place and time, in his poetical creations, which participate in neither. By this assumption of the inferior office of interpreting the effect, in which perhaps after all he might acquit himself but imperfectly, he would resign a glory in a participation in the cause. There was little danger that Homer, or any of the eternal poets, should have so far misunderstood themselves as to have abdicated this throne of their widest dominion. Those in whom the poetical faculty, though great, is less intense, as Euripides, Lucan, Tasso, Spenser, have frequently affected a moral aim, and the effect of their poetry is diminished in exact proportion to the degree in which they compel us to advert to this purpose.

Homer and the cyclic poets were followed at a certain interval by the dramatic and lyrical poets of Athens, who flourished contemporaneously with all that is most perfect in the kindred expressions of the poetical faculty; architecture, painting, music, the dance, sculpture, philosophy, and, we may add, the forms of civil life. For although the scheme of Athenian society was deformed by many imperfections which the poetry existing in chivalry and Christianity has erased from the habits and institutions of modern Europe; yet never at any other period has so much energy, beauty, and virtue been developed; never was blind strength and stubborn form so disciplined and rendered subject to the will of man, or that will less repugnant to the dictates of the beautiful and the true, as during the century which preceded the death of Socrates. Of no other epoch in the history of our species have we records and fragments stamped so visibly with the image of the divinity in man. But it is poetry alone, in form, in action, or in language, which has rendered this epoch memorable above all others, and the store-house of examples to everlasting time. For written poetry existed at that epoch simultaneously with the other arts, and it is an idle inquiry to demand which gave and which received the light, which all, as from a common focus, have scattered over the darkest periods of succeeding time. We know no more of cause and effect than a constant conjunction of events: poetry is ever found to coexist with whatever other arts contribute to the happiness and perfection of man. I appeal to what has already been established to distinguish between the cause and the effect.

It was at the period here adverted to that the drama had its birth; and however a succeeding writer may have equalled or surpassed those few great specimens of the Athenian drama which have been preserved to us, it is indisputable that the art itself never was understood or practised according to the true philosophy of it, as at Athens. For the Athenians employed language, action, music, painting, the dance, and religious institutions, to produce a common effect in the representation of the highest idealism of passion and of power; each division in the art was made perfect in its kind of artists of the most consummate skill, and was disciplined into a beautiful proportion and unity one towards the other. On the modern stage a few only of the elements capable of expressing the image of the poet's conception are employed at once. We have tragedy without music and dancing; and music and dancing without the highest impersonations of which they are the fit accompaniment, and both without religion and solemnity. Religious institution has indeed been usually banished from the stage. Our system of divesting the actor's face of a mask, on which the many expressions appropriated to his dramatic character might be moulded into one permanent and unchanging expression, is favourable only to a partial and inharmonious effect; it is fit for nothing but a monologue, where all the attention may be directed to some great master of ideal mimicry. The modern practice of blending comedy with tragedy, though liable to great abuse in point of practice, is undoubtedly an extension of the dramatic circle; but the comedy should be as in *King Lear*, universal, ideal, and sublime. It is perhaps the intervention of this principle which determines the balance in favour of *King Lear* against the *Oedipus Tyrannus* or the *Agamemnon*, or, if you will, the trilogies with which they are connected; unless the intense power of the choral poetry, especially that of the latter, should be considered as restoring the equilibrium. *King Lear*, if it can sustain this comparison, may be judged to be the most perfect specimen of the dramatic art existing in the world; in spite of the narrow conditions to which the poet was subjected by the ignorance of the philosophy of the drama which has prevailed in modern Europe. Calderon, in his religious *Autos*, has attempted to fulfil some of the high conditions of dramatic representation neglected by Shakespeare; such as the establishing a relation between the drama and religion, and the accommodating them to music and dancing; but he omits the observation of conditions still more important, and more is lost than gained by the substitution of the rigidly defined and ever-repeated idealisms of a distorted superstition for the living impersonations of the truth of human passion.

But I digress. The connection of scenic exhibitions with the improvement or corruption of the manners of men has been universally recognized; in other words, the presence or absence of poetry in its most perfect and universal form has been found to be connected with good and evil in conduct or habit. The corruption which has been imputed to the drama as an effect, begins, when the poetry employed in its constitution ends: I appeal to the history of manners whether the periods of the growth of the one and the decline of the other have not corresponded with an exactness equal to any example of moral cause and effect.

The drama at Athens, or wheresoever else it may have approached to its perfection, ever coexisted with the moral and intellectual greatness of the age. The tragedies of the Athenian poets are as mirrors in which the spectator beholds himself, under a thin disguise of circumstance, stripped of all but that ideal perfection and energy which everyone feels to be the internal type of all that he loves, admires, and would become. The imagination is enlarged by a sympathy with pains and passions so mighty, that they distend in their conception the capacity of that by which they are conceived; the good affections are strengthened by pity, indignation, terror, and sorrow; and an exalted calm is prolonged from the satiety of this high exercise of them into the tumult of familiar life: even crime is disarmed of half its horror and all its contagion by being represented as the fatal consequence of the unfathomable agencies of nature; error is thus divested of its wilfulness; men can no longer cherish it as the creation of their choice. In a drama of the highest order there is little food for censure or hatred; it teaches rather self-knowledge and self-respect. Neither the eye nor the mind can see itself, unless reflected upon that which it resembles. The drama, so long as it continues to express poetry, is as a prismatic and many-sided mirror, which collects the brightest rays of human nature and divides and reproduces them from the simplicity of these elementary forms, and touches them with majesty and beauty, and multiplies all that it reflects, and endows it with the power of propagating its like wherever it may fall.

But in periods of the decay of social life, the drama sympathizes with that decay. Tragedy becomes a cold imitation of the form of the great masterpieces of antiquity, divested of all harmonious accompaniment of the kindred arts; and often the very form misunderstood, or a weak attempt to teach certain doctrines, which the writer considers as moral truths; and which are usually no more than specious flatteries of some gross vice or weakness, with which the author, in common with his auditors, are infected. Hence what has been called the classical and domestic drama. Addison's *Cato* is a specimen of the one, and would it were not superfluous to cite examples of the other! To such purposes poetry cannot be made subservient. Poetry is a sword of lightning, ever unsheathed, which consumes the scabbard that would contain it. And thus we observe that all dramatic writings of this nature are unimaginative in a singular degree; they affect sentiment and passion, which, divested of imagination, are other names for caprice and appetite. The period in our own history of the grossest degradation of the drama is the reign of Charles II, when all forms in which poetry had been accustomed to be expressed became hymns to the triumph of kingly power over liberty and virtue. Milton stood alone illuminating an age unworthy of him. At such periods the calculating principle pervades all the forms of dramatic exhibition, and poetry ceases to be expressed upon them. Comedy loses its ideal universality: wit succeeds to humor; we laugh from self-complacency and triumph, instead of pleasure; malignity, sarcasm, and contempt succeed to sympathetic merriment; we hardly laugh, but we smile. Obscenity, which is ever blasphemy against the divine beauty in life, becomes, from the very veil which it assumes, more active if less disgusting: it is a monster for which the corruption of society forever brings forth new food, which it devours in secret.

The drama being that form under which a greater number of modes of expression of poetry are susceptible of being combined than any other, the connection of poetry and social good is more observable in the drama than in whatever other form. And it is indisputable that the highest perfection of human society has ever corresponded with the highest dramatic excellence; and that the corruption or the extinction of the drama in a nation where it has once flourished is a mark of a corruption of manners, and an extinction of the energies which sustain the soul of social life. But, as Machiavelli says of political institutions, that life may be preserved and renewed, if men should arise capable of bringing back the drama to its principles. And this is true with respect to poetry in its most extended sense: all language, institution, and form require not only to be produced but to be sustained: the office and character of a poet participate in the divine nature as regards providence, no less than as regards creation.

Civil war, the spoils of Asia, and the fatal predominance first of the Macedonian, and then of the Roman arms, were so many symbols of the extinction or suspension of the creative faculty in Greece. The bucolic writers, who found patronage under the lettered tyrants of Sicily and Egypt, were the latest representatives of its most glorious reign. Their poetry is intensely melodious; like the odour of the tuberose, it overcomes and sickens the spirit with excess of sweetness; whilst the poetry of the preceding age was as a meadow-gale of June, which mingles the fragrance of all the flowers of the field, and adds a quickening and harmonizing spirit of its own which endows the sense with a power of sustaining its extreme delight. The bucolic and erotic delicacy in written poetry is correlative with that softness in statuary, music, and the kindred arts, and even in manners and institutions, which distinguished the epoch to which I now refer. Nor is it the poetical faculty itself, or any misapplication of it, to which this want of harmony is to be imputed. An equal sensibility to the influence of the senses and the affections is to be found in the writings of Homer and Sophocles: the former, especially, has clothed sensual and pathetic images with irresistible attractions. Their superiority over these succeeding writers consists in the presence of those thoughts which belong to the inner faculties of our nature, not in the absence of those which are connected with the external; their incomparable perfection consists in a harmony of the union of all. It is not what the erotic poets have, but what they have not, in which their imperfection consists. It is not inasmuch as they were poets, but inasmuch as they were not poets, that they can be considered with any plausibility as connected with the corruption of their age. Had that corruption availed so as to extinguish in them the sensibility to pleasure, passion, and natural scenery, which is imputed to them as an imperfection, the last triumph of evil would have been achieved. For the end of social corruption is to destroy all sensibility to pleasure; and, therefore, it is corruption. It begins at the imagination and the intellect as at the core, and distributes itself thence as a paralyzing venom, through the affections into the very appetites, until all become a torpid mass in which hardly sense survives. At the approach of such a period, poetry ever addresses itself to those faculties which are the last to be destroyed, and its voice is heard, like the footsteps of Astræa, departing from the world. Poetry ever communicates all the pleasure which men are capable of receiving: it is ever still the light of life; the source of whatever of beautiful or generous or true can have place in an evil time. It will readily be confessed that those among the luxurious citizens of Syracuse and Alexandria, who were delighted with the poems of Theocritus, were less cold, cruel, and sensual than the remnant of their tribe. But corruption must utterly have destroyed the fabric of human society before poetry can ever cease. The sacred links of that chain have never been entirely disjoined, which descending through the minds of many men is attached to those great minds, whence as from a magnet the invisible effluence is sent forth, which at once connects, animates, and sustains the life of all. It is the faculty which contains within itself the seeds at once of its own and of social renovation. And let us not circumscribe the effects of the bucolic and erotic poetry within the limits of the sensibility of those to whom it was addressed. They may have perceived the beauty of those immortal compositions, simply as fragments and isolated portions: those who are more finely organized, or born in a happier age, may recognize them as episodes to that great poem, which all poets, like the cooperating thoughts of one great mind, have built up since the beginning of the world.

The same revolutions within a narrower sphere had place in ancient Rome; but the actions and forms of its social life never seem to have been perfectly saturated with the poetical element. The Romans appear to have considered the Greeks as the selectest treasuries of the selectest forms of manners and of nature, and to have abstained from creating in measured language, sculpture, music, or architecture, anything which might bear a particular relation to their own condition, whilst it should bear a general one to the universal constitution of the world. But we judge from partial evidence, and we judge perhaps partially. Ennius, Varro, Pacuvius, and Accius, all great poets, have been lost. Lucretius is in the highest, and Virgil in a very high sense, a creator. The chosen delicacy of expressions of the latter are as a mist of light which conceal from us the intense and exceeding truth of his conceptions of nature. Livy is instinct with poetry. Yet Horace, Catullus, Ovid, and generally the other great writers of the Virgilian age, saw man and nature in the mirror of Greece. The institutions also, and the religion of Rome, were less poetical than those of Greece, as the shadow is less vivid than the substance. Hence poetry in Rome seemed to follow, rather than accompany, the perfection of political and domestic society. The true poetry of Rome lived in its institutions; for whatever of beautiful, true, and majestic, they contained, could have sprung only from the faculty which creates the order in which they consist. The life of Camillus, the death of Regulus; the expectation of the senators, in their godlike state, of the victorious Gauls; the refusal of the republic to make peace with Hannibal, after the battle of Cannæ, were not the consequences of a refined calculation of the probable personal advantage to result from such a rhythm and order in the shows of life, to those who were at once the poets and the actors of these immortal dramas. The imagination beholding the beauty of this order, created it out of itself according to its own idea; the consequence was empire, and the reward ever-living fame. These things are not the less poetry, *quia carent vate sacro*. They are the episodes of that cyclic poem written by Time upon the memories of men. The Past, like an inspired rhapsodist, fills the theatre of everlasting generations with their harmony.

At length the ancient system of religion and manners had fulfilled the circle of its revolutions. And the world would have fallen into utter anarchy and darkness, but that there were found poets among the authors of the Christian and chivalric systems of manners and religion, who created forms of opinion and action never before conceived; which, copied into the imaginations of men, became as generals to the bewildered armies of their thoughts. It is foreign to the present purpose to touch upon the evil produced by these systems: except that we protest, on the ground of the principles already established, that no portion of it can be attributed to the poetry they contain.

It is probable that the poetry of Moses, Job, David, Solomon, and Isaiah had produced a great effect upon the mind of Jesus and his disciples. The scattered fragments preserved to us by the biographers of this extraordinary person are all instinct with the most vivid poetry. But his doctrines seem to have been quickly distorted. At a certain period after the prevalence of a system of opinions founded upon those promulgated by him, the three forms into which Plato had distributed the faculties of mind underwent a sort of apotheosis, and became the object of the worship of the civilized world. Here it is to be confessed that 'Light seems to thicken,' and

> The crow makes wing to the rooky wood,
> Good things of day begin to droop and drowse,
> And night's black agents to their preys do rouse.

But mark how beautiful an order has sprung from the dust and blood of this fierce chaos! how the world, as from a resurrection, balancing itself on the golden wings of Knowledge and of Hope, has reassumed its yet unwearied flight into the heaven of time. Listen to the music, unheard by outward ears, which is as a ceaseless and invisible wind, nourishing its everlasting course with strength and swiftness.

The poetry in the doctrines of Jesus Christ, and the mythology and institutions of the Celtic conquerors of the Roman Empire, outlived the darkness and the convulsions connected with their growth and victory, and blended themselves in a new fabric of manners and opinion. It is an error to impute the ignorance of the dark ages to the Christian doctrines or the predominance of the Celtic nations. Whatever of evil their agencies may have contained sprang from the extinction of the poetical principle, connected with the progress of despotism and superstition. Men, from causes too intricate to be here discussed, had become insensible and selfish: their own will had become feeble, and yet they were its slaves, and thence the slaves of the will of others: lust, fear, avarice, cruelty, and fraud, characterized a race amongst whom no one was to be found capable of creating in form, language, or institution. The moral anomalies of such a state of society are not justly to be charged upon any class of events immediately connected with them, and those events are most entitled to our approbation which could dissolve it most expeditiously. It is unfortunate for those who cannot distinguish words from thoughts, that many of these anomalies have been incorporated into our popular religion.

It was not until the eleventh century that the effects of the poetry of the Christian and chivalric systems began to manifest themselves. The principle of equality had been discovered and applied by Plato in his Republic as the theoretical rule of the mode in which the materials of pleasure and of power produced by the common skill and labour of human beings ought to be distributed among them. The limitations of this rule were asserted by him to be determined only by the sensibility of each, or the utility to result to all. Plato, following the doctrines of Timæus and Pythagoras, taught also a moral and intellectual system of doctrine, comprehending at once the past, the present, and the future condition of man. Jesus Christ divulged the sacred and eternal truths contained in these views to mankind, and Christianity, in its abstract purity, became the exoteric expression of the esoteric doctrines of the poetry and wisdom of antiquity. The incorporation of the Celtic nations with the exhausted population of the south impressed upon it the figure of the poetry existing in their mythology and institutions. The result was a sum of the action and reaction of all the causes included in it; for it may be assumed as a maxim that no nation or religion can supersede any other without incorporating into itself a portion of that which it supersedes. The abolition of personal and domestic slavery, and the emancipation of women from a great part of the degrading restraints of antiquity, were among the consequences of these events.

The abolition of personal slavery is the basis of the highest political hope that it can enter into the mind of man to conceive. The freedom of women produced the poetry of sexual love. Love became a religion, the idols of whose worship were ever present. It was as if the statues of Apollo and the Muses had been endowed with life and motion, and had walked forth among their worshippers; so that earth became peopled with the inhabitants of a diviner world. The familiar appearance and proceedings of life became wonderful and heavenly, and a paradise was created as out of the wrecks of Eden. And as this creation itself is poetry, so its creators were poets; and language was the instrument of their art: '*Galeotto fù il libro, e chi lo scrisse*'. The Provençal Trouveurs, or inventors, preceded Petrarch, whose verses are as spells, which unseal the inmost enchanted fountains of the delight which is in the grief of love. It is impossible to feel them without becoming a portion of that beauty which we contemplate: it were superfluous to explain how the gentleness and the elevation of mind connected with these sacred emotions can render men more amiable, more generous and wise, and lift them out of the dull vapors of the little world of self. Dante understood the secret things of love even more than Petrarch. His *Vita Nuova* is an inexhaustible fountain of purity of sentiment and language: it is the idealized history of that period, and those intervals of his life which were dedicated to love. His apotheosis of Beatrice in Paradise, and the gradations of his own love and her loveliness, by which as by steps he feigns himself to have ascended to the throne of the Supreme Cause, is the most glorious imagination of modern poetry. The acutest critics have justly reversed the judgment of the vulgar, and the order of the great acts of the 'Divine Drama,' in the measure of the admiration which they accord to the Hell, Purgatory, and Paradise. The latter is a perpetual hymn of everlasting love. Love, which found a worthy poet in Plato alone of all the ancients, has been celebrated by a chorus of the greatest writers of the renovated world; and the music has penetrated the caverns of society, and its echoes still drown the dissonance of arms and superstition. At successive intervals, Ariosto, Tasso, Shakespeare, Spenser, Calderon, Rousseau, and the great writers of our own age, have celebrated the dominion of love, planting as it were trophies in the human mind of that sublimest victory over sensuality and force. The true relation borne to each other by the sexes into which humankind is distributed has become less misunderstood; and if the error which confounded diversity with inequality of the powers of the two sexes has been partially recognised in the opinions and institutions of modern Europe, we owe this great benefit to the worship of which chivalry was the law, and poets the prophets.

The poetry of Dante may be considered as the bridge thrown over the stream of time, which unites the modern and ancient world. The distorted notions of invisible things which Dante and his rival Milton have idealized, are merely the mask and the mantle in which these great poets walk through eternity enveloped and disguised. It is a difficult question to determine how far they were conscious of the distinction which must have subsisted in their minds between their own creeds and that of the people. Dante at least appears to wish to mark the full extent of it by placing Rhipæus, whom Virgil calls *justissimus unus*, in Paradise, and observing a most heretical caprice in his distribution of rewards and punishments. And Milton's poem contains within itself a philosophical refutation of that system, of which, by a strange and natural antithesis, it has been a chief popular support. Nothing can exceed the energy and magnificence of the character of Satan as expressed in *Paradise Lost*. It is a mistake to suppose that he could ever have been intended for the popular personification of evil. Implacable hate, patient cunning, and a sleepless refinement of device to inflict the extremist anguish on an enemy, these things are evil; and, although venial in a slave, are not to be forgiven in a tyrant; although redeemed by much that ennobles his defeat in one subdued, are marked by all that dishonours his conquest in the victor. Milton's Devil as a moral being is as far superior to his God, as one who perseveres in some purpose which he has conceived to be excellent in spite of adversity and torture, is to one who in the cold security of undoubted triumph inflicts the most horrible revenge upon his enemy, not from any mistaken notion of inducing him to repent of a perseverance in enmity, but with the alleged design of exasperating him to deserve new torments. Milton has so far violated the popular creed (if this shall be judged to be a violation) as to have alleged no superiority of moral virtue to his God over his Devil. And this bold neglect of a direct moral purpose is the most decisive proof of the supremacy of Milton's genius. He mingled as it were the elements of human nature as colours upon a single pallet, and arranged them in the composition of his great picture according to the laws of epic truth; that is, according to the laws of that principle by which a series of actions of the external universe and of intelligent and ethical beings is calculated to excite the sympathy of succeeding generations of mankind. *The Divina Commedia* and *Paradise Lost* have conferred upon modern mythology a systematic form; and when change and time shall have added one more superstition to the mass of those which have arisen and decayed upon the earth, commentators will be learnedly employed in elucidating the religion of ancestral Europe, only not utterly forgotten because it will have been stamped with the eternity of genius.

Homer was the first and Dante the second epic poet: that is, the second poet, the series of whose creations bore a defined and intelligible relation to the knowledge and sentiment and religion of the age in which he lived, and of the ages which followed it, developing itself in correspondence with their development. For Lucretius had limed the wings of his swift spirit in the dregs of the sensible world; and Virgil, with a modesty that ill became his genius, had affected the fame of an imitator, even whilst he created anew all that he copied; and none among the flock of mock-birds, though their notes were sweet, Apollonius Rhodius, Quintus Calaber, Nonnus, Lucan, Statius, or Claudian, have sought even to fulfil a single condition of epic truth. Milton was the third epic poet. For if the title of epic in its highest sense be refused to the *Aeneid*, still less can it be conceded to the *Orlando Furioso*, the *Gerusalemme Liberata*, the *Lusiad*, or the *Faerie Queene*.

Dante and Milton were both deeply penetrated with the ancient religion of the civilized world; and its spirit exists in their poetry probably in the same proportion as its forms survived in the unreformed worship of modern Europe. The one preceded and the other followed the Reformation at almost equal intervals. Dante was the first religious reformer, and Luther surpassed him rather in the rudeness and acrimony than in the boldness of his censures of papal usurpation. Dante was the first awakener of entranced Europe; he created a language, in itself music and persuasion, out of a chaos of inharmonious barbarians. He was the congregator of those great spirits who presided over the resurrection of learning; the Lucifer of that starry flock which in the thirteenth century shone forth from republican Italy, as from a heaven, into the darkness of the benighted world. His very words are instinct with spirit; each is as a spark, a burning atom of inextinguishable thought; and many yet lie covered in the ashes of their birth, and pregnant with the lightning which has yet found no conductor. All high poetry is infinite; it is as the first acorn, which contained all oaks potentially. Veil after veil may be undrawn, and the inmost naked beauty of the meaning never exposed. A great poem is a fountain forever overflowing with the waters of wisdom and delight; and after one person and one age has exhausted all its divine effluence which their peculiar relations enable them to share, another and yet another succeeds, and new relations are ever developed, the source of an unforeseen and an unconceived delight.

The age immediately succeeding to that of Dante, Petrarch, and Boccaccio was characterized by a revival of painting, sculpture, and architecture. Chaucer caught the sacred inspiration, and the superstructure of English literature is based upon the materials of Italian invention.

But let us not be betrayed from a defence into a critical history of poetry and its influence on society. Be it enough to have pointed out the effects of poets, in the large and true sense of the word, upon their own and all succeeding times.

But poets have been challenged to resign the civic crown to reasoners and mechanists, on another plea. It is admitted that the exercise of the imagination is most delightful, but it is alleged that that of reason is more useful. Let us examine as the grounds of this distinction what is here meant by utility. Pleasure or good, in a general sense, is that which the consciousness of a sensitive and intelligent being seeks, and in which, when found, it acquiesces. There are two kinds of pleasure, one durable, universal, and permanent; the other transitory and particular. Utility may either express the means of producing the former or the latter. In the former sense, whatever strengthens and purifies the affections, enlarges the imagination, and adds spirit to sense, is useful. But a narrower meaning may be assigned to the word utility, confining it to express that which banishes the importunity of the wants of our animal nature, the surrounding, men with security of life, the dispersing the grosser delusions of superstitions, and the conciliating such a degree of mutual forbearance among men as may consist with the motives of personal advantage.

Undoubtedly the promoters of utility, in this limited sense, have their appointed office in society. They follow the footsteps of poets, and copy the sketches of their creations into the book of common life. They make space, and give time. Their exertions are of the highest value, so long as they confine their administration of the concerns of the inferior powers of our nature within the limits due to the superior ones. But whilst the sceptic destroys gross superstitions, let him spare to deface, as some of the French writers have defaced, the eternal truths charactered upon the imaginations of men. Whilst the mechanist abridges, and the political economist combines labour, let them beware that their speculations, for want of correspondence with those first principles which belong to the imagination, do not tend, as they have in modern England, to exasperate at once the extremes of luxury and want. They have exemplified the saying, 'To him that hath, more shall be given; and from him that hath not, the little that he hath shall be taken away.' The rich have become richer, and the poor have become poorer; and the vessel of the State is driven between the Scylla and Charybdis of anarchy and despotism. Such are the effects which must ever flow from an unmitigated exercise of the calculating faculty.

It is difficult to define pleasure in its highest sense; the definition involving a number of apparent paradoxes. For, from an inexplicable defect of harmony in the constitution of human nature, the pain of the inferior is frequently connected with the pleasures of the superior portions of our being. Sorrow, terror, anguish, despair itself, are often the chosen expressions of an approximation to the highest good. Our sympathy in tragic fiction depends on this principle; tragedy delights by affording a shadow of the pleasure which exists in pain. This is the source also of the melancholy which is inseparable from the sweetest melody. The pleasure that is in sorrow is sweeter than the pleasure of pleasure itself. And hence the saying, 'It is better to go to the house of mourning than to the house of mirth.' Not that this highest species of pleasure is necessarily linked with pain. The delight of love and friendship, the ecstasy of the admiration of nature, the joy of the perception and still more of the creation of poetry, is often wholly unalloyed.

The production and assurance of pleasure in this highest sense is true utility. Those who produce and preserve this pleasure are poets or poetical philosophers.

The exertions of Locke, Hume, Gibbon, Voltaire, Rousseau [although Rousseau has been thus classed, he was essentially a poet. The others, even Voltaire, were mere reasoners], and their disciples, in favour of oppressed and deluded humanity, are entitled to the gratitude of mankind. Yet it is easy to calculate the degree of moral and intellectual improvement which the world would have exhibited, had they never lived. A little more nonsense would have been talked for a century or two; and perhaps a few more men, women, and children burnt as heretics. We might not at this moment have been congratulating each other on the abolition of the Inquisition in Spain. But it exceeds all imagination to conceive what would have been the moral condition of the world if neither Dante, Petrarch, Boccaccio, Chaucer, Shakespeare, Calderon, Lord Bacon, nor Milton, had ever existed; if Raphael and Michael Angelo had never been born; if the Hebrew poetry had never been translated; if a revival of the study of Greek literature had never taken place; if no monuments of ancient sculpture had been handed down to us; and if the poetry of the religion of the ancient world had been extinguished together with its belief. The human mind could never, except by the intervention of these excitements, have been awakened to the invention of the grosser sciences, and that application of analytical reasoning to the aberrations of society, which it is now attempted to exalt over the direct expression of the inventive and creative faculty itself.

We have more moral, political, and historical wisdom than we know how to reduce into practice; we have more scientific and economical knowledge than can be accommodated to the just distribution of the produce which it multiplies. The poetry in these systems of thought is concealed by the accumulation of facts and calculating processes. There is no want of knowledge respecting what is wisest and best in morals, government, and political economy, or at least, what is wiser and better than what men now practise and endure. But we let I dare not wait upon I would, like the poor cat in the adage. We want the creative faculty to imagine that which we know; we want the generous impulse to act that which we imagine; we want the poetry of life; our calculations have outrun conception; we have eaten more than we can digest. The cultivation of those sciences which have enlarged the limits of the empire of man over the external world, has, for want of the poetical faculty, proportionally circumscribed those of the internal world; and man, having enslaved the elements, remains himself a slave. To what but a cultivation of the mechanical arts in a degree disproportioned to the presence of the creative faculty, which is the basis of all knowledge, is to be attributed the abuse of all invention for abridging and combining labour, to the exasperation of the inequality of mankind? From what other cause has it arisen that the discoveries which should have lightened, have added a weight to the curse imposed on Adam? Poetry, and the principle of Self, of which money is the visible incarnation, are the God and Mammon of the world.

The functions of the poetical faculty are twofold: by one it creates new materials of knowledge, and power, and pleasure; by the other it engenders in the mind a desire to reproduce and arrange them according to a certain rhythm and order which may be called the beautiful and the good. The cultivation of poetry is never more to be desired than at periods when, from an excess of the selfish and calculating principle, the accumulation of the materials of external life exceed the quantity of the power of assimilating them to the internal laws of human nature. The body has then become too unwieldy for that which animates it.

Poetry is indeed something divine. It is at once the centre and circumference of knowledge; it is that which comprehends all science, and that to which all science must be referred. It is at the same time the root and blossom of all other systems of thought; it is that from which all spring, and that which adorns all; and that which, if blighted, denies the fruit and the seed, and withholds from the barren world the nourishment and the succession of the scions of the tree of life. It is the perfect and consummate surface and bloom of all things; it is as the odour and the colour of the rose to the texture of the elements which compose it, as the form and splendour of unfaded beauty to the secrets of anatomy and corruption. What were virtue, love, patriotism, friendship—what were the scenery of this beautiful universe which we inhabit; what were our consolations on this side of the grave—and what were our aspirations beyond it, if poetry did not ascend to bring light and fire from those eternal regions where the owl-winged faculty of calculation dare not ever soar? Poetry is not like reasoning, a power to be exerted according to the determination of the will. A man cannot say, 'I will compose poetry.' The greatest poet even cannot say it; for the mind in creation is as a fading coal, which some invisible influence, like an inconstant wind, awakens to transitory brightness; this power arises from within, like the colour of a flower which fades and changes as it is developed, and the conscious portions of our natures are unprophetic either of its approach or its departure. Could this influence be durable in its original purity and force, it is impossible to predict the greatness of the results; but when composition begins, inspiration is already on the decline, and the most glorious poetry that has ever been communicated to the world is probably a feeble shadow of the original conceptions of the poet. I appeal to the greatest poets of the present day, whether it is not an error to assert that the finest passages of poetry are produced by labour and study. The toil and the delay recommended by critics can be justly interpreted to mean no more than a careful observation of the inspired moments, and an artificial connection of the spaces between their suggestions by the intertexture of conventional expressions; a necessity only imposed by the limitedness of the poetical faculty itself; for Milton conceived the *Paradise Lost* as a whole before he executed it in portions. We have his own authority also for the Muse having 'dictated' to him the 'unpremeditated song.' And let this be an answer to those who would allege the fifty-six various readings of the first line of the *Orlando Furioso*. Compositions so produced are to poetry what mosaic is to painting. This instinct and intuition of the poetical faculty are still more observable in the plastic and pictorial arts; a great statue or picture grows under the power of the artist as a child in a mother's womb; and the very mind which directs the hands in formation is incapable of accounting to itself for the origin, the gradations, or the media of the process.

Poetry is the record of the best and happiest moments of the happiest and best minds. We are aware of evanescent visitations of thought and feeling sometimes associated with place or person, sometimes regarding our own mind alone, and always arising unforeseen and departing unbidden, but elevating and delightful beyond all expression: so that even in the desire and the regret they leave, there cannot but be pleasure, participating as it does in the nature of its object. It is as it were the interpretation of a diviner nature through our own; but its footsteps are like those of a wind over the sea, which the coming calm erases, and whose traces remain only as on the wrinkled sand which paves it. These and corresponding conditions of being are experienced principally by those of the most delicate sensibility and the most enlarged imagination; and the state of mind produced by them is at war with every base desire. The enthusiasm of virtue, love, patriotism, and friendship is essentially linked with such emotions; and whilst they last, self appears as what it is, an atom to a universe. Poets are not only subject to these experiences as spirits of the most refined organization, but they can colour all that they combine with the evanescent hues of this ethereal world; a word, a trait in the representation of a scene or a passion will touch the enchanted chord, and reanimate, in those who have ever experienced these emotions, the sleeping, the cold, the buried image of the past. Poetry thus makes immortal all that is best and most beautiful in the world; it arrests the vanishing apparitions which haunt the interlunations of life, and veiling them, or in language or in form, sends them forth among mankind, bearing sweet news of kindred joy to those with whom their sisters abide—abide, because there is no portal of expression from the caverns of the spirit which they inhabit into the universe of things. Poetry redeems from decay the visitations of the divinity in man.

Poetry turns all things to loveliness; it exalts the beauty of that which is most beautiful, and it adds beauty to that which is most deformed; it marries exultation and horror, grief and pleasure, eternity and change; it subdues to union under its light yoke all irreconcilable things. It transmutes all that it touches, and every form moving within the radiance of its presence is changed by wondrous sympathy to an incarnation of the spirit which it breathes: its secret alchemy turns to potable gold the poisonous waters which flow from death through life; it strips the veil of familiarity from the world, and lays bare the naked and sleeping beauty, which is the spirit of its forms.

All things exist as they are perceived: at least in relation to the percipient. 'The mind is its own place, and of itself can make a heaven of hell, a hell of heaven.' But poetry defeats the curse which binds us to be subjected to the accident of surrounding impressions. And whether it spreads its own figured curtain, or withdraws life's dark veil from before the scene of things, it equally creates for us a being within our being. It makes us the inhabitants of a world to which the familiar world is a chaos. It reproduces the common universe of which we are portions and percipients, and it purges from our inward sight the film of familiarity which obscures from us the wonder of our being. It compels us to feel that which we perceive, and to imagine that which we know. It creates anew the universe, after it has been annihilated in our minds by the recurrence of impressions blunted by reiteration. It justifies the bold and true words of Tasso—'*Non merita nome di creatore, se non Iddio ed il Poeta*'.

A poet, as he is the author to others of the highest wisdom, pleasure, virtue, and glory, so he ought personally to be the happiest, the best, the wisest, and the most illustrious of men. As to his glory, let time be challenged to declare whether the fame of any other institutor of human life be comparable to that of a poet. That he is the wisest, the happiest, and the best, inasmuch as he is a poet, is equally incontrovertible: the greatest poets have been men of the most spotless virtue, of the most consummate prudence, and, if we would look into the interior of their lives, the most fortunate of men: and the exceptions, as they regard those who possessed the poetic faculty in a high yet inferior degree, will be found on consideration to confine rather than destroy the rule. Let us for a moment stoop to the arbitration of popular breath, and usurping and uniting in our own persons the incompatible characters of accuser, witness, judge, and executioner, let us decide without trial, testimony, or form, that certain motives of those who are 'there sitting where we dare not soar,' are reprehensible. Let us assume that Homer was a drunkard, that Virgil was a flatterer, that Horace was a coward, that Tasso was a madman, that Lord Bacon was a peculator, that Raphael was a libertine, that Spenser was a poet laureate. It is inconsistent with this division of our subject to cite living poets, but posterity has done ample justice to the great names now referred to. Their errors have been weighed and found to have been dust in the balance; if their sins 'were as scarlet, they are now white as snow'; they have been washed in the blood of the mediator and redeemer, Time. Observe in what a ludicrous chaos the imputations of real or fictitious crime have been confused in the contemporary calumnies against poetry and poets; consider how little is as it appears—or appears as it is; look to your own motives, and judge not, lest ye be judged.

Poetry, as has been said, differs in this respect from logic, that it is not subject to the control of the active powers of the mind, and that its birth and recurrence have no necessary connection with the consciousness or will. It is presumptuous to determine that these are the necessary conditions of all mental causation, when mental effects are experienced unsusceptible of being referred to them. The frequent recurrence of the poetical power, it is obvious to suppose, may produce in the mind a habit of order and harmony correlative with its own nature and with its effects upon other minds. But in the intervals of inspiration, and they may be frequent without being durable, a poet becomes a man, and is abandoned to the sudden reflux of the influences under which others habitually live. But as he is more delicately organized than other men, and sensible to pain and pleasure, both his own and that of others, in a degree unknown to them, he will avoid the one and pursue the other with an ardour proportioned to this difference. And he renders himself obnoxious to calumny, when he neglects to observe the circumstances under which these objects of universal pursuit and flight have disguised themselves in one another's garments.

But there is nothing necessarily evil in this error, and thus cruelty, envy, revenge, avarice, and the passions purely evil have never formed any portion of the popular imputations on the lives of poets.

I have thought it most favourable to the cause of truth to set down these remarks according to the order in which they were suggested to my mind, by a consideration of the subject itself, instead of observing the formality of a polemical reply; but if the view which they contain be just, they will be found to involve a refutation of the arguers against poetry, so far at least as regards the first division of the subject. I can readily conjecture what should have moved the gall of some learned and intelligent writers who quarrel with certain versifiers; I confess myself, like them, unwilling to be stunned by the Theseids of the hoarse Codri of the day. Bavius and Mævius undoubtedly are, as they ever were, insufferable persons. But it belongs to a philosophical critic to distinguish rather than confound.

The first part of these remarks has related to poetry in its elements and principles; and it has been shown, as well as the narrow limits assigned them would permit, that what is called poetry, in a restricted sense, has a common source with all other forms of order and of beauty, according to which the materials of human life are susceptible of being arranged, and which is poetry in an universal sense.

The second part will have for its object an application of these principles to the present state of the cultivation of poetry, and a defence of the attempt to idealize the modern forms of manners and opinions, and compel them into a subordination to the imaginative and creative faculty. For the literature of England, an energetic development of which has ever preceded or accompanied a great and free development of the national will, has arisen as it were from a new birth. In spite of the low-thoughted envy which would undervalue contemporary merit, our own will be a memorable age in intellectual achievements, and we live among such philosophers and poets as surpass beyond comparison any who have appeared since the last national struggle for civil and religious liberty. The most unfailing herald, companion, and follower of the awakening of a great people to work a beneficial change in opinion or institution, is poetry. At such periods there is an accumulation of the power of communicating and receiving intense and impassioned conceptions respecting man and nature. The person in whom this power resides, may often, as far as regards many portions of their nature, have little apparent correspondence with that spirit of good of which they are the ministers. But even whilst they deny and abjure, they are yet compelled to serve, that power which is seated on the throne of their own soul. It is impossible to read the compositions of the most celebrated writers of the present day without being startled with the electric life which burns within their words. They measure the circumference and sound the depths of human nature with a comprehensive and all-penetrating spirit, and they are themselves perhaps the most sincerely astonished at its manifestations; for it is less their spirit than the spirit of the age. Poets are the hierophants of an unapprehended inspiration; the mirrors of the gigantic shadows which futurity casts upon the present; the words which express what they understand not; the trumpets which sing to battle, and feel not what they inspire; the influence which is moved not, but moves. Poets are the unacknowledged legislators of the world.

43

DREAM-CHILDREN: A REVERIE

Charles Lamb

Children love to listen to stories about their elders, when they were children; to stretch their imagination to the conception of a traditionary great-uncle or grandame, whom they never saw. It was in this spirit that my little ones crept about me the other evening to hear about their great-grandmother Field, who lived in a great house in Norfolk (a hundred times bigger than that in which they and papa lived) which had been the scene—so at least it was generally believed in that part of the country—of the tragic incidents which they had lately become familiar with from the ballad of the Children in the Wood. Certain it is that the whole story of the children and their cruel uncle was to be seen fairly carved out in wood upon the chimney-piece of the great hall, the whole story down to the Robin Redbreasts, till a foolish rich person pulled it down to set up a marble one of modern invention in its stead, with no story upon it. Here Alice put out one of her dear mother's looks, too tender to be called upbraiding. Then I went on to say, how religious and how good their great-grandmother Field was, how beloved and respected by everybody, though she was not indeed the mistress of this great house, but had only the charge of it (and yet in some respects she might be said to be the mistress of it too) committed to her by the owner, who preferred living in a newer and more fashionable mansion which he had purchased somewhere in the adjoining county; but still she lived in it in a manner as if it had been her own, and kept up the dignity of the great house in a sort while she lived, which afterward came to decay, and was nearly pulled down, and all its old ornaments stripped and carried away to the owner's other house, where they were set up, and looked as awkward as if some one were to carry away the old tombs they had seen lately at the Abbey, and stick them up in Lady C.'s tawdry gilt drawing-room. Here John smiled, as much as to say, 'that would be foolish indeed.' And then I told how, when she came to die, her funeral was attended by a concourse of all the poor, and some of the gentry too, of the neighborhood for many miles round, to show their respect for her memory, because she had been such a good and religious woman; so good indeed that she knew all the Psaltery by heart, aye, and a great part of the Testament besides. Here little Alice spread her hands. Then I told what a tall, upright, graceful person their great-grandmother Field once was; and how in her youth she was esteemed the best dancer—here Alice's little right foot played an involuntary movement, till upon my looking grave, it desisted—the best dancer, I was saying, in the county, till a cruel disease, called a cancer, came, and bowed her down with pain; but it could never bend her good spirits, or make them stoop, but they were still upright, because she was so good and religious. Then I told how she was used to sleep by herself in a lone chamber of the great lone house; and how she believed that an apparition of two infants was to be seen at midnight gliding up and down the great staircase near where she slept, but she said 'those innocents would do her no harm'; and how frightened I used to be, though in those days I had my maid to sleep with me, because I was never half so good or religious as she—and yet I never saw the infants. Here John expanded all his eyebrows and tried to look courageous. Then I told how good she was to all her grand-children, having us to the great house in the holidays, where I in particular used to spend many hours by myself, in gazing upon the old busts of the Twelve Caesars, that had been Emperors of Rome, till the old marble heads would seem to live again, or I to be turned into marble with them; how I never could be tired with roaming about that huge mansion, with its vast empty rooms, with their worn-out hangings, fluttering tapestry, and carved oaken panels, with the gilding almost rubbed out—sometimes in the spacious old-fashioned gardens, which I had almost to myself, unless when now and then a solitary gardening man would cross me—and how the nectarines and peaches hung upon the walls, without my ever offering to pluck them, because they were forbidden fruit, unless now and then,—and because I had more pleasure in strolling about among the old melancholy-looking yew trees, or the firs, and picking up the red berries, and the fir apples, which were good for nothing but to look at—or in lying about upon the fresh grass, with all the fine garden smells around me—or basking in the orangery, till I could almost fancy myself ripening, too, along with the oranges and the limes in that grateful warmth—or in watching the dace that darted to and fro in the fish pond, at the bottom of the garden, with here and there a great sulky pike hanging midway down the water in silent state, as if it mocked at their impertinent friskings,—I had more pleasure in these busy-idle diversions than in all the sweet flavors of peaches, nectarines, oranges, and such like common baits of children. Here John slyly deposited back upon the plate a bunch of grapes, which, not unobserved by Alice, he had mediated dividing with her, and both seemed willing to relinquish them for the present as irrelevant. Then, in somewhat a more heightened tone, I told how, though their great-grandmother Field loved all her grand-children, yet in an especial manner she might be said to love their uncle, John L——, because he was so handsome and spirited a youth, and a king to the rest of us; and, instead of moping about in solitary corners, like some of us, he would mount the most mettlesome horse he could get, when but an imp no bigger than themselves, and make it carry him half over the county in a morning, and join the hunters when there were any out—and yet he loved the old great house and gardens too, but had too much spirit to be always pent up within their boundaries—and how their uncle grew up to man's estate as brave as he was handsome, to the admiration of everybody, but of their great-grandmother Field most especially; and how he used to carry me upon his back when I was a lame-footed boy—for he was a good bit older than me—many a mile when I could not walk for pain;—and how in after life he became lame-footed too, and I did not always (I fear) make allowances enough for him when he was impatient, and in pain, nor remember sufficiently how considerate he had been to me when I was lame-footed; and how when he died, though he had not been dead an hour, it seemed as if he had died a great while ago, such a distance there is betwixt life and death; and how I bore his death as I thought pretty well at first, but afterward it haunted and haunted me; and though I did not cry or take it to heart as some do, and as I think he would have done if I had died, yet I missed him all day long, and knew not till then how much I had loved him. I missed his kindness, and I missed his crossness, and wished him to be alive again, to be quarreling with him (for we quarreled sometimes), rather than not have him again, and was as uneasy without him, as he their poor uncle must have been when the doctor took off his limb. Here the children fell a crying, and asked if their little mourning which they had on was not for uncle John, and they looked up and prayed me not to go on about their uncle, but to tell them some stories about their pretty, dead mother. Then I told them how for seven long years, in hope sometimes, sometimes in despair, yet persisting ever, I courted the fair Alice W——n; and, as much as children could understand, I explained to them what coyness, and difficulty, and denial meant in maidens—when suddenly, turning to Alice, the soul of the first Alice looked out at her eyes with such a reality of re-presentment, that I became in doubt which of them stood there before me, or whose that bright hair was; and while I stood gazing, both the children gradually grew fainter to my view, receding, and still receding till nothing at last but two mournful features were seen in the uttermost distance, which, without speech, strangely impressed upon me the effects of speech: 'We are not of Alice, nor of thee, nor are we children at all. The children of Alice call Bartrum father. We are nothing; less than nothing, and dreams. We are only what might have been, and must wait upon the tedious shores of Lethe millions of ages before we have existence, and a name'—and immediately awaking, I found myself quietly seated in my bachelor armchair, where I had fallen asleep, with the faithful Bridget unchanged by my side—but John L. (or James Elia) was gone forever.

44

OF TRAGEDY

David Hume

It seems an unaccountable pleasure, which the spectators of a well-written tragedy receive from sorrow, terror, anxiety, and other passions, that are in themselves disagreeable and uneasy. The more they are touched and affected, the more are they delighted with the spectacle; and as soon as the uneasy passions cease to operate, the piece is at an end. One scene of full joy and contentment and security is the utmost, that any composition of this kind can bear; and it is sure always to be the concluding one. If, in the texture of the piece, there be interwoven any scenes of satisfaction, they afford only faint gleams of pleasure, which are thrown in by way of variety, and in order to plunge the actors into deeper distress, by means of that contrast and disappointment. The whole art of the poet is employed, in rouzing and supporting the compassion and indignation, the anxiety and resentment of his audience. They are pleased in proportion as they are afflicted, and never are so happy as when they employ tears, sobs, and cries to give vent to their sorrow, and relieve their heart, swoln with the tenderest sympathy and compassion.

The few critics who have had some tincture of philosophy, have remarked this singular phenomenon, and have endeavoured to account for it.

L'Abbe *Dubos*, in his reflections on poetry and painting, asserts, that nothing is in general so disagreeable to the mind as the languid, listless state of indolence, into which it falls upon the removal of all passion and occupation. To get rid of this painful situation, it seeks every amusement and pursuit; business, gaming, shews, executions;

whatever will rouze the passions, and take its attention from itself. No matter what the passion is: Let it be disagreeable, afflicting, melancholy, disordered; it is still better than that insipid languor, which arises from perfect tranquillity and repose.

It is impossible not to admit this account, as being, at least in part satisfactory. You may observe, when there are several tables of gaming, that all the company run to those, where the deepest play is, even though they find not there the best players. The view, or, at least, imagination of high passions; arising from great loss or gain, affects the spectator by sympathy, gives him some touches of the same passions, and serves him for a momentary entertainment. It makes the time pass the easier with him, and is some relief to that oppression, under which men commonly labour, when left entirely to their own thoughts and meditations.

We find that common liars always magnify, in their narrations, all kinds of danger, pain, distress, sickness, deaths, murders, and cruelties; as well as joy, beauty, mirth, and magnificence. It is an absurd secret, which they have for pleasing their company, fixing their attention, and attaching them to such marvellous relations, by the passions and emotions, which they excite.

There is, however, a difficulty in applying to the present subject, in its full extent, this solution, however ingenious and satisfactory it may appear. It is certain, that the same object of distress, which pleases in a tragedy, were it really set before us, would give the most unfeigned uneasiness; though it be then the most effectual cure to languor and indolence. Monsieur *Fontenelle* seems to have been sensible to this difficulty; and accordingly attempts another solution of the phaenomenon; at least makes some addition to the theory above mentioned.

'Pleasure and pain,' says he, 'which are two sentiments so different in themselves, differ not so much in their cause. From the instance of tickling, it appears, that the movement of pleasure, pushed a little too far, becomes pain; and that the movement of pain, a little moderated, becomes pleasure. Hence it proceeds, that there is such a thing as a sorrow, soft and agreeable. It is a pain weakened and diminished. The heart likes naturally to be moved and affected. Melancholy objects suit it, and even disastrous and sorrowful, provided they are softened by some circumstance. It is certain, that, on the theatre, the representation has almost the effect of reality; yet it has not altogether that effect. However we may be hurried away by the spectacle; whatever dominion the senses and imagination may usurp over the reason, there still lurks at the bottom a certain idea of falsehood in the whole of what we see. This idea, though weak and disguised, suffices to diminish the pain which we suffer from the misfortunes of those whom we love, and to reduce that affliction to such a pitch as converts it into a pleasure. We weep for the misfortune of a hero, to whom we are attached. In the same instant we comfort ourselves, by reflecting, that it is nothing but a fiction: And it is precisely that mixture of sentiments, which composes an agreeable sorrow, and tears that delight us. But as that affliction, which is caused by exterior and sensible objects, is stronger than the consolation which arises from an internal reflection, they are the effects and symptoms of sorrow, that ought to predominate in the composition.'

This solution seems just and convincing; but perhaps it wants still some new addition, in order to make it answer fully the phaenomenon, which we here examine. All the passions, excited by eloquence, are agreeable in the highest degree, as well as those which are moved by painting and the theatre. The epilogues of *Cicero* are, on this account chiefly, the delight of every reader of taste; and it is difficult to read some of them without the deepest sympathy and sorrow. His merit as an orator, no doubt, depends much on his success in this particular. When he had raised tears in his judges and all his audience, they were then the most highly delighted, and expressed the greatest satisfaction with the pleader. The pathetic description of the butchery, made by *Verres* of the *Sicilian* captains, is a masterpiece of this kind: But I believe none will affirm, that the being present at a melancholy scene of that nature would afford any entertainment. Neither is the sorrow here softened by fiction: For the audience were convinced of the reality of every circumstance. What is it then, which in this case raises a pleasure from the bosom of uneasiness, so to speak; and a pleasure, which still retains all the features and outward symptoms of distress and sorrow?

I answer: This extraordinary effect proceeds from that very eloquence, with which the melancholy scene is represented. The genius required to paint objects in a lively manner, the art employed in collecting all the pathetic circumstances, the judgment displayed in disposing them: the exercise, I say, of these noble talents, together with the force of expression, and beauty of oratorial numbers, diffuse the highest satisfaction on the audience, and excite the most delightful movements. By this means, the uneasiness of the melancholy passions is not only overpowered and effaced by something stronger of an opposite kind; but the whole impulse of those passions is converted into pleasure, and swells the delight which the eloquence raises in us. The same force of oratory, employed on an uninteresting subject, would not please half so much, or rather would appear altogether ridiculous; and the mind, being left in absolute calmness and indifference, would relish none of those beauties of imagination or expression, which, if joined to passion, give it such exquisite entertainment. The impulse or vehemence, arising from sorrow, compassion, indignation, receives a new direction from the sentiments of beauty. The latter, being the predominant emotion, seize the whole mind, and convert the former into themselves, at least tincture them so strongly as totally to alter their nature. And the soul, being, at the same time, rouzed by passion, and charmed by eloquence, feels on the whole a strong movement, which is altogether delightful.

The same principle takes place in tragedy; with this addition, that tragedy is an imitation; and imitation is always of itself agreeable. This circumstance serves still farther to smooth the motions of passion, and convert the whole feeling into one uniform and strong enjoyment. Objects of the greatest terror and distress please in painting, and please more than the most beautiful objects, that appear calm and indifferent. [Painters make no scruple of representing distress and sorrow as well as any other passion: But they seem not to dwell so much on these melancholy affections as the poets, who, though they copy every motion of the human breast, yet pass quickly over the agreeable sentiments. A painter represents only one instant; and if that be passionate enough, it is sure to affect and delight the spectator: But nothing can furnish to the poet a variety of scenes and incidents and sentiments, except distress, terror, or anxiety. Compleat joy and satisfaction is attended with security, and leaves no farther room for action.]

The affection, rouzing the mind, excites a large stock of spirit and vehemence; which is all transformed into pleasure by the force of the prevailing movement. It is thus the fiction of tragedy softens the passion, by an infusion of a new feeling; not merely by weakening or diminishing the sorrow. You may by degrees weaken a real sorrow, till it totally disappears; yet in none of its gradations will it ever give pleasure; except, perhaps, by accident, to a man sunk under lethargic indolence, whom it rouzes from that languid state.

To confirm this theory, it will be sufficient to produce other instances, where the subordinate movement is converted into the predominant, and gives force to it, though of a different, and even sometimes though of a contrary nature.

Novelty naturally rouzes the mind, and attracts our attention; and the movements, which it causes, are always converted into any passion, belonging to the object, and join their force to it. Whether an event excite joy or sorrow, pride or shame, anger or good-will, it is sure to produce a stronger affection, when new or unusual. And though novelty of itself be agreeable, it fortifies the painful, as well as agreeable passions.

Had you any intention to move a person extremely by the narration of any event, the best method of encreasing its effect would be artfully to delay informing him of it, and first to excite his curiosity and impatience before you let him into the secret. This is the artifice practised by *Iago* in the famous scene of *Shakespeare*; and every spectator is sensible, that *Othello*'s jealousy acquires additional force from his preceding impatience, and that the subordinate passion is here readily transformed into the predominant one.

Difficulties encrease passions of every kind; and by rouzing our attention, and exciting our active powers, they produce an emotion, which nourishes the prevailing affection. Parents commonly love that child most, whose sickly infirm frame of body has occasioned them the greatest pains, trouble, and anxiety in rearing him. The agreeable sentiment of affection here acquires force from sentiments of uneasiness. Nothing endears so much a friend as sorrow for his death. The pleasure of his company has not so powerful an influence. Jealousy is a painful passion; yet without some share of it, the agreeable affection of love has difficulty to subsist in its full force and violence. Absence is also a great source of complaint among lovers, and gives them the greatest uneasiness: Yet nothing is more favourable to their mutual passion than short intervals of that kind. And if long intervals often prove fatal, it is only because, through time, men are accustomed to them, and they cease to give uneasiness. Jealousy and absence in love compose the *dolce piccante* of the *Italians*, which they suppose so essential to all pleasure.

There is a fine observation of the elder *Pliny*, which illustrates the principle here insisted on. It is very remarkable, says he, that the last works of celebrated artists, which they left imperfect, are always the most prized, such as the *Iris* of *Aristides*, the *Tydarides* of *Nichomachus*, the *Medea* of *Timomachus*, and the *Venus* of *Appelles*. These are valued even above their finished productions: The broken lineaments of the piece, and the half-formed idea of the painter are carefully studied; and our very grief for that curious hand, which had been stopped by death, is an additional encrease to our pleasure.

These instances (and many more might be collected) are sufficient to afford us some insight into the analogy of nature, and to show us, that the pleasure, which poets, orators, and musicians give us, by exciting grief, sorrow, indignation, compassion, is not so extraordinary or paradoxical, as it may at first sight appear. The force of imagination, the energy of expression, the power of numbers, the charms of imitation; all these are naturally, of themselves delightful to the mind: And when the object presented lays also hold of some affection, the pleasure still rises upon us, by the conversion of this subordinate movement into that which is predominant. The passion, though, perhaps, naturally, and when excited by the simple appearance of a real object, it may be painful; yet is so smoothed, and softened, and mollified, when raised by the finer arts, that it affords the highest entertainment.

To confirm this reasoning, we may observe, that if the movements of the imagination be not predominant above those of the passions, a contrary effect follows; and the former, being now subordinate, is converted into the latter, and still farther encreases the pain and affliction of the sufferer.

Who could ever think of it as a good expedient for comforting an afflicted parent, to exaggerate, with all the force of elocution, the irreparable loss, which he has met with by the death of a favourite child? The more power of imagination and expression you here employ, the more you encrease his despair and affliction.

The shame, confusion, and terror of *Verres* no doubt, rose in proportion to the noble eloquence and vehemence of *Cicero*: So also did his pain and uneasiness. These former passions were too strong for the pleasure arising from the beauties of elocution; and operated, though from the same principle, yet in a contrary manner, to the sympathy, compassion, and indignation of the audience.

Lord Clarendon, when he approaches towards the catastrophe of the royal party, supposes, that his narration must then become infinitely disagreeable; and he hurries over the king's death, without giving us one circumstance of it. He considers it as too horrid a scene to be contemplated with any satisfaction, or even without the utmost pain and aversion. He himself, as well as the readers of that age, were too deeply inmeshed in the events, and felt a pain from subjects, which an historian and a reader of another age would regard as the most pathetic and most interesting, and, by consequence, the most agreeable.

An action, represented in tragedy, may be too bloody and atrocious. It may excite such movements of horror as will not soften into pleasure; and the greatest energy of expression, bestowed on descriptions of that nature, serves only to augment our uneasiness. Such is that action represented in the *Ambitious Stepmother*, where a venerable old man, raised to the height of fury and despair, rushes against a pillar, and striking his head upon it, besmears it all over with mingled brains and gore. The *English* theatre abounds too much with such shocking images.

Even the common sentiments of compassion require to be softened by some agreeable affection, in order to give a thorough satisfaction to the audience. The mere suffering of plaintive virtue, under the triumphant tyranny and oppression of vice, forms a disagreeable spectacle, and is carefully avoided by all masters of the drama. In order to dismiss the audience with entire satisfaction and contentment, the virtue must either convert itself into a noble courageous despair, or the vice receive its proper punishment.

Painters appear in this light to have been very unhappy in their subjects. As they wrought much for churches and convents, they have chiefly represented such horrible subjects as crucifixions and martyrdoms, where nothing appears but tortures, wounds, executions, and passive suffering, without any action or affection. When they turned their pencil from this ghastly mythology, they had commonly recourse to *Ovid*, whose fictions, though passionate and agreeable, are scarcely natural or probable enough for painting.

The same inversion of that principle, which is here insisted on, displays itself in common life, as in the effects of oratory and poetry. Raise so the subordinate passion that it becomes the predominant, it swallows up that affection which it before nourished and encreased. Too much jealousy extinguishes love: Too much difficulty renders us indifferent: Too much sickness and infirmity disgusts a selfish and unkind parent.

What so disagreeable as the dismal, gloomy, disastrous stories, with which melancholy people entertain their companions? The uneasy passion, being there raised alone, unaccompanied with any spirit, genius, or eloquence, conveys a pure uneasiness, and is attended with nothing that can soften it into pleasure or satisfaction.

45

A FAMILIAR PREFACE

Joseph Conrad

As a general rule we do not want much encouragement to talk about ourselves; yet this little book is the result of a friendly suggestion, and even of a little friendly pressure. I defended myself with some spirit; but, with characteristic tenacity, the friendly voice insisted, 'You know, you really must.'

It was not an argument, but I submitted at once. If one must!...

You perceive the force of a word. He who wants to persuade should put his trust not in the right argument, but in the right word. The power of sound has always been greater than the power of sense. I don't say this by way of disparagement. It is better for mankind to be impressionable than reflective. Nothing humanely great—great, I mean, as affecting a whole mass of lives—has come from reflection. On the other hand, you cannot fail to see the power of mere words; such words as Glory, for instance, or Pity. I won't mention any more. They are not far to seek. Shouted with perseverance, with ardour, with conviction, these two by their sound alone have set whole nations in motion and upheaved the dry, hard ground on which rests our whole social fabric. There's 'virtue' for you if you like!...Of course the accent must be attended to. The right accent. That's very important. The capacious lung, the thundering or the tender vocal chords. Don't talk to me of your Archimedes' lever.

He was an absent-minded person with a mathematical imagination. Mathematics commands all my respect, but I have no use for engines. Give me the right word and the right accent and I will move the world.

What a dream for a writer! Because written words have their accent, too. Yes! Let me only find the right word! Surely it must be lying somewhere among the wreckage of all the plaints and all the exultations poured out aloud since the first day when hope, the undying, came down on earth. It may be there, close by, disregarded, invisible, quite at hand. But it's no good. I believe there are men who can lay hold of a needle in a pottle of hay at the first try. For myself, I have never had such luck. And then there is that accent. Another difficulty. For who is going to tell whether the accent is right or wrong till the word is shouted, and fails to be heard, perhaps, and goes down-wind, leaving the world unmoved? Once upon a time there lived an emperor who was a sage and something of a literary man. He jotted down on ivory tablets thoughts, maxims, reflections which chance has preserved for the edification of posterity. Among other sayings—I am quoting from memory—I remember this solemn admonition: 'Let all thy words have the accent of heroic truth.' The accent of heroic truth! This is very fine, but I am thinking that it is an easy matter for an austere emperor to jot down grandiose advice. Most of the working truths on this earth are humble, not heroic; and there have been times in the history of mankind when the accents of heroic truth have moved it to nothing but derision.

Nobody will expect to find between the covers of this little book words of extraordinary potency or accents of irresistible heroism. However humiliating for my self esteem, I must confess that the counsels of Marcus Aurelius are not for me. They are more fit for a moralist than for an artist. Truth of a modest sort I can promise you, and also sincerity. That complete, praise worthy sincerity which, while it delivers one into the hands of one's enemies, is as likely as not to embroil one with one's friends.

'Embroil' is perhaps too strong an expression. I can't imagine among either my enemies or my friends a being so hard up for something to do as to quarrel with me. 'To disappoint one's friends' would be nearer the mark. Most, almost all, friend ships of the writing period of my life have come to me through my books; and I know that a novelist lives in his work. He stands there, the only reality in an invented world, among imaginary things, happenings, and people. Writing about them, he is only writing about himself. But the disclosure is not complete. He remains, to a certain extent, a figure behind the veil; a suspected rather than a seen presence—a movement and a voice behind the draperies of fiction. In these personal notes there is no such veil. And I cannot help thinking of a passage in the *Imitation of Christ* where the ascetic author, who knew life so profoundly, says that 'there are persons esteemed on their reputation who by showing themselves destroy the opinion one had of them.' This is the danger incurred by an author of fiction who sets out to talk about himself without disguise.

While these reminiscent pages were appearing serially I was remonstrated with for bad economy; as if such writing were a form of self-indulgence wasting the substance of future volumes. It seems that I am not sufficiently literary. Indeed, a man who never wrote a line for print till he was thirty-six cannot bring himself to look upon his existence and his experience, upon the sum of his thoughts, sensations, and emotions, upon his memories and his regrets, and the whole possession of his past, as only so much material for his hands. Once before, some three years ago, when I published *The Mirror of the Sea*, a volume of impressions and memories, the same remarks were made to me. Practical remarks. But, truth to say, I have never understood the kind of thrift they recommend. I wanted to pay my tribute to the sea, its ships and its men, to whom I remain indebted for so much which has gone to make me what I am. That seemed to me the only shape in which I could offer it to their shades. There could not be a question in my mind of anything else. It is quite possible that I am a bad economist; but it is certain that I am incorrigible.

Having matured in the surroundings and under the special conditions of sea life, I have a special piety toward that form of my past; for its impressions were vivid, its appeal direct, its demands such as could be responded to with the natural elation of youth and strength equal to the call. There was nothing in them to perplex a young conscience. Having broken away from my origins under a storm of blame from every quarter which had the merest shadow of right to voice an opinion, removed by great distances from such natural affections as were still left to me, and even estranged, in a measure, from them by the totally unintelligible character of the life which had seduced me so mysteriously from my allegiance, I may safely say that through the blind force of circumstances the sea was to be all my world and the merchant service my only home for a long succession of years. No wonder, then, that in my two exclusively sea books—*The Nigger of the Narcissus*, and *The Mirror of the Sea* (and in the few short sea stories like 'Youth' and 'Typhoon')—I have tried with an almost filial regard to render the vibration of life in the great world of waters, in the hearts of the simple men who have for ages traversed its solitudes, and also that something sentient which seems to dwell in ships—the creatures of their hands and the objects of their care.

One's literary life must turn frequently for sustenance to memories and seek discourse with the shades, unless one has made up one's mind to write only in order to reprove mankind for what it is, or praise it for what it is not, or—generally—to teach it how to behave. Being neither quarrelsome, nor a flatterer, nor a sage, I have done none of these things, and I am prepared to put up serenely with the insignificance which attaches to persons who are not meddlesome in some way or other. But resignation is not indifference. I would not like to be left standing as a mere spectator on the bank of the great stream carrying onward so many lives. I would fain claim for myself the faculty of so much insight as can be expressed in a voice of sympathy and compassion.

It seems to me that in one, at least, authoritative quarter of criticism I am suspected of a certain unemotional, grim acceptance of facts—of what the French would call *secheresse du coeur*. Fifteen years of unbroken silence before praise or blame testify sufficiently to my respect for criticism, that fine flower of personal expression in the garden of letters. But this is more of a personal matter, reaching the man behind the work, and therefore it may be alluded to in a volume which is a personal note in the margin of the public page. Not that I feel hurt in the least. The charge—if it amounted to a charge at all—was made in the most considerate terms; in a tone of regret.

My answer is that if it be true that every novel contains an element of autobiography—and this can hardly be denied, since the creator can only express himself in his creation—then there are some of us to whom an open display of sentiment is repugnant.

I would not unduly praise the virtue of restraint. It is often merely temperamental. But it is not always a sign of coldness. It may be pride. There can be nothing more humiliating than to see the shaft of one's emotion miss the mark of either laughter or tears. Nothing more humiliating! And this for the reason that should the mark be missed, should the open display of emotion fail to move, then it must perish unavoidably in disgust or contempt. No artist can be reproached for shrinking from a risk which only fools run to meet and only genius dare confront with impunity. In a task which mainly consists in laying one's soul more or less bare to the world, a regard for decency, even at the cost of success, is but the regard for one's own dignity which is inseparably united with the dignity of one's work.

And then—it is very difficult to be wholly joyous or wholly sad on this earth. The comic, when it is human, soon takes upon itself a face of pain; and some of our griefs (some only, not all, for it is the capacity for suffering which makes man August in the eyes of men) have their source in weaknesses which must be recognized with smiling compassion as the common inheritance of us all. Joy and sorrow in this world pass into each other, mingling their forms and their murmurs in the twilight of life as mysterious as an over shadowed ocean, while the dazzling brightness of supreme hopes lies far off, fascinating and still, on the distant edge of the horizon.

Yes! I, too, would like to hold the magic wand giving that command over laughter and tears which is declared to be the highest achievement of imaginative literature. Only, to be a great magician one must surrender oneself to occult and irresponsible powers, either outside or within one's breast. We have all heard of simple men selling their souls for love or power to some grotesque devil. The most ordinary intelligence can perceive without much reflection that anything of the sort is bound to be a fool's bargain. I don't lay claim to particular wisdom because of my dislike and distrust of such transactions. It may be my sea training acting upon a natural disposition to keep good hold on the one thing really mine, but the fact is that I have a positive horror of losing even for one moving moment that full possession of my self which is the first condition of good service. And I have carried my notion of good service from my earlier into my later existence. I, who have never sought in the written word anything else but a form of the Beautiful—I have carried over that article of creed from the decks of ships to the more circumscribed space of my desk, and by that act, I suppose, I have become permanently imperfect in the eyes of the ineffable company of pure esthetes.

As in political so in literary action a man wins friends for himself mostly by the passion of his prejudices and by the consistent narrowness of his outlook. But I have never been able to love what was not lovable or hate what was not hateful out of deference for some general principle. Whether there be any courage in making this admission I know not. After the middle turn of life's way we consider dangers and joys with a tranquil mind. So I proceed in peace to declare that I have always suspected in the effort to bring into play the extremities of emotions the debasing touch of insincerity. In order to move others deeply we must deliberately allow ourselves to be carried away beyond the bounds of our normal sensibility—innocently enough, perhaps, and of necessity, like an actor who raises his voice on the stage above the pitch of natural conversation—but still we have to do that. And surely this is no great sin. But the danger lies in the writer becoming the victim of his own exaggeration, losing the exact notion of sincerity, and in the end coming to despise truth itself as something too cold, too blunt for his purpose—as, in fact, not good enough for his insistent emotion. From laughter and tears the descent is easy to snivelling and giggles.

These may seem selfish considerations; but you can't, in sound morals, condemn a man for taking care of his own integrity. It is his clear duty. And least of all can you condemn an artist pursuing, however humbly and imperfectly, a creative aim. In that interior world where his thought and his emotions go seeking for the experience of imagined adventures, there are no policemen, no law, no pressure of circumstance or dread of opinion to keep him within bounds. Who then is going to say Nay to his temptations if not his conscience?

And besides—this, remember, is the place and the moment of perfectly open talk—I think that all ambitions are lawful except those which climb upward on the miseries or credulities of mankind. All intellectual and artistic ambitions are permissible, up to and even beyond the limit of prudent sanity. They can hurt no one. If they are mad, then so much the worse for the artist. Indeed, as virtue is said to be, such ambitions are their own reward. Is it such a very mad presumption to believe in the sovereign power of one's art, to try for other means, for other ways of affirming this belief in the deeper appeal of one's work? To try to go deeper is not to be insensible. A historian of hearts is not a historian of emotions, yet he penetrates further, restrained as he may be, since his aim is to reach the very fount of laughter and tears. The sight of human affairs deserves admiration and pity. They are worthy of respect, too. And he is not insensible who pays them the undemonstrative tribute of a sigh which is not a sob, and of a smile which is not a grin. Resignation, not mystic, not detached, but resignation open-eyed, conscious, and informed by love, is the only one of our feelings for which it is impossible to become a sham.

Not that I think resignation the last word of wisdom. I am too much the creature of my time for that. But I think that the proper wisdom is to will what the gods will without, perhaps, being certain what their will is—or even if they have a will of their own. And in this matter of life and art it is not the Why that matters so much to our happiness as the How. As the Frenchman said, '*Il y a toujours la maniere.*' Very true. Yes. There is the manner. The manner in laughter, in tears, in irony, in indignations and enthusiasms, in judgments—and even in love. The manner in which, as in the features and character of a human face, the inner truth is foreshadowed for those who know how to look at their kind.

Those who read me know my conviction that the world, the temporal world, rests on a few very simple ideas; so simple that they must be as old as the hills. It rests notably, among others, on the idea of Fidelity. At a time when nothing which is not revolutionary in some way or other can expect to attract much attention I have not been revolutionary in my writings. The revolutionary spirit is mighty convenient in this, that it frees one from all scruples as regards ideas. Its hard, absolute optimism is repulsive to my mind by the menace of fanaticism and intolerance it contains. No doubt one should smile at these things; but, imperfect Esthete, I am no better Philosopher.

All claim to special righteousness awakens in me that scorn and danger from which a philosophical mind should be free...

I fear that trying to be conversational I have only managed to be unduly discursive. I have never been very well acquainted with the art of conversation—that art which, I understand, is supposed to be lost now. My young days, the days when one's habits and character are formed, have been rather familiar with long silences. Such voices as broke into them were anything but conversational. No. I haven't got the habit. Yet this discursiveness is not so irrelevant to the handful of pages which follow. They, too, have been charged with discursiveness, with disregard of chronological order (which is in itself a crime), with unconventionality of form (which is an impropriety). I was told severely that the public would view with displeasure the informal character of my recollections. 'Alas!' I protested, mildly. 'Could I begin with the sacramental words, "I was born on such a date in such a place"? The remoteness of the locality would have robbed the statement of all interest. I haven't lived through wonderful adventures to be related seriatim. I haven't known distinguished men on whom I could pass fatuous remarks. I haven't been mixed up with great or scandalous affairs. This is but a bit of psychological document, and even so, I haven't written it with a view to put forward any conclusion of my own.'

But my objector was not placated. These were good reasons for not writing at all—not a defense of what stood written already, he said.

I admit that almost anything, anything in the world, would serve as a good reason for not writing at all. But since I have written them, all I want to say in their defense is that these memories put down without any regard for established conventions have not been thrown off without system and purpose. They have their hope and their aim. The hope that from the reading of these pages there may emerge at last the vision of a personality; the man behind the books so fundamentally dissimilar as, for instance, *Almayer's Folly* and *The Secret Agent*, and yet a coherent, justifiable personality both in its origin and in its action. This is the hope. The immediate aim, closely associated with the hope, is to give the record of personal memories by presenting faithfully the feelings and sensations connected with the writing of my first book and with my first contact with the sea.

In the purposely mingled resonance of this double strain a friend here and there will perhaps detect a subtle accord.

46

BUDS AND BIRD-VOICES

Nathaniel Hawthorne

Balmy Spring—weeks later than we expected, and months later than we longed for her—comes at last to revive the moss on the roof and walls of our old mansion. She peeps brightly into my study window, inviting me to throw it open and create a summer atmosphere by the intermixture of her genial breath with the black and cheerless comfort of the stove. As the casement ascends, forth into infinite space fly the innumerable forms of thought or fancy that have kept me company in the retirement of this little chamber during the sluggish lapse of wintry weather—visions gay, grotesque and sad, pictures of real life tinted with nature's homely gray and russet, scenes in dreamland bedizened with rainbow-hues which faded before they were well laid on. All these may vanish now, and leave me to mold a fresh existence out of sunshine. Brooding Meditation may flap her dusky wings and take her owl-like flight, blinking amid the cheerfulness of noontide. Such companions befit the season of frosted window-panes and crackling fires, when the blast howls through the black-ash trees of our avenue, and the drifting snowstorm chokes up the wood paths and fills the highway from stone wall to stone wall. In the spring and summer time all somber thoughts should follow the winter northward with the somber and thoughtful crows. The old paradisiacal economy of life is again in force: we live, not to think nor to labor, but for the simple end of being happy; nothing for the present hour is worthy of man's infinite capacity save to imbibe the warm smile of heaven and sympathize with the reviving earth.

The present Spring comes onward with fleeter footsteps because

Winter lingered so unconscionably long that with her best diligence she can hardly retrieve half the allotted period of her reign. It is but a fortnight since I stood on the brink of our swollen river and beheld the accumulated ice of four frozen months go down the stream. Except in streaks here and there upon the hillsides, the whole visible universe was then covered with deep snow the nethermost layer of which had been deposited by an early December storm. It was a sight to make the beholder torpid, in the impossibility of imagining how this vast white napkin was to be removed from the face of the corpse-like world in less time than had been required to spread it there. But who can estimate the power of gentle influences, whether amid material desolation or the moral winter of man's heart? There have been no tempestuous rains—even no sultry days—but a constant breath of southern winds, with now a day of kindly sunshine, and now a no less kindly mist, or a soft descent of showers, in which a smile and a blessing seemed to have been steeped. The snow has vanished as if by magic; whatever heaps may be hidden in the woods and deep gorges of the hills, only two solitary specks remain in the landscape, and those I shall almost regret to miss when to-morrow I look for them in vain. Never before, methinks, has spring pressed so closely on the footsteps of retreating winter. Along the roadside the green blades of grass have sprouted on the very edge of the snowdrifts. The pastures and mowing fields have not yet assumed a general aspect of verdure, but neither have they the cheerless brown tint which they wear in later autumn, when vegetation has entirely ceased; there is now a faint shadow of life, gradually brightening into the warm reality. Some tracts in a happy exposure—as, for instance, yonder southwestern slope of an orchard, in front of that old red farmhouse beyond the river—such patches of land already wear a beautiful and tender green to which no future luxuriance can add a charm. It looks unreal—a prophecy, a hope, a transitory effect of some peculiar light, which will vanish with the slightest motion of the eye. But beauty is never a delusion; not these verdant tracts but the dark and barren landscape all around them is a shadow and a dream. Each moment wins some portion of the earth from death to life; a sudden gleam of verdure brightens along the sunny slope of a bank which an instant ago was brown and bare. You look again, and, behold an apparition of green grass!

The trees in our orchard and elsewhere are as yet naked, but already appear full of life and vegetable blood. It seems as if by one magic touch they might instantaneously burst into full foliage, and that the wind which now sighs through their naked branches might make sudden music amid innumerable leaves. The moss-grown willow tree which for forty years past has overshadowed these western windows will be among the first to put on its green attire. There are some objections to the willow: it is not a dry and cleanly tree, and impresses the beholder with an association of sliminess. No trees, I think, are perfectly agreeable as companions unless they have glossy leaves, dry bark, and a firm and hard texture of trunk and branches. But the willow is almost the earliest to gladden us with the promise and reality of beauty in its graceful and delicate foliage, and the last to scatter its yellow, yet scarcely-withered, leaves upon the ground. All through the winter, too, its yellow twigs give it a sunny aspect which is not without a cheering influence even in the grayest and gloomiest day. Beneath a clouded sky it faithfully remembers the sunshine. Our old house would lose a charm were the willow to be cut down, with its golden crown over the snow-covered roof, and its heap of summer verdure.

The lilac shrubs under my study windows are likewise almost in leaf; in two or three days more I may put forth my hand and pluck the topmost bough in its freshest green. These lilacs are very aged, and have lost the luxuriant foliage of their prime. The heart or the judgment or the moral sense or the taste is dissatisfied with their present aspect. Old age is not venerable when it embodies itself in lilacs, rose-bushes, or any other ornamental shrubs; it seems as if such plants, as they grow only for beauty, ought to flourish only in immortal youth—or, at least, to die before their sad decrepitude. Trees of beauty are trees of paradise, and therefore not subject to decay by their original nature, though they have lost that precious birthright by being transplanted to an earthly soil. There is a kind of ludicrous unfitness in the idea of a time-stricken and grandfatherly lilac-bush. The analogy holds good in human life. Persons who can only be graceful and ornamental—who can give the world nothing but flowers—should die young, and never be seen with gray hair and wrinkles, any more than the flower-shrubs with mossy bark and blighted foliage, like the lilacs under my window. Not that beauty is worthy of less than immortality. No; the beautiful should live forever, and thence, perhaps, the sense of impropriety when we see it triumphed over by time. Apple trees, on the other hand, grow old without reproach. Let them live as long as they may, and contort themselves into whatever perversity of shape they please, and deck their withered limbs with a springtime gaudiness of pink-blossoms, still they are respectable, even if they afford us only an apple or two in a season. Those few apples—or, at all events, the remembrance of apples in bygone years—are the atonement which utilitarianism inexorably demands for the privilege of lengthened life. Human flower shrubs, if they will grow old on earth, should, besides their lovely blossoms, bear some kind of fruit that will satisfy earthly appetites, else neither man nor the decorum of nature will deem it fit that the moss should gather on them.

One of the first things that strikes the attention when the white sheet of winter is withdrawn is the neglect and disarray that lay hidden beneath it. Nature is not cleanly, according to our prejudices. The beauty of preceding years, now transformed to brown and blighted deformity, obstructs the brightening loveliness of the present hour. Our avenue is strewn with the whole crop of autumn's withered leaves. There are quantities of decayed branches which one tempest after another has flung down, black and rotten, and one or two with the ruin of a bird's nest clinging to them. In the garden are the dried bean-vines, the brown stalks of the asparagus-bed, and melancholy old cabbages which were frozen into the soil before their unthrifty cultivator could find time to gather them. How invariable throughout all the forms of life do we find these intermingled memorials of death! On the soil of thought and in the garden of the heart, as well as in the sensual world, lie withered leaves—the ideas and feelings that we have done with. There is no wind strong enough to sweep them away; infinite space will not garner them from our sight. What mean they?

Why may we not be permitted to live and enjoy as if this were the first life and our own the primal enjoyment, instead of treading always on these dry bones and mouldering relics from the aged accumulation of which springs all that now appears so young and new? Sweet must have been the spring-time of Eden, when no earlier year had strewn its decay upon the virgin turf, and no former experience had ripened into summer and faded into autumn in the hearts of its inhabitants! That was a world worth living in.—Oh, thou murmurer, it is out of the very wantonness of such a life that thou feignest these idle lamentations. There is no decay. Each human soul is the first created inhabitant of its own Eden.—We dwell in an old moss-covered mansion and tread in the worn footprints of the past and have a gray clergyman's ghost for our daily and nightly inmate, yet all these outward circumstances are made less than visionary by the renewing power of the spirit. Should the spirit ever lose this power—should the withered leaves and the rotten branches and the moss-covered house and the ghost of the gray past ever become its realities, and the verdure and the freshness merely its faint dream—then let it pray to be released from earth. It will need the air of heaven to revive its pristine energies.

What an unlooked for flight was this from our shadowy avenue of black-ash and balm-of-Gilead trees into the infinite! Now we have our feet again upon the turf. Nowhere does the grass spring up so industriously as in this homely yard, along the base of the stone wall and in the sheltered nooks of the buildings, and especially around the southern door-step—a locality which seems particularly favorable to its growth, for it is already tall enough to bend over and wave in the wind. I observe that several weeds—and, most frequently, a plant that stains the fingers with its yellow juice—have survived and retained their freshness and sap throughout the winter. One knows not how they have deserved such an exception from the common lot of their race. They are now the patriarchs of the departed year, and may preach mortality to the present generation of flowers and weeds.

Among the delights of spring, how is it possible to forget the birds? Even the crows were welcome, as the sable harbingers of a brighter and livelier race. They visited us before the snow was off, but seem mostly to have betaken themselves to remote depths of the woods, which they haunt all summer long. Many a time shall I disturb them there, and feel as if I had intruded among a company of silent worshipers as they sit in Sabbath stillness among the treetops. Their voices, when they speak, are in admirable accordance with the tranquil solitude of a summer afternoon, and, resounding so far above the head, their loud clamor increases the religious quiet of the scene instead of breaking it. A crow, however, has no real pretensions to religion, in spite of his gravity of mien and black attire; he is certainly a thief, and probably an infidel. The gulls are far more respectable, in a moral point of view. These denizens of sea-beaten rocks and haunters of the lonely beach come up our inland river at this season, and soar high overhead, flapping their broad wings in the upper sunshine. They are among the most picturesque of birds, because they so float and rest upon the air as to become almost stationary parts of the landscape. The imagination has time to grow acquainted with them; they have not flitted away in a moment. You go up among the clouds and greet these lofty-flighted gulls, and repose confidently with them upon the sustaining atmosphere. Ducks have their haunts along the solitary places of the river, and alight in flocks upon the broad bosom of the overflowed meadows. Their flight is too rapid and determined for the eye to catch enjoyment from it, although it never fails to stir up the heart with the sportsman's ineradicable instinct. They have now gone farther northward, but will visit us again in autumn.

The smaller birds—the little songsters of the woods, and those that haunt man's dwellings and claim human friendship by building their nests under the sheltering eaves or among the orchard trees—these require a touch more delicate and a gentler heart than mine to do them justice. Their outburst of melody is like a brook let loose from wintry chains. We need not deem it a too high and solemn word to call it a hymn of praise to the Creator, since Nature, who pictures the reviving year in so many sights of beauty, has expressed the sentiment of renewed life in no other sound save the notes of these blessed birds. Their music, however, just now seems to be incidental, and not the result of a set purpose. They are discussing the economy of life and love and the site and architecture of their summer residences, and have no time to sit on a twig and pour forth solemn hymns or overtures, operas, symphonies and waltzes. Anxious questions are asked, grave subjects are settled in quick and animated debate, and only by occasional accident, as from pure ecstasy, does a rich warble roll its tiny waves of golden sound through the atmosphere. Their little bodies are as busy as their voices; they are in a constant flutter and restlessness. Even when two or three retreat to a tree-top to hold council, they wag their tails and heads all the time with the irrepressible activity of their nature, which perhaps renders their brief span of life in reality as long as the patriarchal age of sluggish man. The blackbirds—three species of which consort together—are the noisiest of all our feathered citizens. Great companies of them—more than the famous 'four-and-twenty' whom Mother Goose has immortalized—congregate in contiguous tree-tops and vociferate with all the clamor and confusion of a turbulent political meeting. Politics, certainly, must be the occasion of such tumultuous debates, but still, unlike all other politicians, they instill melody into their individual utterances and produce harmony as a general effect. Of all bird-voices, none are more sweet and cheerful to my ear than those of swallows in the dim, sun-streaked interior of a lofty barn; they address the heart with even a closer sympathy than Robin Redbreast. But, indeed, all these winged people that dwell in the vicinity of homesteads seem to partake of human nature and possess the germ, if not the development, of immortal souls. We hear them saying their melodious prayers at morning's blush and eventide. A little while ago, in the deep of night, there came the lively thrill of a bird's note from a neighboring tree—a real song such as greets the purple dawn or mingles with the yellow sunshine. What could the little bird mean by pouring it forth at midnight? Probably the music gushed out of the midst of a dream in which he fancied himself in paradise with his mate, but suddenly awoke on a cold, leafless bough with a New England mist penetrating through his feathers. That was a sad exchange of imagination for reality.

Insects are among the earliest births of spring. Multitudes, of

I know not what species, appeared long ago on the surface of the snow. Clouds of them almost too minute for sight hover in a beam of sunshine, and vanish as if annihilated when they pass into the shade. A mosquito has already been heard to sound the small horror of his bugle-horn. Wasps infest the sunny windows of the house. A bee entered one of the chambers with a prophecy of flowers. Rare butterflies came before the snow was off, flaunting in the chill breeze, and looking forlorn and all astray in spite of the magnificence of their dark velvet cloaks with golden borders.

The fields and wood-paths have as yet few charms to entice the wanderer. In a walk the other day I found no violets nor anemones, nor anything in the likeness of a flower. It was worth while, however, to ascend our opposite hill for the sake of gaining a general idea of the advance of spring, which I had hitherto been studying in its minute developments. The river lay round me in a semi-circle, overflowing all the meadows which give it its Indian name, and offering a noble breadth to sparkle in the sunbeams. Along the hither shore a row of trees stood up to their knees in water, and afar off, on the surface of the stream, tufts of bushes thrust up their heads, as it were, to breathe. The most striking objects were great solitary trees here and there with a mile-wide waste of water all around them. The curtailment of the trunk by its immersion in the river quite destroys the fair proportions of the tree, and thus makes us sensible of a regularity and propriety in the usual forms of nature. The flood of the present season, though it never amounts to a freshet on our quiet stream, has encroached farther upon the land than any previous one for at least a score of years. It has overflowed stone fences, and even rendered a portion of the highway navigable for boats. The waters, however, are now gradually subsiding; islands become annexed to the mainland, and other islands emerge like new creations from the watery waste. The scene supplies an admirable image of the receding of the Nile—except that there is no deposit of black slime—or of Noah's flood, only that there is a freshness and novelty in these recovered portions of the continent which give the impression of a world just made rather than of one so polluted that a deluge had been requisite to purify it. These upspringing islands are the greenest spots in the landscape; the first gleam of sunlight suffices to cover them with verdure.

Thank Providence for spring! The earth—and man himself, by sympathy with his birthplace—would be far other than we find them if life toiled wearily onward without this periodical infusion of the primal spirit. Will the world ever be so decayed that spring may not renew its greenness? Can man be so dismally age-stricken that no faintest sunshine of his youth may revisit him once a year? It is impossible. The moss on our time-worn mansion brightens into beauty, the good old pastor who once dwelt here renewed his prime, regained his boyhood, in the genial breezes of his ninetieth spring. Alas for the worn and heavy soul if, whether in youth or age, it have outlived its privilege of springtime sprightliness! From such a soul the world must hope no reformation of its evil—no sympathy with the lofty faith and gallant struggles of those who contend in its behalf. Summer works in the present and thinks not of the future; autumn is a rich conservative; winter has utterly lost its faith, and clings tremulously to the remembrance of what has been; but spring, with its outgushing life, is the true type of the movement.

47

BED-BOOKS AND NIGHT-LIGHTS

H. M. Tomlinson

The rain flashed across the midnight window with a myriad feet. There was a groan in outer darkness, the voice of all nameless dreads. The nervous candle-flame shuddered by my bedside. The groaning rose to a shriek, and the little flame jumped in a panic, and nearly left its white column. Out of the corners of the room swarmed the released shadows. Black specters danced in ecstasy over my bed. I love fresh air, but I cannot allow it to slay the shining and delicate body of my little friend the candle-flame, the comrade who ventures with me into the solitudes beyond midnight. I shut the window.

They talk of the candle-power of an electric bulb. What do they mean? It cannot have the faintest glimmer of the real power of my candle. It would be as right to express, in the same inverted and foolish comparison, the worth of 'those delicate sisters, the Pleiades.' That pinch of star dust, the Pleiades, exquisitely remote in deepest night, in the profound where light all but fails, has not the power of a sulphur match; yet, still apprehensive to the mind though tremulous on the limit of vision, and sometimes even vanishing, it brings into distinction those distant and difficult hints—hidden far behind all our verified thoughts—which we rarely properly view. I should like to know of any great arc-lamp which could do that. So the star-like candle for me. No other light follows so intimately an author's most ghostly suggestion. We sit, the candle and I, in the midst of the shades we are conquering, and sometimes look up from the lucent page to contemplate the dark hosts of the enemy with a smile before they overwhelm us; as they will, of course. Like me, the candle is mortal;

it will burn out.

As the bed-book itself should be a sort of night-light, to assist its illumination, coarse lamps are useless. They would douse the book. The light for such a book must accord with it. It must be, like the book, a limited, personal, mellow, and companionable glow; the solitary taper beside the only worshiper in a sanctuary. That is why nothing can compare with the intimacy of candle-light for a bed-book. It is a living heart, bright and warm in central night, burning for us alone, holding the gaunt and towering shadows at bay. There the monstrous specters stand in our midnight room, the advance guard of the darkness of the world, held off by our valiant little glim, but ready to flood instantly and founder us in original gloom.

The wind moans without; ancient evils are at large and wandering in torment. The rain shrieks across the window. For a moment, for just a moment, the sentinel candle is shaken, and burns blue with terror. The shadows leap out instantly. The little flame recovers, and merely looks at its foe the darkness, and back to its own place goes the old enemy of light and man. The candle for me, tiny, mortal, warm, and brave, a golden lily on a silver stem!

'Almost any book does for a bed-book,' a woman once said to me. I nearly replied in a hurry that almost any woman would do for a wife; but that is not the way to bring people to conviction of sin. Her idea was that the bed-book is soporific, and for that reason she even advocated the reading of political speeches. That would be a dissolute act. Certainly you would go to sleep; but in what a frame of mind! You would enter into sleep with your eyes shut. It would be like dying, not only unshriven, but in the act of guilt.

What book shall it shine upon? Think of Plato, or Dante, or Tolstoy, or a Blue Book for such an occasion! I cannot. They will not do—they are no good to me. I am not writing about you. I know those men I have named are transcendent, the greater lights. But I am bound to confess at times they bore me. Though their feet are clay and on earth, just as ours, their stellar brows are sometimes dim in remote clouds. For my part, they are too big for bed-fellows. I cannot see myself, carrying my feeble and restricted glim, following (in pajamas) the statuesque figure of the Florentine where it stalks, aloof in its garb of austere pity, the sonorous deeps of Hades. Hades! Not for me; not after midnight! Let those go who like it.

As for the Russian, vast and disquieting, I refuse to leave all, including the blankets and the pillow, to follow him into the gelid tranquillity of the upper air, where even the colors are prismatic spicules of ice, to brood upon the erratic orbit of the poor mud-ball below called earth. I know it is my world also; but I cannot help that. It is too late, after a busy day, and at that hour, to begin overtime on fashioning a new and better planet out of cosmic dust. By breakfast-time, nothing useful would have been accomplished. We should all be where we were the night before. The job is far too long, once the pillow is nicely set.

For the truth is, there are times when we are too weary to remain attentive and thankful under the improving eye, kindly but severe, of the seers. There are times when we do not wish to be any better than we are. We do not wish to be elevated and improved. At midnight, away with such books! As for the literary pundits, the high priests of the Temple of Letters, it is interesting and helpful occasionally for an acolyte to swinge them a good hard one with an incense-burner, and cut and run, for a change, to something outside the rubrics. Midnight is the time when one can recall, with ribald delight, the names of all the Great Works which every gentleman ought to have read, but which some of us have not. For there is almost as much clotted nonsense written about literature as there is about theology.

There are few books which go with midnight, solitude, and a candle. It is much easier to say what does not please us then than what is exactly right. The book must be, anyhow, something benedictory by a sinning fellow-man. Cleverness would be repellent at such an hour. Cleverness, anyhow, is the level of mediocrity to-day; we are all too infernally clever. The first witty and perverse paradox blows out the candle. Only the sick in mind crave cleverness, as a morbid body turns to drink. The late candle throws its beams a great distance; and its rays make transparent much that seemed massy and important. The mind at rest beside that light, when the house is asleep, and the consequential affairs of the urgent world have diminished to their right proportions because we see them distantly from another and a more tranquil place in the heavens where duty, honor, witty arguments, controversial logic on great questions, appear such as will leave hardly a trace of fossil in the indurated mud which presently will cover them—the mind then certainly smiles at cleverness.

For though at that hour the body may be dog-tired, the mind is white and lucid, like that of a man from whom a fever has abated. It is bare of illusions. It has a sharp focus, small and starlike, as a clear and lonely flame left burning by the altar of a shrine from which all have gone but one. A book which approaches that light in the privacy of that place must come, as it were, with honest and open pages.

I like Heine then, though. His mockery of the grave and great, in those sentences which are as brave as pennants in a breeze, is comfortable and sedative. One's own secret and awkward convictions, never expressed because not lawful and because it is hard to get words to bear them lightly, seem then to be heard aloud in the mild, easy, and confident diction of an immortal whose voice has the blitheness of one who has watched, amused and irreverent, the high gods in eager and secret debate on the best way to keep the gilt and trappings on the body of the evil they have created.

That first-rate explorer, Gulliver, is also fine in the light of the intimate candle. Have you read lately again his Voyage to the Houyhnhnms? Try it alone again in quiet. Swift knew all about our contemporary troubles. He has got it all down. Why was he called a misanthrope? Reading that last voyage of Gulliver in the select intimacy of midnight I am forced to wonder, not at Swift's hatred of mankind, not at his satire of his fellows, not at the strange and terrible nature of this genius who thought that much of us, but how it is that after such a wise and sorrowful revealing of the things we insist on doing, and our reasons for doing them, and what happens after we have done them, men do not change. It does seem impossible that society could remain unaltered, after the surprise its appearance should have caused it as it saw its face in that ruthless mirror. We point instead to the fact that Swift lost his mind in the end. Well, that is not a matter for surprise.

Such books, and France's *Isle of Penguins*, are not disturbing as bed-books. They resolve one's agitated and outraged soul, relieving it with some free expression for the accusing and questioning thoughts engendered by the day's affairs. But they do not rest immediately to hand in the book-shelf by the bed. They depend on the kind of day one has had. Sterne is closer. One would rather be transported as far as possible from all the disturbances of earth's envelope of clouds, and *Tristram Shandy* is sure to be found in the sun.

But best of all books for midnight are travel books. Once I was lost every night for months with Doughty in the *Arabia Deserta*. He is a craggy author. A long course of the ordinary facile stuff, such as one gets in the Press every day, thinking it is English, sends one thoughtless and headlong among the bitter herbs and stark boulders of Doughty's burning and spacious expanse; only to get bewildered, and the shins broken, and a great fatigue at first, in a strange land of fierce sun, hunger, glittering spar, ancient plutonic rock, and very Adam himself. But once you are acclimatized, and know the language—it takes time—there is no more London after dark, till, a wanderer returned from a forgotten land, you emerge from the interior of Arabia on the Red Sea coast again, feeling as though you had lost touch with the world you used to know. And if that doesn't mean good writing I know of no other test.

Because once there was a father whose habit it was to read with his boys nightly some chapters of the Bible—and cordially they hated that habit of his—I have that Book too; though I fear I have it for no reason that he, the rigid old faithful, would be pleased to hear about. He thought of the future when he read the Bible; I read it for the past. The familiar names, the familiar rhythm of its words, its wonderful well-remembered stories of things long past—like that of Esther, one of the best in English—the eloquent anger of the prophets for the people then who looked as though they were alive, but were really dead at heart, all is solace and home to me. And now I think of it, it is our home and solace that we want in a bed-book.

48

THE PRECEPT OF PEACE

Louise Imogen Guiney

A certain sort of voluntary abstraction is the oldest and choicest of social attitudes. In France, where all aesthetic discoveries are made, it was crowned long ago: *la sainte indifférence* is, or may be, a cult, and *le saint indifférent* an articled practitioner. For the Gallic mind, brought up at the knee of a consistent paradox, has found that not to appear concerned about a desired good is the only method to possess it; full happiness is given, in other words, to the very man who will never sue for it. This is a secret neat as that of the Sphinx: to 'go softly' among events, yet domineer them. Without fear: not because we are brave, but because we are exempt; we bear so charmed a life that not even Baldur's mistletoe can touch us to harm us. Without solicitude: for the essential thing is trained, falcon-like, to light from above upon our wrists, and it has become with us an automatic motion to open the hand, and drop what appertains to us no longer. Be it renown or a new hat, the shorter stick of celery, or

> 'The friends to whom we had no natural right,
> The homes that were not destined to be ours,'

it is all one: let it fall away! since only so, by depletions, can we buy serenity and a blithe mien. It is diverting to study, at the feet of Antisthenes and of Socrates his master, how many indispensables man can live without; or how many he can gather together, make over into luxuries, and so abrogate them. Thoreau somewhere expresses himself as full of divine pity for the 'mover,' who on May-Day clouds city streets with his melancholy household caravans: fatal impedimenta for an immortal. No: furniture is clearly a superstition. 'I have little, I want nothing; all my treasure is in Minerva's tower.' Not that the novice may not accumulate. Rather, let him collect beetles and Venetian interrogation-marks; if so be that he may distinguish what is truly extrinsic to him, and bestow these toys, eventually, on the children of Satan who clamor at the monastery gate. Of all his store, unconsciously increased, he can always part with sixteen-seventeenths, by way of concession to his individuality, and think the subtraction so much concealing marble chipped from the heroic figure of himself. He would be a donor from the beginning; before he can be seen to own, he will disencumber, and divide. Strange and fearful is his discovery, amid the bric-a-brac of the world, that this knowledge, or this material benefit, is for him alone. He would fain beg off from the acquisition, and shake the touch of the tangible from his imperious wings. It is not enough to cease to strive for personal favor; your true *indifférent* is Early Franciscan: caring not to have, he fears to hold. Things useful need never become to him things desirable. Towards all commonly-accounted sinecures, he bears the coldest front in Nature, like a magician walking a maze, and scornful of its flower-bordered detentions. 'I enjoy life,' says Seneca, 'because I am ready to leave it.' Meanwhile, they who act with too jealous respect for their morrow of civilized comfort, reap only indigestion, and crow's-foot traceries for their deluded eye-corners.

Now nothing is farther from *le saint indifférent* than cheap indifferentism, so-called: the sickness of sophomores. His business is to hide, not to display, his lack of interest in fripperies. It is not he who looks languid, and twiddles his thumbs for sick misplacedness, like Achilles among girls. On the contrary, he is a smiling industrious elf, monstrous attentive to the canons of polite society. In relation to others, he shows what passes for animation and enthusiasm; for at all times his character is founded on control of these qualities, not on the absence of them. It flatters his sense of superiority that he may thus pull wool about the ears of joint and several. He has so strong a will that it can be crossed and counter-crossed, as by himself, so by a dozen outsiders, without a break in his apparent phlegm. He has gone through volition, and come out at the other side of it; everything with him is a specific act: he has no habits. *Le saint indifférent* is a dramatic wight: he loves to refuse your proffered six per cent, when, by a little haggling, he may obtain three-and-a-half. For so he gets away with his own mental processes virgin: it is inconceivable to you that, being sane, he should so comport himself. Amiable, perhaps, only by painful propulsions and sore vigilance, let him appear the mere inheritor of easy good-nature. Unselfish out of sheer pride, and ever eager to claim the slippery side of the pavement, or the end cut of the roast (on the secret ground, be it understood, that he is not as Capuan men, who wince at trifles), let him have his ironic reward in passing for one whose physical connoisseurship is yet in the raw. That sympathy which his rule forbids his devoting to the usual objects, he expends, with some bravado, upon their opposites; for he would fain seem a decent partizan of some sort, not what he is, a bivalve intelligence, *Tros Tyriusque*. He is known here and there, for instance, as valorous in talk; yet he is by nature a solitary, and, for the most part, somewhat less communicative than

> 'The wind that sings to himself as he makes stride,
> Lonely and terrible, on the Andean height.'

Imagining nothing idler than words in the face of grave events, he condoles and congratulates with the genteelest air in the world. In short, while there is anything expected of him, while there are spectators to be fooled, the stratagems of the fellow prove inexhaustible. It is only when he is quite alone that he drops his jaw, and stretches his legs; then heigho! arises like a smoke, and envelopes him becomingly, the beautiful native well-bred torpidity of the gods, of poetic boredom, of 'the Oxford manner.'

'How weary, stale, flat, and unprofitable!' sighed Hamlet of this mortal outlook. As it came from him in the beginning, that plaint, in its sincerity, can come only from the man of culture, who feels about him vast mental spaces and depths, and to whom the face of creation is but comparative and symbolic. Nor will he breathe it in the common ear, where it may woo misapprehensions, and breed ignorant rebellion.

The unlettered must ever love or hate what is nearest him, and, for lack of perspective, think his own fist the size of the sun. The social prizes, which, with mellowed observers, rank as twelfth or thirteenth in order of desirability, such as wealth and a foothold in affairs, seem to him first and sole; and to them he clings like a barnacle. But to our *indifférent*, nothing is so vulgar as close suction. He will never tighten his fingers on loaned opportunity; he is a gentleman, the hero of the habitually relaxed grasp. A light unprejudiced hold on his profits strikes him as decent and comely, though his true artistic pleasure is still in 'fallings from us, vanishings.' It costs him little to loose and to forego, to unlace his tentacles, and from the many who push hard behind, to retire, as it were, on a never-guessed-at competency, 'richer than untempted kings.' He would not be a life-prisoner, in ever so charming a bower. While the tranquil Sabine Farm is his delight, well he knows that on the dark trail ahead of him, even Sabine Farms are not sequacious. Thus he learns betimes to play the guest under his own cedars, and, with disciplinary intent, goes often from them; and, hearing his heart-strings snap the third night he is away, rejoices that he is again a freedman. Where his foot is planted (though it root not anywhere), he calls that spot home. No Unitarian in locality, it follows that he is the best of travelers, tangential merely, and pleased with each new vista of the human Past. He sometimes wishes his understanding less, that he might itch deliciously with a prejudice. With cosmic congruities, great and general forces, he keeps, all along, a tacit understanding, such as one has with beloved relatives at a distance; and his finger, airily inserted in his outer pocket, is really upon the pulse of eternity. His vocation, however, is to bury himself in the minor and immediate task; and from his intent manner, he gets confounded, promptly and permanently, with the victims of commercial ambition.

The true use of the much-praised Lucius Cary, Viscount Falkland, has hardly been apprehended: he is simply the patron saint of *indifférents*. From first to last, almost alone in that discordant time, he seems to have heard far-off resolving harmonies, and to have been rapt away with foreknowledge. Battle, to which all knights were bred, was penitential to him. It was but a childish means: and to what end? He meanwhile—and no man carried his will in better abeyance to the scheme of the universe—wanted no diligence in camp or council. Cares sat handsomely on him who cared not at all, who won small comfort from the cause which his conscience finally espoused. He labored to be a doer, to stand well with observers; and none save his intimate friends read his agitation and profound weariness. 'I am so much taken notice of,' he writes, 'for an impatient desire for peace, that it is necessary I should likewise make it appear how it is not out of fear for the utmost hazard of war.' And so, driven from the ardour he had to the simulation of the ardor he lacked, loyally daring, a sacrifice to one of two transient opinions, and inly impartial as a star, Lord Falkland fell: the young never-to-be-forgotten martyr of Newburg field. The imminent deed he made a work of art; and the station of the moment the only post of honour. Life and death may be all one to such a man: but he will at least take the noblest pains to discriminate between Tweedledum and Tweedledee, if he has to write a book about the variations of their antennæ. And like the Carolian exemplar is the disciple. The *indifférent* is a good thinker, or a good fighter. He is no 'immartial minion,' as dear old Chapman suffers Hector to call Tydides. Nevertheless, his sign-manual is content with humble and stagnant conditions. Talk of scaling the Himalayas of life affects him, very palpably, as 'tall talk.' He deals not with things, but with the impressions and analogies of things. The material counts for nothing with him: he has moulted it away. Not so sure of the identity of the higher course of action as he is of his consecrating dispositions, he feels that he may make heaven again, out of sundries, as he goes. Shall not a beggarly duty, discharged with perfect temper, land him in 'the out-courts of Glory,' quite as successfully as a grand Sunday-school excursion to front the cruel Paynim foe? He thinks so. Experts have thought so before him. Francis Drake, with the national alarum instant in his ears, desired first to win at bowls, on the Devon sward, 'and afterwards to settle with the Don.' No one will claim a buccaneering hero for an *indifférent*, however. The Jesuit novices were ball-playing almost at that very time, three hundred years ago, when some too speculative companion, figuring the end of the world in a few moments (with just leisure enough, between, to be shriven in chapel, according to his own thrifty mind), asked Louis of Gonzaga how he, on his part, should employ the precious interval. 'I should go on with the game,' said the most innocent and most ascetic youth among them. But to cite the behavior of any of the saints is to step over the playful line allotted. Indifference of the mundane brand is not to be confounded with their detachment, which is emancipation wrought in the soul, and the ineffable efflorescence of the Christian spirit. Like most supernatural virtues, it has a laic shadow; the counsel to abstain, and to be unsolicitous, is one not only of perfection, but also of polity. A very little non-adhesion to common affairs, a little reserve of unconcern, and the gay spirit of sacrifice, provide the moral immunity which is the only real estate. The *indifférent* believes in storms: since tales of shipwreck encompass him. But once among his own kind, he wonders that folk should be circumvented by merely extraneous powers! His favorite catch, woven in among escaped dangers, rises through the roughest weather, and daunts it:

> 'Now strike your sailes, ye jolly mariners,
> For we be come into a quiet rode.'

No slave to any vicissitude, his imagination is, on the contrary, the cheerful obstinate tyrant of all that is. He lives, as Keats once said of himself, 'in a thousand worlds,' withdrawing at will from one to another, often curtailing his circumference to enlarge his liberty. His universe is a universe of balls, like those which the cunning Oriental carvers make out of ivory; each entire surface perforated with the same delicate pattern, each moving prettily and inextricably within the other, and all but the outer one impossible to handle. In some such innermost asylum the right sort of dare-devil sits smiling, while men rage or weep.

49

THE FISH REPORTER

Robert Cortes Holliday

Men of genius, blown by the winds of chance, have been, now and then, mariners, bar-keeps, schoolmasters, soldiers, politicians, clergymen, and what not. And from these pursuits have they sucked the essence of yarns and in the setting of these activities found a flavor to stir and to charm hearts untold. Now, it is a thousand pities that no man of genius has ever been a fish reporter. Thus has the world lost great literary treasure, as it is highly probable that there is not under the sun any prospect so filled with the scents and colors of story as that presented by the commerce in fish.

Take whale oil. Take the funny old buildings on Front Street, out of paintings, I declare, by Howard Pyle, where the large merchants in whale oil are. Take salt fish. Do you know the oldest salt-fish house in America, down by Coenties Slip? Ah! you should. The ghost of old Long John Silver, I suspect, smokes an occasional pipe in that old place. And many are the times I've seen the slim shade of young Jim Hawkins come running out. Take Labrador cod for export to the Mediterranean lands or to Porto Rico via New York. Take herrings brought to this port from Iceland, from Holland, and from Scotland; mackerel from Ireland, from the Magdalen Islands, and from Cape Breton; crabmeat from Japan; fishballs from Scandinavia; sardines from Norway and from France; caviar from Russia; shrimp which comes from Florida, Mississippi, and Georgia, or salmon from Alaska, and Puget Sound, and the Columbia River.

Take the obituaries of fishermen. 'In his prime, it is said, there was not a better skipper in the Gloucester fishing fleet.' Take disasters to schooners, smacks, and trawlers. 'The crew were landed, but lost all their belongings.' New vessels, sales, etc. 'The sealing schooner *Tillie B.*, whose career in the South Seas is well known, is reported to have been sold to a moving-picture firm.' Sponges from the Caribbean Sea and the Gulf of Mexico. 'To most people, familiar only with the sponges of the shops, the animal as it comes from the sea would be rather unrecognizable.' Why, take anything you please! It is such stuff as stories are. And as you eat your fish from the store how little do you reck of the glamor of what you are doing!

However, as it seems to me unlikely that a man of genius will be a fish reporter shortly I will myself do the best I can to paint the tapestry of the scenes of his calling. The advertisement in the newspaper read: 'Wanted—Reporter for weekly trade paper.' Many called, but I was chosen. Though, doubtless, no man living knew less about fish than I.

The newsstands are each like a fair, so laden are they with magazines in bright colors. It would seem almost as if there were a different magazine for every few hundred and seven-tenth person, as the statistics put these matters. And yet, it seems, there is a vast, a very vast, periodical literature of which we, that is, magazine readers in general, know nothing whatever. There is, for one, that fine, old, standard publication, Barrel and Box, devoted to the subjects and the interests of the coopering industry; there is too, *The Dried Fruit Packer and Western Canner*, as alert a magazine as one could wish—in its kind; and from the home of classic American literature comes *The New England Tradesman and Grocer*. And so on. At the place alone where we went to press twenty-seven trade journals were printed every week, from one for butchers to one for bankers.

The Fish Industries Gazette—Ah, yes! For some reason not clear (though it is an engaging thing, I think) the word 'gazette' is the great word among the titles of trade journals. There are *The Jewellers' Gazette* and *The Women's Wear Gazette* and *The Poulterers' Gazette* (of London), and *The Maritime Gazette* (of Halifax), and other gazettes quite without number. This word 'gazette' makes its appeal, too, curiously enough, to those who christen country papers; and trade journals have much of the intimate charm of country papers. The 'trade' in each case is a kind of neighborly community, separated in its parts by space, but joined in unity of sympathy. 'Personals' are a vital feature of trade papers. 'Walter Conner, who for some time has conducted a bakery and fish market at Hudson, N. Y., has removed to Fort Edward, leaving his brother Ed in charge at the Hudson place of business.'

The Fish Industries Gazette, as I say, was one of several in its field, in friendly rivalry with *The Oyster Trade and Fisherman* and *The Pacific Fisheries*. It comprised two departments: the fresh fish and oyster department, and myself. I was, as an editorial announcement said at the beginning of my tenure of office, a 'reorganization of our salt, smoked, and pickled fish department.' The delectable, mellow spirit of the country paper, so removed from the crash and whirr of metropolitan journalism, rested in this, too, that upon the *Gazette* I did practically everything on the paper except the linotyping. Reporter, editorial writer, exchange editor, make-up man, proof-reader, correspondent, advertisement solicitor, was I.

As exchange editor, did I read all the papers in the English language in eager search of fish news. And while you are about the matter, just find me a finer bit of literary style evoking the romance of the vast wastes of the moving sea, in Stevenson, Defoe, anywhere you please, than such a news item as this: 'Capt Ezra Pound, of the bark *Elnora*, of Salem, Mass., spoke a lonely vessel in latitude this and longitude that, September 8. She proved to be the whaler *Wanderer*, and her captain said that she had been nine months at sea, that all on board were well, and that he had stocked so many barrels of whale oil.'

As exchange editor was it my business to peruse reports from Eastport, Maine, to the effect that one of the worst storms in recent years had destroyed large numbers of the sardine weirs there. To seek fish recipes, of such savory sound as those for 'broiled redsnapper,' 'shrimps bordelaise,' and 'baked fish croquettes.' To follow fishing conditions in the North Sea occasioned by the Great War. To hunt down jokes of piscatory humor. 'The man who drinks like a fish does not take kindly to water.—Exchange.' To find other 'fillers' in the consular reports and elsewhere: 'Fish culture in India,' '1800 Miles in a Dory,' 'Chinese Carp for the Philippines,' 'Americans as Fish Eaters.' And, to use a favorite term of trade papers, 'etc., etc.' Then to 'paste up' the winnowed fruits of this beguiling research.

As editorial writer, to discuss the report of the commission recently sent by congress to the Pribilof Islands, Alaska, to report on the condition of our national herd of fur seals; to discuss the official interpretation here of the Government ruling on what constitutes 'boneless' codfish; to consider the campaign in Canada to promote there a more popular consumption of fish, and to brightly remark *à propos* of this that 'a fish a day keeps the doctor away'; to review the current issue of *The Journal of the Fisheries Society of Japan*, containing leading articles on 'Are Fishing Motor Boats Able to Encourage in Our Country' and 'Fisherman the Late Mr H. Yamaguchi Well Known'; to combat the prejudice against dogfish as food, a prejudice like that against eels, in some quarters eyed askance as 'calling cousins with the great sea-serpent,' as Juvenal says; to call attention to the doom of one of the most picturesque monuments in the story of fish, the passing of the pleasant and celebrated old Trafalgar Hotel at Greenwich, near London, scene of the famous Ministerial white-bait dinners of the days of Pitt; to make a jest on an exciting idea suggested by some medical man that some of the features of a Ritz-Carlton Hotel, that is, baths, be introduced into the fo'c's'les of Grand Banks fishing vessels; to keep an eye on the activities of our Bureau of Fisheries; to hymn a praise to the monumental new Fish Pier at Boston; to glance at conditions at the premier fish market of the world, Billingsgate; to herald the fish display at the Canadian National Exhibition at Toronto, and, indeed, etc., and again etc.

As general editorial roustabout, to find each week a 'leader,' a translation, say, from *In Allgemeine Fishcherei-Zeitung*, or *Economic Circular No. 10*, 'Mussels in the Tributaries of the Missouri,' or the last biennial report of the Superintendent of Fisheries of Wisconsin, or a scientific paper on 'The Porpoise in Captivity' reprinted by permission of *Zoologica*, of the New York Zoölogical Society. To find each week for reprint a poem appropriate in sentiment to the feeling of the paper. One of the 'Salt Water Ballads' would do, or John Masefield singing of 'the whale's way,' or 'Down to the white dipping sails'; or Rupert Brooke: 'And in that heaven of all their wish, There shall be no more land, say fish'; or a 'weather rhyme' about 'mackerel skies,' when 'you're sure to get a fishing day'; or something from the New York *Sun* about 'the lobster pots of Maine'; or Oliver Herford, in the *Century*, 'To a Goldfish'; or, best of all, an old song of fishing ways of other days.

And to compile from the New York *Journal of Commerce* better poetry than any of this, tables, beautiful tables of 'imports into New York': 'Oct. 15.—From Bordeaux, 225 cs. cuttlefish bone; Copenhagen, 173 pkgs. fish; Liverpool, 969 bbls. herrings, 10 walrus hides, 2,000 bags salt; La Guayra, 6 cs. fish sounds; Belize, 9 bbls. sponges; Rotterdam, 7 pkgs. seaweed, 9,000 kegs herrings; Barcelona, 235 cs. sardines; Bocas Del Toro, 5 cs. turtle shells; Genoa, 3 boxes corals; Tampico, 2 pkgs. sponges; Halifax, 1 cs. seal skins, 35 bbls. cod liver oil, 215 cs. lobsters, 490 bbls. codfish; Akureyri, 4,150 bbls. salted herrings,' and much more. Beautiful tables of 'exports from New York.' 'To Australia' (cleared Sep. 1); 'to Argentina';—Haiti, Jamaica, Guatemala, Scotland, Salvador, Santo Domingo, England, and to places many more. And many other gorgeous tables, too. 'Fishing vessels at New York,' for one, listing the 'trips' brought into this port by the *Stranger*, the *Sarah O'Neal*, the *Nourmahal*, a farrago of charming sounds, and a valuable tale of facts.

As make-up man, of course, so to 'dress' the paper that the 'markets,' Oporto, Trinidad, Porto Rico, Demerara, Havana, would be together; that 'Nova Scotia Notes'—'Weather conditions for curing have been more favorable since October set in'—would follow 'Halifax Fish Market'—'Last week's arrivals were: Oct. 13, schr. *Hattie Loring*, 960 quintals,' etc.—that 'Pacific Coast Notes'—'The tug *Tatoosh* will perform the service for the Seattle salmon packers of towing a vessel from Seattle to this port via the Panama Canal'—would follow 'Canned Salmon'; that shellfish matter would be in one place; reports of saltfish where such should be; that the weekly tale of the canned fish trade politically embraced the canned fish advertising; and so on and so on.

Finest of all, as reporter, to go where the fish reporter goes. There the sight-seeing cars never find their way; the hurried commuter has not his path, nor knows of these things at all; and there that racy character who, voicing a multitude, declares that he would rather be a lamp post on Broadway than Mayor of St Louis, goes not for to see. Up lower Greenwich Street the fish reporter goes, along an eerie, dark, and narrow way, beneath a strange, thundering roof, the 'L' overhead. He threads his way amid seemingly chaotic, architectural piles of boxes, of barrels, crates, casks, kegs, and bulging bags; roundabout many great fetlocked draught horses, frequently standing or plunging upon the sidewalk, and attached to many huge trucks and wagons; and much of the time in the street he is compelled to go, finding the side walks too congested with the traffic of commerce to admit of his passing there.

You probably eat butter, and eggs, and cheese. Then you would delight in Greenwich Street. You could feast your highly creditable appetite for these excellent things for very nearly a solid mile upon the signs of 'wholesale dealers and commission merchants' in them. The letter press, as you might say, of the fish reporter's walk is a noble pæan to the earth's glorious yield for the joyous sustenance of man. For these princely merchants' signs sing of opulent stores of olive oil, of sausages, beans, soups, extracts, and spices, sugar, Spanish, Bermuda, and Havana onions, 'fine' apples, teas, coffee, rice, chocolates, dried fruits and raisins, and of loaves and of fishes, and of 'fish products.' Lo! dark and dirty and thundering Greenwich Street is to-day's translation of the Garden of Eden.

Here is a great house whose sole vocation is the importation of caviar for barter here. Caviar from over-seas now comes, when it comes at all, mainly by the way of Archangel, recently put on the map, for most of us, by the war. The fish reporter is told, however, if it be summer, that there cannot be much doing in the way of caviar until fall, 'when the spoonbill start coming in.' And on he goes to a great saltfish house, where many men in salt-stained garments are running about, their arms laden with large flat objects, of sharp and jagged edge, which resemble dried and crackling hides of some animal curiously like a huge fish; and numerous others of 'the same' are trundling round wheelbarrow-like trucks likewise so laden. Where stacks of these hides stand on their tails against the walls, and goodness knows how many big boxes are, containing, as those open show, beautifully soft, thick, cream-colored slabs, which is fish. And where still other men, in overalls stained like a painter's palette, are knocking off the heads of casks and dipping out of brine still other kinds of fish for inspection.

Here it is said by the head of the house, by the stove (it is chill weather) in his office like a shipmaster's cabin: 'Strong market on foreign mackerel. Mines hinder Norway catch. Advices from abroad report that German resources continue to purchase all available supplies from the Norwegian fishermen. No Irish of any account. Recent shipment sold on the deck at high prices. Fair demand from the Middle West.'

So, by stages, on up to turn into North Moore Street, looking down a narrow lane between two long bristling rows of wagons pointed out from the curbs, to the façades of the North River docks at the bottom, with the tops of the buff funnels of ocean liners, and Whistleranean silhouettes of derricks, rising beyond. Hereabout are more importers, exporters, and 'producers' of fish, famous in their calling beyond the celebrities of popular publicity. And he that has official entrée may learn, by mounting dusky stairs, half-ladder and half-stair, and by passing through low-ceilinged chambers freighted with many barrels, to the sanctums of the fish lords, what's doing in the foreign herring way, and get the current market quotations, at present sky-high, and hear that the American shore mackerel catch is very fine stock.

Then roundabout, with a step into the broad vista of homely Washington Street, and a turn through Franklin Street, where is the man decorated by the Imperial Japanese Government with a gold medal, if he should care to wear it, for having distinguished himself in the development of commerce in the marine products of Japan, back to Hudson Street. An authentic railroad is one of the spectacular features of Hudson Street.

Here down the middle of the way are endless trains, stopping, starting, crashing, laden to their ears with freight, doubtless all to eat. Tourists should come from very far to view Hudson Street. Here is a spectacle as fascinating, as awe-inspiring, as extraordinary as any in the world. From dawn until darkness falls, hour after hour, along Hudson Street slowly, steadily moves a mighty procession of great trucks. One would not suppose there were so many trucks on the face of the earth. It is a glorious sight, and any man whose soul is not dead should jump with joy to see it. And the thunder of them altogether as they bang over the stones is like the music of the spheres.

There is on Hudson Street a tall handsome building where the fish reporter goes, which should be enjoyed in this way: Up in the lift you go to the top, and then you walk down, smacking your lips. For all the doors in that building are brimming with poetry. And the tune of it goes like this: 'Toasted Corn-Flake Co.,' 'Seaboard Rice,' 'Chili Products,' 'Red Bloom Grape Juice Sales Office,' 'Porto Rico and Singapore Pineapple Co.,' 'Sunnyland Foodstuffs,' 'Importers of Fruit Pulps, Pimentos,' 'Sole Agents U.S.A. Italian Salad Oil,' 'Raisin Growers,' 'Log Cabin Syrups,' 'Jobbers in Beans, Peas,' 'Chocolate and Cocoa Preparations,' 'Ohio Evaporated Milk Co.,' 'Bernese Alps and Holland Condensed Milk Co.,' 'Brazilian Nuts Co.,' 'Brokers Pacific Coast Salmon,' 'California Tuna Co.,' and thus on and on.

The fish reporter crosses the street to see the head of the Sardine Trust, who has just thrown the market into excitement by a heavy cut in prices of last year's pack. Thence, pausing to refresh himself by the way at a sign 'Agency for Reims Champagne and Moselle Wines—Bordeaux Clarets and Sauternes,' over to Broadway to interview the most august persons of all, dealers in fertilizer, 'fish scrap.' These mighty gentlemen live, when at business, in palatial suites of offices constructed of marble and fine woods and laid with rich rugs. The reporter is relayed into the innermost sanctum by a succession of richly clothed attendants. And he learns, it may be, that fishing in Chesapeake Bay is so poor that some of the 'fish factories' may decide to shut down. Acid phosphate, it is said, is ruling at $13 f.o.b. Baltimore.

And so the fish reporter enters upon the last lap of his rounds. Through, perhaps, the narrow, crooked lane of Pine Street he passes, to come out at length upon a scene set for a sea tale. Here would a lad, heir to vast estates in Virginia, be kidnapped and smuggled aboard to be sold a slave in Africa. This is Front Street. A white ship lies at the foot of it. Cranes rise at her side. Tugs, belching smoke, bob beyond. All about are ancient warehouses, redolent of the Thames, with steep roofs and sometimes stairs outside, and with tall shutters, a crescent-shaped hole in each. There is a dealer in weather-vanes. Other things dealt in hereabout are these: chronometers, 'nautical instruments,' wax gums, cordage and twine, marine paints, cotton wool and waste, turpentine, oils, greases, and rosin. Queer old taverns, public houses, are here, too. Why do not their windows rattle with a 'Yo, ho, ho'?

There is an old, old house whose business has been fish oil within the memory of men. And here is another. Next, through Water Street, one comes in search of the last word on salt fish. Now the air is filled with gorgeous smell of roasting coffee. Tea, coffee, sugar, rice, spices, bags and bagging here have their home. And there are haughty bonded warehouses filled with fine liquors. From his white cabin at the top of a venerable structure comes the dean of the saltfish business. 'Export trade fair,' he says; 'good demand from South America.'

50

EVERY MAN'S NATURAL DESIRE TO BE SOMEBODY ELSE

Samuel McChord Crothers

I

Several years ago a young man came to my study with a manuscript which he wished me to criticize.

'It is only a little bit of my work,' he said modestly, 'and it will not take you long to look it over. In fact it is only the first chapter, in which I explain the Universe.'

I suppose that we have all had moments of sudden illumination when it occurred to us that we had explained the Universe, and it was so easy for us that we wondered why we had not done it before. Some thought drifted into our mind and filled us with vague forebodings of omniscience. It was not an ordinary thought, that explained only a fragment of existence. It explained everything. It proved one thing and it proved the opposite just as well. It explained why things are as they are, and if it should turn out that they are not that way at all, it would prove that fact also. In the light of our great thought chaos seemed rational.

Such thoughts usually occur about four o'clock in the morning. Having explained the Universe, we relapse into satisfied slumber. When, a few hours later, we rise, we wonder what the explanation was.

Now and then, however, one of these highly explanatory ideas remains to comfort us in our waking hours. Such a thought is that which I here throw out, and which has doubtless at some early hour occurred to most of my readers. It is that every man has a natural desire to be somebody else.

This does not explain the Universe, but it explains that perplexing part of it which we call Human Nature. It explains why so many intelligent people, who deal skillfully with matters of fact, make such a mess of it when they deal with their fellow creatures. It explains why we get on as well as we do with strangers, and why we do not get on better with our friends. It explains why people are so often offended when we say nice things about them, and why it is that, when we say harsh things about them, they take it as a compliment. It explains why people marry their opposites and why they live happily ever afterwards. It also explains why some people don't. It explains the meaning of tact and its opposite.

The tactless person treats a person according to a scientific method as if he were a thing. Now, in dealing with a thing, you must first find out what it is, and then act accordingly. But with a person, you must first find out what he is and then carefully conceal from him the fact that you have made the discovery.

The tactless person can never be made to understand this. He prides himself on taking people as they are without being aware that that is not the way they want to be taken.

He has a keen eye for the obvious, and calls attention to it. Age, sex, color, nationality, previous condition of servitude, and all the facts that are interesting to the census-taker, are apparent to him and are made the basis of his conversation. When he meets one who is older than he, he is conscious of the fact, and emphasizes by every polite attention the disparity in years. He has an idea that at a certain period in life the highest tribute of respect is to be urged to rise out of one chair and take another that is presumably more comfortable. It does not occur to him that there may remain any tastes that are not sedentary. On the other hand, he sees a callow youth and addresses himself to the obvious callowness, and thereby makes himself thoroughly disliked. For, strange to say, the youth prefers to be addressed as a person of precocious maturity.

The literalist, observing that most people talk shop, takes it for granted that they like to talk shop. This is a mistake. They do it because it is the easiest thing to do, but they resent having attention called to their limitations. A man's profession does not necessarily coincide with his natural aptitude or with his predominant desire. When you meet a member of the Supreme Court you may assume that he is gifted with a judicial mind. But it does not follow that that is the only quality of mind he has; nor that when, out of court, he gives you a piece of his mind, it will be a piece of his judicial mind that he gives.

My acquaintance with royalty is limited to photographs of royal groups, which exhibit a high degree of domesticity. It would seem that the business of royalty when pursued as a steady job becomes tiresome, and that when they have their pictures taken they endeavor to look as much like ordinary folks as possible—and they usually succeed.

The member of one profession is always flattered by being taken for a skilled practitioner of another. Try it on your minister. Instead of saying, 'That was an excellent sermon of yours this morning,' say, 'As I listened to your cogent argument, I thought what a successful lawyer you would have made.' Then he will say, 'I did think of taking to the law.'

If you had belonged to the court of Frederick the Great, you would have proved a poor courtier indeed if you had praised His Majesty's campaigns. Frederick knew that he was a Prussian general, but he wanted to be a French literary man. If you wished to gain his favor, you should have told him that in your opinion he excelled Voltaire.

We do not like to have too much attention drawn to our present circumstances. They may be well enough in their way, but we can think of something which would be more fitting for us. We have either seen better days or we expect them.

Suppose you had visited Napoleon in Elba and had sought to ingratiate yourself with him.

'Sire,' you would have said, 'this is a beautiful little empire of yours, so snug and cosy and quiet. It is just such a domain as is suited to a man in your condition. The climate is excellent. Everything is peaceful. It must be delightful to rule where everything is arranged for you and the details are taken care of by others. As I came to your dominion I saw a line of British frigates guarding your shores. The evidences of such thoughtfulness are everywhere.'

Your praise of his present condition would not have endeared you to Napoleon. You were addressing him as the Emperor of Elba. In his own eyes he was Emperor, though in Elba.

It is such a misapprehension which irritates any mature human being when his environment is taken as the measure of his personality.

The man with a literal mind moves in a perpetual comedy of errors. It is not a question of two Dromios. There are half a dozen Dromios under one hat.

How casually introductions are made, as if it were the easiest thing in the world to make two human beings acquainted! Your friend says, 'I want you to know Mr Stifflekin,' and you say that you are happy to know him. But does either of you know the enigma that goes under the name of Stifflekin? You may know what he looks like and where he resides and what he does for a living. But that is all in the present tense. To really know him you must not only know what he is but what he used to be; what he used to think he was; what he used to think he ought to be and might be if he worked hard enough. You must know what he might have been if certain things had happened otherwise, and you must know what might have happened otherwise if he had been otherwise. All these complexities are a part of his own dim apprehension of himself. They are what make him so much more interesting to himself than he is to any one else.

It is this consciousness of the inadequacy of our knowledge which makes us so embarrassed when we offer any service to another. Will he take it in the spirit in which it is given?

That was an awkward moment when Stanley, after all his hardships in his search for Dr Livingstone, at last found the Doctor by a lake in Central Africa. Stanley held out his hand and said stiffly, 'Dr Livingstone, I presume?' Stanley had heroically plunged through the equatorial forests to find Livingstone and to bring him back to civilization. But Livingstone was not particularly anxious to be found, and had a decided objection to being brought back to civilization. What he wanted was a new adventure. Stanley did not find the real Livingstone till he discovered that the old man was as young at heart as himself. The two men became acquainted only when they began to plan a new expedition to find the source of the Nile.

II

The natural desire of every man to be somebody else explains many of the minor irritations of life. It prevents that perfect organization of society in which every one should know his place and keep it. The desire to be somebody else leads us to practice on work that does not strictly belong to us. We all have aptitudes and talents that overflow the narrow bounds of our trade or profession. Every man feels that he is bigger than his job, and he is all the time doing what theologians call 'works of supererogation.'

The serious-minded housemaid is not content to do what she is told to do. She has an unexpended balance of energy. She wants to be a general household reformer. So she goes to the desk of the titular master of the house and gives it a thorough reformation. She arranges the papers according to her idea of neatness. When the poor gentleman returns and finds his familiar chaos transformed into a hateful order, he becomes a reactionary.

The serious manager of a street railway company is not content with the simple duty of transporting passengers cheaply and comfortably. He wants to exercise the functions of a lecturer in an ethical culture society. While the transported victim is swaying precariously from the end of a strap he reads a notice urging him to practice Christian courtesy and not to push. While the poor wretch pores over this counsel of perfection, he feels like answering as did Junius to the Duke of Grafton, 'My Lord, injuries may be atoned for and forgiven, but insults admit of no compensation.'

A man enters a barber's shop with the simple desire of being shaved. But he meets with the more ambitious desires of the barber. The serious barber is not content with any slight contribution to human welfare. He insists that his client shall be shampooed, manicured, massaged, steamed beneath boiling towels, cooled off by electric fans and, while all this is going on, that he shall have his boots blacked.

Have you never marveled at the patience of people in having so many things done to them that they don't want, just to avoid hurting the feelings of professional people who want to do more than is expected of them? You watch the stoical countenance of the passenger in a Pullman car as he stands up to be brushed. The chances are that he doesn't want to be brushed. He would prefer to leave the dust on his coat rather than to be compelled to swallow it. But he knows what is expected of him. It is a part of the solemn ritual of traveling. It precedes the offering.

The fact that every man desires to be somebody else explains many of the aberrations of artists and literary men. The painters, dramatists, musicians, poets, and novelists are just as human as housemaids and railway managers and porters. They want to do 'all the good they can to all the people they can in all the ways they can.' They get tired of the ways they are used to and like to try new combinations. So they are continually mixing things. The practitioner of one art tries to produce effects that are proper to another art.

A musician wants to be a painter and use his violin as if it were a brush. He would have us see the sunset glories that he is painting for us. A painter wants to be a musician and paint symphonies, and he is grieved because the uninstructed cannot hear his pictures, although the colors do swear at each other. Another painter wants to be an architect and build up his picture as if it were made of cubes of brick. It looks like brick-work, but to the natural eye it doesn't look like a picture. A prose-writer gets tired of writing prose, and wants to be a poet. So he begins every line with a capital letter, and keeps on writing prose.

You go to the theatre with the simple-minded Shakespearean idea that the play's the thing. But the playwright wants to be a pathologist. So you discover that you have dropped into a grewsome clinic. You sought innocent relaxation, but you are one of the non-elect and have gone to the place prepared for you. You must see the thing through.

The fact that you have troubles of your own is not a sufficient claim for exemption.

Or you take up a novel expecting it to be a work of fiction. But the novelist has other views. He wants to be your spiritual adviser. He must do something to your mind, he must rearrange your fundamental ideas, he must massage your soul, and generally brush you off. All this in spite of the fact that you don't want to be brushed off and set to rights. You don't want him to do anything to your mind. It's the only mind you have and you need it in your own business.

III

But if the desire of every man to be somebody else accounts for many whimsicalities of human conduct and for many aberrations in the arts, it cannot be lightly dismissed as belonging only to the realm of comedy. It has its origin in the nature of things. The reason why every man wants to be somebody else is that he can remember the time when he was somebody else. What we call personal identity is a very changeable thing, as all of us realize when we look over old photographs and read old letters.

The oldest man now living is but a few years removed from the undifferentiated germ-plasm, which might have developed into almost anything. In the beginning he was a bundle of possibilities. Every actuality that is developed means a decrease in the rich variety of possibilities. In becoming one thing it becomes impossible to be something else.

The delight in being a boy lies in the fact that the possibilities are still manifold. The boy feels that he can be anything that he desires. He is conscious that he has capacities that would make him a successful banker. On the other hand, there are attractions in a life of adventure in the South Seas. It would be pleasant to lie under a bread-fruit tree and let the fruit drop into his mouth, to the admiration of the gentle savages who would gather about him. Or he might be a saint—not a commonplace modern saint who does chores and attends tiresome committee meetings, but a saint such as one reads about, who gives away his rich robes and his purse of gold to the first beggar he meets, and then goes on his carefree way through the forest to convert interesting robbers. He feels that he might practice that kind of unscientific charity, if his father would furnish him with the money to give away.

But by and by he learns that making a success in the banking business is not consistent with excursions to the South Seas or with the more picturesque and unusual forms of saintliness. If he is to be in a bank he must do as the bankers do.

Parents and teachers conspire together to make a man of him, which means making a particular kind of man of him. All mental processes which are not useful must be suppressed. The sum of their admonitions is that he must pay attention. That is precisely what he is doing. He is paying attention to a variety of things that escape the adult mind. As he wriggles on the bench in the school-room, he pays attention to all that is going on. He attends to what is going on out-of-doors; he sees the weak points of his fellow pupils, against whom he is planning punitive expeditions; and he is delightfully conscious of the idiosyncrasies of the teacher. Moreover, he is a youthful artist and his sketches from life give acute joy to his contemporaries when they are furtively passed around.

But the schoolmaster says sternly, 'My boy, you must learn to pay attention; that is to say, you must not pay attention to so many things, but you must pay attention to one thing, namely, the second declension.'

Now, the second declension is the least interesting thing in the room, but unless he confines his attention to it he will never learn it. Education demands narrowing of attention in the interest of efficiency.

A man may, by dint of application to a particular subject, become a successful merchant or real-estate man or chemist or overseer of the poor. But he cannot be all these things at the same time. He must make his choice. Having in the presence of witnesses taken himself for better or worse, he must, forsaking all others, cleave to that alone. The consequence is that, by the time he is forty, he has become one kind of a man, and is able to do one kind of work. He has acquired a stock of ideas true enough for his purposes, but not so transcendentally true as to interfere with his business. His neighbors know where to find him, and they do not need to take a spiritual elevator. He does business on the ground floor. He has gained in practicality, but has lost in the quality of interestingness.

The old prophet declared that the young men dream dreams and the old men see visions, but he did not say anything about the middle-aged men. *They* have to look after the business end.

But has the man whose working hours are so full of responsibilities changed so much as he seems to have done? When he is talking shop is he 'all there'? I think not. There are elusive personalities that are in hiding. As the rambling mansions of the old Catholic families had secret panels opening into the 'priest's hole,' to which the family resorted for spiritual comfort, so in the mind of the most successful man there are secret chambers where are hidden his unsuccessful ventures, his romantic ambitions, his unfulfilled promises. All that he dreamed of as possible is somewhere concealed in the man's heart. He would not for the world have the public know how much he cares for the selves that have not had a fair chance to come into the light of day. You do not know a man until you know his lost Atlantis, and his Utopia for which he still hopes to set sail.

When Dogberry asserted that he was 'as pretty a piece of flesh as any is in Messina,' and 'one that hath two gowns and everything handsome about him,' he was pointing out what he deemed to be quite obvious. It was in a more intimate tone that he boasted, 'and a fellow that hath had losses.'

When Julius Cæsar rode through the streets of Rome in his chariot, his laurel crown seemed to the populace a symbol of his present greatness. But gossip has it that Cæsar at that time desired to be younger than he was, and that before appearing in public he carefully arranged his laurel wreath so as to conceal the fact that he had had losses.

Much that passes for pride in the behavior of the great comes from the fear of the betrayal of emotions that belong to a simpler manner of life. When the sons of Jacob saw the great Egyptian officer to whom they appealed turn away from them, they little knew what was going on. 'And Joseph made haste, for his bowels did yearn upon his brother: and he sought where to weep, and he entered into his chamber, and wept there. And he washed his face, and went out, and refrained himself.' Joseph didn't want to be a great man. He wanted to be human. It was hard to refrain himself.

IV

What of the lost arts of childhood, the lost audacities and ambitions and romantic admirations of adolescence? What becomes of the sympathies which make us feel our kinship to all sorts of people? What becomes of the early curiosity in regard to things which were none of our business? We ask as Saint Paul asked of the Galatians, 'Ye began well; who did hinder you?'

The answer is not wholly to our discredit. We do not develop all parts of our nature because we are not allowed to do so. Walt Whitman might exult over the Spontaneous Me. But nobody is paid for being spontaneous. A spontaneous switchman on the railway would be a menace to the traveling public. We prefer some one less temperamental.

As civilization advances and work becomes more specialized, it becomes impossible for anyone to find free and full development for all his natural powers in any recognized occupation. What then becomes of the other selves? The answer must be that playgrounds must be provided for them outside the confines of daily business. As work becomes more engrossing and narrowing, the need is more urgent for recognized and carefully guarded periods of leisure.

The old Hebrew sage declared, 'Wisdom cometh from the opportunity of leisure.' It does not mean that a wise man must belong to what we call the leisure classes. It means that, if one has only a little free time at his disposal, he must use that time for the refreshment of his hidden selves. If he cannot have a sabbath rest of twenty-four hours, he must learn to sanctify little sabbaths, it may be of ten minutes' length. In them he shall do no manner of work.

It is not enough that the self that works and receives wages shall be recognized and protected; the world must be made safe for our other selves. Does not the Declaration of Independence say that every man has an inalienable right to the pursuit of happiness?

The old-time minister, after he had exhorted the believers at considerable length, used to turn to a personage who for homiletical purposes was known as the Objector. To him he addressed his most labored arguments. At this point I am conscious of the presence of the Objector.

'All you say,' he remarks, 'in praise of your favorite platitude is true to a fault. But what has all this to do with the War? There is only one thing in these days worth thinking about—at least, it is the only thing we *can* think about.'

'I agree with you, courteous Objector. No matter where we start, we all come back to this point: Who was to blame for the War, and how is it coming out? Our explanatory idea has a direct bearing on the question before us. The Prussian militarists had a painstaking knowledge of facts, but they had a contempt for human nature. Their tactlessness was almost beyond belief. They treated persons as if they were things. They treated facts with deadly seriousness, but had no regard for feelings. They had spies all over the world to report all that could be seen, but they took no account of what could not be seen. So, while they were dealing scientifically with the obvious facts and forces, all the hidden powers of the human soul were being turned against them. Prussianism insists on highly specialized men who have no sympathies to interfere with their efficiency. Having adopted a standard, all variation must be suppressed. It is against this effort to suppress the human variations that we are fighting. We don't want all men to be reduced to one pattern.'

'But what about the Kaiser? Does your formula explain him? Does he want to be somebody else?'

'I confess, dear Objector, that it is probably a new idea to him; but he may come to it.'

www.ingramcontent.com/pod-product-compliance
Lightning Source LLC
Chambersburg PA
CBHW051548100726
47898CB00001B/13
* 9 7 8 9 3 5 7 0 2 9 8 4 1 *